Ordinary Violence

Ordinary Violence

Everyday Assaults against Women Worldwide

Second Edition

Mary White Stewart, PhD

 PRAEGER

AN IMPRINT OF ABC-CLIO, LLC
Santa Barbara, California • Denver, Colorado • Oxford, England

05/14/14
LB
$72.50

Library of Congress Cataloging-in-Publication Data

Stewart, Mary White, 1945–
    Ordinary violence : everyday assaults against women worldwide / Mary White Stewart, PhD — Second edition.
        pages cm
    Includes bibliographical references and index.
    ISBN 978–1–4408–2937–6 (hard copy : alk. paper) — ISBN 978–1–4408–2938–3 (ebook)
    1. Women—Crimes against. 2. Women—Violence against. 3. Sex discrimination against women. I. Title.
HV6250.4.W65S79   2014
362.88082—dc23   2013038607

ISBN: 978–1–4408–2937–6
EISBN: 978–1–4408–2938–3

18 17 16 15 14   1 2 3 4 5

This book is also available on the World Wide Web as an eBook.
Visit www.abc-clio.com for details.

Praeger
An Imprint of ABC-CLIO, LLC

ABC-CLIO, LLC
130 Cremona Drive, P.O. Box 1911
Santa Barbara, California 93116-1911

This book is printed on acid-free paper ∞

Manufactured in the United States of America

To my grandmother, Ada Virginia White
1891–1978
Whose powerful presence is with me every day
and
To my grandson, Hudson, whose love makes my world shine

Contents

Preface

Global violence against women is ordinary, mundane, everyday, and unremarkable. Whether we are talking about rape in the Congo or in Bosnia or rape in some backwater town in the United States, whether we are talking about the trafficking of girls and women across borders from the Philippines or Thailand to Germany, Japan, or the United States, whether we are talking about the multibillion-dollar porn industry or female genital mutilation, we are talking about the ordinary. We may, when we hear about or read about these forms of violence, condemn the trafficker, the rapist, the pornographer, or condemn the woman herself. But seldom do we look at the patterns of inequality, sexism, and racism, and the complex interplay of self, place, culture, and society that link all of these seemingly disparate phenomena.

I am carving out only particular forms of violence to investigate, and am focusing on violence against women. That is not to say that there are not atrocities, horrors beyond belief, around the world experienced by men. War, legitimated violence, murder, post-traumatic stress disorder, which itself is an enduring form of violence, are commonplace and unremarkable, timeless it seems, acts of hatred perpetrated by men against men. But I am focusing on those forms of violence perpetrated by men against women, and when I say men, I include the male-run state and the male-dominated institutions such as the family and the workplace in which women are likely to suffer violence ranging from harassment to death.

While I am a sociologist, this book weaves academic and scholarly analysis with journalistic descriptions of violence against women globally and seeks to reveal the similarities between them. It is specifically a structural treatment of the problems rather than an individualistic or psychological treatment. While not denying that there may be individual characteristics or dynamics that spark the specific problem at a particular moment, the focus is on the structural, cultural, political, and economic factors that lay bare the relationships between violence against women and their relative powerlessness in contemporary society. At the same time, I wish to avoid portraying women only as victims or what some call "survivors" by acknowledging their agency, their voluntary participation in some of these forms of violence, recognizing that all of us make choices bounded by the constraints of our circumstances.

I want to acknowledge that there are different perspectives on each of these problems, a great deal of disagreement among academics, feminists, activists, and policy makers about the causes and the solutions to these problems, and sometimes disagreement about whether they are problems at all. Is trafficking the problem, is prostitution the problem, or is migrant labor the problem? This points to my view that while we may develop categories, legal or political, to describe problems, within each of these categories the actual experiences of the women may be vastly different. The trafficked woman, for example, may be kidnapped, duped, or voluntarily engaged, although in this last instance, she may not be considered to be legally trafficked.

I will avoid using a style that speaks only to other academics or an analytical framework—postmodernism, for example, or critical studies—that relies on a language that sometimes mystifies more than clarifies. If sociological analysis of deviance and crime and violence continues on its present course, it may well end up being understood by such a narrow range of critical theorists that it becomes irrelevant. I am convinced that a sociological framework provides the most powerful way for us to understand the global violence against women that has been and remains so ordinary. A focus on social structures and particularly gender inequality as it intersects with race and class inequality provide the foundation for an understanding of these problems. Further, their solution lies in changes in the very foundations of our society and others across the globe. The scope of the problems makes them seem almost intractable. Yet I fear reliance on those types of changes with which we are most familiar and most comfortable, therapeutic interventions and interventions after the fact. They can easily distract us from major and significant transformations in culture and social systems that are absolutely essential if there is to be any real change in women's lives.

Acknowledgments

I am grateful for the opportunity to revise this book and wish to thank readers of the earlier edition for questions and comments that helped in that process. I am fortunate to have had helpful conversations with friends and colleagues and have benefitted from their useful suggestions and criticisms. I am particularly grateful to the students in my Spring 2012 Gendered Violence class who sought out fantastic examples of television shows, movies, MTV, rap, popular songs, and advertisements that illustrated cultural assumption about gender and gendered violence. They were enthusiastic sleuths, and our discussions of these illustrations were very useful and often entertaining. My colleague Cheryl Maes provided good-natured support when it was greatly needed, and her careful reading of the final draft (final drafts, as it turned out) helped me enormously. Thank you to Sylvia Macey, who attended the difficult details of putting all of this together. This edition was made more challenging because of the enormous range and complexity of the forms of global violence against women, because of the need to revisit much of the literature and to absorb new literature on a wide range of topics, some of which were very new to me and which had not been "on the radar" 10 years ago. It was more difficult, however, because each day seemed to bring new reports of rape, bride burning, sexual assault, or sexual harassment as well as outrageous antiwoman political diatribes and legislation here and around the world.

ONE

Introduction

In Bangladesh, spurned suitors throw sulfuric acid on the faces of women who have rejected them; the scars and deformities remain as evidence of their vengeance. In Egypt, Muslim women are killed by their own brothers and fathers if there is a mere suspicion of sexual impropriety. Their murders are commonplace and uninvestigated and deemed necessary to regain or maintain the family's honor. In the United States, women are sexually harassed, raped, and battered every day, by boyfriends, husbands, coworkers, and strangers. Throughout the world, women are valued less than men: they are likely to do more work, receive less pay, and have less to eat. There is nothing extraordinary about the emotional and physical assaults on women. These are ordinary, mundane, everyday attacks, and their very pervasiveness is illustrative of the deeply rooted cultural stereotypes about women and the structural oppression of women around the world. There is no culture in which it is safer or better to be a woman rather than a man. Given the pandemic nature of violence against women, we need to carefully reevaluate those explanations based only on individual psychopathology or dysfunctions in relationships, no matter how comfortable and how comforting these explanations are. We should carefully attend the cultural beliefs, ideas, religions, historically taken-for-granted realities that shape the lives of men and women in every society. We cannot understand violence against women without understanding the power of constructions of masculinity and femininity as they intersect with constructions of class and race. It is important to understand the relationship between these constructions and the structures they reflect, reinforce, and reproduce.

In writing a second edition of this book, I draw on the now 35 years I have been teaching and writing about family violence and violence against women in order to present one view of the interconnected historical, economic, cultural, and structural factors that cause this problem and the many guises it takes. In so doing, I draw on much of the classic work about women's lives and violence against women. This book is an integration of those ideas and a thoughtful analysis of others who have been devoted to this area with my own conclusions. I no doubt make assertions about which there is not universal agreement. My perspective is clearly feminist, although it is fluid and integrative rather than ideological.

We must begin with patriarchy, with the oppression of women economically and culturally and the mutuality of support between these areas of oppression. The concept, patriarchy, has a slightly quaint feel today, being overused and underspecified, like "sex object" and "objectification" and "racism," but it carries an important meaning nonetheless. Patriarchy's essential elements are male dominance, male identification, and male-centeredness; its core values and beliefs center around the idea of the superiority of masculinity and the inferiority of femininity. It is a reification of the gender binary, the construction of men and women as opposites. But it is nonetheless experienced differently across borders of race and class.[1] The values of patriarchal culture fortify and reinforce violence against women, buttress structural inequities, and reproduce gender structure. The matrix of domination resulting from the imposition of patriarchal culture on race, class, and gender determines its impact. Patriarchy is experienced differently depending on one's location in the race/gender/class hierarchy that privileges white, male, upper-class heterosexuals in cultural images and dominant institutions.[2] Women are victims of violence as a result of their historical powerlessness, their dependence on men for survival, and the right and power of men to define women's sexuality, value, and bodies. Hence, men have the right to do with women's bodies as they will, often using the mother or other women as the handmaidens of violence, rendering their power invisible, and constructing the oppression as natural rather than contrived.

Gendered violence takes many different forms, molding itself to the particular outlines of the history, economy, culture, and governmental realities that differ around the globe. Women are kept behind locked doors in Afghanistan, suffer infibulations in Africa, and are beaten and raped in the United States and South Africa: all of these are forms of oppression reflecting male power and women's position of relative powerlessness and in which this powerlessness is masked as a normal state of gender relations. Cultural values and perceptions, when internalized by women and incorporated into the everyday practices of teachers, parents, employers, and lawmakers, legitimate the oppression of women and present their victimization as ordinary, natural, and deserved.

Despite the extreme danger women face in many cultures, there is hesitance to define the dangerous practices (infibulation, femicide, isolation, ritual rape) as violence or crimes against women for fear that we will be self-righteously imposing ethnocentric norms from Western industrialized countries on other cultures. Over 80 million girls, particularly in the Middle East, Africa, and Southeast Asia, have been the victims of FGM (female genital mutilation). Women in Iran are beaten to death for suspected adultery. Women in Pakistan have acid thrown in their faces by spurned suitors, and female infants in India are quietly killed by the midwife who delivered them. To name these as cultural variations and thereby withdraw judgment from them is to support the continued oppression of women. Yet the notion of cultural relativity does just that, and the view that certain behaviors are simply characteristic of certain subcultures or cultures reinforces our avoidance of significant human rights problems. Social science with its emphasis on value neutrality has contributed to the silence of researchers about the oppression of women worldwide, whether we are talking about infanticide in China, the malnutrition of girls in India, or the oppression of women in Afghanistan under the Taliban. Some are even reluctant to intervene in the cultural practice of female "circumcision" among immigrant groups in the United States, although current estimates are that about 10,000 girls in the United States are at risk each year.[3] Only in March 1997, as a result of legislation sponsored by Senator Harry Reid (D, Nevada) and former representative Patricia Schroeder (Democrat, Colorado) did female genital mutilation become illegal in the United States.

While minor adjustments may occur and even particular forms of violence against women may be all but eradicated, these changes will be half steps toward freedom for women. The fact that every city of any size now has a shelter for battered women, for example, while illustrating that we no longer think battery is a family issue, does not mean that women are no longer beaten for many of the same reasons they were in the past. Let us recognize that and stop the pretense. The diversion programs for men who have abused women will not have any significant impact on the most virulent aggression against women; women, as a category, remain dependent on male-dominated state legislatures, Congress, and the courts to make laws that affect their lives, laws in which men have a tremendous stake; the gender structure continues to operate solidly and effectively against women. A critical analysis of the situation, a radical view that demands the transformation of gender relations, is imperative. As Lenore Walker says in *The Battered Woman*: "My feminist analysis of all violence is that sexism is the real underbelly of human suffering. Men fight with other men to prove that they are not sissies like women. Women show passive faces to the world while struggling to keep their lives together without letting men know how strong they really are for fear of hurting their masculine image. And men beat up women in order to keep themselves on the top of this whole messy heap."[4]

Gender is so central to violence against women that it is rendered invisible. We don't "see" it unless there is some gender transgression, and this invisibility both reflects and reproduces the power of sexism. We can't call it unless we can see it, and as Johnson says, "we can't really see it unless we have something to call it. Not only does its pervasiveness prevent us from seeing, it also marginalizes those who remark about it."[5]

Joan Smith in *Misogynies* writes about her reaction to the Yorkshire Ripper, Peter Sutcliffe, who murdered 13 women in England in the late 1970s:

> What I was struck by, I suppose, was the fact that these were crimes directed against *women* .... For many years I have assumed I was living in a society that was unfair to women, an environment that was sometimes hostile to them, but that this was no more than a hangover from history, an unthinking allegiance to an outdated way of organizing everyday affairs ... only a culture which nurtured and encouraged a deep-seated hatred of women could produce a mass killer of his type. When it did, it was hardly to be wondered at that its agents were unable to distinguish him from the mass of its products. The discrimination and denigration and violence that women suffer are no historical accident but linked manifestations of this hatred; I inhabit a culture which is not simply sexist but *occasionally lethal* for women. Misogyny wears many guises, reveals itself in different forms which are dictated by class, wealth, education, race, religion, and other factors, but its chief characteristic is its pervasiveness.[6]

Marilyn French in *The War against Women* sees men's long-standing aggressions against women as taking on a new ferocity, a new urgency, and new veneers as men fight to retain their privilege and power. Patriarchy, or institutionalized male supremacy, never announces its real purpose in its justifications of male assault on females. However men have subjugated women, the justification was the conviction that God or nature made women subordinate to men by endowing men with certain traits (reasonable, logical, intellectual) allowing them to lead and create a stable society and women with traits (emotionally unstable, sexually unbridled) that are subversive of good and proper order. When governments or religious leaders articulate policies that are injurious to women, they rarely mention women directly, focusing instead on other issues and cloaking the destructive policies in euphemisms, the most popular of which is the "protection of the family."[7]

Violence against women is no longer unspeakable; it is not a "dirty little secret." We are, in fact, overwhelmed with endless stories about violence against women. Within hours of the brutal gang rape of a woman tourist in India and the assault against her companion, or as soon as a wave of rapes in Brazil is recognized, the news is circulated. We almost immediately hear of the shooting of Malala Yousafzai, a schoolgirl in Pakistan who was determined to advance the education of girls; and the tragic deaths of over 1,100 people, almost all women, who were crushed in a clothing factory collapse in Bangladesh are broadcast almost as the collapse occurs. Missouri senator Todd Akin's bizarre remark about the female body's ability to shut down the uterus in the case of a "legitimate rape" is immediately aired and condemned. The overwhelming oppression of women under the Taliban in Afghanistan is common knowledge to most Americans, and we are aware, at least minimally, of footbinding, comfort women, sexual slavery, and other historical and contemporary forms of violence against women.

This book is devoted to expanding our understanding of the current pandemic of ordinary and devastating violence against women, as well as of the context for and history of that violence. We will see that women have a long history of being abused in the United States and other countries and have sometimes been stunningly successful in their fight against violence. In far more cases, however, the battles waged against women's bodies and spirits have been overwhelmingly destructive and seemingly endless. An entire decade has passed since I first wrote about the "taken for granted" predictable violence women suffer on a global scale. Rather than being able to look back on a past that fueled a dramatic change for the better, there has been little improvement in many areas. Dowry deaths and honor crimes are more, not less, common than they were a decade ago, wife battery and sexual assault remain problems of staggering proportions, but they have been replaced on legislative and activist agendas with sex trafficking and labor trafficking, problems that deserve attention too. There have been some changes. Women in the "third world" or what has come to be called the "global south" are now communicating with Western

women about FGM and other forms of violence against women and finding ways to work together to solve a problem that has damaged 100 million
women worldwide; and in some villages today, infibulation and circumcision are rare. The existence of shelters in almost every city across the
United States, public programs, media campaigns, and other social
responses to the epidemic of violence against women indicate a sensitivity
to this violence and a desire to eradicate it, or at the very least diminish its
frequency and lethality.

Some problems that faded in the last few years have reemerged with a
vengeance—a recent report by the Pentagon reveals that 27,000 women
in the military have been the victims of sexual assault during the past year
alone.[8]

Throughout this book we look at the forms, variations, and extent of
violence against women. In the chapters that follow, the reader will be
asked to be patient enough not to look for the causes of violence against
women or for the solutions in the psyches of individuals or in some natural
biological order. The oppression of women is a direct outcome of political
and economic decisions supported by a cultural ideology of female inferiority and accompanied by a parallel ideology of male superiority supporting a structure of male power and privilege. This structure and its
ideological support have to be seen as they operate in each instance of violence against women, whether personal or institutional, and the reader
may have to wade through several layers of justification and reasonable-
sounding psychological or individualistic explanations to be able to finally
see the structure. But when it is laid bare, its organization can be seen as
underlying all types of violence against women, taking different forms at
different times and places, but rendering the violence that women face
ordinary and commonplace. This is the structure that needs to be dismantled; its strength is situated deeply in the institutions that spawned and
continue to support it. This is a difficult challenge, but short of having
the will to take it, we continue to support gender relations and sociopolitical systems that perpetuate this violence—overtly through our fear of
reprisal or our overwhelming fatigue, or covertly through averting our
attention and pretending that psychologically deranged persons cause the
problems and that therapeutic fixes will solve them.

NOTES

1. A. G. Johnson, *The Gender Knot: Unraveling Our Patriarchal
Legacy,* Revised and Updated Edition (Philadelphia: Temple University
Press, 2005).

2. P. Hill Collins, *Black Feminist Thought: Knowledge, Consciousness, and the Politics of Empowerment* (Boston: Unwin Hyman Company, 1990).

3. R. H. Jensen, "Mimi Ramsey: For Selflessly Surviving Despite Her Own Pain, to End the Mutilation of Young Girls," *Ms.* 6, no. 4 (1996): 51–52.

4. L. Walker, *The Battered Woman* (New York: Harper and Row, 1979), xi.

5. A. G. Johnson, *The Forest and the Trees: Sociology as Life, Practice and Promise* (Philadelphia: Temple University Press, 2008).

6. J. Smith, *Misogynies* (London: Faber and Faber, 1990), xviii–xix.

7. M. French, *The War against Women* (New York: Ballantine Books, 1992), 17–19.

8. J. Steinhauer, "Joint Chiefs' Answers on Sex Crimes Dismay Senators," *New York Times*, June 5, 2013, A12.

TWO

Lenses on Violence: Seeing Assaults against Women

Perspectives are lenses through which we bring into focus the obscured intricacies of a complex social world. Our efforts to understand our lives and the lives of those around us are shaped by implicit, often hazy and unacknowledged beliefs, ideas, and values. These perspectives are shaped by our culture, language, and the political and economic system in which we live. Thinking of sex as "performance," for example, or an erection as an "achievement," or describing oneself as "spent" after lovemaking has an unmistakable capitalist ring. Similarly, the view of conception most often taught in sex education courses reflects and reinforces a particular view of masculinity and femininity: a complacent, passive ovum being pierced by an aggressive, competitive sperm, fighting its way to the prize. It would be more accurate to perceive the egg as actively selecting the most attractive or appealing of the sperm coming her way, but such a perspective is inconsistent with the cultural view of masculinity and femininity.[1] Menstruation by the same token has consistently been viewed as the process of the uterus shedding its lining if an egg is not fertilized. Margie Profet, an evolutionary biologist, instead proposes that menstruation serves to protect the uterus and fallopian tubes from harmful microbes delivered by incoming sperm. One perspective views women's bodies as constantly preparing for pregnancy and then recovering for the next possible fertilization; the other views the woman's body as protecting itself from "pathogenic intruders."[2] Perspectives are not facts or truths but ways of viewing the world—frameworks for organizing perceptions and understandings. They are, however, generally assumed to be based on truth or fact; they are the "taken for granteds" that permeate our everyday world. Harold Garfinkel introduced this term to indicate the powerful understandings we bring with us to social interactions, the implicit assumptions on which our interactions with others and our understandings of ourselves are based.[3] He suggests, in *Studies in Ethnomethodology,* that these "taken for granteds" are a way of perceiving the world and that the fabric of our lives exists in the everyday, invisible rules and expectations by which we operate rather than the institutions, laws, and policies that are the more visible indicators of these rules. To understand the depth and the power of these taken for granteds, one need only violate an implicit rule, for example, staring at a man's zipper while engaged in a discussion about stocks and bonds, or trying to barter for one's groceries in the supermarket. Reactions to these breaches indicate both the power the rule has over our behavior and the fact that others in our social world share it.

Perspectives are strongly linked to politics and power. C. Wright Mills insisted long ago that the power elite construct points of view, explanation systems, that dominate our society, primarily because those in the position to construct reality are also in the position to control the dissemination of information and ideas.[4] The average person's view of crime includes street crime but not corporate crime, and most people conjure up a young, black, urban male as a criminal rather than a CEO of a major corporation, even today, when the fraud and mendacity of CEOs and bank boards have pushed so many ordinary Americans into financial ruin. Marx laid the groundwork for understanding these points of view in his analysis of the relationship between ideas and values and class position. The ruling ideas, he wrote, are the ideas of the ruling class. The dominant perspectives have a powerful impact on us, and we often incorporate definitions of reality or points of view that not only do not reflect our reality but are oppressive to us.[5] The dominant view of masculinity as aggressive and powerful, for example, is dangerous to women, as is the view that men are naturally sexually aggressive and women sexually passive. This construction of masculinity is also dangerous to men. These cultural ideologies are built on structural inequalities and reinforce them in a pervasive and invisible manner; definitions of male and female sexuality, for example, not only reflect gender inequality but reinforce it.[6]

Underlying explanations about wife battery, rape, or any other form of violence against women are assumptions about the world. Is it there, to be discovered and named by us, or does it come into existence as we differentiate it from other things and name it? From the "factist" perspective, researchers are searching, with more or less luck, for answers, for truths that exist in the individual, the interactions between individuals, or social and structural factors. The factist perspective is based on the assumption that there is an objective reality that can be ascertained and understood best through the scientific method, which will result in the discovery of that truth.[7] The definitionist perspective, on the other hand, assumes that there is no objective reality; we operate in a world constructed by humans and make agreements about reality that shape our experiences and understandings and that we accept as reality.

On a very simple level, a factist perspective would assume that there is such a thing as gang behavior and that this behavior could be studied with the tools of science, providing understanding about gangs—who joins them, why they join, and so forth. A theorist or researcher operating from a definitionist perspective would assume that various experts and interest groups construct particular groups as gangs and develop ideas and information about these groups and people who belong to them that help make sense of the world, often because the ideas are consistent with assumptions and values we bring to the analysis. Both can be true. Indeed, one can see that the definition of a group as a gang is a political one, while at the same time one is aware that persons define themselves as members of gangs and one could study their motivations, the rewards of membership or identification, the interactions among members, and the like.

The constructionist perspective is far more accepted in the academy than among those working with women who are the victims of violence or among the women and men involved in the violence, or those who are perplexed or dismayed by the prevalence of violence against women. It asserts that social problems are created by people who have an interest in their construction. From this perspective, while there are numerous events, some of them physically damaging, what they are is what we call them; those persons who have the most power are most likely to be in a position to name the problem. From this point of view, what something *is* is far more fluid, more a definition of reality, than a "given," and the response to it is shaped to some extent by the interests of those persons who have something to gain or lose as a result of how the event is defined. For example, rape as a legal category carried a "marital exemption" until 1993, but although it is illegal in every state and many countries, it is seldom prosecuted. The underlying question is, "Is there an objective, discernible reality, or is what we perceive as reality a social construction?" Is there "rape," or is it a "definition"? Is there "battery," or is it a "definition"? Both perspectives assume that the behavior exists, but the "factists" assume it is what it is called, while the definitionists assume it is nothing until it is called something.

Most of the research, as well as everyday understandings about violence against women, is based on the assumption that there are certain behaviors that constitute violence. At the same time, most people are aware that whether a particular event is labeled rape or battery depends on a number of decisions on the part of the individuals involved, the police, prosecutors, juries, and others who might be in a position to respond. We operate for the most part in a world that we do not question at every point—a world that we take as given and real, and indeed we experience it as such. When we make an effort to understand or explain violence against women, we may do so by explaining individual behavior, the interactions between the people involved, or assessing characteristics of the institutions such as the family, or structure, such as class, or culture as the factors causing the violence. How we approach this effort reflects our perspective.

We are far more likely to use cultural explanations when attempting to understand other societies' practices, such as genital mutilation or bride burning, and to use individualistic explanations when analyzing problems women face in the United States. Focusing on the individual in an effort to understand behavior reflects our belief in free will and autonomy and is consistent with a competitive capitalistic economy. Most of us incorporate an individualistic perspective on the world without being aware of it. Only when a contrary perspective is presented do we become aware that the ideas and values we accept as given are in fact points of view or assumptions. However, the contrasting or competing perspective is often viewed as a "theory" competing with the "facts" of the individualistic perspective. When we use culture as an explanation, we often, unfortunately, go no further—the concept is left to stand for an array of assumptions, practices, and phenomena. Such a reliance on culture stops analysis in fact and we can leave the topic assuming we know far more than we do. While cultural forces are powerful, and while it is important to understand dominant values and beliefs, it is also very important to not use culture as a "stand in" for structural, economic, religious, and historic factors. Beliefs and values, including political and legal definitions, are tied to structure. Just as hemlines are said to go up and down with the economy, so do dominant perspectives or explanations of social problems are related to periods of economic growth or decline. Individualistic perspectives are likely to be particularly ascendant in conservative times. When the society suffers hard economic times, a focus on individual responsibility, individual choice, and individual characteristics dominates; in more favorable economic circumstances, social intervention to solve social problems is likely to gain precedence.

In fact, the "cause" of a problem often follows available solutions rather than the solution being derived from an assessment of cause. One may perceive "cause" as a construction, a product of interest group activity. In the case of incest, for example, whether the problem is the responsibility of the father (and whether he is sex obsessed, immature, or a pedophile) or results from the dynamic interaction between the mother, the father, and the child who is molested is determined not by "the facts" of the situation, but by the explanations that are familiar and comfortable to those persons involved in identifying and responding to the problem. Social workers and psychologists are likely to look for individualistic or interactional determinants of social or familial problems, whereas sociologists are likely to look at such factors as the structure of the family in which the father is dominant or the cultural definitions of roles of father and mother, and of female and male sexuality. The information we have about any phenomenon is dependent on the questions we ask.

Likewise, whether wife battery results from a dysfunctional relationship or psychological inadequacies on the part of either partner, or whether it is cultural support for male dominance and the economic dependence of women on men that causes wife battery is clearly a matter of "whom you ask."[8] The questions about wife battery have changed over time and reflect the different assumptions held by the people asking. We will turn to these perspectives now, illustrating their value as well as the problems they pose.

THE MEDICALIZATION OF VIOLENCE

The medicalization of violence of all sorts against women is pervasive. This medicalization takes the form of applying a psychological or psychiatric label to either the perpetrator or the victim of the violence, claiming that there are individual genetic or personality characteristics that make violent acts and acquiescent reactions to them understandable. Rather than there being many competing definitions and solutions, the shared cultural definitions and professional socialization usually result in a hegemony of meaning. Doctors, social workers, newscasters and newspaper editorial boards, volunteers, shelter workers, psychiatrists, and psychologists are all likely to have developed the same view of a social problem with which they deal. Their shared perception reflects their shared participation in dominant political and educational institutions and the influence of dominant and pervasive cultural constructions. Solutions they offer then are framed within a shared worldview that provides for communication between the professionals and agreements about cause and cure that are reinforced by one another and offered to clients or potential clients as correct and acceptable.

Although some critical voices insist that we recognize that acts of violence are reflective of culture and systemic oppression rather than mental aberrations, they are neither many nor terribly loud. As Peter Conrad and Joseph Schneider point out in their influential book, *Deviance and Medicalization: From Badness to Sickness*, the medical model has dominated our explanation of devastating personal problems and stigmatized choices for decades.[9] Problems like alcoholism whose cause was situated in "weak will" or the "work of the devil" are now viewed as resulting from medical problems. These problems require treatment by medical professionals and allied professions, even when there is no specific effective medical response.

We have become saturated in medical explanations and are accustomed to solutions that require therapy or drug treatment for the problems of everyday life. In fact, even a "problem" that is clearly social or situational may be addressed medically simply because it can be. Lawrence Diller, a behavioral pediatrician, says he prescribes Ritalin for more and more children, not because they have attention deficit hyperactivity disorder (ADHD) but because they are normal children who are inattentive or disinterested in school and a bit slow to finish their chores—and it works. Ritalin "works" not because the child is suffering minimal brain dysfunction, but because Ritalin allows anyone to focus and attend the task rather than suffer distraction.[10]

The cavalier labeling of hundreds of thousands of children in this country as suffering from attention deficit disorder (with or without hyperactivity) illustrates the degree to which we rely on medical explanations and solutions, and provides an example that parallels the medicalization of wife battery, rape, incest, and other forms of violence against women and girls. The medicalization of violence against women calls for individualized solutions for a problem that is, in fact, based in social and cultural factors and prevents the broad-scale change that is essential to address the problem. Further, by limiting the discourse about violence against women to the individual, therapeutic construction, the oppression of an entire class of people is obscured, transformed into a problem between a couple or within an individual. The language of interaction and focus on personal characteristics in discussion of family violence and spouse abuse conceals the unseen reality of violence against women. In fact the terms "family violence" and "spouse abuse" or "intimate partner violence" ask us to think about the battery of women in interactional and gender neutral terms. The term "battered woman" is a political term that demystifies oppression and names battery as oppression of women by men.[11] To define the problem as "family violence" or, especially, "spouse abuse" is to obscure the reality that many women experience. Efforts to sanitize violence against women, to remove the reality of sexism and male privilege from the mix in order to avoid sounding like a man-hater if one is a feminist, or to seem "blaming" or less than neutral if one is a therapist, deny reality and disempower women. To talk about family violence as if it is the same thing as violence against women not only confuses different problems but prohibits us from dealing responsibly with either effectively. They require different analyses and responses. In fact, the most widely accepted family therapy theories and intervention strategies may not only *not* deal effectively with violence against women but may also help maintain the collective avoidance of a substantial problem.[12]

THE MEDICALIZED VICTIM

The view that both the batterer and the battered woman can be understood in terms of their individual personal characteristics dominates our approach to this problem, even though it has been embroidered by a broader acceptance of interactional, social, and cultural factors. The basic questions asked from this perspective are, "Why does he do it?" and "Why does she stay?," with a good deal more interest, it seems, in the latter. The individualistic or medical perspective on battery views it as a pathology or dysfunction of the individual and searches for the cause within the psyches or backgrounds of the individuals involved. Individualistic explanations of wife battery generally list a number of personality or emotional characteristics that are presented as predicting violence in relationships and are implicitly assumed to be explanations for that violence. Just as in the case of the early research on child abuse, the assumption has been that cultural or structural factors such as poverty or sexism or behavioral factors such as drug or alcohol abuse are "important only to the extent that they act on an individual with a particular constellation of personality traits."[13]

Although some of the research has focused on the characteristics of the perpetrator, including personality and family characteristics, most of the popular discussion and certainly the most common question in the classroom reflect an assumption that there is something wrong with the woman who is the victim. This assumption is potentially devastating for the woman because of its impact on the response to her by friends, family, and particularly the legal system when she seeks help. The tendency to question her behavior reflects a cultural assumption that the man's behavior of hitting her or attacking her is understandable within the parameters of what we know about relationships and the family, or that while his behavior may be bizarre and dangerous, it is her response that is questionable. Although there is a fairly hefty list of characteristics of the batterer that paint him as a less than desirable partner, the response of police, juries, and social workers suggests that they are often most perplexed by the behavior of the woman who is battered. Lenore Walker's work was developed in part to "normalize" the behavior of battered women and to make her behavior understandable within the context of the relationship and the culture.[14]

It is not unusual to blame the victim. William Ryan, in his classic work *Blaming the Victim*, illustrates the degree to which perceptions about the cause of social problems and their solutions blame those who suffer the problem.[15] The outrageous actions of others in all manner of problems, from sexual harassment to honor crimes to the Holocaust, have been blamed on the victims. Such a perspective essentially allows for the avoidance of social, economic, or structural factors, or even the "banality of evil"[16] that would provide a broader and more accurate understanding of social problems and that would reveal the racist and sexist assumptions that fuel such violence.

In the early research on female victims of battery, therapists and researchers tended to describe the women as either dominant and rejecting of the female role or as masochistic or weak and overly dependent and childlike. Some therapists placed the blame on women who were unwilling to acquiesce to the natural dominance of their husbands, challenging his authority or nagging him until he overreacted. Shelter workers and social workers often relied on descriptions of battered women as traditional, uneducated, or suffering from low self-esteem and passivity. The characteristics of battered women were viewed as emerging from troubled or conflict-ridden childhoods. However, in a study of risk markers for victims and perpetrators, only one consistent risk marker was found for women who are battered—witnessing violence as a child or adolescent.[17] Other research found other risk markers, but none consistently in all of the research on battered women. These factors included experiencing violence as a child or adolescent, drug use, low self-esteem, low educational achievement, and traditional sex role expectations. Age, race, low personality integration, high hostility, low assertiveness, and dominance were also listed as markers.[18] Lenore Walker, whose work has been influential among social workers and in the legal system, developed a list of the most common characteristics of women who are battered that went beyond the psychological traits and incorporated their response to their batterer and to others. In addition to having low self-esteem and being traditionalists who adhere to sex role stereotypes, characteristics that are commonly reported, she suggests that they are also likely to believe the myths about battering, such as it is the woman's fault, and they are likely to accept responsibility for the batterer's actions, to suffer guilt and deny the terror and anger they feel. They present a passive face to the world but are strong enough to manipulate the environment to prevent further violence or death, have severe stress reactions and psycho-physiological complaints, use sex as a way to establish intimacy, and believe that no one will be able to help them.[19]

In a series of questionnaires I sent to therapists some time ago, most agreed that there are particular types of men who batter and particular types of women who are victims. Almost every time I give a talk on violence against women, I get that same response from someone in the audience. Abuse is often seen as a problem instigated by the woman, and they suspect that she would leave one abusive partner only to get involved with another. Let us take a moment to reevaluate this supposed pattern, which therapists, social workers, and sometimes police endorse as indicative of an emotional or psychological problem of the woman. A woman who is battered may for a number of reasons (some economic, some emotional) develop a relationship with a man who eventually hits her or mistreats her. She may have chosen the man, but it does not follow that she chose him *because* he promised to be the kind of man who would beat her. Rather, the characteristics that she found attractive may have also included characteristics that led to the abuse. Further, it may be that it is more accurate to assume that there is a wide range of potentially abusive men available than to assume that a woman seeks one out. It may be that there are many men who are abusive or potentially abusive, and finding them is easy rather than difficult. Nevertheless, focusing on her problems, her characteristics, and why she chooses someone who is abusive is characteristic of a culture in which the focus is on individual rather than social factors that cause social problems.

One of the obvious problems with the development of a profile or a list of characteristics of women who are battered is that such a list does not necessarily differentiate them from other women. This is a major problem, particularly because these characteristics are often used to explain why a woman was battered and to "deviantize" her by making her different from other women. In fact, it is clear that many of the characteristics of battered women are also characteristic of women who are not battered. Let us agree, for example, that battered women use sex to establish intimacy. How could that possibly distinguish them from other women, most of whom see a strong tie between intimacy and sex and actively seek to create sex as an intimate rather than a purely physical interaction? In fact, is the establishment and expression of intimacy not one of the purposes of sex? Further, if we accept the assumption of many therapists who worked with battered women in the 1970s that these women rejected "normal, passive, femininity," we would have to agree that normal femininity is passive and dependent, just as Freud and Erickson said. But the past several decades of the women's movement have been devoted to the rejection of that narrow and limiting description and to the acceptance of autonomy, independence, and strength as valuable characteristics for both men and women. And, even if we were to agree that women who are battered are "masochistic," how would that differentiate them from the supposedly "normal masochism" of women proposed by Helene Deutsch?[20]

Another significant problem with much of the ongoing research from the individualistic perspective is that because women are not studied until after they are battered, many of the characteristics attributed to them may come from the trauma and shock of being battered and the fear of living in a dangerous situation. The low self-esteem or nonassertiveness attributed to battered women allows therapists to categorize them as different, perhaps in some way inviting the abuse, and allows them to distance themselves from the battered woman and her experience. Any list of characteristics will reflect only part of the population, generally women who identify themselves as battered, especially women in hospitals or shelters who are willing to be interviewed. Lenore Walker interviewed women who had been hospitalized after severe beatings by their husbands or boyfriends. The experiences they had and their characteristics cannot be seen as representative of all women who are beaten. In addition, the characteristics she discovered were likely to be reflective of their immediate situation, one in which they were often being pressed by their husband, who was contrite and loving (at least for the moment) and wanted forgiveness. By the same token, women in shelters are hardly representative of all women who are beaten.[21]

Michael Johnson's work that distinguishes situational violence from "patriarchal terrorism" has important implications for treatment as well as intervention.[22] Those women who end up in emergency rooms with broken bones and requiring stitches and those women who escape their batterer and find a safe haven in a shelter are women who are the victims of patriarchal violence or sexual terrorism. They are stalked, and beaten, and controlled by men who think they own "their" women. These are misogynist men with traditional values about masculinity and who embrace notions of male superiority and female inferiority. They are also insecure, often violent and volatile, and the woman probably does risk her life by staying with him. The women who escape these men and the physical and emotional abuse they have experienced can rightly be called "survivors." This term suggests that women are fighters who have overcome something devastating—we include cancer survivors or Holocaust survivors and we now include women who have "survived" "patriarchal terrorism" in this company. But the women who engage in common couple violence are not "survivors," and it does neither them nor anyone who works with them any good to label them this way. To do so evokes a particular constellation of experiences they do not share with survivors and distracts us from the reality of interactional and emotional problems suffered by both partners in this type of violence. Neither are the men in this situation the same men as those involved in patriarchal terrorism. The men involved in common couple violence, what Johnson later renamed "situational violence," are men who get in an argument with their wife and solve the disagreement through hitting or slapping or pushing. These are men who Gelles and Straus tap into with the Family Conflict Tactics Scale when they ask if they have slapped their partner, but these are not the men who stab or shoot their wives or partners.[23] Often these are men involved in mutual violence, and both partners need to learn new ways to cope with their anger and their frustration, or get help with alcohol or drug use, but escape or divorce is not necessarily the answer for them.

If all violence is not the same, then the interventions should not be the same. For example, while "anger management groups" might be productive for those men involved in common couple violence who can learn coping skills in educational programs or gain insight through group therapy, anger management will do nothing for men who are what Sheffield calls "sexual terrorists."[24] These men will only learn new justifications and excuses for their behavior, and forcing them to attend such classes will probably only increase their resentment and self-righteous anger. While jail might help those men who are "patriarchal terrorists," a felony assault record will ruin the careers and damage the economic and social situation of those who are involved in common couple violence with no benefit for anyone.

The activists in the battered women's movement were successful in getting police and courts, who often trivialized and ignored the violence, to pay attention to the very real problem of the battery of women. The

Violence against Women Act, reauthorized in 2013,[25] contained a number of provisions that benefitted victims, including providing funds for legal assistance to victims in civil cases, transitional housing assistance and supervised visitation and child exchange. It also established a registry for battered women and required equal enforcement of protective orders in all jurisdictions, helping women who have been victims of severe abuse. At the same time, there have been some unanticipated negative consequences with the net thrown too wide and with the failure to distinguish types of violence and treat them differently. For example, mandatory arrest laws have had the unanticipated negative consequence of increased arrests of women involved in battering relationships in situations where both partners are involved because police are required to arrest someone and the man may have physical injuries such as scratches. Other efforts to address family violence have inadvertently punished battered women who stay with their batterer by characterizing the women as child abusers if they remain in a battering situation. This leads to the unfortunate circumstance in which a battered woman may not seek help because if she can't or won't leave her abuser, she may lose her children. Mandatory arrest laws, have resulted in more women being arrested, and they have only slightly lowered repeat offending rates while at the same time increasing the risk of retaliation by abusers with a prior history of abuse. These policies may also be disempowering to women and discourage them from calling the police, particularly black and minority women who may already have reason to be suspicious of the justice system. The related "no drop" prosecution policies have also caused difficulty, because the victim's participation is not required to prosecute the case. These policies may also potentially disempower the woman by discouraging her from reporting the violence.[26]

In sum, there is no evidence that battered women have a clinically diagnosable character disorder that distinguishes them from women who are not battered. As Walker points out, personality and other differences among battered women should be viewed as a consequence rather than causes of battering.[27] Women in shelters are likely to be desperate, frightened, suffering painful reactions to their experience, and to have been the victims of severe abuse. Their responses reflect not only their extreme situation but also the immediacy of their pain and fear. Were they to be interviewed under different circumstances, their "personality characteristics" might be different as well. Clinical impressions of women who are battered may well be related more to the therapeutic process than to their personality characteristics. The psychotherapeutic model is narrow and inconsistent, and it cannot be relied on to provide a thorough understanding of women who are battered. All battery is clearly not the same, and the successful efforts of activists to assure that police and courts address violence against women more seriously have not always have the desired consequences.

THE MEDICALIZED PERPETRATOR

Characteristics such as low self-esteem, jealousy, emotional dependence, and emotional instability appear repetitively in the literature on psychological characteristics of men who batter.[28] In addition, batterers are often depicted as rigid and unresourceful in problem solving and as people who have difficulty developing and maintaining close intimate relationships. They are also presented as likely to be impulsive, moody, and self-centered. They have been reported to have problems with intimacy and boundaries, exhibiting considerable suspicion and jealousy, an excessive need for control and authority, to be demanding and aloof, to have feelings of inadequacy, and to be unable to express needs in intimate relationships.[29] Walker reports that men who batter are characterized by low self-esteem, believe myths about battering relationships, adhere to stereotypical views of sex roles, believe in male supremacy, blame others for their actions, are pathologically jealous, have a dual personality, have severe stress reactions, often use drinking as a coping mechanism, use sex as an act of aggression, may be bisexual, and do not believe their violence has negative consequences.[30] This is quite a list, covering a wide range of attitudes, perceptions, and proclivities, and, more importantly, it includes characteristics that do not necessarily differentiate these men from the many men who have embraced traditional masculinity or have misogynistic attitudes but who don't abuse their wives or girlfriends.

The psychological literature leads to the conclusion that as a group male batterers have an identifiable set of personality characteristics: dependence, depression, anxiety, low self-esteem, paranoia, disassociation from their own feelings, poor impulse control, antisocial tendencies, and hostility toward women.[31] Yet there seems to be no single psychological syndrome that is consistently associated with wife battering. Nor do these characteristics clearly delineate men who batter from other misogynist men. The characteristics of men who batter are sometimes described as those of borderline narcissistic paranoid or antisocial disorders, although these labels are infrequently applied and are likely to be applied only after the person has engaged in battering behavior.[32]

Various typologies of abusers have been developed as aids to those providing services to batterers and their victims, with the assumption that different treatment strategies work better than others with particular types. The Massachusetts Department of Social Services has developed the Domestic Violence Protocol, one part of which consists of an Assessment of Offender Lethality, based on the assumption that if the offender fits one of three profiles, there is cause for more serious concern than there would otherwise be: (1) the obsessed offender, who is jealous and irrational, monitoring his spouse's whereabouts, threatening to kill himself or her if she leaves or asks for a divorce; (2) the sadistic offender who is vengeful and has a "bizarre, depersonalized" character and whose violence involves inflicting severe pain or torture on the victim, such as forcing sex after childbirth, locking her in a closet, or tying her up for hours or days; and (3) the hyperviolent offender who takes offense easily, feels his masculinity being challenged frequently, and is often violent in situations other than only in the family.[33]

Some of the work on men who batter incorporates social and cultural factors as they influence behavior rather than relying solely on intrapsychic characteristics for explanation. Hope House, established as a shelter for battered women and their children in 1982 in Kansas City, Missouri, has developed a training manual for shelter workers that includes a list of some of the characteristics of abusive males. This list has emerged from their work with battered women, and the characteristics are viewed as situated in a social and cultural climate that fosters violence against women. The list includes: Abusers feel insecure and powerless and cover their feelings with aggressive behavior; they are afraid of showing weakness, which is equated with femininity, and they overcompensate by being "macho"; the batterers are extremely dependent on the wife and will go to great lengths to control her and keep her close. This manual, however, also incorporates some of the other common characteristics of men who batter that are found in other profiles: abusers are excessively jealous, often interpreted by the woman as a sign of caring; they have poor impulse control and cannot tolerate frustration; they project blame for violent acts on others, especially the wife; they witnessed or were the object of violence during childhood; they may or may not use alcohol; they are often "nice guys" but have a "Dr. Jekyll and Mr. Hyde" personality (a statement often made by therapists about batterers); they view their wife as an object responsible for meeting their needs; they have great difficulty expressing their needs or even knowing what they are; and they are likely to label their unexpressed feelings as anger.[34]

Hotaling and Sugarman, who have done extensive research comparing the findings of different authors, report many consistent risk markers for men, but these were experiences rather than psychological characteristics and were so entwined with the battery as to be inextricable.[35] For example, men who battered were found consistently to act in a sexually aggressive way toward their wife or partner, engage in violence toward their children, or to have witnessed violence as a child or adolescent. Low occupational status, high alcohol usage, low income, low assertiveness, and low educational achievement were also consistently related to violence against women. Inconsistent risk markers for men included unemployment, criminal record, low self-esteem, and a need for power and dominance.

Having witnessed violence and having been battered as a child are often reported in childhood histories of male batterers, and in fact the finding that exposure to violence during childhood is associated with later male-to-female violence is almost universal.[36] However, observing abuse may be a more powerful indicator of future marital violence than experiencing abuse directly, and observing paternal violence may be the best predictor. There are several possible reasons for the powerful impact of childhood experiences with violence. One way of understanding this is to recognize that children model themselves on the roles provided by their parents, especially their same-sex parent. Boys who grow up seeing their father abuse their mother might be expected to see that way of relating as acceptable, or at least not unthinkable. The research is not as clear about the impact of such violence on girls. Some research suggests that girls who grew up experiencing no violence at all were particularly vulnerable to abuse, perhaps because they had no skills for coping with conflict. Most sociologists and psychologists place a great deal of importance on socialization. Not only do children learn ways to relate to other people, through reliance on violence or not, for example, but they also learn a great deal about gender, which also shapes their expectations for relationships.[37] Men learn masculine roles of authority, dominance, and control through socialization, while women learn dependence, nurturing, and passivity. This mutual learning results in relationships in which men think they should dominate and control, and they rely on the models of their childhood to enforce their masculine roles. Women, on the other hand, have learned to be responsible for the relationship and to be cooperative and nurturing, roles that make them vulnerable to violence from men and to remaining in violent relationships. The "compulsory heterosexuality" men learn in a culture that demeans women results in a blueprint for violence.[38]

Socialization is important in another way that relates to gender expectations as well as to the potential for violence in a relationship. We learn
to attribute motives to ourselves and others on the basis of our socialization in the family, as that family reflects cultural values and beliefs.
In our culture, for example, men are likely to learn to attribute their successes to internal factors such as intelligence or drive, while they are
likely to attribute their failures to others (e.g., the boss or teacher was
wrong or unappreciative). Women, on the other hand, as a result of their
socialization are more likely to attribute success to luck or to the efforts
of others while they blame themselves for failure.[39] In a battering relationship, this implies that men are likely to blame others for their problems
and to feel justified in absolving themselves of responsibility, whereas
their female partner blames herself for the beating and for violence toward
her. This is perhaps the biggest reason that feminists are critical of couples
therapy in battering situations—the therapy may well reinforce the attri-
butional processes that were so destructive in the first place. While socialization through media, toys, books, and significant others is no doubt
important in the production of what R. W. Connell calls "hegemonic masculinity" and "emphasized femininity,"[40] we need to look beyond the
production of these identities to see the reproduction of inequality that is
its outcome. The social structures in which inequality is embedded are
reproduced and reinforced by the processes that shape men and women
as "opposites," living on different sides of the gender binary and expected
to perform gender in a highly differentiated way that may feed the
potential for violence. Compulsory heterosexuality[41] easily becomes
compulsive masculinity.[42] Timothy Beneke concludes that compulsive
masculinity is inseparable from sexism, which includes the beliefs that
men are superior to women and to men who do not live up the models of
masculinity, men should not feel or express vulnerability, toughness and
domination of others are essential to masculinity, and sex is about proving
manhood and asserting power rather than about pleasure or relating.[43] The
requirement that men prove masculinity through "rehearsals of toughness,
the exploitation of women, and quick aggressive responses"[44] encourages
the same sexism that makes the world a dangerous place for women, in the
workplace, in the street, or in the family.

Despite the fairly heavy reliance on profiles of men who batter or the
depiction of them as unique psychologically, there is no universal agreement that violent men have distinctive characteristics that differentiate
them from the rest of the population.[45] Some researchers view batterers
as "normal, healthy males" who have basically the same psychological
problems as other men but lack adequate coping skills.[46] And others—in

fact, the majority of researchers until the mid-1980s—agreed that psychopathology is present in only a small percentage (10 to 20 percent) of
batterers. Such an argument is consistent with that of Susan Brownmiller
and, more recently, Scully and Marolla, who view rapists as ordinary
men using cultural justifications and stereotypical views of women, men,
and sexuality to justify their behavior rather than suffering a psychopathology.[47] Yet just as with the literature on rape, most explanations of
the batterer's behavior present him as suffering particular characteristics
that, while perhaps not reaching the level of psychopathology, certainly
distinguish his personality from others who do not batter.[48]

Reliance on profiles, lists of traits, or assessments of personalities influences the type of response made to the batterer. If the batterer is psychologically disturbed or emotionally ill, then clearly treatment is in order.
If he is a violent criminal, incarceration may be a more reasonable
response. The widespread acceptance of psychological explanations for
all sorts of social phenomena and social problems carries over into
explanations for wife battery as evidenced by O'Leary's statement,
"Because not all men batter, it is essential to look for individual differences in personality or other variables."[49] These individualistic perspectives deviantize the characteristics of men and women in abusive
relationships while not showing that they are more common in this population than in the general population.

This perspective leaves many questions unanswered. While men who
batter may be angry or jealous or immature, does that distinguish them
from other men? Clearly we are a culture that allows male anger, defining
it as an appropriate male emotion. We also define jealousy as a normal
reaction, in fact, as one that may indicate caring or love. How would either
anger or jealousy distinguish batterers from other men? Why do not all
men who are jealous or immature batter, or what are the conditions under
which they do or might do so? Why do they not batter their boss instead of
their spouse? What characteristics of culture lead them to define women
as appropriate targets? Why do some men develop such extreme hostility
toward women? Why do men feel they need to be macho? Why can they
not express their feelings? Why do they interpret frustration or agitation
as anger? Just because all men do not batter, we cannot conclude that
those who do are emotionally unique or have different personality characteristics from those who do not. Perhaps the distinction lies in situational
or subcultural factors rather than personality characteristics; perhaps it is
a matter of definition of appropriate behavior, so that what looks like jealousy on a psychological assessment is a reflection of subcultural values or
socialization rather than psychological characteristics.

Unfortunately, much of what we know about men who batter we learn from the victims, and they may well have a different view on their behavior than their partner does. The dominant model of male violence tends to ignore or minimize significant cultural, physical, economic, even situational factors shaping the "might makes right" assumptions underlying much of battery.[50]

YOU AND ME, BABE

The deficiencies of the widely accepted medical model are overcome in part by a model that takes into account the dynamic interaction between those involved in the violence rather than the individuals themselves. Rather than seeing individual characteristics, such as poor impulse control or dependency, as critical factors, the interactional model stresses the process of violence between couples, that is, the interplay between the behavior of one actor and the other. Many interactional models look at relationship dynamics and examine the interaction as a positive or negative feedback system. The underlying view is one of an organic, interconnected system in which each part has a dynamic influence on the other. From this perspective, rather than explaining battery between an immature and jealous husband who abuses a dependent and nagging wife, we see abuse as resulting from the ongoing and fluid assumptions and actions of each person as they interact with one another. Lenore Walker's work on the battered woman's syndrome is the best example of this perspective. She introduces the most influential and widely known model of wife battering, the cycle of violence model in 1979 in her pioneering book *The Battered Woman*. Although "battered woman syndrome" was first introduced in *Ibn-Tamas v. U.S.* (1979), it only became part of the public understanding of battery through Walker's work.[51] Although she does conclude that battered women and men who batter have particular characteristics, she also portrays the violence itself as a process that follows a predictable pattern. In fact, she suggests that the process of violence creates particular characteristics in the women who experience it, so that their shared characteristics result from the process of battery and violence itself rather than from childhood or other experiences. Many therapists, shelter workers, and lay people have adopted Walker's description of women who are battered as suffering from "learned helplessness," a trait she says comes directly from the battering experience.[52]

Rather than occurring at random and completely unpredictable times, Walker found in her interviews with women who were battered that violence occurred in three distinct, interrelated phases that might vary in length and duration but generally not in sequence. The first phase is the tension-building phase during which "minor" forms of battering such as throwing things, increased emotional abuse, and increased feelings of fear are typical. The woman tries to prevent the escalation of the violence, often assumes some responsibility if she is unable to do so, and engages in denial of the degree and severity of the problem, minimizing the problem and blaming outside factors, such as alcoholism or employment problems. During this phase the dynamic between the partners is one in which the man escalates his threats and efforts to gain control while the woman minimizes his potential for violence and her fear. She "walks on eggshells" so as to not "set him off," and their communication becomes increasingly nonproductive. The battered woman sees herself as powerless to do anything to stop the escalation, yet her passivity encourages the batterer to escalate. This phase may be of short duration or may last for years; many couples are adept at maintaining this phase because they want to avoid the destructive and dangerous acute phase of battering.

Eventually the woman's efforts to avoid, deny, overlook, and control the environment are not enough to prevent the escalation. It may well be that some external event or situation triggers the escalation or that the woman's coping mechanisms break down. In any case, the man becomes more volatile, critical, condemning, accusatory, and jealous, and the tension becomes almost unbearable. The acute battering phase follows. Walker portrays the batterer as out of control and extremely destructive during this phase. The couple recognizes this phase as different from the first; it is characterized by its severity and its unpredictability. The batterer is easily enraged; the woman suffers a reign of terror, usually lasting from 2 to 24 hours but sometimes for days or weeks. When the acute phase is over, it is usually followed by initial shock, denial, and disbelief on the part of both parties. They often minimize the severity and unpredictability of the attack and frequently do not seek help. Walker reports that many of the women report symptoms such as listlessness, depression, and feelings of helplessness that are similar to those of victims of catastrophe or trauma. She terms this constellation of emotions and reactions "the battered woman syndrome," a diagnosis that is fraught with controversy and difficulty.[53]

Both parties welcome the end of the second phase during which she is battered and the movement into the third phase, characterized by extremely loving, kind, and contrite behavior by the batterer. This phase begins with an unusual period of calm. The tension dissipates, and the abuser begs forgiveness, promising the violence will never happen again.

He cries, proclaiming his love, regret, and shame. He believes he can now control himself or she has "learned her lesson" and he will not "have to be" violent again. Her sense of responsibility, her guilt, and her love for him now trap her in the cycle. During this phase "her victimization becomes complete."[54] She wants to believe that she will not be abused again, and she believes that he can change. She identifies the man she loves as the man she sees during this phase, and she is convinced that he will die or become disabled without her love and support. This "honeymoon period" often does not last as long as the period of tension buildup, which begins slowly and often so insidiously that it is difficult to discern when it actually begins. Usually small incidents begin occurring—minor acts of violence, jealousy, criticism, oppression—and the cycle begins again.

The woman's lack of control over what happens to her, her inability to find a connection between her behavior and the abuse, her increasing inability to respond, and her decreasing sense of well-being culminate in an overwhelming feeling of helplessness, punctuated by reliance on different ineffective strategies to stop the violence. Walker emphasizes that the woman does not respond with total helplessness. Rather, she narrows her "choice of responses, opting for those that have the highest predictability of creating successful outcomes."[55] Walker's theories of learned helplessness and the cycle of violence focus specifically on the symbiotic relationship that develops between the batterer and the victim.

While Walker's portrayal of the abusive relationship has been widely adopted by shelter workers and almost every other expert in the area of wife battery, it is not universally applicable. This model was developed through interviews with a unique population of battered women, those who were severely abused, and it is unlikely that such a model is reflective of everyday or common couple violence. As Michael Johnson suggests,[56] a great deal of the violence that takes place between members of a couple is an escalating coproduction in which both are actively engaged in violence, albeit not as severe as the violence of which Walker writes. It is also a bit of a stretch to apply the concept of cycle of violence equally to phases that last a few hours or a couple of days and those that last years. To use the same concept in these different cases requires a very elastic, and therefore less precise, meaning of such terms as *tension buildup* or *honeymoon phase*.

Battered woman syndrome, the psychological state that results from this learned helplessness, was originally designed as a clinical diagnostic tool, but as the syndrome was gradually introduced in criminal cases of battered women who kill their abusers, it took on a different purpose and meaning and began to be used to explain how a battered woman would "reasonably" think that she was in danger of harm and thereby kill her abuser in self-defense. It usually is used when the woman admits that she killed her husband and claims it was not an accident but a form of self-defense. It has not been a particularly effective way to receive an acquittal from a jury, but has been useful during sentencing in mitigating her sentence from first-degree murder to manslaughter.[57]

There are some real problems with the battered woman syndrome that need to be addressed. First is a problem with the validity and reliability of the syndrome itself. Walker's important work on learned helplessness has provided clinicians and shelter workers, and battered women themselves, with not only a good understanding of the dynamic of the battering process but also an appreciation for why women stay in violent relationships. Yet the empirical evidence supporting the syndrome is mixed. Walker based her research on a nonrandom sample of 110 white middle-class women who had contacted social service agencies, yet the women who contact shelters or clinicians are not representative of all women who are battered. Walker's research suggests that only 65 percent of the cases she studied involved a tension-building stage, and only 58 percent were characterized by the honeymoon phase. So we can conclude that the process so often applied to an understanding of battered women's reasons for staying in these relationships, while characteristic of more than half of the women, was by no means a universal experience. As such, the experience of learned helplessness is not in fact a characteristic of all or even most battering relationships.[58] Many women do leave violent relationships or use coping mechanisms other than those outlined by Walker. However, despite the relatively modest support for battered woman syndrome, it is cited in almost every review of battery and has been fairly well accepted by the legal community. The American Psychological Association has filed amicus briefs in cases (including *State v. Kelly*, 1986), and a substantial number of courts have accepted expert testimony on the syndrome.[59]

One issue that has far-reaching consequences is whether battered women suffer a syndrome that is a diagnosable mental disorder or whether battered woman syndrome is a description of the temporary effect of abuse on a woman. Any syndrome medicalizes women, characterizing their behavior as understandable in terms of their mental condition, their unusual emotional state, rather than a reasonable response to the threat of harm they fear from their abuser. Battered woman syndrome can, unfortunately, replace other stereotypes about battered women and become a new stereotype of the "typical battered woman" that a woman needs to meet. It implies that she is "psychologically paralyzed" and suffering a psychological abnormality or disorder, supported by the fact that when this defense is used in court, psychiatrists or psychologists are those called on to testify.[60] This syndrome, used to make sense of women's response to fear and threat, reinforces stereotypes of women as weak, submissive, dependent, and passive. It thereby introduces stereotypes about appropriate or reasonable female behavior and is inherently vulnerable to class and race bias because the stereotype is not built on the everyday experiences and normal interactional styles of poor or black or other ethnic women. The battered woman syndrome defense medicalizes a response that is a reasonable form of self-defense from the woman's point of view but has not legally been viewed as self-defense. The definition of self-defense is reflective of male experience and male interaction and does not readily generalize to the experiences of women. When "self-defense" is a successful defense for murder, it results in a not-guilty verdict. The elements of this defense require the defendant to "establish that she had a reasonable apprehension of imminent death or grievous bodily harm from her partner at the time of the killing, and that further, the force she used to repel the threat was a reasonable and necessary response."[61] The elements of "imminent danger" and the requirement of "proportionate response" are particularly difficult for women who kill their batterers because they do not reflect the circumstances in which they are likely to kill. Historically, self-defense has referred to two types of circumstances: a situation in which a man is suddenly attacked by a stranger or intruder or a situation in which a dispute or argument between two men "gets out of hand." These requirements of "sudden" and "stranger" obviously disqualify the battered woman from the first circumstance. She usually has been beaten on a continuous basis by an intimate. Further, the situation preceding the killing is often not one in which an argument gets out of hand. Rather, there is likely to be a history of violence or abuse in which the immediate incident is the last straw. She knows her attacker intimately and knows the history of their relationship and that he will batter her again. Perhaps she fears that he will in fact kill her the next time. She kills within the context of protecting herself from a future attack.

Is this behavior reasonable? Is the fact that she felt unable to escape danger and possible death less justifiable as self-defense than had she felt an immediate threat? Does feeling trapped by a force beyond her control, one that threatens her life, seem to justify killing in self-defense? Why is the cumulative impact of battery not as powerful legally as the impact of one situation? The battered woman kills her batterer because she feels nothing short of that will protect her from further harm. Her actions, however, are unlikely to meet the criteria of self-defense because she could have left the situation that posed immediate danger, that is, she did not kill in the heat of the moment and could have responded in a less harsh manner. The *R. v. Duffy* decision provides a good example of the problems a battered woman would face using self-defense as a defense for murdering her batterer. In Duffy, a woman killed her abusive husband while he slept, after a brutal quarrel. She was convicted of murder, and her appeal, based in part on the trial judge's description of "provocation" to the jury, was rejected. The judge defined provocation as an act, or series of acts, that "would cause any reasonable person, and actually causes in the accused, a sudden and temporary loss of self-control, rendering the accused so subject to passion as to make him or her for the moment not master of his mind."[62] The judge further established time as an important factor, indicating that the further removed an incident is from the crime, the less it counts. The requirement of immediacy is damaging to women, but by the same token, if a woman introduces the impact of cumulative violence, she runs the risk of being guilty of an even more serious offense, a "revenge killing."

The development of syndromes to make explicable the behavior of women who are raped, or battered women who kill their husbands, is situated in the more general climate of the increasing medicalization of social problems during the past century. Any number of problems that in the past were defined as evolving from sin or evil have been transformed into the result of sicknesses over which the individual has no control.[63] There is a dark side to the supposed progress science and medicine have brought, as Conrad and Schneider point out, including the consequence that medicalizing and then treating a problem on an individual level allows a particular segment of the community an enormous amount of power over the individual and over public perceptions and definitions of a problem and its causes.[64] Further, a medicalized approach removes our critical analysis from the structures that provide the context for the problem and from the importance and power of such phenomena as sexism, racism, and poverty as significant causes of the problem being addressed. This is as true of other forms of violence in the family as it is of wife battery. Incest, a crime that requires a gendered analysis rather than one focusing only on individual characteristics, provides an illustration of the medicalization of deviance and offers a clear example of the involvement of interest groups in the construction of deviance.

INCEST: THE MEDICALIZATION OF SEXUAL ASSAULT AGAINST CHILDREN

The transformation of incest over the years from a felony offense to a form of misdemeanor child abuse, accompanied by a change in the official reaction from incarceration to treatment, provides another clear example of the reliance on the medicalization of social problems. Incest emerged as a significant problem on the heels of the recognition of child abuse. When mandatory reporting laws for child abuse were established in the mid-1960s, it became clear that incest was a significant problem. The response on the part of the public was outrage, and the perpetrators were generally defined as the worst type of criminal—one even other criminals placed at the bottom of the barrel. However, consistent with the expanding embrace of medicalized explanations for all manner of social problems, incest was also transformed from "sin" to "sickness" by professionals and lawmakers, who adopted a sickness model for this offense. This transformation was easy to follow in Nevada, where during one legislative session, incest became not just a sickness rather than a crime, but a family sickness rather than one afflicting only the perpetrator.[65] A historical review provides details on the claims-making process that transformed sexual assault or rape to incest.

In Nevada, a legislative subcommittee chaired by a pediatrician was established to investigate the extent of the problem of incest and to fashion a response. The committee held hearings and took testimony primarily from social workers but also from police and some physicians. The definition of the problem on the part of the social workers was based on the very popular work of Henry Giarretto, whose model had served as the foundation for incest treatment programs throughout the neighboring state of California.[66] His family systems model viewed the family in which incest occurred as deeply dysfunctional. His view was that all members of the family were sick and that each needed to take responsibility for his or her role in the incest. Incest was neither a crime nor a problem of the perpetrator alone; the daughter had to look at her own behavior, to see how she contributed to the problem, and the mother had to acknowledge her causal role.

While it is clear that social workers and the state and private agencies for whom they worked (what Becker called "moral entrepreneurs"[67]) did have an individualistic perspective on incest, they also had a great deal to gain by a definition of the perpetrator (and the entire family) as sick rather than criminal. Their professional status and their financial situations would be improved by such a redefinition, and they were eager lobbyists. Because of their professional identities, they were not viewed as having a personal stake in the definitional process, and their expert testimony was convincing, particularly to a committee consisting primarily of laypersons. Police and prosecuting attorneys, on the other hand, were unconvincing advocates for the position that incest was a crime and should be treated as such. They were seen as rigid and unprogressive, and found themselves in the distinct minority.

These "claims makers" who espoused a medical definition of what they determined was a sickness consistently supported therapeutic intervention and treatment programs rather than incarceration for incest perpetrators.[68] One social worker asserted, "Unless it is very severe, throwing a parent in jail is about the worst thing you can do—we need the family in treatment." Lengthy therapy was seen as essential to treat the "fragile self-concept" of the perpetrator and victim alike. One therapist reflected the agency view succinctly when she said that "the perpetrator of sexual abuse commits the ultimate act of self-mutilation." These therapists in fact showed much more sympathy for the perpetrator than for the mother of the incest victim. This was because the father admitted he was responsible—his confession a requirement to be accepted into the diversion program. The mothers, on the other hand, were resistant to the demand that they accept responsibility for their role in the incest. They were likely to be viewed as recalcitrant angry, or "in denial."[69]

The view of incest that was codified in law by the establishment of diversion programs for incest perpetrators limited the understanding of the dynamic of incest significantly. Of course, the previous definition of incest as a crime had not been terribly cognizant of social or cultural factors either. But with medicalization, with the acceptance of this individualistic model, the impact of sexism or misogyny could be ignored completely, while all attention turned to the psychological problems of the perpetrator and the other family members. Focus was diverted from the hierarchical structure of the family that gave power over the wife and children to the father and from the cultural definition of females as sexual objects. One need not ask, "Why the daughter rather than the little girls down the street?" or wonder why so many perpetrators were men and so many victims were girls by focusing instead on "sickness." Basically, all of the important structural factors tied to class, race, gender, and the cultural factors related to the oppression of girls and women remained invisible, while therapists probed the psyches of the perpetrator and their equally sick coparticipants. Further, the implicit assumptions of moral equivalency neutralized the deviance of the father and erased the distinction between the man who violated his daughter's body and her trust, and the daughter herself, in a complete denial of reality.

CODEPENDENCE: THE ENABLING WIFE

Another example of medicalization, embedded in the addiction literature and the addiction industry, is codependence or enabling. We have all heard the jokes and stories about the man whose wife drove him to drink and about the alcoholic who relied on the bottle to escape his wife's interminable nagging. Decades after Alcoholics Anonymous (AA) had its first meeting, such terms as alcoholic, enabling, and denial have become part of our everyday language. Wives who attended Al-Anon meetings to help them cope with their alcoholic husbands learned about their contribution to their husband's addiction through their own "enabling" behavior. During the 1970s, this enabling behavior was joined by other traditionally feminine characteristics to create the all-encompassing disease of "codependence." The definitions of codependence generally center around "ill-health or maladaptive, problematic or dysfunctional behavior that is associated with living, working with or otherwise being close to a person with alcoholism" or with letting "another person's behavior affect him or her ... obsessed with controlling that person's behavior."[70]

Usually the term codependent applies to wives and other family members related to the person identified with the problem. It is identified as a medical disease, as serious as dependence, and treatable, sometimes even requiring in-patient treatment. Behavior on the part of wives that had been viewed as appropriate or "wifely" during the 1950s and 1960s came to be redefined as "enabling" during the 1970s and 1980s, reflective of a "primary disease ... which is often worse than alcoholism itself (and which) has its own physical manifestations and is a treatable diagnostic entity."[71] An entire cottage industry of self-help books provided ways to identify the problem of codependency and to get help to overcome it. Black, Wegscheider-Cruse, and Beattie, in their books *It Will Never Happen to Me* and *Codependent No More*, among others, introduced codependency as an illness suffered by people closely associated with alcoholics and others with destructive dependencies and addiction, and they promised recovery through therapy, often through the incorporation of 12-step programs similar to those in AA. These authors view codependency as an objective condition characterized by a wide array of symptoms, ranging all the way from headaches to suicide.[72] The "disorder" has been embraced within the wide arms of psychotherapy, with Cermack, for example, identifying it as a "mixed personality disorder that can be manifested symptomatically as depression, anxiety disorder, hysterical personality disorder, dependent personality disorder or borderline condition" and suggesting that the illness should be included in the DSM (Diagnostic Statistical Manual) used by all psychologists and psychiatrists. Some suggest that the codependent is actually more psychologically damaged than the addict and requires longer and more extensive (and more expensive) treatment.[73]

Codependency has merged in the popular and professional literature with other loosely defined "addictions," such as love addiction, relationship addiction, sex addiction, shopping addiction, and work addiction, all of which are linked by their roots in the "dysfunctional family." The dysfunctional family is often, but not necessarily, characterized by alcoholism and its attendant problems of secrecy, denial, and skewed communication patterns. Therapists and others who write about this addiction explain that all members of the family participate in and are victimized by the disease. This view of the dysfunctional family matches the definition of the "incest family" in almost every way. The view of the family as dysfunctional reflects the stance of neutrality adopted by therapists who diffuse the responsibility for any problem, from incest to shoplifting, to all members of the family. In the literature on codependence, the person identified with the problem virtually disappears, and our sights are trained on the codependent—the enabling wife, the absent wife, the unaffectionate wife, the wife with low self-esteem.[74]

Just as with incest, in the case of codependence, the underlying assumption is one of moral equivalency and shared responsibility, so that the mother who was at work is equally culpable with the father who insisted that his daughter fellate him; the woman who tries to keep the family together is as responsible as the man who blows his paycheck every week and ends up in his own vomit on the front lawn. These labels deviantize women and medicalize them, making them vulnerable to condemnation as well as to intervention. This process of transforming a woman into a codependent, responsible for either her own abuse or the violence of her husband, is the result of a convolution of the illness metaphor and the labeling process.[75] Normal, expected behavior—behavior that is traditionally demanded of women, especially wives—becomes redefined as pathological, and women are encouraged, especially in the most frequently offered forms of therapy, to view themselves and their behavior as aberrant. Normal feminine identity, based on caretaking and resulting from traditional gender socialization, is pathologized.[76]

Not all efforts to understand deviance rely on the medicalization perspective. William Goode's exchange theory as applied to child abuse and wife battery focuses on the family, power, and the state.[77] This perspective asserts that within a social system, such as the family, or an economic system, the greater the resources a person commands, the greater is that person's potential for force. However, the more resources the person commands, the less likely that person is to feel it is necessary to use force because the institutional support underlying the potential for force is so strong. For example, if the state solidly supports a man's authority and power over his children, he is less likely to have to use force to achieve his ends. When his authority is challenged or unsupported by the state, he is likely to rely on force to achieve his goals because his authority is not taken for granted. That is, all social systems, including the family, rest on force or the threat of force. Whether the person actually deploys force depends on the degree to which his position of authority is supported or challenged. This perspective suggests that as women gain more power and develop economic and social choices, men may be more likely to use force to reestablish their position of power in the family. The research that finds that women who have left an abusive man or have filed for divorce are most vulnerable to violence or death supports this perspective; the man can be viewed as relying on force because his underlying social status is threatened. This perspective would also suggest that violence against women is more likely to occur in lower classes in which male dominance is challenged or threatened by unemployment or racism. It assumes that men have power and authority, that this is supported by the social system, and that when this support crumbles, men use force as a resource to regain their position of privilege, never questioning the initial achievement of this position of privilege.

In 1973, Murray Straus introduced a general systems theory (which is not to be confused with family systems theory).[78] Straus views the family as a "purposive, goal-seeking, adaptive social system." Violence is viewed as a system product or output rather than an individual pathology. He specified that feedback in the system can create an upward spiral of violence or maintain or reduce the level of violence depending on the type of feedback. In a comprehensive, all-inclusive incorporation of almost every factor imaginable, Straus outlines structural factors, social and cultural, and interactional factors such as stress and isolation and various precipitating events and the relationships among them, which can escalate or de-escalate violence in the family. When a number of these factors operate on the individual at the same time, one can anticipate violence. This theory differs dramatically from family systems theory; it includes structural factors such as racism, poverty, and oppression, as well as interactional and individual factors. Perhaps the very breadth of this model makes it somewhat cumbersome and unwieldy, but it does bridge the individual level of analysis with the interactional and more structural levels.

A number of other theorists see the family unit or the couple, rather than the individual, as the analytical unit. A family systems model of violence against women, or children for that matter, stresses not the individual, the family structure, or authority patterns but the dynamic relationship between each person in the relationship and their role in escalating the violence. Psychologist Henry Giarretto's influential, and misogynist, model of father-daughter incest served as the model for treatment programs all over the country during the 1980s and 1990s and had a dramatic impact on the lives of tens of thousands of women and girls.[79] In his therapy centers, Giarretto went to great lengths to convince the wife of the perpetrator and the daughter who was the victim of incest of their contribution to the problem. The father was viewed as only one part of a sick system, not necessarily more responsible than anyone else for the incest that occurred. In one illustration, Giarretto demonstrates the dynamic of the dysfunctional family in incest cases by describing a relationship in which the mother finally recognizes that if she had stayed home more, rather than attending night school, the sexual abuse of her daughter would probably not have occurred. I interviewed a number of therapists whose devotion to Giarretto's model was illustrated by their almost cloying appreciation of "my dads," men who were in diversion programs for incest, and their contempt for the mothers who they viewed as "in denial" about their role in the incest.[80]

This view of the "incest family" was easily applied to an analysis of the "battering relationship," switching the focus to each person's participation in maintaining the sickness. The therapeutic goal, based on this analysis of equal responsibility, is generally to save the relationship through altering the response patterns of each person, particularly their expectations and the way they communicate with one another, insisting that each partner has to change to achieve a peaceful relationship. This approach absolves the batterer of his responsibility and places the woman who is battered in the position of being required to make adjustments in order to avoid a beating. The goal of saving a marriage, particularly an abusive marriage, is questionable, reflecting biases that may be dangerous to the woman who seeks help. Furthermore, the therapy process itself can be dangerous, placing the batterer and the battered woman in the same physical space, maintaining the fiction of equality, and implicitly supporting the batterer's position, which is already likely to be one of woman blaming, by insisting that the woman share responsibility for her battery. In addition, imposing a definition of the situation as "therapeutic" conceals the fact that one person is the aggressor and one is the victim. Focus on the "dysfunctional family" or the "battering relationship" also avoids any analysis of patriarchy, sexism, oppositional constructions of gender, economic inequality, or oppression. The family is viewed as an isolated feedback system in which each person makes an equal contribution to the relationship problem, and each person needs to change in order to create a more functional, harmonious, and communicative relationship.[81] To pretend that men and women are equal economically or that sexist expectations for men and women are not important factors in battery is ludicrous. The family is not separable from either the culture or the economic system within which it is situated, and problems experienced in the family must be linked to their position in the wider system.

Numerous theorists and therapists challenge family therapists' responses to women who are battered and insist that therapists must stop colluding with the abuser by ignoring the misuse of power. They must name the abuse and name the abuser. To do otherwise is to continue to violate those with less power and to reinforce the batterer's belief that violence is not really *his* problem.[82] Gus Kaufman insists that males who batter do not have a problem with impulse control or anger, and to encourage them to work on their anger in fact legitimizes their use of anger as an excuse.[83] He concludes that men batter and use other power and control tactics because they have learned to, because it accomplishes the desired results, and because they can, with few consequences. Not only do men who batter use their anger and power to oppress women, therapists often collude with the batterer to mystify the oppression of women. That is, they are likely to assume the legitimacy of the perspective presented by the dominant partner and to devalue that of the woman. Therapists reflect the victim blaming of our culture by identifying with the batterer because he dominates the conversation, has higher status, and it is safer and more comfortable to do so than to identify with the more powerless victim. When therapists agree to keep the batterer's crime private, to explain "the situation" as resulting from intrapsychic characteristics or communication problems or unhealthy couples' dynamics, they deny women's oppression. Therapists are reluctant to challenge the norm of male control and male privilege for fear of being attacked or of losing some of their heterosexist and class privilege.[84] These issues of male control and power, and a therapeutic system that implicitly supports them by focusing on communication and relationship and anger control problems, must be addressed by therapists.[85]

Another perspective that provides useful insight into a battering relationship, particularly in response to the central questions "Why does he do it?" and "Why does she stay?," is exchange theory. While this perspective does not answer all the questions, it does provide a tool for understanding what may seem like very confusing behavior, and understanding it in terms of the people as they are situated in their relationship, and the relationship as it is situated in the broader economic and social context. An exchange-theoretical approach is basically an economic model of costs and benefits asserting that behavior that is too costly compared with the rewards it provides is likely to be discontinued, but behavior that is rewarding, especially compared with its costs, is likely to be continued.[86] This approach assumes that people conduct an informal reward-cost analysis of their behavior or their relationships and engage in, continue, or cease particular behaviors as a result of that analysis. They rely on standards of comparison that may be cultural or familial and also rely on a comparison of the alternatives to their situation in making their decision. This perspective suggests that men batter because it pays off, just as Kaufman suggested; men get the results they want at relatively low cost.[87] Women may stay in a relationship because although it is costly, it provides more rewards than they would have if they left (i.e., economic or social rewards), and the cost of staying is less than the cost of leaving. Women get a number of rewards from being married in addition to economic ones, including status, security, and a sense that they are fulfilling their feminine destiny. One difficulty with exchange theory, however, is that while it may provide an *ex post facto* sense of understanding, it is tautological and relatively useless in predicting behavior. If one stays in a battering relationship, then we assume she assesses staying as less costly than leaving; if she leaves, we conclude that leaving was less costly than staying. Nevertheless, this perspective provides a valuable analytical language from which we can make sense of behavior that may seem strange without relying on intrapsychic explanations or sickness models.

Another theoretical perspective that provides some insight into the greater incidence of violence against women in some social classes and groups than others focuses on subcultural values. The subculture of violence theory generally asserts that in a multicultural, complex society, certain subcultures develop norms and values that justify and encourage the use of violence to a greater degree and at a higher level than is acceptable in the larger, dominant society.[88] When applied to battery, this theory suggests that particular subcultures may be more "macho" than others, justifying male dominance and legitimating battery, while simultaneously limiting women in ways that make them particularly vulnerable. Further, this perspective would suggest that some subcultural values such as machismo or hypermasculinity render violence against women and couple violence more acceptable than among white middle-class groups and reflect a normal interaction rather than violence.[89]

One can immediately see the fallout from such a perspective. In a society that is committed to the ideological position of "melting pot" and warmly embraces the ideology of classlessness and equality, the assertion that behavior varies by subculture rings racist or "classist." When we discuss this relationship between social class or race, and wife battery or other forms of violence in my classes, students are very uncomfortable with acknowledging the power of race and class. Rather, they explain the differences in terms of reporting rates and response rates. While the poor in this country have much less privacy and have many fewer options and are indeed more likely to be arrested or charged with violent crimes, this does not negate differences in values, life experiences, or situations that influence behavior. We are very reluctant to discuss or even acknowledge class or race as significant influences in our lives, when in fact it is undeniable that they powerfully shape every aspect of our lives. Of course, multicultural feminists are not to be included here. This feminist position theorizes the power of social location on identity and experience, and emphasizes difference, particularly in analyzing relations between privileged women and those on the margins.[90]

One risk of attributing different levels of violence against women to subcultural values is that it may justify ignoring this violence, excusing inaction on the basis of "that's the way those people are." Police may use subcultural values as a justification for nonintervention or for not pursuing a complaint, and district attorneys and others in the justice system may follow suit. Hence, a poor black woman is likely to have less protection from the state than does a middle-class white woman based on these assumptions about her culture. In my research on legal responses to rape, I was struck by a black woman's assertion that when she reported being raped, the police responded, "It was a gang thing and if I didn't want to get raped I shouldn't hang around gang members."[91]

Further, a subcultural approach ignores the systemic structural inequality of women and places attention on particular out-groups that are seen as deviant or exceptional. If we can explain violence against Hispanic women as reflective of the machismo of Hispanic culture, then we can minimize white middle-class male violence against wives. Relying on a subcultural explanation may well thwart efforts to intervene because the problem is attributed to particular psychological characteristics or personality attributes resulting from membership in a subculture, thereby leaving relatively powerless people even more powerless.

In another way, however, this perspective is sensitizing. We are not a homogeneous society; rather, we are honeycombed with race, class, gender, ethnic, and cultural differences. We learn the values of our culture and subculture through our early experiences in the family, and these values are embedded in our perception of the world and expressed in our behavior toward others. If subcultural values are of any importance, we cannot expect them not to influence our perception of masculinity and femininity, of relationships, of family, and of acceptable ways to express anger or resolve arguments.

THE CENTRALITY OF CULTURE

The perspectives on violence against women can be more useful if we acknowledge that they emerge from cultural assumptions. The individualistic perspectives or those that are more interactional cannot be viewed as self-contained but rather are emergent from the broader cultural assumptions in which practitioners, theorists, and clinicians are situated. The violence is linked with cultural beliefs and ideas that define men and women as different and reflects the socialization of male and female children into different identities with the expectation that they occupy different positions in the gender hierarchy. This differential socialization is based on cultural values and beliefs about men and women and their relationships, and it reinforces these same values and beliefs. This reproduction of gender inequality is generated through everyday, subtle, invisible, and powerful interactions and expectations. The seemingly innocuous rewards and punishments meted out for particular behaviors are not simply reflections of gender inequality but implicitly and explicitly reproduce and normalize it. These practices are reflective of cultural beliefs and values, "taken for granted" ideas and understandings that are consistent with, and reinforcing of, structural inequality. Cultural traditions that portray women as molded of finer clay, as passive and nurturing, and that portray men as autonomous, decisive, and aggressive, are values that are built into the socialization and educational processes that middle-class males and females experience that are then taken for granted as natural expressions of sex. When women serve as the object on whom the honor of the entire family rests, as in Pakistan or Afghanistan, for example, both women and men learn to condemn any sign of individuality or autonomy exhibited by women and to normalize complete male authority. In the United States, little girls are socialized to play with dolls and stoves, boys with guns and cars; girls learn to be nice and cooperative and to get along, and boys learn to stand out and to win. Parents and other socializing agents, such as music, children's books and stories, and advertising, reinforce these early socialization differences and lead to the normalization of a relationship of inequality between men and women, integrating their assumed differences into a coherent whole. Media messages reinforce this difference as the natural reflection of male superiority and female subjugation, of masculinity as privilege and femininity as degradation. This is particularly dangerous for women because whether she conforms to the expectation of docility and dependence, or whether she rejects these expectations for individuality and independence, she places herself at risk—whether she reinforces male superiority or challenges it, she stands to lose. Talcott

Parson's view of the family, built on the notion that the woman needed to be the socio-emotional leader and the man to be the instrumental leader, one to maintain the home and be responsible for the family and one to bridge the space between family and the economic and political world, was consistent with differential socialization of males and females.[92] Christopher Lasch's view in *Haven in a Heartless World* that the family was suffering from the intrusion of experts and the erosion of the authority of the father also supported the view of natural masculine authority and natural female subservience, a situation that, if maintained, led to happy and healthy children, and if disrupted by outside experts, led to the eventual destruction of the family.[93]

The focus on culture provides valuable insight into the expectations for males and females that might contribute to violence against women, in the home or on the street. Catherine Itzin asserts that "women are conditioned to conform to the stereotyped images of femininity and womanhood in such a way that they are often unaware that they are misrepresented or mistreated."[94] Mary Pipher, in her widely discussed book *Reviving Ophelia*, provides a similar assessment of the damage girls experience as a result of their socialization: "America today is a girl destroying place. Everywhere girls are encouraged to sacrifice their true selves."[95] And women of color are in double jeopardy, receiving messages of both race and gender inferiority. As Joy Peach points out in *Women in Culture*, images of black and Native women are constructed in contrast to images of white women. Women of color are exempted from the range of images applied to white women and instead are dichotomized; Pocahontas, for example, is either the "good princess" or the "bad squaw."[96] The negative images and stereotypes of women have changed little as a result of the women's movement. Black women were either castrating bitches or good sisters in the 1960s and 1970s, and now, except in rap music, where they are mostly bitches and "hos," are "trichotomized" as matriarch, drug addict, or lazy welfare queen. Women's diminished economic status and political power is submerged in the "natural choices" they make to stay home and have children, for example, or their choice to become a teacher rather than a physicist because that occupation better accommodates family needs. Women's choice to stay in a battering environment or return to their batterer is inseparable from their socialization to dependency, or their dominant identity as a wife and mother, or from the economic reality they encounter when trying to both work and raise a family. This doesn't mean women cannot leave, but it does mean that leaving takes place within a complex circumstance of conflicting and powerful forces. The cultural approach to understanding battery places heavy emphasis on constructions of femininity and masculinity and the expected relationships between men and women, as well as the consequences of cultural demands for both men and women. While acknowledging grand-scale differences between cultures, this perspective also recognizes that cultures within one geographic boundary are not homogeneous. For example, the impact of the ideology of sexism confronts women of color differently than it does white women and elicits a different response from within an entirely different context. Sexism suffered by white women is built on the edifice of race privilege so dominant that the connection with women of color is sometimes obscured. For example, bell hooks contends that white women built the feminist movement on the backs of black women and are heavily invested in the maintenance of racist structures, a point about which there is not universal agreement,[97] while Audre Lorde criticizes the women's movement and its definition of sisterhood by pointing out that white feminists ignore the implicit privilege of whiteness and therefore define women in terms of their own experiences that do not represent those of black women.[98] If Lugones and Spelman are correct, and we speak from our own particular social locations, then we can predict that those on the "outside" are unlikely to be represented accurately or included in the representations of those at the center.[99] The "white women's movement" was a reflection of the relative leisure and privilege of those women who started it, and for whom the impetus may have been very different than it would have been for those less privileged. Yet their successful demands for equal pay, equal rights, equal access, women's right to control their own bodies, and their assessment of the institutional sexism inherent in marriage, education, and the workplace were as beneficial to poor women, women of color, and other women at the margins as they were to those more privileged.

Kimberly Crenshaw focuses more on the particular ways in which black women's experience is not taken into account in the analysis of or response to black women who are battered. Black women have, since the black power movement, been encouraged to put black men first, in part because they have been so degraded by the white male system, but this means that there are impediments to them acknowledging and reporting battery by a black partner. Further, she says, the shelter movement and the agency responses are built around assumptions of whiteness and privilege and are not responsive to black women's particular life circumstances.[100] Crenshaw's position is supported by Potter who calls for a criminology that foregrounds race along with gender and recognizes that black women's experiences with intimate partner abuse are embedded in a social system that is very different from that white women experience, requiring the reporting and response to be seen within that framework.[101] Despite the extreme danger women face in many cultures, there is hesitance to define the dangerous practices (infibulation, femicide, isolation, ritual rape) as violence or crimes against women for fear that we will be self-righteously imposing ethnocentric norms from Western industrialized countries on other cultures. Over 80 million girls, particularly in the Middle East, Africa, and Southeast Asia, have been the victims of genital mutilation. Women in Iran are beaten to death for suspected adultery. Women in Pakistan have acid thrown in their faces by spurned suitors, and female infants in India are quietly killed by the midwife who delivered them. To name these as cultural variations and thereby withdraw judgment from them is to support the continued oppression of women. Yet the notion of cultural relativity does just that, and the view that certain behaviors are simply characteristic of certain subcultures or cultures reinforces our avoidance of significant human rights problems. Social science with its emphasis on value neutrality, has contributed to the silence of researchers about the oppression of women worldwide, whether we are talking about infanticide in China, the malnutrition of girls in India, or the oppression of women in Afghanistan under the Taliban. Some are even reluctant to intervene in the cultural practice of female "circumcision" among immigrant groups in the United States, although current estimates are that about 10,000 girls in the United States are at risk each year.[102] Only in March 1997 did female genital mutilation become illegal in the United States. Cultural values and perceptions, when internalized by women and incorporated into the everyday practices of teachers, parents, employers, and lawmakers, legitimate the oppression of women and present their victimization as ordinary, natural, and deserved.

THE STRUCTURAL FOUNDATIONS OF VIOLENCE AGAINST WOMEN

The cultural understandings and the specific perspectives they generate are necessarily situated in the social institutions and structures of society. This is why cultural explanations alone are inadequate and why it is important to see the convergence between legal and political systems and culture. Violence against women is located in the institutions of the family, the economy, education, and politics. Each of these institutions reinforces the other, and together they maintain a system in which men have power and privilege over women. Although the degree of power and privilege men have may vary by race and social class, the ascendancy of male power is undisputed. As Allan Johnson points out in *The Gender Knot,* the fact that so many men do not feel privileged in patriarchy does not contradict its existence.[103] Rather, it reveals the hierarchical nature of a system in which only a few men can conform to the hegemonic ideal, leaving the rest to occupy inferior rungs on the privilege ladder that characterizes the patriarchal system. Further, as is painfully clear in the cases of "blaming the victim" of honor crimes, rape, harassment, or job discrimination, patriarchy is indeed, not a He, a Them, or an US—it is a system in which women participate fully.[104]

While it may be therapeutically useful, or enlightening, for us to understand the faults and foibles of individuals involved in violence or to understand the battering process, this is far from adequate. If we are to understand the basis for the many forms of violence women suffer throughout the world and have any hope of ameliorating the violence, a perspective that analyzes the underlying structural supports of violence against women must be assumed, particularly because so many forms of violence against women are increasing rather than diminishing. The elimination of violence against women requires the destruction of the hierarchy in which men have greater power and privilege than women and in which women see this inequality as natural and right. The institutions of work and family operate together to increase the vulnerability of women to violence in both institutions. In the family, because women are primarily the caretakers and because the socialization they experience prepares them with qualities useful for this activity but not as helpful for participation in the competitive work world, women often depend emotionally on men and the family for their identity and financially on men for their survival. Because they are defined as caretakers and not primarily as workers, they are likely to experience the types of problems in the workplace that increase their vulnerability—lower wages, fewer promotions, and sexual harassment.

Men's dominance over women and their ability to control women have been translated into laws, policies, and cultural messages that reinforce and legitimate this control. Men make the laws and the laws reflect their position of privilege, just as do the media images and expectations in the workplace and family that provide the context within which those laws are made. Men, because of historical factors, such as size and the fact that they do not become pregnant, have achieved dominance and created the social, economic, and political infrastructure to maintain that power. Women are not in the position to have their perceptions of reality accepted as normal or valid by others or, often, by themselves. Instead, they are quite likely to adopt the dominant system views of them and their behavior, a male-constructed view reflective of male power and control, and in so doing they suffer "false consciousness" and the powerlessness it breeds. Women may, for example, blame themselves for being raped or for being abused, accepting stereotypes and myths about their behavior or demeanor as having caused their victimization. Women who have been victimized by corporations through breast implants, diethylstilbestrol (DES), or the Dalkon Shield blame themselves for their "stupidity" and their "carelessness," just as others blame them. They may accept the justifications for their lower wages or limitations in the workplace by embracing the seductive language of "choice" when in fact their inequality is a reflection of the confluence of structural constraints and gender socialization that disadvantage them.

Male domination explains the historical and cross-cultural pattern of violence toward women. Women who are oppressed under the Taliban in Afghanistan are not oppressed because of some quirk of their husband's personality but because they have no power to resist the definitions imposed on them by the male-controlled structure. By the same token, women who are victims of rape in the United States are not raped because they are suffering from some syndrome such as "self-defeating personality disorder" or because some man has some unresolved issues with his domineering mother. Rather, they are victims of rape because of the definitions of femininity and masculinity and because of gendered power relations that encourage and legitimate male dominance and female submissiveness.

It is of little value to develop new therapeutic techniques to use with men who batter or new treatments for codependence or low self-esteem for women who find their way to shelters. Women will be free from systematic violence when they have power and that power is institutionalized; when women make laws that reflect their reality; when women have the right to personal integrity and control over their bodies and their lives; when women define their own values; and when they are not dependent on being chosen by a man in marriage in order to live comfortably or to survive.

The concentration on institutional discrimination against women and structural oppression of women is compatible with placing patriarchy at the center of women's oppression and the violence they suffer. Patriarchy is a "sexual system of power in which the male possesses superior power and economic privilege."[105] It is an "autonomous social, historical, and political force,"[106] transcending particular economic systems as well as race.[107] It is, to be sure, expressed differently in different contexts, so it is not possible to overlay analysis of gender relations in the West on those in the Third World/South. Chandra Mohanty articulates this best: "Patriarchal and racist relations and structures that accompany capital" are most visible and their power most keenly felt as they are expressed in the lives of marginalized, indigenous communities.[108] Those relations must be assessed in their own context, where they are most visible. This is not to say that patriarchy is not expressed differently in different systems, nor would one suggest that race and class are not intricately meshed with patriarchy in creating the life conditions of women and men. But it does privilege patriarchy, as a more fundamental cause of women's oppression than economic conditions or race. Women's oppression comes not just from capitalism as it is expressed through masculinist, racist global politics; their oppression is universal.

R. Emerson Dobash and Russell Dobash situate the violence against women in patriarchy and see these same values incorporated in the institutions and agencies that are organized to help solve the problem.[109] The late Mary Daly, a philosopher at Boston College, was probably the most unyielding and creative proponent of a radical feminist perspective that presents the interplay between patriarchy and structure as a system that maintains and justifies violence against women.[110] In *Gyn/ecology, Beyond God the Father* and numerous articles, she weaves a tale of unremitting male oppression of women through culture, religion, therapy, heterosexuality, and every other component of culture and social structure. Footbinding, genital mutilation, bride burning, witch hunts, and rape, as well as the values and myths on which they are built, are clear reflections of patriarchy, male superiority, and the oppression of women.

The feminist legal scholar Catharine MacKinnon, known to many for her almost successful efforts with Andrea Dworkin to prohibit pornography in Minneapolis during the 1970s, sees male control of women's sexuality as the core fact in the domination of women. Through rape, sexual harassment, pornography, and violence against lesbians, men exercise their domination of women. Heterosexuality is, for MacKinnon, the systematic male oppression of women.[111] While radical feminist theorists acknowledge the importance of class, race, and economy, they also see that women are oppressed in a wide range of economies and in many different class and race structures, and assert that the destruction of a capitalist economy will not result in the elimination of the oppression of women. Women's oppression is built on ideology, on assumptions of male superiority, on male privilege and power, and is universal. Marxism and other theories based on ownership and economics alone fail, from this perspective, to explain the continuing oppression of women in varied economic structures and do not adequately address the emergence and perpetuation of patriarchy.

Some theorists who place great emphasis on patriarchy nevertheless criticize the reliance on patriarchy to the exclusion of class and race differences.[112] While they may agree that all women are victimized by patriarchy, they are critical of the failure of theories of patriarchy to distinguish the impact of race and class as they operate together in systems of oppression. They are also critical of universalizing woman, expanding Western conceptions of gendered oppression on non-Western countries, basically privileging gender over race or class or the power of colonization. Patricia Hill-Collins's analysis of the intersections of race, class, and gender, points to the integration of these qualities as they determine the experience of the individual. We live in a social structure that is raced, classed, and gendered, and these factors come together in a "matrix of domination" that significantly disadvantages those who are "other" in a white male privilege system. It is the historical development of male ownership and control and the ideologies and laws that men have created to maintain that control.

The perspectives presented in this chapter appear again in the following chapters, often as means for the analysis of the topic being discussed, sometimes contrasted with one another for clarity. They are lenses that help us focus. We carry them either implicitly or explicitly, and the way we apply them determines the analysis, even the perception, of a social problem as well as its solution. These perspectives are not equally valuable in clarifying the reasons for violence against women; rather, those that acknowledge the power of institutions, of class, of male historical privilege translated into laws and policies and the impact of these structural elements on the interaction and the individual take us the furthest toward understanding violence against women. These cultural and structural perspectives are the most difficult to apply to everyday services or programs. They do not translate easily into new policies and procedures but call for deep structural changes that are likely to be slow in coming and fiercely resisted. Perhaps this helps explain the preeminence of individualistic solutions despite their questionable value. One can see an impact, no matter how small it is.

THE VIOLENCE AGAINST WOMEN INDUSTRY

The clearest and most dramatic indicator of change in the social and political response to wife battery and family violence is the growth of what can be called the family violence and violence against women industry. As a result of the hard fights and successes of feminist and other activists for women, the number of professionals and volunteers working in the area of violence against women grew, and eventually there were hundreds of thousands of people working with battered women and their children, as well as batterers, depending on this work for their own survival. The interest in rape remained strong as well, and feminists drew the attention of the public and lawmakers to other forms of violence against women, including marital rape and the "marital exception" that existed in most states, leaving women vulnerable to rape by their husbands. The construction of rape so that it was no longer a dark-alley act committed by a stranger but something that happened on a date, or after having a drink with a coworker, or at home in the marital bed, called for a reassessment of the cause of the problem. Acquaintance rape or date rape and the entire continuum of violence against women, including violent imagery in pornography and sexual harassment, were exposed, and the relationships between these seemingly discrete acts were analyzed as reflections of a structure that was hostile to women. This expansion of the area of violence against women called for increasing numbers of professionals and researchers, social workers, shelter workers, psychologists, and volunteers to respond to the problem. The identification of coerced sex as rape and the development of professionals to address this problem in the workplace, in the home, and in school contributed to the emergence of more experts whose livelihoods depended on this expanding problem. These experts joined the affirmative action and sexual harassment experts and counselors to create an industry in which millions of people are dependent on violence against women for their livelihoods and in which most draw on a model of individual or family pathology in their explanations or interventions. The spawning of new professions, and the growth of those already established, was driven home to me during my family violence class one day a couple of years ago. The guest speaker was demonstrating to the students the plethora of public and private resources required to support an abused child through the legal system. She called on volunteers from the class to come forward as representatives of the professionals and organizations involved with the child from the time the abuse case was investigated until the parents' ties were severed and the child was available for adoption. There were relatively few students still sitting when she finished: the necessary personnel included teachers, school counselors, physicians, nurses, psychologists, judges, attorneys, intake workers, placement workers, police officers, secretaries, clerks, shelter workers, and many others. By the time she had finished, 13 people stood in front of the class representing all of the agencies and individuals involved with one child, and she had not included those whose dependence on such a problem is ancillary, such as architects, computer programmers, grant writers, and academics. I was struck not by the need for a volunteer to maintain continuity and communication through this long process, which was the point she was making, but by the number of people whose livelihoods were directly and indirectly dependent on this child. The experts and professionals represented by the students in that class brought home a paycheck because of the legal and social system's response to the pain of one child. The ordinary, everyday, and common-place nature of violence against women and children clearly is an impor-tant resource, as well as a significant problem.

There is no doubt about the power of the medicalized definitions of social problems.[113] Definitions, based in narrow theory and the research it spawns, are assumed (at least by the experts who are those most likely to be heard in the legal, social, and political arena) to be more accurate than the explanations offered by the persons who are being labeled. A theoretical and practical explanation emerging from an accepted system of thought overrides the explanation offered by the layperson, although in many cases the explanations are consistent, given that laypersons develop their explanations and understandings from the media, which present a fairly coherent and closed explanation system.[114] For example, the label "codependent," while introduced in the psychological and self-help literature, quickly grew to become part of the language of everyday life. One heard this explanation offered in 12-step programs, on talk shows, and in everyday conversation to explain why a woman stayed with an abusive husband, how a wife or parent "enabled" the addiction of a family member, or more casually to explain relationship dynamics in gen-eral. Similarly, the battered woman is likely to draw on socially available constructions to make sense of her situation. That is, her reliance on explanations such as "he was drunk" or "he was under a lot of stress because he lost his job" are no better explanations because she offers them than if he were to offer them. They are constructions that reflect the domi-nance of a powerful male reality and ignore the structural and cultural fac-tors that contribute to her abuse.

The family violence industry and the violence against women industry, including all who write about or work with abused women, depend on these women for their well-being. We all participate in an industry built on the pain of women and children, but it is an industry built by well-meaning and often well-trained professionals. This is perhaps more dan-gerous than had it been built by persons with evil intentions. Respected professionals, including researchers and teachers as well as service prov-iders, are immersed in a view of the world, a construction of reality, that determines the questions they ask and the possible solutions they see. Because the field is dominated by those working from a medical model, the focus is on the individual, and the impact of the very powerful forces of economics and gender inequality within the family are slighted. The family's position as a microcosm of the larger system of inequality, racism, and sexism is ignored. Another problem is that the battered woman's reality is rendered invisible, replaced by that of the men who batter or the experts who define her reality.[115] As difficult as it is for the outsider, including the social worker or therapist, the woman's less prestigious or less well-articulated reality must be heard through the din of explanations that blame her or devalue her explanations. It is to be expected that women will be so alienated from their experience and from themselves when trying to understand their situation that they will rely on dominant explanations or ideas, ideas that do not reflect their reality and further estrange them from their own everyday experiences.

ANGER MANAGEMENT AND BATTERER INTERVENTION PROGRAMS

One of the clearest examples of acceptance of an individual or medical model of violence against women can be seen in the reliance of courts all over the country on alternative sentencing programs for men who batter. As a result of the shelter movement, anger management programs were established for batterers and courts began referring men to these programs. They were viewed as a low-cost alternative to jail and as better than doing nothing. As it turned out, these programs were not only ineffective, they were sometimes counterproductive; and today, there is no federal funding from the Office of Violence against Women for programs designed to place offenders in anger management groups. Instead, they may be assigned to counseling or to a batterer intervention program. Batterer intervention programs recognize that anger is not a loss of control but a means of control used by the batterer and also address the underlying sexism and entitlement characteristic of the abuser. At the same time, although not specifically called anger management programs, most of the programs do have a large component on how to manage or control anger. While psychopathology may not be universal among batterers, it is assumed to be characteristic of many men who batter. Some programs are built on the assumption that batterers may not be mentally ill but do have significant behavioral control problems; others stress the socialization of men into the need for power, control, and dominance as the source of the problem.

Until recently, almost all programs assumed men who battered had anger control problems or problems with aggression. Despite the proliferation of anger management groups as diversionary programs for men who batter, the research on the importance of anger as a significant factor in battery is mixed at best. In one study relying on an anger scale, batterers did not score higher than nonbatterers, and in other research on the relationship between rape and anger, there was no indication that anger was more of a problem for rapists than for other offenders, casting doubt on the usefulness of targeting anger in the treatment of rapists.[116] Anger is not the underlying problem in wife battery.

Dollard and Doob introduced the frustration-aggression hypothesis in 1939.[117] Although it has been criticized by such authors as Carol Tavris and others, it has been one of the best-accepted theories of anger expression to date. This theory asserts that when frustration builds up, it is likely to result in aggression.[118] Some clinicians have suggested that an emotional explosion may result, others that the aggression escapes in smaller spurts ("coming out the seams," in a manner of speaking). In either case, this "hydraulic model" assumes that the human organism can accommodate only a particular amount of tension or frustration, and when that level is reached, the tension must find a way to escape. These theorists suggest that the resultant aggression is likely to be targeted at predictable others, others who are not necessarily the person or situation at the source of the frustration. Rather, in the aggression hierarchy, one is likely to select as a target someone who is associated with the individual but who is a safe target. This theoretical approach suggests that in wife battery, the man has become so frustrated (as a result of unemployment, for example, or failure, or rejection) that he eventually explodes, attacking his wife because she is an available and safe target and because she can be perceived as related to the cause of the frustration. Straus, Gelles, and Steinmetz discuss the closely related catharsis theory, which assumes that innate aggressive drives must be expressed or aggression accumulates and will "ultimately burst forth in destructive and violent ways."[119] The ventilation model assumes the value of openly expressing stored-up hostility. The aggression decreases its potential explosiveness by being expressed in a safe environment and thereby is less likely to convert into other symptoms such as insomnia, depression, and passive-aggressive behavior.[120] While legitimating the expression of hostility and anger against a target in therapy is supposed to de-escalate the anger and hostility in other situations, the evidence is overwhelmingly opposed to this theory. It suggests that ventilating aggression or attacking inanimate objects results in an escalation of violence. Research on this topic also shows that among married couples, the more ventilation expressed, the more violence is likely to occur. Straus, Gelles, and Steinmetz found that among those who were least verbally aggressive, the violence rates were lowest, while a clear majority of the top quarter of their sample who expressed conflict through verbal blasts were also physically aggressive.[121]

This catharsis model, popular in the 1970s, has been supplanted by two other approaches: the profeminist models, including most prominently the Duluth program and the Emerge model; and the cognitive-behavioral models. The profeminist models build from a focus on the use of power and control by the batterer, whereas the cognitive-behavioral programs work from the assumption that the batterers have deficits in coping and communication skills. In almost all cases. the men are court ordered to attend programs that last from a couple of months to nine months. Some of the programs are considered treatment, but the profeminist programs are viewed as educational and transformative. Treatment programs for men differ somewhat, but all focus on beliefs, attitudes, assumptions, and learning to manage behavior and expectations whether it is through therapy, education, or reprogramming, and all can be criticized as contradictory, ineffective, or even potentially harmful to the partners of men who take part in these programs. One survey concluded that 90 percent of the treatment programs incorporate some attention to improving ego functioning, describing "increasing self-esteem" as the main treatment goal. Many programs throughout the country model themselves on the Duluth program or the Emerge program, yet even those that focus more on accountability, responsibility, and changing misogynist attitudes of the perpetrators are still likely to incorporate an assumption that domestic violence is primarily a result of a personal disorder or an emotional problem or disability. Only a minority, 14 percent, listed "having the abuser take responsibility for his action" as a top goal.[122]

Because any program for batterers is situated within a larger judicial and social system, it is very difficult to assess its effectiveness. We can conclude, however, that despite the fact that only five states do not have legislative standards mandating treatment for batterers, there is no evidence that they are terribly effective.[123] Feder and Wilson found only a 7 percent decline in the recidivism rates attributable to intervention programs.[124] Similarly, Babcock and colleagues found the recidivism rate only 5 percent lower for those arrested and sentenced to treatment programs than those arrested and sanctioned in other ways.[125] The ineffectiveness of these programs may be due to a number of factors, including the fact that the men are court ordered and resistant to participating in the program. There are also methodological problems, including the small number of programs often considered in any study, as well as definition and measurement problems. Further, a particular program may be efficient and effective in some areas, such as taking responsibility, using egalitarian language, and controlling anger, but less effective in others, such as taking the perspective of the victim, becoming emotionally vulnerable, or abandoning male privilege.[126] One caution has been that women might have a harder time leaving an abusive mate if he is in such a program since he is "trying." Even the research that draws some positive conclusions about the value of treatment programs finds high rates of reassault (41 percent in a study reported by Edward Gondolf).[127]

Clearly all men who are socialized in a sexist, oppressive society do not abuse women. It is understandable that those persons who work with batterers or their victims would want to find characteristics of their clients that would distinguish them from others and to build the appropriate tools to help them work on the problem. While it is understandable that therapists, social workers, and judges would look for effective treatments and would want to avoid the cost of incarceration, the reliance on individual medicalized models not only ignores the underlying structural problems; it can funnel the energies of well-meaning, well-educated persons into repetitive ineffective efforts to "do something" about a problem rather than attack the problem at its source. Profeminist programs that are sensitive to the sexism and gender privilege that underpin violence against women are nonetheless limited by a group therapy approach that centers the individual and his relationship with his significant other—they can try to change him, but they are doing nothing to change the system that produced him. This is about as useful as parking the ambulance at the bottom of the cliff.

SELLING SERVICES

As we add more problems to the rubric of "family violence," we add more experts, agencies, and other persons who need these problems for their everyday survival. We continue to expand the definitions to fit the new situations or circumstances that we define as problems. Child abuse as a problem expands to include incest; then to include repressed memory syndrome, which expands to include false memory syndrome, and the ongoing debates about these syndromes, all requiring attention. Just as the problem areas expand, resulting in deviance labels being applied to every new phenomenon, we also expand the populations to which we can apply these labels. Attention deficit disorder, for example, is often targeted as the culprit in alcoholism, juvenile delinquency, and other crimes and misdemeanors that have traditionally relied on less medicalized definitions. And as we add these problems and expand the populations, we have more services to sell in a society that no longer produces much of anything else.

Daniel Bell, one of the most influential social observers of our time, concludes that the impact of the information revolution on our lives will be as profound as the Agricultural and the Industrial Revolutions.[128] In the information society, the economy no longer centers on the production of goods but on the production of information, knowledge, and expertise. We have shifted from a manufacturing economy to a service and information economy in which most workers are no longer directly involved in the production of goods. Most of the workforce is engaged in research or the provision of services rather than industrial labor. Workers are professionals and technicians rather than labor and management. The new jobs in the United States and other industrialized countries require that workers work with people, ideas, and information rather than with products or goods. Material production has shifted to developing countries with an abundance of cheap labor, particularly cheap female labor, and is dominated by multinational corporations that have few geographic or political boundaries and can shift production frequently in the search for a more docile workforce, ever-cheaper labor, and a larger profit margin.

Just as there is a need for consumers who will buy products, there is a need for consumers who will buy services. The services we produce, whether they are consulting, therapeutic, assessment, evaluation, treatment, or intervention, require audiences of consumers, voluntary or involuntary. In an economy that is dependent on the misfortunes of large numbers of people for our survival—whether they are prisoners, juvenile delinquents, alcoholics and drug addicts, mental patients, or abused children and women—we must necessarily seek out ever-growing populations of people who need our services. In addition to the most obvious service providers—police officers, wardens and guards, addiction counselors, psychologists and psychiatrists—we need to include the printers, the envelope manufacturers, the form makers, the delivery people, the laundries, the phone companies, the computer companies, the construction industry, the teachers and school counselors, and fund-raisers as people whose livelihoods are also sustained by the services required by dependent populations. The judicial system, including arresting officers, investigators, district attorneys, court personnel, judges, anger management counselors, and other entrepreneurs, is also part of the growing circle of people involved professionally with batterers. And there are hundreds of thousands of volunteers at hospitals, in shelters, and on hot lines and networks, as well as their supervisors and staff, who contribute to the efforts to prevent, treat, or otherwise respond to crises in the family. Our medicalization of social problems leads to the support of increasingly powerful insurance companies and their numerous employees, including the clerks who make admission and treatment decisions over the phone. We have inpatient treatment for the more recalcitrant cases (for those with insurance coverage) and outpatient programs and therapy groups for disorders that have become commonplace. We bring onto the professional treatment team nutritionists, play and occupational therapists, aides, and psychiatric social workers. Constructing so many everyday problems as forms of illness that require medical intervention has resulted in a society in which sickness is commonplace but individualized, made unique and deviant, rather than recognized as a phenomenon produced by the structures of oppression in society.

At a time when we seem to be turning again to individualistic, psychological explanations for social problems, we rely increasingly on an economy that produces a greater number of social problems. The growing discrepancy between the haves and the have-nots, the increasing feminization of poverty (although some would criticize this concept as camouflaging the fact that women have always been poor), the social and cultural reactions to women's freedoms (as evidenced by the power of the Taliban in Afghanistan, the murder of female engineering students at the Montreal Polytechnique, the concerted efforts to refuse birth control and abortions to women, and other outrageous acts perpetrated against women daily) create staggering social problems. Rather than address these problems at the level of the structure, which would demand economic realignment or revolution, we produce increasing numbers of professionals whose work it is to identify and mollify, indicate and respond, but not to acknowledge the underlying cause of the problems to which they respond. And for all of them to have jobs, they need to produce increasing numbers of persons needing their help.

As C. Wright Mills said almost 30 years ago and as Alvin Gouldner made clear later in *The Coming Crisis in Western Sociology*, we need the "down and outers," the poor and disenfranchised, the criminal and the insane.[129] Charles Krauthammer argues that for the ordinary bourgeois, the bar defining normality has been raised: "Large areas of ordinary behavior hitherto considered harmless and inoffensive have had their threshold radically redefined up so that once innocent behavior now stands condemned as deviant."[130] Whereas child abuse was earlier identified as severe punishment that resulted in significant physical harm, now child abuse has expanded to include an entire range of relatively benign behavior, the most difficult of which might be the concept of emotional abuse. Now children who miss too much school suffer "educational abuse," and their parents are punished by incarceration or humiliation, being forced to attend school with their child. The populations to which we can expand the label deviant, those for whom we can provide services, are almost endless. Areas of everyday family life and individual behavior previously viewed as personal concerns have become "deviantized," allowing for expert intervention.

However, while being aware of the problems created by raising the bar on deviance, we must not romanticize a return to "the good old days." A return to a time when fathers were kings of their castles carries all sorts of potential damage for women and children. Stephen Pinker convincingly argues that around the globe, violence has decreased during the last millennium and during the last decades. Whether we are talking about war, rape, massacres, sadism, personal vendettas, battery, or homicide, there is a persistent pattern of decline. Pinker attributes this to "civilization," the growing reliance on trade, rationality, increasing cosmopolitanism, literacy, travel.[131]

While we may live in the most peaceful era ever, while overall violence against women may have decreased, we can still look around us, look at the Congo, India, Afghanistan, the United States, and it is there. Rather than see it as an epidemic, a disease that sweeps the country, trapping individual women in its path, instead of relying on the illness metaphor, we need to dismantle the source of the problems that we are treating symptomatically. We need to eliminate sexist culture, pornographic violence, male privilege, and the definition of women as primarily reproducers, nurturers, and bodies to be used. We must not become hopelessly mired in the quicksand of radical constructionism that limits discussion of different definitions of reality, maintains the therapeutic and political stance of neutrality, and limits us to narrow, reductionistic, individualistic explanations for the experiences women have. We must, instead, be open to naming the everyday assaults women experience as direct reflections of their oppression, their lack of value, their "otherness" in all societies in the world. We must be willing to deal with the complexities of structural change and not be satisfied with mopping-up operations in which we merely minister to the wounded. Rather than opening the door to new victims each day, therapists, counselors, doctors, and all of those others who deal with violence against women must work to change the structure that has brought these women to them.

NOTES

1. E. Martin, "The Egg and the Sperm: How Science Has Constructed a Romance Based on Stereotypical Male-Female Roles," *Signs: Journal of Women in Culture and Society* 16, no. 3 (1991): 485–501.

2. M. Profet, "Menstruation as a Defense against Pathogens Transported by Sperm," *Quarterly Review of Biology* 68, no. 3 (1993): 335–86.

3. H. Garfinkel, *Studies in Ethnomethodology* (Upper Saddle River, NJ: Prentice-Hall, 1967).

4. C. W. Mills, *The Power Elite* (New York: Oxford University Press, 1956).

5. R. Quinney, *The Social Construction of Crime* (Boston: Little, Brown, 1970); and K. Marx and F. Engels, *Collected Works* (London: Lawrence and Wishart, 1975).

6. R. W. Connell, *Gender and Power* (Stanford, CA: Stanford University Press, 1987).

7. E. Pfuhl, *The Deviance Process* (Belmont, CA: Wadsworth, 1986). See for an evaluation of the paradigms of fact and definition P. Berger and T. Luckmann, *The Social Construction of Reality* (New York: Doubleday, 1967).

8. M. W. Stewart, "The Redefinition of Incest: From Sin to Sickness," *Family Science Review* 4, no. 1–2 (1991): 53–68.

9. P. Conrad and J. Schneider, *Deviance and Medicalization: From Badness to Sickness* (Philadelphia: Temple University Press, 1992).

10. L. Diller, *Running on Ritalin: A Physician Reflects on Children, Society, and Performance in a Pill* (New York: Bantam Books, 1998).

11. G. Kaufman Jr., "The Mysterious Disappearance of Battered Women in Family Therapists' Offices: Male Privilege Colluding with Male Violence," *Journal of Marital and Family Therapy* 18, no. 3 (1992): 233–243.

12. M. Bograd, "Values in Conflict: Challenges to Family Therapists' Thinking," *Journal of Marital and Family Therapy* 18, no. 3 (1992), 245–56.

13. R. Vaselle-Augenstein and A. Ehrlich, "Male Batterers: Evidence for Psychopathology," in *Intimate Violence: Interdisciplinary Perspectives*, edited by E. Viano (Bristol, PA: Taylor and Francis, 1992), 150.

14. L. Walker, *The Battered Woman* (New York: Harper and Row, 1979).

15. W. Ryan, *Blaming the Victim* (New York: Pantheon Books, 1971).

16. H. Arendt, *Eichmann in Jerusalem* (New York: Penguin Books, 1963).

17. G. Hotaling and D. Sugarman, "An Analysis of Risk Markers in Husband to Wife Violence: The Current State of Knowledge," *Violence and Victims* 1, no. 2 (1986): 101–24.

18. R. J. Sampson and J. L. Lauritsen, "Violent Victimization and Offending: Individual-, Situational-, and Community-Level Risk

Factors," in *Understanding and Preventing Violence*, edited by R. J. Sampson and J. L. Lauritsen (Washington, DC: National Academy Press, 1994).

19. Walker, *The Battered Woman*.

20. S. Freud, *The Standard Edition of the Complete Psychological Works of Sigmund Freud*, revised and edited by J. Strachey (London: Hogarth Press and Institute of Psychoanalysis, 1964); see also E. Erickson, *Youth and Crisis* (New York: Norton, 1969.); J. Sayer, *Mothers of Psychoanalysis: Helene Deutsch, Karen Homey, Anna Freud, and Melanie Klein* (New York: W. W. Norton, 1993).

21. Walker, *The Battered Woman*.

22. M. Johnson, "Patriarchal Terrorism and Common Couple Violence: Two Forms of Violence against Women," *Journal of Marriage and the Family* 57, no. 2 (1995): 283–94.

23. R. J. Gelles and M. A. Straus, *Intimate Violence* (New York: Simon & Schuster, 1988).

24. C. Sheffield, "Sexual Terrorism," in *Women: A Feminist Perspective* (5th ed.), edited by J. Freeman (Mountain View, CA: Mayfield Press, 1994).

25. U.S. Department of Justice, Office on Violence against Women, *The Violence against Women Act of 2000*, Washington, DC: DOJ, 2001, http://www.ojp.usdoj.gov/vawo/ laws/vawa_summary2.htm

26. UK Center for Research on Violence against Women, Top Ten Series, http://www.uky.wsu/ CRVAW, accessed May 30, 2013.

27. Walker, *The Battered Woman*.

28. O. W. Barnett, T. E. Martinez, and B. W. Bluestein, "Jealousy and Anxious Romantic Attachment in Maritally Violent and Non-Violent Males," *Journal of Interpersonal Violence* 10, No. 4 (1995): 473–486. The authors do not find batterers to be more jealous than nonbatterers.

29. S. Hanks, "Translating Theory into Practice: A Conceptual Framework for Clinical Assessment, Differential Diagnosis and Multi-Modal Treatment of Maritally Violent Individuals, Couples, and Families," in Viano, *Intimate Violence* (1992): 157–76; see also Walker, *The Battered Woman*.

30. Walker, *The Battered Woman*.

31. Vaselle-Augenstein and Ehrlich, "Male Batterers," 150.

32. Hanks, "Translating Theory into Practice," 161.

33. Massachusetts Department of Social Services, Domestic Violence. 1995.

34. *Hope House: A Shelter for Battered Women*. Kansas City, MO, n.d., http://www.hopehouse.net/

35. Hotaling and Sugarman, "An Analysis of Risk Markers in Husband to Wife Violence," 101–24.

36. D. J. Sonkin, D. Martin, and L. E. Walker, *The Male Batterer: A Treatment Approach* (New York: Springer, 1985); see also O. Barnett, C. Miller-Perrin, and R. Perrin, *Family Violence across the Lifespan: An Introduction* (Thousand Oaks, CA: Sage, 1997).

37. I. Frieze, J. Parsons, P. Johnson, D. N. Ruble, and G. Zellerman, *Women and Sex Roles* (New York: Norton, 1978).

38. R. W. Connell, *Masculinities* (Berkeley: University of California Press, 1995).

39. M. Horner, "Fail: Bright Woman," in *The Gender Reader*, edited by E. Ashton-Jones, G. Olson, and M. Perry (Needham Heights, MA: Allyn and Bacon, 2000), 365–73.

40. Connell, *Gender and Power.*

41. A. Rich, *On Lies, Secrets, and Silence* (New York: W. W. Norton, 1979).

42. T. Beneke, *Proving Manhood: Reflections on Men and Sexism* (Berkeley: University of California Press, 1997).

43. Ibid., 47–48.

44. M. Kimmel, "The Cult of Masculinity: American Social Character and the Legacy of the Cowboy," in M. Kaufman (ed.), *Beyond Patriarchy: Essays by Men on Pleasure, Power and Change* (New York and Oxford: Oxford University Press, 1983).

45. Vaselle-Augenstein and Ehrlich, "Male Batterers," 150; see also J. Weitzman and K. Dreen, "Wife Beating: A View of the Marital Dyad," *Social Casework* 63, no. 5 (1982): 259–65.

46. Vaselle-Augenstein and Ehrlich, "Male Batterers."

47. S. Brownmiller, *Against Our Will: Men, Women and Rape* (New York: Ballantine Publishing Group, 1975/1993); D. Scully and J. Marolla, "Rape and Vocabulary of Motives: Alternate Perspective," in *Rape and Sexual Assault: A Research Handbook*, edited by A. Burgess (New York: Garland, 1985).

48. D. Loseke and S. Cahill, "The Social Construction of Deviance: Experts on Battered Women," *Social Problems* 31, no. 3 (February 1984): 296–310.

49. K. D. O'Leary, "Through a Psychological Lens: Personality Traits, Personality Disorders and Levels of Violence," in *Current Controversies on Family Violence*, edited by R. J. Gelles and D. R. Loseke (Newbury Park, CA: Sage, 1993), 243.

50. D. Adams, "Treatment Models of Men Who Batter: A Pro-Feminist Analysis," in *Feminist Perspectives on Wife Abuse*, edited by K. Yllo and M. Bogard (Newbury Park, CA: Sage, 1988), 175–99.

51. L. Walker, "The Battered Woman Syndrome Is a Psychological Consequence of Abuse," in *Domestic Violence on Trial: Psychological and Legal Dimensions of Family Violence*, edited by R. J. Gelles and D. R. Loseke (New York: Springer, 1993), 127–54; *Ibn-Tamas v. United States.*1979. 407A 2d 626.

52. L. Walker, "The Battered Woman Syndrome Study," in *The Dark Side of Families*, edited by D. Finkelhor, R. J. Gelles, G. T. Hotaling, and M. A. Straus (Beverly Hills, CA: Sage, 1983), 31–48; see also Walker, *The Battered Woman.*

53. Walker, *The Battered Woman.*

54. Ibid., 65.

55. Ibid., 135.

56. Johnson, "Patriarchal Terrorism and Common Couple Violence."

57. C. P. Ewing, "Psychological Self-Defense," *Law and Human Behavior* 4, no. 6 (1990): 579–94.

58. M. Dell, "Battered Women: Society's Problem," in *The Victimization of Women*, edited by J. R. Chapman and M. Gates (Beverly Hill, CA: Sage, 1978); see also M. Pagelow, *Woman-Battering: Victims and Their Experience* (Beverly Hills, CA: Sage, 1981).

59. R. A. Schuller and N. Vidmar, "Battered Woman Syndrome Evidence in the Courtroom: A Review of Literature," *Law and Human Behavior* 16, no. 3 (1992): 273–91.

60. P. Frazier and E. Borgida, "Rape Trauma Syndrome: A Review of Case Law and Psychological Research," *Law and Human Behavior* 16, no. 3 (1992); see also *State v. Taylor.* 1984. 663 S.W. 2d 235, 236.

61. Schuller and Vidmar, "Battered Woman Syndrome Evidence in the Courtroom," 275.

62. *R. v. Duffy* (1949) 1All ER 932.

63. Conrad and Schneider, *Deviance and Medicalization.*

64. Ibid.

65. M. Stewart, "The Redefinition of Incest: From Sin to Sickness," *Family Science Review* 4 (1991):1–2.

66. H. Giarretto, "A Comprehensive Child Sexual Abuse Treatment Program," *Child Abuse and Neglect* 6, no. 3 (1982): 263–78.

67. H. Becker, *Outsiders: Studies in the Sociology of Deviance* (New York: Free Press, 1963).

68. The work of Joseph Conrad, Peter Schneider, and Erdwin Pfuhl discussed earlier elaborates on this concept.

69. Stewart, "The Redefinition of Incest."

70. M. Beattie, *Codependent No More* (New York: Harper/Hazeldon, 1987); see also C. Black, *It Will Never Happen to Me* (New York:

Ballantine Books, 1991); S. Wegscheider-Cruse, *Another Chance: Hope and Health for the Alcoholic Family* (Palo Alto, CA: Science and Behavior Books, 1989); T. Giermyski and T. Williams, "CoDependency," *Journal of Psychoactive Drugs* 18, no. 1 (1986); and A. Schaef, *When Society Becomes an Addict* (San Francisco: Harper and Row, 1987).

71. Giermyski and Williams, "CoDependency."

72. Black, *It Will Never Happen to Me*; Wegscheider-Cruse, *Another Chance: Hope and Health for the Alcoholic Family*; and M. Beattie, *Codependent No More* (New York: Harper/Hazeldon, 1987).

73. Giermyski and Williams, "CoDependency."

74. P. Steinglass, L. Bennett, S. Solin, and D. Reiss, *The Alcoholic Family* (New York: Basic Books, 1987).

75. J. Haaken, "A Critical Analysis of the Co-dependence Construct," *Psychiatry* 53, no. 4 (1990): 396–406.

76. M. Hagen, "Bad Attitude, Violent Fantasies," *National Review*, July 20, 1998, 38.

77. W. Goode, "Force and Violence in the Family," *Journal of Marriage and the Family* 33, no. 4 (1971): 624–36.

78. M. Straus, "A General Systems Approach to a Theory of Violence between Family Members," *Social Science Information* 12, no. 3 (1973): 105–25; see also R. Gelles, "Violence in the Family: A Review of Research in the Seventies," *Journal of Marriage and the Family* 42, no. 4 (1980): 873–85.

79. H. Giarretto, *Humanistic Treatment of Father-Daughter Incest: Sexual Abuse of Children*, DHHD Publication No.ADM78-30161 (Washington, DC: U.S. Government Printing Office, 1980).

80. Ibid.

81. J. Avis, "Where Are All the Family Therapists? Abuse and Violence within Families and Family Therapy's Response," *Journal of Marital and Family Therapy* 18, no. 3 (1992): 225–32; see also N. Gavey, F. Pezaro, and J. Tan, "Mother-Blaming, the Perfect Alibi: Family Therapy and the Mothers of Incest Survivors," *Journal of Feminist Family Therapy* 2, no. 1 (1990): 1–25.

82. D. Willbach, "Ethics and Family Therapy: The Case Management of Family Violence," *Journal of Marital and Family Therapy* 15, no. 1 (1989): 43–52; see also G. Kaufman, "The Mysterious Disappearance of Women in Family Therapists' Offices: Male Privilege Colluding with Male Violence," *Journal of Marriage and Family Therapy* 18, no. 3 (1992) 233–234.

83. Kaufman, "The Mysterious Disappearance of Women in Family Therapists' Offices."

84. Ibid.

85. M. Bograd, "Family Systems Approaches to Wife Battering: A Feminist Critique." *American Journal of Orthopsychiatry* 54, no. 4 (1984): 558–68; Bograd, "Values in Conflict."

86. P. Blau, *Exchange and Power in Social Life* (New York: Wiley, 1964); see also G. Homans, *Social Behavior: Its Elementary Form* (New York. Harcourt Brace Jovanovich, 1973).

87. Kaufman, "The Mysterious Disappearance of Women in Family Therapists' Offices."

88. M. Wolfgang and F. Ferracuti, *The Subculture of Violence: Toward an Integrated Theory of Criminology* (London: Tavistock, 1967). This has been an extremely controversial theory over the past several decades, but it does pay attention to subculture as a component in the justification of violence against women and is therefore of value in understanding this type of violence.

89. Ibid.

90. M. Lugones and E. Spelman, "Have We Got a Theory for You! Feminist Theory, Cultural Imperialism and the Demand for the Woman's Voice," in *Feminist Theory,* edited by W. Kolmar and F. Bartkowski (New York: McGraw-Hill, 2005), 17–27; b. hooks, *Ain't I a Woman: Black Women and Feminism* (Boston: South End Press, 1981); P. Hill Collins, *Black Feminist Thought* (New York: Routledge, 2000).

91. For a study of the Nevada justice system, I conducted a number of interviews with women who had been raped, asking them about their decision to report or not report the rape and the treatment they received in the justice system. See M. W. Stewart, *Gender Bias in the Sexual Assault Cases: A Study of the Nevada Justice System.* Report for the Nevada Supreme Court Gender Bias Task Force (1992).

92. T. Parsons, and R. F. Bales, *Family Socialization and Interaction Processes* (New York: Routledge and Kegan Paul, 1956).

93. C. Lasch, *Haven in a Heartless World: The Family Besieged* (New York: Basic Books, 1977).

94. C. Itzin, "Pornography: Women, Violence, and Civil Liberties," in *Women in Culture: A Women's Studies Anthology*, edited by L. J. Peach (Oxford, UK: Blackwell, 1998), 62.

95. M. Pipher, *Reviving Ophelia* (New York: Putnam, 1994), 44.

96. Peach, *Women in Culture.*

97. Stewart, "The Redefinition of Incest."

98. A. Lord, "Age, Race, Class, and Sex: Women Redefining Difference," in *Sister Outsider*, edited by A. Lord (Freedom, CA: Crossing Press, 1984).

99. Lugones and Spelman, "Have We Got a Theory for You!"

100. K. Crenshaw, "Mapping the Margins: Intersectionality, Identity Politics, and Violence against Women of Color," in *The Public Nature of Private Violence: The Discovery of Domestic Abuse*, edited by M. A. Fineman and R. Mykitiuk (New York: Routledge, 1994), 93–118.

101. H. Potter, "An Argument for Black Feminist Criminology: Understanding African American Women's Experience with Intimate Partner Abuse Using an Integrated Approach," *Feminist Criminology* 1, no. 2 (April 2006): 106–24.

102. R. H. Jensen, "Mimi Ramsey: For Selflessly Surviving Despite Her Own Pain, to End the Mutilation of Young Girls," 6, no. 4 (1996): 51–52.

103. A. Johnson, *The Gender Knot: Unraveling Our Patriarchal Legacy* (Philadelphia: Temple University Press, 2005).

104. Ibid.

105. C. Talpade Mohanty, "Under and (Inside) Western Eyes: At the Turn of the Century," in T. Mohanty, *Feminism without Borders: Decolonizing Theory, Practicing Solidarity* (Durham, NC: Duke University Press. 2003).

106. M. Anderson, *Thinking About Women: Sociological Perspectives on Sex and Gender* (Needham Heights, MA: Allyn and Bacon, 2000)

107. T. Mohanty, *Feminism without Borders*.

108. Ibid., 90–91.

109. R. E. Dobash and R. P. Dobash, *Violence against Wives* (New York: Free Press, 1979); R. E. Dobash and R. P. Dobash, *Women, Violence and Social Change* (London: Routledge, 1992); see also M. Daly, *Gyn/Ecology: The Meta-ethics of Radical Feminism* (Boston: Beacon Press, 1978); and M. Daly, *Beyond God, the Father, and Meta-ethics* (Boston: Beacon Press, 1978).

110. Daly, *Gyn/Ecology: The Meta-ethics of Radical Feminism*.

111. C. MacKinnon, *Only Words* (Cambridge, MA: Harvard University Press, 1993); C. MacKinnon, *Feminism Unmodified: Discourses on Life and Law* (Cambridge, MA: Harvard University Press, 1987).

112. Hill Collins, *Black Feminist Thought*; T. Mohanty, *Feminism without Borders*; and hooks, *Ain't I a Woman*.

113. J. M. Avis, "Where Are All the Family Therapists? Abuse and Violence within Families and Family Therapy's Response," *Journal of Marital and Family Therapy* 18, no. 3 (1992): 225–32; see also Gavey, Pezaro, and Tan, "Mother-Blaming, the Perfect Alibi."

114. Ibid.

115. D. Willbach, "Ethics and Family Therapy: The Case Management of Family Violence," *Journal of Marital and Family Therapy* 15, no. 1 (1989): 43–52; see also Kaufman, "The Mysterious Disappearance of Women in Family Therapists' Offices: Male Privilege Colluding with Male Violence," June 1991.

116. W. Loza and A. Loza-Fanous, "The Fallacy of Reducing Rape and Violent Recidivism by Treating Anger," *International Journal of Offender Therapy and Comparative Criminology*, 43, no. 4 (1999); see also J. D. Hastings and L. K. Hamberger, "Personality Characteristics of Spouse Abusers: A Controlled Comparison," *Violence and Victims* 3, no. 1 (1988): 31–38 (found that batterers scored either lower on the Novaco 1975 Anger Scale or did not score significantly higher than nonbatterers); and R. Davis and B. Taylor, "Does Batterer Treatment Reduce Violence? A Synthesis of Literature," in *Women and Domestic Violence: An Interdisciplinary Approach*, edited by L. Feder (New York: Haworth Press, 1999).

117. J. Dollard, L. Doob, N. Miller, and R. Sears, *Frustration and Aggression* (New Haven, CT: Yale University Press, 1939); see also M. Howell and K. Pugliesi, "Husbands Who Harm: Predicting Spousal Violence by Men," *Journal of Family Violence* 3, no. 1 (1988): 15–35; O. Barnett, R. Fagan, and J. Booker, "Hostility and Stress as Mediators of Aggression in Violent Men," *Journal of Family Violence* 6, no. 3 (1991): 219–241; and M. A. Straus, "Victims and Aggressors in Marital Violence," *American Behavioral Scientist* 23, no. 5 (1980): 681–704.

118. C. Tavris, *Anger: The Misunderstood Emotion* (New York: Simon & Schuster, 1982); C. Tavris, *Mismeasure of Woman* (New York: Simon & Schuster, 1982).

119. M. Straus, R. Gelles, and S. Steinmetz, *Behind Closed Doors: Violence in the American Family* (Garden City, NY: Doubleday, 1980), 167.

120. L. Berkowitz, "The Case for Bottling Up Rage," *Psychology Today*, July 24–31, 1973; see also J. Hokanson, "Psychophysiological Evaluation of the Catharsis Hypothesis," in *Dynamics of Aggression*, edited by E. I. Megargee and J. E. Hokanson (New York: Harper and Row, 1970), 74–88; and M. A. Straus, "Leveling, Civility, and Violence in the Family," *Journal of Marriage and the Family* 36, no. 1 (1974): 13–29.

121. Straus, Gelles, and Steinmetz, *Behind Closed Doors*, 167.

122. D. Adams, "Counseling Men Who Batter: A Pro-feminist Analysis of Five Treatment Models," in *Feminist Perspectives on Wife Abuse*, edited by K. Yllo and M. Bograd (Newbury Park, CA: Sage, 1988), 180.

123. UK Center for Research on Violence against Women. Top Ten Series.

124. L. Feder and D. Wilson, "A Meta-Analysis Review of Court-Mandated Batterer Intervention Programs," *Journal of Experimental Criminology* 1, no. 2 (2005): 239–62.

125. J. C. Babcock, C. E. Green, and C. Robie, "Does Batterers' Treatment Work? A Meta-Analytic Review of Domestic Violence Treatment," *Clinical Psychology Review* 23, no. 8 (2004): 1023–53.

126. D. P. Schrock and I. Padavic, "Negotiating Hegemonic Masculinity in a Batterer Intervention Program," *Gender and Society* 21, no. 5 (October 2007): 625–49, http://www.nij.gov/topics/crime/intimate-partner-violence/interventions/batterer-intervention

127. E. Gondolf, "A 30-Month Follow-up of Court-Referred Batterers in Four Cities," *International Journal of Offender Therapy and Comparative Criminology* 44, no. 1 (2000).

128. D. Bell, *The Coming of Post-Industrial Society* (New York: Basic Books, 1973).

129. C. W. Mills, *The Power Elite* (New York: Oxford University Press, 1951); A. Gouldner, *The Coming Crisis of Western Sociology* (New York: Avon Books, 1980).

130. C. Krauthammer, "Defining Deviance Up," *New Republic*, November 22, 1993. 20–25.

131. S. Pinker, *The Better Angel of Our Nature* (New York: Penguin Group, 2011).

THREE

Cultural Support for Violence against Women

In April 2013, the multimillion-dollar corporation Reebok fired Rick Ross,[1] a wannabe rapper, as their spokesperson for his lyrics celebrating rape drugs and rape: "Put Molly all in her champagne, she ain't even know it," and when he took her home and "enjoyed that," she was just as "unaware."[2] What was surprising about these lyrics was not their celebration of violence against women carried in a brutal rap cadence, but the fact that a targeted social media campaign by the feminist organization UltraViolet[3] got him fired for them. One might wonder how he thought it was okay to rap about putting a date-rape drug in a woman's drink and then raping her, but his ignorance and insensitivity isn't completely incomprehensible. Dolce and Gabbana ads[4] show a woman pinned down by one man while three look on, and a Calvin Klein jeans ad[5] shows what looks like a back-alley gang rape, one man, pants unzipped, getting ready to penetrate, the other also with bare torso and pants unzipped pulling her hair and holding her down, the third waiting or just finished, one can't tell. No apologies here as there were by Sears[6] when it pulled its t-shirts, some child size, that read "Kick Me in My Fallopian Tubes," or a Ford India ad[7] showing a cartoon of the Kardashian sisters with their mouths taped, legs and hands bound, stuffed in a trunk. The offenses are many and the apologies are few. So Whitechapel's song "Prostatic Fluid Asphyxiation" presents lyrics like "Raping her and hacking, slashing, violated/I'm not sorry" as just a song.[8] Eminem, white rapper darling of the establishment media, writes lyrics condemning the "sluts and bitches" who don't "put out"—who he wouldn't "piss on," finally concluding he will "put anthrax on a tampax, and slap you till you can't stand." This is accepted as a form of artistic expression.[9] Evidently there is no problem as long as the message is uttered as art, not advertising.

There's no shortage of these messages—of course, there is the reliable woman-hating from rappers, but it is everywhere in the media, in ads, movies, television shows. And the fact that it is everywhere seems to render it acceptable. Not only is pornography a form of "free speech," but a range of blistering sexist verbal and visual assaults, language, and images that would never be acceptable if directed at blacks, gays, or other minorities can be hurled at women under the cover of "free speech." To respond too strongly can be condemned as hysteria. It is "just the way things are." And that is precisely the problem.

Here we look at the many ways in which violence against women is encouraged, applauded, and supported in the media. We are not asserting causation or a direct correlation between these images and the actual violence women experience. Not at all. Nor do I want to equate the venomous verbal attacks against women in the media with the hideous war crimes against humanity occurring around the globe, both today and in the past. The media attacks on women are on a different level than, for example, the assaults against women in the east Congo, rapes so violent they cannot be captured by the word "rape" according to Dr. Denis Mukwege, medical director of Panzi hospital in Bukavu. Dr. Mukwege continues, under threats against his life, to repair the fistulas of women who have been brutally raped over and over again, by armies on all sides of a civil war that has left millions of men dead and the lives of millions of women and their children devastated. No, there are probably no billboards with Pabst Blue Ribbon beer pouring into a woman's open mouth, mimicking a "golden shower,"[10] and there are no ads in the Congo for Liquid Plumbr showing a housewife being thrown into paroxysms of pleasure when two dark handsome plumbers come to "snake her drain" with "double impact."[11] There are no lyrics from 816 Boyz and Kutt Calhoun rapping "Told me to bang/like it ain't a thang," then asking if he should pull his "thang" out, or TechN9ne saying they will "bang out" with their "thang out" and put it "right in they mouth."[12] No, the brutality of war doesn't draw on this ugliness, but instead is firmly situated in historical and cultural assumptions that allow for the treatment of girls and women as bodies to be taken, pillaged, ruined, cut, raped, and killed because they are there to be had, for pleasure or for revenge.

We are horrified by the vicious acts of war, the murderous rampages, the slaughter, and the never-ending violence that leaves millions displaced, homeless, sick, dying, and dead. However, we cannot dismiss the cultural degradation of women as acceptable just because it pales in comparison to the horrors of outright war. We need to document the extent of this cultural assault on women and investigate the factors that produce and that legitimate it in mainstream media as well as on the cultural margins. It has not always been thus. Violent images, lyrics, and ads are far more prevalent now than they were at any other time in our history, if by "now" we mean the period since the women's movement emerged in the 1960s. Taking the long view shows us that although violent images have waxed and waned, they have become so commonplace today that they serve as the backdrop of everyday life. They are truly unremarkable.

VOGUE AND VIOLENCE

Few of the young women who buy *Mademoiselle* will buy a cashmere shell for $485 or a jacket for $1,200. The older women who buy *Vogue* and *Bazaar* will generally not buy the $5,000 gowns or the $900 Chanel bags. But they will consume the images, tying themselves to the models and their world though identification. Having some of the things in the magazine—the creams or scents, maybe a scarf, even having the magazine itself—places the buyer on the runway or in the scene with the model in a world of beauty, power, and romance. The reader is not simply a consumer of images, learning to dress or make herself attractive; she absorbs the model's life and clothes into her interior and moves in her world with a dual self. Her own mundane life is fed first from the consumption of the models; once interiorized, it continues to nurture her from the inside—a kind of fashion time-release capsule. She incorporates that image of wealth, power, and perfection from the magazine, seeing herself as changed by buying and using the mascara or face cream advertised by flawless models, expanding her own view of herself, becoming a vision to others as she sees them seeing her.

A review of the portrayal of American women in *Vogue* magazine from the World War II era until 1990 shows how the changing economic and social position of women generates changing cultural mythology about women's value. Advertisements in *Vogue* allow us to trace dominant representations of femininity over 50 years, revealing significant changes in the relationship between women and their social world.[13] During the war years, women were comfortable in the world at large, a world largely absent of men, or "real men," most of them having gone to fight the war in Europe and in Asia. While they were gone, women in *Vogue* worked, "dressed to the nines" in heels and smart little suits, and focused on the business at hand. They were trim, hardworking, no-nonsense women engaged in the serious work of supporting the war effort and keeping America prosperous for the return of their husbands. Sex would seem to be the furthest thing from their minds. The women represent self-sufficiency as well as safety; they are self-contained, focused, efficient, and sincere. The audience was offered a world of security through the pages depicting women on their own, living freely in the world, open to the changes they knew were coming when the men returned.

Much has been written about the dramatic shifts that occurred in the United States after World War II. The "problem that had no name," the malaise that led to the second women's movement germinated in the fecund '50s. Sociologists, psychoanalysts, and preachers lauded the new family form characterized by parents who were biologically and socially constituted to fill contrasting and mutually supportive parenting roles, raising happy, well-adjusted children and soaking up the rewards of post-war economic growth. The sun always shone on Levittown and other suburbs that popped up throughout the country, luring city dwellers with the promise of space, safety, and community. Reflecting this change, the *Vogue* women of the 1950s abandoned their tailored suits and urban sophistication for cute house dresses that matched those worn by their daughters and spent their days making meals in their new Amana or Kenmore kitchens and meeting the all-consuming needs of their well-behaved but demanding children. These *Vogue* women spent a lot of time in their bedrooms, but they were seldom with men. Rather, dressed in "baby doll" pajamas or waltz-length sheer gowns, they sipped tea with other women their age, often accompanied by poodles or other small dogs.[14] Despite the fact that they were married and had children, these suburban women exuded innocence and childishness, their lives seemingly built around their friends, their houses, and their babies. Looking back on the pages of *Vogue*, these women seem a bit old to be having slumber parties, but the innocence of their relationship with other women and the sweetness of their demeanor purify and desexualize them, taking them back to the piety, purity, and domesticity of the cult of true womanhood of generations earlier. These women wanted to please their men, and in fact were admonished to "give your man what he wants." He was, it seems, more likely to want a new hat or a home-cooked meal than hot sex. The women had a nascent sexuality completely tied to their essential commitment to an identity as a wife and mother. Women were the "tender trap"[15] in advertising, song, and film; they captured men with perfume from elegant bottles, kept them on leashes, and, with the Realistic Curl, were likely to achieve marriage and motherhood. However, while their goal was to get their man, their manner was to serve him, to please him, to know what he wanted before he did, and to give it to him. There was not a hint of seductiveness from the woman or any indication of violence in the relationship.

Men were still largely absent in the everyday lives of women and children during the 1950s. Although they were home from the war, they took the early train to their offices in the city and were welcomed back home just in time to shake the martinis and tend the barbecue that evening. While women were almost asexual, men were so carefully dressed and well put together that one imagined their sexual encounters with their wives to be carefully choreographed, cautiously stimulating couplings, conforming to the Freudian and Parsonian expectations for compatible heterosexuality. The 2008 movie *Revolutionary Road*,[16] based on Richard Yates's 1961 novel[17] of the same name, captures the arid emotional landscape induced by the expectations for perfection. Frank and April Wheeler, trapped in the "hopeless emptiness" of their suburban life, finally find a way out of their claustrophobic existence, but when their plans are thwarted by April's pregnancy and Jack's sudden success at work, they see their opportunity evaporate. Empty and predictable affairs punctuate their growing dissatisfaction. April dies as a result of a self-induced abortion, leaving Jack completely bereft, focused now on their children and his work.[18] A pretty bleak picture of the potential destructiveness of postwar suburban America and the traps it set for young men and women pursuing the American dream.

One could hardly imagine the exchange of any bodily fluids between these cardboard figures. Barbie, introduced in 1959, and Ken, who joined her in 1961, would have been very comfortable in that world, unencumbered by differentiating genitalia. The thought of violence in the relationship or violent sexuality was out of the question. The daily lives of women and men, devoted, respectively, to home and work, contrasted greatly with the elegance and sophistication of the evening—cocktails, cigarettes, gowns, and tuxedos. In neither of these worlds was a woman in any danger; there was not one ad in *Vogue* during these years showing a man lurking in a shadow, a dog attacking a woman, a rapist trying to break into a woman's apartment, in part perhaps because women on the pages of *Vogue* were married and lived safely in the suburbs rather than alone in urban apartments.[19]

In the 1960s, women were once more out in the world, often with men, happy, frolicking; women were no longer tied to the kitchen or to children, and their relationships with men were less restrained and role bound than they had been. Men, who had been largely absent during the 1940s and 1950s, were now friendly, fun loving, and happy as well. The word that would best capture the essence of women and men in the 1960s would be *open*, or *free*, or *fun loving*. *Vogue* provided no hint of the social turmoil characterizing the 1960s; the sexual revolution was revealed as trouble-free sexual opportunity, good-natured, high-spirited—good, clean, sexual fun. It was as if men and women had awakened one morning to discover their sexuality and were surprised and delighted by the discovery.

Women in the 1940s were serious and focused, becoming light, airy, and happily sequestered in the home with children in the 1950s. However, by the 1970s, the fun-loving, freedom-seeking women of the 1960s were engaging in some devastating behavior with equally devastating consequences. With the women's movement in full swing and the war in Vietnam having shredded many hopes and any sense of omnipotence on the part of the United States, the world for women and men, alone and together, had changed dramatically. Now the ads portrayed women as both dangerous and in danger. They were victims of rape or murder, stalking, maiming, abuse, and other sadistic acts. Men were no longer hard-working dads and cheerful boys next door; they were rapists, they were enemies, and they were threatening. Men lurked and leered and waited for an opportunity to do women harm, usually at night but sometimes in broad daylight. Women were no longer sheltered from the world, and they were no longer safe, reliable, and trustworthy because they lived in the same world as men and put themselves in positions of danger. Men made the world a dangerous place for women. And while the anonymous stranger posed a threat to women outdoors and in public places, it was just as likely that a woman's dinner date would force his way into her apartment or leave her beaten and bruised on the floor of the restaurant bathroom. Women were masochistic; they loved being beaten "black and blue" by the Rolling Stones or anyone else; they wanted sex, men, and power. They were also dangerous—to men sometimes, but especially to each other as they struggled for the male prize. Women were shown just before being crushed by a train (in a Jordache jeans ad), being followed by a dangerous stranger (in a perfume ad), and fighting off attacking Dobermans. These were not happy women, but they were sexy. They wanted sex; they were going to get sex or be forced to give sex. They were all about sex, not nurturance, fun, not wives and mothers, but bodies to be had or violated.[20]

During the 1970s and 1980s, women and men were often portrayed as enemies, each wanting something from the other and protecting her- or himself from the other. They no longer had babies and backyard barbecues; they were on the street, locked in sexual and physical battle. What do these images tell us about violence against women? They obviously were linked in important ways to the activities of the time—the war, the reunions of families, women being forced out of the marketplace, the anti-establishment youth movements of the 1960s, and the women's movements of the 1970s. However, they also tell a story about self and other, about safety and danger, about who women are together, and about how women and men relate to one another. Women were safe in the 1940s, 1950s, and 1960s not because they were protected by men but because the men were either gone or were hardworking, trustworthy, and non-threatening. These men might have cast a fleeting over-the-shoulder glance at a woman or might have preferred blondes, but they were gentlemen even so, civilized, reliable, and safe.

The upheavals of the 1960s and 1970s perhaps pushed men into aggressive masculinity. White men were threatened by the demands of black men for social and economic access, and sometimes for the right to "their" women as these women began to identify their own oppression with that of black men, transforming white men into a mutual enemy.[21] White men found their position of privilege challenged by the civil rights movement, the war in Vietnam, and the women's movement. Things were stirred up, and someone was going to have to pay. It was likely to be women, and they would pay with their bodies. The confusion emerging from the sexual liberation movement, which insisted that a woman should be sexually active (when a man wanted sex) and should be in charge of her own sexuality (unless her choice was different than his) and had no reason not to have sex when a man wanted (except that she was still likely to be seen as cheap and almost as likely to get pregnant), was minimized in *Vogue* during the 1970s. Women were, plain and simple, sexual. They were sexy. They wanted sex, they had no reservations about it, and they were likely to get raped or beaten in any case, so what they wanted regarding sex was not really all that important. *Vogue* righted the wrongs suffered by men. Even though they might protest "not now," "not here," in real life women in *Vogue* welcomed being taken; they longed to be "had."[22]

Vogue and other fashion magazines backed off somewhat on depictions romanticizing violence against women during the 1990s and beyond, but they surely haven't disappeared. A recent French *Vogue Hommes* yielded outraged comments when its cover depicted a man with his hand around a woman's neck, tonguing his own finger, maybe a "penis," maybe a "gun," his other hand on her breast.[23]

In Lina Wertmüller's classic date-rape film *Swept Away*, embedded in a condemnation of the bourgeoisie, she both presented and ignored

gendered violence and reinforced stereotypical views about rape and violence against women.[24] When the boat carrying a haughty blonde and her
upper-class husband, both reeking of privilege and assumed superiority, is
dashed on the rocks of an isolated island, the deckhand takes the opportunity for class revenge against the wealthy husband by raping his wife.
Predictably, she is initially disgusted by his boorishness, but soon, overwhelmed by his natural animal lust, she revels in the hot, primitive sexuality, transforming the rape into a singular moment of sexual awakening.
Wertmüller not only has the proletariat prevail in this film, she also
reveals the imagined subterranean desire the upper classes have for their
social inferiors—the white slaveholder's lust for the black slave, the society matron's secret fantasy about her driver, the president's wife's yearn-
ing for her bodyguard.[25] Wertmüller's deckhand was sending a message
to the husband, and every other white wealthy man, about the fragile grasp
he had on power, and the damage that could be done when he let down his
guard. Raping the wife rather than attacking the husband was perfect ret-
ribution. The husband's vulnerability was exposed by the violation of his
property and by revealing the wife as bound to the husband only for his
wealth. Her real animal nature desired the lustiness and vigor of life at
the bottom. She was bought but not owned.

　Wertmüller draws on common themes in her movie and illustrates the
power of these cultural constructions. The portrayal of "dark" as lusty,
sexual, and earthy, and "light" as clean, cold, and aloof, coupled with
the theme of lower-class sexuality and upper-class frigidity, especially
for women, dovetails with the theme of rape as punishment, conquest,
and sexual pleasure to construct a story in which the audience is to
applaud the ascendancy of the lower class (good, real) over the upper class
(bad, pretentious). We are to celebrate the revealed sexuality of a woman
too long constrained by the restrictions of wealth and privilege, as well as
her capitulation to the overpowering sexiness of man in his natural, unre-
fined state. These rape themes are common in the media,[26] falling into
predictable categories of revenge, power, lust, and punishment. The work
of sociologists Diana Scully and Joseph Marolla, who studied the
accounts provided by convicted rapists for their behavior, provides a parallel glimpse of the power of cultural constructions, the ways of ordering
the world that allow us to make sense of our behavior and the behavior
of others.[27] The convicted rapists they interviewed, like anyone else
called on to provide an account for his or her behavior, drew on readily
available and widely disseminated messages about women in order to
excuse or justify their behavior. Scully and Marolla found that men who
denied their responsibility were likely to justify their behavior by drawing

on predictable constructions: "Good girls don't get raped," "She eventually relaxed and enjoyed it," "Women say 'no' when they mean 'yes'," and "She asked for it." The minority of men who acknowledged their guilt nevertheless tried to reduce their responsibility by offering excuses such as drunkenness, or being high, or that what they did was bad but not as bad as it could have been.[28] The important point made by Scully and Marolla is not that rapists excused or justified their behavior, but they did so by drawing on readily available cultural constructions, rape myths, and stereotypes that were no different from those relied on by prosecutors, police, and even friends and family members in response to rape.[29] Movies, novels, and music all draw on these same dominant constructions, creating a culture in which even the victim of rape has little choice but to rely on commonplace constructions in her efforts to understand her experience, often to her own detriment. Of course, Wertmüller's arrogant wife not only said "no" when she really meant "yes," she had been humiliating the powerless mate for days, basically "asking for it," and indeed she eventually did "relax and enjoy it," showing that she was in fact not the "good girl" she claimed to be but was "bad" (i.e., sexual) underneath the façade of cool indifference.

Cultural messages about women and violence, whether rape or battery, reflect the thorough saturation of the culture with damaging and dangerous stereotypes of women. The messages range from subtle expressions of sexism such as the ad on the washing label of chinos instructing, "Machine wash warm inside out with like colors ... or give it to your woman. It's her job,"[30] to the blatantly misogynistic Freak dances where girls in junior high and high school bend over with their hands on the ground while a boy stands behind them miming anal intercourse,[31] reflective of the rap song by 2LiveCrew, titled "Face Down, Ass Up, That's the Way We Like to Fuck."[32]

These messages suggest that if woman is valued primarily for her sexuality, then other attributes are of less significance, or if she is presented as intelligent, then her sexuality is called into question. These images, however, frequently clash with one another and with the lived experience of real women. Images of mothers and motherhood are not easy to reconcile with the image of woman as sexually lascivious, leading to the fragmentation and disembodiment of women. This clash between reality and myth was illustrated well in a page from my local newspaper.[33] One photograph depicted the spring fashions in light, frothy colors and frills, the model indistinguishable from a Barbie doll. On the same page, another article revealed the bad news that the majority of women in the United States will have to work until they are age 74 before they can retire as a result of their low wages and work experience. The women portrayed in these two pieces might as well have been different species or lived on different planets for all the similarity there was between them. Similarly, the women who are raped by their boyfriends or beaten by their husbands bear almost no resemblance to the women "asking for it, wanting it, and not able to get enough of it," as shown through the male media gaze. Popular music like Grammy award winner Chris Brown's lyrics, "Uh, fuck um all like a orgy,"[34] various renditions of videogames like "Grand Theft Auto," or ads by companies like *fluid hair*[35] showing a woman dressed for an evening out, sitting on a dirty couch, with a black eye, looking lost, a "madman" type mimicking the suave advertising men on the television program *Mad Men*[36] standing unsmiling behind her, dominate cultural depictions of women's urge for violence in direct contrast to the reality they would so welcome.

While this disconnect between reality and media images is all too prevalent in lyrics and ads, it absolutely saturates music television videos. Here, all the women are young and beautiful, either encouraging rape or violence or enjoying it once they realize they are powerless to prevent it. Real women who are raped are young and old, attractive and plain, married and single; they are raped because they are female rather than for their other attributes or unique characteristics.[37] They are raped to demonstrate male power or female powerlessness, male dominance or female submissiveness, or just because men can. The victims, of course, may be young and attractive, perhaps a college student raped by a classmate at a party when both are drunk, but they are also likely to be poor, tired, plain, and middle-aged. The excitement, thrill, and romance are missing from the rape picture in everyday life, leaving only pain, confusion, humiliation, and physical and emotional wounds.

Constructions of femaleness and female sexuality not only reflect the male fantasy but also carry a strong message to women and girls about the centrality of their sexuality in the definition of their identity and their self-worth.[38] The portrayals in the media submerge women in sexuality, elevating it to their essential characteristic—the one that drives them whether they are taking notes or taking a hike. Fifty years ago, James Bond's women, bearing names like "Pussy Galore,"[39] had no doubt about the place of sexuality in their identity and the power it reflected. Prostitution and emphasized femininity[40] are linked with no contradiction in early films like *Pretty Woman,* as well as the HBO series *Bunny Ranch,*[41] which celebrate childlike, innocence. However, we see less of that today and more depictions designed to humiliate and degrade women, like "Chicken Head" by Rapper Project Pal featuring La Chat &Three 6 Mafia[42] referring to women as oral sex machines pretty similar to Kid Rock intoning in the song "Balls in Your Mouth"[43]

These may be the same women we see in *Jersey Shore*, either "grenades" (big ugly chicks) or "land mines" (thin ugly chicks) who are, or had better be if they want to hang around, always "dtf" (down to f***) with those fun-loving guys who party day and night.[44] Hardee's gets in on the act showing a young, buxom woman licking and sucking on a big juicy burger, the camera caressing her legs and mouth while she caresses the burger, leading some of the viewers to respond on YouTube: "If only I was that burger," or "everybody get a hardee on this," or "I would tear that shit up."[45]

Woman's sexuality is not simply a human characteristic; it is centered as the essence of the female self, serving as the excuse or justification for the violence women experience.[46] Everyday conceptions of violence against women, such as justifications for rape or battery, stem from and are inseparable from their sexuality. There is a seamless relationship between a woman's sexual self and her violated self. Her sexuality either is in need of protection or has been violated, or it is destructive in some way, to herself or others. Woman's natural, inherent sexuality and the destruction it wreaks on her and on the men who love her or with whom she is sexually involved are a familiar centerpiece of film and novel. Her rape in film may be either the focal point around which the story is built, as in *The Accused*,[47] or the point from which the story of revenge and vindication begins. Such highly sexualized, simplistic, and stereotypical portrayals of women are unimaginable as believable storylines for any other group of people. Perhaps the closest we can come to another situation so heavily reliant on stereotypical imagery would be the black-face comedies of the 1930s, or the stereotypes of blacks in such early films as *Gone with the Wind,* or later, during World War II, *Life* magazine's portrayals of the Japanese as "slope heads" or "slant eyes" or the "yellow peril." These portrayals would never be acceptable in mainstream media today, nor should they be. One cannot imagine, for example, a role designed for a black actor dubbed "Big Lips" or "Nappy Head" in a mainstream film, to match the "cunts," and "hoes" and "asses" all over rap music. The cultural scripts produced about women, like cultural constructs of any other group, not only create an environment in which others evaluate and devalue the woman, but they are the constructions the woman herself draws on for her own identity.

We all act toward ourselves to some degree as objects.[48] To be able to do so is to be human, and to do so makes us human. Because the self is social, because we become who we are through our interactions with other people who are important to us, first parents and then peers, the dominant cultural constructions are powerful in shaping the self. The self consists not only of how we see ourselves but also of how we evaluate ourselves, based on our perceptions of how others evaluate us.[49] When we are surrounded by images indicating that the value of a woman comes from her use as an object by men, as occurs in pornography and so often in television and in mainstream literature and film, or as a flawed body and face to be improved and made acceptable through creams and clothes, we are struck by the gulf between the everyday life of women and the images that dominate their world. The images of women supplied by the media are powerful and potentially damaging to women not because they cause men to rape or attack or batter but because they reinforce a view of women as valued or devalued only for their looks or their bodies, and what they have to offer men sexually. Such an image, if internalized by women, is disempowering, if only because no matter how beautiful or flawless she is, she will not always be so. She will have the "bad taste and poor judgment"[50] to age and in so doing will reveal her underlying unacceptable self. Once she can no longer "keep herself up," "makes up" for who she is underneath, she will be discarded, having revealed the truth her lies can no longer conceal. She is necessarily caught in a fight with herself, learning to hate what she will eventually be, hence never being happy with who she is.

Our subjective self, gained through our object status, through being able to view ourselves as others view us, is a reflection of the interactional world in which we construct ourselves.[51] We are clearly not *only* objects, to be viewed or done to by the other, but we are *also* objects, and others' responses to us are shaped by their perceptions of us as much as our own evaluations are shaped by our awareness of how others perceive us.[52] One need not be told verbally that it is important to be beautiful if one is a woman; books, movies, advertisements, MTV clips, and jokes communicate that message to us and those with whom we interact. In what Sut Jhally calls the "male dreamworld,"[53] a construction by men of women, women lose the interiority or subjectivity that reflects the value they know they have in the world.[54] Particularly as they are segmented into parts and pieces—breasts, butts, and legs—they are disembodied and dehumanized. A print ad from "Blender: A concept store with a butcher shop," illustrates this more chillingly than any I have seen: a very thin woman is hanging horizontally from chains, sawed into seven parts with the bone, blood, and muscle showing in each of the vertical cuts. The parts are: her torso and head with her finger placed pensively at her lips, her waist to below her vagina, her upper leg, her thigh and calf, a cut just above her ankle, and her foot wearing six-inch heels.[55] In another example, a Budweiser beer billboard invites us (men, really) to "expect everything." The ad depicts only the area from the waist to the crotch of a woman in tight jeans and an ornate belt standing beside a huge bottle of ice-cold beer, showing just the neck and hip of the bottle.[56]

In many media portrayals, women lose their existence as women with a subjective self and become bodies to be acted on or used for male pleasure. In the dreamworld, men learn that women are hungry for sex; they are always ready, always wanting it, and they are powerless when confronted with the male sexual drive. They also learn that the real world is about men—their wants, their needs—and that women are there to fulfill them, either willingly or under force.

These images are dangerous to girls because they either narrowly subjectify the female self as Timothy Beneke claims or desubjectify the female self, erasing the self as a person with ideas, desires, or goals, making her more of a place on which things occur, on which men act out their fantasies, than a person; a geographical body more than a humanized self.[57] It is not just that the male gaze,[58] the view of women as seen and evaluated by men, dehumanizes women, but that women lose themselves in the male gaze, coming to identify sexuality with debasement, force, violence, or at the very least powerlessness, incorporating into their own identity the male view of their sexuality and their value. When Chris Brown, author of the rap song "Fuck Um All" was convicted finally (after eight or nine incidents) for assaulting his girlfriend, Rihanna, the sympathy and support for him, not for Rihanna, poured out.[59] On *YouTube*, girls wrote, "I'd let Chris Brown beat me up anytime," "Chris Brown can beat me up . . . in the bedroom," and "Any girl that hates on Chris Brown is stupid. Do you realize that it would be an honor if he hit you?"[60] A few years later, he was indeed honored, performing at the Grammy Awards and receiving one himself.[61]

THE DREAMS OF MEN

Sut Jhally outlines the dominant typifications of women in his videos on masculinity themes that characterize MTV, music lyrics, advertising, and prevailing imagery of women in popular film and literature.[62] In the "adolescent male fantasy" that is the impetus for MTV, all that matters about women is their sexuality. They are ravenous, always aroused; they are indiscriminate, willing to have sex with anyone, anywhere, anytime; and they are sexually aggressive. These depictions are reflected in and reinforce the sometimes conflicting and sometimes overlapping themes of violence against women in literature, film, and music. These dominant themes, drawing on gender stereotypes, are saturated with class and race stereotypes that reflect controlling images of black and Asian women and men and the relationships between them. The pervasive negative images of women are of particular concern because they are not shaped by women but shape their lives in ways that reinforce violence or oppression. The themes all, in various ways, reinforce what Beneke calls "compulsive masculinity," the "compulsion or need to relate to, and at times create, stress or distress as a means of both proving manhood and conferring on boys and men superiority over women and other men." It includes the content categories of: that which would hurt anyone; that which poses a psychological danger due to its relationship with manhood, like crying; and that which poses the greatest threat of all—woman.[63]

One dominant theme in the male dreamworld is that of passion and lust—the theme that all women want sex all the time, even though they might act as if they do not. This message is accompanied by the underlying message that women are liars: they act as if they don't want sex, but they actually do. They might pretend to be above it or want it only when accompanied by love or the promise of marriage and babies, but they all really want it. In the video *Dreamworlds3*, Sut Jhally illustrates the impact of the male gaze as it shapes woman's sexuality and her relationship to the male viewer and as it defines for women, and particularly for girls, the paramount value of their sexuality.[64] In the male dreamworld, women are always ready for sex, even when they initially might seem resistant. They are so sex hungry that when men are not around, they search for objects to replace them, like doorknobs or microphones.[65] They love to be looked at and in fact form themselves into objects for the male gaze. For black women, this translates in the male imagination to a fascination with the butt, reinforcing racist stereotypes about black women's bodies for the consumption of white men. Mr. Ghetto's video shows black women happily "bouncing their butts" in tight animal prints while he intones "I'm fuckin' like a wild animal."[66] In this world, the women who pretend to be the coldest, the most aloof and disinterested are in fact often the hottest once awakened. Putting on the face of cool composure to the public, they become hungry animals behind closed doors. They demonstrate this by masturbating, often with any object that is available, and by being transformed into hungry, clutching, wild-eyed creatures when they want sex from the man who is withholding. The message of desire makes every woman the legitimate object of rape. No matter how much she feigns innocence or disinterest, just below the surface lies a willing, even wanton sexuality. One of the convicted rapists interviewed by Scully and Marolla illustrated the danger such a view posed to women: he insisted that the women he raped and killed enjoyed the sex up to the moment right before he killed them.[67]

Another theme is that innocence calls forth men's sexual nature and leads to rape. Perhaps the most well-known contemporary story about female innocence is *Lolita*, remade in 1992 amid great controversy and even prohibited from being shown in some theaters in the United States.[68] The controversy stemmed from the theme of child sexual abuse more than the issue of pornography, however, reflecting a public sensitivity to the implicit approval in the film of a sexual relationship between an older man and a child. Much pornography as well as music videos celebrate this relationship—for example, a classic Britney Spears video[69] presents women as little girls, sexual innocents, in short, plaid schoolgirl skirts and white cotton panties, delectable and sexually available. It may be that as real women become more competent, more independent, and more powerful, girls, or women imitating girls, replace them as idealized sexual partners. The rise in child pornography during the past several decades does suggest that girls and boys carry the innocence that is no longer tied to adult women, making them sexually attractive to men, while grown-up women, being competent adults, are frighteningly unattractive.

While white women are sometimes presented as childlike and innocent, young Asian women dressed as schoolchildren are even more popular. The Japanese male obsession with schoolgirls or women dressed as schoolgirls reveals the juxtaposition of female sexuality and desire with expressed superficial innocence.[70] Girls are virgins, sexual novices, and innocent, and they need to be instructed, sometimes reprimanded. Their youth and innocence create the masterfulness and sophistication of the man. He is wiser and can be the stern but kind schoolmaster. The fact that in Japan, one can buy soiled girls' underwear in vending machines seems somehow linked with this fascination with girls' bodies.[71] The tendency to present young girls as sexually available and attractive is in many ways an extension of the common pattern of courtship and mating in which an older, wiser, more powerful man requires a younger, more innocent woman as a partner. Not only are young girls appropriate targets because their innocence represents passive sexuality, but women dressed as innocents are presented as camouflaging their animal female sexuality just waiting to be awakened by an experienced and skillful older lover (or just an older lover). As one might expect, black women are seldom portrayed as innocents; their sexuality is far more blatant, readily tapped, simmering, smoldering. There exist very few cultural images of black women or black girls as soft, fragile, or vulnerable. As bell hooks writes in "Selling

Hot Pussy," the black woman's body is sexualized and degraded, like the butt of the Hottentot Venus that fascinated all of Europe, even while preserved in formaldehyde.[72] Rap music's construction of women parallels that of nineteenth-century white slaveholders, conveniently mouthed by black rap "artists" who are owned by white corporations, allowing white men to distance themselves from the men who express their sexist views.[73]

The theme that women are weak and stupid and deserve a man's wrath is a theme that allows the most sadistic torture and killing of women. Women are despicable solely because of their femaleness. Their femaleness itself makes them contemptible and legitimate targets of a superior man. A man's superiority is expressed through his debasement and degradation of women. In "The Reunion," hip-hop duo Eminem and Royce da 5'9" of "Bad meets Evil," warn the slut that he's not her husband and if she talks to him like she talks to her husband "I'll fuck you up ... "[74]

Such degradation also reaffirms and advances his masculinity. As Jon Stoltenberg points out in his work on men and sex, men "have a sex," that is, are masculine and know that they are insofar as they are differentiated from women.[75] Acting against women distances them from women and establishes their masculinity.

The theme that women are despicable because of their weakness and deserve to be raped or killed was expressed vividly by Bret Easton Ellis in his controversial novel *American Psycho.*[76] The film of the same name, directed by a woman, Mary Harron, was transformed into a more tasteful depiction of violence against women.[77] The reviews of this film are a trip through fantasyland; the incredible violence against women transformed into a "black comedy," a sophisticated critique of the self-indulgent 1980s. Pat Bateman, the cool, cultivated hero of the story, is dressed in something marvelous, such as "a four-button double-breasted wool and silk suit, a cotton shirt with a button-down collar by Valentino Couture, a patterned silk tie by Armani ... " After dining on "fresh grilled *foie gras* at Le Cirque," which is excellent, and accompanied by "lobster salad which is only so-so," or something similarly marvelous,[78] Bateman systematically destroys the women who are stupid enough to fall for him. They are targets of his disgust, violated by him for their natural insipid inferiority. He despises them, just as he despised and mutilated the homeless or blind person during the hiatus between fulfilling his major fantasies by degrading and killing detestable women—despicable because they are women, disgusting because they are his victims, victims because they are women in a spiral of self-destruction and ugliness almost beyond belief. The women maimed and killed by the well-dressed and sophisticated

Bateman are not violated because of something they did. They are muti-lated and murdered because they are despised, and they are despised because they are women. Their very being is insipid and repulsive to him, and his torture of them is presented as an unremarkable, natural reac-tion to their disgusting, base existence.

An excerpt from *American Psycho* illustrates the acceptability of women as objects of loathing and disgust eventuating in their deserved death. Bateman wakes from a particularly nasty hangover and notes: "Things are lying in the corner of my bedroom: a pair of girl's shoes from Susan Bennis Warren Edwards, a hand with a thumb and forefinger miss-ing, the new issue of *Vanity Fair* splashed with someone's blood, a cum-merbund drenched with gore, and from the kitchen wafting into the bedroom is the fresh smell of blood cooking."[79]

While the foregoing quotation might read like pornography or woman hating, Camille Paglia,[80] self-celebrated "real woman," unafraid of her sexuality, not sniveling and whining about being a victim, as she suggests feminists are, would view it as showing "the deepest truth about sexuality, stripped of romantic veneer."[81] She intones that no one can claim to be an expert in gender studies who is uncomfortable with pornography, which focuses on our rude and crude animality, our primary identity: "Idiotic statements like 'pornography degrades women' or 'pornography is the subordination of women' are only credible if you never look at pornogra-phy," she insists.[82]

The disgust with women expressed by Bateman in *American Psycho* is richly supported by the commonplace and far less violent psychological and academic depictions of femininity. In psychology, foundational theory[83] sets the stage for women's inferiority, dependence and lack of singular identity. Freud concluded that women could not develop as truly moral persons equal in their morality to men because of their inability to separate fully from their mothers. Erickson viewed women as empty ves-sels, waiting to form their identities from the material brought to them by the man they were lucky enough to attract.

Kohlberg assumed that woman's moral development is stunted as a result of her essential entrapment in the web of everyday human relation-ships. She cannot rise above the mundane and emotional to the level of objective reason.[84] In all these unavoidable ways, women are inferior to the standard developed by men that reflects the patriarchal assumptions of male domination, male control, male identification, and male superior-ity.[85] Philip Wylie expressed a predictable hostility toward women in his *Generation of Vipers*, in which he portrayed mothers as overbearing, cas-trating women, destroying their sons' masculinity for their own gratification.[86] Betty Friedan was not much kinder to women, especially those who stayed home to raise their children; they became oppressive, manipulative intruders in their children's lives, having nothing more substantial with which to occupy themselves.[87] Phyllis Schlafly's defense of marriage and opposition to the passage of the Equal Rights Amendment in the 1980s are shot through with distrust—not only of men but also of women.[88] Her picture of the typical marriage shows men and women locked in an embrace of mutual exploitation and distrust, bound to one another in middle age by financial necessity long after affection and sexual attraction have faded. All of these influential authors found women wanting, assessing them as deviating from the male standard of acceptability.[89]

A theme more common in everyday language than in film and music videos is that of a woman needing to be raped to put her in her place, to show her that she is not as tough or important as she thinks she is. This theme blatantly presents rape as deserved punishment, reestablishing the normal hierarchy in which men are at the top and women at the bottom. The woman is raped, assaulted, or killed because she violated the assumption of male superiority, and the male deserves to get revenge against her. She may have challenged his sexuality directly by ignoring, belittling, or criticizing him, or she may have violated his masculinity by sexual allegiance to women instead of men. Women can sometimes violate men's masculinity simply by not responding to their desires, not being what men want them to be. The woman is not raped because of her innocence or because she is property, but because she challenges male superiority; she places herself above or equal to a man, sometimes simply by not attending him, not acknowledging his importance. Man reasserts his position through violation and humiliation or degradation of her. She is subdued and accepts her proper place.

An excellent example from MTV comes from the band Prodigy, whose song "Smack My Bitch Up" showed women being hit and injected with drugs.[90] MTV withdrew the video after a week, not because of the violence but because that was their marketing plan, according to Sheryl Jones, Vice President of MTV Communications. Jones said of the video, "We thought obviously 'Smack My Bitch Up' was a news making and ground breaking video."[91] This remarkable evaluation was of a song that had only two lines of lyrics—one the title and the other a nonsensical inclusion of the rhyming word *pitch*. Along the same lines, a song from Limp Bizkit, "Stalemate," reveals a man getting even with a woman who has scorned him, hunting her down to gain revenge, promising to get "mine" through rape and assault.[92] The wildly popular Grammy-winning Eminem's lyrics in his rap about killing his wife, Kim,[93] are illustrative of this theme of punishing a woman who deserves whatever she gets, up to and including death. They juxtapose the vengeful destruction of the woman who has done him wrong and whom he threatens, viciously assaults, attacks, and benignly observes as she suffers, begs, and bleeds with the innocence of their baby, who is witness to what is presented as a justifiable homicide. Eminem combines vicious misogyny and self-pitying childishness when he sings, "Get the fuck away from me, don't touch me," going on to scream how much he hates her, quickly transforming into a tirade on how much he loves her, blaming her for not loving him enough, moving back and forth between self-pity, virulent woman-hating, self-loathing, and blaming the victim, and ending with (Kim choking) "BLEED! BITCH BLEED! BLEED."[94] One could not hope for a clearer expression of a male batterer's or rapist's self-serving, victim-blaming justification for lethal violence against women.

Thirty years ago one of the most talked about revenge films in America was *Thelma and Louise*.[95] What starts out as Louise shooting the man who is raping her friend on the hood of a car outside a bar, a man who continues to hurl denigrating epithets at them even as he is dying, becomes a wild fantasy of freedom for these women whose newfound power comes from their ability to break all the boundaries of femininity. However, their freedom is fleeting, and they finally choose death over a future imprisoned in an actual prison or in the stultifying lives they have escaped. This illustrates another significant theme, that of female power and powerlessness. While weakness can be despised as "essentially" female, the powerlessness of women takes on a slightly different meaning. The difference between weakness and powerlessness is subtle but strong. Weakness is viewed as a character trait, indicative of inferiority. Powerlessness is a political position, indicating its appropriate place in a hierarchical status system. Women are to occupy a position of "less than" or "one down" in order to be truly feminine. As pointed out by the Brovermans and their colleagues in a classic early study of therapists' assessments of masculinity and femininity, real women, healthy women, are different not only from healthy men but from healthy adults, by being more childlike, less reasonable.[96]

Powerlessness, women's dependence on men for economic and social status, results in vulnerability. This very powerlessness has been transformed into power by men, as well as by some essentialist feminists who view men and women as inherently different and view female dependence as a form of power. Women, with no other symbols of power, find that their sexuality is redefined as power of such strength as to outweigh all others. The fact that women have less economic, political, or physical power is presented as inconsequential in the light of their awesome sexual prowess. Monica Lewinsky, a former White House intern, was portrayed as powerful enough to destroy the president of the United States—the sight of her thong panties, the phone sex, and the allure of her lipsticked mouth rendered the most powerful man in the world suddenly weak-kneed and completely powerless. Redefining her as powerful draws on the cultural constructions of woman's sexuality as dangerous, woman as predator or seductress. I am inclined to believe that this contrivance that women's powerlessness gives them power is more reflective of white men's view of female sexuality than that of black men. The dominant imagery of woman's sexuality controlling men that we see in such phrases as "pussy whipped" is definitely not seen in rap, where men are always in power—women are done to, used sexually, despised and discarded. Black men not only demonstrate their allegiance to white male values of dominance and superiority through their rap, they never concede women's power, never buy into the obviously false notion of "vagina power." Male dominance and control are the only options in rap. LMFAO, for example, raps in "Party Rock," "yo, I'm running through these ho's like Drano."[97] Jay-Z articulates this idea in "Big Pimpin'." "You know I thug em, fuck em, love em, leave em."[98] Later, in an interview about his book *Decoded*, even he was stunned by his lyrics in "Big Pimpin'," saying, "It was like, I can't believe I said that and kept saying it. What kind of animal would say this sort of thing?"[99]

Man's sexuality is conveniently defined as an automatic response system, triggered by external stimuli and uncontrollable once awakened. In his book *Proving Manhood*, Timothy Beneke proposes that men's anger toward women is born in their feelings of powerlessness in the face of women's intrusive female sexuality.[100] Their embarrassment and shame over having an erection when exposed to a woman's thigh or nipples is transformed into self-control and dominance through masturbating to pornography, allowing men to annihilate the powerful female and reestablish themselves as independent, brave men. In researching the Jesus movement of the 1970s, I studied a group with very conservative sexual and social mores. In this group, women who exposed an ankle or thigh were accused of "stumbling the brothers," an offense that could lead to their expulsion.[101] This carries over from the expectation that women are to control not only their own sexuality but that of men as well and to assume responsibility for the man's sexual arousal. This, of course, results in an untenable situation for women. Their nature is provocative; their sexual power accompanies them and is revealed not through their behavior but through the responses and behavior of men. Any power women have is completely derivative, dependent on male response and male definition, so that whatever power men attribute to women as a result of female sexuality is in fact a statement about the ascendance of man—his response, his reaction, his feeling, his body. One cannot help but think of the murder of women in Islamic countries by fathers and brothers whose honor has been damaged by the sexuality of the woman, even if the family member himself was responsible for the rape that dishonored; she is not honorable and has no honor, but she holds the honor of the father and suffers or dies when this honor is threatened by men in the community of men.

Women raped in prisons, hospitals, and mental institutions are brutalized by guards, or orderlies, or nurses who have power over women whose freedoms have already been so circumscribed as to have essentially dehumanized them. The violence they experience is a reflection of institutional sexism and reveals the willingness to assert power and establish a masculine identity through the debasement of women. The women who are raped in prisons or in mental institutions and mentally handicapped girls who are gang-raped are victims of men for whom this powerlessness is both stimulating and safe and who need not call on any motive other than their desire to sexually humiliate or use another human being for their own whims/desires/fantasies.

Women in prison sometimes fight back, and they sometimes win. Jayne Cortez's powerful poem about Joanne Little and Inez Garcia, who killed the prison guards who raped them, peels back any romanticized veneer that might possibly hide the ugliness and brutality of rape, revealing their hatred for their rapist, as they "pumped lead into his 300 pounds of shaking flesh" ... this "repulsive pimple-infested animal, licking 'crabs' from his ass."[102]

Another theme dominant in everyday discourse, not as prevalent as some others in film and music, is "the bitch who deserves it." Although this is similar to the theme of woman being raped to put her in her place, to be punished, it portrays rape as directed at woman's sexual self, her animal sexuality, rather than at something she has specifically done. She is raped not because she is woman and is therefore weak and despicable, as she is in *American Psycho*,[103] but because her animal sexuality calls for it and because deep down, she wants it. She is there for the taking, and whatever pose she affects—strong, independent, good—is simply a camouflage for her hard sexual essence that demands to be mastered. The refrain "She just needs a good fuck" is not uncommon, nor is the notion of rape as punishment for being too dominant, too masculine, too independent, or too self-sufficient. The woman who is sexually free or independent is in danger of being the victim of rape. When she is raped, she is likely to get in touch with her womanhood and like it. Men's power comes through woman's expressed or unexpressed desire for them rather than straightforwardly through their need to hurt or damage. There is always something about the woman that excites the man, that makes him desire her, and this leads to rape, humiliation, and degradation. She can be aloof and demanding, but this has to conceal an underlying sexual heat; a woman with a cold heart is unacceptable even to the rapist. In her review of Spike Lee's film *She's Gotta Have It*, a film he said would portray "a radical new image of black female sexuality,"[104] bell hooks insisted that instead Lee reinforced old norms by showing his sexually free black heroine being raped by her "lover," reduced to losing all ownership of her body. As he is ramming her from the rear, he demands of her, "Whose pussy is this?," and she finally submits, "Yours."[105]

In the film *The Accused*, Jodie Foster's character is brutally raped by several men.[106] She has been drinking with one of them much of the night. They are both sexually excited. However, she insists on going home because she has to work the next day. His lust and desire for her turns to a need, a demand, and an attack, first by him, then the others who have been cheering him on. She is raped because she is sexy and beautiful and drunk, reinforcing the audience's view that being a woman is both desirable and dangerous. The line between lust and destruction is a thin one. I do not know what the real victim in the rape on which this film is based looked like, whether she was beautiful or plain, but a beautiful woman is far more consistent with the romanticization and sexualization of rape victims in the media.

Another twist on this revenge theme embodies hypermasculinity, another characteristic of what Beneke calls compulsive masculinity, as a defense against the feminine self. Hypermasculinity justifies aggression against women as well as homosexuals who share the degraded status of feminine.[107] The presence of the homosexual—his rejection of masculinity, his weakness or femininity—makes him despicable and deserving of rape and, often, death. On May 19, 2013, a young "out" gay black man walking in Greenwich Village, tried to ignore the hate speech thrown at him by a drunk, homophobic person who followed him, the slurs ending in murder.[108] Just the day before, the *New York Times* carried a story about Orthodox priests leading a mob of thousands through the streets of Tbilisi, Georgia, attacking a group of about 50 gay rights demonstrators. This attack reflected the increasing hostility toward gays, led by the Orthodox priests who liken homosexuality to drug addiction and see it as a threat to the conservative majority.[109] The two men who slit Billy

Jack Gaither's throat, bludgeoned him with an axe handle, and threw him on a pile of tires and then set fire to him in Alabama, killing him because "he was a faggot"[110] express this same loathing for and fear of gay men who by challenging hegemonic masculinity lay bare the fragility and tentativeness of masculinity. The two Russian men who tortured to death a 23-year-old with whom they had been drinking and playing pool, sodomizing him with beer bottles, killed him because he was gay,[111] a fact so repugnant, really so threatening to their own masculine identities, that they resorted to murder. Earlier, the two men who killed Matthew Shepherd in Wyoming felt justified—he had been in a bar with them, he was homosexual, he violated all the demands of compulsory masculinity, and he deserved to be punished, hurt, and killed.[112] In *Boys Don't Cry*, the men rape and brutalize the girl who is passing as a boy because she challenges their perceptions; she fools them, illustrating the tentativeness of masculinity.[113] If a frail, sweet-faced girl can be taken for a boy, if she can have sex with "their girls," then what separates them from her? How are they to be comfortable with their masculinity? How can they take anything for granted? She deserves to be brutally beaten and killed.

This theme of hyper-masculinity establishes man as being man, that is, "having a sex," only in juxtaposition to woman, being able to claim masculinity only through opposition to femininity.[114] He can be a man only to the extent that he is not a woman, therefore not feminine, not the dreaded "other." Masculinity is power, but it is "terrifyingly fragile" because it does not exist as a true biological reality, something inside oneself, but as an ideology, as scripted behavior that exists only within gendered relationships.[115] Men then have to be men through gendered interactions that reveal to themselves and others their masculinity, and this is best expressed in acting against anything that is female or feminine.

In *Misogynies,* Joan Smith illustrates this construction of masculinity through the destruction of any hint of femininity in her analysis of Peter Sutcliffe, the mass murderer.[116] He was a man on a search-and-destroy mission, using any woman he encountered to destroy the feminine in himself—a man who grew up a "bit of a sissy, a mummy's boy" in a brutal working-class culture. He could become a man, she suggests, only through ripping, stabbing, mutilating, and destroying women's bodies and annihilating the feminine in himself. This man, who despised women and hated himself for having the devalued characteristics of women, acted against them, not because of what they did, but because of who they were in the broadest sense. As such, he reflects the cultural expectation that women simply *are*, and what they are—their nature, their femininity, their sexuality (all of these being virtually the same thing)—leads to good, or bad, depending not so much on themselves as on the male actor, who is the one who *does*.

Gang rape encompasses this theme, with boys and men signaling their masculinity to one another through the violation or rape of a woman. 2LiveCrew rap about gang rape, playing a game they call *amtrack*, more traditionally known as "pulling a train," in which they all line up and "take our turns at waxing girls' behinds."[117] In *The Accused*, Jodie's Foster's character is the target not of male hatred so much as she is a thing to be violated in front of and for the approval of other men.[118] Hesitation to join in the assault elicits self-doubt; refusal would elicit condemnation by self and others. The harsh, cold violence she suffers illustrates her lack of humanity—the transformation of her from a sexual partner to an object to be f***ed, not for pleasure but to assert masculinity, to assure each man in the circle that he is a man, at least as much a man as the next one. The barroom scene is regularly replayed in fraternities and on the street, a violent conversation of gestures between men reinforcing their fragile masculinity. The Spur Posse, a gang of white middle-class high school boys whose *raison d'etre* was the rape of high school girls, and other similar middle-class gangs fed off the widely held view of women as objects to be used in male competitions. Surprisingly, the parents of the Spur Posse members held no better view of the girls their sons raped than did the boys, and they justified the rapes as "boys will be boys."[119] Gang rape fosters male bonding, the men sharing not only a woman's body but the degradation of her body to establish masculinity as "power over."[120] Rapper Immortal Technique emphasizes this view in "Dance with the Devil" when Billy is called to rape a woman to prove his masculinity. He is joined by all his bros, who rape her repeatedly, kicking her until they cracked her ribs and beat her unconscious. As she lay silent, "Blood leaking through the cloth, she cried silently." And they kept raping her.[121] Such hypermasculine cultures as fraternities and gangs foster a "sexual discourse that rationalizes male sexual aggression against women by defining it as a necessary, indeed natural, ingredient of male sexual expression and heterosexual masculine identity."[122] Some years ago, during a Puerto Rican Day Parade in New York City, reminiscent of the "wildings" in Central Park,[123] groups of aimless, rude men began by throwing water on the women in the crowd and then were transformed into a brutal, cheering mob that sexually attacked at least 22 women within two hours. The terrorized women were first baffled by the behavior, then terrified as the men grabbed them, knocked them down, groped them, and tore their clothes off. Police responded with lassitude to these persistent, ugly attacks against women. Women who reported their assaults to nearby police were treated with indifference; their complaints were minimized and dismissed.[124]

The view of woman as disgusting but having an inherent sexuality that defines her identity is clearly expressed in rap lyrics as well as fighting songs that encourage male bonding. Sexual harassment in the military confirms the historical discomfort men have with women who challenge the hypermasculine world organized around conflict and destruction, but it does not reveal the full extent of the military culture's view of women. That is demonstrated in such ditties as the following, discovered by Christopher Hitchens in the recreational songbook of the 77th Tactical Squadron of the U.S. Air Force.[125]

> The Ballad of Lupe
> Down in Cunt Valley where Red Rivers flow
> Where cocksuckers flourish and whoremongers grow
> There lives a young maiden that I do adore
> She's my Hot Fuckin' Cocksuckin' Mexican Whore
> Oh Lupe, oh Lupe, dead in her tomb
> While maggots crawl out of her decomposed womb
> But the smile on her face is a mute cry for more!!!
> She's my Hot Fuckin' Cocksuckin' Mexican Whore[126]

Hitchens's discomfort with the material prevented him from printing the stanzas that were too tough for him, but he does offer one more, from "I Fucked a Dead Whore" (intercourse with dead women being a fairly common theme).[127]

> I fucked a dead whore by the roadside
> I knew right away she was dead
> The skin was all gone from her tummy
> The hair was all gone from her head.[128]

Sung on marches or after drills, these songs allow men to proclaim their masculinity to one another through their assertion of not being weak, fragile, or feeling. Men who will have to face death, ugliness, and terror in war can reinforce their ability to tolerate such fear and horror through having the strength to meet death and to have sex with it. Anyone can have sex with a woman—maybe even anyone can rape a woman—but it takes a real man to ram a corpse. This is a confrontation, conquering the power of death that tells a man he is a real man, a worthy man, a man who can face anything in war.

Another common cultural theme, perhaps taken for granted in much film and literature, is that of woman as property. Historically, of course, women were the property of first their father and then their husband, so the notion of women as property is almost taken for granted. In *Incidents in the Life of a Slave Girl*, published in 1861, Linda Brent (Harriet Jacobs) portrays her powerless status as property in her relationship with her married doctor owner, who began raping her at 15.[129] "My master met me at every turn, reminding me that I belonged to him, and swearing by heaven and earth that he would compel me to submit to him." It is this same theme, or this assumption, that often is displayed by men who rape their wives. As one legislator is said to have wondered as he expressed his opposition to the imposition of laws prohibiting marital rape, "If I can't rape my wife, who[m] can you rape?"[130] Women are not presented as despised or overly powerful but as owned—sometimes cherished, sometimes not, but nevertheless owned, who can be done with as the owner wishes, with few or no consequences. Historically, in a patriarchal system, women were to do what their husbands said; they were to mind and to bend to the husbands' will because they were dependents. One classic example is Ibsen's *A Doll's House*, in which Nora violates her role as the childlike wife and property, leaving her husband and children to search for her own identity, a choice she felt compelled to make to escape the stultifying constraints of Victorian society. In Charlotte Perkins Gilman's *The Yellow Wallpaper*, the young woman, suffering postpartum depression, does what her husband tells her to do, not questioning his authority but cautiously questioning his wisdom, until she becomes so deranged she is reduced to crawling around in circles on the floor of the nursery to which she has been confined and isolated as a cure for her malaise.[131] The lyrics of the song "Every Breath You Take" by the Police demonstrate the danger that accompanies independence, especially if that involves rejecting a man, implying that being owned is beautiful.[132] In the song "Me and My Bitch" (featuring Puff Daddy) by the artist known as Notorious B.I.G, a similar statement of ownership of "his" woman is offered, and he demands the immediate and automatic compliance of his "bitch": "Yo would you kill for me?," and when she hesitates to agree, he derides her as a "motherfucker" and "bitch"[133] In "Trouble," Bei Maejor punishes "his" woman for not doing as he says, wearing a dress that he finds seductive. He concludes that he thought he had broken his bad habit of "hittin' nigga's girlfriends," but alas, that dress, with her in it, proved him wrong.[134]

RACE AND IMAGES OF VIOLENCE AGAINST WOMEN

Who are the men who rape or violate women in music? Sometimes it is the man whose wife or woman has done him wrong, as is the case in Johnny Cash's song, "Delia's Gone."[135] The "triflin' " woman was tied to a chair and shot, a fate she deserved because of the way she had treated her man. The men sometimes cannot help themselves because they are so overwhelmed by the woman's sexual power. Often they are taking what is rightfully theirs or proving their manhood. In any case, the race of the man is an important indicator of what kind of man he is—how dangerous or how safe. In popular culture, the black man rapes because he is driven by his sexuality, his animalistic impulses, his lack of control over his sex. Black men rape because it is their nature to rape.[136] White men, on the other hand, rape because of particular reasons, often stemming from their flawed childhoods. The white rapist is psychotic or individually flawed; he acts out childhood miseries or traumas in his rape of a woman. His rape is particularistic, specific; he chooses a certain type of woman or rapes with a particular definable purpose or drive.[137] The white rapist must have a motive, whereas the black rapist is acting out his essential nature. Black men, in dominant imagery, are similarly sexually aggressive and are dangerous to both black and white women as illustrated in TYGA's "Make It Nasty" with "Rape til It's Bruising," holding up O. J. Simpson as a role model for murder.[138] Tenderness and vulnerability, generally denied white men, are unthinkable for black men. MacKinnon writes that the portrayal of the sexuality of black men as powerful and uncontrollable justifies their oppression historically and buttresses the fear and punitive reactions of the legal and social responses to them today.[139] Although they were acquitted, the four white officers who claimed self-defense after they pumped 41 bullets into an unarmed African immigrant, Amadou Diallo, as he was standing in the vestibule of his building offer a clear example of the automatic response to the black man as threatening, powerful, and dangerous.[140]

In terms of sexual imagery, Asian women are not hungry or aggressive, but they are good sexual partners because they are compliant and technically skilled, sometimes artful. They take instructions well and are accustomed to and generally accepting of being used for a wide range of sex acts desired by men. They are not particularly sexually excited or interested, but are available, acquiescent partners. If a man wants aggressive sexuality, he must look to a black woman, or even a white woman whose sexuality has been awakened, but if he wants someone who follows orders and does what is asked, he will want an Asian woman (the sexuality of Asian men for the most part simply being denied).

Random violence against women is often portrayed as violence committed by black men. An understanding of the context in which black masculinities are constructed may help us understand these portrayals. Clyde Franklin insists that black men construct their masculinities within a framework of power relations dominated by powerful white males and subordinated minority males. They are immersed in a society in which they experience severe disjunctions between the socially approved goals and the legitimate means for their achievement.[141] Drawing on Robert King Merton's work on anomie,[142] Franklin suggests that one dominant mode of adaptation to the difficulties of this disjunction is innovation, the exaggeration of one aspect of traditional masculinity that can be achieved even though the black man is blocked from legitimate avenues of achievement. Because economic and educational achievements are blocked, innovative black men can embrace the dominant male culture's attitude toward women and exaggerate it as a way of identifying with the success goals of the dominant culture. Some few of these men can simultaneously achieve financial success, the absolute core of the American dream, through identification with patriarchal denigration of women.[143] Sexual explicitness and the debasement of women are two aspects of American masculinity drawn on by such rap musicians as the late Notorious B.I.G. in the aggressive "Me and My Bitch," or the more to-the-point "Fuck You Tonight," or 2 Live Crew in "As Nasty as They Wanna Be."[144] Their lyrics exaggerate the masculine ethic portrayed more subtly but universally in white culture. Rapping against the constrictions of their lives, whether black women, the black family, or white cops, is an avenue to achieving traditional success goals when other avenues are blocked. It might be just as possible to view the content of much rap music not as innovation but as over-conformity to the dominant cultural goals and values.

From NWA (Niggaz wit Attitude) we get such songs as "Findum, Fuckum, and Flee," "To Killa Hooker," and "One Less Bitch," with lyrics about "tying a 'bitch' to a bed, fucking her, then blowing her away with a forty-five." "She Swallowed It" is a lyrical paean to fellatio, likening semen to a vanilla milkshake and demonstrating the willing acquiescence of the singer's "ho" to be raped and sodomized with a broomstick by his friends.[145] Ann Jones, in *Next Time She'll Be Dead*, cites a 1990 rap from the Geto Boys, originally the Ghetto Boys, that chillingly depicts a rape and murder.[146] The woman is brutally beaten, cut, "fucked," and despite her pleas (perhaps because of them) has her throat slit before being raped again.[147] The theme of rape and murder continues in "Dance with the Devil" by Immortal Technique when Billy was made to go first, but each of them took a turn "Ripping her up and choking her until her throat burned."[148] Presented as a cautionary tale about the prevalence and power of evil, it nonetheless layers sex with violence and masculinity, drawing on familiar images of woman as natural victim and man as predator. This is mirrored in crime shows and dramas where, with slight variations on the theme, the victim is always a woman, the rapist or killer a man reflecting and reproducing familiar stereotypes and reinforcing gender hierarchy.

Black rappers draw on cultural misogyny to make their rhymes and in so doing reinforce every stereotype about aggressive, animalistic male sexuality that white men rely on to exclude black men from civilized (white) society. Black men join white men in defining themselves as uncontrollably lustful and sexually driven. Depictions of black men and women as insatiably sexual creatures reinforce the claim of white men to moral superiority and ideologically justify the social control and sexual violence they experience. Membership in the brotherhood of all men is sexually contingent; men must strive to make the idea of male sexual identity personally real by doing things that indicate they belong to the sex that is not female. They objectify women, depersonalize relationships, eroticize rape, and rely on pornography because that is the kind of sex men need in this culture to be real men. Real men are aggressive in sex; real men are cruel in sex; real men use their penises like weapons in sex; real men threaten, hit, and leave bruises. Men have this kind of sex, Jon Stoltenberg suggests in order to achieve and maintain their manhood.[149] Black men became gendered i.e., have been perceived by white culture as having humanity, being masculine rather than male, only in the recent past, so their assertions of masculinity might draw on the most stereotypical constructions of masculinity available. Black males became black men only when they used threats and violence to achieve what they had not been able to achieve through cooperation and negotiation, according to Franklin.[150] But their success in achieving black manhood has been accompanied by the objectification and exploitation of white women. As bell hooks says, if black men cannot also possess that object that white patriarchal culture offers to men as the supreme reward for male achievement, desirable white women, then their success means little. She continues: "In their eagerness to gain access to the bodies of white women, many Black men have shown that they were far more concerned with exerting masculine privilege than challenging racism. Their behavior is not unlike that of white male patriarchs who, on the one hand claimed to be white supremacists, but who could not forego sexual contact with the women of the very race they claimed to hate."[151]

It should not be surprising that in their demand for dominance and power, black males embrace the ideology of the white ruling class. To gain power in the patriarchy requires absorbing or supporting the ideas of those in power. Marx's powerful view that the dominant ideas of any era are the ideas of the ruling class suggests that those desiring power in that system will adopt the dominant ideas—whether they are men or women, black or white. In the case of black rappers, the absorption of white culture's degradation of women is a first step on the ladder to success. And since the degradation can be assumed to be also about black women, the dominant view of black women as sexually depraved can be specifically reinforced, along with the degradation of the wider category "women," to which both blacks and whites belong. And to the degree that hateful lyrics and violent pornography are expressions of anger and hate on the part of those who produce them, they have chosen low-risk ways to express those feelings.

Women and children are safe victims and have been for generations of musicians. The now geriatric Rolling Stones' "Under My Thumb" is almost as degrading toward women as is rap music,[152] and clearly, there are examples in blues, country, rock, and other genres that express and condone violence against women. But short of the marching songs presented earlier and a few other exceptions, like My Morning Jacket's lyric "I love your lack of self-respect, I love my hands around your neck,"[153] and some misogynistic '70s punk rock that's fairly indistinguishable from contemporary rap, such as, "Gonna strangle me a bitch, gonna leave her in a ditch" moving to " chop[ing] off her tits" all of which she deserves because she is a "slut,"[154] rap music carries more violent imagery, is more predictably and more blatantly violent toward women than any other genre. One might see it as reflecting a subculture of violence—a life where everyday violence is commonplace and predictable—but it is also a genre that allows black men unqualified dominance over women. Not only are women, especially black women, safe targets, through violence against women as depicted in music, black men bond with white men in their shared degradation and humiliation of women as a category.

Feminists have been criticized as "demonizing" all rap music, implicitly incorporating the dominant system's racist and "classist" attitudes toward young black men. Indeed, it would be unfair to characterize all rap as hostile toward women. Tupac Shakur, for example, wrote rap that resonates with feeling, vulnerability, sadness, and even hope, as revealed in "Liberty Needs Glasses," "In the Event of My Demise," and other poems from his collection *The Rose That Grew from Concrete*.[155] And Steel Train's "Dakota" promises empathy for young men sexually constrained by the demands of compulsive masculinity, and sympathy for gay guys shot and killed: "Blood washed down him like a faucet," and when he cried for help, nobody came.[156] But lyrics like these are few and far between in rap music, or punk for that matter.

Not all music of a particular genre has to condone or celebrate violence against women in order to illustrate the point that violence against women is commonplace in music and other cultural forms. However, the undeniable ugliness, hostility, hatred, and destructiveness expressed toward women in much contemporary music draws on and "normalizes" a view of women as deserving, needing, or enjoying being beaten, raped, or otherwise brutalized. Linked with less violence, but equally stereotypical, are images of women as stupid, dependent, needy, and vulnerable. Cultural depictions that are consistent, powerful, and omnipresent construct a world in which women are "other," in which they lose subjectivity, in which they are appropriate targets of misogynistic violence because of specific characteristics or, in contrast, because they lack any personhood. TYGA in "Make It Nasty" raps about his Asian "bitch": "Pussy so tight all she do is scream."[157] The literature on television violence, for example, suggests a connection between viewing violence and responding with violence. Malamuth and Check found that exposure to full-length feature films that portray sexual violence as having a positive consequence increased men's acceptance of interpersonal violence against women and increased their acceptance of rape myths.[158] Similarly, Lanis and Covell found that the exposure to sexist magazine advertisements increased men's acceptance of rape myths, stereotypic gender role attitudes, and interpersonal violence against women.[159]

All of these images contribute to the common experience of women in this culture. Images of dependence or stupidity reinforce images of violence, reproducing a culture that encourages rape, battery, and the brutalization of women. The research conducted to date does not allow for a clear conclusion that violent lyrics, violent rape scenes, or mutilations of women actually cause violence against women. At the same time, one would not want to suggest that there is no connection between violent depictions and images and violent behavior. The literature on television violence does suggest a connection between viewing violence and responding with violence.[160] Sexually violent heavy metal rock music has been found to influence men's attitudes toward women, but these images have an influence on women's attitudes as well. St. Lawrence and Joyner found that rap music videos that portray women in sexually subordinate roles (not victims of violence) increased girls' acceptance of teen dating violence, although the videos did not have such an impact on

the boys' acceptance of teen dating violence.[161] Linda Kalof also notes
that exposure to traditional and stereotypical sexual imagery in popular
music videos increases acceptance of interpersonal violence among
women. And even brief exposure to stereotypical images influences
beliefs about the adversarial and exploitive nature of male-female relationships, especially for men.[162]

Disagreements about the impact and importance of the cultural imagery
of women are legion. Whether and to what degree sexist images damage
women, to what extent they shape male response or female expectations,
to what extent they may actually encourage or condone violence against
women are issues that have been vigorously debated for at least
30 years.[163] And the debate continues. Perhaps one difficulty in solving
the differences is that it is hard to target one source, such as television,
as encouraging violence when it is contaminated by so many other images
and depictions that also encourage violence. It is impossible to disentan-
gle all of these threads enough to establish the impact of any one genre,
such as rap music, on violence.

It is clear, however, that whether one wishes to assert cause or not,
images of women are frequently debasing and denigrating; they often
dehumanize, disembody, and dismember women. These images saturate
the cultural air we breathe, influencing our images of ourselves and of
masculinity and femininity. While women in their everyday, practical
worlds often do not recognize themselves in the MTV and advertising
imagery that dominates their world, these images serve as the backdrop
against which decisions about their value as women, workers, and mothers
are made. These decisions have great consequence for them and their
families. If the dominant culture's images of women are skewed, providing a distorted picture of them, the imagery offered in pornography makes
women almost unrecognizable except as a sexually insatiable caricature of
the male fantasy world.

PORNOGRAPHY OR PROTECTED SPEECH

Pornography is what the multibillion-dollar pornography industry produces, according to antiporn feminist activist Gail Dines. Pure and simple.
Pornography is a masturbatory aid. "Men make, distribute, and get rich on
porn. They jerk off to it." [164] Men produce it and they are its primary consumers. It is a men's issue even though the men's voices in opposition to
it, or even in thoughtful conversation about it, are few and far between.
Jackson Katz in *The Macho Paradox* and some few others grapple with
the impact of the pornographic imagination on men and the impact of

pornographic images on women's lives.[165] Some may suggest that it is undifferentiated from erotica, a matter of taste, or that it is what communities label obscenity, but it is, from the radical feminist perspective the sexualization of violence against women.[166] There is no objection to the portrayal of sexual acts or bodies, or lovemaking. The problem with porn is that it humiliates, degrades, and uses women. It narrows women's subjectivity to her sex, and to the way she can be demeaned through it. The themes discussed earlier, themes of power over, degradation, punishment, are magnified in porn. Woman is reduced to her "essential" self that is not a self at all but an object, albeit perhaps a subjectified one, on which men work out their hostility and hatred of women. The reader may protest—it is not working out hostility and hatred but working out sexual desire. Were it desire or lovemaking, it might make some people uncomfortable, but radical feminists would surely not object. The feminist position is that porn is a form of woman hating. Not so, protest the liberal feminists who do not distinguish it from erotica. Pornography is a free expression of woman's sexuality, a reflection of her newfound freedom to be a sexual participant, to be responsible for her own body, her own sexuality. The debates between the proporn and the antiporn feminists have been scorching. Porn is either abhorrent, a purposeful violent degradation of women for male masturbatory pleasure, or it is a reflection of woman's sexual freedom—"we've come a long way … "

Catharine MacKinnon and Andrea Dworkin solidified the classic debate in the 1980s when they drafted a bill prohibiting pornography in Minneapolis in which they defined pornography as "graphic, sexually explicit subordination of women" in pictures or words. They defined pornography not as speech depicting violence against women but as an act of violence against women itself. Included as pornography are depictions in which:

- women are presented as dehumanized sexual objects, things or commodities; or
- women are presented as sexual objects who enjoy pain or humiliation; or
- women are presented as sexual objects who experience sexual pleasure in being raped; or
- women are presented as sexual objects tied up or cut up or mutilated or bruised or physically hurt; or
- women are presented in postures or position of sexual submission, servility or display; or
- women's body parts, including but not limited to vaginas, breasts, and buttocks, are exhibited, such that women are reduced to those parts; or

- women are presented as whores by nature; or
- women are presented being penetrated by objects or animals; or
- women are presented in scenarios of degradation, injury, torture, shown as filthy or inferior, bleeding, bruised, or hurt in a context that makes these conditions sexual.[167]

MacKinnon and Dworkin's bill was passed by the Minneapolis city council in both 1983 and 1984, but the mayor vetoed it each time. A member of the city council introduced a different version of the bill, and while the mayor signed it, the federal district court declared it unconstitutional, defining pornography as a form of speech, which may not be leashed.[168]

Using the criteria for pornography established by Dworkin and MacKinnon, much of rap music also surely qualifies, as does some rock. But focusing on video material here, which is the customary format for pornography, we can see that not only is it here to stay, it is a multibillion-dollar industry that is becoming more violent and more degrading every year. Robert Jensen has concluded that violent pornography, what is called gonzo porn, is on the rise, and appealing to younger and younger audiences.[169] One of the porn producers he interviewed describes himself as doing a public service through porn:

> I'd like to really show what I believe men want to see: violence against women. I firmly believe that we serve a purpose by showing that. The most violent we can get is the cum shot in the face. Men get off behind that, because they get even with the women they can't have. We try to inundate the world with orgasms in the face.[170]

Whatever his other faults, this guy is honest. He depicts porn as purposeful violence against women, imagery that presents women as despicable and degraded, and not only that but as liking it—one of the convenient assumptions of porn is that no matter how degrading or distasteful or disgusting a sex act is, if that's what gets men off, that's what women want to do. Jeff Stewart of the porn company Gag Factor provides a perfect illustration in one of his ads: " '*One of the Biggest Whores Ever!*' Bridgette will probably go down in the annals of porn history as one of the most filthy, disgusting, cumpigs ever to have lived. She'll stuff as many cocks in her mouth, ass, and cunt as is physically possible—and then some!"[171] One can hardly escape the overwhelming sense that these men absolutely despise women. Jensen points out how degraded women are in porn, how the "double anal" and the "ass-to-mouth" are so dominant in porn because, as one of the producers says, they allow men to "watch some girl taking it up the ass and fantasize at that point doing whatever girl happened to be mean to him that particular day . . . "[172] Porn feeds men's anger, their sense of privilege, their need to dominate, assuages their feelings of inferiority. It also, as Beneke suggests, may make men feel they have control.[173] Men who feel violated by women, offended or assaulted by women whose bodies cause them to become sexually aroused can regain a sense of control through masturbating to images of extreme sexual degradation of women.[174] Jensen is very clear about the purpose of pornography—it serves as a masturbatory aid. Not only can men masturbate to it, it provides them with the power and control on which they have such a fragile hold in everyday life.[175]

Not surprisingly, the Christian right supported the antipornography laws, forging an uneasy alliance with feminists that is ongoing. Catharine MacKinnon, the feminist legal scholar who co-introduced this bill, and has written extensively on pornography from a radical feminist perspective, including the book *Only Words*, is clearly uncomfortable with the alliance between feminism and the right, recognizing the disparate sources from which their objection to pornography stems. She makes the important distinction between obscenity laws and pornography laws, insisting that obscenity laws and the right-wing support for them are based on standards of morality that reflect male dominance, while pornography laws are based on standards of politics, particularly politics from the point of view of women. Obscenity is a moral idea; pornography is a political practice based on the powerlessness of one party. Obscenity laws, based on community standards and the average person, are suspect by MacKinnon, who understands the average person to be constructed as a man who is concerned with maintaining community standards that may be detrimental to women.[176] Those who condemn any effort to limit pornographic portrayals of women defend their position as a liberal support of free speech, while those who support antipornography laws reflect the radical perspective that male-defined female sexuality is oppressive and damaging, and all the more so because of its confusion with "normal" as defined to the advantage of men. Camille Paglia is the author who most stridently and viciously attacks women who would prohibit the circulation of pornographic images of women being beaten or killed.[177] Paglia aligns herself with power (i.e., men and masculinity) against the despised weakness of women (femininity), framing protests against degrading and dehumanizing assaults on women as the whimpering of women who are hiding from their natural, vigorous, healthy sexuality behind the skirts of the moralists. Referring to her own dreamworld of erotica rather than the reality portrayed by Bret Easton

Ellis[178] and Max Hardcore[179] and others, she claims: "What feminists denounce as woman's humiliating total accessibility in part is actually her elevation to high priestess of a pagan paradise garden, where the body has become a bountiful fruit tree and where growth and harvest are simultaneous . . . The most squalid images in porn are shock devices to break down bourgeois norms of decorum, reserve, and tidiness."[180]

Robert Jensen provides one example of the porn Paglia would praise: "Max also uses speculums to pry open the fuckholes so you can look deep inside. He'll spray his cum and piss into the gaping tunnels, even making them drink it out of their ass. Whether it's a naïve teen or classy broad, Max delivers the same ruthless treatment."[181] For me, this just doesn't immediately bring to mind being a "high priestess of a pagan paradise garden." Is porn designed to break down tidiness norms? Or is it a depiction of acts of virulent degradation of women?

Foucault makes the powerful point that discourse, the way we talk about everyday things in everyday life, determines what is and what is not.[182] The power of language lies in its ability to construct certain things as being able to be talked about and certain others as not existing. The way we talk about things constructs an orderly universe within which we make sense of our experiences by framing them within a context of meaning. Language provides us with the meanings we attach to our experiences and ourselves. The presentation of freedom of speech as a value shapes a way of seeing the various forms of speech, so that an argument to restrict portrayals of violence against women is construed as an effort to limit and restrict speech rather than to limit and restrict violence. The construction of pornography as freedom of speech forces the analysis of even the perception of daily and gratuitous violence against women, the dismemberment and the attacks, the dehumanization and degradation into the politically powerful bracketed world of free speech rather than into a category of assault, hate crimes, or sex crimes, where it could just as easily fit. The way something is framed determines the discussion about it, and the ability to frame the discussion is more likely to be in the hands of powerful persons in the community than in the hands of the least powerful. Similarly, those who are less powerful are more likely to be those damaged by the framing, their victimization being consistent with the "normal" or "average" view of them by decision makers. Hence, women, with little power in determining the discourse about their sexuality and their selves are the natural targets of degradation and dehumanization in pornography, but are the least likely to be in a position to reframe the discourse as a form of violence against women rather than as an issue of moral prudery.

Jensen's illustration of pornography, especially of the increasingly popular gonzo porn, paints women as such degraded and despicable creatures and men as such ugly, disgusting creatures that it is hard to imagine the debate continuing among feminists.[183] The division Charles Cottle and colleagues draw between the religious right and the antiporn feminists and the proporn feminists seems to be set in a different world than that uncovered by Jensen. Cottle et al. suggest that the traditional religious perspective would define porn as objectionable because of its potential damage to children, the family, and its disavowal of the sanctity of sex within the family for the purposes of procreation.[184] The proporn feminists are the ACLU feminists, the liberal feminists who guard the First Amendment against any possibility of erosion, no matter how vile the expression of free speech might be. The antiporn feminists view porn as pure "violence against women," not because of the images that might lead to violence, but as violence in and of itself.[185] While it is possible that the debate could be reduced to free speech versus violence against women, the arid landscape on which that debate occurs seems far removed from the virulent, woman-hating images of this mainstream, multibillion-dollar industry owned by men, produced by men, and consumed by men.

The vitriol has appeared in other areas also, particularly in social media where the violence displayed in discourse as well as images normalizing hostility to women construct the hostility as an ordinary and everyday accepted manner of presenting women's bodies, value and experience. The images of violence, the ugliness toward women, and the freedom of shock jocks,[186] like Howard Stern, Rush Limbaugh and Tom Leykis, to verbally and dangerously assault women has escalated, joining rap and mainstream advertising in producing imagery and narrative so hateful that it drowns out all but the most lurid and dangerous depictions of female sexuality. Calvin Klein and Dolce and Gabbana both depict gang rape and battery in their advertisements reminiscent of pornography.[187] Duncan Quinn's ad for men's suits shows a woman in underwear, presumably dead, with a noose around her neck being pulled by a man. These ads compete with others for the position of most violent to women so that now only the most extreme ads or statements stand out. The Queen of Mean, Lisa Lampanelli, who uses every filthy misogynist racist epithet in her stand-up performances in venues called insult comedy,[188] stands out, as does Rush Limbaugh's ugly tirade against Sandra Fluke, the Georgetown law student who testified before Congress about access to birth control.[189] One of the worst was radio personality Pete Santillis's recent hysterical tirade against Hillary Clinton, in which he screams: "I want to shoot her right in the vagina and I don't want her to die right away ... I'm supporting our troops by saying we need to try, convict and shoot Hillary Clinton in the vagina."[190]

The messages about women and sexuality and relationships are not particularly important alone or as expressed in one, isolated genre. Their power comes through their omnipresence, their consistent and reinforcing presence in so many cultural forms, from language to music to film. Everyday language that includes far more names for women's body parts than for men's and incorporates many more negative words for women than for men dovetails with other powerful imagery to reflect and reproduce values and assumptions about women that are damaging to women, not just physically as a result of rape or battery, but economically and politically, in ways that reinforce the powerlessness of women, making them vulnerable to everyday violence.

NOTES

1. L. Crook, "Reebok Drops Rick Ross over Lyric Apology Fallout," *CNN Entertainment*, April 12, 2013. http://www.cnn.com/2013/04/11/showbiz/reebok-drops-rick-ross

2. R. J. Cubarrubia, "Rick Ross Issues Official Apology for 'Rape' Lyrics," *Rolling Stone Music*, April 12, 2013. http://www.rollingstone.com/music/news/rick-ross-apologizes-for-pro-rape-lyrics-20130412

3. S. Thomas, *Ultra Violet: Equality at a Higher Frequency*, accessed June 2013, http://www.weareultraviolet.org/about/

4. Pkv vergleich, "Dolce and Gabbana: Fantasy Rape Ad," *GWSS 1001-Gender, Power, and Every Day Life: An Introduction to Gender, Women, and Sexuality Studies* (blog), Spring 2007, accessed November 7, 2011. http://blog.lib.umn.edu/raim0007/gwss1001/2007/04/dolce_gabbana_fantasy_rape_ad.html

5. T. Nudd, "Calvin Klein Ad Banned for Promoting Rape," *AdWeek*, October 21, 2010. http://www.adweek.com/adfreak/calvin-klein-ads-banned-promoting-rape-12033

6. G. Laessig, "Sears Is Selling a Lot of Offensive T-Shirts These Days," *BuzzFeed*, March 6, 2012 http://www.buzzfeed.com/gavon/sears-is-selling-a-lot-of-offensive-t-shirts-these

7. E. Ortiz, "Ford Offers Apology for Ads Featuring Paris Hilton in Car with Kardashians Bound and Gagged in Trunk," *The Daily News*, March 25 2013. http://www.nydailynews.com/news/world/ford-offers-apology-ads-featuring-women-bound-gagged-article-1.1298375

8. Whitechapel, *The Somatic Defilement*, CD. Metal Blade Records, 2007.

9. Eminem (featuring Dina Rae), *The Eminem Show*, Single CD. Eminem and Jeff Bass, 2003.

10. Pabst Blue Ribbon, *Breakfast of Champions, Billboard*, July 2012.

11. M. Thompson, "Liquid Plummer Ad Is Like "WHOA!"," *Of Foxes and Hedgehogs* (blog), February 27, 2012, http://offoxesandhedgehogs .wordpress.com/2012/02/27/liquid-plummer-ad-is-like-whoa/

12. "Bang Out" lyrics, http://rapgenius.com/Tech-n9ne-bang-out -lyrics#lyric; Kutt Calhoun, http://www.lyricattack.com/t/techn9nelyrics/ bangoutlyrics.html; and Tech N9ne, Welcome to Strangeland: Collabos, CD. Seven: Strange Music, 2011.

13. E. Goffman, *Gender Advertisements* (New York: Harper, 1976).

14. C. Jowett, review of *Dogs in Vogue* by J. Watt, October 9, 2009. http://www.express.co.uk/entertainment/books/133069/Dogs-in-Vogue -Judith-Watt

15. *The Tender Trap*, film directed by Charles Walters, starring Frank Sinatra and Debbie Reynolds (Hollywood: Metro-Goldwyn-Mayer, 1955).

16. *Revolutionary Road*, film directed by Sam Mendes, starring Leonardo DiCaprio and Kate Winslet (Los Angeles: BBC Films and Dream Works/Paramount Vantage, 2008).

17. R. Yates, *Revolutionary Road* (New York: Little, Brown, 1961).

18. *Revolutionary Road*, film.

19. See Vogue 365 Gallery July 8, 2013, for a glimpse of the types of photographs that graced the pages of *Vogue* at this time. http://www .vogue.com.au/vogue+magazine/vogue+365/galleries/vogue+365,20573/ galleries/vogue+365,20573?pos=11#top

20. S. Shaw, *Sex & Power,* with reference to "Gender and Hegemony in Fashion Magazines: Women's Interpretations of Fashion Photographs, by D. Crane." *Sociological Quarterly* 40, no. 4: 1999.

21. *Tough Guize*: *Violence, Media, and the Crisis of Masculinity*, film directed by Sut Jhally (USA: Media Education Foundation, 1999).

22. M. W. Stewart, "Images of Women in Advertising, 1945–1985 in *Vogue*," in *Images of Women in the Arts and Mass Media*, eds. V. M. Bentz and P. E. F. Mayes (Lewiston, NY: Edwin Mellen Press, 1993), 19.

23. J. Wong, "Vogue Homme's Choking Cover Spurs Domestic Violence Protest." Styleite, September 18, 2012. http://www.styleite.com/ media/protests-over-choking-vogue-hommes-international-cover/

24. *Swept Away,* film directed by Lina Wertmüller (Italy: Cinema 5 Distributing, 1974).

25. Ibid.

26. *Assisting Venus*, film directed by Charles Huddelston (Los Angeles: Terran Enterprises, 2010); and *Last Tango in Paris*, film directed by Bernardo Bertolucci (Italy: United Artists, 1972).

27. D. Scully and J. Marolla, "Rape and Vocabularies of Motive: Alternative Perspectives," in *Rape and Sexual Assaults*, edited by Ann W. Burgess (New York: Garland, 1985), 394.

28. J. Smith, *Misogynies* (London: Faber and Faber, 1989).

29. Scully and Marolla, "Rape and Vocabularies of Motive."

30. J. Reilly, "'Sexist' Washing Label on Madhouse Chinos Causes Twitter Outrage," *Daily Mail*, March 7, 2012. http://www.dailymail.co.uk/news/article-2110916/Sexist-washing-label-Madhouse-chino-causes-Twitter-outrage.html?printingPage=true

31. F. Harrop, "Freak Dancing Is No Waltz," *Real Clear Politics*, December 12, 2006. http://www.realclearpolitics.com/articles/2006/12/freak_dancing_is_no_waltz.html

32. 2 Live Crew, *Live in Concert,* CD. Effect/Luke Skywalker Productions, 1990.

33. *Reno Gazette Journal.*

34. C. Brown, *In My Zone 2,* Hosted by DJ Drama CD. Chris Brown Entertainment. November 2010.

35. J. Franklin, "City Salon Unapologetic Over Racy Ad," *News Edmonton*, August 28, 2011, http://www.edmontonsun.com/2011/08/29/city-salon-unapologetic-over-racy-ad

36. *Mad Men*, television drama directed by Matthew Weiner (North Vancouver: AMC/Lionsgate, July 19, 2007).

37. F. F. Romeo, "Acquaintance Rape on College and University Campuses," AAETS, Web, November 22, 2010.

38. P. Elam, "Study Reveals That Female Rape Victims Enjoyed Experience," *A Voice for Men: Compassion for Boys and Men*, June 19, 2011. http://www.avoiceformen.com/feminism/study-reveals-female-rape-victims-enjoyed-the-experience/

39. *Goldfinger*, film directed by Guy Hamilton (London: Eon Productions, 1964).

40. R. W. Connell, *Masculinities: Second Edition* (Berkeley: University of California Press, 2005).

41. *Cathouse: The Series,* television series directed by Patti Kaplan (New York City: HBO, 2005)

42. Rapper Project Pat, "Chickenheads" featuring La Chat and Three 6 Mafia, Hypnotize/Loud Records. From *Mista Don't Play: Everythangs Workin'*, CD. 2001.

43. Kid Rock, "Balls in Your Mouth" from *Polyfuse Method*, CD. Continuum Records, 1993. http://www.sing365.com/music/lyric.nsf/ Balls-In-Your-Mouth-lyrics-Kid-Rock/ C52EEB86A21842E24825689D001D41D4

44. S. Salsano, *Jersey Shore*, television reality show developed and produced by Sally Salsano (Burbank, CA: 495 Productions, MTV, 2009–2012).

45. Hardee's, *Mrs. Robinson—The Jim Beam Bourbon Thickburger at Hardee's*, television advertisement, March 2013.

46. Scully and Marolla, "Rape and Vocabularies of Motive"; Sut Jhally, *Tough Guize: Violence, Media, and the Crisis of Masculinity.*

47. H. G. Blumer, http://en.wikipedia.org/wiki/Herbert_Blumer

48. *The Accused*, film directed by Jonathan Kaplan (Hollywood: Paramount Pictures, 1988).

49. H. Blumer, *Symbolic Interactionism* (Berkeley: University of California Press, 1986).

50. E. Melamed, *Mirror, Mirror: The Terror of Not Being Young* (New York: Simon & Schuster, 1983).

51. Blumer, *Symbolic Interactionism.*

52. Ibid.

53. *Dreamworlds 3 (Unabridged): Desire, Sex & Power in Music Video*, film written/narrated/edited by Sut Jhally (Northampton, MA: Media Education Foundation, 2007).

54. Pkv vergleich, "Dolce and Gabbana."

55. Blender Concept Store: Butcher Shop, *Ads of the World*, online advertisement, July 2012. http://ffffound.com/image/262c407558c90 59f851d84aa626cabfa4bc092?c=5920646

56. Budweiser Bud Beer, *Expect Everything*, print advertisement, 2006.

57. T. Beneke, *Proving Manhood: Reflections on Men and Sexism* (Berkeley: University of California Press, 1997).

58. J. Hoffman, "Girls Stand By Their Man," *New York Times*, March 18, 2009. http://www.nytimes.com/2009/03/19/fashion/19brown .html?pagewanted=all; and I hate Rihanna, Facebook. February14, 2005. https://www.facebook.com/...HATE-RIHANNA/ 110199955671163 (No longer available).

59. M. Goldstein, "Chris Brown Hits Rihanna: The Whole Story," February 12, 2009. http://www.spin.com/articles/chris-brown-and -rihanna-whole-story/. http://www.nytimes.com/ 2009/03/19/fashion/19 brown.html?pagewanted=all&_r=0

60. Hoffman, "Teenage Girls Stand by Their Man"; R. Tate, "Why Teen Girls Still Love Chris Brown: Four Theories," *Trendwatch* (blog),

March 19, 2009. http://gawker.com/5174703/why-teen-girls-still-chris
-brown-four-theories

61. "Chris Brown Wins Grammy for F.A.M.E. at the 2011 Grammys,"
http://en.wikipedia.org/wiki/List_of_awards_and_nominations_received
_by_Chris_Brown#Grammy_Awards

62. Jhally, *Dreamworlds 3.*

63. Beneke, *Proving Manhood.*

64. Jhally, *Dreamworlds 3.*

65. Ibid.

66. Mr. Ghetto, *Walmart.* Official Music Video, Walmart, 2011, http://
www.youtube.com/watch?v=VDz9Q9nPA94

67. D. Scully and J. Marolla, "Convicted Rapists' Vocabulary of
Motive: Excuses and Justifications." *Social Problems* 31: 530–44. 1984.

68. *Lolita,* film directed by Adrian Lyne (Hollywood: Samuel Gold-
wyn Company, 1992).

69. Britney Spears, "Hit Me Baby One More Time," Single (New
York: Jive Records. 1998).

70. H. Leukart, "How I Became a Japanese Heartthrob: Japan's
Obsession with Cuteness," *Without Baggage: Travel Fearlessly* (blog),
September 25, 2011, http://withoutbaggage.com/essays/japan-tokyo
-kawaii/

71. La Carmina, "Japanese Dirty Underwear Vending Machines,
Otaku Shopping at Nakano Broadway. Anima Manga Stores Tokyo," *La
Carmina* (blog), September 23, 2011, http://www.lacarmina.com/blog/
2011/09/japanese-dirty-underwear-vending-machines-otaku-shopping-at
-nakano-broadway-anime-manga-stores-tokyo/

72. b. hooks, "Selling Hot Pussy," in *The Politics of Women's Bodies:
Sexuality, Appearance, and Behavior,* edited by Rose Weitz (Oxford, UK:
Oxford University Press, 2002), 112.

73. J. Caramanica, "Rap, Both Good and Bad for Business," *New York
Times,* May 7, 2013, http://www.nytimes.com/2013/05/08/arts/music/
lil-wayne-and-other-rappers-run-afoul-of-propriety.html?pagewanted=all

74. Bad Meets Evil, *The Reunion* from *Hell: The Sequel,* CD. Bonose
TV Productions, Shady/Interscope, 2011.

75. J. Stoltenberg, "How Men Have (a) Sex," in *Refusing to Be a Man*
(New York: Meridian Books, 1990).

76. B. E. Ellis, *American Psycho* (New York: Vintage, 1991).

77. *American Psycho,* film directed by Mary Harron (Vancouver:
Lions Gate Films, 2000).

78. Ibid.

79. Ellis, *American Psycho,* 327–28.

80. C. Paglia, *Sexual Personae: Art and Decadence from Nefertiti to Emily Dickinson* (New York: Vintage Books, 1990).

81. C. Paglia, *Vamps and Tramps: New Essays* (New York: Vintage Books, 1994). Quote retrieved from Internet July 24, 2013, http://izquotes .com/quote/257682

82. Ibid.

83. Foundational Theories are the framework, or perceived set of rules, that children use to describe and explain their experiences of life and their environment. As these are based on personal experiences, many of them may actually be false or fanciful explanations. Example: "My parents get drunk because I'm a bad child."

84. L. Kohlberg, *Stages in the Development of Moral Thought and Action* (New York: Holt, Rinehart and Winston, 1969).

85. P. Wylie, *Generation of Vipers* (New York: Rinehart, 1955).

86. A. G. Johnson, *The Gender Knot: Unraveling Our Patriarchal Legacy* (Philadelphia: Temple University Press, 2005).

87. B. Friedan, *The Feminine Mystique* (New York: Dell, 1963).

88. P. Schlafly, *The Power of the Positive Woman* (New Rochelle, NY: Arlington House, 1977).

89. Ibid.

90. Prodigy, "Smack My Bitch Up" from *Fat of the Land*, CD. Maverick Records, 1997.

91. "MTV Stops Airing Controversial Video," *South Coast Today* (New York: South Coast Today, December 20, 1997), http://www .southcoasttoday.com/apps/pbcs.dll/article?AID=/19971220/NEWS/ 312209952&template=printarthttp://www.southcoasttoday.com/apps/ pbcs.dll/article?AID=/19971220/NEWS/312209952&template=printart

92. Limp Bizkit, "Stalemate" from *Three Dollar Bill, Y'All*, CD. Flip/ Interscope, 1997.

93. Eminem, "Kim" from *The Marshall Mathers LP*, CD. Aftermath/ Interscope, 2000.

94. Ibid.

95. *Thelma and Louise*, film directed by Ridley Scott (Beverly Hills, CA: Metro-Goldwyn-Mayer, 1991).

96. I. K. Broverman, D. M. Broverman, F. Clarkson, P. Rosenkrantz, and S. Vogel, "Sex Roles Stereotypes and Clinical Judgements of Mental Health," *Journal of Consulting and Clinical Psychology* 34, no. 1 (1970): 1–7.

97. LMFAO, *Party Rock*, CD. Interscope Records, 2009.

98. Jay-Z, "Big Pimpin' " from *Vol. 3 . . . Life and Times of S. Carter*, CD. Roc-a-Fella/Def Jam, 2000.

99. J. Jurgensen, "Just Asking: Decoding Jay-Z," *Wall Street Journal*, October 21, 2010, http://online.wsj.com/article/SB10001424052702 30402380457556664417696 1542.html

100. Beneke, *Proving Manhood*.

101. J. T. Richardson, M. W. Stewart, and R. Simmonds, *Organized Miracles, A Sociological Study of a Jesus Movement Organization* (Piscataway, NJ: Transaction Press, 1979).

102. J. Cortez, "Rape," in *The Firespitters* (New York: Bola Press, 1982), 31.

103. Ellis, *American Psycho*.

104. *She's Gotta Have It*, film directed by Spike Lee (Brooklyn, NY: 40 Acres & a Mule Filmworks, 1986).

105. b. hooks, *Talking Back: Talking Feminist, Talking Black* (Toronto: Between the Lines, 1989).

106. *The Accused*.

107. Beneke, *Proving Manhood*.

108. J. Barron, "Two Worlds Collided in Greenwich Village," *New York Times*, May 20, 2013, A17.

109. A. Roth, "Crowd Led by Priests Attacks Gay Rights Marchers in Georgia," *New York Times*, May 18, 2013, A4.

110. "Statement of Steven Eric Mullins re: Homicide of Billy Jack Gaither," *Frontline*, accessed June 18, 2013, http://www.pbs.org/wgbh/pages/frontline/shows/assault/billyjack/statement.html

111. A. Smolchenko, "Russian Gay Man's Death Fuels Fears of Rising Homophobia," *Huffington Post*, May 12, 2013.

112. J. Moore, *Murderer: Matt Shepard Needed Killing*, DenverPost.com, http://www.denverpost.com/entertainment/ci_1346 4996

113. *Boys Don't Cry*, film directed by Kimberly Peirce (Los Angeles: Fox Searchlight, 1999).

114. Stoltenberg, "How Men Have (a) Sex."

115. M. Kaufman, "The Construction of Masculinity and the Triad of Men's Violence," in *Beyond Patriarchy: Essays by Men on Pleasure, Power, and Change*, edited by M. Kaufman (New York: Oxford University Press, 1987), 1–29.

116. Smith, *Misogynies*.

117. 2 Live Crew, *Live in Concert*.

118. *The Accused*.

119. J. Gross, "'Where Boys Will Be Boys' and Adults are Befuddled," *New York Times*, March 9, 1993, http://www.nytimes.com/

1993/03/29/us/where-boys-will-be-boys-and-adults-are-befuddled.html ?pagewanted=all&src=pm

120. S. Brownmiller, *Against Our Will: Men, Women and Rape* (New York: Ballantine Books, 1975); P. Y. Martin and R. A. Hummer, "Fraternities and Rape on Campus," *Gender and Society* 3, no. 4 (1989): 457–73.

121. Immortal Technique, "Dance with the Devil," *Revolutionary Vol.1*, CD. Viper Records, 2001, http://www.youtube.com/watch ?v=qggxTtnKTMo

122. P. R. Sanday, *Fraternity Gang Rape: Sex, Brotherhood and Privilege on Campus* (New York: New York University Press, 2007).

123. C. J. Chivers and W. K. Rashbaum, "Inquiry Focuses on Officers' Responses to Park Violence," *New York Times*, June 14, 2000, A27.

124. Ibid.

125. Recreational songbook of the 77th Tactical Squadron of the U.S. Air Force based outside Oxford, England.

126. C. Hitchens cited in *The War Against Women*, edited by M. French (New York: Ballantine Books, 1992).

127. Ibid.

128. Ibid.

129. H. Jacobs, *Incidents in the Life of a Slave Girl* (Boston: Thayer & Eldridge, 1861).

130. M. D. A. Freeman, "But if I Can't Rape My Wife, Who[m] Can You Rape?: The Marital Rape Exemption Re-examined," *Family Law Quarterly* 15, no. 1 (Spring 1981). See Footnote marked *.

131. H. Ibsen, *A Doll's House* (London: Eyre Methuen, 1974).

132. The Police, "Every Breath You Take" from *Synchronicity*, Vinyl, A&M, 1983.

133. Notorious B.I.G., "Me and My Bitch" from *Ready to Die*, CD. Arista, 1994.

134. Bei Maejor, *Trouble*, http://www.azlyrics.com/lyrics/beimaejor/ trouble.html, digital download, January 4, 2012.

135. J. Cash, "Delia's Gone" from *The World of Johnny Cash*, CD. American Recordings, 1994.

136. P. Hill Collins, *Black Sexual Politics: African Americans, Gender and the New Racism* (New York: Routledge, 2004).

137. Ibid., also see MacKinnon, "Feminism, Marxism, Method and the State," *Signs* 8, no. 2 (1983).

138. Tyga, "Make It Nasty" from *Careless World: Rise of the Last King*, digital download, Universal Republic, 2012.

139. MacKinnon, "Feminism, Marxism, Method and the State," 27.

140. T. Lynch, "'We Own the Night,' Amadou Diallo's Deadly Encounter with NYC's Street Crimes Unit," *Cato Institute's Project on Criminal Justice*, briefing paper, no. 56 (Washington, DC: Cato Institute, 2000).

141. C. W. Franklin II, *The Changing Definition of Masculinity* (New York: Plenum, 1984).

142. R. K. Merton, "Social Structure and Anomie." *American Sociological Review* 3 (1968): 672–82.

143. Salsano, *Jersey Shore*; and Jackson Katz, *Tough Guize: Violence, Media and the Crisis in Masculinity*, video (Northampton, MA: Media Education Foundation, 1999).

144. Notorious B.I.G., "Me and My Bitch" from *Ready to Die*; and 2 Live Crew, *Live in Concert*.

145. NWA (Los Angeles: Priority Records L.L.C., 1991).

146. A. Jones, *Next Time She'll Be Dead: Battering and How to Stop It* (Boston: Beacon Press, 1994).

147. Salsano, *Jersey Shore.*

148. Immortal Techniques, "Dance with the Devil."

149. Stoltenberg, "How Men Have (a) Sex."

150. Franklin, *The Changing Definition of Masculinity.*

151. b. hooks, *Ain't I a Woman: Black Women and Feminism* (New York: South End Press, 1999), 113–14.

152. Rolling Stones, "Under My Thumb," from *Still Life*, Vinyl, Virgin Records, 1982.

153. My Morning Jacket, "Strangulation" from *At Dawn*, CD. Darla Records, 2001.

154. Ibid.

155. T. Shakur, *The Rose That Grew from Concrete*, New York: MTV Books, 1999.

156. Steel Train, *Dakota*, uploaded November 17, 2009. No description available. http://www.youtube.com/watch?v=4pu4WcO0FDw

157. Tyga, *Make It Nasty.*

158. N. Malamuth and J. Briere, "Sexual Violence in the Media: Indirect Effects on Aggression against Women," *Journal of Social Issues* 42, no. 3 (1986): 75–92.

159. K. Lanis and K. Covell, "Images of Women in Advertisements: Effects on Attitudes Related to Sexual Aggression." *Sex Roles* 32, no. 1 (1995): 639–49; and L. Kalof, "Dilemmas of Femininity: Gender and the Social Construction of Sexual Imagery," *Sociological Quarterly* 34, no. 4 (1993): 639–51.

160. N. Malamuth and J. Check, "The Effects of Mass Media Exposure on Acceptance of Violence against Women: A Field Experiment," *Journal of Research in Personality* 15, no. 4 (1981): 436–46.

161. G. T. St. Lawrence and D. J. Joyner, "The Effects of Sexually Violent Rock Music on Males' Acceptance of Violence against Women," *Psychology of Women Quarterly* 15, no. 1 (1991): 49–63.

162. L. Kalof, "Dilemmas of Femininity," and L. Kalof, "The Effects of Gender and Music Video Imaging on Sexual Attitudes," *Journal of Social Psychology* 139, no. 4 (1999): 378–85.

163. J. Savage, "Does Viewing Violent Media Really Cause Criminal Violence? A Methodological Review," *Aggression and Violent Behavior* 10, no. 1 (November-December, 2004): 99–128.

164. G. Dines: *Pornland: How Porn Has Hijacked Our Society* (Boston. Beacon Press, 2010); J. Katz, *The Macho Paradox: Why Some Men Hurt Women and How All Men Can Help* (Naperville, IL: Sourcebooks, 2006).

165. Katz, *The Macho Paradox*; J. Stoltenberg, "How Men Have (a) Sex"; R. Jensen, *Getting Off: Pornography and the End of Masculinity* (Cambridge, MA: South End Press, 2007); and T. Beneke, *Proving Manhood*.

166. A. Dworkin and C. MacKinnon, *Pornography and Civil Rights: A New Day for Women's Equality* (Minneapolis: Organizing against Pornography, 1988); C. MacKinnon, *Feminism Unmodified: Discourses on Life and Law* (Cambridge, MA: Harvard University Press, 1987); C. MacKinnon, "Not a Moral Issue" in *Feminism Unmodified* (Cambridge, MA: Harvard University Press, 1988); and C. MacKinnon, *Only Words* (Cambridge, MA: Harvard University Press, 1993).

167. Dworkin and MacKinnon, *Pornography and Civil Rights*, Appendix D.

168. MacKinnon, *Only Words*.

169. Jensen, *Getting Off*.

170. Ibid., 69.

171. Ibid., 73.

172. Ibid.

173. Beneke, *Proving Manhood*.

174. Ibid.

175. Jensen, *Getting Off*.

176. MacKinnon, *Only Words;* MacKinnon, *Feminism Unmodified*; and MacKinnon, "Not a Moral Issue."

177. Paglia, *Vamps and Tramps*.

178. Ellis, *American Psycho*.

179. Max Hardcore is actor Paul Little, a porn film star who specializes in films that feature actresses portraying young girls. Wikipedia, http://en.wikipedia.org/wiki/Max_Hardcore, retrieved July 24, 2013.

180. Paglia, *Sexual Personae*.

181. Jensen, *Getting Off*.

182. M. Foucault, *Madness and Civilization* (New York: Vintage Books, 1965); and M. Foucault, *The Birth of the Clinic: An Archaeology of Medical Perception* (New York: Pantheon, 1973).

183. Jensen, *Getting Off*.

184. C. Cottle, P. Searles, R. Buerger, and B. A. Pierce, 1997. "Conflicting Ideologies and the Politics of Pornography," in *Gender Violence: An Interdisciplinary Perspective*, edited by L. L. O'Toole, J. R. Schiffman, and M. L. Kiter Edwards (New York: New York University Press. 1997), 383–94.

185. Ibid.

186. Ibid.

187. Pkv vergleich, "Dolce and Gabbana."

188. Lisa Lampanelli, http://www.comedycentrl.com.

189. http://www.youtube.com/watch.

190. http://www.policymic.com, May 21, 2013.

FOUR

The Construction of Violence against Women as a Social Problem in the United States

On June 19, 1983, in Torrington, Connecticut, Tracey Thurman frantically dialed 911. Her husband, Charles "Buck" Thurman, was at her door, threatening to kill her. She had been in this situation before, and despite having a protection order, she knew that Thurman was serious. To escape, she ran outside, with Thurman right behind her wielding a knife. He caught her, beat her with his fists, slit her face and throat, and began kicking her in the chest and head. The police officer leisurely made his way to Tracey's home, even stopping to use the bathroom en route. When the officer finally arrived, he took the knife Buck was using to slice Tracey's face and neck and walked to his patrol car, leaving the enraged Buck plenty of time to continue pummeling her with his fists and kicking her in the head and neck. By the time he was subdued, Buck had stabbed Tracey 13 times, and she was near death. When she could finally leave the hospital, she was permanently paralyzed on one side and scarred for life. She sued the City of Torrington, claiming that she had been denied equal protection under the law because she was married to the man who attacked her. The brutality of this attack and the outrageous negligence of the police stand as one of the low points in the recent history of wife battery. A great deal of media attention focused on the disgraceful response of the police, and activist groups throughout the nation demanded that police respond quicker and more effectively and that communities take physical and sexual attacks on women seriously.

It was reasonable to conclude, given the amount of attention given wife battering and child abuse during the decades of the '70s, '80s, and '90s, that we were experiencing an unprecedented epidemic of wife battering. Whether it was epidemic or whether activist groups finally brought it to the attention of the public is not clear, although the latter seems more probable. And though it no longer enjoys the limelight, violence against women was, and indeed is, commonplace—some would say pandemic— and it has been so throughout history. Perhaps even more important than its prevalence is the response of the community and the police to battery. Tracey's lawsuit changed the police response and galvanized the shelter movement across the country. The shelter movement grew out of the com- pletely inadequate response of the police and courts in dealing with situa- tions of abuse. The response was slow, haphazard, and often dismissive of the woman's complaints. The goal of keeping the family together and not criminalizing the offender was a substantial threat to the health and life of the woman who was being beaten. Until three decades ago, the response of police to domestic violence in the United States reflected the view that men were the head of the household and the state should not challenge the authority of the husband. Violence against women in the family was defined as a private rather than a public matter even though as early as 1871, Alabama rescinded a husband's legal right to hit his wife. North Carolina was close behind but provided the exclusion that "if no perma- nent injury has been inflicted, nor malice, cruelty, nor dangerous violence shown by the husband, it is better to draw a curtain, shut out the public gaze and leave the parties to forgive and forget."[1] This was the generally accepted response for almost 100 years.

The feminist response to wife battery was built on the knowledge that women were both victimized and blamed, that there was often nowhere for them to go to escape a batterer, and that police did not take their fears seriously nor respond to their 911 calls as priorities. Colleen McGrath concluded in the late 1970s that in most cities, "domestic disputes have had a priority with police somewhere just above that of cars stuck in trees."[2] Women experience far more intimate partner violence than do men, with 22.1 percent of women in one survey compared with 7.4 percent of men reporting that they were physically assaulted by an intimate part- ner.[3] Violence against women is no mystery. The gnashing of teeth about why the battered woman returns to her batterer, why she continues to choose men who batter, why she does not "do something" about her situa- tion, if only for the children's sake, and the infrequently asked question "Why does he do it?" are easily answered. It is stopping violence that is difficult. The abuse of women is so much a part of this and other cultures as to be woven into its very social fabric. The answer to "why" is both obvious and complex. It is inseparably connected with the economic, political, historical, cultural, and social experience of men and women. It is complex because all of these institutions are interconnected, and one's everyday experience in each of them is shaped by the other.

Today, while there is no indication that wife battery has declined significantly, interest in it has declined—it is no longer front page news. This may be because of the range of social responses to abuse—the shelters, the laws, the police trainings, the anger management groups, the fundraisers, the victim advocates; or it may be because the problem has become bureaucratized, and the response to it professionalized, compartmentalized, and addressed in a routine manner by what has emerged as the "family violence industry." Perhaps we have become weary of this seemingly intractable problem and replaced it with new, fresh problems, like sex trafficking, which we have some hope of solving.

One of the obvious changes of the past several decades is the redefinition of violence against women from acceptable, or at the very least as an unfortunate occurrence, to a broad-scale and serious social problem requiring the intervention of social agents. Grassroots movements have been replaced by agencies and organizations devoted to this problem, theses and dissertations have been written, government grants have funded research, and a whole cadre of professionals now address the problem in hospitals, in social service agencies, and in the legal system. Each state and the federal government have developed hotlines, laws, organizations, workshops, and trainings to respond to violence against women.

RECENT HISTORY

In Rome, where the first marriage laws were enacted, the husband was the owner and absolute authority controlling all persons and property in his household, and he had the right to punish his wife for any act of disobedience or misbehavior. Under English common law, a woman suffered legal death (coverture) at marriage and had no legal existence apart from her husband, who owned and controlled her. Other British laws reflected the propertied status of women as well. If they were raped, their husbands (or, in the case of unmarried daughters, their fathers) were granted restitution. In Islamic countries, such a definition of women continues, reflected in the fact that a man can avoid conviction for rape if he agrees to marry his victim.

Under English common law, women and children were property of the husband and father; and William Blackstone the influential legal theorist, argued that husbands had a right and a duty to "chastise" their wives or children as they would apprentices for "correctional" purposes.[4] Most people are familiar with the early nineteenth-century rule-of-thumb dictum, attributed to Blackstone, which allegedly allowed a husband to discipline his wife with a rod no thicker than his thumb, a ruling that was later changed to a policy of benign neglect or noninterference in family violence so long as no permanent injury was inflicted on the wife.[5] Some, including Christina Hoff Sommers, writing in *"Who Stole Feminism: How Women Have Betrayed Women,"*[6] challenge this rule of thumb as revisionist feminist history, "feminist fiction," but few deny the relative powerlessness of women in the family.

While not denying the property status of women nor the fact that men had significant control in the family, our history is not one of pervasive and acceptable violence against women in the family. Wife beating has been condemned for most our history, with many groups, including Methodists, Quakers, and Baptists, punishing, shunning and even excommunicating wife beaters, levying fines and whipping or imprisoning them. Family historian Elizabeth Pleck points out that several states in nineteenth-century America, one even predating the American Revolution, passed statutes specifically prohibiting wife beating and establishing severe punishment for the perpetrator.[7] Mildred Pagelow traces these early reforms, pointing out that during the 1870s, a wave of reforms occurred, with Alabama and Massachusetts introducing the first spouse abuse laws that made it illegal to "beat a wife with a stick, pull her hair, choke her, spit in her face, or kick her to the floor."[8] Such reforms nevertheless were embedded in a social and economic system in which women were without significant choices. It is no doubt true that if women were beaten by their husbands, the response of the community and the law was not likely to be swift or severe. But various characteristics of the family, including its significance as a social institution, its central location within the community, and the expectation that the family should be a respite from the demands of work and formal relationships would work against acceptance of violence as an expected and approved behavior. A man struggling for survival on the prairie or the remote ranches of the West, for example, would be poorly served by alienating a woman who was his helpmeet and without whom he might not survive. Just such an unfortunate outcome is captured in the short film *A Jury of Her Peers.*[9] The taciturn farmer's brutish treatment of his wife, merged with the isolation and loneliness she endured on a remote farm, led her to kill him in his sleep. The work-worn women from neighboring farms kept her secret, empathizing with her despair and understanding her desperate solution.

It was not until the Industrial Revolution that the family became a haven, and this required a redefinition of work as something different from and separate from the family, something engaged in by one person who would earn a family wage—enough money to support an entire family. This imagery was white middle class; it did not include the poor, the young, single women, immigrants, or blacks. The separation of work from family has had severe consequences for women. Rather than being producers whose work was core to the survival of the family, their work became private and invisible, and their status, and that of their husband, began to depend on them not doing any visible labor. Women's dependence on men for their economic survival both in fact and in the powerful and determining cultural imagery caused their economic futures to dim considerably. The unpaid labor of women, while necessary for the survival of the family, disappeared as productive and valued labor, and women's value plummeted.

During the early twentieth century, the problem of wife abuse and incest was defined by feminists as resulting from the depravity and brutishness of ignorant, alcoholic, immigrant men. Linda Gordon traces the changes in the response to violence in the family from the child protection movement of the late 1880s when alcohol and ignorance were blamed for family violence to the 1960s when women's innate masochism or denial of femininity and dependence were seen as the cause.[10] Relying on extensive social service records in Boston, Gordon reports that in the late 1800s men were shamed by the organizations from which their families sought help, and they were admonished and threatened with punishment for abusing their wives and children. During the Progressive era, social work became a profession, and its practitioners identified social problems such as poverty and unemployment as the underlying cause of family violence. The focus of the middle-class women who replaced the philanthropists of the earlier decades shifted to the inability of the parent to provide for the child as the main cause of child neglect and other family problems. During the Great Depression, while well-meaning, devoted social workers were quick to note the role played by poverty, lack of education, and what they saw as other cultural deficits in violence against both children and women, they were unwilling to further humiliate men who were unemployed and already emasculated by their inability to provide—men whom they viewed as in desperate enough straits already—and soon switched their attention and blame to mothers for their unwillingness or inability to provide adequately for their children. Little focus remained on violence against women in postwar America, painted as a suburban retreat from the disruptions of World War II and the crowding and poverty of inner cities.[11]

After WW II, violence in the family was not viewed as a significant problem, and what did occur was viewed as having its source in individual pathologies or complexes. Freudian psychoanalytical explanations for wife battery targeted threats to the male ego by domineering and "castrating" wives. The family was constructed as the cornerstone of the postwar society in the United States and was defended in its traditional form as the template on which unfettered progress was to be built. In the post-Freudian, Parsonian depictions of American life at mid-century, the family was a "haven in a heartless world."[12] In postwar America, the family was buttressed by the burgeoning field of advertising, calling women to construct their identity through homemaking and motherhood. A singular view of the family as the most important institution in America was forwarded by political and religious leaders. Any problems that occurred in the family were defined as resulting not from the family as traditionally structured but due to pathological individuals or disturbed relationships within the family. Often, although violence was acknowledged, it was seen as a natural expression of the emotional relationship between husband and wife or as avoidable if women would assume responsibility for changing their behavior.

But after the upheaval of the 1960s, which saw the impact of the civil rights movement, the women's movement, the "sexual revolution," the antiwar movement, and other significant economic and political changes, the family was no longer immune to criticism. The feminist movement, with its analysis of women's inequality and women's oppression in the family, reframed the violence in the family as one more indication of the damage caused by social and structural oppression. The family itself, not just its members, was seen as potentially destructive or troubled. Even Betty Friedan joined the chorus of concern about the family, although her focus was on the potential destructiveness of mothers trapped in the stultifying roles they were expected to naturally enjoy in the family. These social movements of the 1960s and 1970s also raised critical questions about the sanctity of family privacy, the privileged position of the male head of the family, and the importance of family togetherness at all costs. They created an atmosphere in which wife beating, child abuse, and incest could be pulled out of the closet. The view that poverty, poor education, crowding, isolation, and the hierarchical structure of the traditional family caused violence, and the inadequate institutional response resulting from that view, was supplanted by critical analysis of the patriarchal structure of the family and the oppression of women in the workplace and in society. Shelters, support groups, and national feminist organizations put forward definitions of incest and abuse as natural by-products of sexism and discrimination against women. Feminist activists and an increasing number of academic feminists condemned the family itself as a structure in which male power and male privilege resulted in violence to women supported by other male-dominated institutions, including the courts and the church.

It was only with the emergence of the women's movement and the political, legal, and social goals it achieved that the degree and prevalence of violence against women became part of the public consciousness. The feminist perspective has historically focused on the patriarchal family, contemporary constructions of masculinity and femininity, and structural constraints that operate against women who are battered. This analysis depicts violence against women in the family as a microcosm of violence against women in the wider society.[13] Violence, they agree, is a natural by-product of the ownership and oppression of women and of the cultural definitions of masculinity as power and control and femininity as naturally dependent. From this perspective, violence against women cannot be eradicated without the destruction of the sexist system and oppressive institutions that damage women and result in patriarchal terrorism against women. Intimate violence is a product of this system and a form of terroristic control of wives by their husbands, involving the systematic use of violence as well as economic subordination, threats, isolation, and other control tactics.[14]

Accompanying the theoretical discussions and contributing to their development were the grassroots activists involved in the shelter movement and welfare rights movement who were untangling and solving the immediate practical problems that battered women and poor women faced. The women working on these problems found common patterns in the lives of battered women and in the response of the police and legal institutions to these women and their children. Researchers and policy analysts then analyzed these patterns. The interplay between practice and theory contributed significantly to the development of interest in battered women and the research to address the problem at the individual, political, and structural levels.

The first shelter for battered women and their children in the United States, Haven House, opened in Pasadena, California, in 1964, but it was not until Erin Pizzey wrote about the Chiswick Women's Aid refuge for battered women in her 1974 book *Scream Quietly or the Neighbors Will Hear* that the shelter movement in the United States became powerful.[15] One of the earliest shelters to open after Pizzey's book brought the need for shelters to the public's attention was Women's House, opened in 1974 in St. Paul, Minnesota, by the group Women's Advocates. By 1986, there were over 700 such shelters,[16] and by 2010, there were 1,500 shelters in the United States.[17]

Women's organizations were increasingly active in drawing attention to violence against women during the 1970s. The National Organization for Women (NOW) prioritized the issue of battered wives in 1974, and organizations such as the National Coalition Against Domestic Violence, focusing specifically on battered women, fought to establish better social services for battered wives and to force changes in legal statutes that failed to protect women from spouse abuse.[18] A number of other organizations, often with different political and social agendas, combined their efforts to raise awareness about violence against women as a social problem. These included the Displaced Homemakers Network, the National Association of Women and the Law (in Canada), the National Association for Victims Assistance, the National Clearinghouse for the Defense of Battered Women, and the National Council on Child Abuse and Family Violence.

Prior to 1971, the *Journal of Marriage and the Family* published no articles on wife battery or spouse abuse.[19] By the mid-1970s, a number of studies had addressed the problem of violence against women in the family and began to elevate it to a national social problem. Between 1975 and 1980, 44 states passed legislation on domestic violence.[20] Much of the research on family violence was initiated by Murray Straus and Richard Gelles, who focused on characteristics of the family and society that encourage or lead to the acceptance of violence against women. This work was closely aligned with the earlier attention given to child abuse, which led to a revised view of the family—from haven to cauldron of violence. By the mid-1980s, several journals specifically devoted to family violence and violence among intimates had appeared, including *Journal of Family Violence, Violence and Victims*, and *Journal of Interpersonal Violence,* and by the beginning of the new century, hundreds of articles had been specifically devoted to this problem. Rather than providing information about the incidence, prevalence, and characteristics of those involved, researchers could now turn their attention to assessments and comparisons, and the methodological problems that made these comparisons so difficult.[21]

In 1995, President Bill Clinton announced plans for the implementation of the Violence against Women Act, introduced by Senator Joseph Biden of Delaware, to provide states with funds to help reduce violence against women. The Centers for Disease Control conducted a national study in 2000 to assess the "extent, nature and consequences" of intimate violence, and today federal, state, and local governments have established protocols for responding to violence against women and their perpetrators. The federal Violence against Women Act of 1994, recently reapproved by

Congress, provides financial support for shelters, research, and law enforcement. In 2013, the Department of Justice, which implements the Violence against Women Act, allocated $12.6 million to develop programs to address escalating violence, domestic homicides, and dating violence. The Violence against Women Act, however, passed both houses of Congress only after a lengthy battle, fought by activists committed to providing protections for immigrant women, gays and lesbians, and Native American women.

CONCEPTIONS OF THE FAMILY

The family and its members are situated in the larger social structure and are supported by powerful cultural imagery and beliefs about family, work, sexuality, and gender. These structural and cultural factors contribute to the vulnerability of women and children. Feminist researchers writing about violence against women in the family (and on the streets) such as Susan Brownmiller, Andrea Dworkin, Kate Millet, Mildred Pagelow, and R. Emerson and Russell Dobash see violence against women as situated in family structure, hierarchy, and role expectations. In that family as within the broader society, women's subordinate status, lack of political and economic power, and patriarchal traditions create an environment in which they are subject to the control of their husband, either directly or because they rely on him economically or for identity and acceptance. He may never explicitly acknowledge his control and ownership, but he will rely on the culture and the roles he occupies to maintain a position of dominance. He may never hit or verbally abuse his wife, but whether he does or does not is up to him. Ultimately, the restrictions and limited control of their lives that women experience create their vulnerability to battery and abuse.

The family is traditionally conceptualized as a place in which women protect men from the punishing realities of their harsh and demanding economic life and nurture their children in preparation for entering that same world. In this view, men provide for their families, establishing a boundary between the family and the state, and through their position of authority, protect the family and reinforce the legitimacy of the state. During the early days of the feminist movement, conservative social critics such as George Gilder, Christopher Lasch, and Lionel Tiger were alarmed by the feminist critique of the family as an oppressive patriarchal structure. They emphasized the importance of the traditionally structured family and viewed its survival as based on the ability of the man to protect and provide for his family.[22] Phyllis Schlafly successfully led the fight against the Equal Rights Amendment with the powerful, fear-based message that women's strength comes only from their dependency on their men.[23] Men would support women and their children only if they felt this was their one avenue to legitimate manhood, and if they faced severe punishments for not doing so. Conservative commentators today like Lou Dobbs on Fox News mirror this concern, predicting catastrophe not just for the family but for society as a result of women's increasing participation in the marketplace. A Pew survey[24] reporting that women are the sole or primary breadwinners in 40 percent of American families reflects a number of disturbing trends including increasing job polarization, the inadequate structural supports for child support, increasing economic inequality in our society, and the necessity of two incomes for many families, but conservative commentators are most alarmed by what they see as the upset in the natural biologically determined social arrangements and the destruction of male superiority in the family. Like Schlafly 40 years ago, they are terrified by women's increasing economic independence. As she contended, if feminists let men "off the hook" by becoming financially independent, they will free men from their obligatory responsibility for the family, and once untethered, men will run amok, committing, as Gilder said, sexual suicide.[25]

Recent conceptualizations of the family idealize traditional arrangements and present housework as "family work with its basis in moral obligation," asserting that women are providing nurturing and caretaking as well as household work within a moral context, which differs from work in other institutions. These theorists counter the paradigm of housework as demeaning, repetitive drudgery, ascribing moral superiority to unrewarded, low-status jobs generally held by economic subordinates. Traditional views applaud the integrative functioning and division of labor among family members, viewing all tasks as essential and equivalent, eschewing any notion that woman's relegation to the private sphere limits her power in the family as well as in the larger society.[26] Such a view ignores the reality of "the second shift"[27] foisted on women who must provide for their families economically and still provide for all of their other needs. Traditional and conservative views of gender relations that assume that males and females participate organically in an integrated structure in which they provide separate but equal functions are no doubt comforting and attractive to many, providing a sense of historical normalcy and right. But we should remember it was not until the 1950s that the "crummy job of scrubbing the floor was suddenly an honor"[28] and a test of femininity, a convenient social virtue that served to convince women that unattractive jobs were virtuous.

Conservative theorists explained women's dependence on men as a natural condition resulting from the pre-historic gender relations in which men bonded with other men on big-game hunts, leaving women relatively isolated and alone. This bonding resulted in the kind of cooperative competition between men that became the hallmark of a successful capitalist system. As such, women's insistence on disturbing this natural arrangement could only result in a disastrous destruction of the economy. When Christopher Lasch wrote *Haven in a Heartless World*, he insisted that the reduction of the authority of men in the family, coupled with the resulting intervention of "experts" into the sacrosanct male-headed family, had led to the demise of the natural authority relations in the family and triggered chaos in the economic and social world. He called for the reestablishment of the traditional authority system in which men are responsible for their dependent wives and children, and women for relieving men from the punishing realities of economic life and nurturing their children. In Lasch's world, men establish a boundary between the family and the state, and through their authority not only protect the family but reinforce the legitimacy of the state.[29]

Relegating women to the private sphere, asserting the moral rightness of their work in the home, and defining women's tedious and difficult labor as the hallmark of femininity not only denied the real experiences of women in the family but perpetuated an ideology that was dangerous to women. The definition of women as natural caregivers and men as natural providers, of women as dependent and men as independent, of women as cooperative and men as competitive, had severe consequences for women, as did limiting women's natural participation to the private sphere and excluding men as full participants in this sphere, condemning women as unfeminine or unnatural when they rejected its limitations. Charlotte Perkins Gilman's heroine/victim in *The Yellow Wallpaper* exemplified the consequences of the constricted life. She went mad in the attic, succumbing to the ministrations of her doctor-husband who had enforced social isolation and complete rest for the depression she suffered after giving birth. The limitation of women's economic and social participation damages their abilities and their value, and increases the real possibility that women, whether they accept these limitations or try to overcome them, become vulnerable to abuse, often in the workplace but more commonly at home.[30]

Feminist criticism of the oppression of women or discrimination against women has centered squarely on the family: woman's childbearing and child-rearing roles, her status as wife, the low status and powerlessness accompanying the homemaker role, discrimination against her in education and employment resulting from the traditional perceptions of her as wife and mother, and her dependency on a man for her survival and on her children for her identity. Challenges to the traditional were met with enormous resistance from the clergy, academics, and men and women, framed as resistance against radical feminism, man-hating lesbians, and efforts to destroy the family, but devoted to maintaining the traditional masculine and feminine roles in the family. While feminists railed against the oppression of women, conservatives clamored for revitalizing the idealized family form, condemning feminism as destroying not only the family but the economy and the American way of life

Despite strong resistance, women have been increasingly successful in demanding that the state become their ally in fighting the abuse and inequality they experience, although they have clearly not overcome major economic hurdles, like equal pay for equal work, discrimination in the workplace, and sexual harassment. They have overcome powerful stereotypes about themselves as well as about men, and have had to fight a legal system that incorporated the same stereotypes that were so dangerous to them in the first place. There is evidence that women are less likely to be battered today than they were 50 or 100 years ago and have more alternatives and support if they are. And in an increasingly global social world, the rapes and dowry deaths and honor crimes are met by outrage rather than acceptance. Legally and socially, women are not as dependent as they were in the past. In terms of almost any indicator—education, occupation, or income, women's status has improved dramatically. And women in the United States are enormously fortunate when compared with women in many, perhaps most, other cultures. The same could be said for men. To acknowledge these positive changes, however, does not mean the current inequities or current problems women experience are acceptable. Family violence is still an obvious and significant problem; women are still battered and raped, harassed and violated in other ways. And the causes of this violation of women can be found in the structure. The family is the institutional fulcrum on which culture rests. We live and breathe our culture from our experiences in the family, and as we learn language, we learn the expectations for ourselves—the expectations accompanying masculinity and femininity, our identities and value, and what is normal. What is normal translates into what feels right, so it becomes both right and normal for women to marry older and more powerful men, for men to marry younger and less powerful women, for us to marry within our own class and religious group. It is "normal" to establish relationships built on traditional notions of masculinity and femininity; women naturally are better at child rearing and nurturing and most household tasks, while men are naturally more mechanical, more aggressive, and more fit for the competitive marketplace. It is on these bases that patriarchy is reinforced and reproduced. And patriarchy, a system based on the belief that women are inferior, is buttressed by, and in turn reinforces, the economic, political, and social inequality of women. This pervasive system breeds the terrorism that some women experience at the hands of men. Yet this is the system we romanticize, accept as normal, view as right, and that makes us comfortable in our everyday interactions.

The family is highly privatized; it is defined as an entity in which members' obligations to one another are protected by the state and in which members are responsible for one another and free to interact as they wish within certain rather unclear limits. Both political liberals and conservatives are concerned about intrusions into family and individual freedoms by educational institutions and the government, varying only in the type of intrusion about which they are concerned. This view of the family as private and sacrosanct is rather recent. In colonial America, for example, the community could not allow families such autonomy. Survival of the whole required that each family had an obligation to the others to abide by standards that benefitted the whole. Children were disciplined by adults other than their parents, and neighbors were likely to evaluate the behavior of one another in the light of its impact on the community

FROM CHILD ABUSE TO VIOLENCE AGAINST WOMEN

The definition of violence against women as a social problem rather than a personal misfortune is embedded in the work on child abuse published in the early 1960s that grew out of the idealization of the family, resulting in its vulnerability to ever-greater scrutiny.[31] Setting their sights on parents as potentially destructive to their children, child abuse researchers and practitioners exposed the family to increasing analytical and physical intrusiveness. The family was the center of both comfort and destruction, of passion and potential violence. By the late 1950s and early 1960s, Freudian psychology's definition of the family as a cauldron of sexual volatility was well accepted in everyday understandings of relationships between parents and children; *oedipal complex*, *ego*, and *phallic phase* were tossed around with easy authority in casual conversation.[32] Similarly, the functionalist view of the family as a placid, cooperative system in which men and women filled complementary roles in the family and at work, resulting in an integrated, healthy, and productive whole, was adopted by parenting magazines, advertisers, and academics.[33] All were fixed on the family as the centerpiece of society, an institution simultaneously so fragile and so powerful as to hold the future of the country in its hands. The idealized American family of the post–World War II era was viewed as both the emblem of peacetime prosperity and the proof of the unquestioned superiority of capitalism and democracy. Its power as a symbol also focused unprecedented attention on the family and the relationships among its members.

The return of men to the workplace after World War II resulted in both blatant and subtle efforts to encourage women to leave the workplace and go back into the home, and if those didn't work, they were forced.[34] The family, and in particular the role of mother, was catapulted to the place of supreme social significance. Mothers who had been encouraged to leave their children at child care centers, many of them supported by the federal government under the Lanham Act, so they could work in factories and industry to support the war effort were now required to stay home if America was to prosper. After World War II, women were redefined as caretakers, essential to the everyday well-being of their children and the production of a healthy and prosperous future generation. Motherhood and homemaking became their work. Whereas only a few years earlier a woman who could work but who chose to stay home might be viewed as lazy, selfish, or even unpatriotic, a mother who now refused to be at home suffered these same epithets, at least if she was a member of the great middle class. Betty Friedan chronicled the malaise and intangible dissatisfaction and uneasiness experienced by well-educated suburban housewives during the late 1950s, identifying "the problem that has no name," which resonated with so many women. But she also expressed suspicion about the damage women could do while isolated in suburbia, and together these ideas were a powerful impetus for the women's movement of the 1970s.[35] Friedan's *The Feminine Mystique* remains the classic statement of women's dissatisfaction to this day. She described the creative marketing efforts of American corporations that were designed to induce guilt in women who would dream of something other than backyard barbecues and coffee klatches, and to intrude in the lives of high school girls before they had an opportunity to experience anything that might entice them away from a life of cleaning, consumerism, and maternity.[36] Girls in my high school class, graduating in the early 1960s, received a hope chest from the Lane Furniture company in anticipation of the real thing in which they would store the kitchenware and hand-embroidered linens that would accompany them into the "happily ever after." Even as I was college bound, I knew this was to be the real me, my real future.

As motherhood was transformed, so childhood was redefined, expanded, extended, and elaborated. No longer were children left to unfold as natural beings; no longer were they assumed to reflect inborn biological traits. Rather, in order to justify motherhood as a full-time job (which it historically had never been), the physical and psychological well-being of children was redefined as being completely dependent on the constant nurturing presence and tireless vigilance of the mother.[37] Whereas previously motherhood had been understood as a function performed by woman along with her many other responsibilities for the survival of the family, the 1950s inspired a definition of motherhood as woman's natural calling, an expression of her biological self. The "cult of true womanhood," a cult of purity, piety, domesticity, and idealized femininity, was born during the Industrial Revolution.[38] During the 1950s, it reemerged full blown, glorifying woman as homemaker and keeper of the morality of the patriarchal order just as it had in the Victorian era.[39] And just as this stifling definition of woman helped sow the seeds of the feminist revolution of the twentieth century, so it eventually led to the decades of discontent resulting in the second women's movement in this country.

Of course, there were some drawbacks to woman's constant presence in the home—problems stemming from constraining women within such tight and narrow definitions of femininity. As both Philip Wylie and Friedan pointed out, the singular and incessant attention of the mother could become destructive. Wylie concluded in *Generation of Vipers* that domineering mothers were responsible for creating weak young men whose masculinity was not well established, who were vulnerable to the brainwashing efforts of the North Koreans, and who were therefore a potential national security risk.[40] Mothers were suspected of feminizing their sons, emasculating them through their overbearing intrusiveness and manipulativeness, reflecting perhaps their refusal to accept their feminine role and adjust to their natural submissiveness. Friedan suggested that intelligent, potentially productive women, restricted to the drudgery of the home and left with too much time on their hands, placed all of their considerable energies and abilities on their children, becoming overprotective and overbearing, to the detriment of their children. The feminist movement, Friedan asserted, would allow women out of the home, resulting in happier women, healthier children, and a better America. The centrality of the patriarchal family as the cornerstone of America and repository of its dominant values, including patriotism, is reiterated with each change in the traditional hierarchical gendered structure whether the concern is about child care, gay marriage, abortion, or women working outside the home.

The spotlight on the family, especially the role of the mother and the conviction that it was critical to the development of the child, contrasted with the historically more prevalent view of the child as having inherited genetic characteristics and traits that would unfold. During the colonial period, the westward movement, and for most of the time this country was being settled, parents went about their work of survival, relying heavily on the skills and physical energy of their children, viewing their children as developing according to some predetermined plan and viewing themselves as caretakers and overseers of this process rather than as forces responsible for their children's identity. Clearly, parents were responsible for the moral development and physical well-being of their children, as was the entire community, but the child's self was not perceived as fragile, malleable, and constantly at risk, as it became during the 1950s and remains today. One cannot imagine the concepts "toxic parents," "co-dependence," "schizophrenic parent," "refrigerator mother," or "helicopter mother" until the 1950s and beyond, when motherhood became central to a woman's identity. This is not to say that children were not viewed as needing parental supervision; rather, this supervision could be provided by fathers, ministers, or neighbors, as well as mothers, and was an obligation of the community rather than an expression of a woman's natural, essential self. Children were viewed as needing control and training, this often being translated into the view that corporal punishment was essential for their well-being and growth. As late as the colonial period, fathers had the authority to beat, cane, imprison, and even mutilate their children if they thought it was essential for their discipline and development. Certainly the view of children as needing or deserving special attention or love as infants and toddlers emerged only with the Enlightenment.[41]

In *Mother Love*, Elisabeth Badinter reveals just how uncommon the "motherhood instinct" was among middle-class women.[42] In one region of France during the sixteenth century, she reports, not one infant survived to the first birthday. All were sent to wet nurses, many dying on the journey and others dying of malnutrition. Of the children who did survive their first year, many were malnourished, deformed, or crippled, and upon their return home were quickly sent away again to apprentice with a family member or stranger. The institutions of wet nursing and apprenticeship reflected the low value placed on infants and children, especially among the upper-middle classes, and the desire of parents with the privilege of choice to avoid the constrictions and drudgery of child rearing.

The privatized and closed family that characterized the ideal family type during the 1950s and 1960s was a real departure from the family of the past. Over the past 150 years or so, the family has changed from a public institution to a private one, from a microcosm of society to a counter point to it, from large to small, from a work unit to a unit of socialization.[43] These changes had an impact on the attention eventually given to violence against women as a social problem, to some extent as a result of the increased attention given to the lives of children within the family. Christopher Lasch suggests that the family's functions diminished as many of its previous functions were assumed by experts who now were in the position to oversee the family, decreasing the authority of the father.[44] No longer did a father make decisions about punishment; instead, the state intervened. No longer did a father decide when and where his children would go to school; the state did. No longer did a father determine the appropriate level of support and comfort due his family; that burden was transferred to the state. This state intervention reflected the state's investment in children and its right to intervene in order to protect its resources—the children.

While Lasch is correct in portraying the American father as losing his position of authority in the family, he misrepresents the family of the past with a shortsighted perspective. In fact, the family has often been the object of intervention by others, but this intervention was more informal and decentralized than it became after World War II. Before the Civil War, courts and legislators conceptualized childhood as a separate, protected state and defined women as responsible for domestic affairs.[45] In the late nineteenth century, families, especially immigrant and other poor families, along with women who refused traditional family roles, were subject to frequent intrusions by zealous reformers and philanthropists. These reformers imposed middle-class values on the lower classes, maintaining a punitive posture toward those who were unable or uninterested in abiding by middle-class morals and manners. They were, in fact, willing to destroy the families that did not meet their ideals, viewing orphanages and state support as superior to the influences of the wretchedness they saw in tenements and slums. As Stephanie Coontz points out, during the Progressive era, it was sometimes deemed necessary to intervene in the privacy of the family in order to enforce the middle-class norms that social workers and "child savers" demanded be adopted by all.[46] She makes the interesting point that immigrants were suspected of not only living immoral lives but of living cooperatively. State aid was built on the assumption of the superiority of private property, property rights, competition, and the family wage system and was designed to discourage social cooperation and sharing of economic resources. This sharing was punished, and autonomy and independence were rewarded. The war on poverty waged by Presidents Kennedy and Johnson similarly allowed social workers to intervene in the lives of poor families, especially single women and women of color, making support equal to conformity with certain middle-class sexual and family norms. As late as the 1970s, for example, food stamps were denied to any poor family or individual who shared cooking facilities. Social service workers could enter a welfare recipient's home and look for evidence that she was living with or sleeping with a man, in which case, she would be removed from the welfare rolls. The family is an essential ideological adjunct to the state, and the state has a stake in determining what is "normal" or at least acceptable behavior. A woman without a man was to be sexually loyal to the state, or what the welfare mothers knew as "The Man."

This increased permeability of the once-inviolable family and the definition of children as fragile resources led to the possibility of intervention in the family. The definition of child abuse as distinct from ordinary and acceptable punishment followed this intervention, as did an ongoing debate about this definition, its parameters, and whose values it should reflect. Child abuse was initially constructed as an individualistically based medical problem, likely to reflect some "defect in character structure" or individual emotional inadequacy.[47] As Gordon suggests, this medicalization of child abuse followed on the heels of a postwar commitment to defending the conventional family, a commitment that is no weaker today than it was over 50 years ago.[48] Problems in the family were explained as the result of individual complexes rather than cultural or structural arrangements. Henry Kempe's groundbreaking article "The Battered Child Syndrome" introduced the diagnosis of child abuse and firmly established it as a medical epidemic, produced not by cultural or structural arrangements but by parents who were inadequate, neurotic, or otherwise disturbed.[49] Between 1963 and 1965, following the publication of Kempe's article, 47 states passed mandatory child abuse reporting laws. Kempe suggested that abusers may be suffering oedipal anxieties or penis envy, and Steele and Pollock, also major early researchers on child abuse, suggested that characteristics of the child such as prematurity or hyperactivity might place her or him at risk.[50] In contrast to this purely individualistic approach, sociologists writing in this area, including Richard Gelles, Murray Straus, and Suzanne Steinmetz, emphasized the characteristics of the family as an institution, focusing on social structural factors such as isolation and poverty as well as socialization.[51]

A decade after Kempe introduced the concept of "child abuse" in 1962, as this social problem ran its course at both the federal and the state levels, interest switched to the more broadly defined issue of family violence, including not only child abuse and neglect but also wife battering and eventually sexual abuse and incest as well. The family was the designated problem, with child abuse and wife battering being intimately tied to one another and reflecting problems in the family. The women's movement, the changing sexual mores during the 1960s, and increased openness in the discussion of sex, blended with the attention given child abuse to broaden the pathways for criticism of the traditional hierarchical family. This led eventually to a critique of the family as not just the "cradle of violence" but the most dangerous place in the world for women. The very place women were most suited for by nature, according to postwar imaginations, began to be defined as potentially lethal for them. The idealized family of the 1950s became, in the 1960s and 1970s, an institution suspected of doing great damage not only to children but to women. The view of functional integration and role symmetry that characterized earlier analyses of the family was eroded as a result of the women's movement, the discovery of child abuse, and the resultant vulnerability of the family to criticism.[52] The increasing criticisms of the family were themselves sometimes taken as indications of its heightened vulnerability since institutions firmly grounded and accepted as operating properly are unlikely to be subject to great scrutiny or to even be terribly visible to the public. The family again, as it had been sporadically throughout history, was described as an institution both fragile and failing.

Concern about the family was not limited to the potential danger it posed to women. There was also a great deal of concern about the danger women posed to the traditional family itself. As women warmed to the message of Betty Friedan and as young women began to demand more from their brothers in the sexual revolution than the opportunity to make their coffee or "make their day," the alarm about the impact of women's changing lives on the family escalated. The conservative call to return authority to the father was accompanied by a parallel call for the return to the traditional roles of dependence and nurturing for women. In order for man to be the authority in his home, for his home to be his castle, woman had to give up any demand for autonomy or separate personhood. The construction of masculinity and femininity were built on opposite sides of the gender binary; for men to be masculine, women had to conform to traditional femininity.[53] Of course, these constructions of

masculinity and femininity did not include people of color, nor did they
include a large portion of white America, but they were powerful cultural
touchstones, called upon time and again by politicians, columnists, and
ministers. Critics of the women's movement were especially alarmed by
the erosion of male power and what they saw as women's abandonment
of their mandate to provide nurturance and support. George Gilder held
that if women were not willing to be *women*, then men could not be
men; without women's civilizing influence, men would run amok, and
the responsibility for the destruction of the human race would ultimately
be placed at the feet of women.[54] Women's entrance into the workforce
in ever-greater numbers, the increasing divorce rate accompanied by the
increasing poverty of women and children that resulted from pay
inequities and discrimination in the workplace, and women's reassessment of the traditional family and their role within it were among the
many factors leading the family to be viewed as vulnerable, troubled,
and headed for disaster.

Anxiety about the family is, of course, not unprecedented, as Gordon
points out in *Heroes of Their Own Lives*[55]: "For at least 150 years there
have been periods of fear that 'the family,' meaning a popular image of
what families were supposed to be like, by no means a correct recollection
of any actual 'traditional family' was in decline. Anxieties about family
life, furthermore, have usually expressed socially conservative fears about
the increasing power and autonomy of women and children, and the corre-
sponding decline in male, sometimes rendered as fatherly, control of
family members."[56]

Concern about the decline of the family was not matched by the introduction of any significant proposal for new policies or programs to buttress it. While lauded as the cornerstone of American life, each
individual family was left to sink or swim based on its own economic
resources—what was proclaimed publicly as critical to the survival of
American life did not change the fact that the family was to rely on its
own private resources for its survival. This lack of institutional realignment allowed for increased intervention by social workers, physicians,
and therapists into an economically and socially vulnerable family. At
the same time, however, social workers and other professionals (teachers,
physicians) seemed reluctant to diminish further the power of the traditional head of household, whom they conceptualized as male, and so
walked a thin line between recognizing problems in the family and being
willing to intervene. They could only do so by refusing to define characteristics of the traditional family and its attendant roles as problematic
and by maintaining a definition of the family in which violence occurred

as a "troubled family" or a "dysfunctional family." This way, social workers and others who had the authority to intervene could justify "helping" the family in order to strengthen it. By maintaining the view that a particular family was the problem or that troubled families had unique characteristics, there was no need to analyze the structure and dynamics of the family, traditionally built on gender inequality and patriarchal values.

The women's movement, however, was quick to situate many of the forms of oppression that women suffered in the family structure. Hierarchy, male control and ownership, female economic dependence, the demands of motherhood, the political inequality of women, the disjunction between the institutions of work and family, and restrictive cultural constructions of women were attacked as leading not only to limitations on women's lives but violence against women. The discovery of violence against women is indelibly and irrefutably linked most intimately with the emergence of the women's movement. By the early 1970s, theoretical analyses of the status of women in the family and society acknowledged the physical trauma women suffered as a result of oppression or inequality. While there was disagreement about the underlying cause, with radical feminists condemning patriarchy and liberal feminists pointing to economic and political disenfranchisement, feminists shared in the condemnation of violence against women, whether on the streets or in the family.

CLASS, CULTURE, AND THE VULNERABILITY OF WOMEN

The lack of equality in wages, opportunities for advancement, fringe benefits, and the other problems women experience in the workplace are critical components of the violence they experience, for a number of interrelated reasons. First, persons with power are less likely to be the victims of abuse or violence or terrorism than those without power. In our economy, having money, prestige, and status translates into power. Women who have power in their relationship and are not dependent emotionally or financially are less likely to be battered than those who are powerless. Even if battery does occur, the woman with power has the resources and the experience to leave, find housing, and maintain herself and her family, and she has more knowledge and access to legal remedies and other social support. No matter what her choice, she is in a better position to take care of herself outside marriage than is a woman with fewer resources and less work experience, whether that woman is wealthy or poor. Poor women are clearly at a disadvantage economically, but it may be that as a result of connection with social service agencies or other support networks, they may have more access to support outside the marriage than a blue-collar woman does. In addition, subcultural values may influence the woman's perception of choice; a woman used to being on her own, poor or not, may find it easier to make it alone with her children than can a woman in a lower-middle-class family who lives in a world of traditional values shared by her family, her church, and her community. The social and personal factors that might keep her in an abusive relationship may override the importance of economic factors, as Loseke and Cahill conclude in their research on "experts' " explanations for why women stay.[57]

Much of the research has focused on this question of economic dependency because one of the most widely accepted assumptions of shelter workers and others is that women stay in battering relationships because they do not have the resources to leave or to stay away once they have left. The probability of staying in a violent relationship is highest for women whose husbands are the sole breadwinners. Women who work outside the home are far more likely to leave if they are battered.[58] Economic dependence is one of the primary reasons battered women remain with their abusers, and divorce often makes matters worse. Women and children's postdivorce incomes have declined substantially under no-fault divorce laws, in large part because the resources that are divided are inadequate and because women have lost their bargaining power if the husband decides to dissolve the marriage. Also, women almost always have custody of the children, whom they are supporting on lower wages and without full, or any, child support from their ex-husband.[59] Whether a woman works outside the home, the type of employment she has, and the resources she has are also related to whether she stays. Working women are likely to occupy several roles and to have not just economic resources but an identity that is not restricted to the wife-mother role. Women whose occupational role is a significant part of their identity may find leaving a battering husband much less threatening to their identity than would women whose sole source of identity comes from their marriage. Women who are socialized to view themselves as primarily responsible for the family, and culpable if it fails, are perhaps less likely to see leaving as an option than are women for whom the family is only one source of personal identity. Not only individual marriage choices and arrangements but their social and cultural context are significant factors in linking the woman to a marriage that is abusive.

Much is made in the literature on violence against women about battery knowing no class, cultural, or racial bounds. While it is true that violence against women takes place at every class level and in every culture and within all racial and ethnic groups, to assert that it is unrelated to class, race, or culture is wrong. And these factors operate differently in different circumstances; for example, rural women who are isolated and who lack access to health care are likely to experience higher rates of abuse than urban women, although in both instances economic status plays a significant role. Rates of violence among blacks and whites in the same social class are similar, but since a larger proportion of blacks are poor, their overall rates of violence are higher.[60] Every author who has written about the family, from Karl Marx to the more recent work of Annette Lareau, has noted the heavy impact of economic opportunities on life chances and experiences in general.[61] The desire to ignore the reality of a class- and race-divided society and the impact of such a division is reflective of our individualistic, democratic ideology. This desire translates into the medicalization of significant social problems, demanding that we explain them in terms of individual pathology rather than social or structural factors or values that degrade or oppress women.

Some theorists have focused on violent subcultures, indicating that subcultural values may encourage reliance on violence to solve problems or to assert one's will.[62] While sociologists and social workers resist any theories that would suggest they are racist or "classist," the literature nonetheless suggests that our society contains different strata and different cultures and that expectations about appropriate and ordinary behavior differ by subgroup. Almost 40 years ago, Cohen suggested that lower-class parents discipline their children differently than do middle-class parents, relying more heavily on physical punishment, while middle-class parents practice love withdrawal. Studies of parents' attitudes toward punishment in both the home and the school suggest that lower-class parents are more supportive of teachers' using corporal punishment and are more likely to approve of it than are middle-class parents. Not to expect class, culture, and race to make a difference in the area of family violence, when we know that these factors are either determining or contributory in every other arena, would be senseless.

At the same time, as the O. J. Simpson case illustrates, misogyny can express itself in lethal ways at any class level. Simpson owned Nicole just as other wealthy men own their trophy wives. We could expect her to be in almost constant danger, her safety tied to her ability to please him and anticipate his needs. Her only power came from her attractiveness, and her attractiveness gave her power because it demonstrated his status. She was a vehicle through which he communicated his wealth and prestige to an audience, his expression of normative masculinity.

Cultural values and beliefs about the family, masculinity and femininity, husband and wife, are not uniform across race and class categories in this complex, heterogeneous social system. As we move up the socioeconomic ladder, the family becomes less traditional in terms of relationships between the parents and between parents and children. Upper-middle-class families are more likely to be egalitarian, more companionate, and less sex role stereotyped. Working-class families, such as those described by Lillian Rubin in her moving study *Worlds of Pain*,[63] are structured in a more hierarchical manner, are more divided by sex roles, and are more authoritarian. This difference exists for a number of reasons. First, persons with higher educational achievements are less likely to embrace sex role stereotypes, instead espousing marriage roles of greater equality, which allow more flexibility and less authoritarianism in both work and relationships. In addition, because religion is tied to social class, as one moves up the class ladder, religious values become more liberal, less literal, and more supportive of an egalitarian relationship between husband and wife. It may seem contradictory that Christianity as a belief system could be dangerous to women, but Christianity places men at the head of the family, woman being the vessel. Traditional Christianity is a belief system that exalts feminine piety, purity, and docility. Indeed, women in Christian families may be cared for and adored, but they also run heavy risks when they stray from perfection—they may well fall from the pedestal on which their faith places them because they violate the demands of one of the feminine virtues, and if this happens, they may pay the price with their bodies. It is not that fundamentalist Christian men are brutish or woman hating; it is just that if they are, they can find justification for their behavior within their religious belief system. Women are vulnerable to the moods, whims, and expectations of their husband, and this may serve them well or poorly, or may change from time to time. Ultimately the fact that women are not in control of what happens to them, that they are subordinate and dependent, that their value is tied to their role as wife and mother, creates vulnerability and may lead to their battery and abuse.

Social isolation is often presented as an important contributor to violence against women in the home. A good deal of research has suggested that social isolation creates a potentially dangerous situation and may be a precursor to violence or may reflect other problems that result in isolation. One researcher in this area, Garbarino, suggests with his ecological approach that among families in which violence occurs, there is a mismatch between the family and the social environment. The family has been thrust into a situation in which they have little in common with other members of the community, and this isolation from the rest of the community eventuates in stress that may escalate into violence. This situation may be common among military families, other families that move frequently, or families that experience sudden reverses in fortune and are forced to relocate.[64]

Stress caused by poverty, unemployment, or other forms of family disruption is also linked to abuse. In this culture, the family is expected to be a self-sufficient economic unit, equipped to absorb the demands of providing for its members. When there is difficulty in doing this, perhaps as a result of unemployment or illness, the structural provision that men provide for women and children is not met. Men cannot provide unless they have jobs that yield a decent income; their status as breadwinner is threatened by this inability, and both the wife and the husband may understand his abuse of her as reflective of this structural strain. Other stressors, some exacerbated by poverty, are also related to violence in the family. The stress of moving or the illness of a child, parent, or spouse may lead to violence. Family members are most vulnerable for a variety of reasons, including their ready access to one another, the lack of physical or psychological barriers, and the intimacy and knowledge of the other that accompanies it. One can assume that stress would vary by social class, with economic stressors and their consequences most powerful in the lower class. Other forms of job-related or relationship stress and the stress of caring for a sick child or parent are likely to occur at all social class levels.

The legal, social, and physical superiority of men in the family is a powerful factor in the production of violence. Men batter their wives because they can, because it is effective at least in the short term, and because the rewards for doing so outweigh the costs. If a husband has all the resources in the family, her opportunity to leave is limited. By the same token, given that she has few resources, her alternatives are limited as well. His level of resources allows him to suffer few costs if he beats her or controls her actions, while at the same time, his threats of abusive behavior may get the results he wants—whether they are ego gratification or her compliance. His analysis is embedded in an economic and social system in which he is superior economically and has been socialized to assume this superiority is his privilege. She, by the same token, is economically inferior, for all the reasons we discussed earlier, and she is likely to accept this inferiority as a consequence of the choices she has made to be a wife and mother or to select certain types of employment. Her perception of the weight of social forces on these choices is likely to be limited. The institution of marriage and the power relations it establishes lead the husband to expect compliance from his wife and to assert his right to force her compliance if it is not voluntarily forthcoming. From a conflict perspective, battery can be viewed as one technique men use to maintain their power in a relationship hierarchy. Marriage is a structure of inequality, in which the woman at the bottom of the hierarchy desires to gain power, perhaps just to achieve equality, and the man, at the top, works to keep his superior status.

This hierarchical structure of the family reflects the economic, political, and social world that spawns it and, in fact, is a microcosm of that system. Woman's inferiority in the family is supported by her inferiority in the wider social structure, and in both instances, cultural assumptions and beliefs reinforce her inferior status and relative powerlessness. To the extent that she also believes she should occupy an inferior position in the family (and in the larger system) she predictably suffers false consciousness, absorbing the values and beliefs of her oppressor rather than those reflective of her material position in the world. Women are violated because they are relatively powerless, an out-group, unworthy of the same treatment men as a category receive. This unworthiness may be justified with disarming language about how women run the world through their feminine wiles, how they influence and shape the decisions made by men, how they have the power of persuasion, how their softer and more delicate natures are the foundation on which the family is built. But the underlying truth is that as a category (not as a particular individual), women are cast as "the other," as Simone de Beauvoir asserts, and they are not perceived as having the same human qualities as men; their emotions, their physical beings are different and "less than."[65] The definition of them as emotional belittles their emotions, while the definition of men as strong and contained gives great value to their expression of emotion, especially emotions of tenderness or caring. The definition of men as needing power, needing to dominate, leads to understanding his violence when this power or authority is challenged or lost.

The danger women face in their relationships is a result of their position in the social structure as well as in the family. There is no need to look for particular unique characteristics or psychological profiles of men and women that will explain their violence. If this were so, the violence would not be so predictable. Women are more likely to be responsible for family, to earn less when they work, to be portrayed as ready and often willing victims of sexual assault and violence. These factors shape women's lives in their relationships with men and determine their vulnerability to men. This power differential and the cultural imagery that justifies it are at the base of violence against women in the family, the streets, and the workplace.

Women's advocates are often dismayed by the amount of abuse a woman will take before she leaves her abuser. Psychologists several decades ago explained this in terms of the woman's natural masochism and the sadism of the abuser, resulting in a symbiotic relationship rewarding to both partners. The layperson is perhaps most confused by the tendency of women to stay in abusive relationships and least able to understand the choices women make from their perspective. However, it is not difficult to understand why women stay and why they avoid the label of "battered woman" that is proffered by emergency room personnel and shelter workers, who encourage them to see their husband as an abuser and themselves as abused women and who encourage them to leave their relationship. There is a difference between getting in a fight with a spouse or boyfriend, or being hit and being a "battered woman." To be labeled a battered woman and to accept the label is to accept a definition of self as deviant, and the label requires a restructuring of the self. It implies that one is the victim of physical violations, the kind of person who could be victimized, and leads to a potentially very difficult reassessment of the self, the other, and the relationship.

"Wife battery" in this context is a political term, and it implies that the woman is not only beaten but is beaten by a person who should love her, care for her, and treat her with kindness. It implies more than that an argument got out of control or that one had an especially explosive argument. The process of accepting the label is not a simple or straightforward one for the woman who is beaten. She considers this label within a context in which she may blame herself for his behavior and in which others may see her as culpable or at least contributory. What are the implications of her accepting the label "battered woman"? Does she not then have to assess the kind of person she is, ask herself what kind of person would be beaten by her own husband? This is far different from asking oneself what caused an argument or a fight with one's spouse. It demands a reassessment of the self that is not called for if things "just got out of hand." It is no surprise that women have been reluctant to accept this label.

Experts may not have much to offer when attempting to explain why a battered woman does not leave the man who abuses her. Expert opinions fall into two primary camps. The more prevalent assessment is that she is psychologically disturbed, suffering from codependence or learned helplessness or battered woman syndrome. Sociologists are reluctant to accept these explanations, suggesting instead that structural barriers prevent her from leaving, such as lack of child care, lack of a place to live, or lack of economic support.[66] However, it might be perfectly reasonable for her to stay in the relationship. Don't we expect people to work through problems in their marriage? Aren't we to marry for the good times and the bad? Aren't women in particular to acquiesce and maintain the family at all costs rather than to strike out selfishly on their own when the going gets rough? Staying is understandable and predictable; the woman may well love her abuser despite the social worker's assessment that this is dependency disguised in more noble clothing. Whether one is a battered woman or not is not simply a matter of fact. It is a matter of definition, and while there are reasonable motivations for establishing a woman as a "battered woman," there are equally reasonable reasons for denying or avoiding that label.

Women who are battered by their husbands often love them, just as mothers who beat their children may love them. Experts, clinicians, and shelter workers dismiss these expressions of affection as symptoms of emotional disease, but the woman's point of view should not be discounted. It may make a psychologist or a sociologist uncomfortable to hear from a woman sitting before her with bruises or stitches that she loves the man who did that to her, but the therapist's discomfort does not make the woman's evaluations of her feelings invalid. She can both love him and be his victim. By the same token, the fact that he beats her does not mean he does not love her. He may love her, desire her, want her, and yet beat her.

The desire to be loved, however we define that, may keep us in situations that are incompatible with our well-being. Many women and men grow up in families in which some violence is a normal part of their everyday life. It is not necessarily a crisis, nor does it threaten the relationship. It may be that we make a choice: to have love as we know it or to be safe. Maybe we opt for one or the other; maybe we try to have both. Perhaps, we agree, "'Tis better to have loved and lost than never to have loved at all."[67] Violence is part of the fabric of everyday life in many families, incorporated into the day as a disruption but not a threat. In other families, violence is so rare that one incident of slapping or hitting devastates the base on which the marriage is built.

ALL WIFE BATTERY IS NOT THE SAME

All violence against women in the home is not the same; sometimes women are attacked by men who view them as property and want to control them, and in other situations a couple's disagreements or arguments escalate to the point of involving hitting, slapping, or punching. Both may have consequences for the couple and for their children; both may be devastating, but they have different sources, follow different patterns, and have different outcomes. Michael Johnson makes an important distinction between common couple violence or what he later termed "situational violence" and patriarchal terrorism. This distinction helps explain the ongoing, fairly heated, disagreements between the feminist theorists who write about women as victims of male abuse and the family violence theorists, such as Straus and Gelles, who conclude that most violence is reciprocal.[68] Johnson says that the disagreement is, in fact, based on the different methodologies relied upon by these theorists: the family violence theorists rely on national surveys and the Conflict Tactics Scale (which has some built-in problems of its own, such as not including sex abuse), while feminist theorists rely on shelter and hospital populations. These theorists access very different forms of violence and their study populations lead them to draw very different conclusions about violence. The disagreements are in the following areas: escalation, mutuality, frequency, symmetry, and reciprocity. Patriarchal violence is a form of terrorism, a form of control reflective of male privilege and female subordination, of the desire on the part of the man to own and control "his woman." It is fortified by women's economic and political subordination and grounded in the ideology of male superiority and natural gender differences. Patriarchal violence is "a product of patriarchal traditions of men's right to control 'their' women, a form of terroristic control of wives by their husbands that involves the systematic use of not only violence, but economic subordination, threats, isolation, and other control tactics."[69] These violent assaults should be distinguished from the ordinary violence that characterizes so many families. Common couple violence is less gendered and operates as a family dynamic in which arguments or disagreements escalate into conflict or in which couples rely on physical violence to settle disagreements in a particular situation. In sum, the debate about whether men are as likely to be victims of violence as are women, which began in the 1970s when Steinmetz published her article "The Battered Husband Syndrome," can be better understood if we acknowledge these different types of violence.

This debate has reemerged recently as researchers once again examine the prevalence of the violent and abusive wife.[70] The national surveys conducted by Straus, Gelles, and Steinmetz led them to conclude that women were as likely as men to use violence in the family.[71] This conclusion was met with a great deal of criticism, particularly from feminist researchers, and with a great deal of applause from men's groups and others who saw the battered woman movement as a social construction of disaffected women's groups. The media pounced on Steinmetz's article, which presented the group's findings, as a condemnation of the feminist arguments about the violent family. The reaction to Steinmetz's work revealed the degree of emotion underlying the seemingly neutral academic questions and assumptions that provided footing for much of the legal and grassroots response to battered women. She was berated, condemned, and threatened, sometimes by victims and sometimes by advocates. Her colleagues, while supporting her findings about mutual violence, focused on the differential degree of damage women suffered as a result of their smaller size and their lack of familiarity with physical confrontation. Some suggested that while women may also use force in the family, their violence was reactive and self-protective rather than aggressive.

The uproar and current disagreements about this topic underline the importance of differentiating types of violence. There are two sets of researchers examining different populations and coming up with different findings, according to Michael Johnson. Researchers working from a "violence against women" perspective are likely to be feminist scholars, shelter workers, and grassroots activists who rely on findings from questionnaires or interviews with women who seek help from shelters. The women they interview are likely to be the victims of terroristic violence from which they have escaped. On the other hand are social service workers and academic researchers who come from a "family violence" perspective; they rely on national surveys of families and tap into an entirely different dimension of violence in the home. They instead find common couple violence, resulting from escalating arguments between husband and wife, either or both of whom are likely to slap or hit the other. These are the couples engaged in what Straus saw as ordinary violence, viewing it as "American as apple pie." Ordinary violence or common couple violence flows from the organization and dynamic of the family, which make it a breeding ground for violence. These include the intimacy that characterizes the family, the fact that one does not choose one's family members, constant and close proximity of family members, the lack of privacy in the family, and the protected nature of the family, and are reflective of the structure and organization of the family.[72]

Researchers working from the family violence tradition describe a process in which family life produces conflicts that occasionally escalate into violence that "gets out of hand." In these families, there is almost perfect symmetry in the use of violence by men and women against their partners, and these forms of violence take place on the average about once every two months. Furthermore, there is little likelihood of escalation of common couple violence over time. According to findings based on the Conflict Tactics Scale used in the National Family Violence Survey in 1975 and its 1985 replication,[73] ordinary violence is viewed as one end of a continuum resulting at the other extreme in violent assaults. These are viewed not as different forms of violence but as more or less severe and dangerous violence resulting from the same factors.

So, rather than one group of researchers being wrong and one being right, their research is based on different populations and reliant on different methodologies, resulting in different findings. Michael Johnson suggests that the feminist researchers and the family violence researchers are studying entirely different phenomena and that the sampling biases of the researchers led them to study distinct, almost nonoverlapping populations, leading to very different findings about violence. As a result it is possible to get widely varying and conflicting findings. Family violence researchers, using national surveys and a very broad definition of violence, report on common couple violence and find almost no difference between the violence perpetrated by men and women.[74] This may be because the researchers the Conflict Tactics Scale includes "pushing," " hitting," " shoving," "grabbing," "slapping," or "hitting or trying to hit" even once, as classifying that person as a perpetrator.[75] Recent analysis of police files in the United States and Canada yielded similar results.[76] P. J. Kincaid analyzed family court files in Ontario, Canada, and found 17 times as many female as male victims.[77] Melton and Belknap found both real similarities and significant differences emerging from their quantitative and qualitative analyses. Relying on official statistics, they found not only that men far outnumbered women in police reports but that African Americans were significantly overrepresented. Further, men were far more likely to make threats, to push and grab, to pull the victim's hair while women were more likely to hit with an object, a vehicle, or to bite the victim. Men made more serious threats and showed a pattern of threatening that was not characteristic of women. Male attacks were more serious and severe than those of women, and women were more frightened by the threats and actions of the perpetrator. These authors, as did others,[78] found that women were more likely to use violence to resist the threats or assaults against them, whereas men were likely to use violence to control and have power. So, when one looks beyond the different populations family violence and feminist theorist are relying on and mine the material to look at motive and patterns and reactions, real gender differences emerge.[79]

Straus found in his 1990 work that among women who reported being assaulted in the National Family Violence Survey (NFVS), the average number of such assaults per year was six, although for those who used the services of a shelter, the average was 15.[80] Other researchers, however, using the same series of survey questions, found an average annual number of incidents per woman to be between 65 and 68. While family violence theorists did not find violence to escalate over time, shelter researchers found a very different pattern. Mildred Pagelow, for example, concludes that "one of the few things about which almost all researchers agree is that the battering escalates in frequency and intensity over time," a point that is arguable from the perspective of family violence researchers.[81] Both sets of researchers would agree that women, because of their smaller stature and socialization (emphasizing docility and nonaggression), are more likely to be injured during violence, whether it is male perpetrated or mutual violence.[82]

In either case, women are being assaulted in the family. The different populations of women studied by these two groups of researchers help to clarify the differences in their findings. It also makes more understandable the common assertion by shelter workers that class, ethnicity, and race are not significant elements in determining violence against women. I suspect that patriarchal terrorism operates differently from common couple violence in a number of ways. Ownership and control of women is historically embedded in culture and gender relations. Yet ideologies of equality are more characteristic of the upper class than the lower, and there is probably less social support for violence against women as a control tactic. At the same time, control of economic resources and status resources may be more available to men in the upper class than to men in other classes, so they may rely less on physical violence in order to assert control over their wives. Those who have the full threat of the force of the state behind them are unlikely to have to rely on actual force.[83] In the case of both patriarchal terrorism and common couple violence, I would expect less violence in the upper than in the lower classes, but for different reasons. Common couple violence would be less frequent because there would be fewer stresses, more access to resources, as well as socialization and education that emphasize other means of conflict resolution. In the case of patriarchal violence, the man would have other resources to exhibit his power and control and would not have to resort to violence to assert his ownership. When a woman like Nicole Simpson is beaten and killed by her ex-husband, it is likely to be an indication of patriarchal terrorism, which one might expect when the discrepancy in status and resources between the man and the woman in a relationship is great—that is, when he has chosen her as a marriage partner to exhibit his power and status.

Barrie Thorne has referred to the family as a tangle of love and domination.[84] It is both the most intimate and the most dangerous relationship. The ties are not simply roles or expectations for behavior; they cannot be captured with a description of the duties or rights or responsibilities of husband and wife. The ties are deep and complex; they have a history of caring and hurt, disappointment and pain. Husbands and wives have shared illnesses, childbirth, economic crises, the successes and failures of one another and their children and others in their families. The richness, depth, and complexity of the family cannot be captured in the stereotypical view of the family as either a form of legalized prostitution (Engels) or a haven (Lasch). It is more than a structure of ownership, more than a reflection of a capitalist system, more than a misogynist tool of patriarchy. It is also more than an authority structure of roles and relationships in which all is well as long as each member of the family conforms to the traditional expectations. It is neither the cauldron of woman hating nor the prison of motherhood that the late radical feminist Shulamith Firestone describes in *The Dialectic of Sex*.[85] Yet neither is it the placid, cooperative, integrated system that the functionalists present. Each view provides a useful but incomplete and distorted picture of the family. Each is too simple, relying on stereotype and myth rather than the complex interplay of real people in everyday situations. Understanding the battering situation and the battering relationship is promoted by incorporating a number of views. The complex relationship between couples that take place within an institutional structure of marriage, situated as it is within a wider structure characterized by class and race differences, demands complex understanding. Yet while all of these structural and individual factors may be taken into account, and even be understood, the precipitating event may be unpredictable and incomprehensible to the participants as well as to experts.

While love and common couple violence seem not to be incompatible, the relationship between love and patriarchal terrorism is more complex. The man's violence against his wife reflects a pattern of using control tactics to intimidate, threaten, belittle, and demean. Are these efforts incompatible with what he defines as love? Probably not. He loves her as an object—as something he can control and use, but he may love her nevertheless. He also despises her and belittles her attempts to stand alone or to have an identity that is separate from him. He sees her as a legitimate target of his wrath, an outlet for his frustrations, a perfect object against which to rail, an appropriate victim. Women are culturally presented as sex objects, as available to fulfill men's wishes, to meet their needs; surely he can expect no less from "his woman." Women are culturally depicted as good mothers, perfect wives, all giving, responsible for anything that goes wrong in the family; surely his wife is no different. Women (good women, that is) are supposed to be dependent and submissive and to put their own desires and wishes on the back burner—surely he cannot be blamed for expecting this of "his woman." Women are presented culturally as always ready for sex, as owing sex to their husband, providing sex as a service, and that is the least he should be able to expect from "his woman." The ideology, although increasingly divorced from reality, is something like men have a right to a decent meal when they get home from work; after all, they are supporting the family. They are bringing in the income, or the most income, and they should have the most voice in how it is spent. They grew up believing that privilege accompanied masculinity, and there is nothing in their culture that communicates anything different.

Patriarchal terrorism is a reflection of patriarchal culture. The messages men get from the media, religion, and language reinforce male privilege, sometimes blatantly and always subtly. Men do not learn in our culture that women are independent, equal in every way, deserving of respect for their abilities. They may respect particular women, exceptions from the norm, but women as a category are defined as different from and less than. These cultural messages are more carefully camouflaged in the upper classes than the lower, where machismo and hypermasculinity may be more blatant, as evidenced by the wildly popular WWE and the "man shows" on television as well as video games and rap lyrics.

The cultural messages of inequality are so much a part of everyday life that most of us do not perceive them. We insist that we believe in equality, choice, and freedom. It is only when we ask men to give up some of their privilege that we can actually see the privilege structure in which we live. If, for example, we suggest that men stay home with the children, take over the care of the home, make the meals and serve them, ask their wives to "babysit" when they want to go out for the evening, ask permission to go to work or take a class, or that men see women's ideas and conversation as more important than theirs, women's space more valuable than theirs, then we begin to see the privilege structure that men take for granted.

This privilege system is subtle and strong. It is the skeleton on which most relationships between men and women are built and is one with which both are often comfortable. A patriarchal system is not only supported and maintained by men. Women work equally hard to maintain the system that benefits them as long as they play according to the rules of the system. Women are indeed the primary socializers, passing on the dominant cultural messages to their sons and daughters. The structure of the family, and women's place in it, leads women to reproduce the very inequality they experience, and with the best of intentions. Teachers and parents tell little girls to "be nice" and to "act like ladies," to smile and be sweet, so they will be liked and accepted and eventually chosen as marriage partners. Aunts and grandmothers perform mutilating acts on the girls in their villages so they will be marriageable, so they will have a husband, a family, and a place in the community. In China, during the first half of the twentieth century, mothers bound their daughters' feet, breaking their bones and inflicting great pain, not because they wanted to wound their daughters but because they wanted them to make good marriages. It is to be a part of patriarchal society, to be chosen by a man, to be supported, to survive, that these girls were, and sometimes still are, mutilated. In these extreme examples of foot binding or genital mutilation, just as in modern middle-class United States, women are preparing their daughters to succeed, or at least to survive, in patriarchy. They are the messengers, the carriers of culture. They do the dirty work of men, with softer hands, but men are the invisible actors.

Phyllis Schlafly was well aware of the benefits the system of inequality bestowed on women in her social class. She was determined to protect middle-aged, upper-middle-class wives and mothers, women who had been homemakers for 20 years, from the destructiveness of their husbands' midlife crises. Schlafly was willing to trade women's right to equality for women's right to be protected financially by men—not a bad trade for some women, at least in theory. Her fear of the Equal Rights Amendment was that if women gained legal equality, men would no longer have any reason to stay with them. She believed that no man would stay with a 45-year-old woman when he could trade her for his 25-year-old secretary. To keep him, and to keep his financial support, he must be forced to stay in the relationship or have to pay so heavily to get out that he would decide it was not worth it to leave. Schlafly convinced millions of voters that legal equality would be woman's downfall; her place in the family would be threatened, her financial security lost. Women needed to be protected by men, and if they hesitated or declined the privilege, they must be forced.

Schlafly was onto something. Although she idealized the family system under which men had control and economic power and portrayed the realities of divorce inaccurately, she knew that divorce for women, especially women with children who had been out of the marketplace for a decade or so, would be financially devastating. She wanted to force men either to stay married or continue to support their former wives if they bailed out. The demand for equality, when translated into the no-fault divorce laws, was indeed devastating for women. Under the old fault system, divorce laws assumed that marriage was a contract in which the man agreed to be the provider and the woman to be the homemaker, even though this was more true on paper than in reality. Although the couple could divorce, it was only with some difficulty and with someone being to blame for breaking the contract. After the divorce, the man was still expected to support the family, and the woman was still expected to be the homemaker. This arrangement was expected to be a disincentive to divorce, particularly for the man.[86]

No-fault divorce laws codified a presumption of equality between men and women in the family and the workplace that was a fiction. Husbands and wives could agree to "dissolve" the marriage, no fault attached, and the decisions about child custody and financial support were based on the idealistic premise that women could compete with men equally in the marketplace and that the more financially able parent would care for the children. In fact, women were still the ones primarily responsible for the care and custody of the children, and even women who were as educated as their husband, and had professions and occupations that were relatively high status (which was very rare indeed) were still at a disadvantage when it came to providing for their children on their own. Most women were not as prepared educationally, did not have jobs that paid as well as their husband's, and yet most remained responsible for the children. Their financial situation was devastating, while men overall benefitted economically by divorce. Further, men were more likely to get remarried earlier and at faster rates than women, taking on new responsibilities (at least temporarily), even further constraining their support of their previous family.[87] The two-tiered family —one old wife and their children, one new wife and their new children—became more commonplace.

THE SOLUTION AND WHY IT WILL NOT BE ACHIEVED

The eradication of wife abuse, battery, and sexual assault requires the eradication of sexism. This means significant social change, change that is almost impossible to achieve. Herein lies the complexity. The scope and depth of change required to eliminate sexism and the oppression of women require such a thorough reorganization of society, a deep cleaning of cultural beliefs and values that support the economic and social oppression of women, that achieving it would require a staggering amount of effort and commitment. Starting with the proposition that the solution would be simple if one could entirely restructure a society solidly embedded in inequality and the oppression of women, eliminating violence against women as a category, would be addressed by dismantling one institution after the next. Clearly that will not happen. Such broad structural change is unlikely to be achieved; more important, those who would benefit from such a change are often not in a position to effect it. Those who make the laws, the policies, are men, and they are likely to benefit from the structure, not simply because they are men but because they have power and privilege in the system as it is currently structured. They would be reluctant, at the very least, to give it up. In the early 1970s, women naively thought that as soon as they had pointed out the inequities in the family and the workplace and revealed the problems of inequality, men would throw up their hands in alarm and amazement, horrified by their clear advantage based solely on gender, and would clamor to help change the system to make it more fair to women. It did not happen. Women were surprised, then disappointed, then angry.

If sweeping structural change is unlikely to be achieved, it is nevertheless agreed by most theorists in this area that we must change cultural values and family structure if we are to make a significant dent in the problem. This requires altering fundamental beliefs, values, and attitudes and eradicating the normalcy of inequality that is built into patriarchy. And beyond this, since so much violence in the family, violence against women and children both, is a reflection of more systemic inequality, a living wage would go a long way toward addressing the isolation, stress, and conflict tied to poverty.

There are a number of ways in which the family can be changed to reduce family violence, including violence against women. The research team of Straus, Gelles, and Steinmetz summarizes some of the most important:

1. Eliminating the norms that legitimize and glorify violence in the family and society at large. This requires domestic disarmament and stopping violence committed in the name of the state.

2. Reducing the violence-provoking stresses created by society, such as underemployment, poverty, and health problems.

3. Integrating families into a network of kin and community, so that people have someone with whom to share the strains and stresses, to reduce the isolation and alienation they may experience.

4. Changing the sexist character of society and the family. Inequality in the home is a primary contributor to violence between family members. Men's view that they are head of household and responsible for a dependent family and women's view that they are primarily responsible for caretaking create destructive stresses and strains.

5. Breaking the cycle of violence in the family by eliminating the reliance on physical punishment and condemning rather than accepting violence among siblings.[88]

Such violence learned in the home as part of everyday life recreates violence in the next generation.

All of these suggestions would change the relationships between members of the family and would also require dramatic changes in culture. And who is willing? Too many religious organizations, corporations, educational systems, and family structures are built around the current differentiation between men and women, and they would have to be torn down and built again. Perhaps in a Utopian community, one could achieve such major restructuring, but a complex, heterogeneous society such as ours cannot achieve such major change swiftly or smoothly, or maybe at all. There would have to be a will, and clearly most of the problems we have in this society are intransigent: poverty, crime, drug addiction, alcohol abuse, and violence against women and children.

Rather than making the sweeping changes that are necessary for the elimination of violence against women, we often turn our attention to minor alterations and realignments. Not only does this approach seem practical and reasonable, it provides no challenge to the current gender structure and current ideology of oppression. Battery of women remains defined as a personal problem even though it can be seen as a social and structural issue. It befalls families with particular characteristics and women with unique personalities. Entire professions and thousands of agencies and organizations at the local, state, and federal levels are built around studying this problem from the individualistic perspective, developing programs and approaches designed to intervene in the family or provide counseling and education to couples or individuals who are victims or perpetrators. These organizations employ hundreds of thousands of people who are professionalized in a perspective that ultimately maintains the status quo. They are well-meaning in their efforts to reduce the pain suffered by women, but their complete embeddedness in a psychological perspective prevents them from thinking in large, structural terms. The relatively minor changes with which we might be comfortable will probably be of little real benefit, or may even be damaging, to women. The minor realignments we are willing to make are simply institutionalized efforts to maintain the jobs of the middle class, designed to reproduce the institution or agency rather than to eliminate the problems they are designed to address.

The criticisms voiced by women who were struggling for women's rights at the beginning of the twentieth century are still valid. In addition, the different perspectives held by conservative and radical women, involved in different ways in changing women's lives, endure. The equal rights movement resulted in a number of significant improvements for women: the Equal Rights Act, the Equal Pay Act, sexual harassment laws, changes in rape laws and their enforcement. Many other changes have had a clear, positive impact on the lives of women. At the same time, radical feminists still see a culture steeped in the hatred of women; the oppression of women through advertising, music, and the media; and a work-family structure organized around male realities and perpetuating a male privilege system that prohibits women from achieving freedom. Both are right, and efforts from both arenas continue. Some women work for greater participation of women in politics, reducing workplace inequity and improving women's status in the home. Others call for a complete restructuring of the family and the workplace, insisting that as long as women are the primary caretakers, they will remain secondary earners and hence remain dependent and vulnerable to divorce, desertion, and violence. Still others work toward reducing or eliminating the cultural imagery of women in movies, music, and other media that present women as objects, as enjoying rape, as wanting to be hurt or damaged, or simply as powerless beings whose needs and desires matter little or not at all.

These efforts are not contradictory; rather, the changes advocated by each would result in a dramatic reduction of the violence against women, particularly patriarchal terrorism. Were women economically independent and perceived as competent and able persons with clear boundaries and the right to self-determination, the violence against them would be greatly reduced. But this requires changes in men's lives as well—changes in definitions of masculinity that reduce the threat posed by powerful women and that eliminate the assumption of male privilege. As Jackson Katz insists in *The Macho Paradox*, violence is really a men's issue that has been painted as a women's issue.[89] Surely individual acts of violence would occur and couple conflict and couple violence would continue in families isolated and burdened by too many children and bills and too few resources and time, but the predictable violence women face as a result of simply being women would be alleviated.

NOTES

1. S. B. Carter, "Assessing the Veracity of Domestic Violence Allegations in Parenting Disputes," *Florida Bar Journal* LXXVI (November 2002): 70.

2. C. McGrath, "The Crisis of the Domestic Order," *The Socialist Review*, no. 9 (San Francisco: Center for Social Research and Education, 1979), 13.

3. P. Tjaden and N. Thoennes, *Full Report of the Prevalence, Incidence, and Consequences of Violence against Women* (National Institute of Justice and Centers for Disease Control and Prevention, November 2000).

4. T. Davidson, "Wife Beating: A Recurring Phenomenon throughout History," in *Battered Women: A Psychological Study of Domestic Violence,* edited by M. Roy (New York: Nostrand Reinhold, 1977).

5. L. A. Frisch, "Research That Succeeds, Policies That Fail," *Journal of Criminal Law and Criminology* 83, no. 1 (1992): 209.

6. C. H. Sommers, *Who Stole Feminism: How Women Have Betrayed Women* (New York: Simon & Schuster, 1994), 203.

7. E. Pleck, "Wife Beating in Nineteenth Century America," *Victimology: An International Journal* 4, no. 1 (1979): 60–74.

8. M. Pagelow, *Family Violence* (New York: Praeger Publishing, 1984).

9. S. Heckel, *A Jury of Her Peers*, film distributed by Women Make Movies, 1989.

10. L. Gordon, *Heroes of Their Own Lives: The Politics and History of Family Violence—Boston, 1880-1960* (New York: Viking Press, 1998).

11. C. Lasch, *Haven in a Heartless World* (New York: Basic Books, 1977).

12. Ibid.

13. J. Makepeace, *Family Violence: Readings in the Social Sciences and Professions* (New York: McGraw-Hill, 1995).

14. M. P. Johnson, "Patriarchal Terrorism and Common Couple Violence: Two Forms of Violence against Women," *Journal of Marriage and Family* 57 (1995): 283–94.

15. E. Pizzey, *Scream Quietly or the Neighbors Will Hear* (Short Hills, NJ: Ridley Enslow, 1974).

16. R. A. Berk, P. J. Newton and S. F. Berk, "What a Difference a Day Makes: An Empirical Study of the Impact of Shelters for Battered Women," *Journal of Marriage and Family* 48, no. 3 (1986): 481.

17. N. Tracy, *Battered Women's Shelters: What Are They? How to Find One?* Healthy Place: America's Mental Health Channel, http://www.healthyplace.com

18. M. Studer, "Wife-Beating as a Social Problem: The Problem of Definition," *Journal of Women's Studies* 7, no. 5 (1984): 412–22.

19. J. O'Brien, "Women Abuse: Facts Replacing Myths," *Journal of Marriage and Family* 33 (1971): 362–398.

20. H. Wallace, *Family Violence* (Needham Heights, MA: Allyn and Bacon, 1996).

21. O. Barnett, C. Miller-Perrin, and R. Perrin, *Family Violence across the Lifespan* (Thousand Oaks, CA: Sage, 1997), 8.

22. G. Gilder, *Sexual Suicide* (New York. Quadrangle, 1973); Lasch, *Haven in a Heartless World*; and L. Tiger, *Men in Groups* (New York: Random House, 1969).

23. P. Schlafly, *The Power of the Positive Woman* (New Rochelle, NY: Arlington House, 1977).

24. W. Wang, K. Parker, and P. Taylor, "Breadwinner Moms" (New York: Pew Social Research and Demographic Trends, May 29, 2013), http://www.pewsocialtrends.org/2013/05/29/breadwinner-moms/

25. Gilder, *Sexual Suicide*.

26. T. Parsons, *The Social System* (Glencoe, IL: Free Press, 1951); see also Tiger, *Men in Groups*; Gilder, *Sexual Suicide*; and L. Tiger, and R. Fox. *The Imperial Animal* (New York: Holt, Rinehart, and Winston, 1989).

27. A. Hochschild, *The Second Shift: Working Parents and the Revolution at Home* (New York: Viking Penguin, 1989).

28. O. Barnett and C. Rivers, *She Works/He Works: How Two-Income Families Are Happy, Healthy, and Thriving* (Boston: Harvard University Press, 1998).

29. Lasch, *Haven in a Heartless World*.

30. C. P. Gilman, *The Yellow Wallpaper* (New York: Feminist Press, 1975).

31. C. W. Mills, *Sociological Imagination* (New York: Oxford University Press, 1959).

32. S. Freud, *The Ego and the Id* (New York: W.W. Norton, 1960).

33. T. Parsons and R. F. Bales, *Family, Socialization and Interaction Process* (New York: Routledge and Kegan Paul, 1956).

34. B. Friedan, *The Feminine Mystique* (New York: Dell, 1963).

35. Ibid.

36. Ibid.

37. S. Coontz, *The Way We Never Were: American Families and the Nostalgia Trap* (New York: Basic Books, 1992); E. Badinter, *Mother Love: Myth and Reality* (New York: Macmillan, 1981); and A. Skolnick, *Family in Transition* (15th ed.) (Boston: Allyn & Bacon, 2006).

38. B. Welter, "The Cult of True Womanhood: 1820-1860," *American Quarterly* 18, no. 2, part 1 (Summer 1966): 151–74.

39. N. Cott, "Eighteenth-Century Family Life Revealed in Massachusetts Divorce Records," in *A Heritage of Her Own*, edited by N. Cott and E. Pleck (New York: Simon & Schuster, 1979).

40. P. Wylie, *Generation of Vipers* (New York: Rinehart, 1955).

41. Badinter, *Mother Love: Myth and Reality.*

42. Ibid.

43. Coontz, *The Way We Never Were.*

44. Lasch, *Haven in a Heartless World.*

45. Coontz, *The Way We Never Were.*

46. Ibid.

47. H. Kempe, "The Battered Child Syndrome," *Journal of the American Medical Association* 181, no. 1 (1962): 17–24.

48. Gordon, *Heroes of Their Own Lives.*

49. Kemp et. al., "The Battered Child Syndrome."

50. B. J. Steele and C. Pollock, "A Psychiatric Study of Parents Who Abuse Infants and Small Children," in *The Battered Child*, edited by R. Heifer and C. H. Kempe (Chicago: University of Chicago Press, 1968): 89–133.

51. M., Straus, R. Gelles, and S. Steinmetz, *Behind Closed Doors: Violence in the American Family* (Garden City, NY: Doubleday Anchor, 1980); see also M. Strauss and R. Gelles, *Physical Violence in American Families* (New Brunswick, NJ: Transaction Publishers, 1990): 96–98; and R. Gelles, *The Violent Home: A Study of Physical Aggression between Husbands and Wives* (Beverly Hills, CA: Sage, 1972).

52. Parsons and Bales, *Family, Socialization, and Interaction Process.*

53. J. Lorber, *Paradoxes of Gender* (New Haven, CT: Yale University Press, 1994).

54. Gilder, *Sexual Suicide.*

55. Gordon, *Heroes of Their Own Lives.*

56. Cott, "Eighteenth-Century Family Life Revealed in Massachusetts Divorce Records."

57. D. Loseke and S. Cahill, "The Social Construction of Deviance: Experts on Battered Women," *Social Problems* 31, no. 3 (1984): 296–310.

58. M. Strube and L. Barber, "The Decision to Leave an Abusive Relationship: Economic Dependence and Psychological Commitment," *Journal of Marriage and the Family* 45, no. 4 (1983): 785–93.

59. L. Weitzman, *The Divorce Revolution: The Unexpected Social and Economic Consequences for Women and Children in America* (New York: Free Press, 1985); see also M. Garrison, "Good Intentions Gone Awry: The Impact of New York's Equitable Distribution Law on Divorce Outcome," *Brooklyn Law Review* 57, no. 3 (1991): 621–754; B. R. Rowe, and J. M. Lown, "The Economics of Divorce and Remarriage for Rural Utah Families," *Journal of Contemporary Law* 16, no. 1–2 (1990): 301–32;

B. E. Aquirre, "Why Do They Return: Abused Wives in Shelters," *Social Work* 30, no. 4 (1995): 350–54; and I. M. Johnson, "Wife Abuse: Factors Predictive of the Decision-Making Process of Battered Women," *Dissertation Abstracts International* 48 (1988): 3202A (UMI No. 8803369).

60. M. L. Benson and G. L. Fox, "When Violence Hits Home: How Economics and Neighborhood Play a Role" (NCJ 205004) (Washington, DC: National Institute of Justice, September 2004).

61. A. Lareau, *Unequal Childhood: Class, Race, and Family* (Berkeley: University of California Press, 2011).

62. M. Wolfgang and F. Ferracuti, *The Subculture of Violence: Toward an Integrated Theory of Criminology* (London: Tavistock, 1967).

63. L. Rubin, *Worlds of Pain: Life in the Working-Class Family* (New York: Basic Books, 1976).

64. J. Garbarino, "The Human Ecology of Child Maltreatment," *Journal of Marriage and the Family* 39, no. 4 (1977): 721–35.

65. S. de Beauvoir, *The Second Sex* (New York: Knopf, 1952).

66. Loseke and Cahill, "The Social Construction of Deviance: Experts on Battered Women."

67. From Alfred Lord Tennyson's poem *In Memoriam: 27*, 1850: "I hold it true, whate'er befall; I feel it, when I sorrow most; 'Tis better to have loved and lost Than never to have loved at all."

68. M. Johnson, "Patriarchal Terrorism and Common Couple Violence: Two Forms of Violence against Women," in *Family Violence: Readings in the Social Sciences and Professions,* edited by Makepeace; Straus and Gelles, *Physical Violence in American Families.*

69. Johnson, "Patriarchal Terrorism and Common Couple Violence."

70. S. Steinmetz, "The Battered Husband Syndrome," in *Family Violence: Readings in the Social Sciences and Professions,* edited by Makepeace, 252–60; "Spouse Abuse Crackdown Surprisingly Nets Many Women," *New York Times*, November 23, 1999, Al; S. Steinmetz, "The Battered Husband Syndrome," *Victimology* 2, no. 3–4 (1978): 499–509.

71. Straus, Gelles, and Steinmetz, *Behind Closed Doors.*

72. E. Pleck, J. H. Pleck, M. Grossman, and P. Bart, "The Battered Data Syndrome: A Comment on Steinmetz' Article," *Victimology* 2, no. 3–4 (1978): 680–83; see also R. E. Dobash and R. P. Dobash, *Violence against Wives* (New York: Free Press, 1979); R. E. Dobash and R. P. Dobash, *Women, Violence and Social Change* (London: Routledge, 1992); and I. M. Johnson and D. Kurz, "Social Science Perspectives on Wife Abuse: Current Debates and Future Directions," *Gender and Society* 3, no. 4 (1989): 489–505.

73. The widely used Conflict Tactics Scale, developed by Straus, is discussed in M. Straus, "The Conflict Tactics Scale and Its Critics: An Evaluation and New Data on Validity and Reliability," in *Physical Violence in American Families,* edited by Straus and Gelles. See a thorough criticism of the scale in R. E. Dobash, R. P. Dobash, M. Wilson, and M. Daly, "The Myth of Sexual Symmetry in Marital Violence," *Social Problems* 39, no. 1 (1992): 79–91.

74. M. A. Straus, "Injury and Frequency of Assault and the 'Representative Sample Fallacy' in Measuring Wife Beating and Child Abuse," in *Physical Violence in American Families,* edited by Straus and Gelles, 1990.

75. Dobash, Dobash, Wilson, and Daly, "The Myth of Sexual Symmetry in Marital Violence."

76. Dobash and Dobash, *Women, Violence, and Social Change.*

77. P. J. Kincaid, *The Omitted Reality: Husband-Wife Violence in Ontario and Policy Implications for Education* (Maple, Ontario: Learners Press, 1982); see also L. Okun, *Woman Abuse: Facts Replacing Myths* (Albany: State University of New York Press, 1986); J. Giles-Sims, *Wife-Battering: A Systems Theory Approach* (New York: Guilford Publishers, 1983).

78. L. K. Hamberger, J. M. Lohr, D. Bonge, and D. F. Tolin, "An Empirical Classification of Motivations for Domestic Violence,"*Violence against Women* 3, no. 4 (1997): 401–42.

79. H. Melton and J. Belknap, "He Hits, She Hits: Assessing Gender Differences and Similarities in Officially Reported Intimate Partner Violence," *Criminal Justice and Behavior* 30, no. 3 (2003): 328–48.

80. M. A. Straus, "Injury and Frequency of Assault and the 'Representative Sample Fallacy' in Measuring Wife Beating and Child Abuse," in *Physical Violence in American Families,* edited by Straus and Gelles.

81. M. Pagelow, *Woman-Battering: Victims and Their Experience* (Beverly Hills, CA: Sage, 1984).

82. Johnson, "Patriarchal Terrorism and Common Couple Violence."

83. W. Goode, "Force and Violence in the Family," *Journal of Marriage and the Family* 33, no. 4 (1971): 624–36.

84. B. Thorne and M. Yalom, *Rethinking the Family: Some Feminist Questions* (New York: Longman, 1982).

85. S. Firestone, *The Dialectic of Sex: The Case for Feminist Revolution* (New York: Morrow, 1970); see also A. Dworkin, *Woman Hating* (New York: Penguin Books, 1974).

86. Schlafly, *Power of the Positive Woman.*

87. Thorne and Yalom, *Rethinking the Family*.

88. Straus, Gelles, and Steinmetz, *Behind Closed Doors: Violence in the American Family*, 237.

89. J. Katz, *The Macho Paradox: Why Some Men Hurt Women and Why All Men Can Help* (Naperville, IL: Sourcebooks, 2006).

FIVE

Just Tryin' to Make a Livin'

During cotton-picking season, my grandmother went to the fields early every morning with her husband, their older children, and some field hands. She left the field before the others to go home and make the midday dinner for everyone, remaining behind afterward to do dishes and get supper started. She then returned to the fields for the afternoon. After the noon meal, my grandfather, "Pop," and the field hands rested on the front porch for a while, feet up on the rail, smoking and chewing. The boys played and the girls helped "Mom" in the kitchen. At night after supper, "Mom" still had the cleaning, mending, and ironing to do, with the help of her daughters. The garden was her responsibility, as well as the house that was home to the family of seven children. Hard work was ordinary and expected for women and was a necessity for family survival. Women's work inside the home, on farms, in other women's kitchens, and in the factories was essential but was never defined as woman's essence, her fulfillment, her identity. It was just work.

Work before the Industrial Revolution was the means for sustaining the family unit and the entire family was required to generate the necessary resources; the work was an obligation equally shared by family members. But with industrialization, the work of men and women was separated, with men spending long hours in factories and women keeping home and hearth for their family. The family wage system replaced the family work system, and men were to earn enough to support themselves as well as their dependents. Work for a large number of women was confined to the home, and while this "sacred sphere" may have been a relief from the double-duty of the farm, their work was constraining and eventually led them to chafe at the restriction of domesticity. The separation of men as workers from women as keepers of the domicile laid the groundwork for the later dependence of women on men's earnings and finally, in the 1960s, to a revolution against the restrictions of the cult of domesticity.

The first women's movement, which emerged from the realization on the part of women that they were prohibited from even the most rudimentary participation in economic and political life, resulted in gaining the right to vote, but the women compromised other significant economic and social advantages, promising that "the hand that rocks the cradle will never rock the boat." It was not until after World War II that women once again began to chafe against the restrictions they suffered on the basis of their gender and the second women's movement emerged from what Betty Friedan called "the problem that had no name."[1] This problem was ennui and disenchantment and a lack of fulfillment on the part of middle-class and well-educated women. Coupled with the often conflicting demands of younger women, working women, and women who had been involved in the peace and the civil rights movements, the women's movement gathered into a fragmented and impatient movement that rolled across the land. It carried with it the destruction of the assumptions and "taken for granteds" about women's lives that had constrained them for decades.

The post–World War II effort to transform woman's work in the home into a profession, a highly skilled occupation she was uniquely qualified to perform for her children and husband, was a miserable failure. There may have been the temporary titillation of determining her child's success in school by choosing the right breakfast cereal, or guaranteeing her husband's promotion by keeping the toilet bowl sparkling white, or making great Manhattans, but the veneer soon wore thin. Women wanted something with some depth—something to worry about besides the see-through shine on their kitchen floor or getting their whites whiter.

The kind of work women did outside the home was not all that enticing either. They worked as clerks or typists or in service jobs for low pay and few benefits. But this was nothing new; women historically have worked long hours at hard jobs for low wages, worked alongside their husbands and children to support the family, worked at home when their day in the factory or office was finished. They worked when they were exhausted, and sick, and tired, and wanted nothing more than to have one good night's sleep and someone to make breakfast for them in the morning, or do the laundry, or mind the children for a few hours.

The 1950s were unique in the efforts of advertisers and the government to try to transform the meaning of work for women into something completely new: to convince them that the home was their natural place and that they should find happiness and fulfillment there. Separating women from the workplace, reframing the home as women's work, and romanticizing domestic duties for middle-class women eventually led women to identify the problem that had no name; whether it was named boredom, malaise, or depression, it meant that women were unhappy with the way things were. The situation was not getting any better, and something had to change.

The effort to convince women that they belonged solely in the home went counter to centuries of experience. The home prior to the Industrial Revolution was a place of rest and recuperation, a place to take nourishment, to prepare for the next day of work. The family consisted not of parents and children but of parents, and the third cousin who was apprenticed, and one of the mother's sister's daughters, and a couple of farmhands who were there to put in the crops, and sometimes a cow or a pig that needed some warmth or special attention. With the Industrial Revolution, the home was transformed into a haven, the man's castle, while the workplace was transformed into the real world—a rough, ugly, and uncivilized place fit only for men. These men needed replenishment and comfort when they crossed the hearth from the hostile work world to the home, and women were transformed from workers to pious, pure, and domestic creatures, formed of finer clay, particularly fit for the task of mopping the sweat from the brow of their men and providing a sanctuary from the demands of the capitalist system. That was the ideology, of course—one built on the experiences of the middle class. Poor women, women of color, and immigrant women were completely invisible in this fantasy. For them, the factory or someone else's kitchen demanded their presence each day, and the home required their time each evening. They either did not have a husband or were working as many hours as he was to make ends meet. Home was not a profession, nor was it created for women's comfort and delight; it was a place requiring their efforts after they had worked all day for a meager income. It is not possible to romanticize either arena in which they participated. They worked in sweatshops 10 to 12 hours a day, often on Sundays as well, and ensured that meals, clothes, and other essentials were provided for their families the rest of the time. These women were not, at the turn of the century or during the 1950s, those who were clamoring to get back into the workplace. They were eager to get out of the factories and other people's homes and spend their time in their own kitchens, with their own children. These women were not the women encouraged to build their identities around their children and husbands. In fact, their identity was of little import; they were valued for their labor. Their lives were ignored by the mythmakers both at the turn of the century and during the 1950s, and by activists who revealed the problems that led to the sexual revolution and the women's movement.

Today the women who work in the *maquiladoras*, who slave in the duty-free zones established by the United States for American corporations in Mexico and Bangladesh and Central America, live comparable lives to those of immigrant women and poor black women during industrialization. The women are hired at pitiful wages, working under almost unbearable conditions for American clothing and electronic manufacturers. In April 1995, while Nike, the largest supplier of athletic shoes in the world, posted a profit of $298 million, the women making those shoes in factories in Jakarta made less than $2.00 a day.[2] In Bangladesh, almost a decade later in May 2013, factory workers were making less than $40.00 a month, probably the lowest wages in the world. They make sweatshirts and souvenirs for Walt Disney Company that sell for more than they make in a week; they also produce fad fashions for Calvin Klein, Tommy Hilfiger, Walmart, J. C. Penney, and Sears, to name only a few.[3] These women work under terrible conditions because they have no other choice, no other possibility of employment. They are hired because they provide a "docile" workforce, have children to support, and this is the only work available. The trade agreements made between Third World governments and the U.S.-based companies that establish factories in Southeast Asia, South Korea, and Taiwan are based on the lowest wages, the loosest environmental standards, and the worst record for workers' rights—a mix allowing the greatest profits for the companies and the worst situation for the workers. Yet these jobs are coveted. And if workers complain or make any move to organize, these companies move on to find women who will work under even worse conditions for still less. The recent devastating fire and building collapse in Bangladesh, killing over 1,000 people led to demands from across the world for better working conditions and higher safety standards for workers. Yet the economy is so dependent on the mass production and shipment industries that workers would be devastated if they left. The vast majority of the workers are women, as are those in training, with 98 percent of the seamstresses in training in Indonesia's national training center being women.[4] The women are young, usually between ages 16 and 21. They are old by age 23 if they work in electronics, by 27 if they work in textiles. The industries are relatively impervious to the traditional organizing efforts of labor groups in large part because the women who work in the *maquiladoras* are hired not by the manufacturers but by subcontractors. A factory will move into a community, hire the women, and then later cut their pay and any benefits, until the women's already desperate situation becomes completely impossible. Then the manufacturer moves on. The horrible working conditions and the lack of humane treatment are reminiscent of the very worst sweatshops ever to have existed. This system, developed and supported by the U.S. government, is a shameful crime against women.[5]

At the turn of the century, while middle-class women were beginning to organize for the vote and for more sexual and economic freedom, working-class women organized around work issues such as earning a living wage and working decent hours in a safe workplace.[6] Many of the concerns of middle-class or well-educated women seemed of no consequence to working-class women; concerns about the right to control one's own body, sexist language, marriage as legalized prostitution, and the right to be free from the restrictive demands of traditional femininity seemed of little import to these women whose lives were spent working at menial and fatiguing jobs and trying to keep their family fed, healthy, and together. It is small wonder that the women's movement of the 1960s did not speak to the lives of women at the bottom. These women were worrying about the struggle to survive, not searching for meaning or trying to find themselves amid the diapers and cleansers. This is not to say that many of the same issues did not bind women of different classes. The demands on the part of middle-class women to enter the marketplace and be taken seriously as workers, to be paid well and given benefits, eventually led to workplace changes that were equally beneficial to working-class women, just as access to birth control and abortion was every bit as critical for working-class or poor women as it was for middle-class women.[7] The difficulty was that their language was so different that the similarities in their situations and the shared consequences of economic and social limitations were almost invisible. The rift between these groups of women, while wide, was crisscrossed with similar problems hidden below the obvious differences. While the origins of the middle-class women's movement of the late 1960s were in the antiwar movement, they were also in the civil rights movement, and not just for middle-class white women getting their liberal kicks cozying up to black men. Black men's apparent attraction to white women split women further than the objective conditions they shared would have warranted. White women were likely to identify with the oppression of the black man, both of them identifying the white man as the oppressor, but white women had little interest in black women, and black women viewed them as interlopers and a threat to their relationships with black men. Black women had to figure out whether they were women first or black first and what the relationship between those two identities was. Black women had to figure out what they wanted to risk and for whom.

Despite the enormous gulf between the meaning of work and family to middle-class women, and to working-class or poor women in the 1950s, changes in policies and laws during the last half of the twentieth century benefitted everyone. The problems that remain are different in scope but not in the impact they have on women's lives. Since women, middle class and poor, work to survive—either to support themselves and their children or to support their families with their husbands—they are working for essentially the same reasons, and for the same reasons that men work. To say that women work because they need to does not imply that they should work only if it is essential for their survival. Freud and Marx both knew the importance of work in our lives, that meaningful work is essential, and the fact that so few have achieved that should not lead to condemnation of those who do.

Whether women work because they absolutely must for survival or because they enjoy work and find meaning in it, or both, their work should accommodate them to the same extent as it does men. This has never been the case. In addition to other forms of sex discrimination, such as unequal pay or promotion and the double burden of work and family women carry, sexual harassment poses devastating problems for women in the workplace and in educational institutions. Sexual harassment is a form of violence against women covering the gamut from bothersome to assaultive; in each case, it violates the rights of women to pursue work or education unencumbered by discrimination of the basis of their sex.

SEXUAL HARASSMENT

The young women who worked for one of most powerful politicians in New York, Assemblyman Vito J. Lopez, were continually groped by him, told to wear low-cut blouses and high heels, and pressured to stay in hotels with him overnight. They had to fight off his kisses, his demands that they massage him, and his efforts to fondle their breasts and genitals. They were afraid to report him because he could ruin their careers. As one young woman said, "you can't get a dog license in Brooklyn without Lopez's blessing."[8] It was bad enough that these young women endured this sexual violence but worse to discover that the Assembly speaker, Sheldon Silver, and his staff shielded Lopez from public scrutiny, reaching confidential settlements to prevent disclosure of the allegations against the 71-year-old assemblyman.[9] The goal of mitigating damage to the Assembly was evidently more important than investigating or disciplining the assemblyman. Sexual harassment is a form of oppression. It is ordinary and ubiquitous and is still, in instances such as this, a workplace condition women endure if they want to work or advance their career. The protestations of perplexity from men about the meaning of sexual harassment are omnipresent. How often have I heard a male colleague or student say, "I'm afraid even to open the door for a woman anymore for fear that I'll be accused of sexual harassment," or, "You can't even smile at a woman or say you like her hairstyle without being accused of sexual harassment"? Male faculty seem especially bewildered, largely, I would guess, because they have for so long seen their female students as one of the "benefits" of their relatively low-paying jobs. Many of my colleagues dated their students and in fact often married these students. They can hardly identify themselves as the harassers in all the talk about sexual harassment in the classroom.

Sexual harassment of women on college campuses and in the workplace receives much less attention than sexual assault, although both can be devastating and lead to significant psychological and physical problems, interruptions of career and educational plans, job changes, loss of income, and other life disruptions. Dziech and Weiner, in their groundbreaking book *The Lecherous Professor*, list the typical behaviors on the part of male professors that are harassing, including ogling and leering, commenting on the student's personal appearance, touching, flattering, and generally sexualizing the environment.[10] On a more general level, women are harassed as part of normal classroom activity. In classic examples, medical students are subject to jokes about a cadaver's breasts, or professors punctuate their lectures with sexist jokes or material. Men, having constructed the environment in the classroom and university and having kept women out for so long, find it unpleasant to rid the academy of the attitudes that justified their exclusiveness—attitudes that women are body parts or primarily sexual objects available for the gratification of men.

The befuddlement men express is based in part on the reality that sexual harassment laws are probably the only laws governing violence against women that emerge from a woman's perspective, from *her* definition of the situation rather than from the man's. These laws reflect the "reasonable woman's" view of the interaction or speech rather than that of a reasonable man. As Catharine MacKinnon points out, "The legal claim for sexual harassment marks the first time in history, to my knowledge, that women have defined women's injuries in a law."[11] Men and women do see sexual harassment differently; they identify it with different eyes and ears. What women see as sexual harassment, men may see as an ordinary way for men and women to interact and so may be baffled when they are accused of sexual harassment.[12] One study of children concluded that while both girls and boys had experienced sexual harassment in grade school, girls were more likely to have lowered self-esteem as a result and were likely to feel afraid or powerless, while boys were likely to feel flattered.[13] Women and men learn very different lessons about the appropriate context and the meaning of sexuality and sexual interaction, so it is not surprising that their perceptions of the same behavior may differ greatly. In addition, those with power may define sexual remarks or behaviors toward those with less power very differently than those with less power would, again resulting in different perceptions of the same behavior. The unusual thing about sexual harassment is that the law reflects the reality of those without power and assumes the validity of the socialization messages women receive. Women's everyday experiences are incorporated into the law, something that occurs in no other instance.[14]

Rape laws in the past were property laws, and the offense was against the husband or the father, not the woman who was raped. Italy's 1936 Fascist-era law that designated rape as an offense against public morality rather than an act of violence against women was still in effect as recently as 1995, with lenient application and punishment for offenders.[15] Sexual harassment laws, unlike rape laws, emerge from the subtle and blatant sexual offenses against women in the workplace, acts that add insult to the already destructive reality of lower wages and other forms of workplace discrimination.

Sexual harassment is behavior that becomes coercive because it occurs in the context of employment, thus threatening a woman's job satisfaction and job security. The salient factors establishing harassment are that the verbal or physical behavior is sexual in nature, that it is unwanted, and that it is implicitly or explicitly experienced as a threat to the woman's job or ability to perform her work or educational functions.[16] Harassment can be or include acts of assault and physical contact, and is clearly violence within any context. Further, sexual harassment is a threat to woman's physical, emotional, or economic safety. It is a direct statement to her that she is not in control of herself or her environment. It is a direct statement that someone who is her superior, or supervisor, or simply a man who carries male privilege has the ability to impose himself on her. Such an assertion creates an environment in which women are, if not explicitly living under the threat of harm, implicitly adapting to a harmful situation and are responding to the demands of that system in addition to the demands of their work. Experiencing this lack of safety on a daily basis establishes a work environment for women that differs dramatically from that of men.

Loy and Stewart identify four types of harassment: verbal commentary, which includes sexual jokes, sounds, and teasing; verbal negotiation, which includes explicit sexual propositions and negotiation; manhandling, which includes unwanted touching such as patting, brushing against, or pinching; and sexual assault, which involves the use of physical force.[17] Their description covers a wide range of behaviors, and those who deride women who charge harassment as meek whiners always keep their descriptions of sexual harassment comfortably within that first category. Franklin and colleagues prefer the term "gender harassment" to refer to forms of sexual harassment that, like racial and ethnic slurs, are directed at persons the speaker views as inferior, and are designed to humiliate or disparage the person as a woman, rather than to elicit sexual cooperation.[18] Still, sexual innuendo and joking make women uncomfortable *because* it is directed at them to make them uncomfortable or because it is part of an environment that does not take their presence into account, not because of women's delicate moral sensibilities. Laws prohibiting sexual harassment are designed to address the continuing discrimination against women in the workplace, acknowledging the parallels between sex and race as minority group characteristics resulting in work experiences that selectively damage women and other minorities.

The women's movement was in full swing in 1974 when an Environmental Protection Agency employee brought a suit alleging sex discrimination when she lost her job because she refused to have sex with her supervisor. A federal district court dismissed the case, asserting that she lost the job not because she was a woman but because she refused to have sex with her boss. The U.S. Court of Appeals for the District of Columbia reversed the decision and awarded her $18,000 back pay, the first federal court to rule that sexual harassment is a form of discrimination in employment and is illegal under Title VII of the Civil Rights Act of 1964.[19] The grounds for the lawsuit had been laid only a year before in *Williams v. Saxbe*. Until then, despite Title VII, unwanted sexual attention was simply one more condition of work for many women.[20] The inclusion of sex in this act was in fact not a serious acknowledgment of sex discrimination but the result of a ploy on the part of southern senators to scuttle the act. The Civil Rights Act as it was initially written prohibited discrimination based on race, color, religion, or national origin but included no mention of sex. A few southern senators were smugly confident that adding something so ludicrous as sex to an antidiscrimination bill would result in its being laughed off the floor, ensuring its defeat.[21] However, proponents of the bill were able to overlook the inclusion of sex in order to get a bill prohibiting other forms of discrimination passed, a happy accident for women and an unanticipated humiliation for the senators.

This same bill established the Equal Employment Opportunity Commission (EEOC) to oversee the new law and establish regulations and guidelines for its enforcement. Title VII of the Civil Rights Act states that it is illegal for employers, labor unions, and others to "discriminate in the terms, conditions, and privileges of employment" on the basis of (among other things) ... sex.[22] Sexual harassment is a violation of Title VII because it creates a difference in the terms and conditions of employment for women. Sexual harassment in employment is broadly defined as any attention of a sexual nature in the context of the work situation that has the effect of making a woman uncomfortable on the job, impeding her ability to do her work or interfering with her employment opportunities. It can be manifested by looks, touches, jokes, innuendos, gestures, epithets, or direct propositions.[23] However, from 1964, when the Civil Rights Act was passed, until 1975, 11 years later, the U.S. Supreme Court issued only two opinions elaborating on the standards surrounding sexual harassment claims.

Headed by Eleanor Holmes Norton, the EEOC published a landmark series of guidelines in 1980 to help corporations conform with the Civil Rights Act.[24] The EEOC defined sexual harassment as unwelcome sexual advances, requests for sexual favors, and other verbal or physical conduct of a sexual nature in which "(1) submission to such conduct is made either explicitly or implicitly a term or condition of an individual's employment or status in a course, program, or activity; (2) submission to or rejection of such conduct by an individual is used as the basis for employment or educational decisions affecting that individual; or (3) such conduct has the purpose or effect of unreasonably interfering with an individual's work performance or educational experience, or creates an intimidating, hostile, or offensive environment for working or learning."[25]

In her 1979 book *Sexual Harassment of Working Women: A Case of Sex Discrimination*, Catharine MacKinnon illuminated the distinction between quid pro quo and hostile workplace sexual harassment.[26] Both are prohibited as a form of sex discrimination under Title VII. At one extreme, is *quid pro quo*, the direct demand for sexual compliance coupled with the threat of firing if a woman refuses. Quid pro quo harassment involves a more or less explicit exchange of sexual favors for employment or advancement or prevention of job loss. Most cases of quid pro quo harassment that reach the courts involve a situation in which an employer or instructor makes a sexual advance to a woman, she declines his advance, and she is punished in some way—by being demoted, not considered for promotion, or her work life made miserable. Quid pro quo harassment cases were tough to prove, and victims began to point out that supervisors and coworkers could create a very hostile and abusive work environment without actually demanding sex in exchange for benefits. *Vinson v. Meritor Savings Bank* established hostile work environment as a form of sexual harassment.[27]

Hostile work environment significantly broadened the definition of sex discrimination, and most sexual harassment cases fall in this category. It refers to being forced to work in an environment in which, through various means such as sexual slurs, the public display of derogatory images of women, or the requirement that she dress in sexually revealing clothing, a woman is subjected to stress or made to feel humiliated because of her sex. Hostile work environment harassment involves conduct that has the purpose or effect of unreasonably interfering with an individual's work environment and may include sexual innuendo, teasing, jokes, language, posters, and cartoons that degrade women in the workplace. It can be blatant or subtle and is often regarded as normal male behavior or "an extension of the male prerogative of initiation in male-female interaction."[28] Michelle Vinson initially refused her boss's requests for dates. Eventually, however, she relented and had sex an estimated 40 or 50 times with him. In addition, she said he groped her, exposed himself to her, pressured her, and even raped her. She lost her case against him at the district court level, in part because she was not demoted or fired from her job. The Supreme Court's reversal established hostile environment as a form of sex discrimination. In *Meritor Savings Bank v. Vinson*, the Supreme Court upheld the 1980 EEOC guidelines on sexual harassment, ruling unanimously that sexual harassment "sufficiently severe or pervasive to alter the conditions of the victim's employment" could amount to sex discrimination actionable under Title VII. The Supreme Court decision in *Vinson* also established that a voluntary relationship was not necessarily a consensual relationship.

The Supreme Court decision in *Vinson*, while establishing hostile environment harassment, left several areas unresolved, including the issue of "welcomeness," the types of sexual conduct that are actionable, and the standards for holding employers liable.[29] These issues have been addressed and are still being addressed in subsequent decisions.

Two 1999 Supreme Court decisions addressed employer responsibility and created a new set of rules to govern employer liability for harassment by supervisors. The Supreme Court established that an employer can be

vicariously (i.e., strictly) liable for the actionable harassment by a supervisor that involves a tangible employment action. In *Faragher v. City of
Boca Raton*, two female lifeguards sued the city after their supervisor
made lewd comments, touched them in offensive ways, and engaged in
other hostile conduct.[30] The city argued that it was unaware of the behavior of its supervising lifeguard and should not be liable. This case was a
classic example of hostile work environment harassment, meaning that
the plaintiff had to show that the conduct was severe or pervasive, objec-
tively and subjectively offensive, unwelcome, because of the plaintiffs'
sex, and occurring within the relevant time. While plaintiffs must meet
all of these conditions, they are not required to show that the harassment
adversely affected their work performance or inflicted psychological
injury. However, the employer's strict liability depends on whether the
victim suffered a "tangible employment action," defined as a "significant
change in employment status, such as hiring, firing, failing to promote,
reassignment with significantly different responsibilities, or a decision
causing a significant change in benefits."[31] In *Burlington Industries Inc.
v. Ellerth*, the plaintiff worked in a two-person office and was supervised
by her office manager who reported to his supervisor in another city.[32]
The manager made sexual advances to Ellerth, and when she resisted, he
said, "I could make your life very hard or very easy at Burlington." She
wanted to establish the case as a quid pro quo case, but the lower court
held that her claim was a hostile environment claim. Although this case
was different from *Faragher*, the plaintiffs in both cases were required
to meet the conditions of hostile environment sexual harassment. The
exact actions, or the degree of harassment, or the specific consequences
of the harassment are still argued in lower courts. One requirement is that
the harassment has to be based on the person's sex, resulting in the situation in which an "equal opportunity harasser" does not qualify as creating
a hostile workplace.[33] Yet it is clear that sexual harassment law applies to
both men and women. In *Oncale v. Sundowner Offshore Services*, the
Supreme Court ruled that same-sex harassment was against the law as
long as the harassment was based on the victim's sex.[34]

The EEOC has continued to create regulations and refine the definition
of sexual harassment and appropriate employer responses. It holds an
employer responsible for the harassing behavior of its supervisory
employees, regardless of whether the acts complained of were authorized
or even forbidden by the employer and regardless of whether the employer
knew or should have known of their occurrence. Employers also incur
liability for the sexually harassing behavior of nonsupervisory personnel,
coworkers, clients, customers, and members of the general public if they

knew or should have known of the conduct. Employers, though, are able to defend themselves if they have well-established training programs, adequate notice of sexual harassment laws and policies, and a zero tolerance policy, taking prompt remedial action if they are informed of the occurrence of harassment.

The Civil Rights Act of 1991 allowed women alleging sexual harassment the right to a jury trial and the right to sue for compensatory and punitive damages. Prior to this, the law allowed only for reinstatement in one's old job and back pay. In 1995, Peggy Kimzey received a $50 million jury award against Walmart, an award later reduced to $5 million by the judge.[35] The jury held that the continual subjection to degrading and demeaning sexual remarks—in one case, the store manager saying to another employee as Kimzey was bending over a package, "I just found someplace to put my screwdriver"[36]—constituted harassment and she should receive punitive damages.

Hostile workplace harassment is often likely to occur in nontraditional work settings, for example, among firefighters or police officers, on the assembly lines, in factories or construction—settings in which the coworker may not have a great deal of power and may see the woman's presence as a threat to the power and social status he gains from the job. Women doing traditional men's work threaten traditional gender relations and the world of male privilege that men have taken for granted for decades. Offensive sexual remarks or behaviors are designed to make women uncomfortable enough to leave their jobs. Such things as putting sexual posters on women's lockers, telling jokes that demean and sexualize women, pinching, rubbing, leering, and yelling are all tactics used against women who enter man's domain. This kind of environment is not just sexual; it objectifies women, constructing them as things against which men act out sexually. Many women have been so uncomfortable or frightened that they quit. The men, line workers or supervisors, often see sexual humor and a sexualized workplace as a condition of the job and take the position that if women want to work in men's jobs, they had better be "man enough" to handle it.

The military is infamous for sexual harassment. The Department of Defense released a study of the armed forces showing that nearly two-thirds of women in the military and 17 percent of men experienced some form of sexual harassment during the year prior to the survey. Women reported more severe forms of sexual harassment, with 25 percent reporting unwanted touching or cornering, 12 percent reporting pressure to have sex, and 5 percent reporting actual or attempted sexual assault or rape. Women in the Marines report the most harassment at 64 percent, and

women in the Air Force report the least at 49 percent.[37] The widely publicized Tailhook case illustrated the breadth of the problem: At its 35th
annual convention in 1991 in Las Vegas, Nevada, 83 women, over half
of them officers, were assaulted. They reported that they were sexually
abused and harassed in a hotel hallway gauntlet by drunken pilots. Over
100 officers were implicated in incidents of indecent assault, indecent
exposure, conduct unbecoming an officer, or failure to act in a proper
leadership capacity.[38] In this instance, women had entered a formerly
all-male world, and the assaults and sexual harassment were strong messages of their unwelcomeness. Their sexuality was reestablished as their
dominant identity, overriding the importance of their abilities and
achievements. Sexual harassment and sexual assault in the military are
increasing rather than diminishing. A report issued by the Pentagon in
2013 of a survey conducted in 2011 shows that sexual abuse is higher than
it was five years earlier: Approximately one in every five military women
report being the victim of unwanted sexual contact by another service
member. The highest rate was in the Marines, where almost 30 percent
of the women said they experienced unwanted sexual contact.[39]

Other high-profile cases, in addition to the charges brought against
President Clinton by Paula Jones and Monica Lewinsky, include that of
Army Sergeant Major Gene McKinney, who stepped down from his position as Secretary of the Army's Senior Review Panel on Sexual Harassment after being accused by Retired Sergeant Major Brenda Hoster of
improper sexual advances and touching. Although acquitted on all harassment charges, he was convicted of "obstruction of justice," demoted to a
lower rank, and granted full retirement with pay.[40] The next year, Retired
Major General David Hale was charged and faced court-martial for seven
counts of "conduct unbecoming an officer and a gentleman."[41] And in
2000, Lieutenant General Claudia Kennedy, the army's top-ranking
woman, accused Major General Larry Smith of sexual harassment. The
army recommended his appointment to deputy inspector general.[42]

More recently, the sexual harassment problems tied to Herman Cain,
Tea Party activist and Republican contender for president during the
2012 elections Mark Hurd, CEO of Hewlett Packard, and Bob Filner,
mayor of San Diego, reveal the range and prevalence of sexual harassment.[43] Hurd resigned following an investigation by outside legal counsel
into the relationship he had with a former contactor with Hewlett Packard.
Even though the investigation found no violation of HP's sexual harassment policy, it did find a violation of the company's Standards of Business
Conduct.[44] Cain's case was quite different, suggesting that he was either a
bully or that he thought the employees he harassed had signed on for more

than restaurant work. His hope of being seriously considered as a presidential candidate in the 2012 elections was scuttled by his boorish behavior during the period he was president of the National Restaurant Association.[45] Mayor Filner has had some difficulty seeing anything wrong with headlocking women and whispering sexual comments in their ears or with asking one of his employees to not wear underwear to work.[46] It seems unclear to me whether men at the top of the status hierarchy think the laws simply don't apply to them, that they are so powerful they are immune to scrutiny, or if they just think no one will believe the women who complain. It is obvious, however, that these men are not quick studies. Anthony Weiner, disgraced former congressman and failed candidate for New York mayor, says he spent the last two years rehabilitating his reputation and his relationship with his wife after sending photos of his penis to women on the Internet. However, he recently acknowledged that rather than being rehabilitated, he continued his proclivity for displaying his privates to women he met on the Internet well into 2012.[47]

As lawsuits have opened the door of military academies to women, harassment has become a greater problem. The Citadel, the state military college in South Carolina, fought a long court battle to keep women out and capitulated only after the Supreme Court ruled that the Virginia Military Institute had to admit women.[48] The Citadel did not welcome women, and the behavior of male cadets toward the women reflected this displeasure. In 1997, nine cadets at the Citadel were disciplined, and one was dismissed, for harassing female cadets. Two others had resigned earlier, having been accused of setting the women's clothes on fire, putting kitchen cleanser and deodorant spray in their mouths, and pushing one of them against a wall in a lengthy ordeal of hazing and harassment.[49]

Other organizations that are arranged in a rigid hierarchy, with women at the bottom and men at the top, also place women in a vulnerable position, and it seems that they are subject to harassment in high-status, high-prestige fields, in which they also would hesitate to appear weak or victimized. While harassment in primarily or formerly male domains may reflect male resentment of women for threatening the males' economic and social status, much of the harassment that occurs in "women's occupations" reflects the expectation that women's sexual nurturing roles should carry over into their employment position. Women in relatively powerless positions in the workplace, doing the work of serving men, doing for men, giving to men, are sexualized in the same way as wives and girlfriends, and their work role is not differentiated from their wife/ mother roles. Men, having greater power and being in supervisory positions, extend their privilege in work roles to privilege in the personal interactions. When women are defined primarily as sex objects, when their presence sexualizes the environment, they are responded to sexually. In some work roles, nursing, secretarial and clerical work, waitressing, their work is perceived as an extension of their sexual selves, and men respond to them sexually. A woman may not know how to feel about it, much less how to respond. She may feel flattered by the attention, may not want to hurt the man's feelings or his ego, and may not want to make waves in the workplace, all of which she sees herself as doing by "making a scene."

In an interesting article on workers in restaurants, Patti Giuffre and Christine Williams investigated the question of how people define behavior as sexual harassment.[50] In a restaurant, as well as in many other workplaces, a certain level of sexual banter, joking, and interaction is taken for granted. Under what conditions does this sexualized environment become redefined as harassment? In a number of interviews with employees, they found that a good deal of sexual behavior and talk was seen as acceptable but that sexual advances were labeled as sexual harassment under four conditions: (1) when perpetrated by someone who exploited his powerful position for personal sexual gain; (2) when the perpetrator was of a different race or ethnicity than the victim, usually a minority man harassing a white woman; (3) when the perpetrator was of a different sexual orientation than the victim, usually a gay man harassing a straight man; or (4) when violence or the threat of violence was used. Barbara Gutek, a sociologist who has written extensively on sexual harassment, also reports that men and women have very different perceptions of intimidation, hostility, and offensive behavior. She found that 67 percent of the men she surveyed said they would feel flattered if a colleague of the opposite sex propositioned them, while 63 percent of women would be offended.[51] In another survey, conducted by *Redbook* magazine and *Harvard Business Review*, 24 percent of the women believed that a man giving a female worker a "visual once-over" was harassment, while only 8 percent of the men thought so.[52] A case often relied on by those who want to demonstrate how ludicrous the sexual harassment laws are is the case of Jerold Mackenzie. He was fired from the Miller Brewing Company when his coworker, Patricia Best, accused him of sexual harassment after he described a *Seinfeld* episode that indirectly referred to the word clitoris and he showed her the word in the dictionary. The jury concluded that he had been wrongfully dismissed and awarded him over $26 million in damages.[53]

Evidently Senator Robert Packwood, Chair of the powerful Senate Finance Committee, thought that his power and charm made him irresistible to the women employees and campaign workers on his staff. He made the phrase "he just doesn't get it" a household phrase when it became clear that he did not see anything unusual about rubbing, kissing, fondling, forcing his tongue down the throat of an employee, or making lewd remarks to women. Twenty-nine women eventually accused him of sexual harassment—in some cases, sexual assault—and after a two-year investigation, the Senate Ethics Committee in 1996 unanimously recommended that he be expelled from the Senate for sexual and official misconduct. He resigned just before their decision was made public.[54] While there are gender and situational differences in the definition of sexual behavior, sexual harassment laws have provided women who find inappropriate behavior directed against them hostile or intimidating with a definition for that behavior. With laws and policies that define sexual harassment and facilitate the recognition and reporting of sexual harassment, women can at least distinguish certain behaviors as inconsistent with the expectations of the workplace.

Laws prohibiting sexual harassment have been targets of much criticism. One criticism is of the chilling effect sexual harassment laws can have on interaction in the workplace, suggesting they destroy the informal give-and-take sociability that makes the workplace a positive environment. The fear of being accused of sexual harassment is viewed as damaging relationships and denuding the workplace of informality between workers that creates comfort and productivity. Kate Roiphe, in *The Morning After: Sex, Fear and Feminism on Campus*, pokes fun at harassment laws, asserting, along with other pseudo-feminists like Camille Paglia, that these laws turn women into weaklings, denying their robust human sexuality, constructing them as fragile flowers of femininity, unable to hear a curse word or the mention of a sexual act without requiring a fainting couch and smelling salts.[55]

Another criticism focuses on the violation of constitutional rights, particularly the First Amendment protection of free speech. Pornographic images in the workplace, dirty jokes, sexual innuendo, and invitations for sex may all be framed as protected speech, unduly infringed on by Title VII. Ellen Bravo, president of 9 to 5, the National Association of Working Women, replies that we give up a lot of our freedoms at work: "I don't have the right to bring arms to work, or to tell the boss to go to hell. The company can tell you to wear certain clothes, tell you how to behave, say certain phrases when you answer the phone. The idea that it's inappropriate to have boundaries on what people can say at work is pretty amazing."[56]

The dampening impact of sexual harassment laws on sexual talk and behavior cannot be denied; the question is, does this restriction unduly violate the Bill of Rights? A directly related issue is the policy that many institutions, especially universities, now have against relationships between faculty and students or supervisors and workers. These policies, usually called consensual relationships policies, are based on the assumption that relationships between persons with unequal power in an institutional setting are vulnerable to abuse by the person in power.[57] Whether the other agrees to the relationship, even initiates the relationship, if something goes wrong, the person who is the dissertation supervisor, or instructor, or supervisor has the ability to damage the other. In order to avoid this possibility, a consensual relationships policy carves out a contact-free zone in which relationships are prohibited. The ACLU and faculty rights organizations have been critical of such policies, viewing them as not only an intrusion on freedom of speech but also a violation of the constitutionally guaranteed freedom of association and the constitutional right to privacy. In many institutions, these policies are included in ethics statements and are presented not as prohibitions but as risky behaviors that may leave the faculty open to lawsuits and other damaging claims. As a result of changes in the law allowing victims of sexual harassment to receive compensatory damages and some high-profile and expensive cases, more companies and educational institutions not only have workplace policies prohibiting harassment and outlining grievance procedures, but they take these complaints more seriously.[58]

Sexual harassment laws are sex discrimination laws that respond to the significance of work and education in women's lives, and they acknowledge the degradation of women in the workplace that is embedded in our history. The jokes and other acts that sexualize the workplace and maintain discrimination against women at work are not simply light-hearted, innocent interactions. They can be extremely destructive when engaged in by coworkers who are peers, and even more destructive when engaged in by superiors or supervisors. Harassment is very hard to combat, in part because people are reluctant to call it harassment or to acknowledge it as a form of behavior that makes women's experience in the workplace different from that of men. In addition, women want to be team players, to be accepted by their coworkers, to get along. To criticize a joke or refuse to participate in sexual banter can lead one to be labeled unfriendly or cold, with the work and social consequences that come with those labels.

The way Katie Roiphe and Camille Paglia construct harassment is the way men have for centuries constructed rape and other forms of violence against women: women getting even, women changing their minds, women denying they "want it," women trying to save their reputation, women afraid of their bodies and the consequences of sexuality.[59] They assert that feminists have constructed women as pitiful victims needing protection from men. Far from it; feminists have acknowledged that women work and live in a world that men have constructed for their own benefit and want to maintain a privilege system that benefits them. Women demanding a place in the world other than in the role of demure, weak, and dependent need to be strong enough to call harassment what it is: not sexual fun among equals but sexual oppression.

THE EXTENT OF HARASSMENT

Sexual harassment is pandemic, a commonplace experience of women in the workplace and at school. Yet the number of charges filed has declined during the last decade or so with a decrease from 15,889 in fiscal year 1997 to 11,364 in fiscal year 2011. During that same period, the percentage of charges filed by males has increased from 11.6 percent to 16.3 percent, which may reflect an increased willingness on the part of men to report or may reflect increased hostility toward gay men in the workplace from other men.[60]

Monetary awards have also increased during that period. Most surveys reveal that as many as half of all employed women and about 40 percent of all college students have experienced some form of sexual harassment.[61] Among high school and junior high school students, close to 70 percent of girls and 42 percent of boys have experienced some form of harassment at school, either unwelcome touching, pinching, or groping.[62] The vast majority of those who are harassed are women, but an increasing number are men, up from 8 percent 20 years ago to 16 percent in 2010.[63] Very few cases involve women supervisors harassing male employees; most of the complaints from men come from harassment by other men.[64] Women supervisors, however, are frequently subject to harassment by their subordinates. Heather McLaughlin and her colleagues discuss the "paradox of power" in their research. They contrast the "power-threat model," one that suggests that women who pose a greater threat to male dominance are more likely to be harassed, with the "vulnerable victim" hypothesis that suggests that subordinates or people who are lower status, such as women and people of color, are more likely to be harassed. They conclude that men in the workplace use harassment to reestablish dominance and to patrol the gender borders. They subject women who violate gender expectations, through being assertive or powerful, and men who do not comply with "hegemonic masculinity"[65] —such as gay or "effeminate" men—to harassment.[66] Many of the most important harassment cases, including *Meritor Savings Bank v. Vinson*, involved African American women and white male harassers, suggesting that black women, who break both the gender and race expectations, especially for white men, are even more vulnerable to harassment.[67] Monetary settlements not including those reached through litigation by the EEOC rose from $7.7 million in 1990 to over $55 million in 2000, remaining fairly stable thereafter with around $51 million in benefits in 2009. Legal costs, including punitive damages won in lawsuits, have soared.[68] In 1994, the median jury award for sexual harassment was $104,750,[69] but by 2010 it had reached $350,000. Some awards, such as in the Wal-Mart Stores, Inc. case discussed above and in *EEOC v Lutheran Medical Center*, the figures were in the millions.[70] The United Nations reports that sexual harassment is a major problem in all countries in which it has been studied. In Belarus, 26 percent of women report being harassed; in Russia, it is 60 percent. In Poland, 25 percent of the women report being harassed, and the same percentage of Czechs report experiencing sexual harassment. The outlook is even worse in Western Europe, with between 40 and 50 percent of the women reporting harassment. In Australia, it is approximately 28 percent who have experienced harassment at work; in Japan it is 62 percent; and in the United States, the figure is between 40 and 60 percent. The South African figures are very telling—here 76 percent of the women said they had experienced sexual harassment, and a full 40 percent of these had left their jobs or changed jobs as a result of the harassment.[71] Given the severe consequences of harassment and the economic losses experienced by organizations and governments, these figures are extremely disturbing.

Nearly 75 percent of mid-sized and large firms reported sexual harassment claims in 1995, according to a survey reported by the American Management Association in 1996, compared with just over 50 percent in 1991.[72] In 1996, the EEOC sued Mitsubishi Motor Manufacturing of America Inc. in what is probably the largest sexual harassment suit ever prosecuted. The alleged harassment ranged from sexual graffiti, to grabbing women's breasts and genitals, to requiring that women engage in sexual relationships as a condition of their employment. *Forbes* magazine projected that the EEOC's suit against Mitsubishi could have resulted in damages of up to $210 million if every woman employee had received the maximum $300,000 allowed under the 1991 Civil Rights Act.[73] Instead, Mitsubishi settled for $34 million to be distributed among "eligible" claimants.[74] In another case, the EEOC obtained a $10 million settlement with the pharmaceutical company Aetna U.S.A. for claims by employees that they had been fondled, asked for sex, or suffered in a hostile workplace.[75] Three temporary workers who were harassed by a supervisor, and a coworker who opposed their harassment, received a jury award of $1.5 million in back pay, compensatory damages and punitive damages in a case brought by the EEOC against New Breed Logistics in Memphis, Tennessee.[76] Large jury awards continue with the plaintiffs in a sexual harassment case brought by the EEOC against Four Amigos Travel in Largo, Florida, in 2013 being awarded over $20 million.[77]

Most corporate executives recognize that the majority of the complaints they receive are valid and see sexual harassment as a major economic problem for their company. Sexual harassment costs a typical Fortune 500 company $7 million a year in absenteeism, low productivity, and employee turnover. This does not include additional millions in possible court costs, executive time, and damage to the company's image.[78] In 1980, the U.S. Congress commissioned the first extensive study of sexual harassment. The U.S. Merit Systems Protection Board surveyed 23,000 civilian employees of the civilian branch of the federal government, providing a reliable picture of sexual harassment in the United States. This study found that 42 percent of the female federal employees had experienced some type of sexual harassment during the previous two years. Twenty-nine percent experienced "severe sexual harassment," including unwanted letters, phone calls, pressure for sexual favors, unwanted touching, pinching or being cornered, or materials of a sexual nature. Twelve percent were victims of "less severe sexual harassment," which included pressure for dates; unwanted suggestive looks, leers, and gestures; and unwanted sexual teasing, jokes, remarks, or questions. One percent, a full 230 women, had been raped or assaulted at work.[79] A 2008 Harris Poll reveals that 31 percent of female workers and 7 percent of male workers report being harassed at work, but most of these, 62 percent, took no action.[80] This and other studies have suggested that young women, unmarried women, and lower-status women are the most vulnerable to being harassed in the workplace, although McLaughlin and her colleagues report substantial harassment of supervisors, suggesting this supports a "power threat" explanation for organizational harassment.[81]

Cyberbullying and cyber-harassing are increasingly serious problems, calling for changes in training and materials for businesses, universities, and other organizations. Texting is fast replacing the phone and e-mail for conveying information and ideas, and because of the ease with which many people can be included in messaging simultaneously, in chat rooms, on e-mail, on social networking sites, the potential for extensive harassment has increased. The one advantage to the victim may be that an e-trail of evidence is available in this instance, which is accessible by investigators. Cyber-harassment may include the forwarding of messages, music, advertisements, or cartoons that are either specifically directed at a person or simultaneously sent to a large number of contacts. Because the sender of an e-mail blast may not know all of the recipients, and because of the lack of nonverbal cues, the potential for communication to be interpreted as harassment may be increased. Universities and businesses, given their responsibility for the behavior of their employees and students, need to be flexible enough to respond to these rapid changes in technology in order to prevent harassment and to inform and train the personnel within their communities.

Sexual harassment occurs not only in the workplace or in secondary schools and universities, but also in grade school. A mother in Forsyth, Georgia, sued the school her daughter attended, claiming that school officials did nothing when she complained repeatedly that her fifth-grade daughter was being sexually harassed at school by a boy classmate. Aurelia Davis's daughter was consistently and painfully harassed at school, and despite her efforts, the school officials did not respond to her complaints. The mother complained to the teacher, the principal, and the school district, looking for a remedy, and brought suit only when her complaints were ignored.[82] A federal district court dismissed her suit, finding that Title IX does not apply to a student's harassment by a classmate, stating that the school officials had no role in the harassment. An Eleventh Circuit U.S. Court of Appeals panel reversed the district court decision, but the full Eleventh Circuit vacated that decision, ruling that Congress did not intend for schools to be held liable for this form of sex discrimination under Title IX. The U.S. Supreme Court heard this case in 1999, *Davis v. Monroe County Board of Education*, and ruled that the 1972 Title IX Education Amendment's prohibition of discrimination in federally funded educational institutions did include the right to sue for student-on-student sexual harassment and found in favor of Davis. *Drawing the Line: Sexual Harassment on Campus,* a study conducted by the AAUW, demonstrates that harassment in colleges and universities remains a problem, with 62 percent of college students reporting that they have experienced sexual harassment. This survey concludes that men and women are equally likely to experience harassment, but women are more likely to be harassed through physical contact than are men. While student-to-student harassment is the most common, almost one-fifth of the students reported they had been harassed by a faculty or staff member.[83]

RESPONSES TO SEXUAL HARASSMENT

Not only is there reluctance to report, but women may not immediately perceive harassing behavior as harassment. Relatively few of the women who are harassed in the workplace ever complain about it, few who experience behavior that could be legally defined as harassment actually interpret it as such, and even fewer file a formal complaint or bring suit. A 1992 study by Temple University indicated that while 35 percent of female students report they have been harassed by their instructors or professors, few ever lodge an official grievance.[84]

Researchers estimate that as many as 70 percent of employed women have experienced behavior that legally constitutes sexual harassment, but only a fraction of women report this behavior. Mahabeer reports that according to an AOL Jobs Survey, while one in six persons reports being sexually harassed in the workplace, only 35 percent reported it, with women being more likely (47 percent) than men (21 percent) to report.[85] Many do not recognize the harassment as an actionable offense, although women do have a broader definition of what constitutes unacceptable behavior than do men.[86] The discrepancy between the way women think they would respond to harassment and the way they actually respond is unsettling. Most women think they would not tolerate harassment, just as most women think they would not tolerate being beaten and would leave their abuser.[87] The enormous gap between incidents of harassment and reporting was made clear by the U.S. Merit Systems Protection Board survey; only 6 percent of government employees who said they had been harassed filed a formal complaint requesting an investigation.[88] The Women's Legal Defense Fund concluded that between 1 and 7 percent of women overall who are sexually harassed file a formal complaint or seek legal remedies.[89]

There are some predictable patterns of responses to sexual harassment. The power differential in the relationship is important, with a woman being less tolerant of harassment by an inferior and more likely to report the offense.[90] This finding highlights the importance of power, revealing that when women achieve a certain degree of power, it is accompanied by some expectations about appropriate experiences in the workplace, and by a sense on the woman's part that she can control her work environment, at least to some extent. Of course, women are not customarily in a more powerful position than their harasser, and overall, women in the workplace are in relatively powerless positions. Some research suggests that women with higher self-esteem and life satisfaction are more likely to pursue complaints about sexual harassment.[91] This makes sense, because these women would feel more competent and would have an expectation that they could shape their own lives. But knowing the law and knowing her legal rights does not necessarily mean the woman will file a complaint; she may be more apprehensive because of what she knows.[92]

The most common response on the part of women who are harassed is to ignore the behavior and do nothing, hoping it will end. A study of female athletes' responses to sexual harassment indicates that they, like many women in traditionally male-dominated fields, "appear to grow resigned to the frequent acts of verbal and physical harassment."[93] In a study of undergraduate students, women who were harassed by their professors used indirect tactics such as ignoring sexually laden comments or innuendos, bringing a friend with them to any meetings with the professor, pointedly mentioning they had a boyfriend or husband, or avoiding contact during class or office hours.[94] Some women try to adjust their own behavior or attitudes to cope with the harassing behavior, while others are more likely to adapt their work environment to avoid the problem. They may take later lunches, walk down different corridors, take breaks at different times, ask for reassignments, and make other changes that allow them to avoid or diminish contact with the harasser.

In the 1995 Merit Protection Board study, although most women did nothing (44 percent), 88 percent said that asking or telling a person to stop would be the most effective response.[95] Women know what to do; it is the cultural mandates, their own sense of guilt or blame, or the demands of the situation that render them silent and powerless. In this as well as other situations, Pat Heim reports that women try to avoid confrontation and use indirect tactics to stop the behavior.[96] This can require a good deal of thought and planning, and it surely does not erase the discomfort or difficulty posed by a man who harasses. This indirect response leaves the woman continually searching for ways to avoid, adapt, or ignore and creates an environment in which the harasser may become the centerpiece of her experience.

High-profile, high-status women who bring sexual harassment charges against their harassers still do so only after considerable deliberation and careful assessment of the damage it might do to their career. Lieutenant General Claudia Kennedy, age 52, the army's Deputy Chief of Staff for intelligence and the highest-ranking woman in the U.S. Army, brought a sexual harassment complaint against Major General Larry G. Smith for making an unwanted sexual advance toward her. The army substantiated Kennedy's accusation that Smith had touched her in an inappropriate way and had tried to kiss her at the end of a meeting in her office at the Pentagon. But even this high-status woman, well informed about sexual harassment and appropriate responses to it, handled it privately throughout her career in the Army. She did not bring a complaint against Smith until he was to be appointed to a position in which his duties would include investigating accusations of sexual harassment.[97]

The culture and structure of organizations also affect the woman's response to sexual harassment. If women see the norms and values of the organization as causing the problem, they are more likely to address harassment aggressively than if they view individual characteristics as being at the base of the harassment.[98] This interesting finding may reflect the fact that women are likely to be peacekeepers and to focus on maintaining relationships in the workplace, and would therefore be hesitant to respond to another individual in a blaming or disruptive way. The more abstract or less personal organization itself would be an easier target for her displeasure and her efforts at change.

The response of Anita Hill to the harassment she said she suffered at the hands of Clarence Thomas, now a justice on the U.S. Supreme Court, is perfectly consistent with the socialization of women, as well as reflective of the irrelative powerlessness in the organization. Researchers of women's experiences with male violence show that many women use silence as a coping strategy to deal with the shame and self-blame that often accompany these experiences.[99] During the confirmation hearings in October 1991, senators opposed to the confirmation of Clarence Thomas to the U.S. Supreme Court called Anita Hill, a black attorney, to testify about her experiences with Thomas, who had been her superior in two different federal positions. She revealed a pattern of innuendo, joking, sexual slurs, and misconduct on his part that challenged his fitness for the position of Supreme Court justice. The country was both fascinated and divided by this conflict: successful black woman versus successful black man. The hearings were a spectacle of political infighting and finally affirmed the ascendance of a male worldview over that of the woman. The race card made the gender conflict more enticing, more lurid, but it did not camouflage its essential significance. Women, even women as successful as Anita Hill, are socialized to be nice, to not make the environment uncomfortable, to blame themselves if a man solicits sexual favors or harasses them. They learn to overlook and ignore problems in order to survive in the workplace. Hill's acquiescence to Thomas's sexist, misogynistic behavior was understandable from a feminist perspective, and she could perhaps have been forgiven that. But the fact that she called a black man out on his *sexual* misconduct in the presence of powerful white men and the entire country, feeding the stereotype of the "oversexed, animalistic" black man, was unforgivable for many.

The response of the public to Hill in the Clarence Thomas hearings is instructive. Some people proclaimed if she had really been harassed, she would have confronted him on the spot, filed a complaint against him, and would not have moved with him from the Department of Education to the EEOC. Her assertions of harassment were incredible, while the insistence of Thomas that any sexual activity was welcome and mutual was more believable to many. Her response was directly in line, however, with the way most women respond to harassment: ignore it, try to laugh about it, joke or change the subject, try to avoid situations in which it might occur, or think that it will eventually stop when he gets the idea she is not interested.

Many women do not report sexual harassment, or do not report it earlier, because they fear they will not be believed, will be shunned, or will suffer retaliation. Since most complaints are brought against a woman's immediate supervisor or another person with greater power than she has, her fears of retaliation are not unreasonable.[100] Because harassment tends to escalate when the woman finally does complain, her position is weakened because she did not complain sooner. Some may respond to her with disbelief, assuming that if it really happened or the sexual advances were really unwelcome, she would have complained to the harasser or his supervisor or taken some formal action earlier.

Women do, of course, report sexual harassment, file claims or grievances, or bring lawsuits, and sometimes this solves the problem. But too often when they report the harassment, they are ignored, discredited, or belittled. Some go so far as to change jobs as a result of sexual harassment (about 10 percent according to the U.S. Merit Service Protection study in 1981). But even when women take the most assertive stance, even confronting the harasser, 43 percent reported that their most assertive response made no difference.[101] The tendency to blame the woman in cases of sexual harassment is based on stereotypes about masculinity and femininity and on different views about what is acceptable in the workplace between men and women. We can see that even when women complain directly to the harasser, these stereotypes often persist, and their protests are rendered meaningless.

Despite the fact that there are sexual harassment laws and Supreme Court decisions that prohibit harassment, as well as over 500 court cases involving harassment, the laws do not prevent harassment. A woman who is the victim of harassment must have the personal and financial resources to take advantage of the law in order to right the wrong she feels she is experiencing; she has to be willing to suffer the consequences of a long legal battle with an uncertain outcome.[102]

Large settlement costs plague counties, states, and other jurisdictions that ignore the harassing behavior of their employees. The *Press Enterprise* reports that an administrator of health and community programs for Riverside County, California, was consistently ogled, touched, and verbally harassed by her supervisor. Her complaints went unheeded, and she was eventually fired. She sued the county and was awarded a settlement of $490,000.[103] New York State paid out at least $5 million to settle 11 sexual harassment lawsuits in the two years between 2008 and 2010, according to the attorney general's office.[104] The cases involved employees being harassed by other employees. Five of these cases involved the State Department of Corrections, and three involved public universities.[105] In April 2000, a former medical school researcher at Stanford University was awarded $545,000 after a jury concluded that she had been fired in retaliation for complaints of sex discrimination. The maximum award under federal law is $300,000, but the jury tacked on lost salary and benefits and attorney's fees.[106] The case, brought by Colleen Crangel, age 48, was the first time Stanford University had defended itself against such charges in court rather than settling. Dr. Crangel had complained that she was treated like a "Girl Friday" by a fellow researcher who was threatened by her strong opinions, and when she complained to her supervisor, she was told that if she did not like it, she should leave.[107] Major university medical schools, including Stanford and Berkeley, have experienced a good deal of attention for their harassment of high-profile faculty, and there remains significant concern about harassment during medical and nursing school training.[108] Although about 48 percent of the medical school students are women today,[109] medicine remains a gendered world, an environment that is often hostile to women,[110] with at least 96 percent of the women Hinze interviewed reporting that they had experienced sexual harassment during medical training.[111] Hinze says that "men enact gender in formerly male-dominated territory by creating environments hostile to women"[112]—a statement that is as applicable to the sexual harassment and assault that women experience in the military as it is to medicine.

Sexual harassment trainings (as is true, I would say, with sexual assault trainings) overlook the fact that harassment and assault are mechanisms through which "gender boundaries are patrolled and by which deeply held identities are established."[113] At the same time, women residents are resistant to naming sexual harassment as a problem. In her extensive research on women residents, Hinze found that women were likely to wonder if they were "too sensitive," and gave the offender the benefit of the doubt rather than seeing themselves as victims.[114] While they may be extremely uncomfortable and even angry about their treatment, they are still likely to question their own responses to it. Victims of harassment resist acknowledging discomfort, thereby firmly resisting the label of victim. A resident may recognize the behavior she receives as inappropriate but take credit for not letting it hold her back. Ours is a society in which a victim is viewed very negatively—an outsider or as powerless, and it is easier to ignore the behavior than to become a victim. Another way of avoiding being a victim is to "not sweat the small stuff."[115] Hinze provides an example of extremely hostile harassment that was very hurtful and demeaning but that the resident interpreted as sexist behavior that was just part of what women had to go through to become a surgeon. She decided to simply "play along" and not let it become a serious impediment to her.[116] In 1991, Dr. Frances Conley, the first female tenured professor of neurosurgery, resigned her teaching position to protest the promotion of a colleague who had subjected her and her female colleagues to blatant sexual harassment. Further, there had been an undercurrent of gender-based discrimination and harassment at the medical school for years and fear of the subtle and blatant retaliations for reporting it. Although Conley returned a few months later, she wrote a book, *Walking Out on the Boys*, that chronicles her own experience and that of other women in academic medicine, revealing a pattern of discrimination and harassment that accounts for their severe underrepresentation.[117] For example, a woman who brings a grant into the department may be shut out when it is distributed; a woman who asks to lighten her workload to accommodate a crisis in the family finds her career is endangered. This type of workplace discrimination at Stanford, coupled with sexual harassment claims, resulted in a complaint to the U.S. Department of Labor by several dozen women.

Men, understandably, are not pleased by the demand that they change their behavior in the workplace to accommodate women. They insist that if women are going to work in a "man's world," they need to be able to "take it like a man." Such a demand perpetuates discrimination against women. The fact that women have been prohibited from certain occupations fostered the creation of male culture that does not reflect women's experiences, and then when they do have access, they must acclimate to a foreign and demeaning environment. If men at work bring their locker room behavior into the work world and are comfortable with it, fine; if women enter that workplace (albeit with more difficulty and for lower wages), then the workplace needs to change to accommodate their presence. Saying that women need to adjust to the male world is to suggest that since women have been discriminated against in education and work for decades, they need to put up with the attitudes and behaviors that kept them out in the first place. Camille Paglia would agree that women should accommodate themselves to men's "natural" sexualization of the environment, claiming that miserable "old maids" have banished normal, exuberant lustiness from human interaction and replaced it with a sterile system of sexual surveillance.[118] While men may not be pleased by it, a change in the workplace culture is essential for women to participate comfortably and fully. Few women could work well in a situation where they faced "crotch shots" every time they went into the office or were regaled by tales of male sexual prowess during coffee breaks.

CONSEQUENCES

A woman's decision to bring a suit in a sexual harassment case is made in the context of family and personal relationships. Women's lives are profoundly relational, and decisions about litigation often pit the woman's familial responsibilities against her longing for formal justice. For many women, the desire for connection and interpersonal harmony mitigates the desire for formal justice. The laws governing relationships between men and women in the workplace are perceived as resources, but they exist within a complex set of personal relationships, and their usefulness is evaluated in terms of the impact they would have on the relationships women value.

The consequences suffered by women who are harassed can be devastating. It is difficult to overestimate the toll that harassment takes on women's lives. Women are disproportionately represented in the most economically vulnerable segments of the labor market, and women work from financial necessity. Workplace harassment places these women in an intolerable situation. Virtually tens of thousands are forced to tolerate sexual exploitation or run a daily gamut of sexual and emotional abuse as the price of earning a living.[119] Barbara Martin (*Youngstown, Ohio v. Martin*, 1992) tolerated degrading harassment from her boss and co-workers at the wastewater treatment plant where she worked. A supervisor told her, "I don't have oral sex with women because they smell like dead fish," and another time her boss tried to force her to kiss him in a locked car. Despite the fact that she won her suit, she is not sure she would pursue the process again; she said she does not remember Christmases or birthdays for years because they were marred with death threats and other retaliatory acts. "I lost my job, I lost my career." "It took me six years" and "destroyed my marriage and my family."[120] As this case illustrates, the consequences for confronting harassment can be overwhelming, including a sense of loss of control, disruption to daily life, depression, anger, anxiety, feelings of humiliation and alienation, vulnerability, shock, and post-traumatic stress disorder.[121] Especially in unsupportive work environments, women may feel guilt, shame, fear, helplessness, and even empathy for the harasser.[122] Those are the psychological or emotional consequences. The economic consequences for women are severe: quitting their job, being transferred or reassigned, loss of income, loss of seniority, disruption of work history, problems with references. Decreased morale, damage to interpersonal relationships, job dissatisfaction, poor job performance, and lower productivity are also common consequences of harassment.[123] Students often drop a class or drop out of school altogether, change majors, receive lower grades, find their work no longer supported, or are left out of the formal and informal networks so essential to success, particularly for graduate students.

Prior to 1964, when sex discrimination was outlawed by the Civil Rights Act, women were without recourse if they experienced sex discrimination, and simply took it for granted that they would be harassed by their bosses, coworkers, and professors. Their only remedies were personal solutions: quitting the job or the class, avoiding the person, trying to joke about the situation to prevent its reoccurrence, or in some cases complying or cooperating in order to keep their job. While women today use many of these same techniques, with similar consequences, sexual harassment, as a legal category, is part of the cultural framework and provides a structure within which a woman can make sense of, and react to, the offensive behavior. Despite this, however, many women feel guilty and blameworthy when they are sexually harassed, and they tolerate outrageous conditions in order to keep their colleagues, their friendships, or their jobs.

WHY DOES HARASSMENT OCCUR?

The answer to the question "Why?" is an easy one and can be answered at several levels. There is no need to rely on explanations involving the seductive behavior of women, women's inability to acknowledge their sexuality, or women's vengeful and wrongful accusations. Rather, the answer can be found in structure and culture. Men have occupied and continue to occupy positions of authority over women in organizations structured in a hierarchical fashion. These structures are integrated into a culture that normalizes male superiority in authority structures and legitimates gender relations based on assumptions about normal femininity and masculinity that require dominance and aggression on the part of men and submissiveness on the part of women. Women who are in powerless positions are likely to be harassed, reflecting the power of men in the workplace and the institutionalized gender arrangements and authority patterns.

Men who harass have the weight of the culture behind them. Both men and women are familiar with the assumptions of a misogynist culture that defines women in terms of their sexuality rather than their abilities. Women are targeted as "less than" in a number of ways—less serious, less important, less powerful. Further, both males and females are socialized to adapt to relationships of dominance and submission, and sexual harassment becomes a reflection of those assumptions about normal relationships between men and women. Clearly, if males and females are identified as dichotomous beings, and are responded to differently with the expectation that they become different beings, this will have an impact. If men learn not to take women seriously—to value them for their bodies and their sexuality and to be attracted to women who are "less than," as in less educated, less valuable, and less powerful—and if women learn that their drive and spirit should be diminished in order to be acceptable or attractive, a congruence is established that paves the way for the violation of women. By the same token, if men learn that their value lies in their power, their superiority, both physical and economic, and if they learn to be sexually aggressive with women and to value themselves for being what women are not, then it should come as no surprise that men would see women as accessible to them in the workplace. Where men occupy traditional positions, they may rely on sexual threats or epithets when they feel their power and position threatened by a woman who moves out of her expected place.

This is not to say that all men practice sexual harassment. Clearly that is not the case. But as Brownmiller suggested in her controversial book *Against Our Will*, the fact that men allow sexual violence against women to continue creates an environment in which all men benefit from the efforts of the few.[124] Dziech and Weiner suggest that in the academic world, a few professors are likely to be the harassers, and they fall into several predictable categories: the adviser or confidant; the intellectual seducer who impresses the woman with his skills and knowledge; the opportunist who takes advantage of the situation; and the powerbroker who offers jobs or recommendations in return for sex. Harassers, they suggest, may operate in private; they may use their authority to gain private access to the employee or student, or they may be high-profile public harassers, in which case they perform harassing acts in public, assuming that by being observed, they will not be challenged or chastised.[125] These roles allow them to engage in sexually harassing behavior that is difficult for the woman to define or distinguish from the other components of male superiority. She must then see beneath his behavior and his words to the implied meaning.

The ambiguity of the faculty harasser's role allows him to merge assertions of sexual interest with those of professional interest in the student's academic or intellectual qualities. The student may initially be poorly prepared to separate these interests, and once their differences become clearly visible, may be in a poor position to do anything about them without risking a great deal. This is particularly true at the graduate level, where professors and their students work very closely together for long periods of time, usually years. The intimacy and informality that develop in the faculty-student relationship in those instances blur the boundaries between professional helpfulness and sexual interest. Once the sexual interest is on the table, however, the student may be no better off. Now she has to weigh her compliance against the loss from angering or alienating him. She has a great deal invested in the relationship, and if he decides not to be her adviser or withdraws his care, support, and guidance, her professional future may be ruined.

Women who challenge the gender structure by refusing to adopt the feminine pose are also the victims of harassment—in this instance, it being an effort to reestablish the traditional power and authority relations. Women who break the norms, who assert themselves as powerful or competent, may experience harassment from men whose assumption of male superiority and privilege is threatened by such autonomy. On the other hand, women who remain firmly devoted to traditional femininity and its demands for acquiescence, nurturing, and peacekeeping are also likely to be harassed as a consequence of the display of male privilege. Given the pervasiveness of the opportunity structure for harassment of women, it is not surprising that women are victims of sexual harassment, any more than it is a surprise that they are beaten or raped. What is a surprise is that harassment has been defined legally as a form of sex discrimination and that court decisions have supported women's right not to be violated in the workplace.

THE BROADER CONTEXT

The harassment of women takes place within a context of power relations between men and women built not only on assumptions about sexuality and appropriate "places" for men and women, but against a backdrop of daily inequities that culminate in a violation of woman's spirit and productivity. Subtle remarks, sexual suggestions, innuendos, and jokes are so difficult to deal with in the workplace because the organization of relationships at work is built on accepted, taken-for-granted ways of interacting that are detrimental to women. The larger context within which these relationships occur is organized by men, who come to it unfettered by family and relational responsibilities. Women, on the other hand, bring with them the additional obligations of their role as mother, wife, and caretaker. While men's wives may be home caring for the children, women must juggle their commitments and then go home to handle the kinds of responsibilities their colleagues have passed down to their wives.[126]

I looked around my department when I was a graduate student; not only did all the professors have wives at home, those wives had once been the students of the male faculty members, and many of them had given up their own promising careers to assist their husbands. Today, while I have one female colleague who shares child care with her ex-husband, most of my other colleagues either have wives who do not work or who began working only when their children were grown. During their early years in the academy, when they were establishing and proving themselves, they had a great deal of assistance from a full-time homemaker. Seldom is that true for women. They either have no one at home, or they are doing double duty even if they are married. The importance of this arrangement is not only that it provides substantial practical advantages for the man; it also provides an explanation as to why the men involved in those relationships absorb a view of women as fit for certain activities, as different from men, and as more capable of doing certain types of things and less capable of doing others. The women they encounter in their work world are tainted with learned assumptions about femininity and appropriate female behavior that reflect their experiences with women as wives and mothers rather than as colleagues.

These are the men who shape the reality of the university. Their assumptions about everyday reality are translated into the policies and practices of the academy. The way they interact with one another, the form and content of their relationships, excludes women in a myriad of ways that men do not recognize, and that women cannot condemn without being seen as wanting special treatment. Sexual harassment of women, students or faculty, takes place within this context in which women are the nonstandard, the different, those who sexualize the workplace and make gender visible. Because of their peripheral or marginalized status, the reality that women experience is rendered less central and is not incorporated into the routine activities in which both men and women participate. Men participate in these from within a context in which their values are paramount, whereas women engage in these activities from the margins, attuned to their outsider status and its consequences.

This is why equality should never be the goal for women. Equality is the goal of fitting in, of being the same as, of having the opportunity to not be treated differently. Women are different from men. They are the only ones who have babies, and they are, despite the insistence that men are deeply involved in child care and family, the ones who raise the children.

Claiming equality as a goal is not enough. In fact, equality is detrimental to women because it insists that they compromise their complex, relational lives to fit the arid world men have arranged, that they not challenge the professional system in which they struggle. To identify and name the practices that are institutionalized in the academy as sexist does not require a demand for equality. It demands a change of the system, or at the very least, an acknowledgment that the present structure differentially benefits men.

The Massachusetts Institute of Technology's (MIT) report on the status of its women faculty[127] described a number of areas in which women fared more poorly than men as a result of the structures and expectations of the academy that was established for men by men. A committee of faculty assessed the experience of women at MIT and found significant problems, leading to the disenchantment of women faculty, alienation, decreased productivity and job satisfaction, and slower promotions. While the MIT report detailed the problems of women faculty, and at least momentarily focused on some of the subtle forms of violation women experience in the academy, the less visible Status of Women committees in universities throughout the country have been coming to these same conclusions for years. As the MIT report points out, a significant problem exists with the promotion of women to full professor from associate professor. Men are comfortable with women as the junior partner, the person coming to them for help or advice, and with women being second author on professional papers and articles. They are far less comfortable, and so are many women, with women as equals, much less superiors. Men's networks with other men create a chilly climate not just for women students but for women faculty. They are outsiders. While men may suggest to their male junior colleagues ways of moving ahead and may encourage them to do so, the idea of a woman moving ahead is often either a threat or simply is not considered as something she needs or would want. Men may tell their male colleagues about professional meetings, put them in touch with colleagues, and suggest an editor who might be interested in something they are working on, but they do not think of extending these essential mentoring acts to women. While men may encourage a male colleague to apply for promotion, they may suggest to a woman with the same background that she is not yet ready. As one of my colleagues sitting on a promotion and tenure committee said, "The men think of reasons the man is ready and should be promoted, and think of reasons the woman should wait."[128] By the same token, women who necessarily learn the rules as outsiders think the rules are real and they busily, often in isolation, work to meet the guidelines, thinking if they are "good girls" they will be rewarded. Not so. Rewards are based not just on doing the work, but on doing it in the right places, with the right visibility, from the right people.

Getting a promotion from associate to full professor is not just a matter of putting together a good promotion package, although that is the base. It is a political process, requiring a good reading of the members of the promotion committee, knowing who to get letters of recommendation from, and garnering departmental support. In one case with which I am familiar, a college dean encouraged a male professor to apply for promotion and recruited a high-status male colleague from another department to shepherd him through the process. When a female professor in the second professor's own department decided to apply for promotion, he suggested it was worth a try and wished her good luck.

This is the climate that the professors at MIT revealed. It exists in universities across the country.[129] The problems women faculty experience in promotion, tenure, and salaries foster a sense of isolation, self-blame, and even shame. The everyday small, invisible, and often initially unrecognized violations of women erode their confidence and clearly communicate their peripheral and secondary status. Such violations are completely consistent with the subtle illustrations of superiority so often displayed in the workplace. The culture of civility and the presumed ethic of equality in such a place as the university mitigate against blatant sexism and obvious forms of sexual harassment, but lend themselves to the erosion of a woman's sense of self-worth that shadows other, more extreme and visible violations. The very subtlety of the violation, the decency with which it is delivered, and the insistence that the values it imposes are a reflection of an ideal, rather than a political construction, make the naming of it almost impossible. *Institutional* sexism is the right name. This built-in, invisible sexism oppresses women to the same extent, but in a different form, as does physical violence against women. Awareness and action on the part of an administration, such as keeping track of the gender profile of important university committees, can lead to significant changes in the inclusion of women, and this can be accomplished much more rapidly in a university or business than in the larger society.

In an interesting twist, as more male academics take on increasing responsibilities in the home and with child care, there may be a tendency to acknowledge their home/family responsibilities in the workplace by accommodating their schedules and expectations for participation in departmental or organizational life. This adjustment in expectations contrasts with the situation in the 1970s, when women were afraid to even mention that they had children who needed care for fear that they would not be seen as committed employees. Even today, as Sheryl Sandberg points out in her book on women and leadership, *Lean In,* women in organizations were strongly discouraged from even referring to "women in the workplace" for fear that they would be seen as asking for special treatment for those women.[130] When the very few men who had begun to take on some of those responsibilities made it clear that they needed workplace adjustments, the structure began to change to accommodate them, benefiting women as well as men.

As long as men feel powerful and in control, they may not have a need to assert their control in a physical way. They may not feel it necessary to assert their gender superiority in other settings as long as women are not challenging their position. Harassment may come about to keep or put women in their place, to reintroduce their master status as a sex object, and someone not to be taken seriously. On the other hand, in the workplace, men may commit acts of harassment in their daily round of activities because they see women as accessible and available to them, as in the case of some professors; they view female students as one of the bonuses of a relatively low-paying job. That is, they were not sexualizing the environment to make women uncomfortable or to reestablish dominance, but as a taken-for-granted reflection of their assumed superiority and their gender privilege. In a case at my university, a tenured full professor was finally, and with great difficulty, terminated after years of having affairs with his graduate students. This faculty member had support from his department and the faculty rights association, despite the fact that he had persisted in a pattern of sexual harassment for at least 10 years, all of these after the recognition of sexual harassment and the establishment of it as a form of sex discrimination. The policies were in place. The enforcement was a different matter.

Simply having sexual harassment policies on campuses and in organizations does not solve the problem. In fact, some suggest it creates problems. Now men complain they are afraid to offer a compliment or a friendly greeting without being accused of harassment. Let us get one thing straight. Just as with rape, the cases in which a sexual harassment claim is unfounded are extremely rare. In reality, far more cases go unreported than are false reports made. Further, the law does not prohibit civil conversation or politeness among colleagues. Any cursory reading of it would indicate that it is specifically directed to particular types of sexual behavior in the workplace that discriminate against women. The existence of laws alerts employers and employees, students, and faculty to a standard of appropriate and legal conduct and to consequences for breaking it. It does not eliminate the complex legal process and the painful emotional problems a woman may experience when bringing a grievance against a colleague or superior and following through with her complaint. These cases indeed not only damage the people who are directly involved but frequently disrupt the workplace for years. One case that occurred in a small, and previously friendly, workplace continued unresolved for over two years, with hearings and appeals, by the end of which time several people were transferred, some never spoke again, and a couple quit. The office in which the persons worked was so fractured that it virtually ceased to function as a productive workplace. This is not only emotionally extremely difficult to all involved, especially given the importance of the workplace to our social and emotional lives, but it is enormously expensive financially.

Sexual harassment is not just a problem in the workplace. It is a reflection of workplace and dominant culture, and it reproduces that culture. When women are defined primarily in terms of sex and then responded to sexually, either with hostility or with come-ons, then their legitimacy as people is undermined. Their sexuality stands for and replaces them. When women do not respond but suffer in silence because of fear or confusion, they reinforce their oppression. When they respond by filing a complaint against the harasser or the company, they take a step toward self-respect and power, but they take on a good deal of hardship in the process. Successful legal cases that continue to clarify sexual harassment law change the way women are treated and perceived and can have a tremendous positive impact on women's participation and promotion in the workplace. When companies establish strict sexual harassment policies and respond forcefully to harassment, they not only alter women's experiences in the workplace, condemning their discrimination, they also change the definition of woman to include characteristics other than those synonymous with her role as mother, wife, or sex object.

That is a critical step. When women are finally welcome at all levels and in all occupations; when they are not sex stereotyped as assistants, aides, secretaries, or clerks; and when they excel as easily as do men in positions of power, positions reflecting their abilities and interests, then sexual harassment, and the erosion of self-confidence that accompanies it, will not be the malevolent scourge that it is today. Laws prohibiting sexual harassment in work and educational settings not only will eventually ensure a more even playing field for women; in the long run, they will change the perceptions and definitions of women. If women are required to be treated as serious workers or students, then assumptions about their motivations for being in the workplace or educational institutions, assumptions about their inferiority, or about personality characteristics based on their sex or gender will be challenged. Sweeping changes in women's lives in other arenas will emerge from the legal requirement that women not be discriminated against in the workplace or at school.

NOTES

1. B. Friedan, *The Feminine Mystique* (New York: Dell, 1963).

2. C. Enloe, "The Globetrotting Sneaker," Chapter 3 in *The Curious Feminist: Searching for Women in a New Age of Empire* (Berkeley: University of California Press, 2004).

3. S. Greenhouse, "Groups Press Big Retailers on Safety Overseas," *New York Times*, May 17, 2013: B1, B4.

4. K. Bradsher, "After Bangladesh, Seeking New Sources: Western Retailers Scramble for Suppliers, and Find Options Are Few," *New York Times*, May 16, 2013: B1, B6.

5. *The Global Assembly Line*, film produced by L. Gray (Tiburon, CA: New Day Films, 1998).

6. A. S. Kraditor, *The Ideas of the Women's Movement: 1890–1920* (New York: W. W. Norton, 1981).

7. Ibid.

8. D. Hakim, "Report Finds Lawmaker Was Shielded by Leaders," *New York Times*, May 16, 2013: 18.

9. Ibid.

10. B. Dziech and L. Weiner, *The Lecherous Professor* (Boston: Beacon Press, 1984).

11. C. MacKinnon, *Feminism Unmodified: Discourses on Life and Law* (Cambridge, MA: Harvard University Press, 1987), 195; C. MacKinnon, *The Sexual Harassment of Working Women* (Cambridge, MA: Harvard University Press, 1979).

12. L. Farley, *Sexual Shakedown: The Sexual Harassment of Women on the Job* (New York: McGraw-Hill, 1978).

13. S. Murnen and L. Smolak, "The Experience of Sexual Harassment among Grade-School Students: Early Socialization of Female Subordination?" *Sex Roles* 43, no. 1–2 (2000): 1–17.

14. MacKinnon, *Feminism Unmodified*.

15. A. J. Everhart, "Predicting the Effect of Italy's Long-Awaited Rape Law Reform on 'The Land of Machismo,' " *Vanderbilt Journal of Transnational Law* 31, no. 3 (1998): 671–718.

16. S. Martin, "Sexual Harassment: The Link Joining Gender Stratification, Sexuality and Women's Economic Status," in *Women: A Feminist Perspective*, edited by Jo Freeman (Palo Alto, CA: Mayfield, 1984), 57–85.

17. P. Loy and L. Stewart, "Sexual Harassment: Strategies and Outcomes." Unpublished paper.

18. P. Franklin, H. Moglin, B. Zatling-Boring, and R. Angress, *Sexual and Gender Harassment in the Academy* (New York: Modern Language Association, 1981).

19. *Barnes v. Costle*, 1977, 561 F. 2nd 983 (D.C. Cir.).

20. *Barnes v. Costle*; *Williams v. Saxbe.* 1976. 413 F. Supp. 654 (D.C.) *rev'd on procedural grounds* 587 F. 2nd 1240 (D.C. Cir. 1978), *on remand subnom*; and *Williams v. Bell.* 1980. 487 F. Supp. 1387 (D.C.).

21. W. Petrocelli and B. K. Repa, *Sexual Harassment on the Job* (Berkeley, CA: Nolo Press, 1992).

22. It was not until 1980 that the EEOC, in *Guidelines on Discrimination*, explicitly defined sexual harassment under Title VII as a form of unlawful, sex-based discrimination.

23. U.S. Department of State, *Sexual Harassment Policy*, www.state .gov/s/ocv/c14800.htm. Accessed July 17, 2013.

24. Ibid.

25. *Meritor Savings Bank v. Vinson.* 1986. 477 U.S. 57.

26. MacKinnon, *The Sexual Harassment of Working Women.*

27. A. B. Cochran III, *Sexual Harassment and the Law: The Michelle Vinson Case* (Lawrence: University Press of Kansas, 2004): 374–76.

28. R. Sandroff, "Sexual Harassment in the Fortune 500," *Working Woman*, December 1988.

29. *Meritor Savings Bank v. Vinson.* 1986. 477 U.S. 57.

30. *Faragher v. City of Boca Raton.* 1998. 118. S.Ct. 2275.

31. Paul E. Starkman, "Learning the New Rules of Sexual Harassment: Faragher, Ellerth and Beyond," *Defense Counsel Journal* 66, no. 3 (1999).

32. *Burlington Industries Inc. v. Ellerth.* 118. S.Ct. 998, 1998.

33. For a definition of "equal opportunity harasser," see adversity.net/ Terms_ Definitions/TERMS/Equal_Opportunity_Harasser.htm

34. *Oncale v. Sundowner Offshore Services Inc.* 118. S.Ct. 998, 1998.

35. *Peggy Kimzey v. WalMart Stores, Inc.* No. 95-4219, 95-4220. United States Court of Appeals, Eighth Circuit, Feb. 20. 1997.

36. S. Glazer, "Crackdown on Sexual Harassment," *CQ Researcher*, July 19, 1996: 627–28.

37. M. Anderson and H. Taylor. *Sociology: Understanding a Diverse Society* (Belmont, CA: Wadsworth, 2000).

38. J. Zimmerman, *Tailspin: Women at War in the Wake of Tailhook* (New York: Doubleday, 1995).

39. https://www.safehelpline.org/, accessed May 20, 2013.

40. "New Testimony against Army's Top NCO," *Tribune News Service*, July 2, 1997.

41. M. Kilian, "Retired General Faces Court-Martial Related to Sexual Affairs," December 11, 1998, Articles.chicagotribune.com./1998-12 -11news/9812110108_1_

42. S. Myers, "Army Rescinds Appointment of Deputy Inspector," *San Francisco Chronicle,* May 24, 2000: 2B; "Senate Panel Holds Hearing on Military Sexual Harassment," 1997. Available online at http://www.cnn.com/45/9702/04/Army.sex

43. A. Vance, "HP Ousts Chief for Hiding Payment for Friend," *New York Times*, August 6, 2010, http://www.nytimes.com/2010/08/07/business/07hewlitt_html?pagewriter

44. Ibid.

45. P. Bacon and D. Eggars, "Can Herman Cain's Campaign Weather His Latest Sexual Harassment Charges?" November 7, 2007, Articles.washingtonpost.com/2011-11-07/political 35280836_1_sharon -bailek-herman-cain-graphics-allegations

46. *New York Times*, July 23, 2007, http://www.nytimes.com/2013/07/23/us/san-diego-mayor-is-sued-by-an-ex-aide.html

47. D. Chen and J. Hernandez, "Weiner Admits Web Dalliance after Resigning," *New York Times*, July 23, 2013: A1, A18.

48. C. Manegold, *In Glory's Shadow: The Citadel, Shannon Faulkner and a Changing America* (Vintage Books, Random House Digital, 2009).

49. A. Nossiter, "A Cadet is Dismissed and 9 Are Disciplined for Citadel Harassment," *New York Times*, March 11, 1997: A15; see also Feminist News (http://www.feministorg.news).

50. P. Giuffre and C. Williams, "Boundary Lines: Labeling Sexual Harassment in Restaurants," *Gender and Society* 8, no. 3 (1994): 378–401.

51. B. Gutek, *Sex and the Workplace.*(San Francisco: Jossey-Bass, 1985).

52. A. Deutschman, "Dealing with Sexual Harassment," *Fortune.* November 4, 1991: 104–37; *Jarold J. Mackenzie v. Miller Brewing Company and Robert Smith.* Case No. 97-3542. Supreme Court of Wisconsin. Review of a Decision of the Court of Appeals. March 20, 2001.

53. Ibid.

54. U.S. Senate Select Committee on Ethics, Report for Investigation of Senator Robert Packwood, 1995.

55. K. Roiphe, *The Morning After: Sex, Fear, and Feminism on Campus* (Boston: Little, Brown, 1993).

56. Glazer, "Crackdown on Sexual Harassment."

57. B. Dziech, R. Dziech, and D. Hordes, "Consensual or Submissive Relationship: The Second-Best Kept Secret," *Duke Journal of Gender, Law, and Social Policy* 6, no. 1 (1999): 83.

58. M. C. Stites, "University Consensual Relationship Policies," in *Sexual Harassment on College Campuses: Abusing the Ivory Power*, edited by M. A. Paludi (Albany: State University of New York Press, 1996).

59. P. Sanday, *A Woman Scorned: Acquaintance Rape on Trial* (Berkeley/Los Angeles: University of California Press, 1997).

60. U.S. Equal Employment Opportunity Commission, http://www .eeoc/statistics/ enforcement/sexualharassment.cfm

61. A. Thio, *Deviant Behavior* (Boston: Beacon Press, 2009); M. Anderson and H. Taylor. *Sociology: Understanding a Diverse Society*, (Belmont, CA: Wadsworth, 2000).

62. M. Henneberger and M. Marriott, "For Some, Youthful Courting Has Become a Game of Abuse," *New York Times*, July 11, 1993: 1, 14; B. Kantrowitz, "Striking a Nerve," *Newsweek*, October 21, 1991: 38, 40.

63. S. Hananel, "More Men Filing Sexual Harassment Claims: Percentage Has Doubled in Last 20 Years," NBCNews.com, March 6, 2010.

64. Ibid.

65. R. W. Connell, *Masculinities* (Berkeley: University of California Press, 1995).

66. H. McLaughlin, C. Uggen, and A. Blackstone, "Sexual Harassment: Workplace Authority and the Paradox of Power," *American Sociological Review* 77, no. 4 (August 2012): 625–47.

67. J. E. Gruber and L. Bjorn, "Blue-Collar Blues: The Sexual Harassment of Women Autoworkers," *Work and Occupations* 3 (August 1982): 271–98; K. McKinney, "Sexual Harassment and College Faculty Members," *Deviant Behavior* 15, no. 2 (1994): 171–91.

68. Glazer, "Crackdown on Sexual Harassment," 625–648; see also J. Cloud, "Sex and the Law," *Time,* March 23, 1998: 49–54.

69. Glazer, "Crackdown on Sexual Harassment," 640.

70. A. Conte, *Sexual Harassment in the Workplace: Law and Practice* (4th ed.), Aspen Publishers online, June 10, 2010.

71. The Secretary General of the United Nations: In-depth Study on All Forms of Violence against Women, 68, July 2006.

72. American Management Association, *Sexual Harassment: Policies and Procedures*, American Management Association, 1996.

73. Ibid.

74. http://money.cnn.com/1998/06/11/companies/mitsubishi

75. Cloud, "Sex and the Law"; see also Sandroff, "Sexual Harassment in the Fortune 500."

76. *Employment Law Weekly*, May 20, 2013.

77. U.S. Equal Employment Opportunity Commission, Press Release, May 13, 2013.

78. "Sexual Violence in the Workplace" (East Hartford, CT: CONSACS) http://www.connsacs.org/learn/documents/sexualviolence andtheworkplace.doc, accessed July 15, 2013.

79. Glazer, "Crackdown on Sexual Harassment"; U. S. Merit Systems Protection Board. *Sexual Harassment in the Federal Workplace: Trends, Progress, Continuing Challenges* (Washington, DC: United States Government Printing Office, 1981): 34–38.

80. P. Mahabeer, "Sexual Harassment Still Pervasive in the Workplace," AOL Original, February 10, 2011.

81. H. McLaughlin, C. Uggen and A. Blackstone, "Sexual Harassment: Workplace Authority and the Paradox of Power," *American Sociological Review*, 77, no. 4 (2012) 625–647.

82. L. Greenhouse, "Sex Harassment in Class Is Ruled Schools' Liability," *New York Times*, May 15, 1990: Al, A24.

83. AAUW, *Drawing the Line: Sexual Harassment on Campus*, 2005, http://www.aauw.org/resource/drawing-the-line-sexual-harassment-on -campus

84. *Sexual Assault and Sexual Harassment-Resource and Policy Guide* (Philadelphia: Temple University, 1992).

85. Mahabeer, "Sexual Harassment Still Pervasive in the Workplace."

86. P. Giuffre and C. Williams, "Boundary Lines: Labeling Sexual Harassment in Restaurants," *Gender and Society* 8, no. 3 (1994): 378–401; and R. Katz, R. Hannon, and L. Whitten, "Effects of Gender and Situation on the Perception of Sexual Harassment," *Sex Roles: A Journal of Research* 34, no. 1–2 (1996): 35–38.

87. M. P. Koss, L. A. Goodman, A. Browne, L. Fitzgerald, G. Keita, and N. Russo, *No Safe Haven: Male Violence against Women at Home, Work, and in the Community* (Washington, DC: American Psychological Association, 1994). Koss and colleagues, in a 1994 review of the literature, found a wide discrepancy between the way women think they would respond and the way they do. In one study, 60 percent of the respondents who were harassed did not file a formal complaint, usually out of fear of retaliation. In the 1994 Merit Systems Protection Board study, only 6 percent of women who reported being sexually harassed took any formal action.

88. U.S. Merit Systems Protection Board, *Sexual Harassment in the Federal Workplace*; see also Glazer, "Crackdown on Sexual Harassment."

89. Women's Legal Defense Fund, *Sexual Harassment: Legal and Policy Issues* (Washington, DC, 1995); see also Martin, "Sexual Harassment."

90. A. M. Marshall, "Sending a Message: Claiming in Sexual Harassment Cases." Paper presented at the 1998 Annual Meeting of the Law and Society Association, Aspen, CO. She indicates that those women who knew more about their rights might be more willing to confront harassment; but on the other hand, knowing the law might make women apprehensive about using it.

91. U.S. Merit Systems Protection Board, *Sexual Harassment in the Federal Workplace*; see also Glazer, "Crackdown on Sexual Harassment."

92. Marshall, "Sending a Sending a Message."

93. K. Volkwein, et al., "Sexual Harassment in Sport: Perceptions and Experiences of American Female Student Athletes," *International Review for the Sociology of Sport* 32, no. 3 (1997): 283–95.

94. D. J. Benson and G. E. Thomson, "Sexual Harassment on a University Campus: The Confluence of Authority Relations, Sexual Interest, and Gender Stratification," *Social Problems* 29, no. 3 (1982): 236–51; see also U.S. Merit Systems Protection Board, *Sexual Harassment in the Federal Workplace*.

95. J. Horsman, "Riverside County Sexual Harassment Suit Settled for $490,000," *The Press Enterprise*, August 20, 2011, http://www.pe .com/local-news/politics/Riverside.

96. P. Heim, *Power Dead Even Rule and Other Gender Differences in the Workplace* (Buffalo Grove, IL: CoreVision Media, 1995).

97. S. Meyers, "Army Rescinds Appointment of Deputy Inspector," *San Francisco Chronicle*, May 24, 2000: A5.

98. J. E. Gruber and M. D. Smith, "Women's Responses to Sexual Harassment: A Multi-Variate Analysis," *Basic and Applied Social Psychology* 17, no. 4 (1995): 543–62.

99. H. Lenskyj, "Unsafe at Home Base: Women's Experience of Sexual Harassment in University Sport and Physical Education," *Women in Sport and Physical Activity Journal* 1, no. 1 (1992): 19–33.

100. Sandroff, "Sexual Harassment in the Fortune 500."

101. U.S. Merit Systems Protection Board, *Sexual Harassment in the Federal Workplace*; see also Glazer, "Crackdown on Sexual Harassment."

102. Ibid.

103. Horsman, "Riverside County Sexual Harassment Suit Settled for $490,000."

104. U.S. Merit Systems Protection Board, *Sexual Harassment in the Federal Workplace*; see also Glazer, "Crackdown on Sexual Harassment."

105. D. Hakim, "11 Sexual Harassment Settlements Cost the State $5 Million," *New York Times*, October 4, 2012.

106. Ibid.

107. B. Feder and J. Hubner, "Reactions to Call for Gender Equality Differ at Stanford, MIT Female Scholars Pressure Schools," *San Jose Mercury News*. February 18, 2000. 1A. Print.

108. Ibid.

109. K. Chen and J. Chevalier, "Is Medical School a Worthwhile Investment for Women?" http://www.theatlantic.com/health/archive/2012/07/is-medical-school-a-worthwhile-investment-for-women/260051/

110. J. Lorber, *Gender Lens Series: Gender and the Social Construction of Illness* (2nd ed.) (Thousand Oaks, CA. Sage Publications, 1997); and F. Conley, *Walking Out on the Boys* (New York: Macmillan, 1999).

111. S. W. Hinze, " 'Am I Being Over-Sensitive?' Women's Experience of Sexual Harassment during Medical Training," *Health: An Interdisciplinary Journal for the Social Study of Health, Illness* 8, no. 1 (2004): 101–24.

112. Hinze, 111.

113. Ibid., 121.

114. Ibid.

115. Ibid., 114.

116. Ibid.

117. Conley, "Walking Out on the Boys."

118. C. Paglia, *Vamps and Tramps: New Essays* (New York: Vintage, 1994); see also C. Paglia, *Sexual Personae: Art and Decadence from Nefertiti to Emily Dickinson* (New York: Vintage, 1992); and C. Paglia, *Sex, Art and American Culture: Essays* (New York: Vintage, 1992).

119. M. P. Koss, et al., *No Safe Haven.*

120. Glazer, "Crackdown on Sexual Harassment."

121. B. A. Gutek and M. P. Koss, "Changed Women and Changed Organizations: Consequences and Coping with Sexual Harassment," *Journal of Vocational Behavior* 42, no. 1 (1993): 28–48.

122. M. Anderson, *Thinking about Women: Sociological Perspectives on Sex and Gender* (3rd ed.) (New York: Macmillan, 1993).

123. Gutek and Koss, "Changed Women and Changed Organizations."

124. S. Brownmiller, *Against Our Will: Men, Women and Rape* (New York: Simon & Schuster, 1975).

125. Dziech and Weiner, *The Lecherous Professor.*

126. D. Smith, "Women's Perspective as a Radical Critique of Sociology," *Sociological Inquiry* 44, no. 1 (January 1974): 7–13.

127. *A Study of the Status of Women Faculty in Science at MIT* (Cambridge: Massachusetts Institute of Technology, 1999).

128. Personal communication to the author.

129. *Report to the University and Community College System of Nevada Board of Regents* (Reno: University of Nevada, 2000); see also *A Study of the Status of Women Faculty in Science at MIT.*

130. Gutek and Koss, "Changed Women and Changed Organizations."

SIX

Real Victims, Reasonableness, and Rape

SEX, GENDER, AND POWER

On December 16, 2012, in New Delhi, a student returning home with her fiancé after viewing the film *The Life of Pi* was brutally attacked, raped, then impaled by a steel rod shoved through her vagina, destroying her internal organs and leading to her death and to the hospitalization of her fiancé who tried to protect her. The six men who assaulted her were arrested. Indian men and women activists and ordinary citizens were outraged, demanding an end to the backlog of rape cases, demanding protection for women, demanding the resignation of government officials if nothing was done.[1] Rape isn't an event, an occurrence that happens once in a great while; it is a pandemic of violent assaults on women by men. The rapes in India, according to *Hindustan Times* columnist Sagarika Ghose, reflect "[a] profound fear and a deep, almost pathological hatred of the woman who aspires to be anything more than mother and wife," justifying her assault on the grounds of tradition.[2] These men had raped another young woman two weeks earlier, a woman who suffered such physical and emotional damage that she committed suicide days after the assault. Three months later, a Swiss tourist traveling in India with her husband was brutally attacked by six men, all 19–25 years old, an illustration of the rising rate of gang rape, particularly in northern India.[3] These are the most recent, and they have been occurring for some time. In an earlier case, just one of a string of brutal sexual assaults and gang rapes, five drunken men from a village gang-raped a woman and beat her male escort. Lydia Polgreen reports that in these cases, there has been

an "explosive clash between the rapidly modernizing city and the embat-
tled, conservative village culture, upon which the capital [New Delhi]
increasingly encroaches."[4] Men, says Ranjana Kumari, a women's rights
advocate, are not accustomed to seeing so many women in the country
occupying public spaces.[5] Women have made enormous strides in India
during the past decades, but their gender makes them vulnerable to attack
by "a growing sea of unattached and unemployed young men who view
women's success as the reason for their failure."[6] These rapes are the tip
of the iceberg in a country where two million women die each year from
sexual violence, family disputes, infant neglect, female infanticide, and
health and nutritional factors that disproportionately affect women and
girls.[7]

These rapes, as with rape in general, are centered in an acceptance of
wide-ranging male violence against women, female inferiority, and male
control and privilege. It is a logical outcome in a country that tolerates
and diminishes the everyday harassment of women as "eve teasing" and
is exasperated by the entry of increasing numbers of women into educational and occupational positions once filled by men. They are a reflection
of the belief of an ever-growing number of unemployed and unattached
men that women are displacing them from what is rightfully theirs.[8] These
rapes, felt so powerfully by the city, the state, and the world, were not
unique local events—they are just one more instance of global assault
against women. Dr. Denis Mukwege, who administers the Panzi Hospital
in the Congo, was at a loss as to what to call the systematic, brutal, ugly
chronic assaults of women he sees so often, attacks that destroy their
bodies, ruin their lives, and destroy their homes and economic survival.
He knows they are designed as assaults, as aggression, not sex, and sees
them as a form of sexual terrorism.[9] Rape cannot be isolated from the context of women's economic, social, and political inferiority. These high-
profile attacks on women join others—honor crimes, dowry deaths, the
sale of trafficked women, in the global assault on women's lives. The horrible attacks that gain worldwide attention need to be viewed not as an
exception, not as inexplicable, but rather as stark and clear illustrations
of the everyday and ordinary violence against women. Rape is a vengeful
assertion of male power over female, a reenactment of male oppression
expressed on an individual level but coupled with a culturally approved
justification for that oppression. Rape is embedded in the contextual relationship between sex, gender, and power, just as are foot-binding, honor
crimes, genital mutilation, sexual harassment, and every other form of
violence against women.

Rape is a particular type of power statement, different from battery or from shooting or bludgeoning. It is a violation of a woman's sexual self, a self that she has, she holds, but that is accessed legitimately by others she chooses. It is a statement to her that she has no control, that she cannot protect her body. It is a man's celebration of the cultural oppression of women, a reinforcement of a misogynistic gender ideology, and in particular, an illustration of his privilege and power. He knows that his violation of her is a violation of her pleasure, her womb, the body whose sharing means love and vulnerability and a willingness to be open. He forces himself on her not only to oppress but to humiliate, to speak to her and to those who love her about her worthlessness, her inability to protect or control herself, her life. He knows, in the United States but more clearly in other countries, that his attack destroys not only her sense of herself but her relationship with her husband, family, and community.

His attack on her is one he often justifies through a further degradation of her by asserting that she eventually enjoyed it, or by asserting that she would be more of a woman after she had sex with him, or simply that he had the right to do what he wanted. He usurps her right to define herself and defines her as an object to be used and discarded. His rape is an act of power over, of ownership of, of control of her essence. I am not suggesting that woman is only her sexuality. But no matter what else she is, no matter how accomplished or how lost and degraded she is, her body is her last and final source of herself. We identify the body as the self, as "me" and "mine." To violate the body is to violate the self.

It is impossible and pointless to try to unravel the complex relationship between sex and gender. The distinction is not as simple as sex is biology, gender is society. Gender is critical, but it is absolutely melded with sex; gender expectations, such as marrying and having sons, or having dinner on the table, are directly tied to the expectations that exist for women based on their sex, being female with reproductive capabilities. The gender expectations flow from the identification of them as the female sex, and their sex is both debased and feared, leading to the restrictions tied to them. For example, in the case of foot-binding, the female foot is broken and crippled to contain and limit the woman, to make her properly feminine; as this occurs, the foot itself becomes a sex object, sexual, fetishized as it symbolizes powerlessness, dependence, and weakness. The violence that a woman suffered when her feet were bound was based on her sex and the gender expectations that accompany it. She was rendered powerless, reproducing the system that disempowered her in the first place. Her only power was to come through marriage, and to be violated and maimed was to be prepared for marriage. This is no different from the girl who is infibulated in the Sudan to protect the honor of her family through her virginal purity. She is cut and sewn together so she will find a marriage partner and fulfill her childbearing responsibilities. Her sex is seen as potentially powerful and therefore excised. Her sexuality as her own, as specifically hers, is destroyed, mutated into an object for her husband's use. The demand that the Hindu woman be shameful and modest is situated in a cultural definition of her sex (female), her sexuality (dangerous), and her gender (docile and inferior). To protect her family's honor, she must remain inside, hidden, venturing out only if fully covered, accompanied by a close male relative. As one Hindu man interviewed by Steve Derne succinctly described women's life, "women here are not left independent. Women here are not free. They are under control."[10] Wife battery and rape are forms of control based on sex and sexual relations; men who beat their wives and men who rape strangers or neighbors do so within a gendered context in which their masculinity is correlated with their power.

The relationships between men and women are framed by power, and the violence women experience in the family and on the streets cannot be separated from its relationship with power. Power disparities, power inequities, power struggles, and power demonstrations are all tied to the violence women experience from men. Power is not a thing any more than sex is a thing. These are constructions, meaningful only within interactions between people who understand and apply meanings to behavior. One can only challenge a man's power, for example, within a structure in which the participants share an understanding of the term and its meaning; if a man's masculinity is challenged by the wife's decision to work, as it was for the husbands interviewed by Lillian Rubin in *Worlds of Pain*[11] in Oakland, California, it can be threatened only because of the cultural constructions of masculinity and femininity agreed on by the couple and formed within a wider cultural milieu. These men tied their masculinity to being able to provide for their families, to be the head of household— functions that were inseparable from their sex, gender, and sexuality. A woman who works may, through her independence, her ability to provide, her possible autonomy, challenge the superiority of her husband and his status in the family, thereby challenging his sexuality and rendering him less a man. His masculinity is dependent on her femininity as defined by him, and her breach of acceptable femininity easily devastates him. As the poet and social critic Adrienne Rich wrote, "A plain fact cleanly spoken by a woman's tongue is not infrequently perceived as a cutting blade directed at a man's genitals."[12]

MASCULINITY AND FEMININITY

When one talks about masculinity and femininity, one is talking about the relationship between persons and power. The feminine ideal is accomplished through powerlessness. It requires the negation of strength, decisiveness, autonomy, and aggressiveness. In forsaking all of these forms of power, a woman gains power residually, through femininity.

Of course, there have been examples of very high-profile women who do not meet this ideal—women who are powerful, articulate, and wealthy: Margaret Fuller, Hillary Clinton, Madonna, Oprah Winfrey, Madeline Albright, and Margaret Thatcher, to name a few. And there are some who combine power with femininity, merging their sexual identities with their powerful positions—for example, Facebook COO Sheryl Sandberg, author of the much debated *Lean In*; Christie Hefner, former CEO of Playboy; and Yahoo CEO Marissa Mayer. But these women do not challenge the norm. They are exempted from the norm, and their enormous success can put a damper on the complaints of other women who are not so fortunate—if they can do it (no matter the Harvard and Stanford degrees and rich husbands), then why can't you? However, the norm remains in the background, readily available to serve as the standard against which to assess a woman's behavior or measure a woman's value if the circumstances call for it. Simply because women are not, without exception, fragile flowers languishing about the house with fans and ethers does not mean that they are valued for aggressiveness, dominance, power, strength, decisiveness, and control. These qualities, if merged pleasantly with a preponderance of feminine qualities, may ignite femininity, increasing the woman's attractiveness. But heaven help the woman for whom these qualities are dominant, particularly if she is old or homely. The political button available at the California Republican Party Convention illustrates the vitriolic attacks on woman's body if her power threatens male control: "KFC Hillary Special: Two fat thighs, two small breasts, right wing."

Femininity calls for the achievement of power through relative powerlessness for most women, although the exceptions prove the rule. Woman's sexuality is her most essential and legitimate form of power, and just as women are designated as the source of their family's honor while having no honor of their own, woman's sexuality is powerful not because of something she does but because of something she is: a woman. Her power comes through male construction of her sexuality, not through her own control and ownership of her sexual self. Women are portrayed as having a natural sexual power that victimizes men. So powerful is woman's sexuality that her wayward glance can dishonor her family; her clitoris can kill a man or a baby; and the sight of her thong panties can completely undo the president of the United States. Monica Lewinsky was in fact a rather ordinary and average-looking intern, not remarkable intellectually or physically. The reaction toward her reveals the strange and destructive contradictions women face. With little economic or political power, they experience discrimination and sexism daily. They hit a glass ceiling and glass walls, yet their sexual power destroys kings, emperors, and presidents. Who is fooling whom here? The assertion that Lewinsky's potent sexuality brought the president to the brink of destruction accords her the same kind of power as that held by Islamic women whose sexuality can destroy their family yet they are without any power of their own. Male definitions and interpretations of female sexuality, used by men in their conflicts and communications with one another, give men the right and justification for controlling women, obliterating any real power they might ever hope to have.

Male control of women, and through that, their control of other men, is based on the useful fiction that women are uncontrollable sexually and that their sexuality is destructive to men and even entire nations. A sexual misstep by her, or even the suspicion of a sexual violation, results in her beating or death, not because *she* is dishonored (she has no honor, only shame), but because her father and brothers are dishonored. Woman is accorded a power that absolves man of responsibility for sex, while at the same time freeing him to have sex. Her sexuality is implicit and pervasive, making him sexually powerless, while at the same time, it is not truly her own. She is to be controlled and "kept in" so that he can be out of control. To define her sexual organs as dirty or destructive is to remove responsibility from him for what he does to overcome her. Her sexuality can then be destroyed so that his can be expressed. While the Western reader might see this contradiction when presented with analyses of honor crimes or female genital mutilation, it may not be so clear when applied to rape or sexual harassment. But these forms of sex-based violence are more similar than they are different. When a woman is sexually harassed, men, and sometimes women steeped in male ideology, justify their behavior in terms of something she did or said or the way she dressed. There was something about her sexually that drew out assaultive behavior in him; she had not camouflaged her sexuality adequately. He was responding as a man to her essential womanhood and punishing her for expressing it outside the confines he had established for its expression or for expressing it too clearly within those confines. That is, she was either too sexy, or too provocative, and was "asking for it," or she was a "frigid bitch" who "just needed a good lay."

CLARIFYING THE IMPORTANCE OF WOMAN AS SEX OBJECT

While laws regarding rape in the United States reveal the social norms against certain types of sexual assault on women, they also reveal some of the historical changes in the status of women and situate the rape of women within a context of relationships and definitions. It is common knowledge that rape was initially a property offense rather than a crime against the person—the property damaged in this instance being the father's daughter or the husband's wife. The woman had no protection from rape in the family because the husband could do with his property as he wished, particularly within the confines of his home. Punishment for the rape of one's property was reparation of that damage, which could, and still does in some cultures, include the rapist's agreement to marry the victim, thus atoning for his offense to the father's property and preventing future economic loss to the father who would be unable to find a husband for his damaged daughter. The damage to the daughter was especially significant if the girl or woman was chaste and from a wealthy family, increasing the value of her virginity and the danger to her from an attack. Rape of a woman in Afghanistan or Pakistan today places the victim in jeopardy for these same reasons—she dishonors her family and their salvation may come through further punishing her—sometimes only through her death. The relative value of women who are raped is clear today in this country, although she is not as likely to suffer the extreme punishment she might elsewhere. A wealthy white woman who is raped, especially if she is young, is viewed as more violated than a poor young black woman who is raped, a white woman being more sexually valued, not only by white men, but as Eldridge Cleaver has pointed out in *Soul On Ice*, by black men as well.[13]

When Edward I put forth the Statutes of Westminster at the end of the thirteenth century, he permanently severed the distinction between a virgin and a married woman by banning the custom of redemption of the rapist through marriage. Further, for the first time, rape became an offense against the state, a concern of public safety rather than remaining simply a family matter: If the family did not respond legally to the rape within 40 days, the "right to prosecute automatically passed to the crown."[14] With this change, rape became a public wrong rather than a purely private matter. It was not until later that rape became a crime against the person rather than a crime against the public welfare, which it in fact remains today in many countries.

By the 1800s, rape was a crime punishable by a maximum of life imprisonment or death. But the severity of the punishment was accompanied by the requirement of corroboration or supportive evidence, including proof of resistance in order to prove lack of consent. Resistance became the essential distinction between rape and sexual intercourse, a distinction that remains problematic because of the legal burden it places on the woman who has been raped. A more reasonable requirement would be to insist that the man prove that the woman did consent—or better, as University of California psychologist Patricia Rozee says, for him to prove that it was her "choice" to have sex with him.[15] To require that a woman consent to sex implies traditional gender relations, with men aggressively asking for or wanting sex, women resisting or acquiescing. If one uses the requirement of "consent," forcing the woman to indicate that she did not consent rather than forcing the alleged perpetrator to prove that she did consent, the fact that rape occurs in an ordinary, normative way in all societies is missed.

Rozee distinguishes normative from nonnormative rape and indicates that in all societies, some forms of rape are culturally disapproved, but women's sexuality is ordinarily violated on a regular, and regulated, basis. These violations, though they occur without woman's choice, are not considered to be rape.[16] Normative rapes would include punitive rapes, status rapes, marital rapes, ceremonial rapes, and theft rapes. She says that researchers, in their efforts to avoid ethnocentrism, often instead embrace androcentrism, by accepting dominant cultural definitions of rape, which obviously reflect the reality of those who construct the definitions of reality rather than the women who are likely to be its victims.[17] The most important underlying dimension of human sexuality and interaction is choice. If a woman chooses sex unencumbered, she is "making love" or "having sex," whereas if she does not choose, because of cultural impositions or physical force, she is the victim of rape. Historically, neither consent nor choice was an issue. Men were entitled to sex when they wanted it with few exceptions, and women surrendered their right to bodily integrity when they married.

While rape was a common problem for immigrant girls working in factories, poor women working on farms, black women who were slaves, this rape was unapologetically sexual assault—women had absolutely no choice in sexual or other matters. There was no need for subtlety or any facade of agreement on the part of the woman because women were so unvalued and their word worth so little that they were appropriate and safe targets for male sexual attack. These rapes were what Rozee calls status rapes—rapes of social inferiors by social superiors, rapes that were socially condoned even though they violated the woman's bodily and psychic integrity and denied her any choice.[18] Today, women are still likely to be in subordinate positions in the workplace, but they are not considered chattel nor do they have to accept sexual assault as a job requirement. Nevertheless, they are still subject to the subtle pressures of sexual harassment and still seen as complicit in the attacks they suffer.

Rozee's categories don't seem to be quite adequate to incorporate the way rape is used today on a global scale—it is not status, it is not normative, it is hatred and disgust and anger. And, maybe more importantly, it is the simple and total disregard for women as sentient beings, as persons with feelings, with soul, with an identity, with meaning. The horrible rapes of women during war are expressions not of normative acceptability or of status enforcement or privilege, but of men assuming the unquestioned right, assuming that their desire to do this to women, their ability to do this to women, renders them immune from judgment. It is not just men speaking through other men about women as the spoils of war; while it is also that, as Susan Brownmiller says, " It is that during war, when the other is dehumanized, subject to unimaginable atrocities, women's bodies are the recipients of male rage and hatred."[19] When Muslin women in Bosnia are attacked over and over by the Serbian soldiers, when genocide is the goal, when ethnic cleansing is the purpose, women's bodies are not mere objects, they are despised icons of life and liberty and humanity and are slated for destruction of the most vicious kind.

Women's vulnerability to violations of their bodies is generated by their more pervasive powerlessness, including the inability to define their own sexuality. Today, girls in Africa are raped because men believe that sexual intercourse with a virgin can cure AIDS,[20] just as in Europe during the late 1800s, men believed that having sex with a virgin would cure gonorrhea and other venereal diseases.[21] Rape is justified in the United States by men who claim that women who wear provocative clothing or hitchhike are advertising their availability. As recently as 2011, a police officer cautioned women that if they didn't want to be raped, they should avoid dressing like "sluts,"[22] a commonplace sentiment but one seldom pronounced with such assumed legitimacy as was this. Sex, like gender, is social, and the construction of female sex and sexuality creates women's vulnerability to rape and battery, or infibulation and dowry deaths. The dominant cultural definitions of women, constructions that oppress them but that they have not created, are intertwined with the definition of male dominance and sexuality. Male sexuality is taken for granted, unquestioned, and accepted as natural. Masculinity and maleness both demand aggression and control of women. While male sexuality is the standard, female sexuality is stigmatized; woman is "other," both sexually and socially. While both males and females are sexual and gendered, only women are consistently objectified on the basis of their gender.

We are so accustomed to hearing the criticism that women are "objecti-fied" or treated as "sex objects" that it has almost become a cliché, and it has lost force and critical power. But there is no better way to describe what happens to women in pornography, in war, in dowry crimes, honor crimes, or rape. Woman is both a physical and a cultural object. She suffers the violations of her integrity and her honor because of her object status. When she is infibulated, it is because not to do so would reduce her value as a marriageable object even though it would provide her with subjectivity, with selfhood. For her to control her own sexuality, her body, would womanize her, give humanity to her woman self. To infibulate her is to make her an object for commerce, an object transferable between men, a thing subject to barter. A woman whose dowry is inadequate is also a commercial object. Her sex is an economic burden that can be lifted only through marriage. Her object status either enhances the status of the fam-ily into which she is married or acts as a barrier to their success. A kitchen fire removes her and allows for a more satisfying commercial negotiation with another family.

A woman who is raped during war is acted on as an object of war; the rape communicates the superiority of the victor over the vanquished. Her body is turf on which a male war is fought, and her personhood is completely irrelevant. When women are murdered by their family for adultery or sexual misconduct, or even for being the victim of incest or rape, they are killed to regain the honor of the family. They are murdered because their virginity or their sexual purity was tainted; the father or brothers respond the way they must to regain their power and status. They destroy her because of what she stands for, not because of who she is. By the same token, a woman who is sexually harassed is responded to not as a person but as a symbol against which men can identify themselves as mas-culine. She is attacked as a representative of gender to reestablish the privileged status of men in the gender hierarchy.

We need to revisit the "object" status of women, to take it seriously as a statement about the value of woman in this and other cultures. The analy-sis offered by sociologist Edwin Schur in his book *Labeling Women Deviant* is a well-developed discussion of the process and definition of objectification. He makes the important point that as part of her subordina-tion, the value of woman as a unique individual with full humanity is denied.[23] Women are stigmatized, generically devalued, not because of what they do but because of what they are—because of the condition of being a woman. The woman is treated as a case or a thing rather than a person with autonomy and agency. Schur presents a thorough definition of the objectification of woman, both generally as an object and specifically as a sexual object, and he makes it clear that her object status is an indication of her powerlessness in the gender structure in which men are dominant:

THE OBJECTIFICATION OF WOMEN

1. General Aspects of Objectification
    a. Each woman is responded to primarily as "a female," an instance of the category; personal qualities and accomplishments are of secondary importance.
    b. Women are seen as "all alike"; therefore they can be substituted for one another.
    c. Woman's imposed secondariness, as inessential other, and her assumed innate passivity, imply object-like status, compared with the actively engaged subject (male).
    d. Woman's subordination means that things can easily be "done to her," for example, discrimination, harassment, violence. It also means that she can be endlessly studied, advised, converted into "a case."
    e. Similarly, woman can be easily ignored, dismissed, or trivialized; treated as childlike or even as a nonperson.
    f. Her social standing is deemed to attach vicariously, through men; likewise, many of her actions are attributed to her relations with men.
2. Specifically Sexual Aspects of Objectification
    a. Woman is responded to (by heterosexual males) first and foremost, and in almost any context, as an object of sexual attention; men are socialized not to respond to females as full human beings. This leads to perpetual male gaping, routine sexual harassment.
    b. There is cultural preoccupation with women's looks:
        1. Male perception of woman as depersonalized body parts (e.g. "a piece of ass").
        2. Cultural and economic uses of depersonalized female sexuality —media, advertising, fashion, and cosmetic industries, as well as pornography.
        3. Woman as "decorative" and status-conferring objects, to be sought (sometimes collected) and displayed by men.
        4. Women are evaluated according to prevailing narrow beauty standards.
        5. Induced female preoccupation with physical appearance; concern about ascribed deficiencies and continuous efforts to

    conform to "appearance norms," corresponding tendency for
    women to see themselves through male eyes as objects, and to
    respond to other women as competing objects.

  c. Women are "sexual property," to be bought, sold, and "owned" (by
    men). The owner can treat women largely as he wishes; and lack of
    an exclusive "owner" tarnishes woman's "respectability."

  d. Woman is an object in sexual behavior itself (assumed passivity);
    her function is to please a man and her satisfaction is not important.
    She is not supposed to initiate sexual activity.[24]

From this description, one wonders how women forge a definable self at
all. And, while Schur's categories clarify the meaning of the oft-used
"objectification," they more importantly clarify the underlying justification for gang rape and military rape—women are sexual property, women
are there for men, women are an instance of a category, having no singular
identity, really no subjective identity.

Sometimes this view is bent almost to breaking in favor of the man or
boy. In 2013, two young men, the proverbial small-town football stars,
raped a young woman in Steubenville, Ohio. Perhaps the story would have
stopped there, and the young woman would never have pursued charges,
but the young men shared pictures with their friends from their cell
phones, and so were caught, tried, and sentenced to terms as juveniles.
The real outrage came when CNN reporter Poppy Harlow reported on
the trial and conviction; reporting from in front of the courthouse, she
said: "I've never experienced anything like it, Candy. It was incredibly
emotional, incredibly difficult even for an outsider like me to watch what
happened to these two young men that had such promising futures—star
football players, very good students—we literally watched as they believe
their life fell apart." At first it seemed she was talking about the victim, but
it quickly became clear that she was devastated by the fate befalling these
rapists. Ninety thousand signatures were gathered within 24 hours to complain to CNN of the inordinate sympathy for the rapists and the virtual
neglect of the victim.[25]

The United States is one of the most rape-prone societies in the world,
having among the highest rates of any industrialized country of all forms
of violence against women, rape as well as domestic battery and spousal
murder.[26] Between 12 and 35 percent of all American women have been
raped, and another 12 to 20 percent have experienced attempted rape.
One estimate is that between 20 and 30 percent of all girls in the United
States who are 12 years old will suffer a violent sexual attack sometime
during their life.[27] A 2006 National Violence against Women report was

more precise, finding that almost 15 percent of the 8,000 women and 2 percent of the 8,000 men studied said they had been the victim of a completed sexual assault.[28] Findings, though, need to be interpreted with caution. There are reporting problems, classification problems, and definition problems in the data leading to a wide disparity between reports in different studies.

During the 1970s and 1980s, feminists insisted that rape was not about sex; it was about power. We made the point over and over. It was important for rape to be defined as assault, as an attack, a violation, and to be separated from sex so that the role of power, domination, and oppression was made visible. Sex was rape when it was unwelcome, forced, imposed. Activists and scholars who talked about rape as power rather than sex meant that they were forced to have intercourse or to have a man's penis in their mouth, and that was the furthest thing from "having sex" as anything they could imagine. To insist that rape was about power, not sex, demanded that the focus be shifted from woman's body or woman as seductress or woman as doing something to ask for sexual violation to man's behavior. Men's behavior was clearly defined as driven by the desire to control, own, oppress, or punish rather than by sexual needs or animal lust or desire. Power over woman could be achieved through the threat of force, a force that not only assaulted woman physically but assaulted woman's identity.

To redefine rape as about power could ease the discussion away from such constructions and spotlight the force and fear that were so central to it, thus separating it from sex. Rape was completely disempowering, whereas having sex involved participating, wanting, desiring, cooperating, being willing. To identify rape as being about sex would link it with lovemaking, and feminists wanted the police, the press, parents, and husbands to understand that it was a form of violence against women—male power being used against women.

Yet rape is specifically about sex. Women's vaginas, their mouths, are violated, used sexually by a man against their will. Rape is undeniably and clearly about sex, even if it is not only about sex. And it is about sex in several ways. The distinction between sex and gender has been critical in the feminist literature. Sex is designated one's biological identity, whereas gender is viewed as derivative, a product of socialization and gendered relations. In talking about rape, we are talking about being violated because we are female, biologically, with breasts and vagina to be violated by a man's penis, so it is male against female. But male-female sex is different from male-female rape; rape is a social category, an act that differs from "having sex" on the basis of its meaning to the participants. Lyrics by Jayne Cortez about Joanne Little, a prisoner who killed her rapist, probably illustrate how a woman experiences rape as well as anything I have seen. There is no doubt that she is talking about violence rather than about lovemaking or even "having sex" when she refers to the guard's testicles as "claptrap" and his lips as "toilet stool."[29]

So although rape is not sex, it is about sex. Women are raped by men because they are female and because of the meaning attached to sex. And females are raped because they are women, and thus objectified, dehumanized, or depersonified. Women are constructed as wanting sex, asking for it, subconsciously desiring it, deserving it, and these constructions superimpose rape on sex, making rape sexual. The merger of rape and sex is possible because of the way men view sex. For men, sex and rape may not be so far apart; to be masculine is to be aggressive, to take, to be in control, in charge. A man's power and his sexuality are intertwined; as Henry Kissinger once said, "Power is the greatest aphrodisiac." One wonders if Madeleine Albright would make the same observation. Men are sexy because they have power. Women have a different relationship with power; although a powerful woman is not by fiat a sexy woman, a sexy woman is powerful.

One author concludes that men see women's beauty not only as power but as an aggressive force, an invasion on their senses, and they use pornography and fantasize rape to get even with women, to tear them down, to punish them for their power.[30] Their sense that women's bodies are intrusive or aggressive is displayed by the language: "she's a knock-out," a "bombshell," "ravishing," "stunning," "dressed to kill," "a femme fatale." Woman's sexuality draws from men a sexual response over which they have no control. Their response of hostility to women is a reflection of their efforts to regain power and control. The entitlement they feel to women's bodies coupled with their feelings of powerlessness over their response creates a dangerous recipe for rape. Of course, this theory does not explain the rape of women who are less than attractive and seems to support the view that there is a tie between how a woman looks and rape, when in fact, such a tie is more of a media creation (i.e., "beautiful blonde found murdered in motel room") than a fact. Also left unexplained by this theory is the origin of men's sense of entitlement, as well as the reason men view women's attractiveness as a form of aggression against them. Women are raped not because they are attractive but because they violate a man's sense of entitlement. Women are raped because of male power and an ideology that constructs woman as "less than" and as someone who can be "done to," and in the final analysis, as someone who can be owned.

RAPE MYTHS AND STEREOTYPES

Rape is a social construction deeply embedded in social context. The separation of sex from rape can be achieved only through an analysis of meaning, not behavior. The distinction is difficult for the police, district attorneys, judges, and juries for a variety of reasons related to law and evidence rules and the activities that take place in the courtroom and before, but it is equally complex for the woman who claims to have been raped. The definition of an act as rape hinges on a number of possible factors, and these factors are not things so much as they are meanings. With rare exception, the defense in rape cases is consent, which establishes the fact that differing definitions of the situation will be proffered and that one ultimately will be designated as legitimate. The context within which the parties define the situation, as well as the context relied on by others, is permeated by myths and stereotypes about women and men, their sexuality, and their relationship with one another.

Cultural myths and stereotypes are powerful forces in shaping responses to rape victims. The universality and perceived legitimacy of these cultural myths and stereotypes are reflected in the worldview as seen through the eyes of the traditional "reasonable man" rather than the more recently developed and more controversial "reasonable woman" standard. Illustrative of this is a recent statement by a district court judge. "The cutting point is what was the point of the defendant and what he did. The testimony and evaluation of it would lead the court to believe the conduct of groping, lying on top of the victim while spreading her legs, feeling over the victim's clothing of her crotch and breast areas and the aberrant requests for the victim to undress falls short of an attempt of sexual assault."[31]

Common cultural myths and stereotypes about rape include the belief that rape is a sex act rather than an assault, that women lie about being raped, and that women are responsible for their own victimization. Cultural myths tell us that "only bad girls get raped," "women provoke rape by their behavior or physical appearance," "all women really want to get raped," and "women ask for it." These rape myths and stereotypes reflect predominant assumptions about women and their relationships, and they are linked with "rape culture," a culture in which rape and other forms of sexual violence are commonplace, normalized, and trivialized. Definitions of rape reflect not only the stereotyping of women but the stereotyping of men and myths about male sexuality. These myths are dominant because they are reflective of male experiences and are powerful because so many of the experts and other agents women interact with after they have been raped hold these beliefs and opinions.

These myths influence the response to women who are raped, not only by family and friends but by experts on whom the woman must rely for legal or other assistance. Professionals and paraprofessionals who work directly with rape victims are powerful forces in their recovery, and their attitudes and lack of information are alarming. Many of them, for example, believe that stranger rape is more common than acquaintance rape and that women provoke men to rape by their appearance, dress, or seductive behavior. Fewer than half of the professionals interviewed by Colleen Ward in her fine book *Attitudes toward Rape: Feminist and Social Psychological Perspectives* believe that men were actually responsible for rape.[32] These professionals' attitudes are critical for the rape victim because of the important role they play in helping them respond to the trauma they experience from the rape and from its aftermath, including the response of the justice system. Professionals are not immune to rape myths and stereotypes by any means, and, in fact, police may hold more biased and stereotyped attitudes about women and rape than persons who are unfamiliar with law enforcement policies and procedures.[33] In fact, police are more similar to rapists in their attitudes toward rape than to other experienced professionals, a rather startling finding.[34] Research in this area leads to the conclusion that rape myths affect the reaction to women by police, public defenders, and judges, and that jurors' assessments of the woman's credibility are heavily influenced by whether they accept rape myths and stereotypes. Jurors who are older, more conservative, more authoritarian, or more religious are likely to accept rape myths and hence to discount the woman's story in court.[35]

Overall, the acceptance of rape myths is high. One of the common myths might be called the "pedestal myth." This myth incorporates a view of woman as "molded of finer clay," of being morally superior and of a more fragile and gentle nature than men. It holds women to a higher standard of moral conduct than men, much as did the nineteenth-century cult of true womanhood, asserting purity, piety, and domesticity as natural womanly virtues, emphasizing sexual purity. Pedestal myths allow others to believe that victims get what they deserve because they behave in an inappropriately provocative way. The woman is a legitimate victim only when the rape gives the appearance of violating traditional female role expectations.

The interesting point about the perceptions women have of how they will be viewed if they report a rape is that they are absolutely congruent with those held by the police and public defenders, who would have to be the woman's allies in a criminal case. In addition to the victim's perception of whether a rape occurred, she must also determine within a social context whether she is a real victim. She is aware that police and district attorneys would rely on characteristics of her neighborhood, peer group, and social class to determine her credibility. Not only is she aware that others evaluate her behavior in terms of these extralegal factors, but she evaluates her own behavior in these terms, incorporating cultural mythology about rape to her own detriment. If she has been drinking, doing drugs, or has a less than perfect past (and one's past takes a fast tumble in examination by the defense), she loses her balance on the pedestal rather quickly and suffers the condemnation of those who insist on the purity of "true women." As Bumiller says in her work on rape, she will have a very difficult time defending her "heavenly qualities after her fall from grace."[36]

Even women who might not be judged so harshly are reluctant to report a rape. Clearly before a rape can be "founded" by the police or classified as a "real rape," it must be reported to them. The FBI concludes that rape is a seriously underreported crime; some research concludes that there are 3.5 unreported rapes for every one reported, a ratio of actual to reported crimes that is lower than for any other major violent crime.[37] The National Center for Victims of Crime reports that even in forcible rapes, only 50 of 100 are reported, and of those only one-quarter lead to an arrest. The vast majority of sexual assault victims, then, never see their attacker brought to justice.[38] And as Holmstrom and Burgess point out, even when rape is reported, it is reported by the victim herself in only 22 percent of the cases; a friend, relative, or even a stranger is more likely than the victim to report the rape.[39] She often hesitates to report because of her awareness of others' perceptions and her lack of clarity about her own behavior. Did having a drink constitute compliance or consent? Why did she invite him in unless she really thought she might like to have sex? One of the most powerful consequences of rape myths and stereotypes is not how they influence the way a jury or a neighbor will perceive the woman, but rather how they influence the way the rape victim perceives herself and the situation. The cultural imagery and information about rape permeate her consciousness, just as they do that of others, and sorting through all the layers to find a way to trust herself may be fraught with difficulty.

In a series of interviews I conducted with rape victims, the reasons women gave for not reporting the rape reflected their awareness of the social context within which the rape occurred and the power of definitions imposed on them. The three main reasons these women gave for not reporting were: the fear of others' judgments and condemnation, both specific others and the community as a whole; the feeling that they deserved it or asked for it in some way due to their poor judgment; and they simply wanted to put the experience behind them, trying to block it from their thoughts. These women provided reasons such as "I knew I was no saint, and I thought they wouldn't believe me," or "I was new in town and I thought it would be seen as my fault."[40] As one woman said, she did not report because she had a job in a bar, and her attacker was a powerful person in the community, and she did not think others would believe her. Another said she was "drunk, and I knew it would be seen as my fault." Most rapes are not reported by the victim because she second-guesses herself, blames herself for "risky" behavior, and thinks (correctly) that others will blame her as well. Most of the women we interviewed knew their assailants, and their assaults included some risky behavior on their part, which they understood to be a strike against them. Police were likely to take into account the very extralegal factors about which the women were concerned. They classified a case as "unsubstantiated" for a variety of reasons, including a prior relationship with the assailant; delay in reporting the crime; being a prostitute, black, or a welfare recipient; and engaging in "risky behavior," which could include kissing at a bar, having too much to drink, getting into a car with a man, or inviting him into her home. Police we interviewed when presented with these types of cases were likely to tell the woman she did not have a "good" case and were reluctant to send it to the district attorney for prosecution. Overall, the district attorney's responses paralleled those of the police; they relied heavily on extralegal factors, particularly "risky behavior," to determine whether a case should go forward to trial.

When and if a woman finally does report a rape, she may have waited so long to do so that she has lost all credibility. One of the primary indicators of a "real" rape from the perspective of the police is the speed with which a woman reports. Police assume that if a woman really is a victim of rape, she will report it right away. However, very few women who are raped ever report the crime, and those who do often report hours or even days later. In fact, they may not report until coaxed to do so by a parent or friend who helps them sort out the blame and self-doubt.[41] When she finally reports, she is not believed because she did not report immediately but instead relied on someone else who "talked her into it." The shared definition at all these levels is one of the most significant barriers to increasing the reporting of rape and pursuing the cases through the justice system. It is difficult to understand why one would assume that a woman would immediately report a rape. Almost every factor she considers mitigates against that. First, she questions herself and the reality of the rape; then she assesses the ways in which she is responsible; then she thinks of the interpretations others will have of her experience; then she imagines the process of reporting to a string of unsympathetic strangers; and she imagines the impact all of this will have on her life and on her family. Unless the woman is brutally raped by a stranger, it seems completely understandable that she would not report at all. To assume that she should report immediately afterwards is absurd. To reduce the complicated and emotional decision making she goes through before she finally is convinced that she was really raped and that the gain of reporting outweighs the cost to her to a suspicion about the credibility of her report is almost inconceivable.

The common myth that women who claim to have been raped are lying has powerful historical roots and damaging contemporary consequences. Rape laws are unique in the requirement of corroboration. This requirement is usually viewed as a reflection of male fear of false charges that would result in the conviction of innocent men.[42] It is just as likely that it reflects men's awareness of the difficulty a woman would have corroborating her claim since rapes almost never take place in public or have witnesses, at least witnesses who are willing to testify. The corroboration requirement might instead reflect men's concern that the common reaction of not taking no for an answer, or forcing sex on someone who was less powerful or who did not protest strongly enough from his perspective, would be misinterpreted as rape.

The parable of Potiphar's wife captures the essence of the assumptions about woman's nature and man's vulnerability that we see built into the corroboration requirement in rape laws today. Potiphar's wife lusted shamelessly after the slave Joseph, and when he rebuked her she accused him of rape, using the shreds of cloth from a cloak she herself had torn in a rage as proof. Joseph was imprisoned, and although he was able to gain his freedom with God's help, the terrible consequences of false accusation by a woman scorned lived on as a warning to all men.[43] The admonitions given juries prior to deliberation flow from this fear that women frequently accuse innocent men of rape, even though in fact false accusations of rape are very low—about the same as for other offenses. The instruction—named after Lord Hale, who first presented it—stating, "Rape is an accusation easily made and hard to be proved and harder to be defended by the party accused, though never so innocent," was until recently commonly given to juries in rape cases.[44] In "The Rape Culture," Diane Herman includes a quotation that illustrates the institutionalized male fear of women: "Women often falsely accuse men of sexual attacks to extort money, to force marriage, to satisfy a childish desire for notoriety, or to attain personal revenge. Their motives include hatred, a sense of shame after consenting to illicit intercourse, especially when pregnancy results, and delusion."[45]

Sporadic reports of rape accusations leveled against powerful men and then withdrawn fuel these fires. In the summer of 2012, former chief of the International Monetary Fund and front-runner for president of France, Dominique Strauss-Kahn, stepped down and out after being accused of raping a hotel maid, Nafissatou Diallo, in New York City. Charges were subsequently dropped when the judge determined that Ms. Diallo showed a pattern of lies and suspicious behavior, falsely reporting having been gang-raped before migrating to the United States, for example; telling her boyfriend that Strauss-Kahn had a lot of money; and having five cell phone accounts. Nonetheless, Strauss-Kahn later settled a civil suit with Diallo.[46] Such a case pitted feminists who saw the perfect example of sexual harassment and rape in this picture against those for whom Diallo epitomized the tendency of women to lie about being raped.

The psychoanalytic literature of female and male sexuality and much of the early work in the area of marital relations, counseling, and gynecology buttressed the myths and stereotypes about women's sexuality and women's lack of credibility in claiming to have been raped. After initially believing the stories his patients told him about being molested and assaulted as children, Freud finally bowed to the pressure of his colleagues in the psychiatric community and concluded that women could not tell fact from fiction after all. He explained their experiences with incest and rape as wishful thinking resulting from their desire to possess their father sexually, a decision on Freud's part that had powerful consequences for women. It bolstered the position that women really wanted to be raped; they just could not admit to their own sexual desires and urges. Helene Deutsch, a colleague of Sigmund Freud, who also judged women to be naturally masochistic, claimed that "even the most experienced judges are misled in trials of innocent men accused of rape by hysterical women."[47] These psychoanalytical attitudes provided background for the widely accepted view of the well-known researcher Menachem Amir that rape was a victim-precipitated crime. His broad definition included a range of situations in which the victim had (from the assailant's, i.e., the important, point of view) implicitly agreed to intercourse or had allowed herself to be placed in a dangerous or vulnerable situation. Such things as drinking, accepting a ride from a stranger, or not resisting strongly enough illustrated to Amir that "in a way, the victim is always the cause of the crime."[48] I remember how uncomfortable and then how angry his work made me when I was a young graduate student in the early 1970s. Those of us who grew up in the late 1950s knew that to wear provocative clothing, hitchhike, or go home with a stranger was "asking for trouble." But to have a researcher in the 1970s, during the heady early days of the women's movement, validate the claim that if a woman was raped it was her fault reeked of victim blaming, and it fed into every stereotype about male sexual response that the fledgling feminist movement was fighting. We were grappling with the confusion produced by the demands of the sexual revolution pasted onto the backdrop of the preceding years during which we learned that "only cheap girls did it before they got married." Amir's interpretation of research, his taken-for-granted sexist assumptions and conclusions, devastated our sense of freedom. We were catapulted back to the 1950s with his admonition that if we reaped the few benefits achieved by the sexual revolution, we ran the risk of being raped, and rightfully so. We were right back where we started.

The Women's Center at my university recently distributed "Stop Rape" buttons to all students and faculty. The buttons were accompanied by a campaign to educate students about the link between alcohol and acquaintance rape. How different from the "Take Back the Night" marches we had 20 to 30 years ago, when men and women marched through the streets, admittedly in small numbers, to alert people to the danger women faced in public places. Ever so slowly, the image of rape is changing to accommodate the reality that women are more likely to be raped by someone they know, often someone they know intimately, than by a stranger. While stranger rape still makes for popular television programs, and "slasher" movies still sell, these media images belie the reality. On college campuses, women are more likely to be raped by a man they know than by a lunatic leaping from the bushes. In fact, one-fourth of the college men in one survey reported that they would be likely to rape or use force to get sex if they knew they would not be discovered.[49] Nonetheless Katie Roiphe and Camille Paglia attack women who claim to have been raped by someone they know, claiming instead that the women have regrets "the morning after," are being vindictive, are suffering from "victimism," or have wafted into a puritanical swoon, unwilling to acknowledge their own sexual desires. Overall, however, the landscape has changed. College campuses have woken up to acquaintance or date rape and have begun to address the impact of alcohol on judgment, the danger of leaving a drink unattended, vulnerable to a roofie or date-rape drug. Further, while still not addressing the constructions of masculinity and femininity that underpin rape, or unraveling the dominant cultural messages that lead to women's vulnerability to rape, they have begun to acknowledge the complex tie between intimacy and rape.

Before the women's movement and the sexual revolution of the 1960s and 1970s in the United States, sex carried a different meaning than it did afterwards. Sex had severe consequences—Betty Friedan wrote, in the *Feminine Mystique*, that during the 1950s, 25 percent of the women in the United States went to the altar pregnant—marriage was one of the consequences—either that or going to Iowa to visit Aunt Edna for a year and then returning to school, refreshed.[50] Not only was rape terrifying, but sex itself was laced with the potential for danger unless one was married. Girls had a great deal to lose if they became pregnant without being married, not just their reputation but their freedom, their futures. If a girl didn't want to marry Bubba and live in a trailer park in Fernley, Nevada, as in my case, then sex was out of the question. Abortion wasn't available, birth control pills weren't available, and both girls and boys had everything to lose if the girl became pregnant. I am claiming here, of course, that there is a relationship between rape and sex. Rape in the United States is far more likely to be date or acquaintance rape than stranger rape. This is, I submit, one of the reasons juries are so reluctant to convict accused young men of rape. The penalties are severe, with sentences averaging around 12 years and time served around 5, a significant decrease from the possible death penalty in some states until the late twentieth century,[51] and when a case comes down to conflicting narratives on reality, no evidence, no witnesses, and no place for the defense to go except to try to destroy the girl's reputation to win a "not guilty" verdict, it may well be that prosecutors demur. The claim that the boy didn't stop when she refused sex is complicated by the fact that juries see two young people, often acquaintances or people who have had sex before, partying, probably drunk. This commonplace reality is inconsistent with the image of "rape" the jury may be accustomed to. The rape laws in this country are based on the specter of stranger rape, ideally a deranged black man jumping out of the bushes and attacking a young white mother on her way home from work in the late evening. This is at least according to the interviews with police officers and prosecuting attorneys in a study I conducted for the Nevada Supreme Court on gender equity in the courtroom.[52] While a jury could convict on that, the defense of consent being unbelievable, they are unlikely to want to impose too severe a penalty on a young man whose defense of consent is far more believable, if only because of the factors mentioned above.

Fifty years ago, sexual mores in this country would have alerted both parties to the risks of sex, and both knew the potentially severe consequences. There was a long distance between "petting above the waist" and "going all the way," whereas today, sex is tied to hookups, the consequences are minimal, and the "no means no" dictum by which men are supposed to abide can easily be lost in the fog of alcohol and hormones. When it is, the reluctance to prosecute is coupled with a view that women are, after the women's movement, responsible for their own sexuality, have dominion over their own bodies, and have power in their relationships. The gains women have made, in education and economics and overall, politically and socially, speak against the view of women as victim, hence against the view of man as cad and brute, and lean toward equality. Rape in the context of sex, then, is likely to be viewed as an unfortunate, but not surprising, accident of irresponsible and immature behavior on the part of both parties.

Built into this woman blaming were implicit assumptions about male sexuality. In fact, these messages had never gone away; on the other hand, the sexual revolution had demanded that women drop the sorry old excuses they used to use for not having sex when a man wanted it. One assumption is that it is both physically and psychologically devastating for men to become aroused and not to "achieve" orgasm. So women could either deal with the anger and hurt of a man if he became aroused sexually (no requirement that she actually do anything to arouse him), or she could hold herself responsible for the consequences if he was stimulated and then raped her. Note that rape was viewed as a sexual outcome, an unavoidable end result of overstimulation. One physician put it almost lyrically in his 1918 interpretation of a seduction that a woman falsely claimed to be raped:

> From secret loving glances ... to intimate amorous caress, they have, to their mutual satisfaction traversed the whole via voluptatis. At length, the man's erotic sensualism has attained its extremest tension. And he has therefore "suddenly" demanded complete possession—in other words, he has arrived at the natural conclusion of all that has gone before. Now, he asserts, the woman refuses. But this revolt often comes too late. The man is now, in part owing to the woman's own actions, in a state of sexual hyper-excitability which has ... [deprived] him of the power of free, rational self-determination. ... Her sudden return to virtue is ... regarded by him as merely an incomprehensible mood or as an underhand trick. Thus the amorous sport ends in an act of "rape," for which both parties are equally responsible, in the moral sense, but for which legally the man alone has to pay the hard and disgraceful penalty of imprisonment.[53]

Later, in the 1950s and 1960s, the description was far less poetic; she was a "prick tease," and she could be expected to get her comeuppance. If a woman does not want sex, she is expected to make the fact clear, time and again if necessary, in a way that convinces him she does not want it, which means she has to struggle through a minefield of words and gestures. Her success is not gauged on the basis of what she means or says but on what he hears or how he responds to what he hears her say. She supports the confusion by not wanting to hurt his feelings, second-guessing what he really wants, trying to maintain a relationship with him while not going beyond the boundaries she has set. There is, not surprisingly, nothing terribly straightforward about these interactions since they deal with sex, intimacy, and power, but there is a word that carries the information needed to support a victim's or plaintiff's case if it can be found beneath all of the extralegal and situational noise: *No.*

If only it were that simple. The legal definition of rape requires that a woman is forced to have sex without her consent. *No* ideally conveys lack of consent, but it is never uttered without the surrounding, sometimes confusing, context within the parameters of a relationship. Men learn not to hear *no* until it reaches a certain decibel level, but instead try to read the subtext of the woman's behavior. The woman learns to be sexual but not "easy," interested but needing to be convinced. The sex scenario, unless it involves women and men both equally eager for sexual intimacy, demands that he take the role of leader, if not aggressor, and that she acquiesce, more or less or not at all. This process may well involve protestations on her part; "not yet," "no," "we don't know each other well enough," "I can't," "honey, don't." These utterances reflect both the construction of the sexual dance and her awareness of the meaning of sex for her. She comes to this encounter carrying a good deal of cultural knowledge and personal risk, knowing there are consequences to her encounter but not always knowing exactly what they are. The definition of a sexual encounter he brings with him is consistent with masculinity and power; hers is loaded with potential loss. Her expectation that he will pursue and persist is both comforting and frightening. Should he express disinterest too quickly, she will feel rejected; should he become too demanding, she may feel endangered. He understands her expectations, but he also understands that his sexuality is defined as active, forceful, and demanding attention. He can rely on his knowledge of everyday assumptions to justify his continuing pressure, even as she protests. He draws on the cultural language of his race, age, and class to make sense of her responses to his demands and to evaluate his needs in relation to her responses.

Growing up in the 1950s and before, girls learned that it was important to be a virgin at marriage, or at least not to have sex with someone they did not intend to marry. Males and females alike clearly delineated the good girls from the girls who went "all the way." But girls, even good girls, did not want the boy they were with to think they were mean, withholding, or, worse, frigid, so they maneuvered the difficult territory between keeping him interested, happy, and feeling good about himself and her and not having real sex until he asked her to marry him. Girls faced every date with the powerful knowledge that boys had an inexplicable automatic sexual response and that if the girl was not careful (and she often was aware of how careless she had been only after the fact), she would arouse the boy. If she would not then have sex with him, he would suffer physical pain and condemn her for it, or she would have to do something to help him relieve himself, such as masturbate him, an act recognized as "sex" but not as "doing it." While girls were seen as able to control their sexual response perfectly, to know how far to go and when to stop, boys were not. Girls had the responsibility for sex and for what went wrong, such as rape. Fifty years later, girls are more likely to be seen as sexual beings who want sex, have sex, and enjoy sex, even outside marriage. The relationship between a couple is defined less in terms of the uncontrollable needs of one being met or resisted by the other, and more in terms of desires. The consequences a girl experiences from having intercourse are mild, unless she gets a sexually transmitted disease or becomes pregnant.

Interestingly, during the 1950s and for the most part until the 1970s, rape was presented by the media and police and antirape campaigns of various sorts as stranger rape. Women were encouraged to lock their car doors and not roll down the windows even in the summer and to buy a plastic blow-up dummy to sit in the passenger seat on trips or in clear view of the picture window if she was at home. The rapist was portrayed as a madman, a dark and dangerous pervert lurking behind shrubs in dark alleys, pouncing on the unsuspecting. Today the image of the rapist is changing to include "every man"—the average male who may live next door or sit next to you in class or whom you meet at the water fountain.

The myths and stereotypes are powerful not only in determining the perceptions and behavior of the woman victim and the people who interact with her. They serve another very important function in justifying or excusing the rapist. Scully and Marolla conducted extensive in-depth interviews with men who were in prison on rape charges. They focused on the excuses they gave, if they admitted they had committed rape, or the justifications they gave, if they insisted that they were wrongly convicted.[54] These authors found that the rapists drew strongly on constructions about female sexuality that were readily available; they did not contrive reasons that were unique to their own situation. They found that those who offered excuses after admitting rape were likely to rely on the excuse that they were drunk or incapacitated in some way or that they should not be judged on the basis of that one terrible act. The majority of the rapists did not admit and excuse their behavior; they denied and then justified it by blaming the women. These deniers relied heavily on readily available myths and stereotypes about women to deny their culpability in the rape. One was that women are seductresses who provoke rape; they lure unsuspecting men (rapists) into sex with them. Another justification was that women mean *yes* when they say *no*. As one rapist said, "She semi-struggled but deep down inside I think she felt it was a fantasy come true." "Most women eventually relax and enjoy it" was the image presented by a large number of rapists. One said, "She felt satisfied, she wanted me to stay, but I didn't want her." Another readily available cultural image was, "Nice girls don't get raped." The rapists justified their action on the basis of the woman's reputation, insisting that she was "loose" or had had a baby out of wedlock. One man said of his victim, "We knew she was a damn whore and whether she screwed one or 50 guys didn't matter." The view that rape was "only a minor wrongdoing" was relied on by rapists who pled guilty to lesser charges. A rapist who picked up a woman when her car had stalled pulled onto a deserted road to "see how my luck would go." When it did not go as well as he hoped, he said, "I did something stupid. I pulled a knife on her and I hit her as hard as I would hit a man. But, I shouldn't be in prison for what I did. I shouldn't have all this time for going to bed with a broad." The most chilling conclusion to be drawn from this important research is that these rapists easily pulled from readily available cultural constructions of women to justify their violence. They relied on the everyday myths and stereotypes, powerful constructions shared by the rapists, the experts, and often by the women.

Susan Brownmiller emphasizes the impact of ideologies about rape on victims, in the courtroom as well as the community. One of her most controversial conclusions was that was all men benefit from rape. Her point was that rape serves a social function for all men by reinforcing the cultural myths that blame women and keep women aware of their vulnerability and their need to rely on men for safety.[55] While individual men may be outraged or hurt when their loved one is the victim of rape, the image of rape and of women who are raped is one that allows us to avoid confronting the underlying oppression of women as a problem and to rectify it. To continue to define rape as an individual problem and rapists as sick or disturbed, and women who are raped as somehow different from other women—maybe too forward or not careful enough—ignores the impact of the gender structure on women and men. Women would be much less vulnerable to rape and other forms of violence if they were economically, socially, and politically in the position to make laws, construct core cultural beliefs, and participate fully in their society.

The core questions to be answered are why men rape and why women are the victims. Why are men, unless they are in prison, not the victims of rape? Structurally, women are raped because they are in a position of relative powerlessness. Their powerlessness has been sexualized, and they have been defined as sexual in ways that reflect male imagery and desire rather than women's reality. Powerful cultural imagery constructs women as objects to be raped and then blames women for being raped, allowing men access to them with few concerns about the consequences.

It is not women who construct the dominant imagery about women's sexuality. Men do. But not all men are equally able to construct dominant imagery; many men are poor or disenfranchised in various other ways or are members of oppressed groups themselves. But these men are not immune from the power of the imagery, and they in fact may find the incorporation of misogyny to be one of the only avenues of power open to them. Dominant male imagery of women has divided us into parts and against one another. Black women and dark women are characterized as sexually earthy, insatiable, rough, and needing to be overpowered—as wanting hard, raw sex. Light women are portrayed as childlike and innocent sexual partners, women who are relatively powerless and acquiescent, and willing to give a man what he wants. Asian women are not clearly in either category; they have been constructed as docile, servile, and subordinate, but at the same time as imaginative and cooperative in bed. These women are stereotyped as being superficially demure and docile, camouflaging their conniving and manipulative nature. The stereotype separates Asian women from white women just as the myths about black women and white women separate them. The rape of black women was built around imagery of white women as pure and domestic, not equipped physically or emotionally for raw, animalistic sex; black women were considered bestial, voracious, and base and would have no choice but to tolerate whatever the white man did. Black men were constructed as rapists by white men, as a means of oppressing them further, of justifying the beatings and lynchings that kept black men afraid for their lives. The white women served a purpose in the war of white men against black men, just as the imagery of black woman's sexuality reinforced the myth of white feminine frailty and vulnerability. The intersections of race and gender are perhaps clearer here than in any other area.[56]

Why don't women rape men? Of course, you may say that they do, referring to the few scandalous examples you have heard about or read, or you may ask in turn, don't men rape other men? And doesn't that imply that rape is not about gender and power but about sex and sexual gratification? The cases in which men rape men prove the relationship between rape and power: straight men in prison rape other straight men to demonstrate their power, and when gay men rape other gay men, their sexual fulfillment is dependent on their ability to belittle and debase. However, the general case is almost exclusively one in which men rape women.

Women simply do not rape men, except in the rare case in which a woman may sexually violate a boy or several women may assault and sexually attack and humiliate a man. Women do not rape men for a number of predictable reasons related to structure, culture, and socialization. First, women are generally not as physically or as socially powerful as are men. They are not accustomed to viewing their bodies as weapons. Women have a difficult time even making a fist or hitting another person with any accuracy or real vigor. When women harden their bodies through exercise, they do not see themselves as developing a machine for aggression, for war; they see themselves as developing a defensive weapon. Women learn to protect and use their bodies to gain approval, but the approval is gained through male admiration and approval, not the ability of women to do damage or to control. Women are not in positions to control and manipulate men, and men are not often dependent on women for their physical and economic survival. Further, and related to their structural position, what women and men both learn about sexuality and identity reproduces the gender structure: women learn to value themselves for their looks and their attractiveness, or at least acceptability, to men and to value men for their ability to compete and produce. Men learn the same messages, so together they reinforce the gender relations that undergird the gender structure.

Women do not need to own men physically. Women have grown up thinking of men as autonomous beings, not as possessions. Men do not violate women's sense of power and control and ownership when they express a separate identity, when they assert a self. They are men; they are masculine when they are separate. Women do not demand that men do not achieve separateness, that they stay tied to them, that they stay dependent. Women do not learn that it is important to be more than or better than men. Women's years of raising sons, as Adrienne Rich, Sigmund Freud, and Nancy Chodorow have all said in different ways, are devoted to training their sons to separate from them, to leave them, while they keep their daughters close.[57]Women do not insist that men be less than, that they stay inside, have a protector, toe the line. Instead, little girls still learn that their value comes through traditional femininity and dependence, while little boys learn the importance of being strong and decisive. An article in the *Kansas City Star* about the groundbreaking for a battered women's shelter, Rose Brooks, illustrates how little progress has been made in expanding the traditional and dangerous roles for men and women. The article begins, "Aided by little girls in pink fairy costumes and boys wearing plastic construction helmets, Rose Brooks Center broke ground Wednesday."[58] Rose Brooks Center will probably be admitting some of those little girls who have learned their oppressive roles well to their shelter in 20 years.

THE COMPLEXITY OF ACQUAINTANCE RAPE

In the not-too-distant past, girls in the United States learned that their sexuality was a gift to bestow on the man who chose them—a gift they would give once and for all and that would solidify their identity. Historian Anne Swidler writes about this in an analysis of the relationship between love and adulthood in a changing culture.[59] She suggests that if women are to marry once, and only once, and if divorce is viewed as a failure, they are likely to "save themselves" for marriage, which is the culmination of their preparation for adulthood and the opportunity for the solidification of self. However, if women have more than one chance to seek a partner over a lifetime, divorce being a growth experience rather than an indication of failure, they are likely not to guard their virginity as a gift to bestow on some lucky partner. Women are likely to be more sexually free and to view their sexuality as theirs rather than as being held in safekeeping for someone else. (Of course, women in many other cultures are not in any position to choose to have a number of sexual partners, to express themselves sexually as they wish. Virginity until marriage is imposed on them with a penalty of death for its violation.)

The changes in the participation of women in the sexual arena that have come about as a result of the sexual liberation movement in the United States and other Western countries, as well as the achievement of significant educational and economic gains, have led to an environment in which women may be more vulnerable to acquaintance rape than they were in the past. Of course, the definition of rape has changed as well, and the consequences of pregnancy have changed, so these must be taken into account in an understanding of the change in rape rates and the characteristics of rape over time. Going back a few decades, the consequences of pregnancy were sure and immediate for most young women. Legal abortions were almost completely unavailable during the early years of the sexual liberation movement, and women had a great deal to lose by obtaining one, just as they did for having a baby without being married. Middle-class women who were in high school or college were likely to have to quit, at least for a year, and virtually go into hiding until they had the baby and put him or her up for adoption. Another choice open to these girls was to get married.[60] The specter of pregnancy hung over both boys and girls, and the knowledge of the consequences of sex likely stopped many boys from forcing themselves on their girlfriends or dates. With the freedom achieved through the ready availability of birth control, the consequence of sex did not have to be pregnancy, and if one did become pregnant, the availability of legal abortion, achieved in 1973 with *Roe v. Wade*, meant that marriage was not a foregone conclusion. Coupled with and related to this physical freedom from fear, the sexual revolution removed women's legitimate justifications for "saving themselves." Now, women who were cool, modern, and "with it" were women who owned their own bodies and did what they pleased with them. Women who refused sex were viewed as backward, stuck, regressed in some way, limiting themselves in an unnatural and unhealthy way. Perhaps because the stakes are not so high as they once were, men felt that forcing sex was not such a major problem; she was not going to be ruined if she had sex with him, and he probably would not have to marry her—or even tell her he loved her. So, the barrier was lower, and her "loss" was less from his point of view, as well as that of others who might accuse her of overreacting, or of ruining his life for a minor infraction if she claimed to have been forced to have sex. Hence, if he forced her to have sex, she might feel less legitimate than previously in reporting him or defining it as rape. She was contradicting her definition of self as free and equal and sexual and was on the border of seeing herself and being seen as being vindictive or blaming him for something they both wanted.

One would never suggest that acquaintance rape and date rape did not occur in the 1950s. Indeed, some of those marriages based on the girl's pregnancy were probably the result of date rape. But the sexual barriers between males and females were much higher. The consequences of breaking them were lifelong and severe. However, by the 1970s, young women in the middle class at least had few readily acceptable reasons for not having sex with their dates, and sex was certainly not viewed as a prelude to marriage. For many girls, the question was, "Why not?" The motto, "If it feels good, do it," applied to sex as well as drugs. Exploration in both of these areas was applauded. Male and female sexuality was defined differently as well, with females generally learning not to reveal their sexual desires openly but to succumb to the sexual needs of the man, his needs being viewed as irrepressible and not fully within his control. While sex may have been forced on women, their protestations unheeded, this may well have reflected the girl's inability to assert her sexual wants under the circumstances as much as his unwillingness to "take no for an answer."

Girls in the lower class were in a somewhat different position. First, abortion was relatively expensive and therefore unavailable for many of them. Cultural norms supported marriage in the case of pregnancy rather than abortion or adoption, and religious values were likely to define sex before marriage (for girls) as taboo. Lillian Rubin writes about the disastrous sexual dance between lower-class boys and girls.[61] These young people, who dreamed of a life different from that of their parents, removed from the drudgery and limitations of low education and low income, found themselves repeating the pattern their parents had followed. Girls, who dreamed of sun-kissed cottages filled with sun-kissed babies, and boys, who dreamed of adventure and power rather than the dreary, repetitious, often dirty work of their fathers, found themselves right back in their parents' tracks when the girl became pregnant. The class and religious condemnation of birth control and abortion, coupled with the attraction of taboo sexual relations, resulted in these couples getting married when the girl became pregnant, becoming parents before they even got to know each other, and living with the constrictions of limited educational and occupational preparation.

There was, however, at least in the middle class, a difficult relationship between current and past expectations. In fact, the girls who were supposed to feel so free and open and in charge of their own sexuality are the same girls who only a few years earlier were worried about limiting their sexual activity to "petting above the waist" to prevent their boyfriend from becoming too aroused and finding themselves "in trouble." They had grown up clearly aware of the distinction between the good girls and the bad girls, and although the bad girls might have had more fun (smoking, dyeing their hair, and "going all the way"), the good girls had a future married to someone and being cared for and loved. That was worth waiting for. In addition, these boys who were now happily acclaiming the wonders of female sexual freedom were the same boys who divided girls into the "bad" but fun ones, and the "good girls" they would eventually introduce to their parents. They had not forgotten the distinction; they were just celebrating the sudden availability of so many more girls who were willing to be "bad."

Acquaintance rape is such a troublesome concept in part because the questionable behavior (forced sex) takes place within a context that is often extremely confusing. This very confusion—stemming from knowing the other person, if only slightly; the socialization messages of both men and women; and the complexity of the moment creates difficulties not just in interpretation but in the impact of the rape. When women know a man from seeing him in the elevator, the lobby, or around campus, this acquaintance lends an air of familiarity and safety to their encounters. If she then has a drink with him or he takes her home after work, his sexual pressure or sexual advances reflect a very different context than if he were a stranger who pushed himself on her. When she is familiar with him, she is likely to see the sexual advance as part of an ongoing relationship and to respond very differently than she would to a total stranger. There are subtle yet powerful definitions of the situation that operate in this instance in which neither is a stranger nor is it a friend or date. These are situations in which the cues and the anticipated consequences are very different than they would be in stranger rape. Here the woman is responding to a familiar yet unknown person, one with whom she has some past and can anticipate some future, and her responses are likely to be ones that maintain the status quo as much as possible. Women learn early on that they are responsible for the social and emotional environment, that they are to do the emotional work in a situation or a relationship, and they are likely to consider the impact of their reaction on the ongoing situation at work or at school. Women who have been raped by men they know consider not only how others will see their behavior in the situation but also the long-term impact of their reaction in the specific situation on others in their social world. Sociologist Erving Goffman points out that in our everyday interactions, we are likely to avoid talking or behaving in a way that would ruin the interaction; we try to maintain a semblance of normalcy.[62] Women particularly learn to take care of others and to take care of the relationship, so they are likely to make an effort to not "overreact" or "misinterpret," and at the same time, they learn not to trust their own feelings or perceptions and so may respond more slowly or weakly than would be effective. This caretaking tendency can be counterproductive for women because they may be viewed as not adequately resisting sexual advances. And, indeed, given that they may be required to prove physical resistance, they may be viewed as complying.

The fact that acquaintance rape is more complex and multifaceted than the relatively rare stranger rape by no means implies that we cannot differentiate acquaintance rape from consensual sex. Rape or sexual assault is forced intercourse or other penetration. It is the refusal of the man to heed the woman's *no*. Whether she is incapacitated by drugs and alcohol and cannot resist or assert her will, or whether she does and is overpowered by fear or physical force, she is the victim of rape. The person who is raped has had her power destroyed by someone she knows. She has been violated as a person with a separate and identifiable self, a person with integrity, by someone with whom she has a relationship. This violation is not a simple reconstruction the woman conjures up "the morning after," and cannot be reduced to a misunderstanding.

Young women on college campuses today are holding their administrations responsible not only for allowing a climate, in which the occurrence of rape is commonplace, but for minimizing the problem, responding insensitively and inadequately, and implicitly reinforcing violence against women. College students have responded with anger and action—filing complaints against their colleges, including Amherst, Yale, Occidental, and Swarthmore, claiming they mistreated victims of sexual assault and harassment. These complaints have led to numerous lawsuits and to a call for an investigation by the Department of Education and a demand that rape within the context of alcohol and acquaintanceship is still rape and must be responded to seriously.

The difficulty we have as a society dealing with commonplace, ordinary types of violence against women reveals the depth of our stereotypes about masculinity and femininity and about sexual relationships, and demands that we become willing to reconceptualize rape. It is essential to take into account the characteristics of the situation in which the sexual interaction takes place. One cannot apply the rules and expectations that clarify stranger rape to acquaintance rape. These are not simply acts at different ends of a continuum; they are essentially different and are in many ways unrelated. Although both reflect the view that male sexual demands, whether tied to consensual sex or forced sex, must be met, this does not distinguish them from ordinary sex or from one another. Further, both types of rape, like consensual sex, reflect a view of male sexuality as dominant and aggressive and female sexuality as subordinate and passive. They are distinguished because the lines between sex and aggression are blurred in acquaintance rape, whereas they are not in stranger rape. While men who rape strangers may draw on cultural constructions of woman's sexuality or character that allow them to justify their behavior, it is quite clear that these rapes are attacks. Acquaintance rape, on the other hand, dances between friendliness, flirtation, normal and everyday sexual advances and responses, and the shift to extraordinary pressure, force, confusion, and perhaps compliance. There is a point in acquaintance rape when the consensual interaction is transformed into one of resistance and conflict, but the interaction is a complex tangle of ongoing acts that are contextually based. The meaning of the interaction is fluid, preventing the easy separation of choice from force. This process is complicated by the familiarity of the sexual interaction in a consensual setting. The recognition on the part of the woman that it is moving from consent to force comes creeping into her awareness rather than arriving full blown and recognizable.

Just as it is important to distinguish the relatively uncommon stranger assault from the more common acquaintance or date rape, it is also important to recognize that while acquaintance rapes have common elements, they too are very different. It may be possible to place date rape on a continuum. At one end would be the situation in which a woman meets a man at a bar or some other public place, and he takes her home and forces sex on her while in the car. Clearly this is very close to stranger rape; in fact, as one detective I interviewed said about this kind of rape, the rape began when he saw her in the bar, not when he tried to penetrate her. These people did not know each other, their interaction was brief, and the assault was not comingled with the intimacy that characterizes an ongoing knowledge of or relationship with a coworker or fellow student. At another end of this continuum, we would place the woman who has had a sexual relationship with a man but who in this instance does not want to have sex with him. If her resistance, her refusal, and her *no* are ignored, this too is rape.

REASONABLE MAN OR REASONABLE WOMAN: WHAT'S THE DIFFERENCE?

Many legal scholars and feminist scholars have suggested that the issues that are so difficult in rape cases would be better resolved through the use of a legal standard that takes into account the realities women experience. The myths and stereotypes about rape and women who are raped would be tempered were the point of view of women rather than of men to be incorporated into legal judgments. Adoption of a "reasonable woman standard" could have a dramatic impact on the process that victims experience and would allow for the woman's perspective of her own experience to be validated. Such a standard could be expected to diminish the strength of rape myths and stereotypes and to increase both reporting and conviction in rape cases.

The principle of reasonableness dates back at least 140 years and has today gained a prominent position in almost every area of American law.[63] The principle provides a range of allowable departures from a standard of absolute conformity to a social norm. It balances individual freedom with community security, reflecting the nature of the social contract in which individuals agree to conform to community standards.[64] This standard was initially embodied in the now archaic "reasonable man" standard. Historically, the legal status "man" referred specifically to males, since women were legally property or chattel.[65] "Man" reflected a male society in which male values were the standard, women being perceived as both intellectually and emotionally inferior and childlike. For almost 200 years, the legal landscape remained fundamentally male dominated, reflecting a society in which no woman was man's equal and married women were legal nonentities.

During the past several decades, it has become generally accepted that the long-held reasonable man standard excludes women's reality from the courtroom. Against the backdrop of the feminist movement and the Supreme Court assertion of equal protection, the courts began to reassess the male-dominated standards that had pervaded American jurisprudence.[66] As a consequence, many courts began to use a formally gender-neutral reasonable person standard, incorporating social norms and the values of both man and woman in its definition.[67]

However, critics suggest that the reasonable person standard, rather than being objective, is fundamentally flawed, reflecting its deep roots in the reasonable man standard and providing only a cosmetic change rather than a substantive one. In fact, the apparent neutralizing of the reasonableness standard may make it too easy for the courts to overlook woman's experiences and the meaning of these experiences by creating a false impression that these experiences are already included within the general test of reasonableness.[68] That is, the reasonable person standard keeps alive the *illusion* of a universal and unitary subject of the law. The dissatisfaction with the reasonable person standard became the catalyst for a movement to develop a standard of reasonableness that would, in effect, force the courts to recognize the female point of view.[69] The obvious question "Is there a female point of view?" emerges and is certainly worth considering; however, one might ask the same question about the reasonable man standard, which has heretofore escaped such scrutiny. Although there can be no singular women's perspective, given class, race, and other differences, this limitation is not limited to women's perspectives. While there may be no "female" point of view, women's perceptions of certain phenomena such as rape or battery are probably more similar than men's and women's views on these. The research on jury decision making and attribution of blame and responsibility suggests that men and women do evaluate behavior in rape cases quite differently.[70]

Some have suggested that in cases specifically and predominantly involving women, such as rape cases or a battered woman accused of killing her batterer, a reasonable woman standard should be applied. This suggests that in particular situations involving relationships, and women's and men's definition of sexuality, women's views are underrepresented, or not represented, and should be. This also assumes, however, that in other areas, men and women have parallel or compatible perspectives, which is doubtful.

Although courts have been slow to apply the standard, within the past 15 years, the reasonable woman standard has gained a measure of legal force through hostile work environment cases and cases in which women have killed their abusive spouses. A number of recent hostile workplace harassment cases illustrate the application of a reasonable woman standard, concluding that a woman and man might differ in their perception of objectionable conduct.[71] In sharp contrast to battered women cases or those involving women who kill, the reasonable woman standard has proven problematic in rape cases. Some researchers suggest that it might be counterproductive because the standard incorporates assumptions about the "due care" a woman should have exercised. That is, a "reasonable woman" could be expected to know the culture in which she lives and to understand how men will interpret her statements or behavior and should therefore not reasonably place herself in dangerous situations.[72] In this way, the reasonable woman standard in rape cases may perpetuate or reinforce rape myths and stereotypes rather than challenge them, supporting the view that a woman who hitchhikes, has drinks with a man, or invites a man to her home is indeed "asking for it."

The intuitive appeal of a reasonable woman standard is not completely synchronous with the practical concerns that shape its application. It has been criticized as both too broad and too narrow—too broad in implying sameness among women on the basis of sex while ignoring differences in race, class, or ethnicity; too narrow in its depiction of femininity, reflecting cultural images of femininity that cast women in the role of the passive victim. For example, in *Radtke*, the Michigan Supreme Court concluded, "Courts utilizing the reasonable woman standard pour into the standard stereotypic assumptions of women which infer women are sensitive, fragile, and in need of a more protective standard. Such paternalism degrades women and is repugnant to the very ideals of equality that the act is intended to protect."[73] The claim is that the adoption of the reasonable woman standard undermines the effort to establish the moral irrelevance of gender codifying gender inequality. However, it seems more reasonable to assert that a standard acknowledging a woman's reality does not *ipso facto* diminish her. Nor does it seem reasonable to make gender irrelevant in the justice system. Rather, gender is undeniably a dominant social identity, reflecting structural and social characteristics that provide context to social interaction. Gender is one of the most powerful definers of the self, and its relevance cannot be ignored. Nor can wishing it to be so make it so, even in a court of law.[74]

Two alternatives to the reasonable woman standard have been suggested by legal scholars. One is the "modified reasonable person standard," which would take into account the relevant central characteristics and significant group associations of the individuals in question.[75] Another calls for a "contextualized reasonable woman standard," which focuses on the victim's actual reactions and the actual circumstances surrounding the victim's behavior, thereby allowing for each woman's experience to be viewed from her perspective and allowing for the multiplicity of images and voices that exist among women to be expressed and acknowledged.[76]

In an earlier work, my colleagues and I suggest a "situated reasonable woman" standard that requires the reasonableness of both actors' behavior to be assessed within the parameters of the dynamic interaction and its social context.[77] This standard would allow courts to acknowledge the reality of everyday interactions and that people's perceptions shape their behavior in process. The focus on interaction highlights the characteristics that are salient at the moment, including gender, race, age, physical attributes, status, power, and history of the relationship. The "situated reasonable woman standard" acknowledges and incorporates the notion that what constitutes normal behavior is dependent on the situation, the participants, and the social world in which they are embedded. Reasonableness is fluid rather than static.

Most states have revised their rape laws to include several levels of sexual assault with a broader range of penalties. A perpetrator may be charged with first-, second-, or third-degree rape, each with a different maximum sentence. First-degree rape is defined as forced sexual assault with aggravating circumstances. Second-degree rape is forced sexual intercourse, and third-degree rape is nonconsensual intercourse or intercourse with threat to self or property. This calibrated system of rape has increased reporting and probably convictions as well. Another significant change that has occurred as a result of feminist activism has been the inclusion of the man's force or threat of force in determining whether the sex was consensual rather than simply addressing the woman's consent or level of resistance. These changes are important ones and incorporate into the legal system the reality of the rape experience. Still, since most rapes fall into the third category, nonconsensual intercourse, women are still reluctant to report. The process of reporting and prosecuting a case demands an enormous amount of strength and a complete sense of confidence. It also requires an ability to withstand condemnation and criticism. It may be that only if the damage the woman suffers is extreme, or if she has "nothing else to lose," will she risk the humiliation and public scrutiny required to pursue a charge of rape.

RAPE TRAUMA SYNDROME

There is an uneasy fit between women's experience and legal definitions in what is known as "rape trauma syndrome"[78] defense. The usefulness of this defense for women who are rape victims is questionable for many of the same reasons that the battered woman defense is of questionable value. "Rape trauma syndrome refers to a victim's stress reaction resulting from sexual assault." Ann Burgess introduced the syndrome in 1974 after studying victims of forcible rape at Boston City Hospital.[79] The victims were characterized as suffering a two-phase process: the acute phase of disorganization and the long-term phase of reorganization. During the acute phase, which lasts from the first 24 hours to several weeks, a rape victim may experience a wide range of emotions, from fear, anger, and anxiety to calm and control. Physical symptoms may include sleep disorders, nausea, gastrointestinal problems, headaches, and loss of appetite. The Philadelphia Assault Victim Study reported that during the acute stage, common reactions to rape included insomnia, fear of leaving home, guilt and self-blame, restlessness, hyperalertness, crying, distrust of men, and generalized and specific fear.[80] The second phase, which can last for months or years, is characterized by such reactions as phobias, dreams, nightmares, sexual fears, hyperactivity, job loss, anxiety, depression, and gastrointestinal problems. This syndrome has been introduced in legal cases in an effort to make a woman's reaction to rape understandable to a jury, who may not otherwise find her reactions to the rape comprehensible. In the vast majority of rape cases, the defendant acknowledges that sexual intercourse or some other sexual act took place but claims the woman consented to the sex. This defense immediately turns the focus to the credibility of the woman, and the reasonableness of her behavior becomes the concern for prosecutors. While rape trauma syndrome has been widely accepted by the academic, scientific, and psychiatric community, and is included in the American Psychiatric Association's Diagnostic and Statistical Manual of Mental Disorders (DSM) as a subcategory of both acute and chronic or delayed post-traumatic stress disorder, the courts have not wholeheartedly embraced this syndrome as valid and reliable scientific evidence.[81] The potential prejudicial impact of the science on a jury has been the most controversial aspect of rape trauma syndrome, but all aspects of this syndrome evidence have been contested.

Given the history of rape laws and their protection of men from false accusations through requirements of corroboration and proof of force, rape trauma syndrome is an effort to give credibility to the behavior of the rape victim. Because the syndrome illustrates the effect of severe trauma on the victim, it has been useful in giving credence to her reactions that might otherwise seem inconsistent with her rape claim. Courts have admitted testimony in a number of areas for this purpose, including failure to recall details of the assault (*Simmons v. State*, 1987), asking the defendant not to tell anyone about the assault (*Lessard v. State*, 1986), delayed reporting (*People v. Hampton*, 1986), and lack of emotion following the assault (*People v. Taylor*, 1990).[82] However, one of the limitations of the "rape trauma syndrome" and other measures designed to protect women in rape cases, such as the rape shield law and the introduction of evidence addressing the credibility of the victim in court, is that they come so late in the process; long before the case reaches court, if indeed it ever does. Numerous important decisions have already been made by the victim, the family, the police, the district attorney's office, and others in a climate saturated with myths and stereotypes about gender and rape.

During the time I have been teaching about violence against women, I have noticed some positive changes in attitudes and understandings of my students about sexual assault. Of course, university students in my classes are not representative of the general population, nor even of the population of undergraduate students, but changes in their views over time reflect at least some movement forward. Further, there are well-developed and well-instituted emergency room protocols for rape victims, there are shelters and advocates and hotlines. There seems to be a growing understanding that rape victims are not likely to be victims of stranger rape but of rape by an acquaintance or friend. Fewer students blame women for their victimization, and more understand the impact of rape myths and stereotypes on our evaluations. At the same time, however, it is impossible to ignore the increasing sexualized violence against women in mainstream media and in music. No one can listen to popular rap music today without being immersed in a cesspool of virulent antiwoman venom. The contradictory forces of women's increased freedoms and success in every area clash ever more strongly with wildly popular views that women are despicable objects of legitimate male violence. This is a deep and dangerous conundrum.

NOTES

1. Gardiner Harris, "Deadly Rape Turns India's Thoughts to the Hardships Its Women Endure," *New York Times*, January 13, 2013, 6–7.

2. Ibid.

3. L. Polgreen, "Rapes of Women Show Clash of Old and New India," *New York Times*, March 27, 2011, 6.

4. Ibid.

5. Ibid.

6. Harris, "Deadly Rape Turns India's Thoughts . . . "

7. Ibid.

8. Ibid.

9. Press release from Panzi Foundation/DRC on the occasion of the International Day in Support of Victims of Torture, June 27, 2013.

10. S. Derne, "Hindu Men Talk about Controlling Women: Cultural Ideas as a Tool of the Powerful," *Sociological Perspectives* 37, no. 2 (1994): 208.

11. L. Rubin, *Worlds of Pain: Life in the Working-Class Family* (New York: Basic Books, 1976).

12. A. Rich, *Of Woman Born: Motherhood as Experience and Institution* (New York: Norton, 1976), 213.

13. E. Cleaver, *Soul on Ice* (New York: McGraw-Hill, 1968).

14. S. Brownmiller, *Against Our Will: Men, Women, and Rape* (New York: Simon & Schuster, 1975). One of the most controversial aspects of Brownmiller's classic book is her discussion of the relationship between race and rape.

15. P. Rozee, "Forbidden or Forgiven: Rape in Cross-Cultural Perspective," *Psychology of Women Quarterly* 17, no. 4 (1993): 499–514.

16. Ibid.

17. Ibid.

18. Ibid.

19. Brownmiller, *Against Our Will.*

20. M. Koss, "Rape: Scope, Impact, Interventions, and Public Policy Responses," *American Psychologist* 48, no. 10 (1993): 1062–69.

21. E. Mills, "One Hundred Years of Fear: The Danger of Administering Anesthetics without Witnesses," *Medical and Surgical Reporter,* edited by D. G. Brinton, M.D., 46 (1882): 36.

22. See http://www.guardian.co.uk/world/2011/may/06/slutwalking -policeman-talk-clothing, accessed July 29, 2013.

23. E. W. Schur, *Labeling Women Deviant: Gender, Stigma, and Social Control* (New York. Random House, 1984).

24. Ibid.

25. http://news.yahoo.com/blogs/lookout, Retrieved, 4-15-2013

26. P. R. Sanday, "The Socio-Cultural Context of Rape: A Cross-Cultural Study," *Journal of Social Issues* 37, no. 4 (Fall 1981): 5–27.

27. M. Kimmel and M. Messner, *Confronting Rape and Sexual Assault* (New York: Macmillan, 1998).

28. ojp.usdoj.gov, retrieved December 30, 2012.

29. J. Cortez, "Rape," in *Gender Violence: Interdisciplinary Perspectives*, edited by L. O'Toole and J. Schiffman (New York: New York University Press, 1997), 204–5; see also O. Adisa, "Undeclared War: African-American Women Writers Explicating Rape," *Women's Studies International Forum* 15, no. 3 (1992): 363–74; and L. O'Toole and J. Schiffman, *Gender Violence: Interdisciplinary Perspectives* (New York: New York University Press, 1997).

30. T. Beneke, *Men on Rape* (New York: St. Martin's Press, 1982).

31. Fifth Judicial District Court, Nye County, Nevada, cited in *Reno Gazette Journal*, January 11, 1994.

32. C. A. Ward, *Attitudes toward Rape: Feminist and Social Psychological Perspectives* (Thousand Oaks, CA: Sage, 1995).

33. Ibid.

34. Ibid.

35. H. S. Field, "Juror Background Characteristics and Attitudes toward Rape: Correlates of Jurors' Decisions in Rape Trials," *Law and Human Behavior* 2, no. 2: 1978.

36. K. Bumiller, "Fallen Angels: The Representation of Violence against Women in Legal Culture," *International Journal of Sociology of Law* 18, no. 2 (1990): 125–42; see also M. Burt and R. Albin, "Rape Myths, Rape Definition, and Probability of Conviction," *Journal of Applied Social Psychology* 11, no. 3 (1981): 212–30.

37. FBI Uniform Crime Reports: 2006–2010.

38. The National Center for Victims of Crime, http://www.victims ofcrime.org, accessed July 29, 2013.

39. L. Holmstrom and A. Burgess. *The Victim of Rape* (New Brunswick, NJ: Transaction Press, 1991); see also Federal Bureau of Investigation, *Crime in the United States* (Washington, DC: U.S. Department of Justice, 1994); and S. Estrich, *Real Rape* (Cambridge, MA: Harvard University Press, 1987).

40. M. W. Stewart and S. Storman, "Gender Bias in Sexual Assault Cases: A Study for the Nevada Justice System" *Supreme Court of the State of Nevada*, 1992.

41. Holmstrom and Burgess, *The Victim of Rape*.

42. P. R. Sanday, *A Woman Scorned: Acquaintance Rape on Trial* (New York: Doubleday, 1996).

43. M. W. Stewart, S. Dobbin, and S. Gatowski, " 'Real Rapes' and 'Real Victims': The Shared Reliance on Common Cultural Definitions of Rape," *Feminist Legal Studies* 4, no. 2 (1996): 159–77.

44. Justice Matthew Hale's enormously influential judgment quoted in Brownmiller, *Against Our Will,* 413.

45. D. Herman, "The Rape Culture," in *Women: A Feminist Perspective,* edited by J. Freeman (Mountain View, CA: Mayfield, 1984), 32.

46. http://metro.co.uk/2012/12dominique, retrieved April 15, 2012.

47. R. Albin, cited in Ward, *Attitudes toward Rape*; see also J. Strachey, et al., *The Standard Edition of the Complete Psychological Works of Sigmund Freud,* Vol. 22, New Introductory Lectures on Psychoanalysis (London: Hogarth Press, 1933): 112–35.

48. M. Amir, *Patterns of Forcible Rape* (Chicago: University of Chicago Press, 1971), 258.

49. M. Kimmel and M. Messner, *Men's Lives* (2nd ed.) (New York: Macmillan, 1992); see also Kimmel and Messner, *Confronting Rape and Sexual Assault* (this book has excellent discussions of attitudes toward rape and rape victims); and Beneke, *Men on Rape.*

50. B. Friedan, *The Feminine Mystique* (New York: W. W. Norton, 1963).

51. "Prison Sentences and Time Served for Violence," *Bureau of Justice Statistics: Selected Findings*, no. 4, April 1995.

52. M. W. Stewart and S. Storman, *A Study of the Nevada Justice System's Response to Sexual Assault: A Report Submitted to the Supreme Court of Nevada's Gender Bias Task Force,* 1992.

53. F. R. Bronson, cited in Mills, *One Hundred Years of Fear*, 29–62; see also N. Rafter and E. O. Stanko. *Judge, Lawyer, Victim, Thief, Women. Gender Roles, and Criminal Justice* (Boston: Northeastern University Press, 1982).

54. D. Scully and J. Marolla, "Convicted Rapists' Vocabulary of Motive: Excuses and Justifications," *Social Problems* 31, no. 5 (1984): 530–44; see also M. Burt, "Cultural Myths and Supports for Rape," *Journal of Personality and Clinical Psychology* 38, no. 2 (1980): 217–30.

55. Brownmiller, *Against Our Will.*

56. P. Hill Collins, *Black Feminist Thought: Knowledge, Consciousness, and the Politics of Empowerment* (Boston: Unwin Hyman, 1990).

57. N. Chodorow, *The Reproduction of Mothering* (Berkeley: University of California Press, 1978); see also Rich, *Of Woman Born*; and N. Weisstein, "Psychology Constructs the Female," in *The Gender Reader*, edited by E. Ashton-Jones, G. Olson, and M. Perry (Needham Heights, MA: Allyn & Bacon, 2000).

58. *Kansas City Star*, July 13, 2000, and postcard: "Welcome to the New Fairyland."

59. A. Swidler, "Love and Adulthood in American Culture," in *Themes of Work and Love in Adulthood*, edited by N. Smelser and E. Erikson (Cambridge, MA: Harvard University Press, 1980).

60. Friedan, *The Feminine Mystique*.

61. Rubin, *Worlds of Pain*.

62. E. Goffman, *The Presentation of Self in Everyday Life* (New York: Doubleday, 1959).

63. R. Unikel, " 'Reasonable' Doubts: A Critique of the Reasonable Woman Standard in American Jurisprudence," *Northwestern University Law Review* 87, no. 1 (1992): 326–75.

64. M. Gluckman, "Judicial Process among Barotse," in *Lloyds Introduction to Jurisprudence* (5th ed.), edited by D. Lloyd and M. D. A. Freeman (London: Sweet & Maxwell, 1967): 904–10.

65. R. E. Dobash and R. Dobash. *Violence against Wives: A Case against the Patriarchy* (New York: Free Press, 1979); see also Brownmiller, *Against Our Will*; Estrich, *Real Rape*; and M. Daly, *Gyn/Ecology: The Metaethics of Radical Feminism* (Boston: Beacon Press, 1978).

66. Unikel, " 'Reasonable' Doubts"; see also N. R. Cahn, "The Looseness of Legal Language: The Reasonable Woman Standard in Theory and Practice," *Cornell Law Review* 77, no. 6 (1992): 1398–1446; Estrich, *Real Rape*; L. Bender, "A Lawyer's Primer on Feminist Theory and Tort," *Journal of Legal Education* 38, no. 1–2 (1988): 20–21; and M. A. Meads, "Applying the Reasonable Woman Standard in Evaluating Sexual Harassment Claims: Is It Justified?" *Law and Psychology Review* 17 (1993): 208–23 (for a discussion of the history of and challenges to the "reasonable man" standard).

67. R. S. Adler and E. R. Pierce, "The Legal, Ethical, and Social Implications of the 'Reasonable Woman' Standard in Sexual Harassment Cases," *Fordham Law Review* 61, no. 4 (1993): 773 (for a discussion of the gender-neutral standard, the "reasonable person" standard, and the "reasonable woman" standard).

68. K. Abrams, "Gender Discrimination and the Transformation of Workplace Norms," *Vanderbilt Law Review* 42, no. 4 (1989): 1183–1203; see also S. Dobbin, S. Gatowski, M. W. Stewart, and J. Ross, "Reasonableness and Gender in the Law: Moving beyond the Reasonable Person and Reasonable Woman Standards." Paper presented at the Annual Meetings of the International Sociology of Law Research Council, July 10–13, 1986, Glasgow, Scotland.

69. H. Allen, "One Law for All Reasonable Persons?" *International Journal of the Sociology of Law* 16, no. 4 (1988): 419–32; see also Unikel,

" 'Reasonable' Doubts"; and Meads, "Applying the Reasonable Woman Standard in Evaluating Sexual Harassment Claims."

70. Ward, *Attitudes toward Rape.*

71. Meads, "Applying the Reasonable Woman Standard."

72. Cahn, "The Looseness of Legal Language." For a good discussion of this ironic impact of applying a "reasonable woman" standard in rape cases, see Estrich, *Real Rape.*

73. *Radtke v. Everett.* 1991. 47 N.W. 2d. 660 (Michigan Court of Appeals).

74. Unikel, " 'Reasonable' Doubts"; Dobbin, et al., "Reasonableness and Gender in the Law."

75. Unikel, " 'Reasonable' Doubts."

76. Cahn, "The Looseness of Legal Language."

77. M. W. Stewart, S. Dobbin, and S. Gatowski, "The Reasonableness of the Reasonable Woman Standard." Unpublished manuscript, 2000.

78. Burgess, A. (Ed.), *Rape and Sexual Assault: A Research Handbook* (New York: Garland, 1985).

79. Ibid.

80. Beneke, *Men on Rape.*

81. P. A. Resnick, "The Psychological Impact of Rape," *Journal of Interpersonal Violence* 8, no. 2 (June 1993): 225–55.

82. Fifth Judicial District Court, Nye County, Nevada, cited in *Reno Gazette Journal*, January 11, 1994.

SEVEN

Corporate Violence against Women

In recent decades, several high-profile cases, including Love Canal, Exxon *Valdez*, the Ford Pinto case, Three Mile Island, Chernobyl, and more recently the BP oil spill in the Gulf of Mexico, have dramatically expanded public awareness of corporate carelessness and criminality. They have brought to our attention the "socially injurious and blameworthy acts, legal or illegal, that cause financial, physical or environmental harm . . . crimes committed by corporations and businesses against their workers, the general public, the environment, other corporations and businesses, the government, or other countries . . . designed to further the goal of a corporation."[1] While the injuries or damage may be immediately and obviously devastating, as in the case of the BP oil spill, they may also be more insidious and cumulative, as in the case of the devastation at Love Canal, or the impact of the drug diethylstilbestrol (DES) on the daughters of women who took it during pregnancy. Corporate violence is a subset of corporate crime, referring to crimes that cause physical injury to persons or to the environment.[2]

The impact of Agent Orange on Vietnam veterans and asbestos on thousands of workers, as well as the impact of toxic dumping, reveals the breadth of victimization by corporations. Women are not the only ones who are victimized by corporate crime, yet they are particularly likely to be the victims because their bodies are vulnerable to intervention and the resulting damage. Women are barraged with messages about not being good enough and needing to change themselves to be acceptable, and since women bear children and are still responsible for birth control, they are especially vulnerable to abuse from corporate wrongdoing. Corporate crimes of violence against women occur within an invisible and powerful cultural, political, and economic context, just as do individual assaults. These crimes are a product of a culture in which a woman's value has historically been determined by men. Women's bodies continue to be under the control of men—their husbands, lawmakers, business establishments, and the medical industry. Women in the United States still depend on male-controlled federal and state legislative and executive bodies, male-controlled regulatory agencies, and male-controlled corporations that produce medical devices and pharmaceuticals used to maintain their health and appearance or to regulate their reproduction. Women's perspective or sensibility is missing from all of these organizations and agencies; women make up only 4 percent of all corporate directors, up from 2 percent 10 years ago and 14 percent of executive managers, up from 6 percent, and are sorely underrepresented at the top management levels in every country.[3] The fact that the same legislators that rejected requiring coverage of birth control in health insurance plans fell all over themselves to see that Viagra was covered tells us much about the negative impact of male-controlled decision making on women. These same men who thought women should pay for protection against pregnancy and made abortion extremely difficult to obtain (and will probably make it so again) were quick to provide all of us an opportunity to pay for their impotence problems.

The profit motive is probably the most basic and simplest explanation for corporate crime. This motive is supported by two other major factors: a corporate culture that defines questionable actions as being acceptable, even though they may be illegal; and the organizational goals of stability, prestige, and growth. To maximize profits, the corporation must lower costs, create demand, and minimize competition.[4] Clearly costs can be diminished with less lengthy or less careful testing of products, and competition is enhanced by getting the product to the market ahead of other producers, with more features, or at a lower cost, with fewer regulatory restrictions. Corporations may resort to false advertising, consumer fraud, omitting research findings, manipulating data, and other deceptive practices in their efforts to create and expand demand for their products. The importance of the bottom line can obscure or overwhelm considerations of the safety and efficacy of a product. In general, the concerns of the corporate leaders can create a two-tiered system in which the success of the product, and the corporation, are divorced from the tedious requirements for producing a safe product.

In addition to the single-minded focus on profit, corporations possess other social and structural characteristics that discourage challenges or disagreements, thereby creating a climate of civility and cooperation in which corporate crime is transformed into everyday business. In any corporation, norms that provide justifications and excuses for the commission of acts that potentially place the health and safety of consumers in jeopardy develop. In the coffee room, the cafeteria, and the hallways of these attractive corporate buildings, filled with hardworking and pleasant workers, an assumption of cooperative goodwill grows. One risks a great deal by challenging the familiar way of doing business. Much of an employee's time and identity are intimately tied to the workplace, especially for high-status organizational actors. Corporations also serve as a home away from home, a social and cultural center for managers and executives, not simply as a workplace. Corporate culture in fact merges the self with the corporation, involving the person in numerous activities linked not only to production but to affiliation with others and identification with the corporation. Internal organizational goals that determine the prestige and status of corporate executives can outweigh the importance of following strict safety and health guidelines in the process of production.

It is not just the corporation, a bloodless entity that is engaged in crime, it is real people, mostly men, making decisions that affect other people, often women. Not only do men occupy the overwhelming number of corporate positions of power, the characteristics that lead to success are parallel with the characteristics of masculinity.[5] A corporate executive's masculinity is centered around a struggle for success, reward, and recognition in the corporation and community, and "he sees working life as a series of stages leading finally to recognition by the community of individual achievement."[6] Corporate profit is far more important in the male culture of the corporation than is sensitivity or empathy, and the old boy network and the masculine ethic equate the achievement of profit and corporate success with the achievement of masculinity. These characteristics of the corporation and the demands for cooperation and achievements that they embody are of some help in understanding why corporations may engage in activities that are injurious to consumers. In addition, other activities are more directly and straightforwardly linked to corporate demands that place the bottom line before any other considerations, especially before the health consequences to women, for whom their products are designed. Corporate involvement in criminal activities reflects, in part, the separation of behavior from consequences, the dehumanization of the consumer, and the willingness to manipulate, dissemble, lie, and withhold research data in order to achieve financial dominance.[7] The destruction wreaked on women reflects their relative worthlessness compared with corporate practices of competition and achievement and the corporate goal of profitability.

In the corporate system, men become terrorists in the name of masculinity, and women become victims in their service to corporate profits.[8] The notion of sexual terrorism broadens the context of violence against women to include not only direct attacks but the cultural supports, ideology, and system of patriarchy that provide the backdrop for these attacks. The ideology of patriarchy supports a culture in which women experience violence on both an interpersonal and an institutional level where their bodies become either the battleground on which male wars are fought, such as in the case of gang rapes or international conflicts, or the turf that others violate in the corporate quest for profit.

The violence that women suffer at the hands of corporations is less obvious and sometimes less immediate than the violence of sexual assault, sexual harassment, and wife battery. Like these physical attacks and assaults, corporate crime is a form of sexual terrorism.[9] This is a system of cultural and organizational behavior that defines women as appropriate victims (powerless, limited in value to childbearing and related activities, or to being a sexual partner) and operates in universally insidious ways against their bodies and their minds. Corporate excess and manipulation result in serious harm to women, revealing an indiscriminate, arbitrary, and ruthless destruction. Terrorism refers not to discrete and infrequent acts of violence against women but to the cultural climate that makes women fearful and vulnerable to arbitrary and ruthless mistreatment. It relies on "voluntary compliance" rather than sustained violence to achieve its goals.[10] The elaborate system of sex role socialization instructs men to be terrorists in the name of masculinity and women to be victims in the name of femininity. Terrorism does not require immediate and visible violence. Rather, there is a reliance on propaganda in which sexual terrorism is expressed in all forms of popular culture and in the dominant ideas of patriarchy. These include medicine, science, and psychology and are generally effective enough to sustain woman's fear and man's domination and control.

In this chapter, I illuminate the practice and impact of corporate crime through a discussion of four types of crime committed against women. Silicone gel breast implants, DES, the Dalkon Shield intrauterine device (IUD), and Fen-Phen are products that illustrate the cultural and structural bases for the damage women suffer from corporations and reveal the ability of corporations to draw on and reinforce women's sense of inadequacy for profit. These prominent cases of corporate crime against women that have occurred during the past 50 years provide a clear illustration of the relationship between women's bodies and the opportunity for corporate profit making. Silicone gel breast implants, the Dalkon Shield, the drug DES (sold to prevent miscarriage), and the diet drug Fen-Phen are products developed specifically or primarily for women and marketed and sold to women with inadequate safety testing and careless disregard for their impact on health and well-being. They have all been removed from the market as a result of the damage or death they caused. All of this has occurred after the fact, however—after hundreds of thousands of women and their children suffered for the benefit of corporate profits. These are not the only instances of medical or corporate violence; surely the history of hysterectomies and childbirth practices in the United States provides a clear example of women's bodies being used as profit centers for the medical establishment.[11] But these recent cases have much in common and depict corporate practices that have been damaging to women, from the testing and development of the product, through sales and marketing, to influencing regulatory agencies and public perceptions. The activities of corporations rely on cultural definitions of appropriate femininity or reinforce views of women in their natural state as inadequate or incompetent. The manufacturers of these devices and drugs medicalized women's bodies, resulting in illness, disfigurement, disease, and death. Through the discussion of these types of violence against women, it becomes clear that the definition of corporate crime needs to be expanded to include not only the most blatant deceptions but a larger range of activities, such as public relations, influence peddling that reinforces or conceals wrongdoing, and other everyday activities that take place in the ordinary round of corporate life.

THE MEDICALIZATION OF WOMEN AND THEIR BODIES

The corporations that produced silicone gel breast implants, DES, the Dalkon Shield, and Fen-Phen relied on the knowledge that women are perfect victims. Women learn early and well that they are never enough —never good enough, attractive enough, desirable enough, and for most of their lives not young enough.[12] Women are "the other"; they are "born wrong."[13] Women's value is measured not in terms of what they accomplish but how well they succeed as a spectacle. Women's worth is situated in their bodies, most obviously in their attractiveness but secondarily in their reproductive abilities. They are encouraged to view themselves as inadequate objects in need of transformation to correct their implicit inadequacies. Women are to bring themselves into conformity with a cultural ideal, to "do something" to themselves, to "make themselves up" to be acceptable. Convincing women of their inherent inadequacy and need for improvement in order to meet even minimum standards of acceptability is not difficult, and public relations and other marketing efforts of corporations build their appeal on this deficit.

Cultural messages, that condemn women as imperfect while simultaneously demanding that they improve or perfect themselves, increase women's vulnerability to the medicalization of their bodies. Women's bodies have proven to be a mother lode for manipulation, intervention, and control, as is evidenced by the fact that cosmetic surgery is a $450 million per year industry[14] and that the diet drug fenfluramine, also known as Pondimin, alone brought in $150 million a year to American Home Products.[15] It is not just in the area of cosmetic surgery or dieting that women's carefully fortified sense of failure and inadequacy is a boon for industry. Women's reproductive processes have long been a particularly attractive region for the expansion of medical turf resulting in the medicalization of pregnancy, childbirth, lactation, and menopause.[16] Normal body variations and functions are transformed into problematic conditions, and the aesthetic realm becomes legitimate terrain for expansion of medical authority. The female body is defined as a product, and its "salability" is determined by the packaging. Corporations that manufacture and sell products to improve, repair, normalize, or enhance women dip effortlessly into the pool of cultural condemnation of women in their natural state to provide them with solutions to their imperfection and inadequacy. They encounter an almost inexhaustible resource when they market their products to women and the experts who advise them.

Women are locked into a lifelong medical gaze, as Foucault suggests, and their natural, everyday life experiences are transformed into illnesses or disabilities.[17] This medicalization of women simultaneously expands the number of women who are targets for intervention and correction, while trivializing the seriousness of any actual illnesses or symptoms. Doctors and pharmaceutical companies have come to the rescue of premenstrual, menstrual, menopausal, and postmenopausal women (and all women teetering on the edge of one of these conditions) victimized by their wild and raging hormones. In addition, women, defined as emotional and irrational, are not to be taken seriously when they claim damage or illness from the interventions of the medical profession. In each instance we discuss here, the women's pain and the amount of damage they suffered was minimized by physicians, and it was ultimately only when a jury of their peers, not doctors or corporate executives, found that the women had been harmed by a corporation that they were taken seriously.

"The medical-industrial complex," as Judge Bernstein so aptly labeled the interwoven and mutually interdependent pharmaceutical and medical corporations in *Blum v. Merrell Dow*, "preys on women."[18] It draws on everyday popular cultural imagery in an effort to broaden the market, relying on the consistent and tireless media messages to women of their imperfection and consequent lack of worth. The constant vigilance required to overcome the stigma of the female body, a demand that divides the self against itself, has provided fertile soil for the efforts of the manufacturers of birth control devices, pregnancy regulators, breast implants, and diet drugs. For example, women's suspicion of their inadequacy in their natural condition, and their doctor's full support for that position, rendered them ready targets for DES, even when it was known that it did not prevent miscarriage or other problems of pregnancy; and for breast implants to correct what the American Society of Plastic and Reconstructive Surgeons has dubbed the "deformity" of "micromastia," otherwise known as small breasts.[19] Pregnancy in the pro-natal 1950s was transformed from a natural process to a medical condition requiring the intervention of the medical profession, and no middle-class, responsible woman wanted to reject her doctor's advice about achieving an optimum pregnancy. And in the case of the Dalkon Shield, one sees the manifestation of a male culture that demands that women shoulder the responsibility for birth control and punishes them severely if they become pregnant under less than ideal conditions (too young, too old, unmarried, too poor).

Women are far more likely to be the targeted market for drugs specifically for them, and ostensibly for their betterment, than are men. Joan Steinman, professor of law at Chicago-Kent College of Law, notes that her review of multidistrict litigation shows that women are disproportionately affected by harmful drugs and medical devices.[20] Cases based on harm to women include Bendectin (the antinausea drug for pregnant women); DES (the synthetic estrogen for the prevention of miscarriage); the Dalkon Shield and Lippes Loop intrauterine devices; Norplant; tampons; numerous oral contraceptives; oxytocin (to facilitate labor and delivery); and breast implants. Steinman did not find a single mass tort in which men were injured by a product made specifically for men.[21] One cannot help but conclude that there is a real disparity between concern devoted to the safety and efficacy of products designed for women and those designed for general use or for men. Of course, it is true that many of the drugs and devices that have damaged women have been designed to affect their reproductive process in some manner, and this makes them more vulnerable to damage. But it is also true that researchers, most of whom are men, have been disinterested in producing products that affect the male reproductive system, despite its relative simplicity.

Compensatory damages awarded women are lower than those men receive, an indication of women's perceived lower value.[22] This is due in part to the public perception that the "worth" of women is less. Their unpaid, but indispensable, services are consistently undervalued or overlooked, and estimates of loss of future income are based on often false assumptions that women work for different reasons than do men and are likely to leave the marketplace to raise children. Further, women's complaints of pain and injury historically have been dismissed as emotional or hysterical, while men's complaints are taken more seriously. It is more difficult to recover damages for emotional distress than for "pain and suffering." Women's bodies are simply not as valued. A particularly disturbing illustration of this is revealed by the American Medical Association's *Guide to the Evaluation of Permanent Impairment*. In comparing damage to reproductive organs, "an impairment of the penis results in 5-10 percent impairment when sexual function is possible, but there are varying degrees of difficulty of erection, ejaculation, and/or sensation," an evaluation that acknowledges the importance the authors of the guide place on male sexual response. On the other hand, impairment of the vulva-vagina results in a "0% impairment if symptoms ... do not require continuous treatment, the vagina is adequate for childbirth ... and sexual intercourse is possible," an evaluation that again stresses the importance of male sexual satisfaction and defines women as receptacles for sperm and objects for male pleasure.[23]

All of the products discussed here that resulted in violence against women's bodies were designed to exploit women as a vulnerable market, reliant on the medical profession in their efforts to meet the standards of acceptable femininity, whether that was improving their looks, improving the "maternal environment," or protecting themselves from pregnancy. The development, testing, and marketing of these products reveal very similar processes despite differences in the products themselves. The corporations that manufactured or marketed them engaged in a number of activities that are clearly forms of corporate crime. In addition to the obvious crime of manufacturing and marketing products that were inadequately tested for safety and efficacy, and in addition to damaging hundreds of thousands of women with their products, the corporations engaged in more invisible forms of crime to buttress their sales and profits. They engaged in practices designed to conceal information, negative results, and their wrongdoing. They manufactured evidence or bought science by manipulating research through financial payments to supposedly neutral and objective researchers. They pulled out all the stops to influence the Food and Drug Administration (FDA) and other regulatory bodies to allow their product on the market. They attempted to shape public opinion and the opinion of medical professionals through spending millions on public relations and through buying research articles for publication in respected, peer-reviewed medical journals. And when they were finally forced to compensate the women for the damage they had done, they filed for bankruptcy to protect their assets from the women with claims against them.

DES: FOR THE PREVENTION OF MISCARRIAGE DURING PREGNANCY

DES is a synthetic estrogen developed in Britain in 1938 by Sir Edward Dodds and first prescribed in the United States between 1938 and 1945.[24] Because natural estrogen, harvested from mare urine, is difficult to extract in large amounts and very expensive ($30 per gram compared with $2 per gram of the synthetic), DES was met with a great deal of enthusiasm by doctors and pharmaceutical companies who saw its potential to treat symptoms of menopause, suppress lactation after birth, and possibly prevent miscarriage.[25] Dr. Karl Karnaky's experiments with DES on women who came to his clinic with premature labor pains and bleeding led him to conclude in 1942 that DES was an effective treatment for "premature labor, as well as threatened and habitual abortion." He enthusiastically proclaimed, "We can give too little stilbestrol but we cannot give too much."[26] This glowing endorsement of DES was followed by an article published by two Harvard Medical School physicians, George Smith and Olive Smith, who had conducted an experiment in 1946 in which pregnant women were given DES.[27] These researchers concluded that at-risk pregnant women who were given DES were more likely to deliver healthy full-term babies than would otherwise be expected. Based on their study and the complete case history of only *one* woman, these doctors recommended a massive dosage of estrogen for use in the prevention of miscarriage. The lack of any concern about such a recommendation on the part of the FDA or other doctors reflected the prevailing medical and regulatory attitude toward drugs; it emphasized benefits and minimized risks. Although DES was not approved by the FDA for use in preventing miscarriages, the pharmaceutical sales representatives were not restricted in what they could report to or suggest to doctors to whom they marketed the drug. They often urged doctors to experiment with DES on women, including pregnant women for unapproved uses, and their companies supplied the

doctors with drugs for these experiments.[28] DES was promoted as a prophylactic treatment for any pregnancy, with claims that it provided "a
more normal maternal environment at the very start,"[29] a claim revealing
an uncritical eagerness to define the woman's body in its natural state as
needing correction or improvement, illustrating the underlying willingness to accept women's bodies, while constructed for reproduction, as
not adequately constructed, requiring intervention and improvement from
the medical establishment.

Long before the public was aware of any problems with DES, the pharmaceutical companies knew that the safety testing was inadequate. As
early as 1939, there were over 40 articles published in U.S. and European
journals documenting the carcinogenic effects in animals from both natural and synthetic estrogens, including DES, and articles expressing caution from the British developer of the drug himself, Sir Edward Dodds.
The American Medical Association (AMA) Council on Pharmacy and
Chemistry issued a cautionary report on DES in December 1939, warning
that "its use by the general medical profession should not be undertaken
until further studies have led to a better understanding of the proper functions of the drug."[30] Early tests of DES showed that it could cross the
placental barrier and adversely affect the fetuses of pregnant animals.
The drug's developer was adamantly opposed to using DES in conjunction with pregnancy because he thought "the hormone was too powerful
and the female reproductive system too susceptible and complex to be
manipulated by chemicals."[31]

There were other reasons for concern about DES. In 1939 and 1940, a
research team at Northwestern University found that when pregnant rats
were administered DES, an alarming number of their female offspring
developed misshapen uteruses and structural changes in the ovaries and
vagina, and some of the males developed reproductive tract abnormalities.[32] These studies and others, however, did not convince the drug companies that any caution should be used when marketing DES for pregnant
women, nor were the FDA or doctors concerned about such reckless use
of a known carcinogen. Any studies that raised doubt about the efficacy
of the product or suggested concern about the carcinogenic nature of the
drug were simply ignored. Doctors eagerly accepted any information supporting widespread use of DES and just as eagerly ignored indications of
problems with the drug.

DES illustrates the damage that can result because of the relationship
between the FDA and the manufacturers. Based on very limited research
and emphasizing the findings of Karnaky and the Smiths, which were
based on small, unrepresentative samples, the pharmaceutical

corporations applied in 1947 to the FDA to produce and market larger doses of DES for treatment of "accidents of pregnancy."[33] In their push for approval, the pharmaceutical companies did not mention the increasing numbers of studies on DES, of which they were aware, questioning its usefulness in the prevention of miscarriage. They even more assiduously avoided the mention of evidence on carcinogenicity and studies that revealed that the drugs crossed the placental barrier, producing reproductive abnormalities.[34] The FDA, fueled by the atmosphere of reliance on science as the solution to all of humanity's ills and lulled into inattentiveness by the country's romance with postwar pronatalism, provided its approval within only two months.[35]

The FDA was initially reluctant to approve DES because of the number of studies on its carcinogenicity and the cautions raised by the AMA Council on Pharmacy and Chemistry.[36] It indicated to the drug companies that they should withdraw their applications for approval and resubmit them when they had more evidence of their safety. The FDA also suggested that the drug companies working with DES cooperate and submit one application rather than several. Eli Lilly, Squibb, Upjohn, and Winthrop Chemical Company joined forces, led by a doctor from Eli Lilly, and developed a resubmission based on evidence gleaned from anecdotal clinical reports rather than controlled scientific studies.[37] Their application also relied on questionnaires that stressed the benefits rather than the problems, such as carcinogenicity, that had been submitted to preselected pro-DES doctors. Under great pressure from doctors and the pharmaceutical companies, the FDA approved DES in 1941 for four uses—to treat menopausal disorders, to treat gonorrheal vaginitis and senile vaginitis, to suppress lactation, and for use during pregnancy—and notified all physicians to that effect.[38]

Despite the widespread use of DES, increasing evidence indicating that it had no significant effect on preventing miscarriage was accumulating. In 1952, researchers at Columbia University found that DES was "in fact a dismal failure in the general treatment of threatened abortion." They concluded that "the public has been so frequently told of the virtue of this drug through articles appearing in lay journals that it now requires a courageous physician to refuse this medication."[39]

Even though the reports from the manufacturer to the contrary, two studies published in 1953 concluded that DES had no effect at all on pregnancy outcomes. Both studies were larger in scope than earlier studies that had the same results and were more methodologically rigorous. The first study, conducted by Dr. James Ferguson, followed the recommendation of earlier research conducted by the Smiths at Harvard Medical School.

He administered the drug to 184 women and a placebo to 198 women. The results showed no impact of DES. Ferguson's findings specifically refuted the Smiths' claims that DES produced heavier or healthier premature babies.[40]

A larger study, conducted at the University of Chicago Lying In Hospital by Dr. William Dieckmann and colleagues, also followed the Smiths' regimen, giving 840 pregnant women DES and 806 a placebo in a double-blind experiment.[41] They found that the drug did not decrease the number of miscarriages, had no effect on prematurity or toxemia, and did not increase the weight, size, or health of premature babies. In sum, his research refuted each claim that had been made by the earlier research and had been relied on so heavily by pharmaceutical companies.[42] The emphatic conclusion that "DES has no therapeutic value in pregnancy" was completely ignored by the pharmaceutical companies, which by this point should have been well aware that their claims were not substantiated. The companies continued to list "threatened abortions" and "pregnancy accidents" as among the indicated uses of DES in the *Physicians Desk Reference*. Eli Lilly, the major producer of DES, continued to describe the positive indications of DES in preventing miscarriages based on the earlier discredited studies.[43]

Despite their enthusiastic marketing of DES, it was clear to the corporations producing it that it was carcinogenic; resulted in miscarriages and other "accidents of pregnancy"; crossed the placental barrier, resulting in potential damage to the fetus; and did not prevent miscarriages.[44] That is, not only was it dangerous, it was useless. Rather than warn doctors and women of the dangers of DES, remove it from the market, and attempt to mitigate the damage they had done, they continued to market it, ignoring the research that so clearly condemned its use. It was prescribed to hundreds of thousands of women, resulting in damage to them, their daughters, and sometimes their granddaughters. For 18 years after the Dieckmann study, physicians continued to issue an estimated 100,000 DES prescriptions to pregnant women every year. The peak years for sales were from 1954 to 1957, *after* the publication of research showing no effectiveness.[45] Between 500,000 and two million infants and up to two million mothers may have been exposed to DES and its carcinogenic dangers in the United States alone after it was proven to have absolutely no prophylactic value during pregnancy.[46] And it continued to be prescribed through the 1960s in routine pregnancies to "improve the maternal environment" and produce a plumper baby, despite no evidence of its effectiveness.

Although Dieckmann's research, and that of others, clearly indicated that DES had no prophylactic value nor did it improve the chances of giving birth to a plump, full-term baby, there was not yet any evidence that it did significant harm to women or their babies. The fact that it was a known carcinogen seemed to dissuade no one from marketing it and prescribing it to women. Then, in 1971, physicians Howard Ufelder, Arthur Herbst, and David Poskanzer published an article in the *New England Journal of Medicine* revealing their findings of a very rare and sometimes fatal human transplacental carcinogen.[47] These gynecologists had treated a cluster of cases of clear cell adenocarcinoma in young teenage girls who had to undergo radical hysterectomies and removal of their vaginas. Some did not survive. This rare type of cancer was previously unheard of except among women who had gone through menopause, and doctors were shocked to see it in such young women. The only thing these girls had in common was that their mothers had been given DES during pregnancy.[48]

Ufelder and Herbst became aware of other cases in the country with the same characteristic pattern, and other researchers began to trace the history of young women with clear cell adenocarcinoma in their states. Based on this research and follow-up checks of the state cancer registry, the New York State health commissioner, Hollis Ingraham, issued a letter to all physicians in New York State. He warned them about the danger of administering DES to pregnant women and urged them to aid in the surveillance and monitoring procedures they had established.[49] Despite this concern, and their awareness of the convincing data showing the link between DES and cancer in the daughters, the FDA did nothing for eight months.[50]

In November 1971, pushed by Congress, the FDA finally declared DES "contra-indicated for use during pregnancy." As a result of the FDA's inaction, another 60,000 pregnant women received prescriptions for DES during those critical eight months.[51] As a result of their mothers being urged to use this drug by their doctors, many DES daughters suffer cancer or are rendered infertile; their fallopian tubes are misshapen, making an ectopic pregnancy more common; and they have an abnormally T-shaped narrower and smaller uterus space, reducing the likelihood of a fertilized egg's implanting successfully. Their uterus is often too small to carry a normal pregnancy to term, and the hoods and ridges in the cervix make it medically incompetent to act as a plug to hold the developing fetus.[52]

The problems DES daughters encounter are overwhelming. The treatment for clear cell adenocarcinoma is a radical hysterectomy and removal of most or all of the vagina, with a new vagina being reconstructed from skin grafts. Many of the women have radiation treatment, resulting in infertility and radiation burns and scar tissue that affect the bladder and digestive system. These young women often have had their sexual organs removed during a time of sexual maturing, forever maiming them and dramatically altering their conception of self. I have spoken with women who have had hysterectomies without their full knowledge and consent, and the anger and betrayal they feel is akin to that of a woman who has been raped by a friend. The DES daughters suffer anger, humiliation, and fear as a result of the medical problems they have and can anticipate in the future.

Once it had been determined that their product was dangerous, the pharmaceutical companies that had so eagerly experimented with hundreds of thousands of women, basing their safety and efficacy claims on a few flawed studies and knowingly keeping negative information from the FDA, were not in the least interested in the follow-up research. Instead, the research was conducted by the federal government and universities, and in a long-term tracking study of DES women and their daughters, the Collaborative DES Adenosis Project (DESAD), which was established by the National Cancer Institute.[53] In one follow-up study conducted 25 years after the original Dieckmann study, the women who participated were tracked and their records reanalyzed. The results were even more negative, showing a statistically significant increase in the number of miscarriages, premature births, and neonatal deaths.[54]

Public awareness about DES and the continuing research on its impact on the DES daughters and their granddaughters in large part resulted from the efforts of a grassroots advocacy group, DES Action, an organization of DES mothers and daughters. This group pressured the federal government to establish a DES task force, first in 1978 and again in 1985, to evaluate the ongoing research and medical findings and to develop recommendations for medical, educational, and research responses. In 1992, DES Action lobbied Congress to provide appropriations for more education about the drug. DES daughters have been an effective lobbying group, being primarily white, well-educated, and middle- or upper-middle-class. They had the background and the support to advocate research, network effectively, and eventually file a large number of lawsuits. These middle-class women were not reluctant to use the courts or to lobby their legislators and to expect results. Their efforts were fueled by the knowledge that many doctors and many more women were not aware of the seriousness or the extent of the DES problem and that many of the women did not even know they had been exposed to DES. They had simply been given a prescription by their doctor and told to "take this" to help with their pregnancy. Many doctors did not know what to look for in DES daughters or what to do when they found something.

For over 20 years, DES Action has pushed the federal government to do research and to educate women and doctors. It continues to insist on the follow-up of DES granddaughters. While DES was produced and marketed by many pharmaceutical companies, none has acknowledged responsibility for the damage caused by DES. Yet, in the 1970s, a large number of lawsuits against many of these companies led to a landmark 1980 decision of the Supreme Court of California in *Sindell v. Abbott Laboratories*. The court ruled that all manufacturers of DES had liability proportional to their share of the market at the time the drug was consumed by the mother of any particular plaintiff.[55] Juries have been sympathetic to some of the DES daughters, but their daughters (DES granddaughters) have not fared as well in the courts, nor has the National Cancer Institute shown significant increased risks among third-generation daughters and sons.[56]

THE DALKON SHIELD

The Dalkon Shield was developed in the late 1960s, touted as a birth control device for all women—those who were disorganized, those who were forgetful, those who were modern and wanted the latest convenience, as well as those who were likely to be irresponsible.[57] It seemed the perfect birth control device for lower-income and minority women, and they were a significant part of this market. The Dalkon Shield was developed by Dr. Hugh Davis, along with an engineer, Irwin Lerner, who worked to design an IUD that would not easily be expelled from the uterus.[58] The shield was tested on poor women in a family planning clinic at Johns Hopkins University in Baltimore, without their consent. The unique shape of the Dalkon Shield and its downward prongs kept it in place, but also required a heavier string for removal than other IUDs. The string initially developed was uncomfortable for the male partners of the women on whom it was tested, so to alleviate their complaints, a multifilament string was developed.[59] Herein lay the potential for disaster. This string was the cause of the many problems experienced by women with the Dalkon Shield, including pelvic inflammatory disease, the impairment or loss of childbearing ability, spontaneous abortions, recurring health problems and defective babies, and persistent pain and bleeding.[60]

Davis, Lerner, and their attorney formed a company to manufacture and market the device and soon sold it to A. H. Robins, with Davis becoming their well-paid consultant.[61] Davis wrote up the results of his research on the Dalkon Shield, concealing evidence of its ineffectiveness and overestimating the success rate in the prevention of pregnancy. He relied on results from women who had had the device for an average of only six months, failing to indicate that he had advised his patients to use a backup contraceptive method during the first three months after having the shield inserted and ignoring women's complaints of severe cramping, excruciating pain, and bleeding. He also failed to report his financial interest in the Dalkon Shield in his influential articles. He and A. H. Robins took advantage of the fear surrounding the birth control pill to tout the shield as a safe and effective (having no evidence of its safety or effectiveness) birth control device.[62]

Six months before marketing the Dalkon Shield, A. H. Robins knew that the multifilament string presented a potentially dangerous situation to the women who would use the shield for birth control.[63] The string on the Dalkon Shield, running from the device in the uterus through the cervix, to the vagina, which was designed to allow the woman to know she had not expelled it unknowingly and to allow the doctor to remove it, was the source of the problem. The strings on all IUDs beginning in the 1960s were mono-filaments, meaning that the bacteria that are always in the vagina could not enter the sterile environment of the uterus. The Dalkon Shield's string was instead a tiny cylindrical sheath, 0.4 millimeter in diameter, encasing 200 to 450 round monofilaments separated by spaces. Any bacteria that got into the spaces between the filaments would be insulated from the cervical mucus shield, the body's natural antibacterial defense, and would be drawn into the womb by "wicking," a phenomenon similar to that by which a string draws the melting wax of a candle to the flame.[64] Robins was aware that problems were likely to develop with time and initially recommended replacing the Dalkon Shield every two years. However, acknowledging a loss in sales as a result of this inconvenience and expense, they removed their recommendation and failed to inform doctors of the increased risk of deterioration of the string after two years.[65]

Despite their knowledge that the claims they made for the shield's rate of pregnancy prevention were wrong and that the polyfilament string could cause damage, the company never once during the four years the shield was on the market revealed its knowledge to doctors or women, nor did it conduct a study of the problematic "wicking" tendency of the string.[66]

A. H. Robins estimates that approximately 4 percent of the nearly 90,000 women in the United States using the shield were injured.[67] Considering that it is conventional wisdom that adverse reactions to drugs are underreported, we can anticipate that is also true of the injuries from the Dalkon Shield. Hundreds of women who conceived while wearing the shield gave birth prematurely to children with severe congenital defects, including cerebral palsy, blindness, and mental retardation. Other women had stillbirths.[68] Robins had been warned by Dr. Thad Earl in mid-1972 that there were numerous dangerous side effects of the device, but the company suppressed the information. Earl had advised Robins that the "device should be removed as soon as a diagnosis of pregnancy is made" because to leave it in place was "hazardous."[69] Earl and other doctors, including Andrew Latteier at the University of Utah, urged Robins to investigate the problem of infection and septic abortions, yet Robins ignored the warnings altogether.[70]

The animal studies that usually precede clinical trials were a failure, leading Dr. Murphy, director of scientific development for A. H. Robins, to conclude that "we possess inadequate support data from animal studies as to long-term safety of the current Dalkon Shield."[71] A subsequent study with baboons, who have a reproductive tract similar to that of women, resulted in 1 of 8 dying and 3 of 10 suffering a perforated uterus, results that were not revealed to the FDA or to the medical profession.[72]

In addition, a 12-month study of the pregnancy rate of the Dalkon Shield showed it to be five times higher than the rate advertised and promoted by A. H. Robins, a fact well known by A.H. Robins but kept from the women, the doctors, and the FDA. In fact, A.H. Robins specifically sought out studies that were favorable, knowing that the majority were not.[73] Ellen Preston, the company's liaison with doctors, reported in an August 1973 memo that most of her efforts to find favorable pregnancy reports with the Dalkon Shield had failed, with most showing pregnancy rates above the hoped-for 2 percent rate. She warned that Robins needed positive studies to counter the "great deal of unfavorable data," and "to meet this need, studies will have to be accepted on a very selected basis, i.e., those known in advance to be favorable with a pregnancy rate of 2 percent or less."[74] Robins made no pretense of objectivity, recommending that "we engage in at least ten retrospective studies in 1973 for the purpose of obtaining favorable Dalkon Shield data."[75]

Meanwhile, A.H. Robins recognized the necessity of studying the shield for safety and effectiveness in women for very practical purposes; executives believed that Congress would soon enact testing requirements for medical devices, and they wanted to be prepared for compliance. Frederick Clark, the medical director of A.H. Robins, wrote on August 31, 1970: "In light of extreme probability of device legislation in next twelve months it behooves us to commence indicated studies as soon as possible."[76] In fact, Robins never conducted the necessary safety tests and turned down a series of proposals for studies from outside the company (from Medical College of Virginia and the University of Kentucky Medical Center in Lexington) that had the potential to provide an early warning of the pelvic infections.[77]

They need not have worried. It was not until 1976 that Congress adopted the Medical Device Amendments Act which required premarket testing. Prior to this, only drugs, not devices, were subject to premarket approval and proof of safety and effectiveness.[78] Although the FDA eventually abandoned its effort to classify IUDs as drugs, it did make one exception, stipulating that IUDs using any active substance to increase the contraceptive effect, decrease adverse reactions, or provide increased medical acceptability are not generally recognized as safe and effective for contraception.[79] Although A.H. Robins officials and salespersons touted the copper used in the Dalkon Shield to doctors and women as a contraceptive agent and as another advantage of the shield over other IUDs, they were able to convince the FDA that the copper served *only* to make the device more flexible, stronger, and more readily visible under X-ray and insisted that it should remain classified as a device.[80] After a number of disagreements within the FDA, the IUD remained classified as a device rather than a drug.

It was not long, however, until the FDA's interest in the Dalkon Shield was rekindled, having been informed by doctors and women of a suspected association between the shield and an increasing number of septic abortions, deaths, infections, perforated uteri, and other problems.[81] In addition to the damage done from perforated uteruses and pelvic inflammatory disease, injuries that prevented subsequent pregnancy, and required hysterectomies, many women became pregnant while wearing the IUD, and of those, approximately 60 percent miscarried. Most of these suffered miscarriages in the first or second trimester, but at least 248 women in the United States endured dangerous infected miscarriages called septic spontaneous abortions. At least 15 of the women who suffered this type of miscarriage died from the infection.[82] In 1974, the FDA requested that A.H. Robins stop the sale of the Dalkon Shield and recall all devices already sold because of the health hazard they posed. Ongoing panel and advisory committee disputes within the FDA kept it off the market until August 8, 1975. Finally citing ongoing bad publicity, Robins announced it had no plans to market the device again. However, it was not until 10 years later that the device was recalled and women who had been wearing it for years were encouraged to have it removed.

Although it took the FDA over 10 years to recall the Dalkon Shield and to warn women that they should have it removed, the FDA had early and telling experience with IUDs and their regulation. In the late 1960s and early 1970s, there were many IUDs on the market—the Lippes Loop, the Birnberg Bow, the Spring, and the Dalkon Shield among others—all classified as medical devices and all sold to doctors and inserted in the uteri of hundreds of thousands of women without approval of the FDA or any other governmental agency. The FDA's general counsel, William Goodrich, a top authority on the drug act, wrote that the agency "should reconsider our regulatory policy concerning devices" so that anything intended for long-term use in the body, including IUDs, should be classified as a drug, not a device. His view that IUDs should be approved for safety before they were allowed to be marketed was based in part on a comprehensive report of the FDA advisory committee on obstetrics and gynecology, which concluded that there were some serious adverse reactions that, although rare, called for more adequate testing of the IUD.[83]

By 1973, the Centers for Disease Control had conducted a survey of 35,502 medical and osteopathic doctors and discovered that the rate of complicated pregnancies was twice as high for Dalkon Shield wearers as for others, that the rate of infections was higher than with other IUDs, and that five of the women in the study had died from infection.[84] The FDA, in receipt of this report and aware of at least 6 fatal and 70 nonfatal spontaneous septic abortions, recommended the withdrawal of the Dalkon Shield from the market.[85] After extensive lobbying, however, the FDA agreed to allow a voluntary temporary suspension of sales and consider the issue of safety at a subsequent meeting. The FDA advisory subcommittee recommended at that meeting that the moratorium on the sale of the shield be extended until definitive data were in hand, but the FDA commissioner, Alexander Schmidt, simply offered a plan by Robins to sell the device only to physicians who would register new patients and maintain detailed records on them. Subcommittee members were outraged, and Dr. Emanuel Friedman resigned, charging that Schmidt was "protective of the pharmaceutical industry and not of the women at risk."[86] The registry program never got off the ground, and the Dalkon Shield was never placed on the market again.

By 1985, there were thousands of lawsuits against A.H. Robins. The company estimated that 14,330 cases had been filed, and new ones were being filed at a rate of 15 a day. By June 1985, Robins and its former insurer, Aetna Life and Casualty Company, had paid out $378.3 million to dispose of cases and an additional $107.3 million in legal expenses.[87]

Juries had awarded $24.8 million in punitive damages for reckless and wanton behavior.[88] Not only did Robins know of the potential and real hazards of the Dalkon Shield, so did its insurer, Aetna. In 1978, as a result of increasing liability, Aetna decided it would no longer insure the Dalkon Shield.[89] The resulting lawsuit from Robins revealed that the hazard of the Dalkon Shield was so well known to both Aetna and A.H. Robins prior to 1977 that Robins could not acquire additional coverage after 1978—yet both had persistently failed to warn, recall, or otherwise sound the alarm to women.[90]

One of the most lucid voices in the entire history of the Dalkon Shield controversy was Judge Miles Lord, who presided over many of the cases in which women were severely injured, had miscarried, or had given birth to children with severe disabilities.[91] At a settlement hearing, he angrily condemned the CEOs of A.H. Robins for their incredible disregard for women:

> Your company, without warning to women, invaded their bodies by the millions and caused them injuries by the thousands. And when the time came for these women to make their claims against your company, you attacked their characters. You inquired into their sexual practices and into the identity of their sex partners. You exposed these women—and ruined families and reputations and careers—in order to intimidate those who would raise their voices against you. You introduced issues that had no relationship whatsoever to the fact that you planted in the bodies of these women instruments of death, of mutilation, of disease.[92]

A.H. Robins pursued a creative and desperate course of settlement offers with injured women in their efforts to defend themselves in litigation and avoid a class-action suit. After a jury in 1979 awarded Carrie Palmer, who had almost died from a septic abortion with the Dalkon Shield in place, $6.2 million in punitive damages, settlement offers increased from the initial meager $11,000 to about $40,000 per case.[93] However, in 1983, Brenda Strempke, who suffered from infertility as a result of the shield, was awarded $1.5 million in punitive damages, and later, Loretta Tetuan, who had a hysterectomy in her twenties as a result of the damage caused by pelvic inflammatory disease resulting from the shield, won $7.5 million in punitive damages from a Kansas jury.[94] These jury awards and the accompanying negative publicity raised the stakes considerably. In 1983, U.S. district court Judge Miles Lord consolidated the 23 Dalkon shield cases that were on his docket into one trial to speed up discovery and the trials. He demanded that A.H. Robins turn over to the plaintiff all of the documents and memos related to the testing and safety of the Dalkon Shield—documents that showed a pattern of mismanagement, irregularities, and cover-ups and which resulted in the company's decision to seek refuge in bankruptcy court.[95]

Robins's decision to seek bankruptcy protection was designed to settle the cases with as little damage as possible to the stockholders and to bring the case to their hometown of Richmond, Virginia, where they had a friendly relationship with the judge, Judge Merhinge, and where A.H. Robins, maker of Robitussin and Chapstick, was a significant contributor to the economic well-being of the community.[96]

This bankruptcy litigation is important in its own right, but it is also important because the Plaintiffs Steering Committee and Dow Corning and other breast implant manufacturers used it as the model in structuring the bankruptcy settlement before Judge Pointer in the breast implant litigation.[97] In both instances, the women who were damaged were forced to accept a payment structure that gave priority to the least seriously damaged women but provided them with only minimal compensation from the company. Nearly 100,000 women who had Dalkon Shields received a paltry settlement of $725 after being convinced that they might receive nothing if they did not settle or would have to wait years for compensation.[98] During this time, A.H. Robins was sold to American Home Products (AHP), the producer of the diet drug Fen-Phen. AHP agreed to establish a fixed-value trust fund of $2.38 billion to pay Dalkon Shield claimants, and with the unknowns of the bankruptcy and litigation settled, the bankruptcy proved to be a winning financial strategy for A.H. Robins, though not for the women who were injured. Stock value quadrupled from what it was before the bankruptcy, an enormous boon to Robins stockholders, particularly the top corporate executives and the family, who owned the majority of the stock.[99]

During the four years the Dalkon Shield was on the market, Robins sold about 2.86 million of them in the United States, and these were implanted in about 2.2 million women. In addition, about 1.71 million were distributed in 79 countries, approximately 1 million of which were implanted.[100] Although it was finally removed from the market and eventually recalled in this country, Robins dumped Dalkon Shields in some 40 Third World countries. The staggering thing about this has been the involvement of the U.S. Government's Office of Population with the AID. The Dalkon Shield was purchased at discount rates for assistance to developing countries by the Agency for International Development (AID) and, more surprisingly, Robins sold unsterilized Dalkon Shields in bulk packages at a 48 percent discount to AID, an unconscionable move on both of their parts.[101]

SILICONE GEL BREAST IMPLANTS

Breast implants are a particularly lucrative form of plastic surgery, con-stituting almost half of the business at most plastic surgeons' offices and bringing in over $300 million a year.[102] Based on the deep-seated and widely supported view that women are inherently inadequate, the breast implant industry provides bigger, better, perkier breasts in order to help women overcome disability, feel better, compete better in the marriage market, or regain some of the value they lost as a result of aging. Plastic surgeons worked intimately with the manufacturers in the testing and pro-duction of these devices, often ignoring warnings about their potential danger, continuing to implant them in women's bodies with absolutely no assurance that they were safe.

Long before breast implants were developed by enterprising doctors, silicone injections were used, initially by Japanese prostitutes during World War II to attract the American servicemen who were accustomed to larger-breasted American women, and then by dancers and entertainers in Nevada and California. In the early 1960s, after it became clear that liquid silicone caused horrific disfigurement, illness, and sometimes death, it was banned in the United States.[103] Researchers then worked on developing a shell that would contain the liquid silicone and could be inserted into the breast, through the nipple or under the arm, placed either behind the chest muscle or in front of it. This silicone was presented as medical grade, and the implant was touted as a completely safe medical device; if broken, it would spill harmless silicone into the woman's body.[104]

While claiming that these were "lifetime products," manufacturers pri-vately harbored some concerns. For example, an internal memo from the manufacturer 3M in 1977 declared that "virtually no documented safety and efficacy data exist on McGhan's implant product."[105] Not knowing whether they were safe, doctors and manufacturers nevertheless worked hand in glove, trying them out in their women patients to see how they worked. Documents produced during the discovery phase of litigation reveal that the corporations were aware of safety problems; concealed information; misled the FDA, doctors, and women; and directed more effort at keeping these dangerous products on the market than at develop-ing a safe and effective product that met their product claims.

The corporations, some doctors, the AMA, and the American Society of Plastic and Reconstructive Surgeons (ASPRS) worked tirelessly to con-vince the FDA and the public that implants were a health necessity, a claim that the FDA eventually bought. They developed a disease diagnosis for small breasts, micromastia, and submitted that this disease caused significant problems in living for women, requiring the corrective intervention of plastic surgeons. To quote one of the ASPRS documents: "There is a common misconception that the enlargement of the female breast is not necessary for maintenance of health or treatment of disease. There is a substantial and enlarging body of medical information and opinion, however, to the effect that these deformities (small breasts) are really a disease which in most patients results in feelings of inadequacy, lack of self-confidence, distortion of body image and a total lack of well-being due to a lack of self-perceived femininity."[106] In addition, they were able to convince the FDA to weaken the warnings to women about the hazards that implants posed to their health, for example, changing the word *cancer* to *lesion*, and changing "closed capsulotomy must not be performed," in the original consent form, to "while the FDA and manufacturers recommend against closed capsulotomy, some physicians, based on clinical experience, feel that closed capsulotomy is an appropriate treatment in some patients."[107] Closed capsulotomy is a procedure in which a breast is forcefully manipulated and pressed to rupture the scar tissue. It is often extremely painful and can rupture the envelope containing the silicone gel, causing it to leak into the body.

Breast implants provide a good example of the relationship between the FDA and corporate scientists that may be beneficial for the corporations but disastrous for consumers. Manufacturers worked to convince the FDA to keep breast implants on the market by manipulating the safety data and covering up their knowledge that the implants were not safe, but the FDA was reluctant to push the corporations to provide the safety studies that it needed.[108] The manufacturers, the AMA, and the ASPRS convinced the FDA that implants were essential to the health and well-being of women, going so far as to define small breasts as a painful and destructive disease that posed a grave public health threat to thousands of American women.[109] They accomplished this without presenting one study showing that implants were safe. That doctors had a stake in getting implants approved seemed to go unnoticed, but breast implants were a lucrative business, making up about $300 million of plastic surgeons' income in 1992 alone.

For at least 15 years, the FDA and the manufacturers misled the public, particularly women, about the safety of implants. Despite their concerns about safety, the corporations worked assiduously with the ASPRS and the AMA to prevent regulation by the FDA. This involved enormous lobbying and public relations efforts, as well as funding of studies designed to aid the corporations in their litigation by showing no relationship between silicone gel and autoimmune diseases women were claiming to have as a result of their implants. During the years from 1988, when the FDA demanded safety studies from the corporations, to 1992, when the implants were finally virtually removed from the market, the FDA did nothing to demand responsible behavior from the manufacturers. Furthermore, when women began to sue the corporations for their illnesses and disfigurements, the FDA cooperated with the corporations, keeping hundreds of documents about the safety of implants secret until forced to make them public by U.S. district judge Stanley Sporkin in 1990.[110] The cooperative relationship between the FDA and the corporations could reasonably lead to the conclusion that "the regulatory agency appears to be more concerned with the safety of the corporations than the safety of consumers."[111]

When it became clear that the implants were going to be removed from the U.S. market, corporations began dumping the implants on foreign markets just as they had with the Dalkon Shield, Rely tampon, and other products that were more highly regulated in the United States than in other markets.

While the extent of problems caused by breast implants is still unknown, implant manufacturers have long been aware of the possibility of serious consequences, including both local and systemic autoimmune problems.[112] There are a number of local complications tied to silicone gel implants, including hardening of the breast, rashes, disfigurement, numbness, and migration of silicone to the neck, arms, and shoulders. The autoimmune and systemic diseases include joint pain, muscle pain, fatigue, fever, rashes, hair loss, dry eyes and other mucous membranes, and abdominal discomfort. In addition, a number of studies have reported a relationship between silicone breast implants and connective tissue diseases, lupus, scleroderma, arthritis, and rheumatism.[113] Documents produced during discovery in two high-profile cases (*Mahlum v. Dow Chemical*, 1995, and *Merlin v. 3M*, 1996) clearly indicate the degree to which manufacturers purposely concealed problems.[114] In one telling memo of May 20, 1976, Don McGhan of 3M wrote to Dr. Michael Purdue: "Your desire to have a soft mammary implant is getting a bit out of hand—the tissue strength of the bag has been reduced."[115] The Meme brand implant too was inadequately studied, relying on an 18-month follow-up of only 81 Meme implant recipients in one study and one short-cut animal study conducted on beagles in another.[116] In 1976, Congress had toughened the FDA medical device regulations, now mandating that device manufacturers would be required to prove the safety of their products before putting them on the market. This is the regulation the breast implant manufacturers were dreading; they worked against the clock to get their devices marketed before its passage so that they could be grandfathered in and would not have to be tested before being marketed.

The carelessness the manufacturers exhibited in their rush to market is illustrated by the shocking finding that the polyurethane foam used in some implants, touted as safe medical-grade polyurethane, was in fact produced by Scotfoam Corporation for industrial applications, including furniture upholstery, oil filters, and carburetors.[117] Ed Griffith, product manager of Scotfoam Corporation, was alarmed when he discovered this: "My eyes popped out when Powell, a Cooper Surgical Vice President, explained that his company was buying the foam from a jobber in Los Angeles and using it as a covering for a breast implant. They had been using our foam for many years and it was the first time that I or anyone else at the company had heard about it."[118] While manufacturers knew that implants bled (leaked or seeped) and suspected that gel migrating to other parts of the body caused trouble, they continued to stress their strength, durability, and safety, as well as to insist that they would last a lifetime. Most of the research on implants concludes that they actually have a very high failure rate—between 30 and 40 percent by the most modest estimates, compared with, for example, a 2 percent failure rate for knee implants or a 1 percent failure rate for corneal implants.[119]

Internal memos from one of the major implant manufacturers, Heyer-Schulte Corporation, acknowledged that corporations were well aware of other problems: "problems with physical migration, including liver dysfunction and foreign body granuloma in four victims of silicone injection," which would be similar to silicone migrating from the implant to other parts of the body. A 3M memo warned that "histological studies suggest that gel bleed of silicone has been found in the capsule and may be a prime candidate: causing or contributing to capsular contracture."[120] However, reflecting the precedence of profit over safety, 3M/McGhan finally concluded that further safety testing was simply "not worth the effort."[121] The manufacturers seemed to conclude that the low tear strength of the silicone shell used as the envelope for the silicone gel was simply a "regrettable characteristic."[122]

Epidemiological studies designed to assess the safety of breast implants were initiated only as a result of efforts of corporations to defend themselves in litigation in the 1990s, and in the case of Dow Corning, this was only *after* they had decided to cease the manufacture of implants.[123] The studies, conducted decades after the implants were manufactured and sold, were designed as a legal defense measure rather than as a premarket safety study. Corporations involved in litigation not only funded the studies and participated in their design, but then relied on them as evidence in ongoing litigation. As stipulated by James R. Jenkins, Dow Corning's general counsel and vice president, "[Each] external scientific study that Dow funded was only after consulting with legal counsel to determine its impact on the breast implant litigation."[124]

The two studies relied on most heavily to provide the foundation for the epidemiological case against the causal relationship between silicone gel breast implants and autoimmune disease are referred to as the Harvard Nurses Study and the Mayo Study.[125] Dow and other manufacturers gave the ASPRS approximately $7 million, which was funneled to the Mayo Clinic for research on breast implants.[126] On the one hand, Dow claimed that the money was a normal research contribution, while on the other it claimed it as a defense expense in bankruptcy documents. Jenkins revealed, "In order to defend itself against silicone breast implant claims, Dow Corning funded or contributed funding to a number of internal and external studies which were intended to provide the epidemiological data necessary to defend against allegations of breast implant plaintiffs that their breast implants caused certain diseases."[127] Dow also paid consulting fees to authors and reviewers of the Harvard Nurses Study, including Laing, Schur, and Colditz, with Laing serving as a consultant for the defense and Schur agreeing to serve as a witness for implant manufacturers.[128] In depositions, Laing admitted to providing Dow with information about the Harvard Nurses Study while the study was in progress, another indication of involvement on the part of the corporations in the ongoing research that they then presented as neutral science.[129]

While the corporations claim an arms-length relationship with the research, Dr. Jorge Litvak, in the *Journal of the American Medical Association*, argues: "While research from private industry is to be commended, in this particular case, financial support was received from Dow Corning, one of the manufacturers of silicone breast implants. This company has been in litigation regularly in the last few years as defendants in the center of the controversy. The lawyers for the company provide, consistently, as their main arguments, data from published articles that seem to favor their position."[130] The statement of the authors of this study that "these data are compatible with prior reports from other cohort studies that exclude a large hazard" will certainly be used again by the lawyers from the company that supported this study in part.[131]

After several stunning losses before juries and with thousands of women involved in a mass litigation, Dow Corning filed for protection under Chapter 11 bankruptcy just as A. H. Robins had done when threatened by large numbers of lawsuits by damaged women. The reorganization and settlement with the creditors, including the women who had been injured, required a payment plan. This plan compensated women according to their placement on a grid indicating the degree of injury or illness they suffer as a result of implants. Many of the attorneys who represented the plaintiffs agreed to settle the case with Dow Corning in order to get some compensation for the women and for themselves. The federal government and women from Nevada initially refused to support the settlement, insisting through their team of attorneys, Geoffrey White and John White, that the successful Mahlum case against Dow Chemical provided them with the right to opt out of the settlement and to fight their cases in court.[132]

Silicone gel breast implants were allowed back on the market in the United States in 2006.[133] Concerns about the safety of implants have been dispelled for the most part by the results of the long-term safety studies required by the FDA of the breast implant manufacturers. With the 2013 approval of the Natrelle 410 breast implant, there are now three companies manufacturing silicone gel breast implants Allergan, Mentor, and Sientra.[134] The problems reported in the follow-up studies include breast pain, hardening of the implant area (capsular contracture), changes in nipple sensation, rupture, infection and the need for additional surgery. These studies have not reported system diseases, but the likelihood of rupture or leakage has led to the warning that breast implant are not lifetime devices. The FDA points out that many of the changes to the woman's breast as a result of implants are irreversible and that she should remain alert to possible breast changes and problems. The FDA recommends MRI screenings every three years because ruptures may not be noticeable to the patient. The review conducted by the Institute of Medicine concluded that the predominance of the evidence did not show a causal relationship between silicone gel breast implants and particular autoimmune diseases.[135] In addition, the National Science Panel, established by Judge Pointer in the bankruptcy settlement hearings he oversaw between the plaintiffs and the corporations, reached the conclusion that the research did not show a causal relationship between silicone gel breast implants and autoimmune disease.[136] In a thorough review of the research, the Institute of Medicine concluded that the silicone in breast implants does not provide a basis for health concerns. Yet there is reason for extreme caution. Women's bodies have often been subject to the types of dangerous interventions we are discussing, and they are often assured that these are beneficial and safe. The FDA allowed the implants on the market if the companies conducted follow-up studies when a far better plan would have been to follow a cohort of women who had implants from the time they were removed from the market to the time they were being considered for approval in order to specifically trace the health consequences of breast implants. Given the fact that one in five implants has to be removed within 3 years and that most break within 10 to 15 years and that removal and reimplantation are usually not covered by insurance,[137] it would seem sensible to have delayed approval until the results were both better and better known. During my interviews with women who had breast implants, many of them revealed their bodies to me, showing bodies misshapen and disfigured by the implants they had removed because of the various illnesses they suffered. My hope is that other women will use caution in choosing breast implants, recognizing that FDA approval does not mean that the implants are safe, but that the supposed benefits outweigh the risks associated with them.[138] Another hope is that women will begin to depend less on their body for their feelings of self-worth.

THE FEN-PHEN DIET

Most women's magazines have two themes: weight loss and food. A recipe for a mouth-watering dessert shares the cover with the most recent guaranteed way to lose 10 pounds in two days and keep it off. The weight-loss industry in the United States is a multibillion-dollar industry. Americans want a quick, sure, painless, and safe way to lose weight that does not involve the tedium or sacrifice of exercise and reasonable eating habits.[139]

In 1992, Dr. Michael Weintraub completed a four-year study at the University of Rochester in which he concluded that using two weight-loss drugs, fenfluramine and phentermine, together, one in the morning and the other in the evening, would result in greater weight loss than either alone without the side effects of drowsiness and diarrhea that accompanied fenfluramine alone.[140]

The Fen-Phen diet was an immediate success. Drug companies that had been producing these drugs for years with modest profits suddenly saw their profits skyrocket. Fen-Phen was marketed by Interneuron Pharmaceuticals and Wyeth-Ayerst Laboratories, the pharmaceutical division of American Home Products (AHP), under the names Pondimin and Redux. However, the FDA had never approved the combined use of the product.[141] AHP had begun marketing Pondimin in 1989 and was aware of the role of fenfluramine in causing a fatal condition, primary pulmonary hypertension (PPH), a rare but potentially fatal cardiopulmonary disease.[142] The symptoms of PPH include shortness of breath, loss of stamina, and swelling in the lower extremities. In fact, AHP knew of the problems within months of acquiring Pondimin (fenfluramine) from Servier, the French company that initially manufactured fenfluramine, because Servier had specifically notified AHP that the labeling on the product bottle was probably inadequate and needed to be revised.[143] Nevertheless, executives waited several years before updating the warning label on their product. Not only did AHP not indicate to doctors the true number of deaths from fenfluramine, always insisting on 4 rather than the actual 62 of which they were aware, but according to Wyeth's own medical department, they contrived to present findings about the safety of fenfluramine alone, although they knew that the most effective and most frequently recommended use of it was in lethal combination with phentermine.[144] They knew that the Fen-Phen diet was neither effective nor safe for long-term weight loss (over 12 weeks), but they knew that it would be used for months. AHP counted on doctors' inattention to any warnings, suggesting that "a weight maintenance positioning strategy is still possible with a primary pulmonary hypertension warning because physicians may overlook the warning as they currently do with other drugs."[145]

The company avoided reporting the problems tied to Fen-Phen through callous manipulation of their data; they eliminated listing problem areas on their checklist of "Serious Adverse Effects." They removed from or did not include in the safety checklist most of the terms that would call attention to PPH or other heart problems:"valvular heart disease," "aortic insufficiency," "cardiovascular disease," or "mitral valve." They did not have a term in the safety surveillance system for any form of valvular heart disease, so none of these problems could be tracked.[146] AHP took the approach of protecting itself and its profits through telling only the parts of the story that benefitted it.

Shortly after the Fen-Phen diet came on the market, neuroscientists, based on their knowledge of brain cell damage and PPH in the United States and Europe, particularly Belgium and France, were concerned enough to call for an FDA special panel to review the safety data.[147] AHP knew that if the FDA's significant safety concerns about Fen-Phen were translated into a "black box" warning (a caution to doctors about the severe side effects, including death) on the drug, sales would be seriously affected. They were motivated to conceal any problems with the drug given that their market research indicated that consumers were unwilling to accept any risk just to take a diet drug. They therefore withheld knowledge of problems from doctors and their own medical advisers about the potentially life-threatening damage caused by Fen-Phen.[148]

Not only did the manufacturers conceal their knowledge that their drug was likely to cause valvular heart problems, they did no follow-ups on the reports of problems, and they camouflaged the problems of the diet drug by using the term "pulmonary hypertension," a much milder disease than primary pulmonary hypertension, which is inevitably fatal, when discussing problems tied to the drug. The corporation also camouflaged the amount of damage one could expect from their drug with another sleight of hand; they reported their findings on another drug closely related to fenfluramine, dexfenfluramine, when their tests resulted in positive findings, claiming them as generalizable to fenfluramine. But when their studies resulted in negative results, they claimed the drugs were entirely unrelated and the findings from dexfenfluramine could not be generalized to fenfluramine.[149]

Rather than report the potentially deadly problems related to Fen-Phen, the corporations turned their considerable energies to heavily lobbying the FDA panel that Commissioner David Kessler had formed to convince them that restrictions should not be applied. AHP organized a team to convince the FDA not to require a black box warning and boasted of its "tremendous success" despite the fact that scientific studies showed that the incidence of abnormal heart valve function in Fen-Phen users was as high as 25 percent.[150] AHP boasted that it would "neutralize" any FDA officials who sought to impose a black box warning about PPH or other restrictions on Redux. The first FDA panel voted that there were not enough long-term safety data to recommend approval of Fen-Phen. The corporations then maneuvered a second, reconstituted panel and conducted a full-court press to convince the panel to vote for approval. Political pressure and corporate advocacy, including the help of Alexander Haig, former Secretary of State and Interneuron board member, led to an eventual recommendation by the panel that the benefits outweighed the risks of the drug and a narrow six-to-five vote for approval of Redux.[151]

The panel had not, however, received a full report from AHP, which had not reported the accurate number of PPH cases tied to Fen-Phen, and AHP had not conducted adequate testing to determine the long-term efficacy of Fen-Phen, even though it was being prescribed for long periods of time (over a year). By 1995, Dr. Leo Lutwak at the FDA was so concerned with all the media attention given Fen-Phen that he wanted AHP to discourage the combination use of fenfluramine and phentermine.[152] But because this combination use was driving Pondimin and Redux sales, nothing was done to discourage its long-term use. It was not until 1996 that AHP finally took steps to change the labeling on Pondimin, but it still did not use the black box warning that was recommended by the FDA and that was being used in Europe. To accompany its labeling change, it instead published editorials from paid consultants in the *New England Journal of Medicine* and distributed misleading press releases downplaying the risks of PPH.[153] Not until 1997, with the publication of an article in the *New England Journal of Medicine* by Dr. Heidi Connolly describing the heart valve problem tied to fenfluramine, did the FDA act. In response to an estimate that between 20 and 30 percent of the patients taking Fen-Phen had a very rare heart condition and that others had developed a lung disorder, Redux and Pondimin were taken off the market in late summer 1997.[154] By then, thousands of women and men had been damaged by a diet drug that not only caused them harm, but that was not effective in long-term weight loss.[155] Over a thousand people sued AHP for valvular defects and PPH resulting from their use of these products. AHP was willing to cause significant harm to thousands of people in this country alone with a drug it knew to be unsafe and ineffective. The company, with its eye firmly on the bottom line, had ignored warnings from the French manufacturer of the drug, its own medical advisers, and its own in-house counsel, and continued to market its product to doctors and the public without proper warning.

THE MARRIAGE OF CONVENIENCE BETWEEN CORPORATIONS AND REGULATORY AGENCIES

In 1938, the Federal Food, Drug, and Cosmetic Act, a response to a scandal caused when over a hundred deaths were traced to a liquid sulfa drug whose manufacturer had never tested its main component for safety, gave the FDA authority to judge the safety of new drugs. This act strengthened the FDA's control over drugs, requiring that all new drugs be approved by the agency before being sold.[156] The restrictions on drugs were more severe than those on medical devices, and manufacturers had a significant stake in keeping it that way. In 1962, after the tragic results of thalidomide, a sedative given during pregnancy, the FDA's role was strengthened and expanded to include the consideration of efficacy or effectiveness of the drug for different purposes.[157]

However, as long as a product was designated a device rather than a drug, it was the responsibility of the government to prove it was not safe, and this could be done only after it was on the market. The rapid technological advances of the late 1950s and early 1960s meant that such complex and sophisticated things as contact lenses, pacemakers, heart valves, kidney dialysis machines, and other complicated devices were put on the market with no prior approval by the FDA. In 1968, the U.S.

Court of Appeals for the Second Judicial District ruled that a product used
to suture severed blood vessels during surgery was a drug, not a device, a
ruling that established the protection of public health as a justification for
allowing the FDA to expand its regulatory power. In 1976, after the
Dalkon Shield debacle, the FDA gained increased oversight of medical
devices, requiring corporations to submit safety studies. Unfortunately,
however, the FDA still did not determine the safety of devices until they
were already on the market.

The complex ties between corporations and regulatory agencies sometimes result in blatant efforts to manipulate regulations. The FDA has
been severely criticized for its inadequate response to conflicting interests
between its reviewers and manufacturers of pharmaceutical and medical
devices, as well as for its response to manufacturer lobbying to speed the
process of approval of new drugs.[158] Yet, given the intermeshing of the
various regulatory agencies of the state, one can anticipate such a conflict.
Regulatory agencies are often staffed by corporate scientific decision
makers whose sympathies may lie as much with those they are supposed
to regulate as with those they are to protect. Nicholas Regush reviews
the dangers posed to the public as a result of pharmaceutical company
pressure on the FDA in the United States, illustrating this problem by
the slow and inadequate response of the FDA to reports of problems with
Viagra.[159] Charles Edwards, president of Scripps Clinic and Research
Foundation and a former FDA commissioner, reported that the problems
with the FDA's process were so severe that they posed a threat to public
health.[160] We saw in the case of DES, the Dalkon Shield, and breast
implants that the FDA's response to problems was so slow that hundreds,
sometimes thousands, of women were at risk for injury, illness, or even
death before they acted. In fact, Congress had to push the FDA to act in
the case of both the Dalkon Shield and breast implants.[161] Congressman
Ted Weiss and Diane Zuckerman, executive director of the National
Center for Policy Research for Women and Families, were so concerned
with the FDA's sympathies for the corporations and their reluctance to
release information to the public about silicone gel breast implants that
they conducted an investigation of the FDA, concluding that its response
was inadequate to protect the safety of the women and children affected
by these implants.[162]

Despite the regulatory powers of the FDA, the interdependent networks
that so closely link corporations, government, and law in the United States
have a powerful impact on the willingness and ability of the FDA to regulate consumer products and often result in harmful products being allowed
on the market, only to be removed after they have proven harmful.

Voluntary recalls of products are usually more cost-effective than presale testing of products, providing little motivation to ensure product safety before they hit the market.[163] When anticipating a recall, a company may reasonably delay as long as possible in order to get rid of its stock of product, weighing the delay against the potential costs of lawsuits. For example, "the harm done by the anti-inflammatory drugs Oraflex and Zomax finally led them to be withdrawn from the market and provoked congressional criticism of the FDA's drug approval process. In both cases, the manufacturers acted only after adverse reactions and looming publicity made continued marketing infeasible."[164]

Corporations have long been successful in having their views integrated into dominant political ideology, thereby shaping the way the state defines and responds to crime: "It is in the best interest of the state to protect and preserve the dominant means of production—the corporate system."[165] We can see the meshing of corporate interests and regulatory reluctance to limit commerce in our acceptance of the concept "on-the-job accident" or "nuclear accident" when it might be more reasonable to see these outcomes as related to negligence on the part of the corporation, or cost-cutting efforts, or resistance to responding to plant weaknesses and signs of danger because of potential vulnerability to lawsuits, as seems to have been the case in the recent nuclear incident at the Fukushima Daiichi nuclear plant run by the Tokoyo Electric Power Company. In this instance, a tsunami and severe earthquake resulted in extreme flooding, leading to damage to the plant and reactors causing chemical explosions and reactor core meltdowns, resulting in the evacuation of over 300,000 people as a result of radioactive contamination. Cleanup of the contaminated area will take decades and will cost over $100 billion.[166]

Each year, thousands of U.S. workers die in job-related accidents, and hundreds of thousands die of work-related illnesses.[167] These deaths result from unsafe working conditions, job demands for increased production, and damaging work environments, and they disproportionately affect racial minorities, who end up in the dirtiest, hardest, and most dangerous jobs. To call them accidents resulting from carelessness of the employee, as is so often done, ignores the characteristics of the unregulated labor market that allow for such hazardous work conditions. But "the ability of corporations to deflect responsibility and accountability is a direct consequence of the economic and political power they wield."[168] It is in the best interest of the state to protect and preserve the dominant means of production, which is the corporate system, and when the pursuit of profit is the overriding interest of a corporation, negative consequences of such a pursuit are likely to be seen as accidental or unavoidable outcomes rather than corporate crime.

It is not only in the United States that governmental regulatory agencies are intertwined with the corporations they are supposed to regulate. Controversy within the Canadian Health Services was widely publicized and proved a clear demonstration of the intimate ties between regulatory agencies and corporations. Six scientists at the health protection branch, who were guardians of the biomedical products of the nation, complained that their superiors tried to force them to approve the genetically engineered bovine growth hormone despite their concerns about its safety.[169] Monsanto, the manufacturer of the hormone, was accused of offering health department officials research money they interpreted as a bribe, an allegation the company denies. The Royal Canadian Mounted Police are also investigating Health Canada, the health protection branch responsible for regulating the blood donor system, about the tainted blood tragedy of the 1980s in which thousands of Canadians were infected with the AIDS virus and hepatitis C. They are investigating the destruction of key documents by Health Canada officials, including a report from the federal information commissioner finding that officials destroyed what might have been critical evidence as a result of pressure from the Red Cross, which feared victims would use the documents to support their lawsuits. Health Canada is also being investigated to determine whether officials approved the Meme breast implant despite their knowledge of significant safety problems. A grievance filed by the six scientists, who claim that pharmaceutical manufacturers have too much influence in the drug approval process, mirrors earlier complaints about Health Canada. Scientists charge that their careers are threatened if they stand in the way of approval of a drug they do not believe is safe and that managers without scientific experience regularly overrule their decisions about drug approval. They complain that Health Canada is presenting the industry as the client to be served rather than the consumer. Margaret Haydon, one of the six scientists bringing the grievance against Health Canada, told of her files being broken into after she recommended against drug approval. And Michelle Brill-Edwards, a physician who quit the health protection branch in 1996, said that scientists who raise questions about new drugs are viewed as troublemakers, while those who quietly approve them are promoted. She charged that the health protection branch was putting the interests of the pharmaceutical companies ahead of public safety.[170]

An investigation of the "regulatory-industrial complex" in the United States concluded that regulatory agencies ignore corporate crime because: (1) industry entertains agency personnel; (2) formal advisory groups, which are arranged by the agency but consist mainly of corporate representatives, advise against pursuing charges; (3) lobbying efforts are successful; (4) personnel interchanges occur between corporations and agencies; and (5) corporations make political contributions to legislators able to influence agency appropriations and appointments.[171] Further, as was true in the Health Canada scandal, the Review Panel on Drug Regulation in the United States found that the FDA was managed by individuals who had consciously decided that the agency would be cooperative with, rather than adversarial toward, the pharmaceutical industry.[172] The review panel concluded that dissenters were effectively suppressed, primarily by resorting to involuntary transfers.

The FDA has incurred a great deal of criticism from both manufacturers and pharmaceutical companies who insist that the tedious process of regulation prohibits beneficial and potentially lifesaving medical devices and drugs from being made available to an eager public. They are also criticized by those who see the FDA as tainted by its associations with its applicants and subject to influence peddling from the corporations. In each of the cases examined in this chapter, the FDA's relationship with the corporations that manufactured or marketed the drugs or devices can be criticized for seriously jeopardizing the concerns of consumers in favor of the interests of the corporations. A corporation willing to use concealment, deception, and distortion can manipulate and defeat the regulatory mechanisms of the government, while using the government to cover up corporate wrongdoing, relying on the FDA's friendly relationship and intimate ties with those corporations.[173]

CORPORATIONS AND THE MEDICAL PROFESSION

The power of corporations can also be seen in the intimate ties they have with physicians. In each of the cases we are discussing, the medical establishment was involved with the corporations in the testing and marketing of their products. Their involvement was somewhat different in each case, and their relationship with the corporate manufacturer varied, but they were mutually interdependent in the process of delivery of the product to the patient. The corporations were sensitive to the response of physicians to their products, because it is on them that they depend for their sales. Hence, for example, the attention on the part of AHP to the endocrinologists whose view that obesity was an inherited disease could be helpful in the sale of Pondimin and Redux.

From the very beginning, physicians used women as a testing ground. Rather than test the Dalkon Shield, DES, or breast implants for safety, the process of introducing chemicals and foreign objects into women's bodies was one of cooperative give and take between physicians and manufacturers. In the case of breast implants, plastic surgeons worked closely with Dow Corning and other manufacturers not only in the production process but also in the effort to convince the FDA to keep silicone gelfilled breast implants on the market. While some doctors reported severe problems of rupture and bleed with breast implants, the medical profession as a whole, including the AMA and the ASPRS, fought on the front lines with the manufacturers to keep silicone breast implants on the market and to convince the women, the FDA, and eventually juries that they were well tested, safe products.[174] Manufacturers worked with plastic surgeons to perfect the implants, taking suggestions from surgeons about the problems their patients were experiencing back to the drawing board, refining or redesigning the implants, and again providing them to the doctors to test. One plastic surgeon, Dr. Richard Grossman, author of an early text on how to perform breast augmentation surgery, notified the FDA that "for years it has been the custom and practice of manufacturers to modify the implants based on ideas of surgeons and then try out these custommade prototypes on women to 'see how they worked.' "[175] Doctors relied heavily on the manufacturers' sales materials and asked for little independent verification. They were, after all, making the majority of their income from implants in many instances and would be motivated to ignore problems. Some doctors, with the knowledge of the manufacturers, even cut open the implant and inserted the silicone gel directly into the woman's body, knowing that liquid silicone had been outlawed decades earlier.[176]

A similar intimacy between doctors and pharmaceutical companies is revealed in the case of the Fen-Phen diet, which damaged so many women. Doctors exhibited an unbridled enthusiasm for the diet products Pondimin and Redux, relying without careful scrutiny on sales representatives' presentations and manufacturers' advertising. Although the longterm effects of these drugs had not been studied and their combined use and interactions with other drugs had not been analyzed, between May and September 1996, as a result of a multimillion-dollar promotion of Redux in medical journals and over 285,000 visits by representatives of AHP to physicians' offices, doctors were writing 85,000 prescriptions a week. During this three-month period, approximately 18 million prescriptions for Redux and Pondimin were written, with the hope for annual sales of Redux of more than $1 billion. These drugs were removed from the market a year later, but only after hundreds of thousands of people had been exposed to cardiopulmonary damage.[177]

The relationship between A. H. Robins and the physicians in the case of the Dalkon Shield was an exception to the way the corporation usually worked with doctors. In this instance, the corporation claimed that the women's problems had nothing to do with the IUD, despite the fact that the shield had many more problems than any of the other IUDs on the market. Robins claimed that the women's problems were a result of negligence on the part of the doctors; doctors had perforated the uterus or introduced bacteria into the uterus or caused other damage to the woman during the insertion of the device. This tactic caused Robins some significant problems during litigation.[178]

Institutional responses to women who are victims of corporate or individual crime are inadequate and destructive. Just as district attorneys and police detectives often do not believe the woman when she charges rape and accuse her, especially if she is poor, black, a prostitute, or in some other way unacceptable, of revenge or lying, women with implants who are sick are often accused of malingering or exaggerating. In a review of physicians' responses to these women, I found that doctors frequently viewed these patients as hysterical, menopausal, exaggerating, or mentally ill. In each of these instances, the woman's response was invalidated, often through infantilizing her, often through discrediting her complaints or symptoms.[179] Attorneys too, many of whom made a small fortune on the breast implant litigation, grew weary of the losses and found it increasingly difficult to encourage women to litigate. Women who had horrible infections and pain from their IUDs were often dismissed by their doctors. Doctors initially accused the women of poor hygiene, or of exaggerating their pain, or, in some instances in which the IUD had been expelled, of pulling it out themselves. And DES daughters are often perceived by the medical profession as having emotional rather than physical problems. These second- and third-generation DES daughters face fear or illness on an ongoing basis and harbor anger about their infertility or the pain and physical deformities they have suffered, characteristics that make them vulnerable to rejection and criticism by others, including their physicians.

ADVERTISING AND PUBLIC RELATIONS

Manufacturers spend significant amounts of money on public relations campaigns, first to sell their product to women and doctors and then to defend themselves in court or to improve their public image. Corporations wish to convince the public that their products are safe and that they are following the demands of the marketplace by offering an important product. Early in the breast implant controversy, Dow Corning hired Burson-Marstellar, the largest PR firm in the world, to help with its public relations crisis.[180] The firm developed strategies to generate support for

Dow in the media and in public opinion before the 1991 congressional hearings to determine whether implants should be restricted. Burson-Marstellar worked intimately with the ASPRS to protect Dow's main product, silicone. It launched two major studies, at New York University and the University of Michigan; held private meetings with influential breast implant surgeons; and spoke at meetings of breast implant surgeons warning them of the possibility of FDA restrictions. It developed a grass-roots program to influence Commissioner David Kessler and the FDA, establishing the goal of "getting women angry about having the right to make their own decision about implants taken away from them."[181] It outlined several strategies for accomplishing these goals. One was to work with patient groups, especially breast cancer support groups, because they "engender more sympathy."[182] Grassroots campaigns such as this are a PR "strategy which uses corporate wealth to subsidize orchestrated mass campaigns that put seemingly independent citizens on the front lines as activists for corporate causes."[183] Dow Corning trained patients to write letters to the FDA and Congress and local newspapers and to speak to local groups about the importance of keeping implants on the market. Burson-Marstellar planned a "fly-in" to Washington for the FDA hearings in November 1991, paying the expenses of women from cancer support groups such as Y-Me and the Susan B. Komen Foundation to testify before the FDA and to lobby their congressional representatives.[184] In addition to these direct efforts to influence decision makers, Burson-Marstellar advised Dow to hire Griffin Bell, former U.S. attorney general under President Carter, to perform an "independent review" of the company. They wanted it to be "somewhat tough" on the corporation, asserting that such a review would allow the company to demonstrate that it has "credibility, responsiveness, a willingness to change."[185]

After the FDA restricted the manufacture and sale of implants, corporations increased their public relations efforts in an effort to get the products back on the market. Burson-Marstellar advised that Dow would need to produce scientific data from seemingly independent "third-party" sources that it could point to as proof that silicone was safe.[186] It also flooded the newspapers with advertising, letters to the editor, and articles reviewing studies favorable to the corporation. Dow ran ads on television and in newspapers highlighting its "corporate citizenship." One ad focuses on a young girl with a life-saving silicone shunt in her brain. Her mother says, "Silicone is not the problem. The personal injury lawyers and their greed is the problem."[187] Significant losses, including punitive damages in some very high-profile jury trials, influenced their media efforts at the national level and locally to create a more positive environment prior to trials.

A. H. Robins advertised the Dalkon Shield heavily to doctors, who were responsible for insertion and removal of the device. At the same time, the shield was promoted to women through a publicity program directed by Richard L. Wilcox of Wilcox & Williams, a Manhattan public relations firm.[188] The approach was to have women's magazines and major newspapers carry articles and columns on the shield or highlight it in special articles on contraception or women's health. As was the case with breast implants, when A. H. Robins was hit hard by significant punitive damages, it turned its attention to media efforts that would have a positive impact on the litigation.

In its "Prelaunch Marketing Plan" for Redux, AHP outlined the target audiences for its antiobesity drug. It viewed the younger "vanity-driven" potential consumers and the older "worried/health driven" groups, both of whom consisted primarily of women, as their most likely audience. It established an annual budget, including a publication budget of $50,000, speakers' training of $100,000 to change professional attitudes about weight loss, and $150,000 in educational programming (targeting the American Diabetes Association, the American Heart Association, the American College of Obstetrics and Gynecology, and the American Association of Family Practice).[189]

The main professional targets were primary care physicians, internists, obstetricians and gynecologists, and endocrinologists. Endocrinologists accounted for only a small percentage of the prescriptions generally but a higher percentage of Pondimin, and were viewed as having an important role in the commercial success of dexfenfluramine because of their view that obesity is a metabolic disease requiring "continuous care." AHP saw the managed-care business as presenting an obstacle in marketing, primarily being affected by the "risk of primary pulmonary hypertension and the price."[190]

The marketing plan acknowledges that price and potential danger were also concerns of primary care physicians. The marketing division was well aware that primary care physicians are "inclined to use the product for longer terms than other currently used agents and longer than the short term indicated," and they were also aware that their "willingness deteriorates significantly when there is a warning of primary pulmonary hypertension," clearly indicating the problems with a black box warning. While 40 percent of consumers declared they were willing to try dexfenfluramine, this declined to only 7 percent if it was accompanied by risks.[191] AHP therefore created a public view that Redux and Pondimin were safe and effective, issuing highly positive statements about the drugs, never disclosing the heart valve risks of which they were well aware.[192] It continued to mislead the public and its own stockholders by withholding evidence of heart valve abnormalities in patients taking Redux. As a result of misleading statements made in its annual report to stockholders, Interneuron stockholders brought a class-action suit against the company in 1997.[193]

Overall, the most important single source of information about drugs and medical devices for doctors is the pharmaceutical company's sales representatives, although doctors also rely on promotional materials received in the mail, journal advertisements, meetings, conversations at cocktail parties, and conferences. Not surprisingly, Braithwaite writes of corporations as "pushers" in the drug industry, defining problems such as depression as widely as possible, "constructing" new diseases for which a drug is available, and heavily promoting their drugs to doctors, through advertising and expensive perks, such as all-expenses-paid "conferences" in exotic vacation spots, kickbacks, and gifts.[194] Plastic surgeons relied almost exclusively on manufacturers' sales reps' representations to them and advertising brochures in their evaluation of breast implants and passed on to women the false information that the implants were safe, accepting what they heard from salespersons rather than requiring any documentation of their safety. This inexcusable carelessness would prove devastating for thousands of women.

The dissemination of research on medical devices and drugs takes place in powerful peer-reviewed journals, among them the *Journal of the American Medical Association* and the *New England Journal of Medicine*. Articles appearing in these journals are picked up by the national press and are widely disseminated through television and radio news, making these journals important players in the public relations activities of corporations.[195] This is particularly true when authors or editors are also involved in the public and legal debates about the use and meaning of scientific research, as was the case with Marcia Angell, editor of the *New England Journal of Medicine*, and several of the authors of the very influential Mayo and Harvard studies discussed earlier. Prestigious medical journals rely heavily on advertising from pharmaceutical companies. For example, the *New England Journal of Medicine* and the *Journal of the American Medical Association* "had display advertising revenues last year of $19 million and $21.4 million respectively, the vast bulk of it from drug companies."[196] Law professor Joseph Sanders concludes that "it may be that [corporate defenders] are able to buy themselves something that should not be for sale."[197]

Not only do medical journals sometimes have less than an arm's-length relationship with corporations that support them through advertising, the articles published in these journals are sometimes written for the corporations under the guise of neutral scientific reports. Wyeth-Ayerst provides a perfect example; while ignoring the danger tied to its product in conjunction with the efforts to strong-arm the FDA, it was also producing articles for publication in peer-review journals that would support the sales of the product. This corporation, as part of its normal business practice, paid medical ghostwriters to write articles favorable to its drug for doctors for publication in peer-reviewed journals. Dr. Jo Alen Dolan, medical monitor for Wyeth Laboratories, producer of Pondamin and dexfenfluramine, indicates that their marketing efforts were designed to portray obesity as a disease, to influence medical opinion about obesity by having articles published in respected journals, specifically the *American Journal of Medicine* and the *Southern Medical Journal* and in *Business and Health Solutions in Managed Care*.[198] The targeted audiences were managed-care businesses, pharmacists, primary care physicians, nurse practitioners, cardiologists, and physicians assistants. These articles were written by Excerpta Medica for a fee of $20,000 each and attributed to a cooperating doctor who received an honorarium of $1,500 for the use of his name.[199] Never were the laboratories of Wyeth-Ayerst tied to the articles by the authors, although the articles touted the safety and efficacy of drugs the laboratory produced and marketed. And Excerpta Medica did a good job. In fact, Atkinson praised one of the papers "authored" by him, under this agreement in which he received an honorarium for the use of his name, on dexfenfluramine: "I am impressed at the level of understanding of the topic. Perhaps I can get you to write all my papers for me."[200] He did offer one modest reservation: "This piece may make dexfenfluramine sound better than it really is."[201] His concerns were evidently not great enough to outweigh the honorarium he received for attaching his name to an article written by someone else. The reliance on medical ghostwriters hired by the corporation to write articles favorable to their products to increase sales is clearly stated in the following note from Dr. Dolan to Dr. Albert Stunkard accompanying an article that was published in the February 1996 issue of the *American Journal of Medicine*: "Attached please find a review article on obesity authored by Dr. Albert Stunkard which was written by Excerpta Medica under contract with Lederle."[202]

The distinction between professional journals and mainstream media is not as great as it once was. The enormous progress made just during the past decade in such things as mapping the human genetic system and the concerns of Americans with diabetes, obesity, and depression translates almost immediately into news. Certainly the breast implant litigation has been widely discussed in the popular media, as has the Fen-Phen litigation. Some critics believe there is a growing preoccupation on the part of medical journals with grabbing the attention of mainstream media. "Newspapers, magazines, television and radio offer the journals not only a pipeline to the public with a seemingly insatiable appetite for health news, but they also are a source of prestige for the journals and for scientists looking for fame as well as funding. More and more journals are supplying reporters with free or advance copies and mailing out news releases and tip sheets translating into English from 'medicalese' the hottest research of the upcoming issue."[203]

Medical journals, particularly the *Journal of the American Medical Association* and the *New England Journal of Medicine*, are relied on heavily by physicians for information in both article form and advertisements. Just as with *Vogue*, *Glamour*, and other women's magazines, the pages of medical journals are dominated by advertising, with about 85 percent of the journal being advertisements.[204] A glance at these journals reveals the unquestioned assumption that every human emotion, problem, desire, or difficulty can and should be treated medically. Pfizer, for example, promotes a tranquilizer, Vistaaril, for children who are frightened by "school, the dark, separation, dental visits, and monsters."[205] Women, though, are far more likely to be portrayed as needing medical help, particularly help with eating disorders, depression, and other mood disorders. The corporations that manufactured breast implants relied heavily on the view that women's mental health could be improved by these devices. And they were safe. Dow Corning, in a full-page ad in the *Annals of Plastic Surgery* featuring the implant it introduced in 1962, boasted: "By the way, our first implants are still in place today."[206]

The AMA and the Pharmaceutical Manufacturers Association (PMA), the lobbying group for the manufacturers of drugs and devices, form a powerful mutual admiration society, and their ties with the ostensibly neutral peer-reviewed journals can result in the publication of articles solicited by drug companies and supported by them, even as the articles are presented as "science." According to a study conducted by the *Los Angeles Times*, the world's top-ranked medical journal and a leading voice in biomedical ethics, the *New England Journal of Medicine*, violated its own ethics policy numerous times in the past three years by publishing articles by researchers with ties to drug companies and not disclosing the potential conflicts of interest. In an analysis of 36 drug therapy review articles since 1997, the *Los Angeles Times* identified eight articles by researchers with undisclosed financial links to drug companies that marketed treatments evaluated in the articles.[207]

Journals that publish articles or letters supportive of particular drugs can expect to have the advertising support of the corporations. On the other hand, articles critical of their products result in the removal of advertising.[208] The same is true for newspapers that support or condemn companies in their editorial policies or statements. For example, when the *New York Times* ran a series of articles on medical incompetence, including the misuse of prescription drugs, the companies retaliated by canceling half a million dollars' worth of advertising in the *Journal of Modern Medicine*, owned by the *New York Times*, saying, "You don't feed people who beat you up."[209]

The corporations need not become overly concerned. Most newspapers in the United States are owned by corporations and are dependent on corporations for their advertising revenues. The alliance between these corporate structures and corporations that produce or market medical devices and pharmaceuticals is a natural one, as is the allegiance between the corporate media and the major corporate owners of manufacturing companies that have moved to Mexico or the Pacific Rim in the search for cheaper labor and bigger profits.

Journalists for the most part have accepted without question the view that corporate-funded research is the only real science, adopting the manufacturers' framing of the safety and efficacy of drugs and devices. The question for most journalists is not whether women's health is at risk, as one might expect, but whether the corporations are being unfairly treated. Businesses, like Dow and other manufacturers of medical devices and pharmaceuticals, benefit from a "presumption of innocence." "There is no media presumption that a product ought to be proven safe before it is put into a woman's body."[210] For example, the AHP press releases about the safety findings on Fen-Phen products were accepted without question by the press, even though they were full of misrepresentation of the research findings and contained misinformation that the public and physicians relied on, to their extreme detriment.

CIRCLING THE WAGONS

Corporations and physicians respond to the claims of the women just as one would expect: with denial, defense, and blame. One of the most despicable forms of defense used by the corporations is blaming women who have been made sick or disfigured by their product for causing their own problems. This happened in every one of the instances discussed in this chapter, with minor variations on the theme. Women who had breast implants were already easy targets. In this culture in which women are

valued for their bodies, it is still a simple matter to condemn them for trying to improve their bodies. Women are devalued if they are not attractive,
yet if they take advantage of a "safe" procedure to make themselves more
attractive and have the misfortune of becoming sick or disfigured, they are
deprecated. Not only do attorneys for the defense persecute and attempt to
humiliate the women who bring suits against them, the injured women are
reviled by academic research. The *Journal of the American Medical Association* has published a study contrasting several lifestyle factors of
women with implants and those without. Two of the authors of this study
have been expert witnesses for Dow Corning Corporation.[211] They link
lifestyle factors to the illnesses suffered by women with breast implants,
suggesting that women with implants are "hard livers" who drink more,
have more sexual partners and more abortions, and even dye their hair
more often (and, quite likely, less expertly) than other women.[212]

Women who experience problems related to breast implants often
encounter what can only be called a climate of disbelief: their symptoms
are viewed as illustrative of their emotional or mental weakness or are
seen as reflective of the aging process and menopause. Sometimes the
constellation of problems women experience is inexplicable to the doctor,
or symptoms are so numerous that the doctor simply discounts their
account of the situation. Women who continue to insist to their doctors
that they are sick or demand further tests or attention are often met with
hostility and rejection severe enough to dissuade all but the strongest or
most insistent women.

The DES daughters faced a similar situation: they were interrogated
about their sexual habits and history.[213] Despite their severe physical
problems, they are often met by a medical establishment that views their
problems as emotional rather than physical. Their fears of not getting
pregnant and then of what pregnancy brings them are significant. Their
anger about infertility or their pain and physical problems are viewed as
their problem rather than these problems being acknowledged as the cause
of their fear and anger. Each Pap smear causes enormous anxiety, the
women wondering if this will be the time that they are diagnosed with
cancer. They are likely to be infertile; if they do get pregnant, they may
face a pregnancy characterized by fear of a miscarriage or premature
delivery. They are often confined to bed for months or have surgery to
stitch the cervix closed. The number of severely premature deliveries to
DES daughters has caused significant problems for their daughters, creating what has become known as the "third generation of DES victims."[214]

Attorneys for the women who were damaged by the Dalkon Shield grew
accustomed to what they called the "dirty questions." The defense

claimed that the women who experienced septic abortions, miscarriages, stillbirths, deformed and damaged babies, and even death were promiscuous or did not practice good hygiene. They were asked about the numbers of sexual partners they had, the type of sex they engaged in, the number of abortions, the number of out-of-wedlock births, and the direction in which they wiped, with the implication that they had created an unclean or infected internal environment.[215] Many women were discouraged from pursuing their cases because of the embarrassing and humiliating questions they knew they would encounter during deposition and trial. In the Norplant litigation,[216] a similar process occurred with the effort to discredit the women as promiscuous and bringing their injuries on themselves. The effort to dichotomize the women as "good" or "bad" is made relatively easy because the drug under consideration is a form of birth control, just as was the Dalkon Shield, and women who use birth control, especially if they are not married and have multiple partners, are easily disparaged, even while they would be condemned if they became pregnant. Women likely to have Norplants are particularly vulnerable to condemnation because they are likely to be young, poor, or minority women, but all women are vulnerable. When women buy the very products that are designed for them, they are subject to accusations of being unhygienic, hysterical, or in some other way blameworthy.

A large segment of the market population for Fen-Phen was the "vanity market," consisting primarily of women concerned about their desirability and acceptability. These women were prescribed a legal and ostensibly safe substance for their obesity, which had handily been defined as a form of treatable illness. However, as with the other women, when they developed primary pulmonary hypertension, they were viewed as complainers, malingerers, and as bringing this on themselves for having "let themselves go" or, alternately, for "being so vain." A fat woman is not an especially desirable client to take before a jury, who will likely offer her little sympathy and will be quick to condemn her for her slovenliness.

If the corporation is not successful in its defilement of a woman's character in medical journals and academic treatises or in its condemnation of the woman during her deposition or trial, there are still legal tactics available. In some instances, after the corporation has caused damage to women and then denied any responsibility, it then asserts that the woman should have been aware of the problems caused by the product in the first place. The corporations producing Fen-Phen as well as those producing implants claimed protection under Comment k to the Restatement of Torts. Comment k is a proposed immunity for manufacturers of

unavoidably unsafe products and is predicated on a policy that the social
necessity of the product (the benefit) outweighs the unavoidable, inherent
risks of the product.[217] In the breast implant litigation, for example, Dow
Corning assured women and doctors for decades that implants were safe,
fighting tooth and nail to prevent the FDA from classifying them as a
Class III device requiring safety and efficacy testing. Yet it turned around
in an appeal of the Mary Anne Hopkins case and insisted that it should be
protected under Comment k of the Restatement of Torts. Breast implants,
it asserted, were "unavoidably dangerous," and Hopkins should have
cared enough about her body to reject her doctor's advice and seek out
the obscure journals in which negative scientific findings were published.[218] However, the appeals court upheld the punitive damages
awarded by the jury in that case, asserting that Dow had knowingly
exposed thousands of women to a painful and debilitating disease, knowing full well that long-term safety studies were needed, that it concealed
from the public negative conclusions from the few studies it did conduct,
and that it continued to market implants despite knowledge that they were
not safe.[219] Comment k would apply, one would think, only if the manufacturer provided warnings of the health risks so that the user was aware
of the potential danger of the product and could make an informed choice
about its use. But corporations knew that many consumers, if properly
warned, would be unwilling to assume such a risk with their health.

In other instances, the corporations claim that when a woman first suspected that a given product might be causing her problem, she should have
done something about it, despite their denial that there were reasons for
concern, and despite the doctors' assertions that there was no relationship
between her physical complaints and the product and their condemnation
of the women for even wanting them removed, sometimes charging them
twice as much to remove them as they had charged to put them in, according to the video *Completely Safe*.[220] There was so much public sympathy
for the women damaged by DES, however, that legal barriers were
removed so they could pursue their case against the manufacturers. First,
because women could not possibly have known they were damaged at
the time the damage was done, the statute of limitations was eased to
allow them to sue much later, after the relationship between DES and
the damage to the daughters was established. Second, since so many
records were lost (doctors had died, clinics had closed) and the women
did not know which manufacturer had made the product they took, the
companies' share of the damages were prorated to reflect their market
share, and cases were brought against the companies as a whole.

CONCLUSION

The violence perpetrated against women by corporations is essentially the same as the violence women suffer at the hands of individual criminals. The impact of corporate violence and medical violence on the lives of women is at least as powerful as that of rape, harassment, and battery. Women are held responsible for the violence they suffer, and they are often rendered ineffective because they feel responsible for the crime or assault; they incorporate the cultural definitions of blame and responsibility to their distinct disadvantage. Judge Miles Lord acknowledged the extent of medical and corporate sexism in his speech to the highest-level executives of A.H. Robins about responsibility for damaging thousands of women who had used the Dalkon Shield: "I dread to think what would have been the consequences if your victims had been men rather than women, women who seem through some strange quirk of our society's mores, to be expected to suffer pain, shame, and humiliation."[221] The shift from corporate responsibility to blaming the victim is swift and sure, even in the case of diet drugs, where the blame is more diffuse and insidious than in the other cases. Just as with rape and battery, not only are women blamed by others, they blame themselves. The medical sexism to which women are exposed, and the corporate violence they experience as a result, creates an unsafe environment for women at a time when their safety should be of the utmost concern. The health-care industry persists in assaulting women, intensifying the already hostile climate women endure on the streets, in their homes, and in the workplace.

NOTES

1. Nancy Frank and M. Lynch, *Corporate Crime, Corporate Violence: A Primer* (New York: Harrow and Heston, 1992), 17.

2. J. Gerber and S. Weeks, "Women as Victims of Corporate Crime: A Call for Research on a Neglected Topic," *Deviant Behavior: An Interdisciplinary Journal* 13, no. 4 (1992): 325–47.

3. http://www.catalyst.org/knowledge/2011, retrieved July 9, 2013.

4. Ibid. R. W. Connell, *Masculinities* (Berkeley: University of California Press, 1995).

5. R. Sims and M. Spencer, "Understanding Corporate Misconduct: An Overview and Discussion. A Look at Corporate Crime," in *Corporate Misconduct: The Legal, Societal, and Management Issues*, edited by M. Spencer and R. Sims (Westport, CT: Quorum Books, 1995), 1–21.

6. A. Tolson, *The Limits of Masculinity* (New York: Harper and Row, 1977).

7. J. Kilbourne, "Killing Us Softly 3," produced by Sut Jhally (Los Angeles: Media Education Foundation, 2000).

8. C. Sheffield, "Sexual Terrorism," in *Women: A Feminist Perspective* (5th ed.), edited by J. Freeman (Mountain View, CA: Mayfield Press, 1994).

9. Ibid.

10. Ibid.

11. B. Ehrenreich and D. English, *For Her Own Good* (Garden City, NY: Anchor-Doubleday, 1978); see also C. K. Reissman, "Women and Medicalization: A New Perspective," *Social Policy* 14 (1983): 3–18.

12. Kilbourne, "Killing Us Softly 3."

13. S. de Beauvoir, *The Second Sex* (New York: Knopf, 1949); see also A. W. Schaef, *When Society Becomes an Addict* (San Francisco: Harper and Row, 1987); and E. Tseelon, *The Masque of Femininity: The Presentation of Woman in Everyday Life* (Thousand Oaks, CA: Sage, 1995). Interesting discussions on the construction of femininity.

14. N. Regush, "Toxic Breasts," *Mother Jones,* January-February, 1992: 24–31.

15. Almost all of the information for the section on the diet drug Fen-Phen was summarized from court documents obtained during the litigation against American Home Products. Specifically, the reader may refer to proceedings of Mealey's Fen Phen Litigation Conference, as well as the Supplemental Materials, presented at the St. Regis Hotel, October 18–19, 1999, King of Prussia, PA.

16. B. Ehrenreich and D. English, *For Her Own Good: Two Centuries of the Experts' Advice to Women* (New York: Anchor Books, 2005).

17. M. Foucault, *The Birth of the Clinic: An Archaeology of Medical Perceptions* (New York: Pantheon, 1973).

18. *Blum v. Merrell Dow.* 1996. Court of Common Pleas of Philadelphia County, 1027.

19. J. Zones, "The Political and Social Context of Silicone Breast Implant Use in the United States," *Journal of Long-Term Effects of Medical Implants* 1, no. 3 (1992): 236.

20. J. E. Steinman, "Women, Medical Care, and Mass Tort Litigation," *Chicago-Kent Law Review* 68, no. 1 (1992): 409–29; see also L. Finley, "A Break in the Silence: Including Women's Issues in a Torts Course," *Yale Journal of Law and Feminism* 41, no. 1 (1989): 51–52.

21. Steinman, "Medical Care and Mass Tort Litigation."

22. E. S. Pryor, "Flawed Promises: A Critical Evaluation of the American Medical Association's Guides to the Evaluation of Permanent

Impairment," *Harvard Law Review* 103, no. 4 (1990): 964; see also Steinman, "Medical Care and Mass Tort Litigation," 425.

23. American Medical Association, "Guide to the Evaluation of Permanent Impairment" in M. W. Stewart, *Silicone Spills: Breast Implants on Trial* (Westport, CT: Praeger Press, 1998).

24. L. Finley, "The Pharmaceutical Industry and Women's Reproductive Health: The Perils of Ignoring Risk and Blaming Women," in *Corporate Victimization of Women*, edited by E. Szockyj and J. Fox (Boston: Northeastern University Press, 1996). Finley was an invaluable resource for this section. I also drew heavily on R. Meyers, *DES: The Bitter Pill* (New York: Seaview/Putnam, 1983).

25. Meyers, *DES*.

26. American Medical Association Council on Pharmacy and Chemistry. "Silbestrol: Preliminary Report of the Council," *Journal of the American Medical Association* 113, December 23, 1939: 2312; Finley, "The Pharmaceutical Industry and Women's Reproductive Health," 6.

27. G. V. Smith, O. W. Smith, and D. Hurwitz, "Increased Excretion of Pregnanadiol in Pregnancy from DES with Special Reference to the Prevention of Late Pregnancy Accidents," *American Journal of Obstetrics and Gynecology* 51 (1946): 411–16.

28. Finley, "The Pharmaceutical Industry and Women's Reproductive Health," 64; see also Silbestrol, "Preliminary Report of the Council."

29. Finley, "The Pharmaceutical Industry and Women's Reproductive Health," 62.

30. Ibid.

31. Meyers, *DES*.

32. Finley, "The Pharmaceutical Industry and Women's Reproductive Health," 66.

33. Ibid., 63.

34. Ibid., 66.

35. Ibid.

36. Ibid.

37. Ibid.

38. Ibid., 63.

39. Ibid., 66.

40. Ibid.

41. W. J. Dieckman, M. E. Davis, L. M. Rynkiewicz, and R. E. Pottinger, "Does the Administration of Diethylstilbestrol during Pregnancy Have Therapeutic Value?" *American Journal of Obstetrics and Gynecology* 66, no. 5 (1953): 1062–81.

42. The Dieckman study conducted at the University of Chicago revealed that earlier research on DES provided inaccurate results on effectiveness. While the medical profession's willingness to ignore research showing the ineffectiveness and danger of DES is shocking, it is even more shocking to note that researchers continued to use pregnant women in experiments, knowing the potential for harm. Tyler Smith, personal communication, July 2000.

43. D. B. Dutton, *Worse Than the Disease: Pitfalls of Medical Progress* (Cambridge: Cambridge University Press, 1998); and R. J. Apfel and S. M. Fisher. *To Do No Harm: DES and the Dilemmas of Modern Medicine* (New Haven, CT: Yale University Press, 1984).

44. Dutton, *Worse Than the Disease.*

45. Ibid. see also Finley, "The Pharmaceutical Industry and Women's Reproductive Health," 67.

46. Dutton, *Worse Than the Disease.*

47. A. L. Herbst, H. Ufelder, and D. C. Poskanzer, "Adenocarcinoma of the Vagina: Association of Maternal Stilbestrol Therapy with Tumor Appearance in Young Women," *New England Journal of Medicine* 284, no. 16 (1971): 878–81.

48. Ibid.

49. Finley, "The Pharmaceutical Industry and Women's Reproductive Health," 69.

50. Ibid.

51. Ibid., 67; see also Dutton, *Worse Than the Disease.*

52. Finley, "The Pharmaceutical Industry and Women's Reproductive Health," 72.

53. Jeffrey Goldberg. *DES Update Current Information.* Grand Rounds Presentation, CDC's DES Update. www.cdc.gov/DES, no date.

54. Finley, "The Pharmaceutical Industry and Women's Reproductive Health," 69.

55. *Sindell v. Abbott Laboratories.* 26Cal 3d 588, 1980.

56. Goldberg, *DES Update Current Information.*

57. A good deal of the information on the Dalkon Shield included in this chapter came from M. Mintz, *At Any Cost: Corporate Greed, Women, and the Dalkon Shield* (New York: Pantheon Books, 1985); see also K. Hicks, *Surviving the Dalkon Shield IUD: Women v. the Pharmaceutical Industry* (New York: Teachers College Press, 1994); S. Perry, and J. Dawson, *Nightmare: Women and the Dalkon Shield* (New York: Macmillan, 1985); and R. Sobol, *Bending the Law* (Chicago: University of Chicago Press, 1991).

58. Mintz, *At Any Cost.*

59. Ibid.

60. Ibid.

61. Finley, "The Pharmaceutical Industry and Women's Reproductive Health."

62. Ibid.

63. Mintz, *At Any Cost.*

64. Ibid.

65. Ibid.

66. Perry and Dawson, *Nightmare.*

67. Ibid.

68. Ibid.

69. Ibid.

70. Ibid.

71. Mintz, *At Any Cost.*

72. Ibid., 122.

73. Mintz, *At Any Cost.*

74. Ibid.

75. Ibid., 117.

76. Mintz, *At Any Cost,* 121. This is from a memo from Dalkon Shield project coordinator Kenneth Moore.

77. Ibid., 116.

78. Ibid., 117.

79. Mintz, *At Any Cost.*

80. Ibid.

81. Perry and Dawson, *Nightmare.*

82. Mintz, *At Any Cost.*

83. Ibid.

84. Ibid.

85. Ibid.

86. This discussion of the history of the IUD and the FDA draws heavily on the work of Mintz, *At Any Cost.*

87. Finley, "The Pharmaceutical Industry and Women's Reproductive Health."

88. Ronald J. Bacigal, *The Limits of Litigation: The Dalkon Shield Controversy* (Durham, NC: Carolina Academic Press, 1990); and Hicks, *Surviving the Dalkon Shield IUD.*

89. Sobol, *Bending the Law.*

90. Ibid.

91. Sheldon Engelmayer, "Lord's Justice: One Judge's War against the Infamous Dalkon Shield," http://query.nytimes.com.gst/fullpage .html?, retrieved July 7, 2013.

92. Lord Miles, cited in Stewart, *Silicon Spills.*

93. Finley, "The Pharmaceutical Industry and Women's Reproductive Health."

94. Ibid.

95. Sobol, *Bending the Law.*

96. Ibid., 89; J. Braithwaite, *Corporate Crime in the Pharmaceutical Industry* (Boston: Routledge, 1984), 258.

97. M. Stewart, *Breast Implants on Trial* (Westport, CT: Praeger, 1998).

98. Finley, "The Pharmaceutical Industry and Women's Reproductive Health."

99. Ibid.

100. Mintz, *At Any Cost.*

101. Braithwaite, *Corporate Crime in the Pharmaceutical Industry.*

102. I drew heavily on my book *Silicone Spills: Breast Implants on Trial* (1998) for this section of the chapter. Some of the same ground is covered by M. Angel, *Science on Trial: The Clash of Medical Evidence and the Law in the Breast Implant Case* (New York: Norton, 1996), although the perspective is very different from mine. The reader would get a proplaintiff and a prodefense perspective from reading both of these books.

103. Stewart, *Silicone Spills.*

104. Ibid.

105. U.S. Congress, House of Representatives, *The FDA's Regulation of Silicone Breast Implants,* Committee on Government Operations,102nd Session (Washington, DC: U.S. Government Printing Office, 1992).

106. Zones, "The Political and Social Context of Silicone Breast Implant."

107. U.S. Congress, *FDA's Regulation of Silicone Breast Implants.*

108. Stewart, *Silicone Spills.*

109. U.S. Congress, House of Representatives. *The FDA's Regulation of Silicone Breast Implants.* Committee on Government Operations. 102nd Session (Washington, DC: U.S. Government Printing Office, 1993).

110. Stewart, *Silicone Spills.*

111. L. J. Rynbrandt and R. C. Kramer, "Hybrid Nonwomen and Corporate Violence: The Silicone Breast Implant Case," *Violence against Women* 1, no. 3 (September 1995): 206–27.

112. *Mahlum, C. and M. Mahlum v. Dow Chemical.* CV 93-0585941. Second Judicial District Nevada 1995; *Merlin, Mildred v. 3M/McGhan.* CVN 95696HDM. U.S. District Court 1996, District of Nevada; W. C.

Cutting, "Toxicity of Silicone," *Stanford Medical Bulletin* 100, no. 1 (1952): 23–26 (Record no. 0789).

113. J. Claybrook, "Women in the Marketplace: Targets of Corporate Greed," in *Corporate Victimization of Women*, edited by Szockyj and Fox, 111–40.

114. *Mahlum, C. and M. Mahlum v. Dow Chemical*; *Merlin, Mildred v. 3M/McGhan*.

115. A. J. Pardue, Letter to Don McGhan, McGhan Medical Corp., September 27, 1976.

116. Regush, "Toxic Breasts," *Mother Jones*.

117. Ibid.

118. Stewart, *Silicone Spills*, 33.

119. F. Vasey and J. Feldstein, *The Silicone Breast Implant Controversy* (Freedom, CA: Crossing Press, 1993).

120. Memo from J. R. Jenkins referring to *Dow Corning v. Hartford Accident and Indemnity*. Case #93-325788CK.

121. A number of letters and memos were produced by the manufacturers during the discovery phase of litigation. Here I refer to several by their identifying numbers: Baxter: 83650-83652, 3M 4960-4962, and Plaintiff's Response to Defendant, 1996, 4.

122. Memo from J. R. Jenkins referring to *Dow Corning v. Hartford Accident and Indemnity*.

123. The two most powerful studies, both financially supported by Dow Corning, are S. Gabriel, W. M. O'Fallon, L. Kurland, M. Beard, J. Woods, and J. Melton, "Risk of Connective-Tissue Diseases and Other Disorders after Breast Implantation," *New England Journal of Medicine* 330, no. 24 (1994): 1697–1702, known as the Mayo Study; and J. P. Sanchez-Guerrero, P. H. Schur, J. S. Sergent, and M. H. Laing, "Silicone Breast Implants and Rheumatic Disease: Clinical, Immunologic, and Epidemiologic Studies," *Arthritis and Rheumatism* 37, no. 2 (1994): 158, known as the Harvard Nurses Study. These articles are frequently referred to in court by the corporation as the science showing no relationship between silicone gel breast implants and connective tissue disorder. They have been criticized as methodologically flawed studies that do not address the problem of nonclassical autoimmune disease, or diseases that do not conform to the symptoms of arthritis and rheumatism.

124. Affidavit of James R. Jenkins, *Dow Corning v. Hartford Accident and Indemnity*. 2.

125. Stewart, *Silicone Spills*.

126. Ibid.

127. Affidavit of James R. Jenkins, *Dow Corning v. Hartford Accident and Indemnity*.

128. See note 123 above.

129. Stewart, *Silicone Spills.*

130. J. Litvak, Letter to the Editor, *Journal of the American Medical Association*, July 10, 1996.

131. Ibid.

132. Geoffrey White represented over 100 women in the breast implant litigation and was cocounsel with Rick Ellis and Ernie Hornsby in *Mahlum v. Dow Chemical Company, Case 28600.* John White Jr., bankruptcy attorney, joined Geoff White and successfully defended the right of Nevada women to opt out of the multibillion-dollar settlement with Dow Corning.

133. FDA: U.S. Food and Drug Administration, http://www.fda.gov/newsevents/newsroom/ pressannouncement/2006/ucm108790

134. http://fdagov/NewsEvents/Newsroom/Press Announcements

135. FDA Consumer Update Information, http://www.fda.gov/NewsEvents/Newsroom/Press Announcements, retrieved July 23, 2013.

136. Ibid.

137. Martha Burk, Chairperson, National Council of Women's Organizations on C-Span Breast Implant Regulation, http://www.c-span.org/program/188398-1 August 9, 2005

138. The National Institutes of Health conducted a long-term study of the effects of silicone gel breast implants. Louise A. Brinton, chief of the Environmental Epidemiology Branch in its Division of Cancer, Epidemiology, and Genetics, was the principal investigator. This was the largest study of implants ever conducted, with 13,500 women who received implants before 1988 included. Although these women were not at increased risk for most cancers, they had higher rates of brain and lung cancer than women undergoing other types of plastic surgery. Another study conducted by Lori Brown of the National Institutes of Health found that ruptured and leaking silicone implants were significantly linked to painful connective tissue and soft tissue diseases, including fibromyalgia, pulmonary fibrosis, dermatomyositis and other debilitating diseases; M. Kaufman, "Breast Implants Linked to Fibromyalgia," *Washington Post*, A12, 2001.

139. Almost all of the information for the section on the diet drug Fen-Phen was summarized from court documents obtained during the litigation against American Home Products. Specifically, the reader may refer to proceedings of Mealey's Fen-Phen Litigation Conference as well as

the Supplemental Materials, presented at the St. Regis Hotel, October 18–19, 1999, King of Prussia, PA.

140. *Privet v. American Home Products*. Plaintiff's Response to Opposition to AHP's Motion for Summary Judgement, re: Punitive Damages, Case # CV9900753, 2nd Judicial District Court, Nevada, February 29, 1999.

141. Mealey's Fen-Phen Litigation Conference as well as the Supplemental Materials, presented at the St. Regis Hotel, October 18–19, 1999, King of Prussia, PA.

142. *Privet v. American Home Products*.

143. This information came from documents produced during discovery in the case *Privet v. American Home Products*.

144. A. Mundy, "Weight-Loss Wars," *U.S. News and World Report*, February 5, 1999, 42.

145. See note 143 above.

146. *Privet v. America Home Products op. cit.*

147. *Privet v. American Home Products*; see also another Fen-Phen case: *Oran v. Stafford*, U.S. District Court, New Jersey. CA 97-4513 (NHP) (John Stafford is the president and CEO of American Home Products.)

148. Ibid.

149. See note 139.

150. See note 147.

151. *Privet v. American Home Products*.

152. Ibid. see also *Oran v. Stafford*.

153. Ibid.

154. Ibid.

155. *Privet v. American Home Products*, 6.

156. Finley, "The Pharmaceutical Industry and Women's Reproductive Health."

157. Ibid.

158. Regush, "Toxic Breasts."

159. Ibid.

160. Summary of Physicians and Managed Care Organizations Report on Quantitative Research, in re: Diet Drugs Liability Litigation: MDL 1203. Deposition of Jo Alen Dolan, January 14, 1999, 142–43.

161. Stewart, *Silicone Spills*.

162. Ibid.

163. H. C. Barnett, "Corporate Capitalism, Corporate Crime," *Crime and Delinquency* 27, no. 1 (1981): 4–13.

164. C. H. Foreman, *Plaques, Products, and Politics: Emergent Public Health Hazards and National Policy Making* (Washington, DC: Brookings Institution, 1994), 96–97.

165. Szockyj and Fox, *Corporate Victimization of Women.*

166. Fukushima Report: Key Points in Nuclear Disaster Report, July 5, 2012. http://www.bbc.co.uk/news/world-asia 18718486

167. J. Messerschmidt, *Capitalism, Patriarchy, and Crime: Toward a Socialist Feminist Criminology* (Lanham, MD: Rowman & Littlefield, 1986); and David J. Maume, "Glass Ceilings and Glass Escalators," *Work and Occupations* 26, no. 4 (1999): 483–509.

168. Szockyj and Frank, *Corporate Victimization of Women*, 5.

169. A. McIllroy, "Parliamentary Bureau," *Globe and Mail*, November 18, 1988.

170. Ibid.

171. R. C. Fellmeth, "The Regulatory-Industrial Complex," in *With Justice for Some*, edited by B. Wasserstein and M. J. Green (Boston: Beacon Press, 1970).

172. Ibid.

173. Braithwaite, *Corporate Crime in the Pharmaceutical Industry.*

174. Stewart, *Silicon Spills.*

175. U.S. Congress: House of Representatives, "The FDA's Regulation of Silicone Breast Implants. Committee on Government Operations," 13; see also Stewart, *Silicone Spills.*

176. Stewart, *Silicone Spills.*

177. *Oran et al. v. American Home Products*, U.S. District Court. New Jersey. Class Action No. 97-4513 (NHP).

178. Finley, "The Pharmaceutical Industry and Women's Reproductive Health."

179. Stewart, *Silicone Spills.*

180. Ibid.

181. Memo from Burson-Marstellar to Brody Cole, and others; correspondence from Ilena Rose, August 20, 1999.

182. J. Matthews, "Burson-Marstellar Memo, September 9, 1991," accessed at http://trimaris.com/~ussw/media/bm_bull.html

183. Mediawatch: Confidence Game: B-M's Plan for Silicone Breast Implants, accessed online at http://www.trimaris.com/~ussw'media/prwatch.html

184. U.S. Congress: House of Representatives, "The FDA's Regulation of Silicone Breast Implants," Committee on Government Operations.

185. Stewart, *Silicone Spills.*

186. Mediawatch: Confidence Game: B-M's Plan for Silicone Breast Implants.

187. R. B. Schmitt, "Can Corporate Advertising Sway Juries?" *Wall Street Journal*, March 3, 1997, Bl.

188. Mintz, *At Any Cost*, 90.

189. *Privet v. American Home Products;* see also *Oran v. Stafford.*

190. Memo from R. Notvest to unspecified others at Wyeth Ayerst, June 29, 1995, including Redux Prelaunch Marketing Plan, June 23, 1995, exhibit 24 in *Privet v. American Home Products.*

191. *Privet v. American Home Products*; see also *Oran v. Stafford.*

192. Redux Prelaunch Marketing Plan, Exhibit 24.

193. *Privet v. American Home Products*; see also *Oran v. Stafford.*

194. M. Silverman and P. R. Lee, *Pills, Profits and Politics* (Berkeley: University of California Press, 1974); see also Braithwaite, *Corporate Crime in the Pharmaceutical Industry.*

195. Schmitt, "Can Corporate Advertising Sway Juries?"

196. Ibid.

197. Ibid.

198. In re: Diet Drugs Liability Litigation, MDL 1203. Deposition of Jo Alen Dolan. January 14, 1999, 26.

199. Ibid.

200. Ibid.

201. Ibid., 24.

202. Ibid., 25.

203. J. Pekkanen, quoted in Braithwaite, *Corporate Crime in the Pharmaceutical Industry*, 245.

204. Stewart, *Silicone Spills.*

205. See note 203 above.

206. Stewart, *Silicone Spills.*

207. T. Monmaney, "Review of 36 'Drug Therapy' Articles since 1997," *Los Angeles Times*, October 9, 1999, 2A; and S. Gottlieb, "Medical Societies Accused of Being Beholden to the Drug Industry," *British Medical Journal* 319, no. 7221 (1999): 1321.

208. Braithwaite, *Corporate Crime in the Pharmaceutical Industry*, 259.

209. R. Hughes and R. Brewin quoted in Braithwaite, *Corporate Crime in the Pharmaceutical Industry*, 221.

210. L. Flanders, "Beware: P.R. Implants in News Coverage," *Extra! The Magazine of FAIR*, 9, no. 1 (1996): 11.

211. L. S. Cook, J. R. Darling, L. F. Voight, et al., "Characteristics of Women With and Without Breast Augmentation," *Journal of the*

American Medical Association 277, no. 20 (1997): 1612–17; see also the response to the article, L. Cook, J. Stanford, L. Brinton, et al., "Character-istics of Women With and Without Breast Implants," *Journal of the American Medical Association* 278, no. 10 (1997): 818–19.

212. Cook, et al., "Characteristics of Women with and without Breast Augmentation."

213. Meyers, *DES*.

214. Finley, "The Pharmaceutical Industry and Women's Reproduc-tive Health," 73.

215. Ibid.

216. In some instances, judges have given women convicted of child abuse or drug use a choice between Norplant and jail time, causing con-cern about the infringement on the rights of poor women. See J. Persels, "The Norplant Condition: Protecting the Unborn or Violating Fundamen-tal Rights," *Journal of Legal Medicine* 13, no. 2 (1992): 237–62.

217. Finley, "The Pharmaceutical Industry and Women's Reproduc-tive Health."

218. *Hopkins v. Dow Corning Corp.*, No. C-91-2132, 1991. U.S. Dis-trict LEXUS (N.D. Cal. May 17, 1992).

219. Ibid.

220. Absolutely Safe: A Documentary Film, C. Ciancutti-Leyva, Pro-ducer and Writer. New York: Amaranth Productions, 2008.

221. Miles Lord, chief U.S. district judge for Minnesota, judge in the class-action suit against A. H. Robins by the women injured by the Dalkon Shield, in Hicks, *Surviving the Dalkon Shield IUD,* 19. See also his court-room statement, February 29, 1984, to three officers of A. H. Robins Co., E. Clairborne Robins Jr., President and CEO; Carl D. Lumsford, Senior Vice President for Research and Development; and William F. Forrest Jr., Vice President and General Counsel. In Mintz, *At Any Cost*, 264–69.

EIGHT

Trafficking

Trafficking is nothing new. Neither is slavery. Yet in the second decade of the twenty-first century, trafficking has reemerged in the public eye with a vengeance. Movies, documentaries, magazine exposés, newspaper articles and analyses, books, and the Internet roll out the drama and details of this sorry tale. Almost every state in the United States has followed the federal government in establishing laws, often several laws, to address trafficking—from mandating service to victims, to punishment and fines for the johns, and criminal punishment for the trafficker.

Trafficking today is presented as a growing global problem of almost unbelievable proportions, relying on complex relationships between countries, governments, traffickers, business people, politicians, lawmakers, and ordinary people. When asked where it is occurring, advocates reply, just walk down any street, eat in any restaurant, go into any shop or factory—it is there. The U.S. imagery has primarily been of young innocent victims sold into prostitution both as depicted in the Trafficking Victims Protection Act (TVPA) of 2000[1] and in the legislation passed by the states. Research on trafficked women in Asia, Latin America, and Africa portray the typical victims as young, poor, and uneducated, reflecting the general conditions of a majority of the population. In contrast, many of the women trafficked from Russia have college degrees, reflecting the lack of opportunity in the post-Soviet economy for those who anticipated upward mobility.[2]

The United States currently estimates that between 800,000 and 900,000 people are trafficked across international borders each year, many of them women and children destined for sale as sex workers.[3] Earlier the State department had reported that 700,000 to two million women and children were trafficked globally each year, but increased this figure to four million in 2003, then later revising it downward to 600,000 to 800,000 victims of all types of trafficking, with "hundreds of thousands" being trafficked into prostitution.[4] Kotrla, in discussing the numbers, says there are currently at least 100,000 domestic minor sex trafficker victims (DMST victims) in the United States with 325,000 more being at risk.[5] If poverty is one of those risk factors, as many suggest,[6] one would think the number would soar into the millions. State Department figures indicate that 100,000 Latin Americans are trafficked internationally each year, many coming from the Dominican Republic and Colombia and being trafficked to Spain, Italy, Portugal, the United States, and Japan. Mexican drug cartels are also estimated to be heavily involved in the trafficking of persons as well as drugs.[7] The figures on trafficking are wildly fluctuating, and as the State department acknowledges, "no one U.S. or international agency is compiling accurate statistics."[8] In the absence of clear numbers to communicate the extent of the problem, there is a heavy reliance on anecdotal horror stories to "demonstrate the gravity of a targeted evil."[9]

Methodologically, there are many issues related to understanding the women who are trafficked and the trafficking process; ethics, safety, sampling, who do you talk to, what stories are they expected to tell, and how might you endanger the women by talking to them? Much of the information about trafficking and the experiences of the women that reach the West come from the nongovernmental organizations (NGOs) that are devoted to ending prostitution and maintaining the support of the various government entities and interest groups that fund them. The women they encounter in their efforts, and the women who seek them out for safety and shelter, may not be representative of all trafficked women. It may be that these women are more likely to be kidnapped or taken against their will, that they have been brutalized, raped, and forced into prostitution, than other women who are more "softly" recruited. The shelters operated by NGOs may then provide a very skewed sample of all trafficked women, and further, since only some shelters will allow access to the women, we may be hearing from the same women over and over. It may be that their stories are the extreme—we have no idea of the stories of all of the women, only those who will talk, and they may well not be representative of all trafficked women. There is also the ethical issue of revealing the women's identities, and the risks they incur by being "saved" by brothel busters and others looking to help the women, or to create moving documentaries or news stories. For example, both Aaron Cohen and Nicholas Kristof have been criticized for carelessly putting some of the women at risk by participating in the trafficking process through buying the freedom of a few women, organizing raids on brothels that they video-tape, and publicizing the whereabouts and identities of the women.[10] Roxana Galusca even suggests they are voyeurs, the epitome of the white western male colonizing brown women's bodies for the sake of publicity and ego.[11]

During the last several years, a great deal of attention has been paid human trafficking, meaning prostitution, depicted as "sexual slavery" or "modern day slavery." Some of this is what we should be calling "com-mercial sexual exploitation," while some of it may be slavery or sex work. We need to use a language that more precisely reflects what we mean. The U.S. government has been as guilty as anyone in using confusing and imprecise language, failing, for example, in their policies for providing funding to NGOs to differentiate sex trafficking and prostitution, practices that are highly distinguished in the countries in which the NGOs operate. Using the term "trafficking" indiscriminately does not reflect the reality of trafficking, the relationship between the people involved, or the enor-mous discrepancy between the numbers of victims that exist at the rhetori-cal level and the small number who are identified in practice. The "modern melodrama" of trafficking is simple and narrow, a "moral crusade" against a "social evil,"[12] evading the complexity of the process and the underlying structural problems that cause it, drawing instead false dichotomies between participants,[13] the good West, and the evil other,[14] and eroding the nuances of relationships, purpose, and process.

While the public conception and the media portrayal of trafficking emphasize sex trafficking and draw on racialized stereotypes of the victim as innocent, young, attractive, and brown as well as positing horrendous working conditions, entrapment, violence, and abuse, the picture that emerges from the research is much more complex. In this chapter, I hope to both describe this social problem as it is experienced at its worst, and then stand back from the exaggerations and extreme caricatures to chal-lenge and complicate "what we know." While we need to understand the economic and social and cultural underpinnings of sex trafficking, we must also keep in mind that this is a very problematic area, one in which hyperbole sometimes outweighs reality. We have to be careful about drawing on essentialized notions of race and gender and recognize the underlying political forces that fuel the concern over sex trafficking. Most of what people know about trafficking is from sensationalized media reports in newspapers and television and the news,[15] highlighting the perfect innocent victim being duped into the sex trade. The trafficking process, Kimm and Sauer point out, is "much more complex and ambiguous than suggested by the image of the seduced girl forced into slavery-like conditions under false pretenses by a male trafficker."[16] Misinformation, extreme stereotyping, and social activism have resulted in a "moral crusade" in which participants have been reduced to caricatures and the problem to a simple binary of exploited and exploiter. As Zhang suggests, "imagination seems to have taken the place of sound empirical studies."[17] The problem is far more complicated and nuanced than the crusaders make it out to be. It is situated historically and in contemporary geopolitical relations, it reflects ongoing debates about prostitution, and it complicates the relationship between the agent and the victim subject.

Trafficking is built on and inextricably embedded in global inequality between the developing and the developed countries.[18] Income and wealth inequality globally is extraordinarily great and increasingly visible, resulting in women from a very wide range of countries being at risk for trafficking. When the USSR dissolved in 1991, hundreds of thousands of people, many of them women, were left in far worse condition economically than they had been under Russian rule. Many of these women were educated, professional women who lost their ability to provide for themselves. In addition, in the Baltic countries, civil wars and invasions left millions homeless, displaced, and suffering from hunger, illness, and the effects of violence, often ethnic cleansing and rape. The Serbians' systematic rape and murder of the Muslim Bosnians left them devastated, but also vulnerable to rape and assault by the UN forces assigned to protect them. Moldova seems to be the country providing the most women to the international trafficking conduits, reflecting their abject poverty and civil chaos. The women from Bangladesh, India, and Pakistan may place themselves at risk for trafficking to escape their daily oppression, or they may be sold by their parents to pay debts or so that there is one less mouth to feed. Those from Thailand and the Philippines, often displaced from their rural villages, may already be prostitutes in the cities looking for a way out through jobs abroad such as nannies, barmaids, or dancers.[19] Trafficking is built on inequality and poverty and displacement by war or through the loss of subsistence agricultural support. Sex trafficking is fueled by the intersections of these structural problems with the global devaluation of women. The clear objectification and commodification of women, the view of women as men's property, and the hierarchical gender arrangements that convince men that they have the right and the privilege of sexual access to women if they can pay drive sex trafficking at both the global and the local levels. It is not just their superior economic ability that leads men to the brothels or to seek sex on the streets and in bars and brothels. It is the assumption of male privilege—the assumption that male sexual desire justifies its fulfillment. Kotrla discusses the role played by the normalization and promotion of commercial sex across America[20] that glamorizes pimping and prostitution, giving as examples the television show "Pimp My Ride"; a video game called "Keep Pimpin' " in which the player can "slap your hoes, pimp the streets, kill the companion . . . "; and "It's Hard to Pimp out Here," a song that won Best Original Song at the 78th Academy Awards.[21]

Further, while women throughout the world are unequal to men, when one intersects male privilege with white privilege, those women who are brown or black are even more vulnerable than those who are white. Those "like us" are less likely to be commodified than those who can be sexually and racially "othered." Very little has been published about the experience of Native American young women who experience commercial sexual exploitation, but the research on them reveals social and economic problems that are probably more generally experienced by trafficked women.[22] Rather than the problem being "innocent girls" sold by "sick perverts," these women are likely to be sold by a family member or boyfriend. The boyfriend, who becomes legally a pimp, uses either "finesse" tactics, such as the opportunity to be a model or a dancer or to go on shopping trips, to lure the girls off the reservation, or "guerrilla" tactics, such as physical violence, force, or threats.[23] Often, those who threaten the girl are other girls, members of a gang. The underlying problem for the Native American girls studied by Pierce was being homeless, abandoned, or forced to leave their family, which made them vulnerable to offers of affection, safety, and work.[24] Further, just as with international trade in women, such as between Nepal and India, the frequency and visibility of prostitution in the neighborhood increased the risk of girls being prostituted.[25] In her interviews with Native American girls in cities in Minnesota and Alaska, Pierce found that the high number of pimps (both male and female) the girls were in contact with, the frequency of drug and alcohol use, physical abuse, and mental health problems were linked with the increased vulnerability of these girls to being trafficked.[26] Rather than there being a completely exploitative relationship between the pimp and the girl, both were caught in a vortex of isolation, poverty, addiction, and homelessness, and the pimps pushed, threatened, or cajoled girls into prostitution for survival and benefits.[27]

One can start the analysis of sex trafficking at several levels; the first question I usually get from my students is "how could any parent sell their daughter to a trafficker?" Questions such as this remind me of the first question I usually get from an audience after delivering a lecture on wife battery: "Why does she stay?" It is not that these are completely inappropriate questions, but their prominence reflects assumptions that go unquestioned: assumptions about why men beat women and why men buy women. These are the larger questions of power and privilege that we need to attend if these many forms of violence against women are to be addressed. At the same time, the process of buying and selling women, the mechanics—details of these transactions in human suffering—need to be uncovered and the roles of the many players understood in order to unravel the many linked ties that encourage and perpetuate this problem. If poverty were not rampant, if women were not defined as sexual objects for the fulfillment of male pleasure, and if men's sexuality were not embedded in a powerful privilege system, women and girls would not be vulnerable to traffickers preying on them and sex tourists buying them for a few pennies. If women were seen as subjects they would not be bought as commodities.

THE PALERMO PROTOCOL

The Protocol to Prevent, Suppress and Punish Trafficking in Persons, Especially Women and Children, usually referred to as the Palermo Protocol, is a supplement to the 2000 UN Convention Against Transnational Organized Crime and contains the first widely accepted definition of trafficking; it is today "the most important international legal instrument on human trafficking."[28] The Palermo Protocol defines trafficking as:

> The recruitment, transportation, transfer harbouring or receipt of persons, by means of the threat or use of force or other forms of coercion, of abduction, of fraud, of deception, of the abuse of power or of a position of vulnerability or of the giving or receiving of payments or benefits to achieve the consent of a person having control over another person, for the purpose of exploitation. Exploitation shall include, at a minimum, the exploitation of the prostitution of others, or other forms of sexual exploitation forced labour or services, slavery or practices similar to slavery, servitude or the removal of organs.[29]

While human trafficking is defined specifically in the "Palermo Protocol,"[30] much is left unspecified, reflecting the negotiations underlying the protocol and the different goals and purposes and commitment of the

signers. The ambiguous language of the protocol itself allows for disagreements in interpretation and meaning. Trafficking is equated with
debt bondage, illegal immigration, modern-day slavery, the sexual exploitation of women, violence against women, and particularly, prostitution.
O'Connell Davidson takes issue with "the idea that 'trafficking' can be
clearly marked off from other violations of human and labour rights."[31]
Similarly, Kimm and Sauer posit that there is an unfortunate mixing of
concepts such as trafficking, forced prostitution, sex work, and migration
that muddies the discussion significantly.[32] For example, Ribando Seelke
says that while orphan children are particularly vulnerable to trafficking,
many trafficked children live with their families and use their earnings
from commercial sex activity to contribute to household income.[33] This
is a confusing usage of the term "trafficking." In fact, 57 percent of the
children who were interviewed in a study conducted in 2002 by Zoila
Gonzales de Innocenti were found to live either with their parents or a
close relative.[34] Smit reports that most trafficking in human beings is for
labor, not sex, and consistent attention to sex trafficking misrepresents
the problem.[35] She also suggests the media coverage of sex trafficking
perpetuates the stereotype that trafficking is primarily of girls and
women,[36] a view that seems to have found its way into policy, for even
though the TVPA includes trafficking for labor, there is a clear and consistent elaboration of sex trafficking in women and girls that overrides all
other forms.[37] The Trafficking Victims Protection Act, for example,
emphasizes the trafficking of women and children for sexual purposes,
claiming trafficking to be "an evil requiring concerted and vigorous
action . . . ,"[38] but it retains a focus on international crime. In practice, this
act has been translated by states to emphasize "internal trafficking" with
primary focus on children, usually meaning girls under 18 years of age,
who are exploited by their pimp. The conditions established by the protocol, such as fraud or coercion, do not have to be met in this instance,[39] and
"organized crime" has given way to concentration on the girl's pimp.[40] It
seems clear that the distance between the protocol as established by the
United Nations and the current interpretation and enforcement efforts by
the state has reached great proportions.

Interestingly, some authors suggest that the UN Protocol does not, by
definition, require movement across international borders, or an illegal
contract, unlike smuggling, while others stress that transnational movement is required.[41] The Palermo Protocol, perhaps because the focus of
the protocol is on transnational organized crime, specifies that it applies
to "offenses [that] are transnational in nature, involving an organized
criminal group,"[42] and involving coercion (differentiating it from

smuggling).[43] Hence a person entering the United States illegally on a tourist visa, for example, and only later being coerced into illegal forms of labor would not, according to this interpretation, be trafficked nor would the protocol apply to a person within a country who is violently, coercively, or illegally exploited, according to Kaneti.[44] Not all authors agree with this interpretation, although it is clearly listed as one of the stipulations of the protocol. This internal or domestic trafficking, like cross-border trafficking, occurs mainly for labor and most commonly in construction, "sweatshops," agriculture, manufacturing, janitorial services, hotel services, and domestic work.[45] Although sex trafficking has received far more media attention, more investigations, and more prosecutions than labor trafficking, non-U.S. citizens are more likely to be found in labor trafficking than in sex trafficking.[46]

Another problem with the protocol is that it is based on a framework of criminality and illegal migration with little emphasis on human rights, although the protocol reads to many as a human rights document,[47] and is therefore expected to address problems of exploitation and violence among laborers. Despite this interpretation, it is a tool to aid in the prevention of illegal migration rather than to either prevent exploitation or to provide support services for trafficked persons. The protocol's emphasis on legality and criminality, rather than individual rights, allows states to use a "moral lens" in developing national policies that address only specific segments of the problem, such as sexual exploitation.[48] This "law enforcement" approach is clearly insufficient, leading many governments to move toward the development of a human rights approach that incorporates victim rights. This has created an interesting dilemma—governments have felt compelled to pass legislation to prevent trafficking but have not felt equally compelled to pursue traffickers as criminals. While there is universal awareness of the Palermo Protocol and its requirements, and while 40 percent of the governments have passed domestic antitrafficking legislation since the Palermo Protocol, most have yet to enforce those laws and convict a single trafficker.[49] Some governments, especially those that wanted to enter the European Union or to look progressive to their neighbors, may well have been more interested in appearance than in investigation and prosecution of traffickers.[50] Even in the United States, where there are an estimated 1,800–1,950 victims of labor trafficking a year, there were only 103 convictions in 2007.[51]

The definition of organized crime is problematic. Despite the fact that the protocol is a component of the UN Organized Crime Convention, trafficking is often more likely to involve a loosely organized and temporary group of family members or friends,[52] which meets the formal definition of "organized crime" but does not conform to the general view of "organized" crime. Despite the rhetoric about the involvement of organized crime, we actually have very little information on the traffickers themselves, in part because of research difficulties and in part because the emphasis has been on the victims. The evidence is simply too scarce to validate the idea that trafficking involves large scale, complex, well-organized transnational crime.[53]

Another area in which there is disagreement about the protocol is the degree to which fraud or force must be used. The common denominator for many authors, more important than "the use of force, fraud, or coercion to exploit a person for profit," is exploitation.[54] This interpretation means that migration and smuggling would be a problem if the person, no matter the mode of entry, were exploited for sex or labor.[55] Smuggling, which is viewed as consensual, is differentiated from trafficking by the issue of consent, a distinction that may itself create problems for the victim. For example, Kimm and Sauer in their comparative analysis of discourses on sex work at the World Cup and the European Championship say that workers, including sex workers, may migrate quite willingly and may voluntarily choose sex work, so that what begins as migration may end as exploitation.[56] In contrast, however, there are authors who see intent as being at the core of trafficking rather than the exploitation of labor in itself,[57] suggesting that drawing the line between exploitation that is illegal and that which is an ordinary and predictable feature of labor relations is difficult.

O'Connell Davidson says, however, that exploitation, lack of consent, or intent should not be viewed as the defining characteristics of trafficking, but rather that violence should be seen as the real evil in trafficking. She asserts that the criterion of violence is so essential to the definition because exploitation is a characteristic of many economic relationships, not just trafficking. Exploitation is explicitly built into many economic relationships, making it difficult to justify as the defining characteristic of trafficking.[58] Female sex workers, particularly those who are coerced or forced into sex work, are very likely to be the victims of violence, she says. In one study, Silverman found two out of five women reported that they were forced or coerced into sex work, and their incidence of HIV infection as a result was high.[59] In addition, those who were trafficked clearly had less control of their lives, more violence (75 percent compared with 54 percent), and relied more on alcohol to endure their lives (69 percent compared with 52 percent)[60] than those who voluntarily entered sex work.

Despite a good deal of disagreement about the definition of trafficking, the importance of organized crime, international transport, and the experience of the people who are trafficked, basic agreements can be reached about the necessity of addressing trafficking as a global problem. In 2000, the Trafficking Victims Protection Act was passed by the United States to combat trafficking both in the United States and abroad. It was strengthened in 2003 and expanded in 2013. This act also established the Office to Monitor and Combat Trafficking in Persons (State Department) that publishes an annual report dividing countries around the globe into three tiers according to how committed they are to the elimination of trafficking from, to, or through their countries, mandating withdrawing most nonhumanitarian aid from those countries in Tier Three. Countries in Tier One are those that are actively fighting trafficking and include Austria, Belgium, Ghana, Germany, the United Arab Emirates, the United Kingdom, and about 20 other countries in all parts of the world.[61] Those in Tier Two do not fully comply with the TVPA but are making significant efforts to do so. These include Mexico, Romania, Portugal, El Salvador, Estonia, Ghana, Belarus, and others. Tier Three, those not responding to trafficking with any effectiveness, includes fewer countries than the others; Congo, Eritrea, Yemen, Kuwait, Saudi Arabia, and Sudan are among them.[62] Critics argue that the tier system is manipulated by the United States, which treads very lightly around countries like Japan and Saudi Arabia and countries from the former Soviet Union because they are important allies of the United States in the war on terrorism or other interests in the region. Katherine Chon, codirector of the Polaris Project, suggests the tier system of evaluating countries in terms of their progress in addressing trafficking favors those countries that are political allies, treating them with "kid gloves" and using the tier system to justify withholding aid from others.[63] For example, some antislavery groups are outraged that Mauritania, a country known for chattel slavery, is treated as a "special case,"[64] a country lifted from Tier One to Tier Two to avoid the necessity of imposing sanctions, basically "given a pass" even when their response to trafficking is minimal or cynical.

As we can see from the above disagreements in interpretation and focus, the phrase "trafficking in persons" can be likened to a Pandora's box: once opened, this term gives life to a multitude of misunderstandings, preferences and rationalities.[65] Trafficking is an international border enforcement issue. It is a human rights concern, although the United States and Britain and other Western states, while including the language of "rights" in the protocol, make the provision of services optional, only recommending access to "rights-based services" and ending automatic deportation for undocumented people who were trafficked.[66] It is also a health issue with sex workers being the group at greatest risk for HIV infection, particularly during the first few months of initiation into sex work, due to the greater likelihood of violence and sexual brutality.[67]

Definitional problems help explain the enormous discrepancy between the numbers of victims of trafficking that exist "in rhetoric" and the small number that are identified and assisted in any country. While the Palermo Protocol guides the definition at the international level, the definitions differ among nations, with some countries having no antitrafficking legislation at all. Some countries, such as the United States, include people under the age of 18 engaged in commercial sex as a severe form of trafficking, while in other countries children are defined as those below 16, leading to inconsistencies in the number of children involved in trafficking. Further, although the protocol expands its definition of trafficking to include cross-border movement, the annual Trafficking in Persons report does not require that a person be physically transported to fall within the definition of trafficking. Another reason it is difficult to get accurate data on the scope of the problem is that the definition is operationalized from different perspectives depending on the research interests, so that labor, migration, and criminal justice approaches approach data and data collection differently. Other problems related to inaccurate and contradictory findings about numbers and processes are methodological, including access to trafficking victims, their unwillingness to respond, reliance on stereotypes, inadequate record keeping, and reliance on data produced by those with vested interests.

THE SOCIAL CONSTRUCTION OF TRAFFICKING

Human trafficking, like other social problems, is constructed as a *problem* through the efforts of interest groups who have a stake in a particular framework or definition. This is not to say that individuals who are exploited, coerced, or forced to engage in labor do not experience a significant and painful personal problem. But this personal deprivation or violation does not constitute a social problem. In order for a personal problem to become a *social* problem, various parties have to successfully stake a claim on this problem, constructing its parameters, definitions, and possible responses to it, although there is still room for negotiating these details.[68] As is the case with prostitution and pornography, those who collaborate on the construction of the problem of trafficking are not readily predictable. Radical feminists, followed by more liberal feminists, have collaborated with the neoconservatives and the religious right in framing trafficking as sex trafficking and in the construction of the "perfect victim."[69] In addition, white, wealthy male investigative journalists—"slave hunters"—join popular films, documentaries, and books to depict the trafficked woman as young, sexually alluring, innocent, and vulnerable.[70]

Trafficking, as a legal and social construct, represents the convergence of the efforts of strange bedfellows, the religious right and the "radical" feminists, who see women's oppression as resulting from patriarchy, as male ownership and control of the female body. This is an interesting collaboration in itself, but it is also interesting that this radical branch of the women's movement has not been relegated to the political fringe but has joined middle-of-the-road and conservative women's groups in this cause. Conservative lawmakers have also firmly embraced this cause, championing the rights of women, even as they remove women's freedoms in other areas, like the right to bodily integrity through access to birth control, the right to privacy and abortion, the right to affordable and nondiscriminatory insurance coverage. All of these actors, including feminist activists, neoconservative activists, the religious right, NGOs, law enforcement, the judiciary, policy makers, and legislators, are involved in different ways and with different agendas in the construction of trafficking. They advanced trafficking as a threat to public health (tying it to the AIDS epidemic), as a threat to the economic and political well-being of states, as a form of violence against women and children in particular, and as a form of human slavery. While not always agreed upon by all actors, this attention has led to a consciousness about trafficking at the local and global level that has shunted aside other social problems.

THE EMERGENCE OF A SOCIAL PROBLEM

Trafficking has, during the past 10 years, become the unchallenged new global scourge, replacing violence against women generally and more specifically child abuse, family violence, elder abuse, and marital rape. Violence against women emerged in the early 1970s as a grassroots movement central to the larger women's movement, and while that movement has quieted and violence against women has been largely bureaucratized as a minor industry, it is, other than the recent wrangling in Congress about passing the Violence against Women Act, fading as a major social problem. Child abuse and elder abuse have also been institutionalized into state and federal agencies. These problems no longer garner the outrage they once did, and have become so firmly entrenched in the social welfare system that they are no longer seen as needing the activist energies of feminist, legal, and legislative bodies. They are being rapidly replaced by human trafficking, now presented as the most critical problem facing women in this country, the latest blight on our society and much of the world, requiring our vigilance and requiring that we fight it at every level.

There are a number of reasons trafficking has become so visible even though there is no evidence that trafficking itself has increased dramatically. One reason may be that it is organically linked with global violence against women more generally, including honor crimes, female genital mutilation, and dowry deaths. Attention to it reflects a tendency for media to look beyond our borders to find social problems "over there," or when looking internally, to see the intrusions of the foreign, to see "aliens" as bringing those problems to our shores. It may reflect increased attention to problems tied to immigration, particularly illegal or irregular immigration, with traffickers representing the vilest of these "aliens." It provides countries with a justification for employing harsh measures against irregular immigration (configured as organized crime) yet allows for the avoidance of human rights protections as required by international agreement. It may represent fatigue in the fight against the seemingly intractable problems of battery, sexual assault, and child abuse and provide a fresh form of violence around which activists can coalesce. And trafficking as a social problem offers a new platform on which to ignite the debate about the meaning of prostitution: is it inherently violence against women based on the fact that it violates a woman's integrity and is embedded in a patriarchal and oppressive society, or is it a form of labor that is not itself problematic but becomes so through the violation of a woman's labor rights or the imposition of work conditions that are inhumane and degrading?

This "new" social problem has deep and conflicting roots in ideologies about the third world, in the ethic of human rights and protection, in governmental interest in border control, in constructions of slavery, and in constructions of gender, particularly those about women's bodies. As such, there are many competing voices, and while some are ascendant, they have not gone unchallenged. Trafficking can be situated as a problem of violence against women, as a problem of prostitution specifically, as a problem related to the avoidance of harm and the protection of innocents, as a problem of organized crime, and as a problem of illegal immigration, to name a few. Further, there is tension between police responses to international migration and a rights-based approach to trafficking, revealing the tension between measures developed to enforce immigration rules established to manage migration and approaches that focus on recognizing and protecting the victims of trafficking.[71] Enforcement of immigration controls has in some instances been recast as the protection of human rights, the rights of immigrants, and the prevention of harm.

In such instances, the prevention of harm can be enshrined as the center-piece of the immigration enforcement regime, camouflaging the state's responsibility for the establishment of relations of dominance and subordination through its immigration controls.[72]

The reader might see the words "trafficker" or "victim of trafficking" in the above paragraphs but is likely to read this to mean "sex trafficker" or "victim of sex trafficking" or "sexual slavery." This is no surprise given that sex trafficking has received the lion's share of attention from the media in every form (news, film, documentaries, television programs) as well as women's groups, legislative bodies, police, and social activists. While the trafficking protocols at both the international and state level include the far larger problem of labor trafficking and other forms of exploitation, and while sex slavery is only a small segment of overall trafficking in persons, sex trafficking is a far more visible and attention-getting problem, calling forth much greater outrage than labor trafficking, debt bondage, chattel slavery, and other forms of trafficking that affect far more people.[73] Legislation at the federal level (Trafficking Victims Protection Act) draws from the Palermo Protocol and has been relied on in the development of antitrafficking legislation in the United States where over 40 states now have antitrafficking laws. Although the TVPA itself does not separately define domestic sex trafficking of minors, this is the topic that increasingly is highlighted by legislators and law enforcement as seems to have captured the attention of the media and activist groups.

"Severe trafficking" as described in the U.S. federal VTVPA (Victims of Trafficking and Violence Protection Act, 2000) refers to: "(a) sex trafficking in which a commercial sex act is induced by force, fraud or coercion, or in which the person induced to perform such act has not attained 18 years of age, or (b) the recruitment, harboring, transportation, provision or obtaining of a person for labor or services, through the use of force, fraud or coercion for the purpose of subjecting to involuntary servitude, peonage, debt bondage, or slavery."[74] The Trafficking Victims Protection Act initially made a distinction between "sex trafficking," which could be voluntarily entered into, and "severe trafficking" relying on force, fraud, or coercion, or involving persons under 18 years of age.[75] A conviction of trafficking can result in a prison term of 20 years. And conviction of severe trafficking allows federal authorities to charge traffickers under the RICO antiracketeering law.[76] This makes it easier for trafficked victims to find refuge in the United States and to sue their traffickers in civil court,[77] although it is difficult to imagine that many trafficked people, often desperate to leave poverty and hardship, have the financial wherewithal and legal knowledge to pursue a case in civil court. Despite the attention, money, and laws, only 111 persons were charged with severe trafficking between 2001 and 2004.[78] This distinction between severe trafficking and trafficking was opposed by the abolition lobby, including Melissa Farley, Donna Hughes, religious activists, and some NGOs, who, along with mainstream feminists (Gloria Steinem and NOW),worked to convince President Clinton to merge the two types of trafficking.[79]

While the UN Palermo Protocol, the EU Framework, and the U.S. law (TVPA) all present labor trafficking as the dominant category of trafficking, the focus on sex trafficking, often embedded in the more historically resonant "sex slavery" or "modern day slavery," results from tireless efforts of feminist and religious interest groups. The trafficking discourse has narrowed to ignore larger human rights concerns, concentrating instead on border and immigration control, or on the exploitation of children. Trafficking has been presented by the media and incorporated into legislation by Congress and an increasing number of states, as a "special evil," to quote former President George Bush,[80] requiring an immediate response at all levels, explaining this is a "multi-billion dollar underground of brutality and lonely fear . . . ."[81] The plethora of new state laws designed to address trafficking (40 states have antislavery legislation) and the imaginaries of most people about trafficking are built on extreme stereotypes of the trafficker and the victim. They are designed to address a small segment of a larger problem and as such, either by design or by fiat, avoid addressing the universal problem of human slavery and the critical structural conditions that produce trafficking opportunities, as well as the involvement of first world countries in the construction of these problems.

HISTORY

Following the history of international concern about trafficking is valuable, although in the past, as in the present, the lines between trafficking as a broad term and the more narrowly construed sex trafficking often intersected or were blurred. The definition as well as the emphasis on trafficking in human beings has shifted over time. The concept of "white slavery," so prevalent in the 1880s, reflected concern about "innocent," young European women, primarily from Belgium, Germany, and Great Britain, being trafficked within Western Europe for work in brothels.[82] In 1904, the International Agreement for the Suppression of the White Slave Traffic was signed,[83] focusing again on the recruitment of women for prostitution through deception or force.[84] The White Slave Traffic

Act (the Mann Act) was passed by the U.S. Congress in 1910. It prohibited unmarried women from crossing state lines for immoral purposes and, more to the point, criminalized interracial couples.[85] More specifically, it prohibited the "knowing transportation of any person for the purpose of engaging in prostitution or other sexual activity."

Then, almost a half a century later, in 1949, the UN Convention for the Suppression of the Traffic in Persons and of the Exploitation of the Prostitution of Others superseded earlier agreements and required that states punish a person who "procures, entices or leads away, for the purposes of 'prostitution' of another person," even with that person's consent.[86] Only a few states ratified it because it took an abolitionist approach to prostitution.[87] This approach is reflected in U.S. policy that until very recently demanded that countries and organizations receiving aid or support maintain a strict antiprostitution stance, disallowing the position that there is such a thing as legitimate sex work and that prostitution should be separated from forced prostitution. At the same time, the United Nations called for the decriminalization of prostitution and the enforcement of laws against those who exploit women and children in prostitution.[88] The proposal, read to the UN General Assembly by Eleanor Roosevelt, was ratified by more than 50 countries, but not by the United States.[89]

It was not until the decades of the 1990s and beyond that trafficking reemerged as a significant problem, this time firmly focused on sex trafficking and fueled by concerns about HIV/AIDS, international sex tourism, and changing sexual mores. Abolitionist discourse characterized trafficking as sexual slavery, and this "sexual domination discourse" intrinsically linked trafficking, prostitution, and sexual slavery.[90] On the other hand, the sex work approach did not define prostitution per se as a problem, instead focusing on work conditions that could be exploitative or degrading.

In 1993, the Vienna Declaration and Programme of Action of the World Conference on Human Rights specifically condemned forced prostitution and trafficking rather than prostitution,[91] and in 1995, the Platform for Action[92] again emphasized fighting forced prostitution and trafficking.[93]

The 2000 Palermo Protocol, a supplement to the UN Convention against Transnational Organized Crime,[94] changed its focus to the threat of transnational organized crime, emphasizing the "proximity of this issue to other irregular migration issues and illicit cross-border activities."[95] It reframed trafficking as a "law and order" issue connected and linked to the protection of borders. The European Union adopted an agreement similar to the protocol,[96] but it clearly specifies that trafficking can be both national and transnational and can be linked to organized crime as well as to small, rather "disorganized" crime. The central underlying concept is "exploitation" by whatever means, with trafficking being viewed as a form of human slavery.

SLAVERY

> "With its compelling narrative of sexual danger, drama, sensation, furious action, wild applause, and most important, clearly identifiable victims, villains, and heroes, the anti-trafficking melodrama remains highly fascinating and effective in mobilizing public opinion."[97]

The language of the TVPA of 2000 illustrates this melodramatic narrative, defining trafficking[98] as a degrading form of modern-day slavery that exists worldwide. It is spoken of as "human slavery," "sex slavery," "modern slavery," leading one to conclude that the purpose of the act is to fight all human slavery. But some scholars conclude that, contrary to the rhetoric of political leaders, human rights activists, feminist abolitionists, and religious leaders,[99] the protocol and the TVPA are of "marginal significance" in the fight against modern slavery. Others, such as James Hathaway of the Melbourne Law School, conclude that usurpation of the term "slavery" by the antitrafficking activists has actually *created* a number of problems, including, most importantly, drawing attention away from worldwide slavery. Framing the antitrafficking efforts of the United States and international governments as a fight against an "unspeakable form of slavery, an unspeakable and unforgivable crime ... "[100] or as Condoleezza Rice suggests, an "abolitionist movement,"[101] raises "real human rights concerns."[102] Hathaway actually sees antitrafficking legislation as a significant *retreat* from the already agreed-upon prohibitions of slavery. In 1926, the Slavery Convention adopted a legally binding definition of slavery that committed to a broad mission: to bring about the complete abolition of slavery. The problem with redefining trafficking as slavery is that the resultant antitrafficking efforts privilege a very small subset of slaves, allowing activists to ignore this seemingly intractable problem of culturally ingrained, endemic slavery. Of the approximately 27 to 30 million slaves in the world today, only about 3 percent or about 750,000 are actual victims of human trafficking.[103] Antislavery activists are concerned that narrowing the definition of slavery, which is a human rights concern of enormous proportions, to trafficking not only allows for greater migration control and potential human rights abuses, but contributes to the perception that world-wide slavery is being addressed rather than leading to a real and effective humanitarian response.[104]

For example, rather than addressing exploitation itself, we narrow our concern to the transport of people for exploitation. The construction of antitrafficking efforts within the framework of human rights or antislavery concerns denies the fact that these efforts actually may increase the risks to people throughout the world and violate their human rights, such as their effort to escape oppression and seek refuge.[105] And the constructed image of the "trafficked sex slave" that has so much cachet works to the advantage of conservative moral agendas on prostitution, gender, and sexuality, and in support of more restrictive border and immigration control[106] while not addressing the larger problem of global human exploitation. The definition of trafficking today as "modern slavery" allows us to engage in moral condemnation of traffickers while simultaneously not condemning the many forcible restrictions on those deemed to be "free."[107] The UN focus on raising the profile of the trafficking problem allows for a sense of complacency, redirecting our attention so that there is a real loss in our effort to eradicate slavery.

The practice of slavery remains commonplace even though it has been outlawed by every nation in the world. It is most prevalent in those countries that are poorest; in South Asia it is estimated that 15 to 20 million people are kept in bonded labor in India, Pakistan, Bangladesh, and Nepal making bricks and carpets, rolling cigarettes, farming, or harvesting salt in the marshes.[108] In sub-Saharan Africa, especially the Sudan and Mauritania, the Anti-Slavery Group estimates that at least 200,000 people are kept in bondage.[109] In Uganda and Congo, children are likely to be enslaved as soldiers for rebel fighters in war zones, having to choose between death and murdering others.[110] The majority of the approximately 30 million slaves alive today are trapped in the traditional debt bondage systems of South Asia or the chattel slavery systems in parts of Africa, particularly the Sudan. Bales reports that most slaves are held under the debt bondage systems in Southeast Asia, a system in which debt can be handed down from generation to generation and in which debt grows as those indebted borrow to make required payments.[111] Millions of slaves, including children, in Africa experience chattel slavery, embedded so deeply in a culture of control and obedience that it need not be enforced through violence.[112] Some of these children are forced to work for organized criminal groups, or are adopted to serve as domestic servants, or in agricultural and mining industries, vulnerable to physical and sexual abuse.[113] In Latin America, forced labor, another form of slavery, is relatively common in rural areas and cattle ranches, logging and mining camps and plantations where beans, corn, cotton, and sugarcane are produced and thousands are trafficked into the mahogany, brick-making and gold-mining industries in the Peruvian Amazon.[114] Undocumented Haitians are lured to the Dominican Republic each year to work in the sugarcane fields.[115] And there are in the United States 1.5 million seasonal farm workers who live in extremely poor working conditions, receive wages below the legal minimum wage, and have no legal protection or access to medical care or social services.[116] An increasing number of slaves are trapped in the "new slavery," an efficient system by which owners control the labor of people but do not have responsibility for the person—they do not own them outright. This allows the owners to ignore those who are nonproductive—infants, the feeble, or the elderly need not be maintained or supported, and people can be controlled for a season but not maintained throughout the year if that works to the advantage to the owner.[117]

Despite the enormity of the problem of slavery, the discourse on trafficking allows the separation of the exploitation and restrictions suffered by one set of people, who are the victims of global economic and political inequality, and another set of people, who are trafficked, privileging this group over others and creating a "hierarchy of victimhood."[118] As O'Connell Davidson writes, "the discourse on 'trafficking as modern slavery' closes down, rather than opens up, possibilities for effective political struggle against the restrictions, exploitation and injustices that many groups of migrants experience."[119] This discourse "inspires and legitimates efforts to divide a small number of 'deserving victims' from the masses that remain 'undeserving' of rights and freedoms."[120] Legitimate victims are depicted as women or girls needing protection from evil men, often "a barbaric foreign national who has associations with organized crime."[121] The separation of the "deserving" from the "undeserving" has the undesirable consequence of denying justice for the many ("undeserving") who migrate for work and have their rights and dignity violated.[122]

Global inequalities ensure the efforts of people to cross borders.[123] Not only is this a reasonable choice for the individual, but the remittances received by the country from which people migrate are extremely beneficial to that country, leading to the conclusion that these remittances are the "single most effective tool of economic and social rights empowerment, dwarfing the impact of official foreign aid programs."[124] The Palermo Protocol, from the point of view of critics, does not seek the amelioration of the root causes, the growing global inequity of opportunity and income, does nothing to address the conditions of being exploited, and does not require any remedies for the victims other than that they are provided with *access* to systems to seek compensation.[125]

Hathaway concludes that if we do not address the underlying conditions that spawn the desire to migrate, even under the worst of circumstances, we only ensure that increasing numbers of people are tempted into the hands of smugglers.[126] Not only that, but the criminalization of smugglers and those relying on smugglers, converts smuggling into a highly risky trafficking situation, thereby increasing both the cost and danger of cross-border crossings.[127]

ORGANIZED CRIME AND TRAFFICKERS

The fact that the UN Protocol is a supplement to the UN Convention against Transnational Organized Crime rather than a supplement to an antislavery convention reflects the intention of the protocol to prosecute criminals rather than to protect victims. Its "law and order" orientation encourages the development and enforcement of border control tactics that might otherwise be defined as violating international human rights agreements.[128] Hathaway sees the trafficking protocol as an effort to increase border control under the cover of promoting human rights, translating domestic law designed to protect states' borders into transnational legal obligations in which all states become agents of the first world, committed to protection of their borders.[129]

The concept of trafficking evokes several assumptions—that trafficking is nonconsensual, that borders are significant in shaping the flow of immigrants, that trafficking is operated by organized crime groups, and that its profits are enormous, even exceeding that of drug trafficking.[130] Trafficking is reported to be the third most lucrative form of organized crime in the world, after drugs and weapons ($9.6 billion a year according to U.S. State Department documents).[131] Others, including Kotrla, estimate that trafficking realizes a profit of between $32 billion and $91 billion a year for its entrepreneurs,[132] while antitrafficking activist Donna Hughes suggests the number is between $7 billion and $12 billion.[133] These authors caution that the revenues need to be understood within the context that, unlike drugs, the trafficked person can be sold again and again, becoming more valuable each time, or if held in bondage, becoming more indebted and trapped each time. Trafficking is usually presented as underpinning a thriving sex industry in which exploiters need to generate a supply for the ravenous market of men ready to consume fellow human beings as sex commodities. Yet these claims contrast with the reality that the government has failed to establish transnational trafficking as the blight it is presented as being, instead relying on inaccurate and fluctuating figures and anecdotal horror stories instead.[134]

Estimates of the extent of trafficking vary wildly from year to year and place to place. Even using numbers from one source, the U.S. State Department, there is great confusion in the numbers: in 2000, the annual trafficking report estimated between 45,000 and 50,000 persons were trafficked into the United States each year, but just one year later, the estimate was 18,000 to 20,000.[135] In 2005, the estimates declined again to 14,400 to 15,500 into all labor sectors[136] after a scathing report from the Government Accountability Office in 2006[137] about the inconsistencies in estimates. Even more interesting, however, is the finding that between 2007 and 2011 only 611 victims were identified nationwide.[138] Similar fluctuations are found in the State Department's estimates on global trafficking; in 2000, it estimates that 700,000 to 2 million women and children were trafficked, with this number rising in 2003 to 4 million. By 2005, the figures "inexplicably" fell to 600,000 to 800,000 victims of all types of trafficking, with "hundreds of thousands" said to be trafficked into prostitution.[139] These statistics are the grossly unreliable and exaggerated figures states and activists rely on as they push to have antitrafficking laws passed. While there is outrage over sex trafficking and, in particular, domestic minor sex trafficking, reliable estimates of the number of victims are unavailable as well. In one review of the various studies regarding the number of suspected domestic minor sex trafficking victims, Smith and Snow found such incompatible data-gathering techniques, definitions, and time periods that comparison by place was impossible.[140] In Dallas, Texas, for example, 150 suspected victims were reported in 2008, and in San Antonio, Texas, only three or four between 2005 and 2008.[141] In Las Vegas, Nevada, 5,122 victims were reported, but the time period was 1994–2007.[142] The conclusion reached by the Ohio Trafficking in Persons Study Commission on the scope of human trafficking within Ohio seems reasonable and seems generalizable to all states: "due to the very nature of human trafficking, it is virtually impossible to determine the exact number of victims . . . at any given time and with any degree of certainty."[143] Further, by its very nature, trafficking is clandestine and records are not made available to officials. Carole Vance has cautioned us to be wary of the extreme claims made by antitrafficking activists, a caution that would surely apply to a recent estimate that there were over 300,000 children in the United States at risk for trafficking.[144]

The numbers offered by the United States not only widely vary but they differ substantially from estimates of sex trafficking into Great Britain, where the range is reported to be between 142 and 1,420 annually. However, even these numbers, discrepant as they are, may be inflated.[145] As an illustration, in London in 2003, during a raid of massage parlors and

saunas, 295 illegal immigrants were found, but only 5 of them were identified as victims of trafficking.[146] This must have been a disappointingly
small number, given Britain's Home Office estimates of the numbers of
girls and women being trafficked into prostitution. But these small numbers are still presented in the context of millions of girls and women being
"at risk."[147]

It is clearly very difficult for the government to arrest and prosecute
traffickers, particularly if they traffic across national borders. The Bush
administration, despite estimating that there were over 50,000 victims of
trafficking and spending $150 million, eventually identified only 1,362
such victims.[148] Not only is it difficult to find victims of trafficking, it is
almost impossible to prosecute and convict the traffickers. The U.S.
Justice Department prosecuted only 131 persons for sex trafficking
offenses and obtained only 99 convictions between 2001 and 2004, a
low figure but five times higher than for the previous four-year period.[149]
And while there may be between 1,800 and 5,950 victims of labor trafficking in the United States each year, only 35 people were charged with trafficking in 2005, 99 in 2006, and 103 in 2007; and of these, the conviction
rates were abominable—only 10 were convicted in 2005, 38 in 2006, and
17 in 2007.[150] The efforts to find and rescue trafficking victims and to
prosecute traffickers have obviously been disappointing at best, with only
53 human trafficking cases charged by the Civil Right and the U.S.
Attorneys' Offices in 2010 (although this is an increase from previous
years).[151] Either the millions of dollars poured into enforcement are woe-
fully inadequate, or there is a significant problem with the estimates.

Until the mid-1990s, trafficking was often viewed as a variation of
smuggling, the illegal transport of people across borders. It was viewed
as illegal migration rather than a form of exploitation of human beings.
Smuggling, however, is an activity in which both parties are willing participants in a criminal consensual transaction, while trafficking specifically targets the trafficked person as an object of criminal exploitation.[152]
Traffickers may be part of a loosely organized criminal network, sometimes small operations called "popcorn" traffickers, or well-organized
criminal groups, sometimes both as they collaborate as needed to get the
girls or women across borders and into the hotels, brothels, or homes
where they will be prostituted. Police and other officials have to be
recruited to participate in the trafficking network in order for it to operate.
Often the police, who are to be enforcers of the law, act as accomplices of
the traffickers, protecting the businesses, bars, dance halls and brothels
from raids, informing the owners of efforts to enforce the law in advance,
paid both in coin and in access to the girls and women they are to protect.

In terribly poor countries, the amount to be earned from organized criminal gangs can keep a man and his family alive whereas his wages cannot—trafficking can make the difference between constant need and a decent living. Border guards, immigration officials, baggage handlers, and others along the way have to be paid in order for trafficking to succeed. Even in Western countries, while the police may have to be paid more, there is still a great incentive for them to look the other way or become embedded in the criminal gang. As long as wages are low, relative to the country, and rewards for breaking the law are great, especially when the person can see himself as only indirectly involved or only involved in one small piece of the process, the likelihood of official corruption is great. For all of those involved, the cost-reward analysis and the ease of transport become key factors in trafficking. Kara looks at the economic analysis engaged in by traffickers and suggests that the penalties must be elevated to reduce profit and increase cost if trafficking is to be effectively addressed.[153] Currently, it is a relatively "low-risk" business, leading Bales, for example, to suggest that the modern sex trade needs to be made more dangerous for the traders.[154]

Who are the traffickers? It certainly depends on how you define traffickers. As in prostitution, if a pimp is one who benefits from the sale of a woman's body, the definition of trafficker could be expanded to include a wide range of people from hotel and bar owners to taxicab drivers, in addition to the man who actually manages the woman on a personal level. Traffickers work at every level, from the man down the street to the embassy officials and the immigration officers at the airport. While the imagery of the organized criminal is powerful, traffickers are likely to be neighbors, kin, acquaintances, or former trafficking victims who recruit new people in order to help pay off their own debt. They are people easily corrupted by money thrown their way because their lives are so miserable, or they are people at the top of the organizations who live a luxurious lifestyle on the backs of the women they sell. Sometimes the traffickers are also involved in gun and drug running but team up for their mutual benefit or move into trafficking because it is extremely lucrative and relatively low risk compared with other forms of smuggling.[155] An individual cannot simply transport a woman illegally from one country to another without the help of a whole array of people along the way. In order to get from her village in the Ukraine to Israel or from Moldova to her destination in Western Europe, the girl or woman may change hands many times, being handed off to ever more sophisticated traffickers as she goes. She may be sold, time and again, or she may accrue a debt of bondage as she is moved down the line, culminating in a debt so great that she can never pay it off.

Dikov has examined the trafficking of women from Bulgaria to Western European countries with a focus on the organization of trafficking and the process of managing, transporting, and investing large sums of money.[156] Her study provides an excellent example of the organization of trafficking. Most human trafficking from Bulgaria (85 percent) is for the purpose of sexual exploitation.[157] With the easing of visa restrictions in the European Union, people with criminal contacts in Europe, as well as those from Roma groups, traveled more widely, and they effectively became the dominant traffickers in Western European countries including Belgium, Germany, and the Netherlands.[158] Bulgaria, Ukraine, Romania, Russia, Nigeria, and Moldova are the primary source countries of prostitution in Eastern Europe, but Bulgaria, with a small population of only 7.5 million people, outdistances its neighbors and competitors in the number of women it sexually exploits.[159]

The traffickers require means to manage, control, and distribute their illicit profits gained through trafficking. Petrunov studied the money laundering activities of traffickers taking women from Bulgaria to Western Europe for the purpose of prostitution—a prostitution market, controlled by organized crime, was already active in Bulgaria before the collapse of the communist regime, but this allowed for more frequent travel and greater contact with organized criminal groups elsewhere.[160] In Bulgaria, there were four main groups of traffickers identified: loners (prostitutes moving around on their own), independent pimps who controlled two to five women (sometimes relatives), partners that were associations of pimps and the women they controlled working together. and large, multilayered organizations, organized in hierarchy and often engaged in other illicit activity. Those acting independently or in smaller groups were likely to have to connect with these larger organizations to remain profitable—they receive the lion's share of the market and have the greatest influence on the other institutions, like the police and the immigration.[161]

Molland challenges the emphasis on the profit motive in trafficking, saying that very few of those involved in the process operate like capitalists. In fact, looking at the Thai-Laos border as an example, he concludes that the distinction between those who move consensually and those who are moved nonconsensually does not result in significant economic differences.[162] Just as with trafficking from Colombia, employment and recruitment are based on informal or extended kin networks—personal alliances are more important than formal relationships, and the offering of commissions for helping others is commonplace, even in government and private business, so that the practice among sex workers of taking a commission for recruiting others is consistent with the larger cultural practice of patronage.[163] Richard Staring reports that traffickers are often part of small, ethnically homogeneous networks in which personal relationships play an important role; recruiters are often acquainted with their victims, looking for women in their circle of friends or in bars and restaurants they frequent.[164] Most of the trafficking networks he studied in the Netherlands consisted of only a few traffickers who ran all aspects of the organization and did not conform to the picture of "organized crime" so dominant in the antitrafficking discourse.[165]

Further, the dominant discourse in the U.S. government—particularly the Trafficking in Persons Office—of the evil predator and innocent victim that cultivates moral outrage and requires intervention distorts the relationship between those involved.[166] Trafficking is often built on friendships and kinship networks; small, informal groups; and the active participation of the person being moved. While some of the women are trapped in a system of human bondage for which they could not possibly be prepared, many are self-motivated and fully aware that they will be providing sexual services.[167] In addition, the "innocent victim" is often aware of the necessity of depicting herself in a particular way in order to get the kind of help she needs and not to be deported or treated like a prostitute. As Hua and Nigorizawa point out, the trafficked women must conform to the typification of the innocent victim, and hence, present themselves as culturally backward, innocent, or as cruelly victimized in acknowledgment of the VTPA's distinction between victims, "illegal immigrants," and "sex workers."[168]

TRAFFICKING: A PROCESS

There is high global demand for domestic servants, agricultural laborers, sex workers, and factory labor. Political, social, or economic crises or natural disasters; discrimination against women and girls; limited economic and educational opportunities for women; well-established trafficking networks; public corruption (especially of border agents and police); restrictive immigration policies in destination countries; and government disinterest are some of the "push" factors. Trafficking may also result from internal policies, such as the increased prices of permanent residence status in Beijing and Shanghai, for example, and other cities that limit the number of rural migrants who can even apply for residence The increasing cost of using a registered employment agent to assist in finding work may increase reliance on a friend or acquaintance that may result in trafficking.[169] Trafficking also relies on governmental corruption at both the national and local level. The women from Thailand who are trafficked to the Tier Two country of Japan provide a good example. Here the Yakuza, an organized crime group made up of Japanese and Thai men, as well as Thai women married to Japanese men, controls the sex trade.[170] The women who are recruited are pushed from Thailand by economic desperation, and once in Japan find themselves in a country where they do not speak the language, where they experience economic discrimination, and often do not have the means to return to Thailand, thus relying on informal arrangements that result in their vulnerability to organized criminals.[171]

The face of trafficking varies by location, with South Asia, Eastern Europe, and Africa being locations from which most trafficked persons come, and with the United States, Western Europe, and the wealthy Arab republics being countries of destination. The UNODC Trafficking in Persons Global Report of 2006 reports as key origin countries: Albania, Belarus, Bulgaria, China, Lithuania, Nigeria, Republic of Moldova, Romania, Russian Federation, and Thailand. In Latin America, the primary source countries are Colombia, Dominican Republic, Guatemala, Haiti, Honduras, Mexico, Nicaragua, and Paraguay, with Argentina, Bahamas, Barbados, Brazil, Chile, Costa Rica, Mexico, Netherland Antilles, Panama, St. Lucia, Trinidad, and Tobago being the primary countries of destination.[172] Although global economic inequality underpins trafficking as well as smuggling and illegal migration of every sort, there is not an absolutely clear relationship between degrees of poverty and other measures of inequality such as the gender gap and low human development among poor countries and their likelihood of being a country of origin.[173] Victims of cross-border trafficking, in fact, are often more likely to come from countries other than those at the absolute economic global bottom. Eight of the top 10 countries of origin for trafficked persons are transitioning from centrally planned to market economies in Southeast Europe, China, or the Commonwealth of Independent States, including Russia, Moldova, Georgia, Ukraine, Armenia, and Bosnia, and these are not the least developed countries in the world today.[174] Many countries act both as countries of origin and destination, and the relationships between countries, changing borders, war and displacement, and changing political systems provide for a fluid and sometimes erratic system of border crossing that does not fit the commonly presented "origin, transit, destination" framework.[175] Trafficking occurs in the context of international and national movements that are increasingly being undertaken owing to economic globalization, the feminization of migration, armed conflicts, the breakdown or reconfiguration of governments, and the transformation of political boundaries.

Not all trafficking crosses wide expanses; there are many global border crossings that involve short distances, and this ease of land access to the destination country is more important from the point of view of Jac-Kucharski than any other factor, including corruption and visa requirements. The trafficking of women from Nepal to India to take advantage of the legal and prospering sex industry there is greatly enhanced by the shared 1,740-mile open border between these two countries.[176] Deane reports over 200,000 women and girls have been trafficked to India's red-light district reflecting a serious problem with a lack of enforcement of regulations and the easy flow of women across borders.[177] The conditions that characterize trafficking from Nepal to India illustrate the underlying problems globally. While there are many prohibitions against trafficking in Nepal, there is no commitment to the implementation of the laws, and there is a public and cultural blaming of women who have been trafficked that discourages them from seeking help or returning to their families, thereby making them vulnerable to retrafficking.[178]

The movement of people from Nepal to India also illustrates some of the other factors that shape trafficking. These include a demand for cheap labor that pushes a demand for child labor in the informal economic sector, low wages, poverty and conflict-induced displacement, as well as a desire on the part of women to escape the restrictions of their home country and their families. The willingness of families to sell their daughters since they are an economic burden, the market for child marriages in India, and the high poverty and unemployment rates in Nepal make the rapidly developing, urban modern cities of India very attractive.[179]

The imagery of trafficked victims varies substantially depending on the country of origin. On one hand, the women who are trafficked from Russia and other post-soviet states are depicted as marginalized, unemployed, homeless, prostitutes, or orphans,[180] while at the same time, many of the women trafficked from Russia are said to have college degrees, their unemployment or poverty reflecting the lack of opportunity in the post-soviet economy.[181] Still others are depicted as representative of the general female population within a particular age group in Russia.[182] The U.S. imagery of trafficked women and girls as depicted in the TVPA of 2000 and the legislation passed by the states has primarily been of young innocent victims being sold into prostitution. Research on trafficked women in Asia, Latin America, and Africa portrays the typical victims as young, poor, and uneducated, although, in fact, these characteristics wouldn't clearly differentiate trafficked women and girls from the majority of the population in these countries. Ribando Seelke lists poverty and unemployment as significant factors contributing to the vulnerability of people to traffickers but also lists illiteracy, homelessness, gang membership, drug use, and a history of sexual abuse.[183] In addition to oppression, lack of opportunity and poverty, weak family or social support networks, and willingness to take risks for short-term rewards might be a push factor for some women.[184] Undeniably, one of the key push factors for migrants in general, and specifically for those who are trafficked, is lack of employment opportunities and low wages in their country of citizenship. Sixty percent of the women and more than half of the trafficked men were lured by the promise of a job, with another 36 percent lured by other false promises such as educational opportunities, tourism, or marriage.[185] Studies in India, Africa, and the Netherlands conclude that women are more likely to be trafficked for sex to areas in which prostitution is already commonplace and in which there are all of the supportive and ancillary services such as escort services and the Internet that provide intrastructural support for prostitution.[186]

Danailova-Trainor and Laczko assert that to understand the reasons for trafficking, we need to look to development rather than simply assume that poverty pushes people into trafficking. They indicate the importance of understanding the "meaning" of poverty rather than assume that a push-pull is based purely on economic factors. Poverty may, in fact, be an impediment to movement, and movement may only occur with "rising expectations."[187] They report from Surtees that women and girls who were trafficked were not actually poorer than those who were not, but perceived themselves to be. Further, those stuck in poverty may be more at risk not just because they are poor, but because they don't have access to information that would help them avoid trafficking, leading to more risky behavior.[188]

The social context, including social, economic, and familial factors, shapes the choices of those involved in trafficking as they do for everyone. The class and gender constraints, the limitations on income and education, and the kin and extended connections within the community all exert an influence on the woman's perceived choices. Her behavior may be seen as a survival adaptation to her difficult economic and social environment.[189] Many of the women know that they are going to be engaging in prostitution in the country of destination and make what Jones et al. refer to as "adaptive choices," seeing this as an opportunity to escape rural oppression and the lack of opportunity for women, who are often expected to sacrifice their own futures to support their families.[190]

While Molland describes informal relationships of mutual benefit that are not necessarily driven by greed as underlies much trafficking of persons, some researchers have stressed the organizational sophistication of trafficking operations characteristic of organized crime syndicates and criminal cartels.[191] The complicated tiered system of Bulgarian traffickers, complete with many checks and balances that deliver substantial resources to the regional and national bosses, is a clear example of this organized crime model.[192] The profits they reap, which are eventually filtered into both legitimate businesses and a life of great luxury, are built on the work of the prostitutes at the very bottom of the economic ladder. Somewhere between 10 and 50 percent of the profits go to the prostitutes, almost all of whom are promised far more than they ever realize.[193] Their incomes are generally spent not on improving their own conditions but on supporting their families in Bulgaria.[194] This expectation that girls and women support their families contributes to their vulnerability to trafficking in other instances as well. Thailand's development policies, for example, created a large pool of women who were not only poverty stricken but also responsible for the welfare of their families, making them a ready reserve of workers willing to migrate and vulnerable to being drawn into sex work by local crime groups with links to global organized crime. Jones et al.[195] report on four case studies reflecting the contribution of this expectation to trafficking: Pom, who returned to her village after three years of work in a massage parlor, was shunned by her family when she refused to cooperate with a trafficker in the recruitment of other village girls. Similarly, Kwan, at the age of 12, took work in a massage parlor after her father died in order to help her family, saying that "our living conditions forced me to sacrifice myself."[196] Villagers often encourage the girls to leave for more lucrative work, claiming that they have friends or daughters who have preceded them and they will find the work good and lucrative.[197] The expectation that women support their families dovetails with the recruiters' efforts—some of the women, as discussed by Molland and Jones et al., were already involved in sex work in Thailand, and in other instances, moved from working as cleaning girls in beer bars or massage parlors to sex work because they could make more money.[198]

Recruitment in Bulgaria relies on what Petrunov describes as "soft methods"—the women are not kidnapped or forced but are often the victims of psychological and emotional abuse and manipulation on the part of the traffickers, thus becoming "willing" participants in the traffickers' scheme.[199] This is a common pattern of trafficking, one in which the trafficker initially befriends the woman who "falls in love with him" and trusts him enough to follow him when he suggests they leave the country. Another common means of recruitment is through women who are already sex workers who can recruit friends and acquaintances in the

villages. In Thailand and Laos, according to Molland, the fictive kin relationships and the patron-client relationships that are commonplace smooth
the way for exploitative relationships.[200]

Rather than there being a perpetrator-victim relationship, the relationship between the trafficker and the trafficked woman is often depicted as
a "helping" or friendship relationship, offering the opportunity for income
that can reduce the stigma tied to prostitution and ease the condemnation
of a young woman who may find herself stigmatized for having premarital
sex. The recruiters and the bar owners who participate in this system often
describe their involvement as "helping" and entice mostly uneducated,
rural, young women into a life that seems attractive for its freedom, nice
clothes, and material possessions. The women create a network in which
friend recruits friend, both seeing their future as one with "good pay"
and an opportunity to escape poverty or difficult family situations. Other
women are more likely to think they are entering work that pays well in
a legitimate business, but may soon find themselves selling sex because
it is more lucrative and less difficult than the work they are recruited
into.[201] These women are usually not forced, nor, Molland suggests, are
they lacking in agency and completely victimized, although they are
caught in the convergence of deception and helping.[202] Both they and
the recruiters are engaged in a process, not an event, one in which definitions of reality are slippery, and euphemisms, used by the recruiters and
the owners of businesses, can soften the entry of young women into the
trade. The trafficked and the traffickers both engage in acts of bad faith
in order to successfully complete this process. Both rely on the "unfulfilled desires for modernity" that encourage the migration of young
women to migrate and provide a rationalization of the recruiters.[203]

Further, the relationships between trafficker and trafficked are more
ambiguous than much of the literature, especially that of the antitraffickers
and those involved in the training of police, law enforcement officers, border guards, and those who use a "check list approach" to the identification
of victims and traffickers, would suggest.[204] Instead, the social relationships are intricately nuanced. Depicting them as polarized and antagonistic
clouds the picture and undercuts efforts to address the problem. The traditional organized crime model doesn't fit this business of low-level pimps,
thugs, transporters, and owners of businesses who cooperate when necessary and compete when it is to their advantage. Warren, in a study of
Colombian trafficking patterns, points out that the "morally derived absolute distinction between traffickers and their victims is deconstructed" by
the lines of evidence presented during trial.[205] Colombian trafficking networks are transnational kinship organizations. Based on domestic

partnerships, combining the efforts of a boss and his girlfriend, mother-daughter dyads, sometimes involving former trafficked women who have moved up in the organization and sometimes a combination of these arrangements, these alliances are transient and flexible as relationships change.[206] Women often work as labor recruiters, and the distinction between sex worker and supervisor turns out to be relatively fluid, contrasting with the image of the "predatory male stranger common in anti-trafficking media."[207] These familial transnational kinship organizations allow for fluidity and flexibility and help protect the bosses at higher levels. The reality presented in the courtroom when these traffickers are brought to trial contrasts with the media coverage that focuses on dramatic brothel raids and heavy police activity; it also illustrates how the complexity of the relationships makes it very hard to convict human traffickers.

Nor does recruiting friends or family into sex work always entail negative moral sanctions—rather, it can be a way of fulfilling reciprocal obligations or climbing the social ladder (moving from controlled prostitution to being in charge). As a result of these relationships and processes, recruitment into sex work takes on the connotation of helping—helping them out of poverty, helping them move up the social ladder, and helping them afford nice clothes and makeup and eventually to be able to send money home (at least half of Laotian immigrants to Thailand send remittances back home).[208]

While trafficking is described as an enormously lucrative business, pure profitability alone is not enough to explain trafficking, at least along the Thai-Lao border.[209] Rather, a mixture of capitalist logic and patron-client relationships allows for the migration of women. As such, the traditional methods of combating trafficking, such as awareness raising, income generation, and victim support, are compromised if they do not take into account the importance of these informal and often close social relations. Concentrating on profitability alone ignores the "subsistence ethics" of those involved and the fact that success (more clothes, higher status) can erase the stigma of sex work—hence the involvement of former sex workers in recruitment.[210] Women who are trafficked operate within a limited set of circumstances and find ways to talk about and characterize their work that minimizes the degree of exploitation or coercion they experience. Further, there is a nuanced flow of people across borders, such as Thailand and Laos by women who often value the noneconomic benefits of their work, like freedom, modernity, and the lack of supervision more highly than the income it generates.[211]

Sex trafficking is often presented as the trafficking in resalable human commodities, a growing international enterprise, involving organized criminals, syndicates, and hundreds of thousands of girls and women, duped or forced into sex slavery. We read that since the mid-1990s, governments, NGOs, and human rights activists have studied, deplored, and legislated against this "scourge." Girls and women are spirited across borders by rogue "popcorn" traffickers or systematically transported through a complex weave of organized crime syndicates and the cooperation or willing ignorance of police, politicians, guards, immigration officials, and numerous other bit players. The women are then delivered to legal and illegal brothels, resold to free agents, constrained in suburban homes, driven to consignments in hotels and parks, owned and controlled by their keepers. The women end up in brothels, bars, strip clubs, or engaged in pornography.[212] Yet, while this may be true for some women, despite her best efforts, Hughes found only six cases of women trafficked for stripping between 1998 and 2005. On the other end of the spectrum, in Cambodia, a country where there are probably more sex workers than in most countries, a USAID report estimated that there were approximately 18,256 sex workers, most of whom were neither underage nor trafficked.[213]

It is not always easy to differentiate those who cross borders voluntarily from those who are forced or threatened, but our notions of victim lead us to emphasize a faceless passivity. The focus of trafficking activists and lawmakers assumes a lack of agency and passivity on the part of the trafficked person, imposing an inaccurate and romanticized victim identity.[214] Such a definition is very problematic for women who may in fact have voluntarily migrated but who then are severely exploited once they have arrived. A woman may have a very hard time proving that she did not voluntarily consent to work in prostitution either because she knew what she was going to do or because she was afraid for herself or her family if she admitted that she was coerced.[215] Women are often reluctant to self-report or to cooperate with the authorities in trafficking cases. One illustration of that is the reluctance of women to call a 1-800 call center established by the U.S. National Human Trafficking Resource Center.[216] Police indicate that there are very few calls for help (a high of 239 when first established, dropping to 174 six months later), and that, when separated from labor-related calls, the calls related to sex trafficking made up only 1 percent of the total calls.[217]

A study of Vietnamese migrants in Cambodia reported that out of 100 women interviewed, only 6 had been duped, and the rest knew that they would be working in a brothel in Cambodia before they left Vietnam.[218] Another study of trafficking from Eastern Europe to Holland concludes that most of the women were also aware they would be involved in sex work in their country of destination and that a large number had previously worked as prostitutes.[219] The women leave their homes to make what is considered a substantial amount of money, in a short period of time, to experience personal and social freedom, and to avoid rural life and agricultural labor.[220] One study reported that many of the Vietnamese women working in Cambodian brothels were recruited by their mothers and aunts.[221] And as Smit points out, since trafficking is most likely to occur where there is the greatest migratory movement, it is sometimes difficult to differentiate those who are trafficking victims from those who are helping their fellow countrymen or family members.[222] This finding is consistent with Zimmerman and Watts, who argue that "it should not be assumed [. . .] that all women who have been trafficked are victimized, consider themselves victims, detest their captors, or wish to escape or go home."[223] We are not really talking about "organized crime" for the most part, but about networks of people, family members, criminals, and others who cooperate in the trafficking effort.

Assumptions about trafficked women also include cultural imagery as it unfolds in the narratives about trafficking. Hua and Nigorizawa point out that women trafficked from Asia are trapped in "racialized colonial frameworks" that depict them as culturally backward, whereas the women from Soviet nations are viewed as representing a temporary diversion from progress due to economic instability.[224] These very different constructions justify differential treatment of trafficked persons as either "worthy" or "unworthy." Those (brown) people trafficked from Asian and African countries are "orientalized" as representing backward, more primitive countries and are not as welcome as those (white) from "modern" progressive states.[225] This "moral divide" allows for some trafficked persons to be constructed as "innocent victims" for the wider public, human rights activists, service providers, and the state, thereby contributing to the economic success of NGOs and subcontractors in the fields of human rights and justice who rely on this image for their support.[226] These constructions deny the subjectivity and agency of the women migrants, while at the same time blaming the trafficked people for their victim status. Warren, for example, describes trafficking victims as forced into marginal positions on the fringes of society and denied the "universal" human rights enjoyed by others.[227] Similarly, in Russia, both men and women are likely to blame victims of trafficking, who are rejected by both society and their own families.[228] The belief, reflecting reality, that many women who are trafficked for prostitution are either already prostitutes hoping to make more money abroad or are aware of the nature of their potential employment when they sign contracts to work as dancers, waitresses, or *au pairs*, renders them unsympathetic to the public.[229]

Women who have been trafficked are vulnerable to retrafficking for a number of reasons: the poverty they were hoping to escape is still there; they may feel shame about what they have been doing and blame themselves; they may be rejected by their friends and families and thus, because of all the negatives tied to being returned to their country of origin, they may be unlikely to cooperate with law enforcement or to testify against their trafficker. They may not want to be "rescued." Some authors see this as reflecting their psychological dependence on their captor, although it is also possible to see this as a realistic assessment of their situation and an awareness that the law-and-order approach to trafficked doesn't include an interest in the well-being of the trafficking victim.[230]

CONCLUSION

Carole Vance proposes a number of ways to "do nothing about trafficking while pretending to," acknowledging the real complexities of this social problem.[231] She suggests that we have no solid data and that we rely on grossly exaggerated numbers to justify new laws and interventions. She suggests that the hyperbole, the language about "ultimate evil" and "sex slavery," is distracting rather than helpful.[232] There is indeed global slavery; slavery is a real and ongoing problem with millions of people either in debt bondage or chattel slavery, but calling sex trafficking slavery both diminishes the real problem of slavery and paints a picture of trafficking that is wholly inaccurate. Vance's critical work condemns framing trafficking as a human rights concern and then not requiring adequate and accessible services for the trafficking victims, instead subjecting them to a criminal justice system that itself sometimes violates their human rights.[233] She joins others[234] in criticizing the extreme focus on sex trafficking and trafficking into forced prostitution rather than labor trafficking. She also sees the government as duplicitous—presenting itself as compassionate to victims yet, for example, often forcing them to testify in order to obtain services. The government also severely limits the number of T-Visas it approves, visas that would allow victims to remain in the United States—giving only 1,591 T-Visas between 2002 and 2009 when it had the authority to grant 40,000 during that same period.[235] She also criticizes the focus on young, innocent girls and the painting of traffickers as evildoers that results in the denial of the powerful forms of structural oppression that drive the desire to migrate. And she condemns the government response when the media hysteria and government alarm over transnational trafficking fail to result in the discovery of a large number of trafficking victims, traffickers, or billions of dollars in profits. In this instance, focus is switched from transnational trafficking to domestic trafficking, targeting girls and their boyfriends but reconstructing them legally as victims and pimps.[236] Based on Vance's powerful criticism of the current constructions of trafficking, and not to engage in hyperbole myself, I am reminded of this country's near-obsession with the "satanic ritual abuse" hysteria of the 1970s. The lives of innocent people were devastated by false accusations and the unbelievable gullibility of public figures and the public. The suspects were ostracized, jailed, convicted of heinous crimes—Virginia McMartin and her family including Raymond and Peggy Ann Buckey; Margaret Kelly Michaels who worked at the Wee Care child care center in New Jersey; a group of people accused of running a satanic sex ring near Bakersfield, California; Doug Nagle; and, others—are some of the better-known cases. A number of authors describe and try to explain this travesty. People were imprisoned, and some are to this day, on the basis of outrageous tales of Satan worshiping and fantastic stories of sexual abuse. Some of the claims included a child being turned into a mouse, children abused in a tractor at the day care center, teachers rolling around with them naked, children taking trips on airplanes, being taken to see a devil with horns, children urinated on and forced to eat "poop," and babies dismembered on church altars. Otherwise perfectly sane people, including prosecuting attorneys, judges, jurors, and therapists, accepted these completely absurd, outrageous claims about child sexual abuse under the banner of "believe the children."[237] And, of course, these stories were not true, but were instead reflections of social angst about the family, changing sexual mores, changing gender expectations, class issues, and widespread guilt about children and child care. While the claims might not be as outrageous in the area of trafficking, it is clear that trafficking, especially transnational trafficking in persons, has not been nearly the horrendous problem so many people have described it to be, not a more lucrative business than traffic in drugs and weapons, not the multibillion-dollar organized criminal sex enterprise it was expected to be, not one involving hundreds of thousands of innocent young girls kidnapped and kept in slavery. The data in all of these areas are sketchy, and there is more hype than proof about the extent and damage of trafficking, not that that has stopped legislatures across the country and law enforcement and Congress and NGOs, activists, and the media from the relentless pursuit of traffickers and trafficked victims—a search that has been, in a significant number of cases, narrowed now to prosecution of men for pimping their girlfriends. Just as Zhang says: "imagination seems to have taken the place of sound empirical studies."[238]

In the final analysis, trafficking is a result of a great discrepancy between the "haves" and the "have-nots," a reflection of the effort on the part of people who are disadvantaged economically to make a better life for themselves, an effort that may make them vulnerable to lies, deception, force, or fraud. It is better understood in these terms than in terms of predators lurking on dark street corners or in bars or posing as boyfriends in small villages luring innocent young girls into a life of prostitution and hell. It is the intentional exploitation of persons who want to be where they are not, either because of the money they can make, the freedom they can buy, the surveillance they can escape, the obligations they feel toward their families, or the naiveté they possess. These are people who, because of their desperation or their dreams, are vulnerable to the control and manipulation of others or take enormous risks to overcome the limitations of the lives they are trying to escape.

NOTES

1. R. Weitzer, "The Social Construction of Sex Trafficking: Ideology and Institutionalization of a Moral Crusade," *Politics and Society* 35, no. 3 (August 27, 2007), http://pas.sagepub.com/, 462; A. Siskin and L. S. Wyler, "Trafficking in Persons: U.S. Policy and Issues for Congress," *Trends in Organized Crime* 14, no. 2–3 (May 2011).

2. S. Stoecker and L. Shelley, *Human Traffic and Transnational Crime* (Lanham, MD: Rowman & Littlefield, 2005), 337.

3. D. Masci, "Human Trafficking and Slavery," *The CQ Researcher* 14, no. 12 (2004): 273–96.

4. Siskin and Wyler, "Trafficking in Persons," 267–71; R. Weitzer, "The Social Construction of Sex Trafficking."

5. K. Kotrla, "Domestic Minor Sex Trafficking in the United States," *Social Work* 55, no. 2 (April 2010): 181–87; R. Estes and N. Weiner, *The Commercial Sexual Exploitation of Children in the U.S., Canada and Mexico* (Philadelphia: University of Pennsylvania, 2002); H. Smith, "Sex Trafficking: Trends, Challenges, and the Limitations of International Law," *Human Rights Review* 12, no. 3 (2011): 271–86; and D. Hughes, "Modern-Day Comfort Women: The U.S. Military, Transnational Crime, and the Trafficking of Women." D. M. Hughes, K. Y. Chon, and D. O. Ellerman, published in *Violence against Women* 13, no. 9 (2007): 901–22.

6. M. Kaneti, "Project Trafficking: Global Unity in Addressing a Universal Challenge?" *Human Rights Review* 12, no. 3 (2011): 345–61.

7. C. R. Seelke, "Trafficking in Persons in Latin America and the Caribbean," *Trends in Organized Crime* 14, no. 2/3 (2011): 272–77.

8. Weitzer, "The Social Construction of Sex Trafficking," 462; Siskin and Wyler, "Trafficking in Persons."

9. Weitzer, "The Social Construction of Sex Trafficking," 463.

10. R. Galusca, "Slave Hunters, Brothels Busters and Feminist Interventions: Investigative Journalists as Anti-Sex-Trafficking Humanitarians," *Feminist Formations* 24, no. 2 (Summer 2012): 1–24.

11. Ibid.

12. Weitzer, "The Social Construction of Sex Trafficking."

13. J. O'Connell Davidson, "New Slavery, Old Binaries: Human Trafficking and the Borders of 'Freedom,' " *Global Networks* 10, no. 2 (2010): 244–61.

14. Galusca, "Slave Hunters, Brothels Busters and Feminist Interventions."

15. Y. Tverdova, "Human Trafficking in Russia and Other Post-Soviet States," *Human Rights Review* 12, no. 3 (2011): 339.

16. S. Kimm and B. Sauer, "Discourses on Forced Prostitution, Trafficking in Women, and Football: A Comparison of Anti-Trafficking Campaigns during the World Cup 2006 and the European Championship 2008," *Soccer & Society* 11, no. 6 (2010): 818.

17. S. Zhang, "Beyond the 'Natasha' story—A Review and Critique of Current Research on Sex Trafficking," in *Global Crime*, Vol. 10 (New York: Routledge, Taylor & Francis Group, 2009), 185; B.C. Oude Breuil, D. Siegel, P. van Reenen, A. Beijer and L. Roos, "Human Trafficking Revisited: Legal, Enforcement and Ethnographic Narratives on Sex Trafficking to Western Europe," *Trends in Organized Crime* 14, no. 1 (2011): 30–46.

18. L. Jones, D. Engstrom, P. Hilliard, and D. Sungakawan, "Human Trafficking between Thailand and Japan: Lessons in Recruitment Transit and Control," *International Journal of Social Welfare* 20, no. 2 (2011): 203–11.

19. Ibid.

20. Ibid., 183.

21. Kotrla, "Domestic Minor Sex Trafficking in the United States," 184.

22. A. Pierce, "American Indian Adolescent Girls: Vulnerabilty to Sex Trafficking, Intervention Strategies," *American Indian and Alaska Native Mental Health Research* 19, no. 1 (2012): 37–56.

23. Ibid., 39.

24. Pierce, "American Indian Adolescent Girls."

25. Ibid.

26. Ibid.

27. Ibid.

28. Oude Breuil et al., "Human Trafficking Revisited," 34–36.

29. S. George, "The Strong Arm of the Law Is Weak: How the Trafficking Victims Protection Act Fails to Assist Effectively Victims of the Sex Trade," *Creighton Law Review* 45, no. 3 (April 2012): 563.

30. Secretary-General United Nations, *Protocol to Prevent, Supress and Punish Trafficking in Persons, Especially Women and Children, Supplementing the United Nations Convention against Transnational Organized Crime.* United Nations, 2000; S. Molland, " 'The Perfect Business': Human Trafficking and Lao-Thai Cross-Border Migration," *Development and Change* 41, no. 5 (2010): 831–55.

31. O'Connell Davidson, "New Slavery, Old Binaries," 245.

32. Kimm and Sauer, "Discourses on Forced Prostitution, Trafficking in Women, and Football," 815–28.

33. Seelke, "Trafficking in Persons in Latin America and the Caribbean."

34. Ibid., 275.

35. M. Smit, "Trafficking in Human Beings for Labour Explotation: The Case of the Netherlands," *Trends in Organized Crime* 14, no. 2/3 (2011): 184–97.

36. Ibid.

37. Ibid.

38. U.S. Government, Department of State. Public Law 106-386—Victims of Trafficking and Violence Protection Act of 2000, October 28, 2000, 1466.

39. Ibid.

40. Ibid.

41. B. Anderson, "Where's the Harm in That? Immigration Enforcement, Trafficking, and the Protection of Migrant's Rights," *American Behavioral Scientist* 56, no. 9 (2012): 1241–57.

42. United Nations, UN Convention against Transnational Organized Crime and the Protocols Thereto Adopted by the General Assembly in 2000 with Two New Protocols, One on Smuggling Migrants and One on Trafficking People, 3.

43. Ibid., 329.

44. Kaneti, "Project Trafficking."

45. Smit, "Trafficking in Human Beings for Labour Exploitation."

46. U.S. Department of State Trafficking in Persons Report 2010; Siskin and Wyler, "Trafficking in Persons," 267–71.

47. J. Hathaway, "The Human Rights Quagmire of 'Human Trafficking.' " *Virginia Journal of International Law Association* 49, no. 1 (Fall 2008): 1–59.

48. Kaneti, "Project Trafficking," 349.

49. Smith, "Sex Trafficking."

50. Ibid.

51. R. Uy, "Blinded by Red Lights. Why Trafficking Discourse Should Shift Away from Sex and the 'Perfect Victim,' " *Berkeley Journal of Law & Justice* 26, no. 1 (March 2011): 204–219.

52. Oude Breuil et al., "Human Trafficking Revisited."

53. Ibid.

54. D. Coghlan and G. Wylie, "Understanding Global Migration: A Social Transformation Perspective." *Journal of Ethnic and Migration Studies* 36, no. 10 (2010): 41.

55. Ibid.

56. Kimm and Sauer, "Discourses on Forced Prostitution, Trafficking in Women, and Football."

57. Molland, " 'The Perfect Business.' "

58. J. O'Connell Davidson, "Will the Real Sex Slave Please Stand Up?" *Feminist Review* 83, no. 1 (2006): 4–22.

59. J. Silverman, A. Raj, D. Cheng, M. Decker, et al., "Sex Trafficking and Initiation—Related Violence, Alcohol Use, and HIV Risk among HIV-Infected Female Sex Workers in Mumbai, India," *Journal of Infectious Diseases* 204, no. 1 (2011).

60. Ibid.

61. Masci, "Human Trafficking and Slavery."

62. Ibid.

63. Ibid.

64. Ibid.

65. Kaneti, "Project Trafficking," 349.

66. C. Vance, "States of Contradiction: Twelve Ways to Do Nothing about Trafficking While Pretending To," *Social Research* 78, no. 3 (Fall 2011): 937.

67. Silverman et al., "Sex Trafficking and Initiation."

68. M. Spector and J. Kitsuse, *Constructing Social Problems* (Menlo Park, CA: Cummings Publishing, 1977); J. Best, *More Damned Lies and Statistics: How Numbers Confuse Public Issues* (Berkeley and Los Angeles: University of California Press, 2004); J. Best, *Deviance: Career of a Concept* (Belmont, CA: Wadsworth, Cengage Learning, 2004); L. Kelley, *Context and Leadership in the Remote Environment* (Halifax, Nova Scotia: St. Mary's University, 2005).

348   Ordinary Violence

69. Uy, "Blinded by Red Lights," 205.

70. *See* R. Galusca, "Slave Hunters, Brothel Busters and Feminist Interventions," on "brothel buster" Aaron Cohen.

71. A. Balch and A. Geddes. "Opportunity from Crisis? Organisational Responses to Human Trafficking in the UK," *British Journal of Politics and International Relations* 13, no. 1 (2011): 28.

72. Anderson, "Where's the Harm in That?" 1242.

73. Smit, "Trafficking in Human Beings for Labour Exploitation."

74. Public Law 106-386.

75. Weitzer, "The Social Construction of Sex Trafficking," 461.

76. Masci, "Human Trafficking and Slavery."

77. Ibid., 280.

78. O'Connell Davidson, "Will the Real Sex Slave Please Stand Up?"

79. Weitzer, "The Social Construction of Sex Trafficking."

80. President George W. Bush, Address to the United Nations General Assembly September 23, 2003, http://www.un.org/webcast/ga/58/statements/usaeng030923.htm

81. Ibid.

82. Oude Breuil et al., "Human Trafficking Revisited"; K. Kempadoo, J. Sanghera, and B. Pattanaik, *Trafficking and Prostitution Reconsidered: New Perspectives on Migration, Sex Work, and Human Rights* (Transnational Feminist Studies) (St. Paul, MN: Paradigm Publishers, 2005); M. Segrave, S. Milivojevic, and S. Pickering, *Sex Trafficking: International Context and Response* (Andover, UK: Willan Publishing, 2009), 32.

83. Oude Breuil et al., "Human Trafficking Revisited," 32–33.

84. Oude Breuil et al., "Human Trafficking Revisited," 33.

85. P. Saunders and G. Soderlund, "Traveling Threats: Sexuality, Gender and the Ebb and Flow of Trafficking as Discourse," *Canadian Woman Studies* 22, no. 3–4 (2003): 35–46; M. C. Desyllas, "A Critique of the Global Trafficking Discourse and U.S. Policy," *Journal of Sociology & Social Welfare* 34, no. 4 (2007): 61.

86. Oude Brueil et al., "Human Trafficking Revisited," 33.

87. Oude Breuil et al., "Human Trafficking Revisited."

88. P. Alexander, "Sex Work and Health: A Question of Safety in the Workplace," *JAMWA* 53, no. 2 (Spring 1998): 77–82.

89. Oude Breuil et al., "Human Trafficking Revisited."

90. Ibid., 33.

91. Oude Breuil et al., "Human Trafficking Revisited."

92. United Nations Fourth World Conference on Women—Beijing, 1995.

93. J. Outshoorn, "The Political Debates on Prostitution and Trafficking of Women," *Social Politics: International Studies in Gender, State and Society* 12, no. 1 (Spring 2005): 141–55.

94. O'Connell Davidson, "Will the Real Sex Slave Please Stand Up?"

95. Segrave, Milivojevic, and Pickering, *Sex Trafficking,* 18; Oude Breuil et al., "Human Trafficking Revisited," 46.

96. *See* Oude Brueil et al., "Human Trafficking Revisited" for The Framework Decision of the European Union on Combating Trafficking in Human Beings, July 19, 2002, PbEGL 203.

97. Vance, "States of Contradiction," 939.

98. See Sec. 102 (b).

99. Hathaway, "States of Contradiction."

100. Ibid., 3.

101. Ibid.

102. Ibid.

103. See K. Bales, *Disposable People: New Slavery in the Global Economy* (Berkeley and Los Angeles: University of California Press, 2012 [1999]), 8–9.

104. O'Connell Davidson, 2010.

105. Ibid.

106. J. Doezema, "Forced to Choose: Beyond the Voluntary v. Forced Prostitution Dichotomy," in *Global Sex Workers: Rights, Resistance and Redefinition*, edited by K. Kempadoo and J. Doezema (New York: Routledge, 1998); O'Connell Davidson, "New Slavery, Old Binaries," 244.

107. O'Connell Davidson, "New Slavery, Old Binaries," 244.

108. Masci, 290.

109. Masci, "Human Trafficking and Slavery."

110. Ibid.

111. Bales, *Disposable People. New Slavery in the Global Economy.*

112. Ibid.

113. R. Seelke, "Trafficking in Persons in Latin America and the Caribbean."

114. Bales, *Disposable People: New Slavery in the Global Economy.*

115. Ibid.

116. R. Seelke, "Trafficking in Persons in Latin America and the Caribbean."

117. O'Connell Davidson, "New Slavery, Old Binaries."

118. Ibid., 257.

119. Ibid., 245.

120. O'Connell Davidson, "New Slavery, Old Binaries."

121. Ibid.

122. Ibid.

123. Hathaway, "The Human Rights Quagmire of 'Human Trafficking.' "

124. Ibid., 12.

125. Ibid., 25.

126. Ibid., 12.

127. Ibid., 5.

128. Hathaway, "The Human Rights Quagmire of Human Trafficking."

129. Ibid, 10.

130. S. Molland, "The Value of Bodies: Deception, Helping and Profiteering in Human Trafficking Along the Thai-Lao Border," *Asian Studies Review* 34, no. 2 (2010): 213.

131. Ibid.

132. Kotrla, "Domestic Minor Sex Trafficking in the United States."

133. Molland, "The Value of Bodies."

134. Weitzer, "The Social Construction of Sex Trafficking."

135. Ibid.

136. Ibid., 463.

137. Vance, "States of Contradiction," 395.

138. Weitzer, "The Social Construction of Sex Trafficking," 462.

139. Ibid.

140. Siskin and Wyler, "Trafficking in Persons."

141. L. Smith, S. Vardaman, and M. Snow, *The National Report on Domestic Minor Sex Trafficking: America's Prostituted Children* (Vancouver, WA, and Arlington, VA: Shared Hope International, May 2009). Also cited in Siskin and Wyler, "Trafficking in Persons."

142. Ibid.

143. C. Williamson, S. Karandikar-Chheda, and J. Barrows, cited in Siskin and Wyler, "Trafficking in Persons," 271.

144. See http://www.policymic.com/articles/37225/300-000-children-enter-the-sex-trade-annually

145. O'Connell Davidson, "Will the Real Sex Slave Please Stand Up?"

146. Ibid.

147. Ibid., 5; Weitzer, "The Social Construction of Sex Trafficking," 474.

148. O'Connell Davidson, "New Slavery, Old Binaries," 252.

149. Attorney General Report, 2004, cited by Weitzer, "The Social Construction of Sex Trafficking," 20.

150. Uy, "Blinded by Red Lights."

151. U.S. Department of Justice, Civil Rights Division, 2010:6 cited by Vance, "States of Contradiction," 937.

152. A. Jac-Kucharski, "The Determinants of Human Trafficking: A US Case Study," *International Migration* 50, no. 6 (2012): 150.

153. S. Kara, "Designing More Effective Laws against Human Trafficking," *Northwestern Journal of International Human Rights* 9, no. 2 (Spring 2011): 123–47.

154. O'Connell Davidson, "New Slavery, Old Binaries," 254.

155. Bales, *Disposable People.*

156. E. Dikov, "Export of Prostitution and Human Trafficking: Trafficking in Women," in O. Shentov, B. Todorov, and A. Stoynov, *Organized Crime in Bulgaria: Markets and Trends* (Sofia: Center for the Study of Democracy, 2007), 108–33.

157. G. Petrunov, "Managing money acquired from human trafficking: case study of sex trafficking from Bulgaria to Western Europe," *Trends in Organized Crime* 14, no. 2–3 (2011): 165–83.

158. Ibid., 167.

159. Ibid., 168.

160. Ibid.

161. Ibid.

162. Molland, "The Value of Bodies."

163. Ibid., 222.

164. R. Staring, "Human Trafficking in the Netherlands: Trends and Recent Developments," *International Review of Law* 26, no. 1 (2012): 59–72.

165. Ibid.

166. K. Warren, "Troubling the Victim/Trafficker Dichotomy in Efforts to Combat Human Trafficking: The Unintended Consequences of Moralizing Labor Migration," *Indiana Journal of Global Legal Studies* 19, no. 1 (2012): 107.

167. Ibid.

168. J. Hua and H. Nigorizawa, "US Trafficking, Women's Human Rights and the Politics of Representation," *International Feminist Journal of Politics* 12, no. 3/4 (2010): 403.

169. R. Seelke, "Trafficking in Persons in Latin America and the Caribbean," 273.

170. Jones et al., "Human Trafficking between Thailand and Japan," 204.

171. R. Seelke, "Trafficking in Persons in Latin America and the Caribbean."

172. Ibid., 272.

173. G. Danailova-Trainor and F. Laczko, "Trafficking in Persons and Development: Towards Greater Policy Coherence," *International Migration* 48, no. 4 (2010): 49.

174. Ibid., 51

175. Danailov-Trainor and Laczko, "Trafficking in Persons."

176. Jac-Kucharski, "The Determinants of Human Trafficking."

177. D. T. Deane, "Cross-Border Trafficking in Napal and India-Violating Women's Rights," *Human Rights Review* 11, no. 4 (2010): 491–513.

178. Ibid.

179. Ibid.

180. Kleimenov and Shamkov, cited by Tverdova, "Human Trafficking in Russia and Other Post-Soviet States," 336.

181. Stoecker, cited by Tverdova, "Human Trafficking in Russia and Other Post-Soviet States." 337.

182. Shelly, cited by Tverdova, "Human Trafficking in Russia and Other Post-Soviet States." 336.

183. R. Seelke, "Trafficking in persons in Latin America and the Caribbean."

184. Ibid.

185. Danailov-Trainor and Laczko, "Trafficking in Persons," 49.

186. Danailov-Trainor and Laczko, "Trafficking in Persons."

187. Ibid.

188. Ibid.

189. Jones, et al., "Human Trafficking between Thailand and Japan."

190. Ibid.

191. Molland, " 'The Perfect Business.' "

192. Petrunov, "Managing Money Acquired from Human Trafficking."

193. Ibid.

194. Ibid.

195. Jones et al., "Human Trafficking between Thailand and Japan."

196. Ibid., 206.

197. Jones et al., "Human Trafficking between Thailand and Japan."

198. Ibid.

199. Petrunov, "Managing Money Acquired from Human Trafficking."

200. Molland, " 'The Perfect Business.' "

201. S. Molland, "'I am helping them': 'Traffickers' 'anti-traffickers' and economics of bad faith," *The Australian Journal of Anthropology* 22, no. 2 (2011): 236–254.

202. Molland, " 'The Perfect Business.' "

203. Ibid., 114.

204. Molland, " 'The Perfect Business' "; Molland, "The Value of Bodies."

204. Ibid.

205. Warren, "Troubling the Victim/Trafficker Dichotomy in Efforts to Combat Human Trafficking," 113.

206. Warren, "Troubling the Victim/Trafficker Dichotomy in Efforts to Combat Human Trafficking."

207. Ibid., 114.

208. Molland, " 'The Perfect Business.' "

209. Ibid.

210. Ibid.

211. Ibid.

212. D.M. Hughes, "Enslaved in the U.S.A.: American Victims Need Our Help" *National Review Online*, July 2007. http://www.nationalreview.com/articles/221700/enslaved-u-s/donna-m-hughes

213. T. Steinfatt, "Measuring the Number of Trafficked Women and Children in Cambodia: A Direct Observation Field Study." Sponsored by USAID, October 6, 2003, 11; Weitzer, "The Social Construction of Sex Trafficking," 474.

214. Doezema and Kempadoo, "Global Sex Workers: Rights, Resistance and Redefinition"; Doezema, "Forced to Choose"; O'Connell Davidson, "New Slavery, Old Binaries," 244.

215. Doezema, *Global Sex Workers*.

216. A. Lange, "Research Note: Challenges of Identifying Female Human Trafficking Victims Using a National 1-800 Call Center," *Trends in Organized Crime* 14, no. 1 (2011): 47–55.

217. Ibid., 51.

218. J. Busza, S. Castle, and A. Diarra, "Trafficking and Health," *British Medical Journal* 328, no. 7452 (June 5, 2004): 1369–71; Weitzer, "The Social Construction of Sex Trafficking," 453.

219. L. Agustin, "Migrants in the Mistress's House: Other Voices in the Debate," *Social Politics* 12, no. 1 (2005): 98–101. in Weitzer, "The Social Construction of Sex Trafficking," 453.

220. Weitzer, "The Social Construction of Sex Trafficking," 453.

221. Steinfatt, "Measuring the Number of Trafficked Women and Children in Cambodia"; Weitzer, "The Social Construction of Sex Trafficking," 454.

222. Smit, "Trafficking in Human Beings for Labour Exploitation."

223. C. Zimmerman and C. Watts (2003) in A. Brunovskis and R. Sutees, "Untold Stories: Biases and Selection Effects in Research with

Victims of Trafficking for Sexual Exploitation," *International Migration* 18, no. 4 (2010): 2–3.

224. Hua and Nigorizawa, "US Trafficking, Women's Human Rights and the Politics of Representation."

225. Ibid., 414.

226. Hua and Nigorizawa, "US Trafficking, Women's Human Rights and the Politics of Representation."

227. Warren, "Troubling the Victim/Trafficker Dichotomy in Efforts to Combat Human Trafficking," 117.

228. Buckley, cited in Tverdova, "Human Trafficking in Russia and Other Post-Soviet States," 335.

229. Kleimenov and Shamkov, cited in Tverdova, "Human Trafficking in Russia and Other Post-Soviet States," 335.

230. See Tverdova, "Human Trafficking in Russia and Other Post-Soviet States."

231. Hua and Nigorizawa, "US Trafficking, Women's Human Rights and the Politics of Representation."

232. Vance, "States of Contradiction."

233. Ibid.

234. For example, see Vance, "States of Contradiction."

235. Vance, "States of Contradiction."

236. Ibid.

237. D. Rabinowitz, "From the Mouths of Babes to the Jail Cell: Child Abuse and the Abuse of Justice: A Case Study," *Harpers*, May 1990, 52–63; E. Loftus and K. Ketchamin, *The Myth of Repressed Memory* (New York: St. Martin's Griffin, 1994); and R. Ofshe and E. Watters, *Making Monsters: False Memories, Psychotherapy, and Sexual Hysteria* (New York: Charles Scribner and Sons, 1994).

238. Zhang, "Beyond the 'Natasha' Story."

NINE

Traversing Global Borders for Sex

THE TRAFFICKING NARRATIVE

A young girl meets a man in her village. He woos her, convincing her of his love, and promises to help her escape her dire circumstances and live happily ever after with him in another country. He actually sells her to a brothel or into bondage, and she is trapped for life in misery and loneliness. This is, very briefly, the outline of the films, articles, and activists' accounts of the trafficked victim. This narrative is quickly being supplanted by another, with another perfect victim; the young American girl who is either captured or duped by an older boyfriend into prostitution, convinced of his love for her until much later, when she realizes he is living off of her body. These imaginaries of trafficking fill our newspapers and conferences, but there is reason, based on the careful research on trafficking, to question these heart-rending depictions. This is a complicated story, populated by strange bedfellows and situated in unproven assumptions, stereotypes, and near hysteria, particularly as trafficking has morphed into prostitution. We need to review the assumptions underlying trafficking narratives and place this problem in a larger sociopolitical context. We need to question the media hysteria about this and recognize the conflicting assumptions that fuel the debates. It is important too to see the links between trafficking and other processes in which the sale of women's bodies simultaneously fulfills the sexual fantasies and desires of men and provides for the economic support of the women they buy.

There are several dominant patterns of trafficking. One pattern involves selling, kidnapping, seducing, duping, drugging, threatening, basically forcing women in one of a number of ways into trafficking. Another path is voluntary—young women are convinced by an acquaintance that their miserable lives will change dramatically for the better if they take a job abroad. Or the young women answer an ad for dancers or entertainers in a Western country and sign up to go, sometimes paying their own way, often being "bought" and operating as a bonded slave until the time when their ever-increasing bond will be paid off. Or they may meet a man at a dance or a coffee shop and he feigns love for them, telling them he will marry them, take care of them, if they will come with him to another country. Once they have left their home or village, he reveals his motives, sometimes raping them before handing them off to another trafficker up the line so that they will not want to return home and so that they will be "broken in" for sex work. In Jones's study, the women were assured that they would be provided with travel documents and airfare with no financial obligation on their part.[1] Instead, they were held liable for all of the expenses incurred by their traffickers, sinking into debt bondage from which they could hardly extricate themselves. Once women arrive at their destination, they may be taken to someone's home where an older woman, herself once trafficked, will introduce them to the rules and regulations. They may be subject to rape and assault, broken in and broken down, and convinced through their brutal treatment that there is no escape and no reason to try. They may be then taken to various locations to provide sex to men for their handler, never being paid. One story recounts the young girls taken from their confined space in a suburban house near Los Angeles to Disneyland and handed off to men there—the color of their dresses signaling their status as a victim for sale. Or they might be kept in a basement or the back of a bar, confined except when they are serving drinks or servicing men. Or they may be taken directly to a brothel, where they are broken in by the bodyguards or their trafficker. They are either owned outright and treated as commodities or they are told that they owe a certain huge sum to their trafficker and must work until they can pay it off. However, they may be sold again for a higher price to another trafficker before they can pay off their original debt and then have a still higher price to pay, never realistically being able to free themselves from debt. And these women may face other dangers. One theory about the hundreds of young women from Ciudad Juarez, whose murders have not been solved, is that they were trafficked and tried to escape or refused to leave or cooperate with their handlers who wanted them to act as "mules," carrying drugs across the border from Mexico to the United States.[2]

Sometimes the first stop is intermediary and the woman will be sold to another trafficker; sometimes she will stay at her first station, serving drinks, cleaning, tending bar, dancing, and, of course, providing her body to men. These men do not pay her—they pay the madam or the proprietor, who indicates he is putting the money toward her debt or is using it to repay the man who brought her there. If she has legal documents, they are usually confiscated. If she tries to escape, there is nowhere to turn. The guards and local police as well as other officials are paid to cooperate with the traffickers, often paid off to aid in keeping her.[3] This scenario is played out in every country into which women are trafficked with slight variations on the theme. One example is provided by Kathryn Bolkovac, a police officer from Nebraska who in 1999 uncovered a ring of locals, UN Peacekeepers, and DynCorp employees who collaborated in the trafficking of women. Through her book *Whistleblower* and the film based on it, she brought the attention of the world to the involvement of individual officers and embassy officials, corporations, the U.S. government as well as the United Nations in the multilayered structures that supported trafficking in Bosnia and as a result was fired from her job.

Trafficked women may be taken individually across borders, or they may be taken in groups, from Mexico to the United States in vans, for example, or on planes from Moldavia to Mexico City, accompanied by a handler who closely watches for signs that they are trying to escape or get help. Often, however, this oversight is not necessary since the trafficker knows their family and threatens to murder them if the victims don't cooperate. Some of the women, even when they escape their handlers, even when they avoid local police, find that when they turn to officials at the state or national level, they receive no help, but are instead returned to their trafficker or reported so that they can be picked up, beaten, raped, and put back into slavery. Especially when women and girls are in countries where they do not speak the language, where they know no one, and where they have been terrified through brutalization or through being told that they will be arrested if they leave the safety of the compound or brothel or house, they are likely not to seek help. Their fear of the unknown is greater than their fear of the known. They have no way of knowing who to contact, and with no money or legal papers or identification, they have no way to get home. While the United States, Italy, and the United Kingdom have provisions allowing a grace period for women who have been trafficked to stay in the country under certain conditions, mainly if they cooperate with prosecutors, those victims of trafficking in the former Soviet Union and other countries, who escape their captors are likely to be found in violation of immigration laws and returned to their home countries.[4] The Trafficking Victims Protection Act (TVPA) of 2000 establishes a process of certification that leads to the official designation of a person as a victim of "severe trafficking," separating the "legitimate victim" from illegal immigrants and sex workers. It basically establishes the difference between the good and vulnerable woman and the woman deserving of punishment or ouster since the response to trafficked subjects is framed through a victimization and rescue paradigm.

In Jones's research, the women were given fake passports and were accompanied by an escort and monitored to make sure they followed orders—they were given lessons on how to deceive immigration officials, and when they arrived at their destinations, were met by members of the smuggling organization that was responsible for supervising them and placing them in bars or brothels.[5] This depiction of the process is so consistent with the media image that one wonders if the women Jones interviewed learned from nongovernmental organizations (NGOs) and from their rescuers what they were supposed to say in order to be treated as victims or whether the NGO representatives selected women for interviews who conformed with the picture of the innocent victim. The process of verification relies on the victim presenting herself as a victim in the false dichotomy between voluntary and involuntary victims, and being able to construct herself as such in a convincing manner. Her account may include medical evidence, witnessed statements made by the victim, or physical evidence. But the critical component is her willingness to cooperate with law enforcement if she is to be eligible for the coveted T-visa that will allow her to remain in the United States and receive government assistance for food, shelter, and legal assistance.[6] Hua and Nigorizawa provide the example of Petrova, who knew she was being smuggled from Russia to New York for the purpose of sex work and did not see herself as in need of being saved. She refused to construct herself as a victim, to frame her story as one of victimization, even when she was threatened with imprisonment. She asserted that she was forced by U.S. law enforcement to provide inaccurate information about the defendants, that she was threatened by U.S. authorities, and had a nervous breakdown as a result of their treatment. The courts nonetheless ignored her contentions and certified her as a victim, providing her with legal and financial assistance.[7]

Petrova's story is astounding, particularly given that the standard for qualifying for a T-Visa is very high. It is very unlikely to be met by a woman who is afraid of her trafficker or who is involved with her trafficker as friend or family. Vance reports that one way the government has tried to resolve the implicit contradiction between hostility toward illegal immigrants and "compassion for the sympathetic victim" is through imposing limits on the number of permissions to stay (T-Visas) and making them difficult to obtain.[8] Between 2002 and 2009, a tiny proportion of the available T-Visas were granted.[9]

Once home, women who have been returned are not necessarily likely to be welcomed with open arms. They may in some instances have disgraced their family, brought dishonor on them, which is an ultimate sin, possibly leading to death or banishment. They may not be welcome because they are simply an economic expense for the family. They may have suffered so much torture, such degradation and physical and emotional pain, that they cannot regain their sense of self, their place in the family, and live the rest of their lives emotionally isolated and adrift. Or they may be reentering an economic and social environment that was so oppressive and unbearable that it led them to leave in the first place.

There is a striking similarity between current representations of victims of trafficking (prostitution) and those made a century ago about "white slaves," a problem that was largely mythical: "today's stereotypical 'trafficking victim' bears as little resemblance to women migrating for work in the sex industry as did her historical counterpart, the 'white slave.' "[10] The depictions remove any agency from the women and paint them as the perfect victim. Globally, the nineteenth-century sex slave was portrayed as a white woman victim of the "animal lusts of the dark races."[11] More recently they have been depicted as passive, unemancipated women from the developing world. This "orientalism" contrasts with the depiction in the United States in the 1880s of Chinese women and other women of color as overly sexual, deviant, and promiscuous.[12] Trafficked women from Southeast Asia today are more likely to be typified as young, brown, innocent, poor, delicate, and vulnerable, a depiction that is not wholly supported by the data.[13] McDonald concludes that the antitrafficking campaign has "capitalized on one of the most powerful symbols in the pantheon of Western imagery, the innocent, young girl dragged off against her will to distant lands to satisfy the insatiable sexual cravings of wanton men."[14]

Even though most of the very hyped media attention to trafficking remains on the victim depicted as the innocent, young naïf, there is now increasing attention to the "demand" side of the economic supply and demand model that dominates the trafficking literature. In the United States, similarly to some other Western countries, those who have been able to shape the TVPA are increasingly turning attention to the men who buy sexual favors. Sweden, for example, soon followed by Finland and Norway, targets the demand side by making the purchase (but not the sale) of sexual services illegal.[15]

THE PROSTITUTION DEBATE

In 2000, when the Trafficking Victims Protection Act was passed, Bill Clinton was president. Passage of the act created the Office to Monitor and Combat Trafficking in Persons. Clinton's administration distinguished between forced and voluntary prostitution, but did not link prostitution to trafficking, did not claim that legal prostitution increased trafficking into the country, and resisted mandatory sanctions against nations with poor records in combating trafficking. However, under President Bush, the unexpected collaboration of feminist abolitionists and right-wing religious leaders like Charles Colson of the Prison Fellowship Ministries and Richard Land of the Southern Baptist Convention formed a "moral crusade"[16] that fused with government positions, leading Bush to declare prostitution as "inherently harmful and dehumanizing," and buttressing the linkage between trafficking and prostitution.[17] Religious organizations, including the Salvation Army, continue to pressure the Church and the government to do more to fight the ideology that underlies trafficking as well as prostitution. They see the separation of sex from love, responsibility, and children as presented by the "media elite" as fueling these evils.[18]

Whether prostitution is, by its very nature, a form of exploitation of women and children or whether it is a legitimate form of labor is a matter of much disagreement. If it is legitimate labor, the concern is with the work and compensation factors that may harm or exploit a woman, but if it is *ipso facto* exploitation, then it is a human rights issue or a human slavery issue. As Desyllas writes, "The abolitionist approach asserts that prostitution is a violation of human rights, analogous to (sexual) slavery"[19] and "an extreme expression of sexual violence."[20] The abolitionist position is that prostitution *in and of itself* is a form of violence against women.[21] Women who are trafficked for prostitution are by definition victims of violence. There is no stronger voice assessing the relationship between trafficking and brothels and legalized prostitution in the United States than that of Melissa Farley. Farley jumps with both feet into the debate on the side of the abolitionists, viewing prostitution as violence against women. Abolitionists argue forcefully that no woman would ever voluntarily consent to sell herself, and any woman who engages in prostitution must be a victim who requires help to escape sexual slavery.[22] And since prostitution has been redefined as trafficking, any trafficked woman is a victim.

Feminists who see violence against women when they see prostitutes focus on the significant constraints under which women operate in house or brothel prostitution as well as on the street, their risk of assault, their lack of control over their working conditions and their money and health-care choices, their lack of freedom of movement, and their risk of being raped by their clients. They further assert, especially Melissa Farley, that legalized prostitution establishes a climate that encourages illegal prostitution.[23] She insists that whether it is legalized, decriminalized, or responded to in any other way as acceptable, any legitimation of prostitution is a cruel lie since not only are prostitutes subject to great violence, such as assault and rape, they also are likely to go into prostitution as a result of violence, such as child sexual abuse or battery. They suffer anxiety, post-traumatic stress disorder, drug and alcohol problems, and other emotional and psychological problems as a result of their "work."[24]

The sex workers' rights approach contrasts mightily with the abolitionist approach. It views "prostitution as a choice women make in order to survive, and is based on the belief that women have the 'right to sexual determination,' the right to work in safe labor conditions, and the right to migrate for sex work wherever they choose."[25] Prostitution is labor, and it should be respected rather than stigmatized.[26] Women have the right to sexual determination, to migrate for sex work to have safe labor conditions—it is not the work itself but the unsafe working conditions, the deprivation of freedom, debt-bondage, and violence that are the problem. Trafficking for sex work is viewed as a form of labor migration, and the protections needed by prostitutes are viewed as similar to those needed by people trafficked to work in the service industry, agriculture, mining, or any other form of labor.

The sex worker position was forwarded early on by Margo St. James, who, with her COYOTE (Call Off Your Old Tired Ethics) organization, lobbied for the legalization of prostitution as a social service. She describes prostitution as a work choice, just as any other.[27] Priscilla Alexander addresses the question of whether one would want their daughter to be a prostitute, a question offered as a standard against which to judge this work.[28] She responds that there are a number of things one wouldn't want their daughters to do, but choice is constrained by education, class, and other factors, and the choice to sell sex is a choice, as are these others. Sex workers' rights should be protected, they should be able to organize for worker's rights, should be able to ply their trade without fear of being limited by the man—arrested by the police or threatened or owned by their pimps. From this perspective, sex work should not be illegal, nor should it be legalized; it should be decriminalized, allowing other laws to protect the prostitute, including assault laws, laws against theft, etc.[29]

It has been possible for most NGOs and international organizations, whether religious, political, or social service, to frame prostitution as a human slavery issue and hence portray the women as innocent victims of violence, a definition that the sex worker advocates view as disempowering women, positioning the West against the global South and stereotyping women as passive objects.[30] GAATW (the Global Alliance against Traffic in Women) is one of the few NGOs that draws the line between coercion and choice and does not see all women engaged in prostitution as exploited or trafficked.[31]

This is a complicated debate, not only because of the different feminist views but because of religious and political positions that hardly seem compatible occupying the same side of this debate. The feminist NGOs' position that women who are trafficked are sex slaves melds beautifully with that of the religious NGOs who want to save the women from their victimization. The debate about whether prostitution is sex work or violence is neither insignificant nor local. Its centrality is reflected in U.S policy that until June 2013 required that all countries and organizations receiving aid or support maintain a strict antiprostitution stance, disallowing the position that there is such a thing as legitimate sex work and that prostitution should be separated from forced prostitution. The policy in fact defined prostitution and sex trafficking as the same thing, which is exactly what the antitrafficking advocates do in other instances regarding these two distinct phenomena. The U.S. Supreme Court ruled against the government's requirement that the NGOs pledge allegiance to its policy of eradicating prostitution, saying that the policy violated the NGOs' First Amendment rights, although the government can still limit the use of government funds for programs or advocacy the government opposes. The U.S. position on prostitution places it in an awkward position globally—prostitution is illegal in only 40 percent of the 99 countries actively involved in trafficking. The majority, 84 percent, do have laws against pimping, but only 25 percent have laws against soliciting a prostitute.[32] Politics makes strange bedfellows.

There is much money to be made in illegal prostitution, most of it not by the prostitutes but by cab drivers, valets, hotel owners, restaurants and bars, and pimps. Farley cites the plethora of flyers and ads for massage parlors and entertainers and strippers in Las Vegas, for example, and the "what happens in Las Vegas, stays in Las Vegas" marketing scheme as incentives to skirt the law in a city where legalized prostitution is just a stone's throw away.[33]

One thing that is pretty clear in this debate is that the construction of prostitute is very different from the construction of "victim of trafficking," one eliciting a certain disapproval or disgust and the other sympathy; so that reframing prostitution as trafficking can result in more public interest, sympathy, and more response from lawmakers. Even in a conservative Catholic and Mormon state such as Nevada, where prostitution is legal outside the urban areas, and where brothel owners are powerful and effective lobbyists as well as lawmakers, there is great support for antitrafficking legislation. This is not as inconsistent as it might initially seem— prostitutes working in brothels are seen as making a choice, whereas trafficking victims are viewed as coerced, forced, or underage.

MAIL-ORDER BRIDES

No matter what the particulars of the historical, economic, political, and cultural context of the buying and selling of women's bodies, there are some truths that remain self-evident. These forms of violence are built on inequality. Often the inequality is global, as in the case of trafficking or mail-order brides (another name for trafficking, according to some scholars).[34] Often the inequality is societal, with women suffering oppression in marital, economic, and cultural arenas (bride burning and female genital mutilation). Often the inequality is expressed in rage against the woman in a relationship or in the family, with battery or honor crimes; and in the case of rape, harassment, and other forms of violence, inequality is the centerpiece. The mail-order bride business as well as sex tourism and prostitution are mired in the intersection of poverty and gendered assumptions. While recognizing this, it is also possible to examine the cultural assumptions and practices and structural factors that underpin the violence, not because they allow us to "other" those who are its victims, but because the violence is tangled in an intricate web that needs to be pulled apart. So, while we could agree that patriarchy does not stand as the sole explanation for violence against women except at the broadest and most abstract level, patriarchy expresses itself in the everyday workings of the world such that they can be seen and untangled.

All of the problems included in the area of violence against women here are complex, and there is a great deal of debate about them, sometimes beginning with the questions of whether they are really problems or not. All of them are situated in global inequality, cultural differences, and concerns about who has the right to define the problem and who has the right to intervene—if anyone does. Female genital mutilation (FGM) is a good example of this complexity, from its definition—mutilation? cutting? circumcision?—to whose voices have the right to be heard in any discussion—should Western women have a voice here? Similarly, one may ask whether prostitution is sex work or violence against women—a question that can be asked in the area of trafficking and mail-order brides as well—what about female agency—when are women victims and when are they agents acting to better themselves, even if it is within sometimes limited circumstances? And what role does culture play—how should its role be assessed—in FGM, in "honor" crimes? How should immigrant communities be responded to when values conflict with those of the dominant culture? And how do oppressive assumptions about gender express themselves in everyday and predictable ways across the globe, whether we are talking about harassment, rape, battery in the United States or honor crimes in Pakistan or Turkey?

Should this particular topic, "mail-order brides," even be included in a book on violence against women? How is this economic transaction between two adults one that could be perceived as a form of violence? Is it necessarily so, or is it the case that it might become so? It is impossible not to see parallels between the arguments between activists and scholars about "mail-order-brides" and prostitution, as well as trafficking. Many of the same issues are at play, and many of the assumptions held by those on either side of the arguments are the same.

Simply put, some authors, especially those who come from a clearly feminist perspective, view the mail-order bride business as one reflecting global inequality and the economic and social oppression of women. Just as they assume that no woman could really agree to sell her body, and would only do so within the complex intersection of sexism, poverty, power differentials, and misogyny, so the same would be true for women who agree to be part of the global marriage brokering system. On the other hand, just as some authors view prostitution as a form of sex work and see the women as having the freedom to do with their body what they wish, viewing them as persons with agency-making decisions that should be regarded as choices, these authors also would view "mail-order-brides" as making rational economic choices based in values of family and individual desire for improvement. In both cases, the women are viewed as having agency rather than being victims of violence. In fact, in the case of trafficking, one sees this same dualism—are women who are "trafficked" for sex necessarily the "subject victims" so often portrayed in the media, or are they women making choices about employment and opportunity?

Some scholars, however, have viewed the whole mail-order bride system as fitting within the tradition of arranged marriages, going back centuries, so the involvement of commercial agencies does not seem strange or inappropriate in the matchmaking process. In this country, particularly in the West and in Hawaii during the late 1890s and early 1900s, a system of "picture-brides" was established in which go-betweens brokered a marriage between a Japanese or Korean woman and a Japanese or Korean man working abroad. U.S. immigration laws and antimiscegenation laws prohibited these Asian men from marrying white women, leading them to seek brides from home. Their communication was minimal, and the one-way ticket the women received often led to them being trapped in a country with a man who was much older, and quite often less attractive than the man in the only photo they had of him. The broker described the women and the men to one another, and the marriage was arranged when the groom's family approved.[35] The women were often motivated to escape their economic circumstances for the same reasons women from the East Coast of the United States were propelled to the frontier to become teachers and to find a husband—the underlying motive was freedom from the constraints of the patriarchal family system, from the narrow definition of femininity and for a better and more fulfilling life. In both instances, the men wanted women who could help them with their work; provide them with a family; and, in the case of the Japanese workers, an identity consistent with American norms; and the women wanted the economic betterment and freedom they hoped marriage would offer them. Sometimes the women were encouraged by their families, either because they were burdensome to support or because they could earn money or marry well enough to send money home to help the family. This is reflective of the "cultural heroes" sent by the Philippine government to work abroad, the government depending heavily on the women's remittances for its own economic survival.[36] So, while the women were not being described or bought on the Internet, the marriage brokerage system was reflective of the tradition of arranged marriages and allowed for both parties to uphold cultural norms of marriage and success.

The mail-order bride business has become an important means of international migration with a dramatic rise since the 1970s overall, and in several Asian countries since the 1990s.[37] Its expansion is linked specifically to the increase in global Internet access and sophistication. It may be defined as an online recruiting network were pictures, body measurements, and descriptions of advertised women are provided.[38] Donna Lee provides a slightly more politicized definition: "the organized business of capitalizing on women's disadvantaged position in pursuit of profit for the benefit of male consumers."[39] In the United States, the rise in demand for mail-order brides coincides with the rise of the women's movement, something that most scholars suggest had such an impact because Western women no longer conformed to the image of ideal femininity that many men had grown to expect, perhaps especially men who had entered adulthood during the complacent, orderly 1950s.

In her study of mail-order bride agencies, Zabyelina provides a typology of the advertising displays of mail-order brides offered on websites: (a) indicative portraits that are nonsexual close-up photos of the woman's face, showing her emotional state, or indicative posing, which are photos taken from a greater distance and showing her full body; (b) erotic images that are revealing, seductive poses; and (c) porn that presents the women as subjects to excite the viewer. Over time, the websites have become increasingly sexualized, representing women as sexual objects who are easily accessible, compliant, and complacent, presenting them in positions of subordination to their "consumer-husband."[40] This may be due to the competitive nature of these businesses that increasingly rely on attention-grabbing visual materials and more flashy, blatant presentations of the women who are for sale.

Some scholars have focused on the commodification of women in the mail-order bride system, seeing this as one more reflection of the global gender inequality and patriarchal values and structure that limit women's life chances.[41] It is a highly unregulated business, although there are now laws in most countries, including the United States, that make certain requirements of the brokers, particularly because of immigration concerns of governments and the wariness about the possibility of trafficking women for sex or forced marriage. As such, marriage brokers are primarily controlled through immigration rules. In the United States, for example, foreign spouses may enter the country on a fiancée visa and then must meet various requirements before being able to apply for citizenship. They must prove that there is a bona fide relationship and that the marriage is not simply a ruse for gaining entry to the United States: the couple must live together for two years, the citizen husband must support the application for citizenship, and then the couple must undergo an interview with Immigration Services before the women are allowed to become citizens.[42] Similar restrictions exist in other countries, in all instances reflecting border control concerns as well as the dominant values of marriage and family.

The pro-family immigration policies that favor the traditional family unit have benefitted the mail-order bride industries and fueled the migrant marriage business. In 1986, Congress passed the Immigration Marriage Fraud Amendment (IMFA) to prevent foreigners from marrying only to obtain legal immigration in the United States.[43] Various amendments to the Immigration Act have taken into account the possible hardships imposed by the immigration laws, leading to changes that allow women or children who are victims of crimes or abuse to apply for an exemption to the requirement for a joint application for citizenship under the Violent Crime Control and Law Enforcement Act and then further expanded protections under the Victims of Trafficking and Violence Protection Act of 2000 and other provisions.[44] The law was amended in 1990 to protect women from battery and other forms of violence against women, providing a waiver to the joint filing requirement listed in the 1986 law if the marriage was entered in good faith and the spouse or child is the victim of battery. These protections are not perfect by any means; in this instance, the woman must be able to prove that she entered the relationship in good faith and must prove that abuse was the primary reason she is seeking divorce. Women may also have difficulty escaping abusive relationships due to language problems, fear of deportation, the stigma of returning home, and fear of the legal system in the United Sates. In 2001, immigration law addressed the activities of the marriage brokers, now requiring that they provide information to potential mail-order brides about the battered spouse waiver and immigration rights, although penalties for nonconformance are minimal—$20,000 for each act.[45]

The laws designed to protect immigrant women, however, do not change the conditional immigration status of the women, and they cannot overcome the problems these women face in the community as immigrants. Nor does the existence of laws guarantee their enforcement or speak to their effectiveness. The Philippines has made the mail-order bride business illegal, giving six- to eight-year sentences for violations, but enforcement has been so lax that the law has been virtually meaningless.[46] Perhaps this is due to the high demand from the United States and other industrialized countries with legitimate businesses that can aid in skirting the law. In Vietnam and Taiwan, neither government has officially recognized the legal status of cross-border marriage agencies, but both have taken a rather "hands off" approach, asserting that people should be free to marry whomever they wish.[47] The brokerage system between these two countries is multilayered and complex, moving from the small matchmaker to larger, more organized businesses that also incorporate other ancillary actors necessary for the transaction to proceed.

One cannot help but be reminded of the trafficking in women when looking at this system, organized in a similar fashion, requiring significant sums (approximately $7,500–$10,500, to be paid by the customer).[48] Wang and Chang, who study the cross-border marriage business between Taiwan and Vietnam,[49] suggest that there is a fine line between the marriage marketing system and trafficking in women as cross-border marriage become more intensely competitive and as family groups drop out to be replaced by multilevel marketers.[50] Belleau simply refers to the mail-order bride system as trafficking, saying that "the Mail Order Bride System is a flourishing and lucrative industry involving the trafficking of women from the Third World to husbands in the First World."[51]

Korea, which experienced a significant influx of foreign brides, especially Chinese women but also Japanese, Filipina, and Vietnamese, views the mail-order bride business as both a partnership and a citizenship issue, one complicated by the fact that international marriages historically were associated with the invasion of Korea by other countries or because Korean women were viewed as the spoils of war, to be taken by conquering invaders.[52] Korean women who married foreign men—for example, men in the U.S. military—were condemned as "betrayers of the nation," and both they and their children were stigmatized. Since the children's citizenship followed the citizenship of the father, they were not considered citizens, and the women faced significant economic and social security problems, being excluded from the social and medical security system in Korea.[53]

Perez indicates that, worldwide, 100,000 to 150,000 women are advertised for marriage.[54] Cherry Blossom, one of the oldest and largest marriage brokerage businesses, lists over 6,000 women as available at any given time, and over 1,000 men a month access their services.[55] Racialized stereotypes that underlie the demand for Asian women have fueled this multimillion-dollar industry, encouraging offensive stereotypes for profit. Vietnam is one of the poorest countries in the world, and women there not only face poor educational and occupational opportunities, but war and migration have skewed the sex ratio against them. Wide Angle reports that 80,000 Taiwanese men have traveled to Vietnam in the last decade to "buy brides" often for as little as $8,000, and the women, who are desperate to escape poverty, are willing to take a foreign partner, in part because they can send money home to their families after their marriage.[56] Their families, often eager to have them married to a Taiwanese, bring them from poor rural areas to brokers in the cities, expecting not only to reduce their financial obligations but also to receive some small remuneration for their daughter.[57] The growth of the industry and the increasing number of intermediaries in the business increase the commodification of the women, who are then required to accept reduced prices and to be less selective in partners and conditions of the marriage. This lends support to Perez's belief that, similar to the slave trade, this industry "reprehensively profits from trade in human bodies."[58] The commodification of women is reflected in their presentation in the catalogs and websites of the mail-order bride agencies. For example, a system of numbering and codes rates women, showing some as of higher quality (prettier and younger) than others. The fact that men can search by category, such as age, height, and location, and "browse, select, and proceed to check-out, just as one would do on any on-line shopping site, reveals commodification of the women as salable objects available for purchase."[59] Such a view is supported by the experience of Kristoffer Garin, a journalist who looked at the business from the inside, joining a tour of men looking for brides in the Ukraine. He found his male companions eager to meet as many women as possible, have sex with as many as possible, and basically enjoy the " stock"[60] who were brought to the hotels and convention centers for the men to evaluate. The work by Chang and Wang points out the importance of these women making a good impression on the men—if a woman can't be married off within a brief period, maybe three months, she will be discarded by the company and required to reimburse the broker for all of the expenses incurred.[61]

The women reflect interrelated and multiple inequalities, usually being from poor countries in which women suffer disproportionately, have few rights, little education, experience patriarchal control, endure arranged or unhappy marriages because divorce laws are so strict, and in general are treated as social, political, and economic inferiors.[62] They overcome the local constraints through negotiating their options within a transnational migratory space—blurring distinctions between marriage and labor migration and the many roles a woman might play—mother, wife, mistress, worker, daughter. Filipina women are fairly representative of other mail-order brides who look to the West with idealized visions of their futures, holding highly unrealistic expectations about marriage.[63] Not only are they motivated to escape the hardships of rural poverty and gender discrimination and other structural factors, they imagine realizing their dreams of upward mobility and family happiness in the West. Going abroad for Filipinas is not only freedom, but is consistent with the long tradition of sending Philippine citizens abroad. These "new heroes" who can provide income for their families who remain behind, substantially supporting the Philippine economy.[64]

Lee suggests that the fact that women participate in the mail-order bride system does not indicate a lack of agency on their part but instead may suggest their willingness to take risks for the betterment of themselves and their families, a very American value.[65] Marriage agencies are seen by some authors as a positive force, where the demand for foreign wives is not necessarily a desire to dominate or colonize and the women who take advantage of this opportunity are in fact exhibiting feminist ideals (even while they would eschew the label) by escaping an oppressive set of expectations and definitions in search of greater gender equality.[66] Although, as Wang and Chang point out, at least in the Taiwan/ Vietnamese marriages, while not all women are brokered by a business entity, these agencies are increasingly dominating the cross-border marriage market. They suggest that even the "friends and family" ties that bring couples together are part of a larger economic transaction.[67] Both feminist scholars who condemn the buying of women as commodities through the mail-order bride system[68] and other scholars who are not so critical view the women as seeking a better life, one not so oppressive, not so male dominated, but they interpret the choice made by the women quite differently. In one instance, putting oneself on the market can be seen as taking the opportunity for advancement, even finding a way to escape oppression, while on the other, it can be viewed as akin to prostitution as a last resort.

The contradictions inherent in the mail-order bride system are potentially destructive to the couple's relationship as well as potentially dangerous to the alien bride. Women in poor countries, with little opportunity, may view marriage to an American man as the most obvious way out, not only of the restrictions on their life but the traditional expectations for women. They may be seeking not only a way out of the prospect of a miserable local marriage, or dreaded "spinsterhood," but may also be seeking modernity, which they situate firmly in the West.[69] They are, in many ways, escaping tradition, a tradition that disallows divorce, that narrows women's options, that subjects her to shame but leaves her no solution if her husband is abusive, a drunk or a philanderer, subjecting her to the status of "second wife."[70] She sees a modern marriage, revealing, yes, a reliance on family for her identity and meaning, but not an acceptance of oppression or subjection. The man she is likely to marry, however, is a man seeking tradition, seeking a woman who has not be ruined by the individualistic goals of the women's movement.[71] Christine So points out that discursively, the mail-order bride is located in the traditional narratives of race, gender, and imperialism.[72] She asks, why is there such sensationalist portrayal of the mail-order bride, why is the "language of capital" such a dominating force?[73] So articulates the complex relationship between our response to this issue and what it represents for us. She says that while we are willing to exploit "third world women's labor through consumption of products sewn, assembled, and manufactured by these women, the transfer of that labor directly to the American home has signaled a collision between the needs of capital and U.SA. ideologies surrounding home, family, and nation."[74] The mail-order bride is a symbol of the dangerous seduction and excess of global capitalism, linking sexuality to economic profit, something that capitalist societies are more comfortable leaving obscured. From So's perspective, the mail-order bride stands for our anxieties about global inequality, about the exploitation of others, especially those who are brown or black, and makes visible the very economic underpinnings of family relationships that we have romanticized.[75]

The mail-order bride is, from the perspective of Bealleu, caught in the trap of "bilateral sexism." Her willingness to fulfill the sexist dreams of men in the West results from being trapped in a system highly favorable to men in her own country, where she is subject to arranged marriages, stereotyped as an "old maid," caught in a dowry system, essentially reduced to a breeder, beset by economic hardship. She is thereby required to look where some of the very qualities that limit her in her own country are sought after—docile, hardworking, submissive, appreciative, and powerless.

We are concerned with the economic inequality we see as underlying the mail-order bride business but seem equally unconcerned with this very inequality in our other global economic and political transactions. So answers her question about the sensationalist response to mail-order bride by suggesting its symbolic value—it exposes the gendered, racial, and economic inequalities that characterize all interactions between first and third worlds.[76] It further supports the traditional American family system through reliance on non-Americans, revealing the inequality in that system that remains so politically and socially central. The mail-order bride reveals the economic value of labor in the home—the economic reality becomes transparent in the business exchange, and it is something romantically obscured in the United States.[77] When Geraldo Rivera refers to a mail-order bride as a "household appliance with sex organs," he places her outside the domain of the U.S. family, although he is in fact specifically revealing the power hierarchy of the normative family system.[78] And this is a system supported by the mail-order bride. Indeed, mail-order brides do not threaten the traditional family structure in the least, but rather support it and uphold its values. She, characterized as small, timid, traditional, affectionate, and devoted to her husband, reaffirms the traditional gender structure.[79] She, given her morality and devotion to family and morality, conveys traditional family arrangements and can save him from his immorality, his devotion to economic success.[80]

Men who peruse the catalogs, use the chat rooms, and sign up for the tours offered by the mail-order bride tour groups are looking for something they can't find at home. U.S. men, from the point of view of Donna Hughes, are seeking nonthreatening, compliant women,[81] natural women,

unspoiled by feminism and individualism,[82] docile, submissive, and subservient brides,[83] the "oriental Butterfly,"[84] an unrealistic, idealized
image built on racist images. In any case, they are looking for women
who are different from those they have found so unattractive or unavailable at home. They are sometimes angry and bitter after a divorce or disgusted with the independence of American women. They are likely to
view themselves as traditional men, good guys who just want a nice home
and family. As Kristoffer Garin found when he accompanied 30 other
men on a "Foreign Affair" tour through the Ukraine on a bride hunt: "what
they really wanted, and what most imagined they would find
in Ukraine, was a fusion of 1950s gender sensibilities with a twenty-
first-century hypersexuality"—"a vision of Madonna and *puttana* rolled
together, an American male desire shaped in equal parts by the Promise
Keepers and Internet porn."[85] The men Schaeffer and Gabriel studied
who toured for mail-order brides in South America were looking for younger, better-looking women than they could find in the United States, given
their age and social status. For them, Latin women represented spiritual
rejuvenation and purifying the boundaries of the self, the family, and the
nation—they were looking for natural women, uninhibited women,
women who they say represent the "last pure frontier," bodies that promise to rectify the crisis in masculinity and the breakdown of the family.[86]
They are looking for women who are more docile and tractable, women
who will make better mothers. They are hoping to escape the dominance
of white women to find the pristine women of other countries.

Belleau views the men seeking mail-order brides as "embittered" and
sexist,[87] and Garin describes them as disillusioned and angry.[88] It is perhaps a stretch to say that the men are looking for women to dominate
and oppress, women who have no real value and who can be used and
abused. Nonetheless, their view of American women as too bossy,
demanding, individualistic, competitive, and selfish and their quite frequent anger and bitterness toward them lead these men to look elsewhere.
They seem to be looking for a woman who can shore up their sense of self,
their definition of themselves as a man—the trouble being that many of
the women they have met or been married to in the United States don't
support their very traditional view of masculinity, especially given that it
includes some pretty real restrictions and stereotypes about femininity.
The women they are looking for are women who they view as remaining
more natural, more real, and unspoiled than Western women, and they
are often brown and racialized as hardworking, reliable, sexy, undemand-
ing, appreciative, maternal, and childlike.[89] They are imagined as women
who will support a traditional masculinity, who will appreciate and

understand gender hierarchy, and who will be satisfied with what they have rather than nagging and cajoling for more or threatening to leave for something or someone better.

There is a safety in seeking women from outside, because of their legal immigration status but also because they are often isolated in the dominant community, stigmatized in their own ethnic community, relatively uneducated, often do not speak the language well or drive, and so they are dependent on their husbands. But the men also view themselves as "good guys" who can rescue the poor women who are unappreciated or abused by their own men, or by the poverty in their country.[90] These are the "White men ... saving brown women from brown men" about whom Spivak wrote, men who can offer the women of Latin America or Thailand the "American dream" and position themselves as the moral good guys.[91] This positioning as the moral good guys and the sensitive male in opposition to the macho male of the women's country of origin may be hard to maintain, however, when the man returns home with his wife and she now wants a job, her own friends, and permanent residency—she is no longer the one who is saved and therefore beholden and appreciative but one who has a voice and may begin to sound a lot like the women he was escaping when he chose her.[92]

While there are similarities between the competitive marriage brokering system and arranged marriages in some countries, this is not so in the United States. There no doubt are many similarities, including the fact that men who are unable or unwilling to find brides in their own country because of ideology or economic factors look elsewhere. There are also similarities globally in the fact that the women may experience isolation and stigma as overseas brides, but this is not always the case, and in some instances, those foreign brides going to Korea, for example, may have more power to negotiate and more flexibility than others. But in the United states, there is an unfortunate convergence of men wanting traditional wives who will be submissive and shore up their masculinity with women trying to escape the very dependence and traditional inferiority the men are wanting. But everything is relative, as the saying goes, and those women who seek Western husbands, whether Asian or Eastern European, often see them as more modern and progressive than the men in their own countries who would be available[93]

SEX TOURISM

Highly sexualized, dehumanized, "othered" women occupy the brothels, the bars and the bedrooms of hotels frequented by sex tourists.

Women were trapped in "comfort stations" during W.W. II, and are today trafficked and ordered from catalogs or on the Internet. One is struck by the similarities between these forms of sexualizing women; the assumptions about femininity, sexuality, and masculinity; the economic inequality, discrimination, and blatant misogyny that are so foundational; and the intersections of race, gender, and class that characterize gendered violence. The Japanese soldiers who forced Korean and Japanese girls and women and women in other occupied territories to serve as rape slaves, completely dehumanized the women, visiting unspeakable horrors on their bodies and souls. This is different by degree from the use of prostitutes near military bases, and from some of these other forms of sexual exploitation, but it is informed by the same sentiments, the same sexual structures, the same ideologies and constructions. Sex tourism relies on economic inequality just as does the mail-order bride business, but here the men are not looking for a wife or mother for their children or someone to iron their shirts and soothe their egos battered by American women's claims for equality. Here, instead, men are looking to women or girls in other countries, women in their native settings, natural women to shore up their masculine identities, to reestablish the gender binary with men as real men and women as subordinate and sexy.

Sex tourism has a long history, relying on the patterns of sexual exploitation established during World War II and the Vietnam War. When the troops left, when the bases were dismantled, the potentially devastating hole left in the economic infrastructure was filled by new waves of men from Germany, Japan, Canada, and the United States in particular, men who were accustomed to viewing women as consumables and themselves as legitimate buyers.[94] Conforming to the same assumptions about masculinity and the familiar tropes about "oriental" women, these men embarked from planes rather than ships, in small groups rather than by the thousands, but with the same constructions of First and Third World and the same expectations for privileged masculinity and servile femininity. Development agencies encouraged the governments of Thailand and the Philippines to develop their tourist industries, to take advantage of their natural resources, including women's bodies, in order to position themselves for loans and to improve their economic system.[95] Women who had lived on farms and in villages before finding work as prostitutes and bar girls during the 1970s had paved the way for the next generation of women who saw the potential for a better life in the cities, perhaps a man who would marry them, provide for them, and their families. Economic inequality laced with racial stereotypes and gendered assumptions fueled this industry and continues to do so. Sex tourism is, of course, not limited to Southeast Asia. Many men find what they define as the earthier, natural, robust sexuality of women from Central America and Mexico an attractive alternative to the independent and individualistic women of their home country.[96] What looks like "nature" and a willingness to submit and serve born of biologically natural, unspoiled femininity is, of course, a contrivance by the women to meet the raced and gendered stereotypes of the men who are their ticket to economic survival.[97] The merger of their needs and their astute awareness of men's needs creates a fantasy world of mutual benefit. Yet this fantasy world is built on deep gender and economic inequality that remains intact long after the tourist, sexually sated and emotionally remasculinized, returns to Emporia or Chicago to once again face a world in which masculinity itself is not an automatic badge of success and superiority.

The parallels between military prostitution and the sex tourism that it helped establish are clear, and the constructions of the women, especially given that they are women from the same locales, are strikingly similar. The difference is in the depiction of the relationship between the sex workers and the men who use them: Military men need sex with objectified women to maintain the gender divide that buttresses military masculinity; global sex tourists need sex with objectified women to maintain a masculinity threatened by increasing gender equality that frays the edges of the gender divide. In both cases, women constructed as docile and servile provide the necessary services to keep masculinity intact.

Internationally, sex tourism is a huge business, bringing men from western and developed countries to those on the economic margins. Travel companies package hotels, meals, and women into an attractive vacation for men who eroticize and romanticize the Asian women as docile, submissive, compliant, and childlike.[98] They are very different from the real women in their everyday lives, at home or in the workplace, who might clamor for equality or expect "help with the dishes or children." The women in highly sexualized tourist destinations are defined in relation to the needs of the men—the men are white, the women dark; they are rational, the women emotional; they are wealthy, the women needy; but mostly they are able to perform white supremacy in relation to the dark inferiors, who not only are "othered" racially, but whose sexuality is defined in terms of the needs or desires of the men.[99] The constructions of women for militarized sex and sex tourism are similar to the constructions of women in pornography and often serve the same purpose. Beneke suggests that porn offers not images of "whole, erotic, autonomous women, but rather subjectified bodies of women, that is, bodies whose putative consciousness and subjectivity, as manifest through facial expression and body posture, refer, and are a complement to, their viewability as bodies to be fantasized about by men."[100] The women are constructed in porn, as in military sex and sex tourism, for consumption by men and are made intelligible as products that meet these needs. A john in the 1991 porn movie *The Good Woman of Bangkok* expresses this perfectly: "You can't beat the attitude of these girls. There's no girl in the world that will give you a shower, give you a blow job, fuck your brains out, and fold your clothes with a smile on her face. Dammit, nowhere."[101]

Another view is that men seeking sex with women who are racialized and sexualized as "other" as in other than white, other than dominant, other than demanding, are seeking not just sex, not just servility and docility, but romance.[102] Hungry for the kind of masculinity idealized in film and dominant cultural imagery, they want women who want them, admire them, who desire them, with no strings attached, and they are able to see these women and their sexual availability and vulnerability as naturally different in a convenient way from the women they know.[103] What they fail to see is that the representation of these women as dependent and vulnerable is built on a system of economic inequality in which white men have what brown women need and want—money, money for their own survival and money for their families. So the women romanticize the relationship, build a fantasy the men will pay for, reinforcing the men's views that they are simply having sex with women willing to please them because of their natural open sexuality.[104]

One of the attractions of the racialized "oriental" woman is her childlikeness, her innocence. Drawing on this construction, tourist junkets for men seeking sex can provide the real deal; not a woman but a child. What might be seen as unthinkable in the United States or perhaps "thinkable" but not "doable" can be accessed through the redefinition of children as "different" in a "different culture." The cultural overlay of children as eroticized, deemed natural, undeveloped, open, unconstrained by the rational-legal impediments of Western society, loosens adherence to the norms of decency in the country of origin. When colonized or non-Western men are feminized by the West and when the women and children are rendered unprotected in their eyes, as well as demarcated as "essentially different," then they too become subject to male desire. These men are not really DSM-certifiable pedophiles, consuming underage children for their sexual satisfaction—that is, unless we are willing to agree there are millions of pedophiles in Japan, Germany, Canada, and the United States who travel to the sex mecca, Thailand, for sex. Rather, they have reconceptualized childhood innocence and availability as sexual willingness. They have severed the constructions of child from those of children from their own neighborhoods and in their own families, children who are, because they are children, sexually off-limits, both legally and morally.

CONCLUSION

The push of poverty, the hope for something better or just for survival that characterizes the women who are engaged in prostitution, who fill the glossy pages of mail-order bride catalogs and who wait in bars or populate internet sites seeking a Western man, do not belie the fact that these women have agency. As is the case with trafficking more generally, many of these women are the most industrious, most ambitious, relying on whatever resources they have to become a valued object in a gendered marketplace. Working a capitalist system to their advantage, they rely on the highly sexualized and stereotyped constructions of femininity to strike the best deal they can for themselves and their families. Whether we are talking about sex work, military prostitution, mail-order brides, or sex tourism, the underlying dynamic is one of global inequality driven by gendered and raced assumptions and opportunities.

NOTES

1. L. Jones, D. Engstrom, P. Hillard, and D. Sungakawan, "Human Trafficking between Thailand and Japan: Lessons in Recruitment Transit and Control," *International Journal of Social Welfare* 20, no. 2 (2011): 206.

2. M. Olivera, "Violencia Femicida: Violence against Women and Mexico's Structural Crisis," *Latin American Perspectives* 33, no. 2 (March 2006): 104–14.

3. G. Petrunov, "Money Laundering from Human Trafficking for the Purpose of Sexual Exploitation." Originally published in Bulgarian in: *Izpirane na pari ot trafik na hora* [Money Laundering from Human Trafficking] (Sofia: RiskMonitor and National Investigation Service, 2009), 17–31.

4. Y. V. Tverdova, "Human Trafficking in Russia and Other Post-Soviet States," *Human Rights Review* 12, no. 3 (2011): 329–39.

5. Jones et al., "Human Trafficking between Thailand and Japan."

6. S. George, "The Strong Arm of the Law Is Weak: How the Trafficking Victims Protection Act Fails to Assist Effectively Victims of the Sex Trade," *Creighton Law Review* 45, no. 3 (April 2012): 563–80.

7. J. Hua and H. Nigorizawa, "US Trafficking, Women's Human Rights and the Politics of Representation," *International Feminist Journal of Politics* 12, no. 3 (2010): 404.

8. C. S. Vance, "States of Contradiction: Twelve Ways to Do Nothing about Trafficking While Pretending To," *Social Research* 78, no. 3 (2011): 937.

9. U.S. Attorney General's Annual Report 2010: 37–38; Vance, "States of Contradiction," 937.

10. J. Doezema, "Loose Women or Lost Women? The Re-Emergence of the Myth of White Slavery in Contemporary Discourses of Trafficking in Women,"*Gender Issues* 18, no. 1 (Winter 2000): 23–50.

11. K. Kempadoo and J. Doezema (Eds.), *Global Sex Workers: Rights, Resistance, and Redefinition* (New York and London: Routledge, 1998): 44.

12. M. C. Desyllas, "A Critique of the Global Trafficking Discourse and U.S. Policy." *Journal of Sociology and Social Welfare* 34, no. 4 (December 2007): 61.

13. R. Weitzer, "The Social Construction of Sex Trafficking: Ideology and Institutionalization of a Moral Crusade," *Politics and Society* 35, no. 3 (September 2007): 447–75.

14. W. McDonald, "Traffic Counts, Symbols & Agendas: A Critique of the Campaign against Trafficking of Human Beings," *International Review of Victimology* 11, no. 1 (2004): 143–76.

15. G. Ekberg, "The Swedish Law That Prohibits the Purchase of Sexual Services—Best Practices for Prevention of Prostitution and Trafficking in Human Beings," *Violence Against Women* 10, no. 10 (2004): 1187–1218; V. Munroe, "Stopping Traffic? A Comparative Study of Responses to the Trafficking in Women for Prostitution," *British Journal of Criminology* 46, no. 2 (2006): 318–33.

16. Weitzer, "The Social Construction of Sex Trafficking," 447.

17. Ibid., 461. Weitzer lists the NGOs and Christian organizations that helped write the bill.

18. Napp Nazworth, "To Fight Sex Trafficking, Fight the Ideology That Creates It, Expert Says," *Christian Post Reporter*, February 25, 2013, http://www.christianpost.com/news/to-fight-sex-trafficking-fight -the-ideology-that-creates-it-expert-says-90694/; J. Katz, *The Macho Paradox: Why Some Men Hurt Women and Why All Men Can Help* (Naperville, IL: Sourcebooks, 2006).

19. J. Bindman with J. Doezema, *Redefining Prostitution as Sex Work on the International Agenda* (Toronto: Anti-Slavery International, Network of Sex Work Projects, 1997).

20. J. Outshoorn, "The Political Debates on Prostitution and Trafficking of Women," *Social Politics: International Studies in Gender, State*

and Society 12, no. 1 (Spring 2005): 145; Desyllas, "A Critique of the Global Trafficking Discourse and U.S. Policy."

21. Bindman and Doezema, *Redefining Prostitution as Sex Work on the International Agenda.*

22. Outshoorn, "The Political Debates on Prostitution and Trafficking of Women," 59.

23. M. Farley, *WakePeopleUp.com*, February 24, 2011, http://www.wakepeopleup.com

24. Ibid.

25. Outshoorn, "The Political Debates on Prostitution and Trafficking of Women," 145.

26. Ibid.

27. C. Jaget (ed.) and M. St. James, "What's a Girl Like You . . . ?" in *Prostitutes: Our Life*, edited by C. Jaget (Bristol, UK: Falling Wall Press, 1980).

28. P. Alexander, "Prostitution: A Difficult Question for Feminists," in *Sex Work: Writings by Women in the Industry*, edited by F. Delacoste and P. Alexander (San Francisco: Cleis Press, 1987).

29. Ibid.

30. Ibid.

31. M. Kaneti, "Project Trafficking: Global Unity in Addressing a Universal Challenge," *Human Rights Review* 12, no. 3 (2011): 351.

32. K. Farr, *Sex Trafficking: The Global Traffic in Women and Children* (New York: Worth Publishers, 2004), 235.

33. Farley, *WakePeopleUp.com.*

34. M.-C. Belleau, "Mail-Order Brides in a Global World," *Global World*, 2003, file://E:/paper/Mail-Order.htm, accessed November 17, 2004.

35. V. B. M. Vergara, "Comment: Abusive Mail-Order Bride Marriage and the Thirteenth Amendment," *Northwestern University Law Review* 94, no. 4 (2000): 3.

36. G. Chang, "The Global Trade in Filipina Workers," in *Dragon Ladies: Asian American Feminists Breathe Fire*, edited by S. Shah (Cambridge, MA: South End Press, 1997).

37. H. Lee, "International Marriage and the State in South Korea: Focusing on Governmental Policy," *Citizenship Studies* 12, no. 1 (2008): 107–23.

38. V. L. de Cortemiglia, in Y. Zabyelina, "Mail Order Brides: Content Analysis of Eastern European Marriage Agencies" (Saarbrücken, Germany: VDM Verlang, 2010): 87.

39. Zabyelina, "Mail Order Brides," 89.

40. Ibid., 87.

41. For example, see H. Wang and S. Chang, "The Commodification of International Marriages: Cross-Border Marriage Business in Taiwan and Viet Nam," *International Migration* 40, no. 6 (2012): 93–114.

42. Belleau, "Mail-Order Brides in a Global World."

43. Ibid.

44. Ibid.

45. B. E. Perez, "Woman Warrior Meets Mail-Order Bride: Finding and Asian American Voice in the Women's Movement," *Berkeley Women's Law Journal* 18, no. 1 (2003): 231.

46. Ibid.

47. Wang and Chang, "The Commodification of International Marriages."

48. Ibid.

49. Ibid.

50. Ibid.

51. Ibid., 1.

52. Lee, "International Marriage and the State in South Korea."

53. Ibid.

54. Perez, "Woman Warrior Meets Mail-Order Bride."

55. Ibid.

56. C. Chang, "In the Market for Love." Wide Angle photo essay *Foreign Policy*, no. 151 (November/December 2005): 72–76.

57. Wang and Chang, "The Commodification of International Marriages."

58. Perez, "Woman Warrior Meets Mail-Order Bride."

59. Zabyelina, "Mail Order Brides."

60. K. A. Garin, "A Foreign Affair on the Great Ukrainian Bride Hunt," *Harpers*, June 2006: 73.

61. Wang and Chang, "The Commodification of International Marriages."

62. Belleau, "Mail-Order Brides in a Global World."

63. A. Lauser, "Philippine Women on the Move: Marriage across Borders." *International Migration* 46, no. 4 (2008): 85–108; Belleau, "Mail-Order Brides in a Global World."

64. Chang, "The Global Trade in Filipina Workers."

65. Lee, "International Marriage and the State in South Korea."

66. Zabyelina, "Mail Order Brides," 89.

67. Wang and Chang, "The Commodification of International Marriages."

68. Perez, "Woman Warrior Meets Mail-Order Bride."

69. Lauser, "Philippine Women on the Move."

70. Ibid.

71. Garin, "A Foreign Affair on the Great Ukrainian Bride Hunt."

72. C. So, "Asian Mail-Order Brides, the Threat of Global Capitalism, and the Rescue of the U.S. Nation-State," *Feminist Studies* 32, no. 2 (2006): 395–419.

73. Ibid., 397.

74. Ibid., 398.

75. So, "Asian Mail-Order Brides, the Threat of Global Capitalism, and the Rescue of the U.S. Nation-State."

76. Ibid.

77. Ibid.

78. Ibid., 403.

79. So, "Asian Mail-Order Brides."

80. Ibid.

81. Zabyelina, "Mail Order Brides," 88.

82. F. Schaeffer-Gabriel, "Planet-Love.com: Cyberbrides in the American and the Transnational Routes of U.S. Masculinity," *Signs: Journal of Women in Culture and Society* 31, no. 2 (2006): 331–356.

83. Belleau, "Mail-Order Brides in a Global World."

84. Perez, 2003.

85. Garin, "A Foreign Affair on the Great Ukrainian Bride Hunt," 74.

86. F. Schaeffer-Gabriel, "Planet-Love.com," 339.

87. Belleau, "Mail-Order Brides in a Global World," 606.

88. Garin, "A Foreign Affair on the Great Ukrainian Bride Hunt."

89. G. C. Spivak, "Can the Subaltern Speak," in *Marxism and Interpretation of Culture*, edited by C. Nelson and L. Grossberg (Urbana: University of Illinois Press, 1988), 90; Schaeffer-Gabriel, "Planet-Love.com."

90. F. Schaeffer-Grabriel, "Planet-Love.com: Cyberbrides in the Americas and the Transnational Routes of U.S. Masculinity," *Signs: Journal of Woman and Culture* 31, no. 2 (2006): 331–356.

91. Spivak, "Can the Subaltern Speak," 396.

92. Schaeffer-Gabriel, "Planet-Love.com."

93. Lauser, "Philippine Women on the Move."

94. J. Nagel, "States of Arousal/Fantasy Islands: Race, Sex, and Romance in the Global Economy of Desire," *American Studies* 41, no. 2/3 (Summer/Fall 2000): 159–81.

95. Ibid.

96. Schaeffer-Gabriel, "Planet-Love.com."

97. Ibid.

98. Wang and Chang, "The Commodification of International Marriages."

99. Nagel, "States of Arousal/Fantasy Islands."

100. T. Beneke, *Proving Manhood: Reflections on Men and Sexism* (Berkeley: University of California Press, 1997), 97.

101. C. P. Shimizu, *The Hypersexuality of Race: Performing Asian American Women on Screen and Scene* (Durham, NC: Duke University Press, 2007), 185.

102. Schaeffer-Gabriel, "Planet-Love.com."

103. Ibid.

104. Wang and Chang, "The Commodification of International Marriages."

TEN

Military Violence against Women in Historical Perspective

THE RAPE OF NANKING

When Iris Chang published *The Rape of Nanking* in 1994, it was met with immediate acclaim and immediate condemnation. She had known little about this atrocity committed by the Japanese Imperial Army until she attended a conference in Cupertino, California, where survivors, journalists, and historians revealed the almost unimaginable horror visited on between 200,000 and 300,000 Chinese civilians and at least 90,000 soldiers during a period of six weeks between 1936 and 1937 in the city of Nanking, China. The victims were, as is so often the case, the poor, those who were unable to leave the city that had been abandoned by the elite and middle classes, the foreigners, and finally the government.[1] It was what Chang called "the forgotten Holocaust."[2] The 50,000 Japanese troops that descended on Nanking were tired, angry, frustrated, and fueled by hatred of the Chinese. Schooled in the ideology that one never surrenders, they despised the Chinese soldiers who had surrendered and systematically tortured and murdered them, often capturing the moment on film. They then turned their wrath on the women and children, raping and then murdering, forcing families to turn against one another, fathers to rape their daughters, sons to rape their mothers, sparing not even the pregnant women who they gang-raped and whose fetuses they then ripped from their bodies with bayonets. The inhumane treatment reflected the Japanese sense of superiority to the "inferior" Asian races, a view that was soon to be reflected in the assaults on women's bodies by soldiers in comfort stations.

The diaries of John Rabe detailed in eight volumes the day-by-day horror experienced by the Chinese.[3] His diaries were published in 1997 just a few years after the publication of *The Rape of Nanking*. A businessman and member of the Nazi party, Rabe led the team, using his party affiliation to negotiate with the Japanese for the survival of the citizens. Eventually, about 20 Americans and Europeans who had remained behind established an International Safety Zone in which, through sheer bravado and tireless effort, they provided what food, medical care, and safety they could to thousands of Chinese civilians.[4] The diaries of Minnie Vautrin, the American who is credited with saving 10,000 civilians by sheltering them in Ginling College, were published later.[5] Vautrin, who was the acting president of Ginling College when the Japanese invaded, kept a diary from 1937 to 1940, describing endless, brutal killings and vicious rapes. Her diaries describe a bone-weariness and hopelessness that eventually led to her "nervous breakdown" in Nanking.[6] Returning home, she was institutionalized and treated with electroshock therapy. She never recovered from the horrors she experienced and finally, foreshadowing the suicide of Iris Chang over 60 years later, took her own life a year to the day after she left Nanking.

The atrocities at Nanking laid the groundwork for the Imperial Army's development of the comfort system only a few years later, one of the most extreme and most large-scale forms of violence against women ever perpetrated by the state. When the Japanese Imperial Army entered Nanking, they pillaged the city, they tortured and brutally raped approximately 80,000 women and girls.[7] The comfort system was to stem the tide of the violence they had visited on innocent women, to impose a measure of order on the army, to meet the soldiers' demands for sex, and to reduce the contempt in which the conquered communities held their captors.[8]

"COMFORT WOMEN" IN JAPAN DURING WORLD WAR II

When Japan entered World War II, the government established what it called comfort stations for the soldiers to provide them with what they saw as necessary sexual release and to prevent the atrocities that had occurred in Nanking. The comfort women were offered as a gift to the Japanese Imperial Army by Emperor Hirohito.[9] The number of comfort stations and comfort women is difficult to ascertain, but there were, in Okinawa alone, 126 sites of *ianjo* (comfort stations) or what McDougal calls "rape centres."[10] The same view of masculinity and femininity that permeates the sale of women's bodies for the sexual pleasure of men today underpinned the government's cynical calculation to use women, some Japanese prostitutes but mostly Korean and Burmese women. They were held at locations near military bases and forced to have sex with soldiers, servicing as many as 30 men a day.[11] The Japanese soldiers were unlikely to get leave time to return to their homes and families during the war, so the comfort stations were established to provide sexual "comfort" for them, with women whose bodies could be used over and over again as dumping grounds. The comfort women were local women recruited or taken from their homes in the occupied territories or women taken by boat, bus, or truck from their homes to the comfort stations Japan had established in the South Pacific. The virgins were delivered to the officers who initiated them through rape, often for days, keeping the light-skinned women for themselves and turning over the darker women to the enlisted men. Those that protested too much were shot. Hank Nelson explains in his research on the "comfort system" at Rabaul in New Guinea that the women were designated "Special Naval Personnel" and divided into categories reflecting the status of the officers and soldiers who would have access to them.[12]

The existence of comfort women only came to light as the result of the work of women involved in the Korean Women's Movement who assisted prostitutes in military "camptowns," or *kijich'on*, who were victims of debt bondage used by American servicemen in Korea.[13] These activists discovered and publicized a connection between the Japanese, U.S., and Korean governments.[14] They found that the Camptown women had been kidnapped, given fraudulent promises, or were coerced by traffickers who had promised them good jobs or education. These women were often initiated into the system through rape. They were held in a debt bondage system by their managers or pimps or by the owners of the clubs where they worked, a system that was regulated and sustained by the official policies and practices of both the U.S. and the Korean governments.[15]

Kirsten Orreill presents four factors that led to the establishment of the comfort system:

- First, to avoid repetition of the horror of the mass rape and slaughter that had occurred in 1937 in Nanking China by the Imperial Army.
- Second, to provide leisure to the men, releasing them from the strict military discipline under which they operated, boosting morale, and compensating for the lack of leave.
- Third, to contain the rapid increase of venereal disease among the Japanese soldiers, among whom the rate of infection was between 30 and 40 percent.

- Fourth, to prevent espionage by keeping careful check on which soldiers used which *Ianfu* so that their subsequent behavior could be monitored if suspicions about them arose.[16]

These reasons are similar to those justifying colonial practices that sent
women to accompany the male workforces sent by the British, the Span-
ish, and others to establish far-flung colonies, providing for their sexual
needs along with food, water, and shelter.[17] Indigenous women were also
forced into the position of sex servants to ensure the commitment of the
laborers to their work and to reward and distract them.[18] The comfort station system is also directly parallels the German military brothels established in World War II and the brothels established by the Nazis in death
camps. Just as with comfort stations, the Nazi brothels were used as a
means to control inmates, encourage collaboration, and prevent riots and
escapes, but in addition they were used to cure gay inmates of their "afflic-
tion" by forcing them to have sex with women inmates.[19]

The comfort women were usually poor, rural women or girls who were
systematically recruited by their teachers and other community leaders to
be taken from their homes to the camps. The comfort women were, in fact,
often only girls, between 11 and 14, and they were usually virgins. They
were cajoled into providing a "service" during wartime or were duped into
believing they were going to do other labor.[20] The recruitment process
reflected the fact that sexual expectations for middle- and upper-class
Korean women differed significantly from those from the lower classes,
who were sometimes sold into prostitution to help their families survive.
These women were both powerless to resist Japanese demands and targeted because they were so defenseless and poor.[21]

Although Japan had a well-established prostitution system, and while
some Japanese prostitutes were used as comfort women, they were not
ideal recruits.[22] First, many of them were older, between 20 and 40 years
old, and many had sexually transmitted diseases. And second, such
women would not make a proper gift to the Imperial Army. The number
of women trapped in the comfort system is widely debated. When Japan
realized they were losing the war, they burned as many documents as possible for fear of war crimes prosecution, leaving very few records of this
system.[23] Further revisionist historians have made a point of downplaying
the numbers. The historian Yoshaiki Yoshimi first brought this issue to the
attention of the public, estimating that between 50,000 and
200,000 women were enslaved as comfort women, while others, including
the International Commission of Jurists, suggest 100,000 to 200,000.[24]
Most authors conclude that the majority of the women came from Japan

and Korea, although others came from the Dutch East Indies, the Philippines, Taiwan, Burma, Indonesia, and other territories occupied by the Japanese.[25] So many came from Korea for a number of reasons: because of its geographical proximity to Japan; because it was a colony, therefore seen as culturally inferior; and because it had little power to resist.[26]

Some authors, such as Hayashi Hirofumi, disagree that the majority were Korean and provide a documented history of Japanese use of local women in the establishment of comfort stations. Citing official documents, Hirofumi reports that in Kuala Lumpur, as in Malaya, Indonesia, and the Philippines, the majority were locals or Chinese, reflecting the ethnic mix of these locations and the fact that by 1942, "comfort houses had been set up in almost every city where Japanese troops were stationed."[27] It seems that a contingent of soldiers went ahead of the rest, establishing the comfort houses and working with local city officials to recruit or convince local women to work in the comfort houses.[28]

The women were recruited in a number of ways:

- Because Korea was a colony, Japan had already established a trafficking system with it and could rely on these brokers to provide women.
- The recruitment was sometimes entrusted to former Japanese prostitutes, who were then often established as managers of the houses.
- Local leaders were often ordered to provide women for the comfort house. This was the case in Malaya, the Philippines, and Indonesia as well as some other countries.
- Women were sometimes recruited through advertising. Sometimes they were aware of the nature but not the full expectations of the job.
- Fraud was sometimes used in the recruitment, and once recruited the women were the victims of force and violence.
- Reliance on forcible abduction was not unknown. In Malaya and the Philippines, for example, comfort women were being abducted at the same time as large-scale massacres were occurring.[29]

The comfort system and the establishment of comfort stations for the Japanese Imperial Army in countries invaded by Japan reflect almost perfectly the problem of sex trafficking that receives so much attention today. The only difference is that government agents were behind these comfort stations and colluded with military go-betweens to dupe, threaten, kidnap, or fraudulently convince women to leave their homes to become military sex slaves. The methods were the same as those used all over the world, with women being told they will have good jobs and make money to send back to their families or that they would escape the oppression and constraints of village life in a patriarchal household. In reality, they soon discover, they are confined, beaten, raped, starved, and dehumanized. The comfort women were guarded 24 hours a day and kept in wood shacks, their bare rooms equipped only with a bed and a bucket of disinfectant. And they were required to service between 10 and 30 men a day.[30] Kentaro Igusa, a naval surgeon assigned to inspect and treat the "love girls," found some of the women were so badly swollen from the constant rapes that they "cried and begged for help," but "the women [were forced to] work through infection and severe discomfort."[31] Many of the comfort women died from infection, or as a result of sexual and physical violence, and many others were so severely injured that they would never have children. Some tried to escape, but because they had been taken from distant other countries, they were unfamiliar with the local language, the customs, and the geography, which either forced them to return or led to their capture. When captured as escapees, they were often beaten or killed. Orreill includes the story of one woman who had escaped and was buried in sand up to her neck and then decapitated in front of the other women.[32]

DEMANDS AND DENIAL

A half a century later, these women, now old, began to demand apologies and reparations from the Japanese government. To this day, once a week, the Korean comfort women protest in front of the Japanese embassy.[33] Many of the women have died, and most of those who are still alive waited until their families died before coming forward to speak about the atrocities they experienced.[34] If they were not killed or abandoned after the Japanese were defeated, most of them returned to their homes, unable to reestablish a meaningful life after their return. Suffering mental and emotional problems, severe physical injuries, and abandoned or rejected by their families, neighbors, and community, some turned to prostitution, others sold vegetables or scraps, doing whatever they could to eke out a miserable existence, sometimes depending on their neighbors for survival.[35] These women could not return to their families, could not marry, and if they did marry, were often infertile and were soon divorced. They were shamed and stigmatized by a society that devalued them from the beginning and then despised them for having been sexual slaves. These women, having taken such brave steps to confront their government rapists, have not only been denied justice, but have been dishonored by their own country, abandoned by the Korean government, which, in order to protect its financial and economic relationship with Japan, has refused to press the comfort women's demand for official government compensation for the war crimes they endured.

Pyong Gap Min makes it clear that while the colonial status of Korea may have made the women much more vulnerable to being trafficked into comfort stations, the fact that they were poor and female in a gender-based hierarchy in a class-based system visited 50 additional years of misery on them.[36] As one surviving former comfort woman, Kim Soon-duk, said: "I am unhappy with the Korean government also. They asked us to come out from hiding and to speak out to let people know the truth, So I did. I spoke out my past that had been hidden even from my mother, Now I wish the Korean government would be more forceful in representing our interests, and help us to regain our dignity."[37]

Only about 30 percent of the original Korean comfort women survived.[38] Many were murdered, many were forced to kill themselves when Japan was defeated, many were killed outright after the defeat rather than becoming an embarrassment to Japan or encumbering the Japanese retreat, many died of infection or injury or starvation, and others were left to die when the Japanese abandoned their positions in occupied territories.[39] There are only a handful of these women still living, some still too ashamed of the violations they suffered to come forward, to be able to acknowledge what happened to them. Human rights activists remain their best ally, demanding not only that the comfort women be recognized as victims of a human rights violation but that rape be recognized as an act of war, no matter where or when it occurs. It cannot be tolerated as ordinary violence.

The Japanese government initially denied its involvement in the creation of comfort stations, insisting instead that the women were prostitutes who followed the soldiers to make money. But historian Yoshaiki Yoshimi, discovered an incriminating document, "Regarding the Recruitment of Women for Military Brothels," in the archives of Japan's Defense Agency showing that the military was directly involved in running the brothels.[40] This discovery led to extensive media attention to comfort women, finally resulting in the Chief Cabinet Secretary, Yohei Kono, in 1993, issuing a statement but not an apology.[41] The Japanese government recognized that: "the Japanese military was directly or indirectly involved in the establishment and management of the comfort stations and the transfer of the women ... and that the military had worked with private recruiters to recruit women, many of whom were recruited through 'coaxing and coercion.' "[42]

In 1995, Prime Minister Tomiichi Murayama specifically apologized, but Japan has continued to deny legal liability for the comfort women

and has consistently refused to provide government-supported reparations. Instead, in 1995, the government established an "Asian Women's
Fund" consisting of private funds to distribute to the women.[43] Most of
the women have refused this offer, saying it would be like reprostituting
themselves. They demanded that the government take responsibility for
its complicity in their misery.[44] The documentary *Silence Broken: Korean
Comfort Women* follows the women into the current period, interviewing
the few women remaining about their experiences in the comfort stations,
and subsequently, revealing the depression, loss of family, and hopelessness of most of the women who survived.[45]

In 2007, Japanese Prime Minister Shinzo Abe denied Kono's acknowledgment, saying that there was no "evidence to prove there was coercion."[46] Revisionist historians and journalists have downplayed the
problem of comfort women or denied Japanese government responsibility,
instead suggesting that the women were prostitutes who willingly serviced
the soldiers. Nishio Kanji, a literature professor, and Ikuhiko Hata, a history professor at Nihon University, are among the well-known revisionists. Hata estimates the number of comfort women to be very small, and
insists that none of the women was forcibly recruited.[47] Kobayshi Yoshi-
nori, the popular Japanese comic book artist, also a member of the Japanese History Textbook reform group that wished to eliminate references
to comfort women in junior high school textbooks, produced a popular
comic in which he depicts the *Ianfu*, or comfort women, as prostitutes.[48]
Fujioka Nobukatsu, an education professor at the University of Tokyo,
joins a number of these other educators and historians who are devoted
to presenting a positive image of Japan, which includes rewriting history
books to erase accounts of the atrocities committed during World War
II, such as forcing women into prostitution.[49] Hata also asserts that the
comfort women were Japanese prostitutes, who not only volunteered for
such duty but were very well compensated.[50] These Japanese historians
and authors join others, including legislators, claiming to be "Assenters,"
or supporters of *The Truth about Nanjing*, a film designed to correct the
inaccuracies of *The Rape of Nanking* and to deny the government's role
in the comfort system.[51] They claim that the women were volunteers and
that the government had no responsibility for them. One of the most
revolting revisionists, a cheerleader for rape, assault, and murder, former
education minister Nariaki Nakayama expressed pride that the
conservative Liberal Democratic Party, Prime Minister Abe's party, had
succeeded in having most references to "wartime sex slaves" removed
from authorized history textbooks for junior high schools. He then went
on to say that the women who were victimized should be proud of being

comfort women: "Those women deserve much sympathy, but (being forced to provide sex) is not so much different from what was commonly seen in poor rural Japanese communities in the past, where women were sold to brothels. It could be said that the occupation was something they could have pride in, given their existence soothed distraught feelings of men in the battlefield and provided a certain respite."[52]

The surviving comfort women and even the government of South Korea were outraged when, in 2007, Prime Minister Shinzo Abe indicated there was no documentary evidence to prove the coercion of the women by the government. The reaction to this was swift and strong: the U.S. House of Representatives passed House Resolution 121 denouncing the "Japanese military's enslavement of Asian and Pacific Island women during World War II."[53] A full-page ad in the *Washington Post* called for the Japanese government to formally apologize and compensate the surviving comfort women.[54] Other countries, including Canada and the Netherlands, joined the United States in condemning Japan's refusal to take responsibility for these war crimes.[55] Under pressure from the United States and other countries, he revised his statement later that month to express his regrets for the violation of the human rights of the comfort women.[56] The back and forth remains, but the Japanese government continues to be pressured by the United States, the Netherlands, Canada, and 27 member states of the European Union to provide a formal apology and government reparations to the women. NGOs such as the Japan Accountability Caucus still work to hold the government accountable to the women and to their signatures on the Beijing Conference in which they agreed to further the human rights of women, in particular reproductive health and rights, by addressing issues of domestic violence, sexual harassment, sexual exploitation, and "comfort women."[57]

The United Nations Commission of Human Rights and the International Commission of Jurists have both demanded that Japan recognize its actions during the war in the Pacific as militarized sexual slavery that should be prosecuted as a human rights violation.[58] The reluctance of the government to take full responsibility for the military sexual slavery led to Amnesty International calling on the government to:

- accept full responsibility for the "comfort women" system in a way that publicly acknowledges the harm that these women suffered and restores the dignity of the survivors;
- apologize fully for the crimes committed against the women;
- provide adequate and effective compensation to survivors and their immediate families directly from the government;

• include an accurate account of the sexual slavery system in Japanese educational textbooks on World War II.[59]

This is an issue that will simply not disappear. Most recently, in 2103, Prime Minister Abe said he would not get into the political position of reviewing the 1993 apology offered by then Chief Secretary Yohei Kono.[60] In May 2013, Toru Hashimoto, populist party leader, found himself trying to quell an uproar over his statement that sexual slavery in Japan was a necessary evil during World War II. He had explained: "When soldiers are risking their lives by running through storms of bullets, and you want to give these emotionally charged soldiers a rest somewhere, it's clear that you need a comfort women system"[61] He made another point that will no doubt make other governments uncomfortable, stating that Japan was not alone in the use of comfort women during the war—Britain, France, Germany, the Soviet Union, and the United States were guilty of similar violations of women's rights.[62]

While the comfort system is extreme in both scale and brutality, the use of women's bodies for sexual release of soldiers is a long-standing global practice. While ancient soldiers may have been cautioned against having sex with a woman before battle, for fear that bodily reserves would be drained, diminishing the man's readiness for battle, it is more often the case that soldiers are viewed as needing sex. This is for a number of reasons—to remain battle ready, to help maintain order and cohesiveness, to protect local women during battle (there being no evidence that it actually does), and to reward men for their sacrifices and bravery. Women are provided as objects in service to their country, bodies on which men can relieve themselves, safe targets of male brutality.

Japan is not the only government that has forced women into prostitution, and the comfort system established in WW II was not the first time Japan used them.[63] In addition to the German military, as mentioned earlier, the commander of the British forces in Tripoli, Libya, during WW II authorized brothels and classified them for use according to the rank of the officers as well as by race, separating the black and white soldiers.[64] And during the occupation of Japan, in consideration of the needs of the conquerors, the Japanese government provided comfort houses for the exclusive use of U.S. soldiers.[65]

The military has historically demanded women for sexual service, both as a reward for their successes and because men are defined as needing sex the same way they might need food and water. In fact, sex is listed as one of several basic needs in Maslow's hierarchy of needs, along with food, water, air, warmth, shelter, and sleep.[66] But rather than establishing comfort systems, as a rule, military forces have regulated prostitution in and around military bases. During WW II, the U.S. Army established a leave system in which men could either visit their families or visit brothels, and during that same war, the United States and allies supervised the local prostitution industry in order to protect their soldiers from venereal diseases.[67] During the Vietnam War, the U.S. military organized "rest and recreation" leaves in Thailand, the Philippines, and South Korea for American soldiers serving in Vietnam, establishing a sex industry that later became one of the early economic lynchpins in the tourism industry. Sindon describes the huge aircraft carriers bringing soldiers from Vietnam during the 1970s for R&R in Southeast Asia, disgorging 7,000 to 10,000 soldiers at one time.[68] The reward of drink, dancing, and sex was an enticement for the men to keep fighting as well as a distraction from the unpopular war they were forced to fight. After the war in Vietnam ended, the Philippines was still used as a military staging area until 1992, and thousands of Americans remained, paving the way for the development of the sex tourism industry that followed. In fact, sex tourism became a major source of foreign investment, and the World Bank and the International Monetary Fund encouraged the development of this trade, exploiting the "natural resource" of women for sex along with the other natural resources that make Thailand and the Philippines such attractive tourist destinations. Similar patterns may be developing in the "global south" including Kenya and other African countries.[69]

Military bases have a dramatic impact on the economy and culture of the countries they inhabit. Huge multimillion-dollar establishments with thousands of military personnel and their families and support staff are a small city in themselves and a major force in the area where they are located.[70] The United States has hundreds of these spread throughout the world. There are 95 military bases and installations in South Korea alone, staffed by approximately 37,000 troops and service personnel.[71] In Japan, where they are not completely welcome, most of them are on the island of Okinawa, establishing it as one of the many "libidinal locations" of which Nagel writes.[72] These bases are "permanent features of the geopolitical landscape,"[73] and the prostitution that grows up around them is a stable industry. It is the scale of these operations, rather than the engagement in combat, that determines the amount of sexual involvement of the military personnel with local women and that shapes the types of involvement, from coercive to cooperative.[74] Nagel reports that since the Korean War of 1950–1953, over a million Korean women have served as sex providers for U.S. soldiers.[75] Of course, not all are prostitutes, and over 100,000 Korean women have immigrated to the United States after marrying servicemen.[76] But prostitution is a staple around military bases, an "ethno-sexual" interface[77] in which the local women are almost always of a different racial or ethnic background than the soldiers. Given where bases are located, the women are readily sexually stereotyped as compliant, eager, docile sexual partners, and they construct themselves accordingly, for survival or profit.[78] This imagery masks the reality of women's lives, the poverty and sexual abuse to which they, like most prostitutes, are subjected. Lynn Thiesmeyer writes that the "western image of the Asian female, the Asian body, and Asian sexuality has been reproduced, yet scarcely updated for centuries." Asian women are "racialized" and "sexualized" as the hyperfeminine, sensuous, promiscuous, and untrustworthy exotic "other." Constructed as "servile sexual availability,"[79] this image leaves her vulnerable to abuse and assault.[80] As such, she becomes the perfect body on which to deposit male angst about the demands of masculinity for combatants and resentment about the challenges to it both in the military and in civilian life.

RAPE AND WAR

Rape is rape, it is a violation, it is men violating women's bodies, but we need to able to make distinctions not because we want to diminish the importance of acquaintance or date rape, or even to treat stranger rape in this country with less seriousness, but because the order of magnitude in military rape and rape in war is so great that there do seem to be different levels of terrorism and hatred attached to these acts. While acquaintance rape clearly reveals disrespect of women and male privilege and power, it is a violation several degrees lower than that suffered by a woman who is brutalized by soldiers and left to die, or the woman in New Delhi who died from the injuries of a brutal gang rape—her internal organs destroyed.[81] The rape of women in the Congo, often referred to as the "rape capital of the world,"[82] or Bosnia or in any number of places where women live in constant terror is a violence of a different order. Women in these locations live with the constant threat of violence—every time they collect water or firewood, they risk being raped or killed; when they finally find safety and food in a relocation camp they risk being raped, not only by the men in the camp, but by the UN troops who are to act as their protectors.[83] They live in a state of siege unparalleled in the United States or any other Western country.

There are similarities in that women's bodies are violated, women's lives are ruined, and not only are men the perpetrators but a male justice system minimizes the seriousness of the offense. Sheffield's phrase "sexual terrorism" seems more fitting in the latter instance than the others.[84] Women in the United States may curtail their activities after dark, avoid certain places and people, live in a state of watchful vigilance, but this is entirely different from the sheer terror of never knowing when the janjaweed[85] will sweep through the village killing the men and boys, raping the women and babies, and doing so within a "culture of impunity" according to Lisa Jackson in her film *The Greatest Silence*.[86] Soldiers who were interviewed explained that they were just doing what everyone else did, that they had been in the jungle too long, and concluded, "we know it's not a good thing, but what do you expect?"[87] Their view was very matter-of-fact, including the notion that the raped women are even helping the war effort, providing sexual satisfaction to the men, many of whom could not remember how many women they had raped—15, maybe 25?[88] The Congolese government army is the single largest group of perpetrators, but there has been in the last few years a significant increase in rape by civilians as well.[89] Dr. Margaret Agama, the DRC's representative to the UN Population Fund, says: "Initially, rape was used as a tool of war by all the belligerent forces involved in the country's recent conflicts, but now sexual violence is unfortunately not only perpetrated by armed factions but also by ordinary people occupying positions of authority, neighbours, friends and family members."[90]

Rape was officially designated a "weapon of war" by the United Nations in 2008, in recognition of the enormity of the problem—40 women are raped every day in the DRC's South Kivu province, for example, leading Major-General Patrick Cammaert, former commander of UN peace-keeping forces in the eastern Congo, to say, "It has probably become more dangerous to be a woman than a soldier in armed conflict."[91]

The military is the ultimate masculinist machine, honoring strength, stoicism, independence, hierarchy, authority, and bravery. Just as sexual harassment is likely to be more prevalent in all-male or mostly male workplaces where women are seen as violating the male culture, or diminishing the value of the organizations through feminizing it, so harassment in the military as well as sexual assault are almost predictable. Perhaps as more women enter the military, men fear the erosion of the identity and ideology that shore up their masculinity, leading to their sense of disempowerment and vulnerability and an increase in violence against those, women, who are viewed as threatening. The dramatic increase in the number of women in the military began in the 1970s when the 2 percent cap on enlistment of women was canceled. At that time, fewer than 30,000 women were in the military (only 1 percent), but by 2005 this had grown to over 200,000 women or about 15 percent.[92] This has not been a comfortable growth, and in military academies, basic training camps and in combat, women were, and are, subject to severe harassment and sexual assault. When there were just a few women, when the door was barely open, the men reacted with hostility, but these women could be viewed as interlopers, gay, masculine, misfits—marginalized women who would not change the culture of the military. But now, as the military not only accepts large numbers of women but gays as well, masculinity, always fragile, becomes more threatened. If masculinity is built against femininity, if power and strength are built against dependence and weakness, when these qualities can no longer be hooked on women, masculinity itself is challenged.

Sexual assault in the military is on the rise—while young men reacted with extreme hostility to women when military academies were required to admit women, harassing them in all of the usual ways, through offensive language, pictures, songs, and behavior, they have more recently upped the ante, relying on physical assault to maintain the boundaries. And efforts on the part of the military to address sexual assault have been half-hearted at best and clearly inadequate and ineffective. This was made ludicrously clear by the arrest of Jeffrey Krusinski on May 5, 2013, for sexual battery after drunkenly groping a woman's breasts and buttocks in a parking lot in Arlington County, Virginia.[93] Krusinski wasn't a mere enlisted man or low-ranking officer. He was the lieutenant colonel responsible for sexual assault prevention programs in the United States Air Force. In fact, he had completed his sexual assault victim training just before the attack.[94] His arrest highlighted the ongoing concerns about the startling increase in sex crimes in the military and the military's inadequate response to sexual assault, as well as the military's rigid insistence that military procedures rather than reliance on the federal court system are the best way to handle these assaults.

Women fear retaliation if they report being sexually assaulted, and this is no idle threat. Women are often assaulted by the very men they are supposed to report to, and because the military has a powerful stake in covering up assault in order to retain important senior officers and maintain morale, a woman who reports sexual harassment or assault may well suffer severe consequences such as demotion, pay cuts, or loss of employment altogether.[95] A lawsuit brought by 17 veterans and active-duty officers against the Department of Defense in February 2011 claimed that retaliation and lack of accountability were part of a culture that fails to protect women from rape and sexual assault, thus violating their constitutional rights.[96] The suit provides an example of such a culture including an account of "a soldier stripping and dancing on a table during the intermission of a class on sexual assault prevention and the videotaping and circulation of the rape of a female soldier by two male officers."[97]

Krusinski's arrest was a perfect illustration of the serious problem of sexual assault in the military. It came during the same week the Pentagon published a report in May 2013 revealing a stunning 37 percent increase in sexual assault in the military in one year with 26,000 women and men being victimized during fiscal year 2012.[98] Not 2,600—but 26,000. And not only are they victimized, they are often subject to victim blaming, just as is the case when women are raped in civilian life—what did she expect in such an environment, and what did she do to cause it? There is one positive—as Maureen Dowd reports—three of the six Senate Armed Services subcommittees are chaired by women, a significant change that may well make a difference in the response to this report and to the outrageous assaults by Krusinski and others.[99]

Assaults in the military are perfectly predictable. Rape and war are linked at their base, both being firmly grounded in notions of traditional hegemonic masculinity. It is this foundation as well as the hierarchical organization of the military and other characteristics reflective of the intersection of military values and military structure that normalize this problem and that make it so intractable. Eileen Zurbriggen writes that military rape will be commonplace as long as the military is dependent on and built on an infrastructure of hegemonic masculinity.[100] She presents a model that links the socialization of men in the military with the rape culture that characterizes it, based on five key values that are taught and rewarded in military training and practice. Military values are based on status and achievement, toughness and aggression, restricted emotionality, self-reliance, and dominance/power and control. While these values are foundational for men in dominant society, their expression varies by age, ethnic and racial group, and class, and there is a less rigid and universal adherence to them than is required in the military. Further, these values reflect lower- and working-class masculinity, one limited by educational restrictions and occupational limitations. Unlike in the military, the range of expressions of masculinity in dominant culture vary widely and are significantly expanded by the privileges of class, degrading the rigid adherence to lower-class masculinity.[101] These values are interwoven at every level in the hierarchical organization of the military structure, a strict system of dominance and subordination, unquestioned obedience, and restricted, highly ritualized relations of ruling. Women's presence encroaches on their highly masculinized space, challenges the natural superiority of men and the hierarchical order that has long privileged men over women. A highly sexualized environment in which senior officers are often the assailants and in which they communicate the permissibility of assault on women creates a dangerous work environment.[102]

The attacks on women in the military result from the confluence of several factors: the hierarchical structure of the military; the dominant, highly masculinized ideology of the military; and, as Zurbriggen suggests, the socialization of men in the rigid military system.[103] The problem is surely exacerbated by the policies and procedures that tightly control the reporting of sexual assault and the military legal response to it, from the investigation to the trial and beyond. Secretary of Defense Chuck Hagel, despite the horrific increase in sexual assault, still supports keeping the investigative and prosecutorial processes within the military, even though this procedure seems rife with problems—the officers have no legal training, the superiors are often those who are the perpetrators, and there is a great potential for conflicts of interest.[104] This, the military insists, is necessary to maintain good order and discipline. One wonders how "good order and discipline" is defined when thousands of women are subject to violence as an ordinary event built into the military structure. But I believe there is another critical factor. While it is true that in the 1970s women made up a tiny fraction of the military, there was also a military draft, pulling men from all walks of life into battle and into immediate physical contact with others. The values of the military were the same as they are now, these values being deemed important for building camaraderie, preparing men for war, maintaining order. But the men came from a range of social classes and had a range of values around masculinity and femininity before entering the military. Today, while there are more women by far in the military, it draws from a much narrower band of men, those who are poorly educated, whose life chances are limited, and who may cling more desperately to the small rewards provided by adherence to rigid norms of masculine behavior and masculinist values espoused by the military. These values are built into compulsive masculinity, a set of assumptions around which all men negotiate their identities.[105] Compulsive masculinity is completely intertwined with sexism. It consists of the following assumptions:

- Men and women are inherently different.
- Real men are superior to women and superior to men who do not live up to models of masculinity.
- Activities normally associated with women are demeaning for men to engage in.
- Men should not feel or express vulnerable or sensitive emotions; the manly emotions are lust and anger.
- Toughness and the domination of others are essential to men's identity.

- Sex is less about pleasure or relating and more about proving manhood and asserting power.
- Gay men are failed men.[106]

For men who have little, the divide between genders may be the only divide in which they fall on the right side, the powerful side. The values of the military merge perfectly with and reinforce the values these men grew up with in the lives they are now trying to escape. These values are embraced by and elaborated on by higher-status men, men they aspire to be, men who are rewarded for their adherence to them. These men, while maintaining allegiance to traditional masculine ideals, compulsive masculinity, have also been successful in the sociopolitical world that requires polish and nuance, reinforcing the values but displaying them with less brutishness, more finesse.

These values easily bleed into misogyny since the masculinity they support is oppositional to the femininity they denigrate. Masculinity is defined not by itself but as built against femininity, as the other side of the gender binary, so that what is masculine is not feminine.[107] The women who enter the military carry femininity by fiat no matter how strong, how fit, how primed for battle—they are not men, so no matter how they perform masculinity, they taint it. The dilemma for the military, then, is that this value system so tightly wound around masculinity is challenged by femininity as women enter this bastion of masculinity, diminishing its value, leading to hostility and resentment. Kori Cioca, a victim of military sexual assault, provides a perfect example during an interview: "And he didn't rape me because I was pretty or that he wanted to have sex with me; he raped me because he hated me and . . . he wanted to show that I wasn't as great as I thought I was, the great Ko-C that I thought I was, and he was going to make sure of that."[108]

This is a conundrum. The values of masculinity are the values of war. The military is dependent on these values, values that are openly hostile to femininity and by extension hostile to women.[109] From this perspective, the sexual assault workshops or sensitivity trainings, and sexual harassment workshops cannot overcome the military cultural milieu—they are a tiny sliver of gender equality in a deep, vast sea of values that are its antithesis. Lieutenant Colonel Krusinski was not on duty when he assaulted the woman in the parking lot, but he is a perfect example of the ineffectiveness of the efforts to place a layer of civility and reason over a structure built from the bottom up on compulsive masculinity.[110] These values wait just below the surface, coiled for action, endangering women.

Performances of masculinity, such as sexual harassment and sexual assault, ogling, lewd comments, disparaging remarks, offensive behavior, are directed at "woman as object," while forging connections with other men around hegemonic masculinity.[111] The behavior in which men engage in the context of hypermasculinity is not a reflection of a lack of understanding the rules regarding sexual harassment or knowing the parameters. It is, rather, designed to reinforce gender boundaries, to establish masculinity as superior, to communicate the inviolability of masculine privilege. When the desire to aggressively patrol gender boundaries is merged with the culture of hypermasculinity built against devalued (and in the military, perhaps, despised) femininity, violence against women is predictable and almost normative rather than aberrant.

The solution to violence against women in the military lies in finding a way to maintain battle readiness, camaraderie, courage, strength, commitment, but to expand their embrace. When we talk about what Americans value, words like individuality, independence, strength, commitment, success, competition, and autonomy come up. We fail to recognize how masculine these terms are, how they don't include the nurturing, caring, caregiving, warmth, cooperation designated as feminine values. Men are judged by other men on the basis of their adherence to these values and are punished by other men for not embracing them.[112] So the military needs to reassess its values—expand their reach or include values that allow for community and caring, values that also seem essential to maintaining emotional and physical health and safety and survival of men and women in the military. In fact, such military values as loyalty, community, and teamwork could be recognized as including values traditionally viewed as feminine such as nurturance, an ethic of care, cooperation, so that the gender value divide might be reduced. Sexual assault "training" cannot be layered on a misogynistic, sexist system that fears and denigrates values that are defined as feminine and still be expected to be effective—masculinity has to expand to include a masculinity that is not built on a virulent subjection of women that serves as the foundation on which men build and maintain heteronormative masculinity.

CHARITY GIRLS AND B GIRLS—PROTECTING MEN FROM THEMSELVES

The novel *Charity Girls* by Michael Lowenthal introduced me to a phenomenon with which I was completely unfamiliar—the U.S. government's forcible incarceration and quarantine of thousands of young women during WW I.[113] These were "charity girls," young women suspected of having syphilis and other venereal diseases. The protagonist, Frieda Mintz, is a young Jewish girl working as a bundle wrapper in a major department store in Boston in 1917. A one-night stand with a U.S. soldier leaves her with a venereal disease, and she is tracked down, forced to undergo a gynecological exam, and then dumped in a "girl's home" with prostitutes and other "loose" women. Little has been written about charity girls, but the fact that the U.S. government felt compelled to protect soldiers from young working-class women during WW I reveals a view of lower-class female sexuality as dangerous and destructive. These girls were dangerous, not only to the health and well-being of the young men who might escort them, buy them drinks and have sex with them, but they were also potentially dangerous to the country through the physical corruption of soldiers. "Charity girl" was the name given to the young, urban, immigrant women by middle-class reformers and social workers who were offended by the rather freewheeling lifestyle built around entertainment and fluid sexual norms.[114] These young women were factory workers, making inadequate wages and using all of their money either to pay for food and board in a tenement or to help their families survive—receiving a small allowance in return. Entertainment was impossible in the close quarters of stuffy and overcrowded family homes and shared rooms or in the tenement walk-ups they occupied, so their socializing took place on the street and in the dance halls and social clubs that welcomed them. These young women made themselves as attractive as possible to young men through the clever use of dress and the development of a flirtatious personality. In order to go out, to dance or socialize or drink, these young women needed to be "treated," and this system was one in which they exchanged sexual favors ranging from innocent flirtation to kissing and petting to sexual intercourse for the small gifts and favors the men had to offer.[115] They were distinguished from prostitutes by not accepting money for sex or company, but their lifestyle was nonetheless offensive to more "upright" young women as well as to middle-class social workers whose concern about these young women was mixed with a strong desire to control their sexuality.[116] As the attitude toward "loose women," especially prostitutes, changed from sympathy to condemnation, seeing them as sources of disease, newly oppressive policies were instituted, not only toward prostitution but toward any young woman who was seen as a sexual threat. The social purity movement brought together the interest of the military and the medical establishment in preventing sexually transmitted diseases resulting in the quarantine of thousands of women without due process. David Pivar indicates that police rounded up tens of thousands of women off the streets and incarcerated more than 15,000 of them.[117]

These women were forcibly subjected to gynecological exams and were placed in quarantine in government-funded institutions, many of them for more than a year, until they could be declared free of disease.[118]

The use of police power in the name of "protecting the nation" during war[119] violated the rights of thousands of vulnerable women during WW I. The sexual double standard easily supported the incarceration of women, especially lower-class women who were suspected of being dirty or dangerous while soldiers who stood for the safety of the nation were medically treated and returned to their ships or stations.[120] Class and gender stereotypes merged to allow for the stigmatization of these women—not only were they dangerous to the men with whom they had sex, but as a result, they were seen as dangerous to national safety, both at home and abroad. Women are relied on to maintain the moral edifice of the nation while men are at war, and to match the sacrifice of the men with their own. These women, forerunners to the dangerous women who threatened the family, hence capitalism and the American way of life, during the Korean War, threatened the double standard of sexual morality that buttressed the American family.

Amanda Littauer has investigated the intersection of sensationalist media reporting, political posturing, and definitions of male and female sexuality as played out in San Francisco, California, where immoral "B-girls" were condemned as a threat to innocent and unsuspecting men.[121] The women, dressed demurely and conducting themselves with reserve, often presented themselves as women waiting for a friend or as secretaries or working girls stopping off for a nightcap before returning home to their lonely apartment. They engaged in sexual flirtation, some sexual contact like necking, kissing, or groping, to encourage the man to continue to buy drinks. His were overpriced as were hers, but hers were water or soda or tea posing as alcohol while his, while weak, led him down the amorous path of desire, a path ending abruptly when he stopped buying her drinks.[122] While this was not a commonplace pursuit, newspapers, and the newly available television, relying on a crime-reporting format, tantalized the public with descriptions of these women and their wanton ways, fanning the flames of outrage at manipulative, immoral women who would defraud innocent American men, especially soldiers.[123] Newspapers printed exposés about B-girls, feeding the desire of the new suburbanites to read about the lascivious leisure activities they had left behind in the urban core.[124]

A B-girl was specifically defined as a "woman employed by a bar, nightclub or the like, to act as a companion to male customers and to induce them to buy drinks, and usually paid a percentage of what the customers spent."[125] They were working girls, making a scant living off the watered-down drinks men bought them in exchange for company and a little sexual diversion. Yet, during a time when the United States was enamored of the newly reestablished postwar traditional family, with men and women charged with upholding traditional American values, these women were suspect as posing a threat to the stability of the family and to normative sexual mores, this time threatening postwar America.[126] Their behavior may have seemed innocent enough to some, just as had the activities of the charity girls, but the B-girls harkened back to the "percentage girls" on the Barbary Coast during the 1850s, who sold themselves to the gold miners after work.[127] And they were too similar to prostitutes from the perspective of the city, the police, and the papers.

The B-girls created a political and social mix of concern about women's morals, the American family, and the democratic nation.[128] During the 1930s, police and social workers were concerned about the welfare of the young women who were "white slaves," forced into prostitution and needing to be saved from evil brown men, much as is the case today with trafficked young women and girls. But during the war, attitudes shifted toward these girls and others, variously known as "khaki wackies, barflies, seagulls (for preying on sailors), victory girls, and prostitutes" and they faced harassment, arrest, and quarantine as suspected threats to the moral fiber of this country and carriers of venereal diseases.[129] Special women's courts were established to deal with the thousands of women who were arrested for drunkenness, promiscuity, lewdness, and other behaviors deemed inappropriate and immoral for women. Just as the "charity girls" had been during the First World War, suspect women were subjected to involuntary gynecological exams and were quarantined for six months or more in special detention centers, a violation of their civil rights.

The concern was as much about appropriate female sexuality as it was about venereal diseases. There was particular consternation over young white women who broke not only the gender boundaries but the race boundaries as well in a still-segregated society, and police paid particular attention to young white girls with sailors who were men of color.[130] The overriding concern with immoral behavior and inappropriate female sexuality faded postwar into apprehension among local and state officials over sexualized commercial fraud. The B-girl trade flourished in part because prostitution was so heavily regulated and because the San Francisco Board of Equalization, which was the enforcement agency, was so lax in its oversight.[131] The visibility of the B-girls came to symbolize urban corruption, and the political furor over the lack of enforcement of the law became fodder for allegations of payoffs and even participation in organized crime. Littauer describes the San Francisco papers, especially the *Examiner*, as creating an atmosphere of suspicion and blame through its ongoing, sensationalist "above the fold" coverage of what could reasonably have been a back-page story.[132] The governor, police chief, head of the Board of Equalization, even the legislature got involved in this sordid affair, condemning one another, the bars, their owners, and the B-girls. The newspapers loved the fight. Where were the men in all this, besides those busy moralizing about the wanton women? They were being constructed as innocent victims of conniving, dishonest women, seduced by them, fleeced by them, left with their hopes dashed, their pockets empty, and their sexual desires unfulfilled. Governor Warren opined that the B-girls directly threatened the well-being of the public: "The manner in which these girls . . . work affects the moral welfare of the community . . . [through duping] the youngsters in the military service."[133] The image of innocent, young American men led astray by sophisticated and sexually tantalizing women grounded the demand to address the problem in sexual politics. Officials drew on tried and true stereotypes of women, the jezebel, the whore, the seductress whose sexual prowess overwhelmed the man whose nature prevented him from resistance. As one Board member said: "The vagaries of human nature being as they are, the patrons of cocktail bars are peculiarly susceptible to the importunings of the 'female of the species.' This weakness is well known to the licensees of this regulated industry and it is the duty of the Department of Alcoholic Beverage Control to prevent . . . this exploitation of bar patrons."[134] It was the Adam and Eve story set in mid-century San Francisco.

Not all of this story about the B-girls is about violence against women. Surely mass arrests and forced gynecological exams and quarantines violated their person, their integrity, and their legal rights. But the story Littauer tells is a lesson in the power of stereotypes about female and male sexuality.[135] Linked with the themes discussed in this book, female sexuality is seen as dangerous, as devious and powerful, potentially ruinous, while male sexuality is conveniently defined as unregulated and responsive at the biological level to the social cues provided by the manipulative woman. These images reflect the responses of juries to women who are victims of rape and their assailants, and they justify the "fits of fury" that excuse husbands murdering their daughters and wives in Turkey as well as the mitigation conferred by "crimes of passion" in courtrooms across the United States.

THEMES

The themes laid out in these early forms of violence against women are woven throughout the atrocities of the late twentieth century in Serbia-Herzegovina, in Rwanda, in the Sudan, in Somalia, and in other war-torn countries around the globe that use rape and torture as weapons of war. These egregious, and now commonplace, violations of human rights, these genocides carried out against men, women, and children, evoke the themes of violence against women that underpin this book and that are threaded through every form of gendered violence experienced by women. Whether we are looking at sexual harassment or at pornography, sexual assault, comfort women, mail order brides, or prostitutes servicing the military installations, we see the intimate ties between violence and women, one never far removed from the other. These themes are mundane and predictable—establishing the backdrop for "gonzo porn" as well as for the desire of Western men for "mail order brides" and the women they can buy on sex tours. They underpin the catcalls women endure in street harassment and the 70 or 80 cents on the dollar women make compared with men. And while the kinds of violence women experience in the West are different in form and, in most cases, in degree, from what women in South Asia, the Middle East, and Africa experience, they draw on the same economic and political structures, sentiments, and enduring definitions of masculinity and femininity. These are the themes that tie what seem like a wide-ranging and diverse set of violent practices together.

Economic inequality, and hence the dependence on men, is a major theme driving violence against women. It serves as the impetus for the practices that make them "marriageable" such as female genital mutilation or cutting as well as, historically, bound feet; and it drives their need to bring dowry to their marriages, the obsession with their purity and obedience. Economic need and the corollary of economic inequality and discrimination keep them in jobs where they are harassed, encourage them to get breast implants, and keep them in relationships and marriages where they are abused and belittled.

Objectification, so prosaic as to not raise an eyebrow, is another theme. When women are dehumanized, when they become objects rather than humans, when their value resides only in their purity or the dowry they can produce, when their humanity is commandeered in pornography or rape, they are reduced to palettes on which others paint their desire or their need but on which they are invisible. Women who are victims of "honor crimes" have been reduced to representatives of their family's honor and their father's ego and have lost their singular humanity, standing for rather than being. Women who are stolen, duped, captured, and forced to serve as "comfort women" or sexual objects for male tourists are bodies not people. Women who are raped or victimized in pornography serve only as things to the men who use them. The everyday objectification of women, the ordinary treatment of women as bodies or receptacles for male desire, is the doorway to the violence women experience that depends on their dehumanization—their lack of a subjective self.

Closely related, almost inseparable, is the commodification of women. When mail-order brides are displayed in catalogs and on Internet sites, their age, breast size, height, hair coloring, and a few details about their personality are laid out for men in the United States and Germany to compare with other available women, eager to leave the constraints or limitations of their lives in Eastern Europe or the Philippines, they are reduced to commodities. Women who are trafficked are purely commodities, bought and sold and sold again for the benefit of their trafficker just as are those women who are so indebted that they are a continuing source of money for the nail salon or bar where they work. And women who are valued for their ability to enhance the masculinity of their partner through their conformity with essentialized femininity are also commodified, and for that the price is often battery or rape.

Women are often reduced to a sexuality that overrides and replaces any other characteristics that would provide them humanity. Their sexuality is at the heart of their identity in the workplace or the military where their male bosses see them first sexually and then perhaps in terms of their other qualities, a problem not only for the women's physical integrity but for their economic survival. Their identities as women, mothers, and selves disappear into male control over their vaginas in the case of FGM, male hysteria about sexual purity in the case of honor crimes, their sex becoming the justification for assault in the case of rape.

Women are blameworthy is a theme most clearly illustrated by honor crimes when they are killed to protect the family honor if there is so much as a rumor about sexual impropriety. It is also built into the public and private response to women who are raped or battered—what did she do, why didn't she do something else? And, not surprisingly, given the power of cultural constructions of gender, women themselves accept responsibility for the violence visited upon them.

Women in their natural state are dirty. Their inherent vileness justifies removing their clitoris and labia and sewing them up, or justifies the pornographic depictions of them celebrated in rap music and pornography, the obsession with their "purity," and the rape of Korean and other Asian comfort women, and Chinese women during the Rape of Nanking, despised for their inferiority by the Japanese Imperial Army. During World War I, the charity girls, lower-class, immigrant girls, could be rounded up and forced to have gynecological exams in order to protect American soldiers from the sexual diseases they were presumed to have, and the B-girls were an affront to postwar America, a reification of woman's destructive sexuality and man's inability to withstand the force of innate female seductiveness. The B-girls posed a danger to men and the American way of life. Women, whose power is lacking in almost every area, are provided this one area of power over men, by men, which then justifies male control of the female body. Women's sexuality is dangerous, both to them and to men. We see this in so many areas—FGM is justified by the belief that the woman's clitoris will sting and kill the man if it touches him, that it will kill her baby during birth, and that if not controlled can destroy a village. The purpose of foot-binding, as expressed in interview after interview, was to keep women home, to keep them from "galavanting" all over, bringing destruction to them and condemnation to their families.

And, as Simone de Beauvoir wrote, women are "other."[136] They are the backdrop, not the center, not the standard; they are the affiliates, the dependents, those who accompany and support, not the main show. Women are punished when they become "too much," raped when they humiliate a man by not putting him first, sought after for sex by Western men who find Western women to be too independent, too resourceful, too accomplished, and who impose their racist stereotypes on women they see as more natural, more dependent, more feminine. Being the "other" means not asking for too much (or any)—too much money, too much sex, too much recognition, and it means living life in the shadow of a man, risking rejection or risking death, as do women in Turkey, Pakistan, Afghanistan and elsewhere when they want their own lives, when they want to be central rather than a satellite.

The construction of femininity itself is remarkably similar around the globe, built against masculinity. The binary paints men as powerful, authoritative, decisive, rational, and in control, against which women are constructed as weak, dependent, and nurturing. These are not just ends of a binary, they are the descriptions of superior (man) and inferior (woman), buttressed by the structural inequality around the globe that places women as secondary in the family as well as in the workplace (if she is even allowed in the workplace).

The degradation of women is another theme. Underlying men's use of prostitutes and their sexual harassment and reliance on pornography for sexual stimulation is a view of women as degraded. Sut Jhally shows men throwing bologna at women's bare bodies, men having anal then oral sex with women in porn, women being violated in porn, "giving men what they want."[137] When men sexually harass women, rap about them as bitches and "hoes" and "cunts" the degradation is explicit—when they judge them as body parts and "pieces of ass," the degradation is implicit, no matter how positive the evaluation.

The themes of masculinity are parallel to themes of femininity, and only in understanding their relationship with one another can we understand violence against women. Men are economically and politically superior to women. They are the faces in the boardroom, in the halls of parliament, the mayor's office, the legislature. As George Bush so eloquently put it, men are "the deciders,"[138] reflecting a history of gender inequality reinforced by sexist socialization and constraining definitions and expectations for women, and structural inequality. The laws governing rape and honor murders, the policies establishing comfort stations, the organization of the workplace, and the male-controlled hierarchy in the military, privilege men and disadvantage women. Such practices as female genital mutilation and foot-binding are performed by women in service to a social system that privileges men and in which women can only attain status and economic security by complying with "cultural" mandates for disfigurement.

Masculinity is defined as control and superiority, and it is centered on privilege, so that for men, the objectification of women as comfort women and as rape victims and as targets of harassment and battery is not aberrant but natural. Men have made the rules of the workplace and have controlled the corporations that reinforce male control and female subordination, so reestablishing that sense of control or superiority when it has been challenged, or outright opposed, may seem like the natural thing to do—to take back what is rightfully theirs. Men who are sexual terrorists, who assault their wives and girlfriends, view themselves as regaining the power that is rightfully theirs. A man who rapes a woman who says "no" is asserting what he sees as his right. A man who sets his wife on fire because she didn't produce an adequate dowry or because now he wants more is a man claiming what is "rightfully his." The murder of his wife, an impediment to his success, is a reasonable thing to do, especially within a social climate in which men and women both view wife beating as a normal form of discipline and maintenance of patriarchal control.

Just as women are to deliver sex, to be available for sex, men need and demand and think they have a right to sex. And not just sex, but sex the way they want it. As the DKE fraternity at Yale put it, "No Means Yes." "Yes means Anal."[139] This same view fueled Emperor Hirohito's gift to his Japanese Imperial Army when he led the establishment of "rape centers" for men who needed sexual release. The gang rape of these women and their injuries and death were simply the "unfortunate" outcome of the need to meet male desire. When men rape women who are drunk or drugged, women who have no ability to protest, they view it as a minor loss for the woman, a natural need fulfilled for them. The prostitution that grows up around the multibillion-dollar military complexes the United

States and its allies have flung across the globe attest to the need for men's sexual desires to be fulfilled as did the U.S. establishment of sex tourism in Thailand and the Philippines during World War II and the Vietnam War.

Men can buy women. The commodification of women is illustrated by the millions of men who frequent prostitutes, whether in brothels or on the streets, the men who buy trafficked girls in bars and hotel rooms, and the men who take sex vacations to South America or Asia. These men are seeking sex with women and girls they define as naturally there for their sexual pleasure, the now familiar "little brown fucking machines."[140] Mail-order brides chosen from glossy catalogs or tours designed to maximize the number of offerings in the minimum amount of time reveal men as having resources where women have none. The economically driven relationships that can emerge from this, like those developed by the B-girls and the charity girls, the mail-order brides and those women who are the targets of sex tourism, reflect this inequality. All of these relationships are subject to the risks associated with such differences in privilege.

What about patriarchy? Allan Johnson makes it clear that patriarchy is a system, not an individual characteristic of either "a He, a Them, or an Us," revealing the way in which both men and women shore up patriarchy by simply following the status quo.[141] As Adrienne Rich says, women participate in our own oppression.[142] We all participate in a privilege system in which few are privileged, but in which those who are privileged are straight white men. This of course leaves a lot of men—men of color, gay men, and poor men—feeling unprivileged or underprivileged. Some of these men who have failed to benefit from a system of male privilege are the most threatened by women's success in that system and pose the greatest danger.

NOTES

1. C. Gluck, "The Rape of Nanking: How 'the Nazi Buddha' Resisted the Japanese," *Times Literary Supplement*, June 27, 1927.

2. I. Chang, *The Rape of Nanking: The Forgotten Holocaust of WW II* (New York: Penguin Books, 1997).

3. J. Rabe, *The Good Man of Nanking: The Diaries of John Rabe* (New York: Knopf, Doubleday, 2000).

4. M. Vautrin, *Terror in Minnie Vautrin's Nanjing: Diaries and Correspondence, 1937-38*, edited by Suping Lu (Urbana: University of Illinois Press, 2008).

5. Ibid.

6. Ibid.

7. Chang, *The Rape of Nanking.*

8. G. J. McDougal, "Contemporary Forms of Slavery: Systematic Rape, Sexual Slavery and Slavery-like Practices during Armed Conflict" (New York: United Nations Commission on Human Rights, 1998).

9. Ibid.

10. Ibid.; Y. Yoshimi, "Comfort Women: Sexual Slavery in the Japanese Military during World War II," *Asia Perspectives*, translated by S. O'Brien (New York: Columbia University Press, 2002), 91.

11. P. G. Min, "Korean Comfort Women: The Intersection of Colonial Power, Gender, and Class," in *Gender and Society* 17, no. 6 (December 2003): 938–57.

12. H. Nelson, "The Consolation Unit: Comfort Women at Rabaul," *Journal of Pacific History* 43, no. 1 (June 2008): 1–21.

13. K. Moon, "South Korean Movements against Militarized Sexual Labor," *Journal of Asian Studies* 39, no. 2 (April 1999): 473–500.

14. Ibid.

15. Ibid.

16. K. Orreill, "Who Are the Ianfu (Comfort Women)?" *New Faces*, November 13, 2012: 128–52, http://newvoices.jpf-sydney.org/2/chapter7.pdf

17. C. Sindon, "Sex Trafficking in the Philippines and Russia: History, Globalization, and Resistance," unpublished thesis (Reno: University of Nevada, May 2003).

18. Ibid.

19. H. Hirofumi, "Japanese Comfort Women in Southeast Asia," *Japan Forum* 10, no. 2 (1998): 211–19, http://plaza18.mbn.or.jp/~modernH/13eng.htm; see also H. Hirofumi, "Government, the Military and Business in Japan's Wartime Comfort Woman System," *Asia-Pacific Journal: Japan Focus*, http://www.japanfocus.org/-Hayashi-Hirofumi/2332, 1998: 214.

20. Min, "Korean Comfort Women."

21. Ibid.

22. Orreill, "Who Are the Ianfu?"

23. Yoshimi, "Comfort Women," 91.

24. Ibid.

25. Ibid.

26. Min, "Korean Comfort Women."

27. H. Hirofumi, "Japanese Comfort Women in Southeast Asia"; see also H. Hirofumi, "Government, the Military and Business in Japan's

Wartime Comfort Woman System," *Asia-Pacific Journal: Japan Focus* 6, no. 4, http://www.japanfocus.org/-Hayashi-Hirofumi/2332

28. Ibid.

29. Ibid., 213–14.

30. Min, "Korean Comfort Women."

31. Nelson, "The Consolation Unit," 31.

32. Orreill, "Who Are the Ianfu?"

33. K. Soon-duk, *Comfort Women Speak: Testimony by Sex Slaves of the Japanese Military*, edited by S. C. Schellstede (New York: Holmes & Meier Publishers, 2000).

34. Ibid.

35. Min, "Korean Comfort Women."

36. Ibid.

37. K. Soon-duk, "Comfort Women Speak."

38. Orreill, "Who Are the Ianfu?"

39. Ibid.

40. J. Choi, "Comfort Women: Japan's Unpaid Reparations," Bologna Journal of International Affairs, 11 (2008): 125–37.

41. Y. Kono, "Statement by the Chief Cabinet Secretary Yohei Kono on the Result of the Study on the Issue of 'Comfort Women,'" August 4, 1993, http://www.mofa.go.jp/policy/women/fund/state9308.html

42. Ibid.

43. Choi, "Comfort Women."

44. Ibid.

45. D. S. Kim-Gibson and C. Burnett, *Silence Broken: Comfort Women of Korea.* Documentary (Dai Sil Productions/Public Broadcasting Services, 1999).

46. Choi, "Comfort Women," 130.

47. Orreill, "Who Are the Ianfu?"

48. Ibid., 147.

49. Orreill, "Who Are the Ianfu?"

50. Ibid.

51. Ibid.

52. T. Castellani, *Defining Comfort Women: Japan Focus.* Introduction: *History of Comfort Women* (JugunIanfu), http://www.slideshare.net/tessac/comfort-women-final-version, accessed June 30, 2013.

53. Choi, "Comfort Women," 131.

54. D. Struck, "In Japan, Victims' Families Expect a Personal Apology," *Washington Post*, February 27, 2001, 8.

55. Castellani, *Defining Comfort Women.*

56. For comments on Abe's retraction and Mike Honda's resolution, see G. Rozman, editor, *U.S. Leadership, History and Bi-lateral Relations in Northeast Asia* (New York: Cambridge University Press, 2011), 135.

57. *Beyond Promises: Governments in Motion One Year after the Beijing Women's Conference* (New York: Women's Environment and Development Organization, September 1996), 42.

58. Ibid.

59. Amnesty International News, November 3, 2008, http://www .amnesty.org/en/news-and-updates/good-news/japan-urged-restore-dignity -wwii

60. H. Tabuchi, "Japanese Politician Reframes Comments on Sex Slavery," *New York Times*, May 28, 2013, A5. http://www.nytimes.com/ 2013/05/28/world/asia/osaka-mayor-wartime-brothels.html?_r=0

61. M. Cucek, "A Rising Star's Self Destruction," May 30, 2013, http://latitude.blogs.nytimes.com/2013/05/30/toru-hashimotos-self -destruction/?_r=0

62. Tabuchi, "Japanese Politician Reframes Comments on Sex Slavery."

63. Hirofumi, "Japanese Comfort Women in Southeast Asia."

64. Ibid.

65. Ibid., 217.

66. A. H. Maslow, "A Theory of Human Motivation." *Psychological Review* 50, no. 4 (1943): 370–94.

67. Sindon, "Sex Trafficking in the Philippines and Russia."

68. Ibid.

69. S. Sassen, "Global Cities and Survival Circuits," in *Global Woman: Nannies, Maids, and Sex Workers in the New Economy,* edited by B. Ehrenreich and A. R. Hochschild (New York: Metropolitan Press, 2003).

70. J. Nagel, "Sex and War: Fighting Men, Comfort Women, and the Military-Sexual Complex," chapter 6 in *Race, Ethnicity and Sexuality: Intimate Interactions, Forbidden Frontiers* (New York: Oxford University Press, 2003).

71. Ibid.

72. Ibid.

73. Ibid., 187.

74. Ibid.

75. Nagel, "Sex and War."

76. Ibid.

77. Ibid., 179.

78. E. C. Childs, *Fade to Black and White: Interracial Images in Popular Culture* (Lanham, MD: Rowman & Littlefield, 2009).

79. L. Thiesmeyer, "The West's 'Comfort Women' and the Discourse of Seduction," in *Transnational Asia Pacific: Gender, Culture and the Public Sphere*, edited by S. G. Lim, L. E. Smith, and W. Dissanayake (Urbana: University of Illinois, 1999), 81.

80. Childs, *Fade to Black and White*, 74.

81. "Trial Begins as Indian Rape Victim's Boyfriend Speaks Out about Brutal Attack," http://www.news.com.au/world/indian-rape-victims-boyfriend-speaks-out-about-brutal-attack/story-fndir2ev-1226547941419, retrieved June 30, 2013.

82. "UN Official Calls DR Congo 'Rape Capital of the World,' " http://www.news.bbc.co.uk/2/hi/8650112.stm, accessed July 17, 2013.

83. C. Lynch, "UN Faces More Accusations of Sexual Misconduct," *Washington Post*, March 13, 2005, A22.

84. C. Sheffield, "The Invisible Intruder: Women's Experiences of Obscene Phone Calls," in *Violence against Women: The Bloody* Footprints, edited by P. Bart and E. Moran (Thousand Oaks, CA: Sage, 1993), 73.

85. Janjaweed is an Arabic colloquialism that means "a man with a gun on a horse." See B. Koemer, "Who Are the Janjaweed? A Guide to the Sudanese Militiamen," July 19, 2005, http://www.slate.com/articles/news_and_politics/explainer/2004/07/who_are_the_janjaweed.html

86. L. Jackson, director, *The Greatest Silence: Rape in Congo* (New York: Jackson Films, 2008).

87. Ibid.

88. Ibid.

89. Ibid.

90. UNFPA. "Campaign Says 'No' to Sexual Violence That Rages in DRC," November 26, 2008, http://www.unfpa.org/public/News/pid/1012

91. http://www.ohchr.org/en/newsevents/pages/rapeweapowar.asp

92. L. Feitz and J. Nagel, "The Militarization of Gender and Sexuality in the Iraq War," chapter 10, in *Women in the Military and Armed Conflict*, edited by H. Carreiras and G. Kümmel (Wiesbaden, Germany: VS Verlag fur Sozialwissenschaften, 2008), 201–13.

93. "The Military's Sexual Assault Crisis," Editorial in *The New York Times*, May 8, 2013: A26. http://www.nytimes.com/2013/05/08/opinion/the-pentagons-sexual-assault-crisis.html

94. Ibid.

95. E. Zurbriggen, "Rape, War, and the Socialization of Masculinity: Why Our Refusal to Give Up War Ensures That Rape Cannot be Eradicated," *Psychology of Women Quarterly* 34, no. 4 (December 2010): 538–49.

96. A. Saenz, *17 Veterans Sue Pentagon over Mishandled Rape Cases*, ABC News, February 15, 2011, abcnews.go.com.

97. Ibid.

98. J. Steinhauer, "Sexual Assaults in Military Raise Alarm in Washington," *New York Times*, May 7, 2013, http://www.nytimes.com/2013/05/08/us/politics/pentagon-study

99. M. Dowd, "America's Military Injustice," *New York Times*, Wednesday, May 8, 2013, A23.

100. Zurbriggen, "Rape, War, and the Socialization of Masculinity."

101. Ibid. 542–544.

101. R. W. Connell, *Masculinities* (Berkeley: University of California Press, 1995); J. Lorber, *Paradoxes of Gender* (New Haven, CT: Yale University Press, 1994).

102. A. G. Sadler, B. M. Booth, B. L. Cook, and B. N. Doebbeling, "Factors Associated with Women's Risk of Rape in the Military Environment," *American Journal of Industrial Medicine* 43, no. 3 (2003): 262–273.

103. Zurbriggen, "Rape, War, and the Socialization of Masculinity."

104. Ibid.

105. T. Beneke, *Proving Manhood: Reflections on Men and Sexism (Men and Masculinity)* (Berkeley: University of California Press, 1999), 47.

106. Ibid, 47–48

107. Lorber, *Paradoxes of Gender.*

108. *The Invisible War.* Chain Camera Pictures. 2012.

109. See M. Kimmel, *Manhood in America* (New York: Free Press, 1996).

110. Beneke, *Proving Manhood.*

111. M. Kimmel and M. Messner, *Men's Lives* (2nd ed.) (New York: Macmillan, 1992).

112. J. Katz, *The Macho Paradox* (Naperville, IL: Sourcebooks, 2006).

113. M. Lowenthal, *Charity Girl* (New York: Houghton Mifflin, 2007).

114. K. Peiss, "Charity Girls and City Pleasures," *Organization of American Historians Magazine of History* 18, no. 4 (July 2004): 14–16.

115. Ibid.

116. D. Pivar, *Purity and Hygiene: Women, Prostitution and the "American Plan," 1900–1930* (Westport, CT: Greenwood Press, 2005).

117. Ibid.

118. Ibid.

119. Ibid.

120. Ibid.

121. A. Littauer, "The B-Girl Evil: Bureaucracy, Sexuality, and the Menace of Barroom Vice in Postwar California," *Journal of the History of Sexuality* 12, no. 2 (April 2003): pp. 171–204.

122. Ibid.

123. Ibid.

124. Ibid.

125. From *The Random House Historical Dictionary of American Slang* (New York: Random House, 1994), 139–40.

126. Littauer, "The B-Girl Evil."

127. Ibid.

128. Ibid.

129. Ibid.

130. Ibid.

131. Ibid.

132. Ibid.

133. "The B-Girl Evil," *Sacramento Bee*, July 3, 1953, 1; Littauer, "The B-Girl Evil."

134. See ABC Appeals, file A-130, 4 in Littauer, "The B-Girl Evil."

135. Littauer, "The B-Girl Evil."

136. S. de Beauvoir, *The Second Sex* (New York: Knopf, 1952).

137. S. Jhally, *Dreamworlds II: Desire, Sex, Power in Music Video* (Northampton, MA: Media Education Foundation, 1997).

138. W. Safire, *Safire's Political Dictionary* (Oxford/New York: Oxford University Press, 2008), 171.

139. http://bigthink.com/focal-point/no-means-yes-yes-means-anal-frat, accessed May 25, 2013.

140. S. Falconberg, *The Raped Vagina: A Military Prostitute's Story* (Bloomington, IN: iUniverse, 2009), 151.

141. A. Johnson, *The Gender Knot* (Philadelphia: Temple University Press, 2005).

142. A. Rich, *Compulsory Heterosexuality and Lesbian Experience* (London: Onlywoman Press, 1980).

ELEVEN

It's Just a Different Culture

Marzouk Abdel Abesh, a Cairo tile maker, stabbed his 25-year-old daughter to death and then chopped off her head. He killed her to restore his honor and the honor of his family. He served two months in prison. "Honor," he said, "is more precious than my own flesh and blood."[1] In Jordan, the law "exempts from punishment a man who kills a female relative after 'discovering her committing adultery,' and provides for a reduced penalty if he kills her after finding her in 'an adulterous situation.' "[2] After the Taliban gained control in Afghanistan in 1996, women were required to remain indoors, the windows of their houses painted so they could not be seen. They ventured out only when accompanied by a male relative and then had to be covered from head to toe by a burqa, a long garment covering the entire body, with a mesh screen at the eyes; they could not be seen or heard and were required to wear shoes that were soundless. Women were not allowed to attend school, male doctors were prohibited from treating women, and women were no longer allowed to work. The rate of depression skyrocketed, and the suicide rate among women climbed dramatically.

Hannah Koroma of Sierra Leone recounts her experience with another type of common and devastating violence: genital mutilation. When she was 10 years old: "I was forced to lie flat on my back by four strong women, two holding tight to each leg. Another woman sat on my chest to prevent my upper body from moving. A piece of cloth was forced in my mouth to stop me screaming. The pain was terrible and unbearable . . . . I was badly cut and lost blood. Afterwards, I hemorrhaged and became anemic. I suffered for a long time from acute vaginal infections."[3]

In Madhogarh, India, in 1998, Hansa pleaded with her parents on her wedding night: "I want to go to bed. Please, Mama, Papa. Let me sleep!" Hansa was 4 years old, and her wedding to a 12-year-old boy was one of many that take place each year in this northern state, where the women are among the most socially disadvantaged in India.[4] In 1999 alone, the Indian government reported 3,260 "dowry deaths" or "stove burnings" in which women are doused with kerosene and ignited because their dowries had proven inadequate or because the husband wished to marry a new wife. In India, despite the fact that dowries have been banned since 1961 when Mohandas Gandhi led India toward independence, thousands of young women die in dowry fires every year, killed by their husband's family because the dowry they brought was not adequate.[5] Is this a less than charming custom, or is it murder? Honor crimes in which women are killed because their behavior dishonors the men in their family, even if they have been the victim of rape or incest, are seen as either cultural quirks or human rights violations. And the paralyzing restrictions placed on women under the Taliban are either relatively benign cultural practices or unacceptable forms of torture and murder.

While some would call these practices gender apartheid, or gynocide, or crimes of violence against women, or human rights violations, some would tremble at the idea of bringing judgment. How can an academic engaged in the pursuit of truth through science afford the luxury of judging the behavior of people in different cultures? The Cultural Survival group at Harvard University and what Fran Hosken calls the male anthropology fraternity support these traditional cultural practices by refusing to differentiate them from cultural curiosities.[6] Anthropologists have long enticed students into the academic world of cultural relativity —describing cultures in which ants are a delicacy, or in which rings to elongate the neck mark a woman's beauty, or in which the fatter the woman, the more desirable she is. For cultural relativists, judgments made by members of one culture about the practices of another are ethnocentric, ignoring the variability among cultures while imposing Western views on them. Ethnocentrism blinds us to the relative nature of the norms and practices, culminating in condemnations of behaviors that are simply different rather than wrong.

Value neutrality is one of the most defining characteristics of the scientific method and has been adopted by social scientists as their hallmark. The scientific method touted by social scientists is built on the assumption of value-free, neutral, unbiased investigation. Scientists are seekers of truth, abandoning all values except for the importance of the truth. Their personal values and biases are to be put behind them, banished from the purified search for the facts. One researcher in this area, Harriet Lyons, illustrates the devotion to the assumption of "value-free" research and simultaneously illustrates how ludicrous it is to assert that a traditional or accepted approach is value free, when she asks, "Can we continue to see the removal of women's chief organ of sexual response as non-sexual, and thus remain value-free?"[7] The reader might understandably wonder how viewing woman's clitoris and labia as nonsexual is value free, any more than seeing women's genitals as sexual is value laden. The radical feminist philosopher Mary Daly gets to the heart of the issue when she claims that anthropologists and other academics cover up woman hating by their insistence on the superiority of cultural relativity as a philosophical and methodological stance.[8]

Cultural relativism demands context. Mindless relativism is as danger-ous as any other ideology requiring adherence to a party line. To hold one position to be true and all others to be inferior has resulted in untold destruction in the past and threatens the lives and health of millions of infants and girls each year. Yet to see all "truths" as equally valid is dehu-manizing and an abdication of responsible scholarship and citizenship, implicitly supporting horrendous crimes against women based on sex. In his thoughtful work, Stephen James calls the philosophical position that would allow for no judgments except those from within a culture "moral isolationism."[9] He suggests that one need not abandon the notion of uni-versal human rights in the face of cultural relativism. Rather, there are supranational norms that are clearly violated by such practices as female circumcision, bride burning, sex slavery, "honor crimes," and female infanticide.

Among feminists, the debate about cultural relativism has been compli-cated by self-analysis and critique of the relationship between women in international context. Feminists who write about women's experiences based on their gender and who are not sensitive to differences women experience in different cultures are likely to be condemned as essentialist and as insensitive cultural imperialists. For example, Robin Morgan's anthology *Sisterhood Is Global*[10] was harshly condemned by Chandra Mohanty for presuming that women share "universal sisterhood" dis-played in suffering inflicted by a universal "patriarchal mentality."[11] Mohanty would claim instead that First World women who embrace a notion of international sisterhood erase critical historical, power, and privilege differences among women. They ignore the differences in privi-lege caused by the "proletarianization of Third World women by corporate capital based in the United States, Europe, and Japan."[12] Awa Thiam criticizes Western feminists and others who would impose their values on other cultures as "people who understand nothing of ritual practices" and "must beware of attacking them, especially when they base their judgment on criteria which bear no relationship to the mentalities of people under consideration. The women of Black Africa have suffered enough from these colonial and neo-colonial attitudes."[13] Such well-known figures as the author Alice Walker are criticized as ethnocentric, and academic feminists who condemn female genital mutilation (FGM) as violence against women are sometimes viewed as cultural imperialists. In a critique of U.S. feminist legal scholarship, Nesiah concludes: "It should be of no great surprise to anyone when we reject a feminism that uses Western social and economic systems to judge and make pronouncements about how Third World women can become emancipated. Feminist theories which examine our cultural practices as 'feudal residue' or label us 'traditional' also portray us as politically immature women who need to be versed and schooled in the ethos of Western feminism. They need to be continually challenged."[14]

Some authors, for example, Julia Wood, describe the pain and damage of FGM but hesitate to condemn the practice, comparing it instead to ear piercing and other practices in the United States, and recognizing that women gain status in their community from this practice.[15] The World Health Organization (WHO) and the United Nations Children's Fund (UNICEF), while concerned about the practice of FGM, were, for decades, reluctant to study ways to eradicate the practice, reluctant to impose international standards of dominant members on other countries, stating that these operations are "based on social and cultural backgrounds, the study of which is outside the competence of the WHO."[16]

UNICEF's inability to protect girls in Kenya and other countries who are being circumcised in clinics supported by the Ministry of Health today is shocking. Many activists, however, insist that a "woman's right to bodily integrity cannot be sacrificed in the name of cultural sanctity."[17] Activist feminists have been able to organize on an international scale to develop policies prohibiting violence against women that are justified on the basis of tradition or cultural values. The Committee on the Elimination of All Forms of Discrimination Against Women (CEDAW) works throughout the world, translating discrimination into a universal human rights issue and demanding that governments cease protecting those members of their society who violate women's human rights. The International Women's Conference in Beijing's Program for Action demanded a rejection of "cultural justifications for violating women's human rights," recognizing that women in every country are greatly affected by laws and customs having to do with women's reproduction, sexuality, and marriage rights. The Program for Action specifies, "Any harmful aspect of certain traditional, customary or modern practices that violates the rights of women should be prohibited and eliminated."[18] Some Third World feminists as well as those from the industrialized countries together demanded to be rid of the cultural excuses for women's oppression that "have plagued us for so long."[19] Karp's conclusion that "no matter how one labels it, FGM involves large-scale tortuous conduct by private individuals backed by state endorsement"[20] is equally applicable to such practices as bride burning, "honor crimes," and sex slavery. These are war crimes or acts of terrorism directed specifically against women.

Those who would condemn cultural traditions such as FGM as hideous or barbaric are sometimes criticized as value laden and are vulnerable to being labeled biased, pursuing their own agendas rather than the pursuit of truth. They are criticized as blinded by sympathy and outrage, emotions inconsistent with finding truth. However, to refuse to judge, to insist on only difference, and to reject evaluation includes a refusal to empathize. Setting oneself apart from the responsibility of judgment results in moral numbing. While the radical cultural relativists pat themselves on the back for objectivity, neutrality, and seeking pure truth, they simultaneously, even if only implicitly, condone the large-scale destruction of human beings based on their gender. Their value neutrality is not, after all, appreciation of diversity and complexity; it is a smug separation of the scientific self from the rest of humanity. Under the pretense of eschewing judgment, this neutrality is really an unwillingness to empathize, to humanize, to identify with the "other." So firmly situated in the center are most anthropologists and academics that the trip to the boundaries is a long and dangerous one. It would require judging the dominant values and the privileged conceptions of reality, and would demand identification with the victim, an enterprise bound to lower the status of the investigator. The assertion of value neutrality, in fact, is a support of the status quo and the dominant values supporting oppression.

The practices of FGM, foot-binding, Indian suttee, bride selling and bride burning, honor crimes, female infanticide, and the impositions of the Taliban are particularly offensive and destructive practices that demand our attention and our support for their eradication. This stance abandons value neutrality, and instead, asserts the primacy of human rights and embraces the right to bodily integrity for all women and girls. Mindless relativism, amoral scientism, is a refusal to make any judgment, and this refusal leaves us awash in confusion, indecisiveness, and ambivalence.

We live in a global economy, a world community, a world in which efforts are made daily to overcome ignorance, death, and disease. Medical researchers from around the globe fight AIDS in Africa and the West, and the eradication of smallpox worldwide has been accomplished (with the unfortunate side effect that it has become a powerful weapon). We now view human slavery in the United States, once an acceptable cultural practice, as a shameful part of our history, and we have finally apologized to Japanese Americans for the racist destruction of their lives during World War II. It is completely contradictory to shudder at the catastrophic horrors of the Holocaust yet not condemn the kind of physical and emotional devastation that infants and girls experience because they are viewed as property and inferiors. We cannot on the one hand express horror at the vicious Nazi description of Jews as rats and pigs deserving to die, and on the other hand accept another culture's view of females as so degraded and unclean as to require their bodies to be mutilated.

How does one really separate a custom from an atrocity? Who does the defining? A letter to the editor of the *New York Times* supporting nonintervention in such culturally valued activities as female circumcision describes the value of the ritual surrounding the event and concludes, with no evidence whatsoever, "There is little doubt that for the girls it was a joyous occasion."[21] Whether cutting a girl's genitals out and sewing her vagina together is a joyous ritual or an unspeakable horror is a matter of continuing disagreement. Even international organizations such as the U.N. Sub-Committee on the Prevention of Discrimination and the Protection of Minorities, while recognizing that female circumcision is a violation of human rights, has adopted a resolution that did not condemn the practice but called on the human rights system to work with the Sudan and other cultures that practice FGM to persuade them to stop performing the operations.[22]

While some insist that international law should be used to hold practitioners of FGM, parents of children who are mutilated, and state leaders responsible for crimes against women, others suggest that legislative change imposed without support from a majority of the population is ineffective, as has been evident in legislation prohibiting the dowry system.[23] These practices are driven underground, resulting in even more damage to the people the new laws are designed to protect. As a Sudanese judge stated in 1950, during the public outcry against legislation that outlawed FGM:

These events brought to mind the risks involved in the rigid application of the new law without first preparing the people .... No social reform could be properly and righteously affected by legislation,

particularly when that legislation was imposed by a foreign ruler . . . .
The ordinary, modest, bashful Sudanese male, for whose supposed
satisfaction women are performing this operation in secret, would
not tolerate his womenfolk being dragged into jail for doing what
their ancestors had been doing without hindrance for over ten
centuries . . . the only effective way for eradication of that bad and
cruel custom is by education of both male and female Sudanese
alike.[24]

Some activists and numerous lawmakers view the issue not as a human
rights one but as a health issue, insisting that the imposition of laws will
do little to change historical patterns of interaction.[25] Rather, people need
to be educated about the risks inherent in some of the cultural practices
and the death and destruction resulting from traditional values that hold
women in such low esteem. This approach would have Western women
become more sensitive to the cultural nuances that lead both women and
men to support some of the practices that are dangerous to women and
to find ways to convince women who perform the acts of destruction to
become allies working for social change. Rather than imposing their
Western values on women in Africa and the Middle East, Western women
can work with women in other cultures, through the village system and
through religious and educational leaders, for a change from the bottom
up. Obviously there is no agreement on the best approach, but there is at
least growing evaluation of cultural crimes against women and girls as
unacceptable in a global community.[26] Foot-binding serves as an example
of one form of violence against women that was situated in economics,
marriage systems, and cultural definitions of femininity that has been
eradicated. This provides some hope that FGM, which is a similar normative practice, could be eliminated in a similar fashion.[27]

FOOT-BINDING

There are "two central facts of footbinding: that it caused prolonged
agony, and that at least half of the little girls forced to endure it had to
be beaten into submission by their elders."[28] As many as 10 percent of
the girls died from gangrene and other infections that accompanied the
hideous process in which the four smaller toes of the foot were bent back
into the flesh, breaking the arch and pulling the heel into the foot. The foot
became putrid, having to be washed several times a day and rebound. The
cloth that shaped the stump was slowly tightened over time. An adult
woman was not free of the need to attend her feet—they must remain

tightly bound to prevent the excruciating pain that would result from having no arch and no ankle support. Special shoes, which covered only the
heel and the toe, allowed her to walk on her heel, her "leg skirts" covering
the "ugly overspill" so characteristic of bound feet.[29] The process was
long and painful, often beginning when the girl was about six and taking
at least two years.

Foot-binding began among the elite in China and diffused to the commoners, a process that mirrors that of female genital mutilation and the
practice of dowry that puts so many women at risk of death. Most authors
agree that foot-binding emerged during the Ming Dynasty and spread to a
wide swath of women in all segments of society during the Sung Dynasty
during which "tenets of female chastity, seclusion, and subordination
emerged and came to reign."[30] The most common story is that it was introduced by a favorite palace dancer, Yao-niang, in the court of "poet-aesthete
Li Yu, Emperor of the Southern T'ang dynasty (961–975 A.D.)."[31] Consistent with Mary Daly's claim that gynocidal torture spreads from the elite
to the lower classes, foot-binding began in the imperial class, radiating
first to other courtesans and then to commoners, moving from the urban
capitals to the rest of the empire, from the north to the south. It became
a compelling and self-enforcing convention, socially obligatory, and practiced even by those who opposed it.[32]

Why would such a painful, disfiguring (from Western eyes), and crippling practice emerge in the first place, and what accounts for its spread
to all classes and its variation among them? Some Western feminists have
situated the practice in patriarchy, a system of male superiority and control
of women's bodies and identities. Mary Daly, for example, surely does this
in *Gynecology*, relying on poetry and pornography to illustrate men's
sexualized infatuation with the bound foot and obsession with purity,
fueled by the ideology of male domination.[33] The commonplace view of
the foot fetish reflects the distaste and fascination Westerners have with
Chinese pornography and erotica, and disgust at the sexualization of
deformity.[34] Some authors have suggested that among the elite, particularly as Chinese men became fashionably delicate, the tiny foot demarcated gender. But the fetishization of the foot—the "golden lotus" and
the "three inch golden lilies"[35]—is reflective of a small segment of the
population, the leisure classes rather than the workers. While much has
been made of Chinese men's foot fetishes, Gates found that most erotica
and pornography, whether narrative, figurine, painting, or woodcut, was
not directed to the foot.[36] It was a rather specialized literature, as Dorothy
Ko points out, referring to the literature that details the erotic attraction of
men to the bound foot as "Chinese connoisseurship literature," revealing,

she says, not the popularity of foot-binding but of its demise since this sort of vulgar writing about the bound foot would have been unthinkable when foot-binding was a normative practice among the elite.[37]

Foot-binding has been presented by "foreign missionaries, Chinese nationalists and feminists of all backgrounds and ideologies as a symbol of China's backwardness and shame."[38] Ko, however, viewing its meaning through the shoes themselves, sees it as a mundane, decidedly unglamorous, procedure designed to discipline the body, creating a highly eroticized illusion of desire. Her reliance on the shoes, their intricate and beautiful patterns and embroidery and rich fabrics, situates any construction of the foot as erotic in the exclusive imperial world of fashion rather than in the villages and on the farms where this practice occurred with much less loveliness.[39]

The control of women's sexuality and government intrusion into women's bodies characterize China today, illustrated well by the horrors experienced by women who violate the one-child policy, who risk being forced to have an abortion as late as the ninth month of pregnancy.[40] But such control, existing now as it did before the Revolution, cannot alone explain the emergence of foot-binding and its variations by time, region, and class. Foot-binding may be seen not as a monolithic whole but as having different meanings for different groups at different times and serving different purposes. Some authors see foot-binding as a practice that consolidated and reproduced the kinship system in which women were expected to marry their social superiors.[41] It established ethnic identities and demarcated geographic regions and regulated relationships between individuals and groups. It may initially have served to separate the cultivated, "us," from the savages, "them," marking the cultural divide between the elite Chinese females during the Ming period from the barbarians. In southwestern Taiwan, for example, some villages were identified as Plains Aborigine rather than Hoklo despite their shared ancestry and other shared customs, with only foot-binding separating them.[42] The absence of foot-binding among these Aborigines marked them as non-Han, therefore less civilized, more culturally backward than Han, thereby regulating the marriage and kinship patterns between them. One reason the meanings attached to foot-binding may have been so diverse is that it was not necessarily seen as a manipulation of the body but as a kind of attire, in the same category as the robes that men wore, hairstyles for both men and women. The body, Ko writes, was less an entity, less a corporal being, than attire, in intimate process with nature and the cosmos and could therefore be manipulated to display political allegiance or political identity.[43]

From the little information available about foot-binding among commoners, it is clear that the practice is far more likely to have been an elite custom differentiating genders or ensuring female subservience and male control than a fetish. Foot-binding maintained the traditional authority of the family and kept married women in their tightly circumscribed place: "It 'kept women from gadding about' as well as meeting customary gendering expectations."[44] Foot-binding, while signaling the woman's desirability and plans for marriage, also reflected the very clear view that girls were submissive to the family and the community, that their own identities as separate beings were inconsequential, and that their allegiance to authority was paramount. It taught young girls obedience and established their place in a family structure in which they were valued for their fertility and their ability to contribute economically to the family, either directly through labor or indirectly through heirs, and in which their sexual or other desires were of little significance.[45] It was not simply a matter of the wealthy binding their daughters' feet for a life of leisure and to assure their marriageability with the poor girls being left unbound to tromp through the woods or wade in the rice paddies. Rather, whether feet were bound or not, and when, depended on the type of labor expected of the girl.[46]

Gates's work clarifies the economic factors tied to foot-binding and minimizes the importance of foot-binding as reflecting erotic desire or foot fetishes.[47] The fact that it was not universally practiced reflects the role women played in the economy. The contribution Chinese women made to their households has been dramatically underestimated because their work has been absorbed in family and the devaluation of unpaid labor, what Gates has called the "curious assumption that only wage-work generates value for households."[48] Women's work is rendered invisible because it occurs in the form of "obedience" as subordinated kinswomen—that is, as daughters and daughters-in-laws "help" their mothers and, as wives, "help" their husbands. The expected contributions of women to the household are directly related to foot-binding, which both demonstrates the use of female labor as it occurs differently in different places and helps explain the enormous variation in the prevalence of foot-binding throughout China. In addition to the variations in the percentages of women bound in various districts, there was also variation in the average age of binding and whether women unbound their feet after marriage. Regional variations depended on the kind of family and work life the girl was expected to face.

Binding a girl's feet drew a bright line between her as a woman who was expected to marry and the nonbound woman who was to become a maidservant. While the binding might have been enormously painful, the unbound woman would face a lifetime of pain as a servant. Binding identified, from Gates's point of view, the woman as a kinswoman, a daughter, a daughter-in-law, one who would be protected by family.[49] The foot-bound woman could engage in light labor, while the heavy work of collecting fuel, work in rice paddies, and heavy lifting and carrying were impossible with bound feet. In regions where girls were expected to engage in heavy or wet work, most were not bound at all as they were in regions where girls did the spinning and weaving. In both instances, foot-binding contributed to the heavy parental control over the girls' labor.

In some areas, where the women engaged in light physical labor, including oyster picking and opium harvesting, girls were not likely to be foot-bound. This may have been because the labor was seasonal or because the girls were needed in agricultural production or because they might marry into other villages where tiny feet would be a disadvantage. In communities that relied heavily on portage for survival, few of the women had bound feet because they could not have traversed the rough mountains and river crossings carrying paper and other materials if they were bound. The direct relationship between foot-binding and the type of work expected of the girls can be illustrated by the change in Tong'an. Gates reports that when the work of spinning and weaving, the work of young girls, was replaced by oyster picking, the number of foot-bound girls declined substantially; only 32 percent of the living informants had been foot-bound, whereas 92 percent of their mother's generation had been. Similarly, in Hua'an, where portage became the alternative to a declining textile industry, only 17 percent of the informants were bound, whereas 91 percent of their mothers had been. The type of labor expected of the girls also influenced the timing of the binding: Tong'an girls were bound at the average age of 10.3 years, compared with the Hua'an, whose feet were bound at 14.6 years of age,[50] revealing that the girls' labor was more valuable to her family than a "good" marriage.

THE END

By 1949, foot-binding in China had virtually disappeared. A few women living today still hobble on bound feet, but for the most part, it is their sons and daughters who carry the memories of their mothers' feet. There are several explanations for the rather abrupt end of foot-binding and several factors that probably influenced it. Of course, it ended coincident with the Communist Revolution in 1949, during which political, economic, and ideological changes discouraged it.[51] But it had already ended in some regions with the overthrow of the Manchu Dynasty. The new leaders were committed to eliminating foot-binding and were very successful in some regions. For example, in one province, a 1929 survey showed that only 2.3 percent of the girls born before 1910 had unbound feet but 95 percent of those born after had unbound feet, a dramatic and immediate shift. It seems clear that industrialization, Western intrusion, and outside efforts to eradicate it, as well as other changes in the economy, all played a role in the discontinuation of foot-binding. It was only in the twentieth century, however, after many different attempts to banish it, "when domestic and foreign assaults brought the magnificent empire to its knees, that footbinding lost its prop and became superfluous."[52]

Greenhalgh suggests that foot-binding ended as a result of expanding employment and educational opportunities in addition to improved transportation that pulled women away from the patriarchal family and toward the labor market. Increased industrialization accompanied by challenges to the ideologies supporting the traditional family system, particularly intrusions from the West that ridiculed the practice, contributed to this change.[53] Gates agrees with Greenhalgh in suggesting that the dramatic decline in foot-binding was far more a reflection of a change in the economic realities encountered by villagers than it was a response to dicta from the capital. When the household production of cotton and hemp gauze mosquito netting was replaced by spinning and weaving machines, families ceased foot-binding their daughters because they needed their help in heavier labor.[54] The consideration was between the girl's value in marriage and her value as a laborer, with political and government campaigns against foot-binding having little effect. The critical element in the disappearance of foot-binding was a change in the production demands: whereas one weaver needed many little spinners, girls as young as five or six who could learn spinning and who could be proficient at seven or eight, when fuel-driven spinning replaced the girls, their labor value evaporated. Suddenly many fewer were bound, and of those who were, many had their feet let out. In some instances, binding continued, but it was done much later, in preparation for marriage.[55]

Gerry Mackie sees the demise of foot-binding as related to the purposes it served initially and the redefinition of, and challenges to, those purposes.[56] It carried several meanings, such as signaling availability for marriage, acting as an ethnic marker, controlling women, supporting the dominance of the patriarch and imposing obedience, exaggerating the difference between the sexes, and enhancing sexual pleasure. These purposes and the props that supported them contributed to it becoming a self-enforcing tradition, practiced universally, even by those who opposed it, just as is female genital mutilation (FGM).[57] From Mackie's position, people were trapped in a belief system, a self-enforcing convention. Their views changed only as they acted collectively to abolish the practice, which any one of them acting individually and privately would have continued to support. Mackie identified three forces that led to the elimination of foot-binding. First, in 1895, the anti-foot-binding reformers carried out a modern education campaign showing that China was alone among nations and that it was losing face as a result of this backward practice, ridiculed throughout the West. Second, the education campaign explained the advantages of unbound feet and the disadvantages of bound feet; and third, they formed natural-foot societies, whose members pledged publically not to bind their daughter's feet and not to allow their sons to marry a woman with bound feet.[58]

At the end of the discussion, I am still, of course, wondering about the underlying question, the same question that remains about honor crimes, dowry deaths, and comfort women—how did it happen that women were those damaged and crippled, linking families through purity and obedience—why women? Why were *they* mutilated rather than men? Why did they provide the human cultural markers? Why were their feet necessarily involved in the marriage transaction? Why were their feet the object of desire? Whether we approach these many forms of violence against women from a cultural perspective, an economic perspective, or a medical perspective, we are still left with the fact that women were and remain today, the perfect victim. This is the case as we turn to contemporary forms of global gendered violence.

THE POLITICS OF FEMALE GENITAL MUTILATION (FGM)

The issues just touched on can be illustrated by a careful consideration of the practice of FGM. The debate about naming this practice reflects the very different points of view regarding it. Western feminists are likely to view the cutting, removal, and suturing of women's genitalia as a virulent form of violence designed to control women's sexuality and to call it female genital mutilation.[59] Others, such as James and Robertson, see this name as sensationalistic and are more likely to view this as a cultural practice that, while designed to control women's sexuality, also incorporates important identity and community dimensions.[60] It is not entirely clear when it first began, although there is mention of it in Egypt in 163 BCE. Perhaps the first thorough descriptions of infibulation were provided by Pietro Bembo (1470–1547), but there are numerous accounts, some rather detailed, from explorers and historians, even psychoanalysts in the early nineteenth century.[61]

This practice, sometimes inappropriately called female circumcision and sometimes called genital surgery or genital cutting, came to the attention of activist women in 1980 at the United Nations Conference on Women in Copenhagen.[62] But much earlier, during the colonial period, Christian missionaries in Sudan had made an effort to educate people against the practice. As early as 1946, the British colonial government had passed legislation regulating *sunna* circumcision and banning the practice of infibulation, but such laws did more to make these practices invisible than to eradicate them.[63] During the 1970s and 1980s, the Decade of the Woman, European and American feminists began to publicize and condemn this practice, leading to international disputes over the enforcement of human rights and the appropriate response of the United Nations to FGM. The issue drove a wedge between Western women and African women. African women defended the practice as a functional cultural practice allowing their daughters to find marriage partners and increasing the status of women. It was viewed as a private family matter, not a human rights issue. Western women condemned the "myth about the importance of cultural traditions that prepared the female sex for a life of suffering," a life "of pain and powerlessness, unquestioning submission to social norms defined by men."[64]

By the next UN Women's Conference in Nairobi, the discussions between Western and African women were less contentious, and by the time of the Beijing Conference in 1995, both African and Western women agreed that FGM is a violation of human rights. Focus on FGM as both a human rights issue and a health issue has had a positive impact on the response to it. Kenya condemned FGM in 1982 and passed formal legislation banning it in 1990. Sweden was one of the first nations to condemn it, prohibiting health professionals from performing the operation in 1982. Australia, Tasmania, France, and the Netherlands have also made FGM a punishable offense, and the United States and Canada have designated it a type of harm that could qualify a person for political asylum under the Refugee Act.[65] Today, FGM is recognized as a human rights issue at the international level, a form of violence against women that cannot be overlooked or justified on the grounds of culture or tradition.[66] The fact that girls and women are the only people who suffer this mutilation, and that the purpose is to desexualize them, marks FGM as a form of violence against women.

The 1993 United Nations Declaration of the Elimination of Violence Against Women (which the United States has not signed) affirms that FGM is a form of violence against women (Article 2[a]) disproportionately affecting the human rights of women.[67] The UN Office of Human Rights in Geneva, the 1993 UN Human Rights Conference in Vienna, the World Health Assembly in 1993, and the Fourth World Conference on Women in 1995 all have condemned FGM as a violation of human rights. Still, the practice remains commonplace in many African and Middle Eastern countries, even in countries that have ratified the international conventions and passed domestic legislation to prohibit it.[68] Margareth Etienne argues that the United Nations has failed women because it has failed to use its global leverage to attack the practice of FGM head-on; for example, allowing CEDAW (UN Committee to Elimi-nate All Forms of Violence Against Women) to let FGM-practicing coun-tries exempt themselves from the jurisdiction of the World Court.[69]

An estimated 130–150 million girls and women in more than 20 African and some Asian countries have undergone female genital mutilation,[70] and the World Health Organization estimates that 3 million girls are at risk annu-ally.[71] That number has grown over time with increased attention to the problem. Female mutilation, a practice that is deeply rooted in traditional culture, dating back over 2,000 years to Egypt, affects more girls and women than any other practice targeted at the mutilation of women, now or ever. The prevalence is almost inconceivable. If, as some authors have suggested, wife beating is not epidemic but pandemic, an entirely new word is needed to describe the extent of the practice of female genital mutilation.

Female circumcision, while physically devastating to the girl or woman, protects the honor of her family through ensuring her sexual purity. With-out infibulation, a Sudanese girl is not marriageable; the tighter her infibu-lation, the higher the potential bride price. After childbirth, reinfibulation renews her virginity, ensuring her husband greater satisfaction during sex-ual intercourse. Among the Sande, infibulation provides enhanced status to the woman or satisfies men that their wives are not enjoying sex with another man (or, in fact, with them, due to the loss of the clitoris). Circum-cision, in patriarchal and patrilineal societies such as the Sudan, separates the decent and protected women from the prostitutes and slaves. Any "transgression on the part of the woman disgraces her entire family and only the most extreme measures, from divorce, to casting the woman out, to her death will restore the family's honor."[72] The honor of the family is measured by the chastity and purity of the women, and because women are defined as sexually lascivious, voracious, and promiscuous, removal of their clitoris and labia is designed to diminish their desire and sexual sensitivity significantly. Infibulation is justified as preventing rape, although, of course, if the girl or woman is raped, she is likely to be torn, just as she is expected to be torn by her husband on her wedding night.

The debate today in the United States about the wisdom and necessity of male circumcision perhaps encourages us to equate these two. Certainly in the case of male circumcision, there is pain; there is often a medical or hygienic justification for male as well as female circumcision, although the view of women's bodies as unclean and therefore needing to be circumcised is not transferred to males. The pain for males is momentary, experienced in infancy; never are the man's genital organs mutilated, removed, or rendered useless. The hygienic justifications seem to have been overridden by recent research showing no increase in cervical cancer rates among women whose sexual partners were not circumcised, and recent studies indicate that remaining uncircumcised may be beneficial to a man's sexual stimulation and performance. The foreskin may protect the head of the penis, thereby making it more sensitive and improving arousal and erection. While there seems to be no good reason for male circumcision, the consequences are not devastating to men. Women, on the other hand, face a lifetime of pain from urination, menstruation, childbirth, and intercourse. They suffer infections throughout their lives. And, predictably, their sexual pleasure is greatly diminished. Hysteria, madness, aggression, homoeroticism, "unrestrained female sexuality," and "immoral lust" have been viewed as situated in an overly large clitoris or, for some, just a clitoris: Jean Riolan, an anatomy professor at the University of Paris during the seventeenth century, recommended "clitoridectomy on all women as a way of disciplining unrestrained female sexuality."[73] During the Victorian era, there was almost a moral panic over "self-abuse for both men as well as women and they were seen as risking mental retardation, gonorrhea, fainting, epilepsy, growth retardation and infertility among other possibilities."[74] Johnsdotter reviews the differing European and Western views and practices and concludes that cutting procedures can be observed from radically different perspectives, leading her to call for a "balanced view of today's cutting practices, both in the West and in Africa."[75] By this she means that the feminist perspective, which views traditional cutting and earlier practices in this country as only efforts to maintain patriarchy and oppress women sexually, should be informed by an understanding that they have long been practiced in this country for medical and hygienic reasons, inappropriate as they might have been. They reflected views about the body and about male and female sexuality that are not terribly far from those of countries where it is still practiced, including the United States where clitoroplasty, vaginoplasty, and labiaplasty for nontherapeutic purposes are still acceptable surgical procedures.

Mutilation is a powerful word, implying permanent crippling, deformity, and disfigurement; as such, it reveals the degree of destruction of tissue, the pain, the suffering, and the possible death of the victims. The ritual performance, the type of circumcision, and the age at which it is performed vary widely. The girl is usually cut with a razor, a kitchen knife, or a pair of scissors, sometimes even with a sharp stone. She is rarely anesthetized in any way and experiences extreme pain. When she is infibulated, her legs and ankles are bound together, and she cannot move for several weeks while scar tissue closes the vagina almost completely. She is likely to suffer severe physical effects, including bleeding, infection, tetanus, shock resulting from the severe pain, dysmenorrhea, hemorrhage, damage to other internal organs, and septicemia. And a significant danger of contracting AIDS is posed by the instruments used in the process. The lifetime damage is dramatic, including chronic pelvic infection, sterility, vulva abscesses, sexual dysfunction, and obstetric complications. Charles Foster reports that menstrual blood is often trapped behind the artificial wall created by infibulation, causing "spectacular urogenital tract infections."[76] While life-threatening immediate and chronic conditions result from FGM, the women also suffer reduced sexual satisfaction. Women who had undergone female circumcision of any type were found to have a significantly lower quality of sexual life than were controls, with women who were sexually active who had undergone FGM differing the most from sexually active controls in a study conducted by SHA Andersson.[77] In addition to the physical effects, women may suffer psychological disabilities such as chronic depression and anxiety.[78] In some countries, almost 100 percent of the girls suffer this mutilation; in many others, it is between 70 and 80 percent.[79]

Female genital mutilation takes four major forms, each more intrusive than the one before, and these vary by place and tribe:

- *Sunna circumcision* (*sunnah* means "tradition" in Arabic)—the removal of the prepuce or hood of the clitoris and the tip of the clitoris. This form of mutilation is the mildest form.
- Excision/clitoridectomy—the removal of the clitoris and labia minora.
- *Pharaonic circumcision*—the removal of the clitoris and labia minora and the incision and stitching together of the anterior two-thirds of the labia majora.
- *Removal of the clitoris and labia minora* plus the incision and stitching together of all of the labia majora to cover the urethra and the entrance of the vagina with a hood of skin.[80]

The first two types of female genital mutilation are considered clitoridectomies, and the second two are considered infibulations (referring to stitching together). The stitches are ripped apart by the groom on their wedding night and are repeatedly torn during intercourse, sometimes causing the woman weeks of agony before the scar tissue sealing the labia is finally destroyed. This sexual assault is a test of the man's manhood; if he is unable to force through the scar tissue, he will seek the help of a midwife, usually in secret and with shame. Clitoridectomies are more common than infibulations, which are practiced widely only in the Sudan, Somalia, and Mali. Pharaonic circumcision is practiced widely among Muslims and Coptic Christians, the wealthy and the poor, and in both urban and rural areas.[81]

In every society in which FGM is practiced, the unmarried woman has no economic or social rights, and without circumcision she cannot marry. All forms of FGM involve the excision of some or all of the exterior female genitalia, and all facilitate the disempowerment of women. While Muslim scholars acknowledge that the Koran does not impose circumcision on women, the custom and tradition of African Muslims in particular demand this practice, which demonstrates and reinforces women's powerlessness and debasement. Women are seen as either impure and vile, or as sexually insatiable animals, or even as potential murderers, all of which can be undone by excising what Mary Daly calls their only "purely sexual, purely female organ."[82] Woman's sexuality is dark, destructive, and powerful, and to castrate her, denying her sexual self, is to control her and maintain male superiority and the superior value of male sexual pleasure.

JUSTIFICATIONS FOR CUSTOMARY GENITAL ASSAULTS

In the 1860s in the United States, there was a brief fad of clitoridectomies following the introduction of the operation by the English physician Isaac Baker Brown.[83] The purpose was to control female personality disorders, and while many doctors frowned on the practice, they thought it might be necessary in cases of nymphomania, intractable masturbation, or "unnatural growth" of that organ. The historian J. Barker-Benfield listed the indications for the more invasive oophrectomy as "troublesome, eating like a ploughman, masturbation, attempted suicide, erotic tendencies, persecution mania, simple 'cussedness,' and dysmenorrhea (painful menstruation), while the most significant indication was a 'strong current of sexual appetitiveness.' "[84] The overall goal was to smooth women's emotional upheavals, making them more complacent, easier to be with, and more controllable.

The justifications for female circumcision today are many. One premise is that females are naturally sexually insatiable and aggressive, and girls left uncircumcised will become wild, craving sexual satisfaction from men. Illustrating the degree to which women themselves incorporate the view that circumcision is necessary, one woman expressed the idea that "it will help us control our emotions."[85] In one study, 95 percent of the women who were asked for the reasons for mutilation answered that it was for cultural and traditional reasons, with 49 percent saying it was to prevent promiscuity.[86]

One Ethiopian man saw the practice as having an educational function: "When you circumcise a woman, they're less active sexually and more interested in their schoolwork."[87] One young woman's mother told her that it protected her from boys. The clitoris is perceived as the center of desire and excision reduces the risk of a man's being shamed by his lecherous wife, his honor being more important than his wife's safety or health.[88]

Another reason for performing circumcision or infibulation is the fear that the clitoris will become like a penis, and men would be unable to have intercourse with a woman. Some tribes even fear that if the clitoris is left alone, it will grow until it drags on the ground. A widespread assumption that clitorhypertrophy (an exceptionally large clitoris) characterized many Ethiopian and Arabic groups probably grew out of Westerners seeing ritual clitoral elongation, but there is no clear evidence for such a problem. The clitoris is the woman's sexual organ, and removing it is instrumental in desexualizing her, thereby erasing the man's unspoken fear of the powerful, evil, sexual woman who has the power to kill men when they are between her legs or to render them impotent.[89]

Some cultures that practice mutilation of females believe that circumcision aids in menstruation and childbirth, although quite the opposite is true. Many women suffer extreme dysmenorrhea, to the extent that they are so swollen with blood trapped in the uterus that they appear pregnant. These women are sometimes suspected of being pregnant and are killed or banned. Childbirth requires that the infibulated woman be deinfibulated to prevent severe perineal tearing or fetal death. It is ironic that infibulation is sometimes done for hygienic and health reasons, when in fact it is likely to cause physical trauma; infections of the uterus, ovaries, and urinary tract; infertility; abscesses; injuries during intercourse; and problems in childbirth including infection, prolonged delivery, higher infant mortality, and brain damage.

The fear of many African women is that if their daughter is not circumcised, no man will want her; she will not marry and will remain a burden on her family for her lifetime. One of the women interviewed by Alice Walker in her video *Warrior Marks* recounted the devastation she felt when her fiancé left her because she would not be infibulated.[90] Her father banished her mother from their home because he thought she helped the daughter avoid circumcision, and then he divorced her. Divorce had grave consequences for the wife, in much the same way that not marrying spelled disaster for the daughter.

GEOGRAPHY OF THE DESEXUALIZED FEMALE SELF

Ritual clitoridectomies are performed sometimes on infants, frequently on young girls between ages five and eight, sometimes on a woman, as late as in the seventh month of pregnancy (in which case the purpose is to prevent the infant from dying during childbirth as a result of touching the mother's clitoris), and as late as after the birth of the first child.[91] In some societies, there remains a good deal of secrecy around this practice. For example, among the Sande in Liberia, the ceremony is held in great secrecy and is carried out by a *Zoe*, an older, respected woman who is an instructor in the Sande society.

In Malay, although circumcision was at one time performed ritualistically when the girl had reached puberty, it is now often conducted when she is much younger; some parents wish to circumcise their daughters at infancy because they feel it is easier and less painful. While in the past, a feast and ceremony were held at the time of the circumcision, now often a family simply calls a midwife to perform the operation for a fee. It is less of a cultural ritual, steeping the community with solidarity, and more of a routinized act of violence against girls and women.

Female genital mutilation occurs primarily in Africa. The prevalence is very high but varies substantially between countries. Heather Simpsa and her colleagues reviewed the current practices and beliefs in Western Africa, finding that about 90 percent of the women in the Sudan, Mali, Djibouti, Egypt, Ethiopia, Somalia, and Eritrea have been mutilated with infibulation being most common in Mali, Somalia, Sudan, Djibouti, the south of Egypt, and in Eritrea. In other countries—Niger, Ghana, and Togo, for example—fewer than 6 percent of the women and only 1 percent of their daughters had been circumcised.[92] The practice also occurs in at least 35 other countries, including France, Canada, Brazil, Sweden, the United Kingdom, and the United States.[93] While it is difficult to determine the exact number of women who have been circumcised, rough estimates suggest that half of the women of Africa have been circumcised: in Somalia, the rate is nearly 100 percent; in Ethiopia, the percentage is over 90; and in Egypt, approximately 50 percent of the women have been circumcised. Most writers on the subject recognize it to be widespread in Oman and South Yemen, and it is well documented in Eastern and Southern Libya and in the far south of Algeria.[94]

This practice in some form is almost universal in Muslim northern Sudan, although it is relatively rare in the non-Muslim south.[95] Although in some countries—Ghana, Niger, and Togo, for example—it is decreasing, and increasing numbers of women believe the practice should be discontinued and are not having their daughters circumcised, there is still a very concerning finding that younger women, those having less education and those who are poor and married, are likely to believe the practice should be continued.[96] It is more common among Muslims where the Islamic customs and traditions (the *sunnah*) that have existed over many centuries have come to constitute Muslim laws. *Sunnah* refers to tradition passed from generation to generation and consists of the words of Mohammed and the customs during the time of Mohammed. Much of what is taken as *sunnah* depends on the opinions of Muslim scholars whose interpretations are morally binding (although not legally binding) on Muslims. So while it may be that the Koran does not prescribe female circumcision, tradition and custom guarantee continuance of the practice to the present day, and there is in many areas virtually no distinction drawn between religion and tradition. Many people believe that a woman cannot be a true Muslim if she is not circumcised; she cannot marry or go to mosque, or in some instances even associate with other members of the community.[97]

In many countries, not to be circumcised is unthinkable. Among the Sande societies in Liberia, an uncircumcised girl cannot attend the powerful bush school system and therefore is prohibited from becoming a "wise" woman or a good wife who is a good adviser to her husband and a political and economic asset to her community. Although there is no religious basis for the tradition of circumcision, an uncircumcised woman is denied the power other Sande women enjoy and cannot be considered part of society, hold important positions, or participate in village initiations. She is also unlikely to be accepted into the social community of women or to find a mate.[98] No matter what the justifications or the current impact on the social and economic opportunities of women, the practice of mutilating women is so common, so widespread, and so devastating that it should be recognized as a "genitort," an offense aimed directly at the annihilation of women's sexual being—a kind of war crime or act of terrorism against women.[99]

MEDICAL AND LEGAL ISSUES

The response of some countries to the health concerns related to genital mutilation has been to regulate the practice, acknowledging its significance as a deeply embedded social and cultural practice. In Malay, the practice, involving excising a small piece of the prepuce of the clitoris with a razor blade on girls between the ages of 2-1/2 and 6, has become modernized and medicalized. The rituals have been abandoned, and a government midwife is increasingly likely to perform the surgery, using anesthetics, antibiotics, and better septic techniques, reducing the risk of infection and death.[100]

Similarly, in Holland, in the early 1990s, there was a significant debate about medicalization, with many children's rights advocates and feminists demanding a prohibition of female circumcision altogether, while advocates for the increasing number of immigrant women, particularly from Somalia, supported cultural traditions. They claimed that a small incision in the foreskin of the clitoris should be regarded as non-mutilating and that it might prevent more mutilating forms of circumcision and should therefore be allowed. The Ministry of Foreign Affairs, however, condemned any form of female genital mutilation, including a small nick of the clitoris, and has prohibited this practice in clinics and health centers or by doctors or specially trained health workers.

In 1982, the World Health Organization (WHO) finally issued a statement categorically opposing the medicalization of FGM and unequivocally advised that it should not be practiced by any health professionals.[101] In the United States, the debate about medicalization has been quieter but not absent, pitting advocates of safe and sanitary circumcision among immigrants against those who insist that to regulate is to lend state support and legitimacy to a practice that in this country would be considered child abuse at the very least. The debate continues because the underlying disagreement is much broader, incorporating opposing views about cultural relativity and its limitations, particularly the right of countries, including the United States, that do not practice FGM to intervene in those cultures that do.

Adam Karp suggests that a strong case could be made for FGM to be tried as torture under international law, a violation of the law of nations because the actions violate a universal, definable, obligatory norm.[102] The law of nations overrides an individual state's objection to international consensus of what constitutes a human rights violation. For example, in the case of genocide, the Kadic court found "universal jurisdiction" over genocidists and war criminals guilty of murder, rape, and torture. This case, however, did not reconcile the distinction between torture and war crimes. "In order to breach the law of nations, torture required state action while war crimes and genocide did not."[103] There is a genuine distinction to be made between systematic, mass torture and incidental acts of torture, and Karp suggests that an argument could be made to classify FGM as "gynocide" (a mass-organized extinction of female sexuality, self-esteem, and bodily integrity) or a crime committed during the undeclared "war of violence against women."[104] Or, he suggests, it could forge its own category as "mass torture" committed during peacetime or could be established as torture directed solely toward children.

Several countries, including Holland, the United Kingdom, and the United States, have laws prohibiting female circumcision or female genital mutilation. In the United States, FGM became illegal when President Clinton signed the Department of Defense appropriations bill on March 29, 1997. Representative Patricia Schroeder (D-Colorado) and Senator Harry Reid (D-Nevada) introduced the legislation that led to this law, which also required data collection on the prevalence of the procedure and provides outreach to immigrant groups that traditionally practice female mutilation. Prior to the enactment of this law, only a few states had defined it as a felony.[105] In France, the first mutilation trial took place in 1983. Linda Weil-Curiel, a prosecutor and the country's leading crusader against FGM, calls the practice "butchery invented to control women." Her work has resulted in 15 trials involving more than 30 families, making France the first nation to bring criminal charges against those who perform female genital mutilation. Weil-Curiel asserts, "If immigrants cut off a girl's ear in the name of tradition, there would be an outcry, but here the sex of a future woman is cut off and people are willing to defend it or turn away."[106]

As a result of the UN Conference in 1995 that defined FGM as a human rights violation, African women were empowered to challenge the practice and to get political support for their challenge. As a result, some countries such as Nigeria and Ghana have issued legal mandates against it, and the United States has allowed asylum to women and girls to protect them from this human rights violation. In 1994, a Nigerian woman living in Portland, Oregon, became the first woman to gain permission to avoid deportation because the judge ruled that it could subject her American daughters to ritual female genital mutilation. Lydia Oluloro, an illegal alien who had been infibulated as a child in Nigeria (where the State Department estimates about 50 percent of the women are mutilated), feared that her daughters would suffer the same fate. The judge, acknowledging tradition, nevertheless proclaimed the operation as cruel and allowed her to remain in the United States.[107]

Alice Walker's film *Warrior Marks* and her novel *Possessing the Secret of Joy* have brought FGM to the attention of many thousands of persons who would otherwise probably see it as a rather rare and exotic cultural practice. She starkly presents the ritual in her film in which the screams and sobs of young girls lined up bleeding on the floor, their legs and ankles bound, reveal the reality of this practice.[108] Walker's book unearths the long-term psychological trauma suffered by a woman mutilated in her village when she was a child. Her life in Paris, her marriage, and her feelings about herself reflect the mutilation she has experienced, and she eventually returns to her birthplace to kill the woman who mutilated her, knowing her own life will be over as a result.[109] Walker's portrayal is in direct and stark contrast to some more appreciative anthropological and other academic analyses. Maynard Merwine, a history instructor at Lehigh County Community College, illustrated a fairly typical perspective in a letter to the *New York Times*: "Western peoples [should] try to understand the importance of these traditions to those who practice them: The importance of the ceremony among traditional Kikuyu cannot be understated, for each girl showed by her act of courage that she was ready to be married."[110] In opposition to these attitudes, immigrant women in various countries have joined forces to fight the tradition among their compatriots in these countries and to influence women in their homelands. They are talking about the experience they have long suppressed, acknowledging their humiliation when a doctor expressed horror at their bodies, their anger at having been irreversibly damaged, and sometimes their shame at having done the same thing to their own daughters.

The international efforts to eradicate FGM during the last two decades have not been notably successful. One approach has been to convince the "cutters" to lay down their tools, to give up their practice. In a ceremony, in the port city of Berbera in Somalia, labeled a "Disarmament Celebration," six women put down the "weapons of war against girls," apologizing for the harm they had caused and were backed by men speaking out in support.[111] Another approach has been to educate the young women and men about the practice, to show them, through video and discussion, what happens to the woman and how dangerous the practice can be. Yet another is to convince religious leaders to detach the practice from religion, convincing local religious leaders of its lack of support. Successful intervention in Somalia, where almost 100 percent of the women are mutilated, is more difficult than in some other countries, like Uganda, where the practice is ritually tied to the transition to womanhood. UNICEF suggests advocacy and the mobilization of the communities, engaging with families, youth, and opinion leaders to reduce the demand.[112] In the short run, the hope is to raise awareness, and the long-term goal is to change social norms. At the same time as this hard work is going on, some countries are reducing their efforts—the Sudan legalized the Sunna type of female genital mutilation in February 2009, for example, to take into account the fatwa that differentiates it from the "harmful" form.[113]

In Kenya, under the auspices of CARE, youth have been given soccer balls with "liberate girls from FGM" stamped on them and bright t-shirts with the slogan: "I will marry an uncircumcised girl."[114] The involvement of boys and men is critical since they are the gatekeepers of religious leaders and the custodians of the culture. The conclusion reached by those who would intervene is similar to the findings in the case of dowry deaths. This practice is deeply held and justified by tradition, even among young people where there has been a slight decrease in acceptance in some places. Efforts have to respond to the particular religious, economic, and traditional context in which the change is being attempted—what may work in Sudan may not work at all in Kenya, for example. Different approaches must be taken in different regions and villages. When there are so many countries in which FGM is practiced, many of which mutilate almost all of the girls, and in which there is such deep support for the practice, eradicating it, no matter what the means, will be extremely difficult. The efforts of CARE, WHO, UNICEF, the UN, and many NGOs, hospitals, and other local organizations have made some inroads but have found resistance to be strong. There are many levels on which the fight must be fought: first, and most importantly, lobby the governments to pass laws making FGM illegal. This is a place where international support might be especially useful. Other avenues to change would be through sensitizing frontline health-care workers, sensitizing the community, developing a permanent media presence and engaging in research, monitoring, and documentation. Intractable as it may seem, there has been progress in the eradication of this violation of the human rights of millions of girls and women, with activists from the countries in which FGM is practiced taking the lead.

BRIDE BURNING

In India, a father is eager to be rid of his daughter; her economic contributions are limited, especially in castes above the lowest, and she is a financial burden to her family. She may cripple the family financially, especially if there are other daughters, and she may be viewed as a traitor since she is required to leave her family and go to that of her husband. The father must find his daughter a husband who is of a higher status, well educated, or a professional. In return for allowing their son to marry her, his family requires a dowry, which consists of money or motorcycles or other material benefits, often to be given over a period of time. In their eagerness to be rid of the daughter, her family may overestimate their wealth and their ability to provide a dowry, or they may not give as much as the husband's family wants. The husband's family too may ask for more as time goes on or may condemn as unacceptable the quality of some of the materials and goods provided, demanding replacements.

The daughter is vulnerable to suicide or murder in this situation. She has left her father's home and often the town or city where her family lives and has joined her husband's family, often including not only his parents but other brothers and their wives and children. She becomes the lowest-status person in her new family and is often isolated and alone. Frequently the husband's mother is rejecting and cruel to the daughter, aligning herself with her son against the intruding wife. The young wife may resent the mother-in-law's power and her own powerlessness and be miserable. She cannot return to her home without bringing shame and financial hardship to her family. Edward Gargan quotes a Mr. Murti, who laments, "Why this trouble. If we didn't give birth to girl children, we wouldn't have these problems. What flows out of our eyes is not just tears, but blood."[115] In a dowry death, the husband and his mother will arrange to douse the wife's clothing with the kerosene that is kept in the kitchen for cooking, and then set her on fire, resulting in her death, which is explained as accidental. A daughter whose husband's family rejects her or demands more of her family will sometimes choose to commit suicide rather than bring such dishonor and financial suffering to her family. These daughters know they will not be welcome at home; they know that their chances of remarriage are virtually nil and that their lives will be lived in poverty and rejection. Compared with the life she faces, suicide does not seem a particularly unappealing option to a young, miserable, isolated woman.

This crime against women is built on the dowry system and is situated within a highly stratified society that is patriarchal and characterized by a joint family system. Caution in the interpretation of the joint family system and the stratification system is necessary, however. Although a good deal of attention has been given the role played by the mother-in-law in dowry deaths, suggesting that she resents the young bride and fears that her son's support will dissipate, the research actually indicates that the joint-family system may protect women, particularly in rural areas where there is communication between the families. Visaria found that 53 percent of the women in joint families and 73 percent in nuclear families reported abuse.[116] Jejeebhoy found that in rural areas where the bride and groom's family remained in the same village or nearby, the presence of the mother-in-law protected the young woman, but did not find that her presence either increased or decreased violence against the daughter where village exogamy is practiced.[117]

Marriage is a process by which two families evaluate each other, and the outcome of the negotiations between them is an expression of the relative worth of their respective families. The amount of dowry given is an expression of prestige and can increase the potential for upward mobility. The estimation of worth is expressed in marriage expenditures that take the form of cash gifts, gifts of household goods, and expenditures on the wedding ceremony and celebration. The daughter's marriage transfers the authority over her from her father to her husband and links her family with a higher-status family. The powerlessness and inferiority of Indian women, particularly Hindu women, and the need of their families to arrange a marriage to a suitable higher-status husband who can support them, creates their vulnerability.

Bride burning, or dowry death, is a crime against women built into the dowry system in which young women are killed by their husbands or his family or commit suicide due to severe harassment. Although it was made illegal by the Dowry Prohibition Act of 1961 (amended in 1984 and 1986) in India as part of Mohandas Gandhi's effort to lead India toward independence, it is nevertheless far from rare, with estimates of between 8,000 and 10,000 victims each year.[118] The difficulty in obtaining good estimates stems from several things: efforts to camouflage the type of crime, failure to report, defining the death as suicide or attributing it an accidental kitchen fire, the victim's fear of telling the truth or her inability to do so. In many instances, both the community and law enforcement turn a blind eye.[119] And even if they do attend this problem, some authors such as Judith Greenberg suggest that criminalizing this practice is less than useful.[120] She outlines the problems tied to the criminalization of dowry deaths and suggests that a civil solution might be more useful and protective for the women. During the 1960s and 1970s, there was a great deal of economic dislocation in India, fomenting action for social change. However, at about the same time, the government declared an emergency, prohibiting criticism of the state. Bride burning, Greenberg suggests, arose as a social problem because it could be individualized rather than viewed as a result of government corruption or inaction. This "private problem" could be widely reported in the media since it did not place blame on the government. A focus on dowry through the dowry prohibition acts could thereby deflect attention from the flaws of the state and avoid the recognition of systemic problems of the economic, social, and political powerlessness faced by women.[121] Although, the Dowry Prohibition Act made it illegal to give or take a dowry, it did allow the giving and taking of wedding gifts when "such gifts are of a customary nature and the value thereof is not excessive having regard to the financial status of the person by whom, or on whose behalf, such presents are given."[122] This same act established the concept of dowry death, which is explained as: "where the death of a woman is caused by any burns or bodily injury or occurs otherwise than under normal circumstances within seven years of her marriage and it is shown that soon before her death she was subjected to cruelty or harassment by her husband or any relative of her husband for, or in connection with, any demand for dowry, such death shall be called 'dowry death' and such husband or relative shall be deemed to have caused her death."[123] Changes in the legal code were also made to allow for the presumption of guilt in these instances and for special investigations into a suicide of a wife within seven years of marriage if requested by her family.

Some analysts conclude that the act has proven singularly ineffective. It has been called "utterly ineffective" and a "near total failure" of the law.[124] Rebecca and R. Emerson Dobash report that in urban Maharashtra and greater Bombay, nearly a quarter of the deaths of women between the ages of 15 and 44 are due to "accidents" caused by burns.[125] In Delhi, Parliament reported 452 deaths by burning for women between the ages of 16 and 30, and there were 1,319 cases reported nationally in 1986. By 1998, this figure was 6,913,[126] and by 2011, the National Crime Records Bureau of India shows 8,301 cases of reported dowry deaths.[127] This crime and the related violence of female infanticide are both grossly underreported. In fact, the age-old practice of female infanticide still flourishes in India's poorest states. In Dewa, one of India's poorest villages, a midwife earns about 50 cents and a sack of grain for each live delivery of a girl and about twice that plus a sari if it is a boy. She earns $5 for getting rid of a newborn girl.[128] And although the use of ultrasound to determine the sex of a fetus is illegal, the Indian Medical Association estimates about three million female fetuses are aborted each year; some place the estimate as high as five million.[129] There is implicit acceptance of the practice of sex-selection abortion, and it is heavily advertised in urban areas.

Greenberg reports that there are four predictable problems tied to criminalizing dowry deaths and suggests that feminist successes in getting laws passed in the 1980s (both the 1983 "anti-cruelty" statute and the 1986 "dowry death" statute) have not really forwarded the cause of women who are potential victims.[130] First, the justice system is likely to focus on the bride's difficulties "adjusting to marriage" at the personal level, ignoring the political and structural problems brought by marriage. This leads to a reliance on counseling centers that even further disempower and marginalize women since the cases are shunted off into conciliation centers rather than being given the full scrutiny of the law.[131] The courts and police have been reluctant to view dowry crimes as a particular manifestation of domestic violence, only one component of a much larger problem of violence and hostility toward women and the desire on the part of men to control women. The women themselves, as well, tend to believe that discipline at the hands of their husband is completely appropriate and are unlikely to report abuse by him. Women agree that they should honor, obey, and respect their husband, not displease him, and that he has the right to punish and control them.[132] A second major problem is that criminalizing dowry deaths implies that other forms of violence against women are acceptable. The courts have "repeatedly found no liability for abuse that does not involve the wife's death and does not include allegations of dowry violence," asserting that "stray incidents" of violence are insufficient.[133] Yet Visaria reports that among the rural women she studied, inadequate dowry accounts for only 1 percent of the violence,[134] and others report that only about 15 percent of the violence against women is attributable to dowry problems, and also point out that 72 percent of the first-person accounts of violence do not even mention dowry.[135] Research by Visaria on women in rural Gujarat supports the conclusion that violence against women is built into the system. Two-thirds of the women in their survey reported some sort of abuse, and 42 percent identified these as physical beatings or sexual assaults.[136] In one village in Punjab, 75 percent of the women from scheduled households (those that are historically disadvantaged and recognized as such in the Constitution) reported regular beatings,[137] consistent with Visaria's finding that illiterate women married to illiterate men were at greatest risk.[138] A third problem with criminalizing this problem is that it leads to blaming "outsiders" rather than seeing cultural and structural characteristics of India as the underlying cause. The culprits are likely to be either the mother-in-law or, in some instances, colonial or Western influence—providing defenses and rationalizations for the husband of the victim.[139] The criminalization of dowry violence encourages the search for socially marginalized people and external forces that can be blamed while obscuring the role of the men who dominate the family as well as the legal and political system.[140]

Because criminal law is individualistic in nature, it does not allow for the interrogation of the structural problems that lead to dowry deaths and other forms of violence. Problems within the institution of marriage and the marital family, the demand that women marry and the stigmatization of unmarried women, the lack of educational and occupational opportunity, the stigma tied to divorce, all of these should be considered as major factors in dowry deaths.[141]

Bride burning and wife beating are more common in the north of India where women have restricted mobility and autonomy, limited inheritance rights and control over their economic resources, and limited support from their natal family after marriage, in part because they are married at a young age to distant families.[142] In the south, women have more autonomy, closer ties with their family, are less secluded, and are more likely to work and to have some control over their economic resources.[143] Violence against women, particularly beating, seems to be more commonplace and more accepted in rural areas, although even in these areas, there is variation on the basis of various measures of social development such as literacy rates, infant mortality, fertility, and mortality in general.[144] Differences between Hindus and Muslims are less determining in shaping domestic power relations than is region. Jejeebhoy, in a study focusing on correlates of violence against women, found that well over three in four women consider wife beating a justifiable behavior. It is viewed not only as acceptable but as right and appropriate in a variety of conditions, including neglect of household duties and failure to obey one's husband. There seemed to be consensus among the women interviewed that if women "misbehave," they deserve a beating.[145]

Bride burning, like violence against women, broadly speaking, is more commonplace in rural and poor areas, yet it is also prevalent among the middle and upper classes, particularly in the north, where brides seek grooms from higher-prestige groups within their own caste. However, the practice has recently spread to the untouchables, who did not traditionally give dowries, and has grown dramatically among the middle classes. In Bangalore, for example, referred to as India's "Silicon Valley," a growing city of high-tech computer enthusiasts and a newly entrenched middle class, approximately 80 percent of the 150 new cases of violence against women each month involve either beating or dowry deaths, including not only burns but suicides from drowning, poisoning, and hangings.[146] The deaths accompany systematic abuse of women in which they are beaten severely by their husband for not providing more money or goods after the marriage.[147] In less than a year, the Herat burn hospital in Afghanistan treated more than 75 women, many of them self-immolations, others made to look that way.[148] Farzana was one of those women, engaged at 8 and married at 12. At 17, after suffering years of abuse from her husband and in-laws beginning on their wedding night, she handed her husband her nine-month old baby and set herself on fire. Young women like Farzana resort to suicide because they feel trapped, they are furious at their situation, and they want to shame their husbands.

Van Willigen and Channa situate the problem of dowry deaths in the interrelated characteristics of Indian social and family structure.[149] Women were until recently excluded from holding property, particularly in the north, where dowry deaths are far more common, and they do not participate in agricultural production as they do in the south.[150] Dowry reflects a class system in which social status can be enhanced through marriage, but one that nonetheless leaves the bride relatively powerless and a tradition in which the bride's family is economically inferior to the groom's.[151] There is increasing pressure on families to make good marriages for their daughters as the caste system disappears, resulting in more families vying for men in higher-status positions. Further, the practice of hypergamy or marrying up into higher-status group, once more characteristic of the north, is becoming more dominant throughout India.[152] The function of marriage as a status move also requires the careful attention to the daughter's virginity, her purity, an issue that emerges time and again in dowry deaths because any question about her moral character can be used as a defense by her husband's family.

For some, the dowry is viewed as transferring property to the daughter before the death of the father, since she is unable to receive property after his death. She receives "movable" property such as saris, jewelry, and appliances rather than land, as do her brothers. While this may be true in other countries, Stone and James claim that in India the property is never truly seen as the woman's. Rather, she is a "pass through"—a vehicle for transferring property from one family to the other: "Women in the Indian dowry system should be seen as vehicles of property transmission rather than as true inheritors."[153] The fact that her jewelry may be incorporated into her husband's sister's dowry is a clear indication that she serves as a vehicle of transmission.[154] Although legally women can now inherit from their father, in practice, their brothers are often able to talk them out of taking their portion, or they are required to sign over their portion upon marriage.[155] This form of discrimination against girls and women is reflected in their lower educational rate, higher death rate, and lower likelihood of getting food and care from the family.

Another important characteristic of Indian society that is seen as contributing to violence against women and helps explain a jump in dowry deaths is the economic transformation of the society.[156] High inflation and rapid economic change make it very difficult for the family to accumulate acceptable gifts and sometimes to produce the gifts promised at marriage. At the same time, the girl's father views the husband's future earning power as a predictable and solid benefit to the daughter, and her father is willing to pay as much as he can because her other avenues for earning are so limited. A third important contributor to dowry deaths is the elimination of local control.[157] While one might expect dowry deaths to be more common in the more traditional rural areas, where women are more oppressed and have fewer life choices, violence against women overall is more frequent in urban areas, where the individuals and the families are less subject to social constraints than in rural areas. In the villages, the dowry system was self-regulating, overseen by the local councils and by the joint families themselves, but in urban areas, state and national laws are less effective in regulating everyday practices. In addition, the daughter is unlikely to have the same kind of support networks she would have if she were living in a neighboring village, where people share kinship ties and intimate knowledge of one another.

Another factor that has been related to the increase in dowry deaths, again tied to female power, is the changing participation of women both in production and reproduction. When women are valued as producers, such as in cultivation, when they have income-producing opportunities, they are likely to be somewhat protected from violence. Stone and James expand this point to suggest that one of the reasons dowry deaths may be increasing is that women's contribution to household income relative to men has also declined. With the urbanization and consumerism characterizing India today, women have not shared in access to new economic opportunities with men.[158] But they go on to point out that this decline in women's production and the rise of consumerism place women in even greater jeopardy because their one traditional source of leverage, their fertility, has diminished in value. No longer are children, even male heirs, protection against violence in a cultural context that emphasizes consumption rather than production.[159]

The practice of child marriage in India also adds to the concern about dowry harassment and dowry deaths. Although the legal age of marriage is 18 for women and 21 for men, many are married much younger. In a survey of 5,000 women living in the northern state of Rajasthan where the practice of child marriage is deeply rooted, 56 percent of the women had married before age 15. Of those, 3 percent married before they were five, and another 14 percent married before 10. Barely 18 percent were literate.[160] Tradition requires that a child who marries spend a few days with her new relatives and then return to her own home until puberty. However, in many instances, the girl's value as a servant or a field hand for her in-laws means that she is not returned, so a girl as young as age six or seven may be removed from her family forever. She will not have access to education, nor will she be likely to have any form of birth control available. This situation is not necessarily viewed as a tragedy by the girl's father.

The father of a four-year-old Hansa cheered on the night of her wedding: "Tonight I am a free man again! Thanks to God, the heaviest of my burdens has been lifted."[161] The National Commission for Women in India has urged the government to require the registration of all marriages in order to prevent underage marriages and to protect girls from dowry deaths and virtual enslavement by their husband's family. However, the government has refused to do so, stating: "It has been the consistent policy of the government not to interfere in the personal laws of the distinct communities unless the initiative comes from the communities themselves."[162]

The concept of dowry death was first established only in the 1970s and only legally in the 1980s.[163] Since that time, bride burning in India appears to be on the rise, although some suggest this only reflects increased attention to the problem. In the mid-1980s, around 400 cases of dowry deaths were reported compared with 5,800 a year by the mid-1990s, with recent estimates being placed at over 8,000 a year. Some have put the number much higher.[164] Marilyn French, in *The War against Women*, reports that hundreds of thousands of women have been victims of bride burning, condoned by a culture in which these cases are not investigated.[165]

Dowry deaths can be viewed as a barometer of the value placed on women in Indian society and need to be viewed in the larger context of wife battery, rape, and harassment. In some instances, violence against women reflects a deep-seated hostility and anger directed toward women, rage on the part of men who feel their power and their privilege being usurped by women. Brutal rapes in India have been in the news numerous times in recent months. Following on the heels of two women who were raped, one of whom died from her injuries, is the report of a five-year-old girl in New Delhi raped and left in critical condition by a neighbor.[166] The growing outrage expressed by men and women against these rapes and their underlying causes, both in India and across the globe, is the only thing that might suggest something positive could result from this brutality. The brutal gang rapes of women, the sexual and verbal assaults minimized as "eve-teasing," are representative of this type of violence. But wife battery and dowry deaths are more situated in family and economic patterns, sometimes deeply traditional, sometimes reflecting the economic changes tied to globalization. In a study on the relationship between female autonomy and wife battery, Jejeebhoy found that a few factors play a very powerful role in influencing wife beating and that these vary by region.[167] Education protects women from beating overall, but in the highly patriarchal setting of Uttar Pradesh, a region she compared with

Tamil Nadu (both rural, both poor), the woman had to achieve a higher educational level to benefit from its protection. Autonomy, while protecting women in the south, had less of an impact in the more patriarchal north where women were more likely to be secluded.[168] More generally, many studies suggest that Indian women are denied the opportunity to build their own social support systems but must rely on their husbands' families instead, a practice that dovetails with the emphasis on keeping the family together at all costs, no matter the frustrations and difficulties.[169] Women who had control of their resources including their dowry were less likely to be beaten than those who did not. This speaks to the importance of the meaning and definition of income, as pointed out by Nazli Kibria in a study of female factory workers in Bangladesh. Kibria found that urban working-class women pooled their income with other family members, leaving them with no control and also ideologically justifying the patriarchal structure of the patriarchal family structure. Yet lower-middle-class women working in these same factories who did maintain control of their money nonetheless supported the view of their husbands as having the ability to fulfill their provider roles by defining their income as "extra" or "supplementary." Simply put, it is not the money but the meaning attached to the money that makes a difference in women's autonomy in the family and in society.[170] While female autonomy plays an important role in preventing violence, it is much more powerful when there are culturally supported egalitarian relationships between women and men.

Dowry deaths, then, occur against a backdrop of patriarchal power, a joint family system, changes in the economic conditions globally, changes in class and caste systems, religion, culture and tradition, and geographic location. Within this context, Natarajan suggests that we should also pay attention to characteristics at the familial and personal levels.[171] The arranged marriage system brokered by third parties—bringing together two people who hardly know each other, often separating the woman from her social supports, maintaining her and her family as subordinates—contributes to the problem.[172] Added to that is the possibility that a woman's family, desperate to make a good match, may promise more than they can deliver, and the man's family, knowing they have other options, and wanting to compensate for the money they have invested in his educational and economic success, may press the bride's family to keep giving or to give more. Further, the personal characteristics of the couple and their living situation may contribute to the problem. The woman is young, has little experience with autonomy or independence, and he may be weak, have low self-confidence, a drinking problem, or be emotionally dependent on his family. If he drinks, harasses her, abuses her, has affairs, is generally disagreeable, she may not feel she has any options—to return to her family is to disgrace them, to leave him is to make herself unmarriageable in a country where unmarried women have extremely low status, she may not have a place to go or any money, and so her unbearable stress and misery could lead to her taking rat poison or committing suicide through hanging or drowning. Or he may douse her in kerosene and light her on fire. He runs a low risk of being apprehended, and if apprehended, he is unlikely to be punished or to have a long sentence; thus, murdering her solves family problems as well as economic ones.[173] After the death of his wife, the man is free to improve his material position by marrying another woman with a more attractive dowry.

The root cause of violence, beneath all of these other factors, both structural and personal, is women's powerlessness, and while there may be variations by geographical region, religion, and economic status, this remains a powerful predictor of assaults on women, whether they result in dowry death or whether they simply continue in marriage as a pattern of violence.

HONOR CRIMES

"Honor crimes" are a form of state-sanctioned murder of women. Like FGM, these atrocities committed against women are based on their sexuality and what that means to men. Women are seen as hypersexual beings who have to be controlled and oppressed in order to protect the social system. Their base sexuality is viewed as easily destroying the power of the men in their families. Sexual relations with an unacceptable man or even gossip about the woman's behavior brings dishonor to the family and can bring death to the daughter. Even when the woman or girl is the victim of rape or incest committed by her father or a brother, she is the person dirtied and the one who is viewed as destroying the family's honor.

Perhaps the most widely known case of an honor crime was that of Amina Lawal, a young woman who was condemned to death for committing adultery by a northern Nigerian Islamic high court, a sentence that was upheld by the Nigerian Supreme Court in 2003. She was to be buried up to her neck and then stoned to death, a sentence that was heartbreakingly delayed for a month so that she could continue to nurse her baby. She had the baby daughter more than nine months after divorcing her husband, a clear indication of nonmarital sex. The presumed father denied any relationship with her and was acquitted for lack of evidence. Amid international outrage, Amnesty International led a campaign to save her life.[174] Her attorney decided to return to traditional Islam courts in search of justice, and her conviction was overturned on the basis that she was not given the opportunity to properly defend herself. In a unique defense, her attorney offered the explanation of "sleeping embryo" to the court, which they evidently saw as possibly explaining how her husband from whom she had been divorced for two years could have been the father.

Why is the effort to control female sexuality and the obsession with female sexual purity so widespread and virulent? One author, in an informal and thoughtful discussion of this topic, situates the efforts to control in the system of patriarchal hypergamy in which she serves as a bridge between her family and a higher-status family.[175] In a wide range of societies, the purity of women reflects the honor and status of their families, resulting in extreme limitations on the women and severe punishments for breaking social and sexual controls. These controls are embedded in the highly stratified state as lower-status families seek upward mobility through the marriage of their daughter to a higher-status man, leading to the obsession with women's honor. This system of hypergamy, in which lower-status women almost always marry higher Status men, creates vertical alliances in stratified societies between male-headed groups[176] and requires the purity of women to enhance their economic value. The virginity of women stands for their inner worthiness, symbolizing exclusiveness and inaccessibility, and more importantly, the purity of women stands for the worthiness of their family.[177] Her status as pure or polluted either allows the male head of the family to make the desired vertical moves in the stratified system or prevents him from doing so.

Since a family's honor is confirmed by a daughter's marriage into a family of the appropriate status, the behavior of unmarried girls is strictly monitored by the girl's father. Steve Derne interviewed Hindu men who talked with him about their control of women.[178] They point out that in order to protect the marriage prospects of their daughters, they severely limited their interactions with unrelated boys and men. Often as early as age five or six, the daughters are prohibited from playing with boys; they must "remain inside the home. The outside is closed to them."[179] One of the reasons girls are married so young, often resulting in severe health and reproductive problems, is the anxiety their fathers have about their virginity. They are, as a result, often married to much older men, have babies at a very young age, and experience severe complications.[180] Fathers of girls who are married off at young ages say they do that to protect them from pollution from unacceptable males or in some instances to prevent them from being raped by men with AIDS, who believe that having sexual intercourse with a "fresh girl" will cure AIDS and other venereal diseases.[181] Such a justification for rape as "the Virgin Cure" is widespread not only in India but also in South Africa today, resulting in rape being a virtual death sentence for millions of women.[182]

In his study of honor crimes in an Arab Muslim society, Kressel situates the honor demands on the woman, based on her purity, within the context of a stratification system in which the purity of the daughter is a matter of importance in reference to groups above or below the family on the status scale.[183] Mobility of family groups comes through matching in marriage, and since the kin group forms the infrastructure of the social, political, and economic activities, the family group has a significant economic and status stake in the propriety of the daughter. In fact, their restrictions and control of her become stronger and more restrictive as mobility and change occur in the hierarchical positions of the family. Social change or the possibility of change then increases the importance of the girl's purity to the family, and the surveillance of her becomes greater and the consequences for breaking the norms more sure and more severe. Kressel suggests that when a family is actively competing with others for superior social standing, the family's honor, and consequently the daughter's life, is most at risk.[184]

It is, of course, true that with all the concern over the woman's honor, she does not in fact really have honor as such. When she is violated or when she acts or is suspected of acting in a sexually inappropriate manner, it is the honor of her father and her brothers that is damaged. When she is killed by them, it is not her honor but their honor that is regained. While they are responsible for maintaining the honor of the family or clan, they can only do so through control of her behavior.[185] Women's and girls' sexual modesty and chastity are therefore essential components of a family's honor but not their own honor, of which they really have none separately.

Kressel provides a context within which to see the obsession with woman's honor and moves us away from a strict functionalist argument into an analysis of the situation.[186] He describes honor murders as rare, carried out by the members of the woman's or girl's family, and planned by the group whose honor has been violated by her behavior or by something that happened to her (like rape).[187] The reason for the murder is forbidden association with a man, not specifically the protection of virginity, although the test of virginity is critical, and not a few women have been put to death immediately after their weddings because they were suspected of not being virgins. The only certain way of restoring a family's honor is murder, a private act carried out by the family that sends a signal to the community and is influenced by aspirations of social mobility. Murder can enhance the prestige of the family and can be likened to a "planned investment in improving" rather than maintaining social status.[188] Family members must execute the killing in such a way that it communicates to the public that the killing is an honor killing, but so that they are nevertheless protected from arrest and imprisonment. Hence, it is constructed as an accident, leaving signs that can be read by the community as murder. Kessler suggests that honor crimes are almost always premeditated, based on economic and prestige considerations.[189] The law in some of the countries in which honor crimes take place seems to acknowledge these types of crimes and to separate them from another form of honor crime in which a man or brother is simply outraged and emotionally out of control at the knowledge that his female relative has been or is being adulterous.[190] In these cases, some states, such as Jordan, simply forgive the crime.[191] Premeditated honor crimes are taken a bit more seriously but are understandable to the court and treated as a minor offense.

Most women in traditional societies are not beaten or killed for damaging the honor of their family or husband. Rather, the honor code communicates to all women the power of the male and legitimates violence against women, institutionalizes it so that women control their own behavior to avoid the fate that awaits them if they damage family honor. Honor justifies patriarchal family arrangements and male control of women's bodies and lives. And women are very likely to uphold the dominant values even as they are likely to be their victims.

Rana Husseini, an activist reporter in Jordan, which has the highest recorded rate of honor killings in the world,[192] interviewed both old and young women, including the sisters of a young woman who had been murdered by her father and brother. The neighbors, the parents, and the sisters all found her guilty and deserving of death because she had run away with her boyfriend, of whom her parents disapproved.[193] An exception to this attitude is the case of the female relatives of Hamda Abu Ghanem, an 18-year-old girl living in Ramla, Israel, killed by her brother for refusing to marry a man her family had arranged for her. Her female relatives, including her mother, broke the silence, going to the police. The case may go unsolved, however, since the eyewitness who initially came forth has disappeared. Hamda's mother said, even if the son could not be convicted of the murder as a result, she would not have him back. She needed "ten years for my soul to dry out."[194]

While the theories presented by Kressel and by Ortner provide an understanding of why the girl is vulnerable to death when she violates the strict sexual norms, they do not adequately explain the preliminary question: Why is the value of a woman tied so intimately to her purity, and why is the family honor dependent on her purity rather than, for example, her intelligence or the father's ability to arm-wrestle his opponent to the ground?

Baker, Gregware, and Cassidy remark that "honor" is a useful fiction in preserving male dominance.[195] It justifies repressive control measures for women inside the home and restricts their participation outside the home. Women are critical symbols of group identity, and their honor defines group boundaries; it holds the males in a community together and establishes their commonality against outsiders.[196] An article in the *San Francisco Chronicle* clarified the role women play in maintaining the relationship between members of a kinship group and others outside that group.[197] An 18-year-old woman was to be part of the compensation provided a clan in return for killing another clan leader. She refused. She wanted to finish high school, to "learn to be a typist." She took refuge from her angry relatives in another city. In the Konumbuka clan of New Guinea, of which she is a member, women are a commodity, an object, but as one archaeologist insists, a "sacred object."[198] He explains that the mother is the base of the family tree, with the brothers being root people. The daughter is a cutting when given in marriage, and when she has children, one or more of them is expected to be returned to the original family. It is owed, or she is owed back to the base family. Her refusal to go challenged the entire social order of the tribe. Her attorney sees this as a landmark case in women's rights. "Women," she says, "are not animals."[199] The young woman, in breaking custom, defying tradition, asserts herself as a valuable person rather than a commodity to be bartered.

Some have argued that honor is gender neutral since men are sometimes the victims. However, Rupa Reddy argues, women are treated much more harshly than men, are much less able to escape, to leave the situation, and since the woman is often sought out first, the man has time to effect an escape.[200] Further, the complicit man may be collateral damage in the perpetrator's need to regain honor—killing him would not reinstate honor. And since masculinity is constructed in terms of male honor and female chastity, his honor is reflected in her shame, which can only be washed away by the eradication of the woman, the source of the shame.[201]

Cultural beliefs, we have seen, are powerful determinants of behavior. One can assess the power of culture while still not dismissing cruelty in its name. One can see the power of culture while not advocating that it be used as justification for sexual terrorism against women. In Jordan, Kulwicki reports, of the women who were murdered in one year, all of them were listed as "honor crimes." And the impact of culture on the legal system can be seen in the penalties meted out to the defendants: the lightest sentences went to those whose victims were pregnant. These penalties ranged from no penalty whatsoever to a maximum of six months in prison.[202] Some people have likened these murders of women who have committed adultery or who have become pregnant out of wedlock as akin to crimes of passion as they are codified in the law in the United States.[203] There are some similarities, both allowing the defendant to claim some form of "temporary insanity," but while this may lead to a reduced sentence in the United States, the Jordanian law excuses the murderer if he sees the wife or daughter having sex. While the United States may excuse the husband, Jordanian law expands the number who can be offended to include brothers, sons, even cousins.[204] While the crime of passion defense in the United States reflects sexist beliefs about marriage and masculinity and femininity, it stops short of the law in Jordan that excuses men who kill.

Honor crimes stand at the intersection of multiple political and social dynamics and are, in keeping with Third World feminist critique, not simply a reflection of culture.[205] Dicle Kogscioglu argues that when these crimes are attributed to codes of honor or tradition, analysts lose sight of institutional structures that support them. Once tradition is invoked, the role of the institutions is diminished, and inquiry need not be made into the way institutions function to support such crimes.[206] This view is shared by Reddy, who suggests that if the courts, in particular, view "honour crimes" as a cultural tradition rather than gender-based violence, the wider spectrum of gender violence and the rights of women can be ignored.[207] With the "utterance of tradition," questions about violence against women fade,[208] yet it is only within the context of patriarchal violence against women that honor-based murders can be understood.[209] Gill concludes that "men victimize and abuse women in their communities entirely to sustain their dominance within the social system."[210] In Turkey, legal codes, such as article 462 and article 51, have allowed leniency if a family member kills a woman suspected of sexual misconduct. Article 51 allows a reduction in sentence by two-thirds if a suspect committed murder because of "uncontrollable grief" or as a result of "provocation," and article 462, which was revoked in order for Turkey to join the European Union, allowed that it was provocation if the perpetrator had discovered or was convinced that one of his first-degree relatives was involved in an illicit relationship.[211] The emphasis placed on "family honor" as opposed to the woman's life and well-being is made clear in text and legal practice allowing the legal system to be complicit in upholding or promoting the view of honor as purely cultural.[212] And cultural stereotyping and disregard for patriarchal norms leads to miscarriages of justice in other countries where the immigrant perpetrator almost always relies on a culturally based defense. Reddy provides an interesting example of a court case in the United Kingdom. Shabri Hussein killed his sister-in-law, Tasleem Begum, by running over her with his car and then reversing over her body. The judge said, "something blew up in your head that caused you a complete and sudden loss of control—something deeply offensive to someone with your background and your religious belief." He then gave Hussein a reduced sentence as a result of these "mitigating factors."[213]

While "honor" and purity and shame all figure powerfully in cases of murder for honor, Phyllis Chesler warns that we need to differentiate two types of honor.[214] Fifty-eight percent of the women who are murdered worldwide are murdered for being "too Western," she says, or for resisting or disobeying cultural and religious expectations. These women are young, with the average age being 17. These young women, Chesler says, are too independent, not subservient enough, not willing to wear Islamic clothing, wanting educations and careers, choosing their own boyfriend or not willing to marry a cousin or someone else chosen by their family, or perhaps, leaving an abusive husband. Of course, the men are welcome to adopt Western dress and practices, such as using cell phones, driving, flying, and hanging out on the streets or in cafes. These women are likely to be killed by a member of their family, the father almost always being involved, and they are likely to be tortured as well. Fewer than half of the murdered women worldwide were killed for committing an alleged "sexual impropriety,"[215] such as being raped or having an extramarital affair or being promiscuous, while 57 percent of those in Muslim countries were murdered for this reason.[216] These women were likely to be older, the average age being 37, and were less likely to be tortured by their family. These killings, she says, are more likely to resemble Western-style domestic femicide. Although Chesler sees these two categories as different, and there is a significant age gap between them, it seems clear that both are based on the desire to maintain male power and privilege and reinforce the subordination and powerlessness of women. The difference she sees between honor crimes and murder of women, especially wives, in the West is that in the West these murders do not so blatantly reflect a cultural and religiously justified isolation and subordination of women. Yet, I would argue that while murder of a wife, indeed, may be an uncommon extreme, when it is committed out of a desire to own or control, it does reflect cultural values of male superiority and control, even though these are far more likely to be promoted through battery, harassment, rape, and assault.

In each of the areas discussed above, we have seen that reliance on the justice system may be ineffective or in fact dangerous to women. In the case of Amina Lawal, the Sharia court imposed a death sentence for adultery, and the Nigerian Supreme Court upheld it.[217] Kogscioglu noted this same problem in Turkey,[218] and Greenberg too suggests that overreliance on the justice system in the case of dowry deaths is not only ineffective but can be dangerous to women, drawing on assumptions about marital maladjustment, providing conciliation courts, ignoring the vast majority of battery.[219] Similarly, overreliance on the criminal justice system, in the case of honor crimes, ignores the convergence of social, political, and economic structures that lead to the systemic devaluation of women that puts them in danger in the first place. Focus on the criminal justice system also ignores women's particular vulnerability within immigrant communities situated in a dominant culture where police may not offer necessary protection.

CONCLUSION

All of these forms of violence against women are acts of terrorism. And while there is hope for change, especially in the area of female genital mutilation, in other instances the problem remains or is growing. The case can be made that these forms of violence are on the rise and that the increase is not only due to increased attention or increased reporting but to changes in global political and economic factors. The cultural relativist cannot claim them as mere cultural variations or expressions. The fact that girls and women are the targets of such practices as infibulation and murder in the name of family honor and dowry deaths makes them specifically crimes against women. The patriarchal organization of these societies, the powerlessness of women economically and politically, and the cultural beliefs that claim women's bodies as symbols of male power maim and kill girls and women. Any discussion of cultural practices that does not specifically address the misogyny that undergirds these practices is at the very least dishonest.

Women who are the victims of dowry deaths and honor crimes are plagued by the indiscriminate response to their offense and the ability of others to minimize the atrocity and trivialize its impact. In the case of female mutilation, women are vulnerable not because of something they have done or are suspected of doing but because they are women. The impact is the same: the overwhelming destruction of woman based on her sexuality. Sexual terrorism when practiced as a custom by a state, or when commonplace within a state despite legal restrictions or prohibitions, is terrorism taken to a new and more dangerous level and should be, as Karp suggests, named a *genitort* rather than a cultural idiosyncrasy.[220]

Despite the extreme danger women face in many cultures, there is hesitance to define these dangerous practices as violence or crimes against women for fear that we will be self-righteously imposing ethnocentric norms from Western industrialized countries on other cultures. Over 80 million girls, particularly in the Middle East, Africa, and Southeast Asia, have been the victims of genital mutilation. Women in Iran are beaten to death for suspected adultery. Women in Pakistan have acid thrown in their faces by spurned suitors, and female infants in India are quietly killed by the midwife who delivered them. To name these as cultural variations and thereby withdraw judgment from them is to support the continued oppression of women. Yet the notion of cultural relativity does just that, and the view that certain behaviors are simply characteristic of certain subcultures or cultures reinforces our avoidance of significant human rights problems. Social science, with its emphasis on value neutrality, has also contributed to the silence of researchers about the oppression of women worldwide, whether we are talking about infanticide in China, the malnutrition of girls in India, or the oppression of women in Afghanistan under the Taliban. Some are even reluctant to intervene in the cultural practice of female "circumcision" among immigrant groups in the United States.[221] Cultural values and perceptions, when internalized by women and incorporated into the everyday practices of teachers, parents, employers, and lawmakers, legitimate the oppression of women and present their victimization as ordinary, natural, and deserved. The violence they experience is thus both ordinary and unspeakable.

NOTES

1. D. Jehl, "Arab Honor's Price: A Woman's Blood," *New York Times*, June 20, 1999, 9, http://www.nytimes.com/1999/06/20/world/for-shame-a-special-report-arab-honor-s-price-a-woman-s-blood.html?src=pm

2. "Reports From Africa and Middle East: Jordan; Finally a Campaign Against 'Honor Killings,'" *Women's International Network*, 25, no. 4 (1999): 54.

3. S. Rajalcaruna, *Report on FGM for the UN Special Rapporteaur on Violence against Women* (Unpublished working paper, 1999): 1.

4. J. Burns, "Though Illegal, Child Marriage Popular in Parts of India," *New York Times*, May 11, 1998: A8.

5. A. Hitchcock, "Rising Number of Dowry Deaths in India," World Socialist Web Site. July 4, 2001, http://www.wsws.org/articles/2001/jul2001/ind-j04.shtml, retrieved July 5, 2013.

6. F. Hosken, "Women, Violence and Human Rights," *WIN News* 18, no. 2 (1992): 1.

7. H. Lyons, "Anthropologists, Moralities, and Relativities: The Problem of Genital Mutilations," *Canadian Review of Sociology and Anthropology* 18, no. 4 (1981): 499–517.

8. M. Daly, *Gyn/Ecology: The Metaethics of Radical Feminism* (Boston: Beacon Press, 1978).

9. S. James, "Reconciling International Human Rights and Cultural Relativism: The Case of Female Circumcision," *Bioethics* 8, no. 1 (1994): 1–26.

10. R. Morgan (ed.), *Sisterhood Is Global: The International Women's Movement Anthology* (New York: Feminist Press, 1996).

11. C. Mohanty, "Feminist Encounters: Locating the Politics of Experience," cited in "Feminism, Women's Rights, and Cultural Differences," *Hypatia—A Journal of Feminist Philosophy* 13, edited by S. Okin (1998): 42–52.

12. Ibid., 43.

13. Quoted in Rajalcaruna, *Report on FGM*, 209.

14. Ibid., 11.

15. Ibid., 1

16. Ibid., 17.

17. Rajalcaruna, *Report on FGM.*

18. S. Okin, "Feminism, Women's Human Rights, and Cultural Differences"; see also A. Karp, "Genitorts in the Global Context: Female Genital Mutilation as a Tort under the Alien Tort Claims Act, the Torture Victim Protection Act, and the Foreign Sovereign Immunities Act," *Women's Rights Law Reporter* 18 (1997): 315–22.

19. Okin, "Feminism, Women's Human Rights, and Cultural Differences."

20. Karp, "Genitorts in the Global Context."

21. Letter to the Editor, *New York Times*, November 24, 1993.

22. S. Garkawe, *The Impact of the Doctrine of Cultural Relativism in the Australian Legal System,* 1995, http://www.murdoch.edu.au/elaw/issues/v2nl/garkawe.txt

23. Karp, "Genitorts in the Global Context."

24. S. McLean, "Female Circumcision, Excision, and Infibulation: The Facts and Proposals for Change: Minority Rights Group," in *Report*

to the U.N. Sub-Committee on the Prevention of Discrimination and the Protection of Minorities, 1980.

25. See Federal Prohibition of Female Genital Mutilation. H.R. 3247. Introduced by Patricia Schroeder, 1993.

26. See, for example, UNICEF's Innocenti Research Centre's work, including G. Mackie and J. LeJeune, "Social Dynamics of Abandonment of Harmful Practices: A New Look at Theory," *Innocenti Working Papers. Special Series on Social Norms and Harmful Practices.* 2009 (IWP 2009-06).

27. G. Mackie, "Ending Footbinding and Infibulation: A Convention Account," *American Sociological Review* 61, no. 6 (December 1996): 999–1017.

28. H. Gates, "Bound Feet: How Sexy Were They?" *History of the Family* 13, no. 1 (2008): 58–70.

29. Ibid., 62.

30. Mackie, "Ending Footbinding and Infibulation," 1000; S. Greenhalgh, "Bound Feet, Hobbled Lives: Women in Old China," *Frontiers: A Journal of Women Studies* 2, no.1 (Spring 1977): 7–21, p. 8 cited.

31. Mackie, "Ending Footbinding and Infibulation."

32. Ibid., 1010.

33. Daly, *Gyn/Ecology.*

34. Gates, "Bound Feet: How Sexy Were They?"

35. Ibid., 61.

36. Gates, "Bound Feet: How Sexy Were They?"

37. D. Ko, Cinderella's Sisters: A Revisionist History of Footbinding, (Berkeley: University of California Press, 2007).

38. D. Ko, "Cinderella's Sisters: A Revisionist History of Footbinding." Reviewed by Charlotte Furth, The China Quarterly, 189, March (2007): 219.

39. Ko, *Cinderella's Sisters.*

40. M. Jian, "China's Barbaric One-Child Policy," *The Guardian,* May 5, 2013, http://www.guardian.co.uk/books/2013/may/06/chinas -barbaric-one-child-policy

41. Greenhalgh, "Bound Feet, Hobbled Lives."

42. M. Brown, "Changing Authentic Identities: Evidence From Taiwan and China." *Journal of the Royal Anthropological Institute* (N.S.) 16, no. 3 (2010): 459–79.

43. Ko, "The Body as Attire."

44. Gates, "Bound Feet: How Sexy Were They?"

45. H. Gates, "Footloose in Fujian: Economic Correlates of Footbinding," *Comparative Studies in Society and History* 43, no. 1 (January 2001): 130–48.

46. Ibid.

47. Ibid.

48. Ibid., 130.

49. Gates, "Footloose in Fujian."

50. Ibid., 144–45.

51. Gates, "Footloose in Fujian," 147.

52. Ko, "The Body as Attire," 5.

53. Greenhalgh, "Bound Feet, Hobbled Lives," 16.

54. Gates, "Footloose in Fujian," 157.

55. Ibid., 140.

56. Mackie, "Ending Footbinding and Infibulation."

57. Ibid., 1010.

58. Ibid., 1011.

59. For example, see C. Foster, "On the Trail of a Taboo; Rajalcaruna," *Report on FGM*; and A. Karp, "Genitorts in Global Context."

60. S. M. James and C. C. Robertson, eds., *Genital Cutting and Transnational Sisterhood: Disputing U.S. Polemics* (Urbana: University of Illinois Press, 2002).

61. S. Johnsdotter, "Projected Cultural Histories of the Cutting of Female Genitalia: A Poor Reflection as in a Mirror," *History and Anthropology* 23, no. 1 (March 2012): 91–114.

62. A. Bunting, "Theorizing Women's Cultural Diversity in Feminist International Human Rights Strategies," *Journal of Law and Society* 20, no. 1 (1993): 6–22.

63. Ibid.

64. Ibid.

65. Rajalcaruna, *Report on FGM*, 10.

66. Ibid.

67. Ibid.

68. Ibid.

69. M. Etienne, "Addressing Gender-Based Violence in an International Context," *Harvard Women's Law Journal* 18 (1995): 143–44.

70. D. Williams and W. Acosta, "Female Genital Mutilation in the United States: Implications for Women's Health," *American Journal of Health Studies* 15, no. 1 (1991): 47–52.

71. H. Mohamed, in "A Future without Female Genital Mutilation." September 2, 2009, *World Pulse*. http://worldpulse.com/node/12114

72. H. Lightfoot-Klein, "The Sexual Experience and Marital Adjustment of Genitally Circumcised and Infibulated Females in the Sudan," *Journal of Sex Research* 26, no. 3 (1989): 375–92.

73. Johnsdotter, "Projected Cultural Histories of the Cutting of Female Genitalia," 103.

74. Ibid., 104.

75. Ibid., 108.

76. C. Foster, "On the Trail of a Taboo: Female Circumcision in the Islamic World," *Contemporary Review* 264, no. 1540 (1994): 244, 246.

77. S. Andersson, J. Rymer, D. W. Joyce, C. Momoh, and C. M. Gayle, "Sexual Quality of Life in Women Who Have Undergone Female Genital Mutilation: A Case-Control Study," *British Journal of Gynaecology: An International Journal of Obstetrics and Gynaecology* 19, no. 13 (December 2012): 1606–11.

78. N. Toubia, *Female Genital Mutilation: A Call for Global Action* (New York: Women Ink, 1994).

79. R. H. Jensen, "Mimi Ramsey: For Selflessly Striving, Despite Her Own Pain, to End the Mutilation of Young Girls," *Ms.*, January-February, 1996: 51–52.

80. N. Toubia, *Female Genital Mutilation.*

81. L. Kouba and J. Muasher, "Female Circumcision in Africa: An Overview," *African Studies Review* 28, no. 1 (1995), 95–110; see also L. Lindsey, *Gender Roles: A Sociological Perspective* (Upper Saddle River, NJ: Prentice-Hall, 1997): 153–54.

82. M. Daly, *Gyn/Ecology,* 159.

83. B. Ehrenreich and D. English, *For Her Own Good* (Garden City, NY: Doubleday-Anchor, 1978): 111.

84. Ibid., 111–12.

85. L. Burstyn, "Female Circumcision Comes to America," *Atlantic Monthly*, October 1995, 30.

86. I. Utz-Billing and H. Kentenich, "Female Genital Mutilation: An Injury, Physical and Mental Harm," *Journal of Psychosomatic Obstetrics & Gynecology* 29, no. 4 (2008): 225–29.

87. Burstyn, "Female Circumcision Comes to America," 34.

88. Foster, "On the Trail of a Taboo."

89. Ibid.

90. A. Walker and P. Parmar, producers, *Warrior Marks.* Film directed by Pratibha Parmar (New York: Women Make Movies, 1993).

91. H. Simpsa, "Female Genital Cutting: Current Practices and Beliefs in Western Africa," *Bulletin of the World Health Organization* 90, no. 2 (2012): 120–27. F.doi 10.2471/BLT.11.090886

92. Ibid.

93. Ibid.

94. Ibid.

95. Foster, "On the Trail of a Taboo."

96. Simpsa, "Female Genital Cutting."

97. N. Toubia, "Female Circumcision as a Public Health Issue," *New England Journal of Medicine* 331, no. 11 (1994): 712–16; see also Toubia, *Female Genital Mutilation.*

98. L. P. Wiefueh, "Spread and Distribution of Female Genital Mutilation in Liberia: Genital and Sexual Mutilation of Females," *WIN News* 19, no. 2 (1993): 46.

99. Karp, "Genitorts in the Global Context."

100. M. Cooper, "Women and Human Rights: Is the Global Anti-Violence Campaign Succeeding?," *The CQ Researcher* 9, no. 16 (April 30, 1999): 353–376.

101. F. Hosken, "Female Sexual Mutilation," *WIN News* 19, no. 1 (1993): 34. Hosken is one of the most outspoken and widely published writers on FGM; see also F. Hosken, "Actions to Stop the Spread of FGM," *WIN News* 19, no. 4 (1993).

102. Karp, "Genitorts in Global Context."

103. *Kadie v. Karadzic,* 70 F. 3rd 232 (2nd Cir. 1995) petition for rehearing, denied. 74 F. 3rd 377 (2nd Cir. 1996), p. 321 in Karp, "Genitorts in Global Context."

104. Karp, "Genitorts in the Global Context."

105. C. Dugger, "Congress Bans Genital Rite," *New York Times*, October 12, 1996, A1.

106. M. Simons, "Mutilation of Girl's Genitals: Ethnic Gulf in French Court." http://www.nytimes.com/1993/11/23/world/mutilation-of-girls-genitals-ethnic-gulf-in-french-court.html

107. S. Wasserman, "Mutilation Fear Wins Halt to Deportation," *USA Today,* March 24, 1994, 3A.

108. Walker and Parmar, *Warrior Marks*, film.

109. A. Walker, *Possessing the Secret of Joy* (New York: Simon & Schuster, 1992).

110. M. Merwine, "How Africa Understands Female Circumcision," *New York Times,* November 24, 1993, A14.

111. "Eradication of Female Genital Mutilation in Somalia," http://www.unicef.org/somalia.Retrieved July 5, 2013.

112. Ibid.

113. Sudanese Government Legalized the Sunna Form of Female Genital Mutilation. E-joussour.net/en/node/3705

114. Web post by Eirin, "Efforts to Eradicate Female Genital Mutilation (FGM)," http://itbeginswithme.wordpress.com/2009/10/23/efforts-to-eradicate-female-genital-mutilation-fgm/ (Oct. 23, 2009).

115. E. Gargan, "For Many Brides in India, a Dowry Buys Death," *New York Times*, December 20, 1993, A5.

116. L. Visaria, "Violence against Women in India: Evidence from Rural Gujarat" in *Domestic Violence in India: A Summary Report of Three Studies.* International Center for Research on Women, Washington, D.C. (1999): 9–17.

117. Ibid., 12.

118. Point No. 17, Dowry Deaths, http://www.ncrb.nic.in/cii2008/Statistics2008.pdf&page=17

119. Government of India.1986. The Dowry Prohibition Act. 1961 (Act no. 28 of 1961) and Connected Legislation (as January 15, 1986). New Delhi: Government of India.

120. J. G. Greenberg, "Criminalizing Dowry Deaths: The Indian Experience," *American University Journal of Gender, Social Policy & the Law* 11, no. 2 (2003) 801–846, http://222.lexisnexis.com.innopac.library.unr.edu

121. Ibid.

122. Ibid.

123. Ibid.

124. M. N. Srinivas, *Some Reflections on Dowry* (Delhi: Oxford University Press, 1984); see also N. R. M. Menon, "The Dowry Prohibition Act: Does the Law Provide the Solution or Itself Constitute the Problem?" in *Social Audit of Dowry Legislation,* edited by S. C. Bahtia (Delhi: Legal Literacy Project, 1988), 11–26.

125. R. P. Dobash and R. E. Dobash, *Women, Violence and Social Change* (New York: Routledge, 1992).

126. J. Van Willigen and V. C. Channa, "Law, Custom, and Crimes against Women: The Problem of Dowry Death in India," *Human Organization* 50, no. 4 (1991).

127. "Disposal of Cases by Court," National Crime Records Bureau Report, retrieved June 20, 2013.

128. M. Jordan, "Female Infanticide Remains Common in Indian Villages," *Wall Street Journal*, May 9, 2000, 1.

129. M. Jordan, "Among Poor Villagers, Female Infanticide Still Flourishes in India," *Wall Street Journal*, May 9, 2000, Al, A12

130. Greenberg, "Criminalizing Dowry Deaths."

131. Ibid.

132. Ibid., 822.

133. Ibid., 819.

134. Visaria, "Violence against Women in India."

135. "Is Dowry the Real Killer," *Manushi* 5 (1989): 8.

136. Visaria, "Violence against Women in India."

137. Mahajan in Visaria, "Violence against Women," 2.

138. L. Stone and C. James, "Dowry, Bride Burning, and Female Power in India," *Women's Studies International Forum* 18, no. 2 (March–April 1995): 125–94.

139. Greenberg, "Criminalizing Dowry Deaths."

140. Ibid.

141. Ibid., 14.

142. S. J. Jejeebhoy, "Wife-Beating in Rural India: A Husband's Right? Evidence from Survey Data," *Economic and Political Weekly* 33, no. 15 (April 11–17, 1998): 855–62.

143. Ibid., 855.

144. Stone and James, "Dowry, Bride Burning, and Female Power in India."

145. Jejeebhoy, "Wife-Beating in Rural India," 857.

146. R. Kandath, "Wife Beating: The Statistics Tell a Story of Pain," *The Times of India*, August 22, 2001.

147. Gargan, "For Many Brides in India, a Dowry Buys Death."

148. Kandath, "Wife Beating: The Statistics Tell a Story of Pain."

149. Van Willigen and Channa, "Law, Custom, and Crimes against Women."

150. Ibid.

151. Stone and James, "Dowry, Bride Burning, and Female Power in India."

152. Ibid.

153. Ibid., 126.

154. M. Kishwar, "Dowry—To Ensure Her Happiness or to Disinherit Her?" *Manushi* 34 (May–June 1986): 6–7.

155. Ibid

156. Van Willigen and Channa, "Law, Custom, and Crimes against Women."

157. Ibid.

158. Stone and James, "Dowry, Bride Burning, and Female Power in India."

159. Ibid.

160. J. Burns, "Though Illegal, Child Marriage Is Popular in Parts of India," *New York Times,* May 11, 1998, A8. The extent to which a girl is a burden in the family is revealed by the number of female infanticides that occur in India and the devastation suffered by widows; see also J. Burns, "Once Widowed in India, Twice Scorned," *New York Times*, May 9, 2000, Al.

161. J. Burns, "Female Infanticide Flourishes in India's Poor Villages," *Wall Street Journal*, May 9, 2000, Al.

162. Burns, "Though Illegal, Child Marriage Popular in Parts of India."

163. Van Willigen and Channa, "Law, Custom, and Crimes against Women," 371.

164. http://www.wsws.org/articles/2001/jul2001/ind-j04.shtmlis

165. M. French, *The War against Women* (New York: Summit Books, 1992).

166. G. Harris, "Rape of 5-Year-Old Girl Sets Off New Furor in India," *New York Times*, April 21, 2013: A4. http://www.nytimes.com/2013/04/21/world/asia/reports-of-rape-of-5-year-old-in-india-set-off-furor.html

167. Jejeebhoy, "Wife-Beating in Rural India: A Husband's Right?"

168. Ibid.

169. D. Jacobsen and S. S. Wadley, *Women in India: Two Perspectives* (New Delhi: Manohar, 1987).

170. N. Kibria, "Culture, Social Class, and Income Control in the Lives of Women Garment Workers in Bangladesh," *Gender and Society* 9. no. 3 (June 1995): 289–309.

171. M. Natarajan, "Victimization of Women: A Theoretical Perspective on Dowry Deaths In India," *International Review of Victimology* 3, no. 4 (1995): 297–308.

172. Ibid.

173. Van Willigen and Channa, "Law, Custom, and Crimes against Women."

174. Amina Lawal's story. "Nigerian Woman Is Acquitted," *New York Times,* September 26, 2003, A3.

175. S. Ortner, *Making Gender: The Politics and Erotics of Culture* (Boston: Beacon Press, 1996).

176. R. Husseini, "Murder the Name of Honor." OneWorld Oxford, 2009: 101–56.

177. M. Roulet, "Dowry and Prestige in North India," *Contributions to Indian Society* 30, no. 1 (May 1996): 89–107.

178. S. Derne, "Hindu Men Talk about Controlling Women: Cultural Ideas as a Tool of the Powerful," *Sociological Perspectives* 37, no. 2 (1994): 203–27.

179. Ibid.

180. Ibid.

181. "HIV/AIDS, The Stats, The Virgin Cure and Infant Rape," http://www.science in Africa.com.

182. Rajalcaruna, *Report on FGM.*

183. G. Kressel, "Sororicide/Filiacide: Homicide for Family Honour," *Current Anthropology* 22, no. 2 (1981): 141–58.

184. Ibid.

185. F. Hoskin, "Jordan: Killings of Women for Traditional 'Family Honor,'" *WIN News* 25, no. 1 (1999): 51.

186. Kressel, "Sororicide/Filiacide."

187. Ibid.

188. Ibid.

189. Ibid.

190. Husseini, "Murder in the Name of Honor."

191. Ibid.

192. "Reports from Africa and Middle East: Jordan." 54.

193. "Saheri's Choice," Videotape on file with Gleeson Library, University of San Francisco (Films for the Humanities, 1998).

194. I. Kershner, "Defying a Clan Code of Silence on Unspeakable Crimes," *New York Times*, April 20, 2008: A4. http://www.nytimes.com/2007/04/20/world/middleeast/20honor.html

195. N. V. Baker, P. R. Gregware, and M. A. Cassidy, "Family Killing Fields," *Violence against Women* 5, no. 2 (February 1999): 164–84.

196. Ibid.

197. S. Mydans, "Bartered Papua Bride Opts Out," *San Francisco Chronicle*, May 7, 1997.

198. Ibid.

199. R. Reddy, "Gender, Culture and the Law: Approaches to 'Honor Crimes' in the UK," *Feminist Legal Studies* 16, no. 3 (2008): 305–21.

200. Ibid.

201. Ibid.

202. A. D. Kulwicki, "The Practice of Honor Crimes: A Glimpse of Domestic Violence in the Arab World," *Issues in Mental Health Nursing* 23, no. 2 (2002): 77–87.

203. Ibid.

204. Ibid.

205. D. Kogscioglu, "The Tradition Effect: Framing Honor Crimes in Turkey" *Differences: A Journal of Feminist Cultural Studies* 15, no. 2 (2004): 118–151.

206. Kogscioglu, "The Tradition Effect," 121.

207. Reddy, "Gender, Culture and the Law."

208. Ibid., 121.

209. A. Gill, "Honor Killings and the Quest for Justice in Black and Minority Ethnic Communities in the United Kingdom," *Criminal Justice Policy Review* 20, no. 4 (2009): 475–94.

210. Ibid., 479

211. Kogscioglu, "The Tradition Effect."

212. Gill, "Honor Killings and the Quest for Justice."

213. Reddy, "Gender, Culture and the Law," 314.

214. P. Chesler, "Worldwide Trends in Honor Killings," *Middle East Quarterly*, 2010. http://ehis.ebscohost.com, accessed December 4, 2012.

215. Ibid., 2.

216. Chesler, "Worldwide Trends in Honor Killings."

217. Ibid.

218. Kogscioglu, "The Tradition Effect."

219. Greenberg, "Criminalizing Dowry Deaths."

220. Karp, "Genitorts in the Global Context."

221. Hosken, "Women, Violence and Human Rights."

TWELVE

Conclusion

The battery of women is pandemic. The rape of women is an ordinary, ritualized, and regulated form of violence. Sexual harassment costs women their jobs, their educations, and their economic futures every day. Thousands of women suffer physical mutilation, poverty, and slavery and live in wretched dependence on their husbands or fathers. Millions of women face mutilation in the name of sexual purity, thousands risk being murdered by their brothers or fathers in the name of honor, and hundreds face a fiery death so their husband's fortune is increased. Some women are so spiritually degraded and physically isolated by systematic oppression that they slide into severe depression or commit suicide. These are not inexplicable horrors visited on a tiny proportion of the population. These are not rare and despicable acts performed by deranged misfits. These are everyday, commonplace acts of ordinary violence visited on millions of women.

If only a few women were maimed or killed by their husbands every year, if only one tiny tribe in Africa practiced female mutilation, if only one woman was stoned to death or beaten in the streets because of her family's perverse sense of honor, these would be horrible and destructive deviations from the norms of a civilized society. If a baby girl died of malnutrition or was killed at birth by the midwife, or if an autocratic husband refused to allow his daughters or his wife to venture outside the house, many of us would feel sympathy, much as we do when we hear of other types of misfortunes. But these are not unusual or unique experiences, rare disruptions in an otherwise civilized existence. These acts of violence are not even disruptions; they are not even particularly noteworthy in the cultures in which they occur. They are often accepted as cultural variations by laypersons and sophisticated academics alike. Violence against women is embedded in the structure and culture of every society, and although it takes many different forms and expresses itself in different degrees, it is omnipresent and ordinary. It is this commonplace, taken-for-granted character of violence against women that is at once so overwhelming and so pervasive.

I have been teaching courses in the sociology of gender, family violence, and violence against women for almost 35 years. During that time, academic feminists progressed from "discovering" violence against women in the family as a shocking social problem to recognizing violence against women as entrenched, global, and ubiquitous. Today when I teach these courses, students for the most part want to hear about individual deviance and psychological cause and correction. They want to hear about the pitiful backgrounds of vicious rapists and serial murderers rather than see a picture of mundane and unremarkable violence. They resist discussion of solutions based on eradicating poverty, improving education or access to employment, or, more important, changing the structure of the family or the workplace. They prefer to talk about what they see as more relevant responses and more direct approaches, like anger management groups and therapy. They are firmly devoted to an individualistic and medical approach to this universal problem and are reluctant to accept the view that such responses are of little value to abused women or to the problem of abuse more broadly. They remind me of the views held by many women in the early days of the feminist movement, when feminists naively assumed that once we had pointed out all the problems women experience based simply on gender, the world would shift to accommodate us. Once men realized that it was unfair for women to do all the housework, they would pitch in. Once it was clear that when women were divorced midlife, they were likely to sink into poverty, the divorce laws would be changed to undo this inequity. Once it was clear that the family structure benefitted men rather than women, both men and women would want to change that. Once we had identified the disadvantages suffered by girls and women, there would be a rush to right these wrongs.

What were we thinking? In fact, of course, few saw it as we did. Some did not see a problem at all; some saw one but thought it was of little consequence—certainly not worth the investment of significant resources. And some were threatened by the prospect of change and fiercely fought to maintain the status quo. During these early years of growing awareness and increasingly sophisticated analysis, at least in sociology, we remained pretty parochial. Our sights were fixed firmly on women in the United States, and too often on middle-class women. The benefit was that it led to the development of consciousness on the part of women with resources, time, money, and knowledge who could put their considerable energies behind change in law, policy, and perceptions. The real disadvantage was that there was a tendency to maintain a rather cavalier attitude about change—to assume that what was good for middle-class white women was good for everyone. It is true that many of the struggles, such as the struggle for control of one's own body and reproduction, economic fairness, equity in divorce, and expanded access to education and the workplace, resulted in benefits to all women. However, the analyses presented by feminists sometimes ignored the real structural and material differences among women, and as such, failed to propose the deep, revolutionary changes that are essential if women's lives are to improve significantly.

Because the mainstream, or equal rights, women's movement saw the problems suffered by women as soluble through legal and policy adjustments and through change in formal and informal socialization of girls and boys, the deep chasm between men and women that was the foundation of the economic structure and buttressed the damaging cultural beliefs and practices was not adequately considered. Researchers and other academics placed faith in the value of adjusting extant structures to be more inclusive and in removing barriers to women's full participation. They focused on helping women learn to take leadership roles, encouraging men to become more nurturing, imposing affirmative action and sexual harassment policies on the workplace and educational institutions, and, more specifically in the case of violence against women, working to improve the response of the courts and police to women who were raped, battered, or beaten. These responses were not wrong by any means. They were simply not enough—not deep enough, not wide enough, not radical enough. They fostered the development of individualistic and reductionistic explanations and solutions: women needed to become less dependent and develop more self-esteem, through sports or through a change in the way parents brought them up. Men, by the same token, needed to get in touch with their feminine side, become more nurturing, and learn to treat women as equals.

In fact, the problems go far beyond the socialization experiences of boys and girls, beyond making minor adjustments to accommodate women in the workplace and men in the home. A global perspective not only alerts one to the enormous variety of devastating violence against women, but the obvious connection with economics and related cultural beliefs provides the avenue for an analysis of violence in the United States as intricately intertwined with the gender structure. This structure, woven through class, race, and culture, is the root cause of the commonplace violence against women, and the many efforts that individuals, organizations, and governments make to address this problem that fall short of radical restructuring of the society are bound to have limited or temporary value at best. In the introduction to this book, I addressed the problems we encounter by our failure to uncover the roots of violence against women in the economy and in the gender structure it reproduces. It is not entirely cynical to assert that if we are unwilling to restructure our gender relations, then we must simply accept violence against women, from poverty to death. On the other hand, to concede hopelessly to a world in which millions of girls and women are victims of violence because of their economic, social, and political oppression seems too wretched to accept. It is perhaps necessary instead to acknowledge the limitations, see the harsh parameters that frame violence against women, and keep those at the center of any effort to reduce such violence. That means asking some uncomfortable questions of those who offer services or support— questions about the long-term or deep impact of their efforts, questions about the benefits and the real recipients of those benefits.

Violence against women is deeply rooted, growing from social, political, and economic inequality. Lack of access to birth control, lack of education, lack of legal rights are all forms of oppression of women. Women, who are victims of honor crimes, die because they are the pawns in a struggle between families for status in a tightly structured system of scarce resources. Women, who are infibulated, enduring lifelong infection or suffering enormous pain with intercourse or childbirth, are mutilated by their mothers and aunties because not to do so is to condemn them to a life of poverty and exile. Women who are harassed in the workplace are victims of men's power in the economic structure, just as women who are raped are the victims of male privilege and female oppression.

At the base of the violence women experience, and the source of its ubiquity, is the deeply rooted historical and material inequality of women. As long as women do not have economic power and do not have control over their own bodies, as long as they gain their sense of worth from men and from "being" feminine rather than from "doing," and as long as they are prevented from or are punished for "doing" as they are today in Afghanistan, for example, they will be vulnerable to abuse by their family members, in the workplace or at school, or in the streets. As long as women are the "other," degraded and devalued because they are female rather than male—which is to say as long as women do not have power ascendant over or equal to that of men in the economic, political, and social realms—they will be abused, violated, and killed by commonplace and completely unremarkable assaults on their bodies and their souls. If, in fact, we want to eliminate the commonplace occurrence of infibulation, kitchen fires, honor crimes, female infanticide, rape, battery, sexual harassment, corporate violence, and the degradation and devaluation of all that is female, political and economic restructuring that lead to cultural changes in beliefs, definitions, and attitudes must be achieved. Short of that, we can study violence against women and understand its scope and cause, but must accept it, ignore it, or admit that we are powerless over it. The choice is ours, and the choice is obvious.

Index

454, 456; male supremacy, 4, 21; in nineteenth-century America, 118; in Progressive era, 119, 131; in WW II, 119, 393, 401–2, 409, 412

Family violence, 2, 15, 48–50, 60–62, 64–65, 118–19, 122, 126, 133, 137, 143–46, 151, 154–55, 157, 320, 472; as byproduct of patriarchy, 121; as cauldron of, 122; as an industry, 50; as reflecting traditional family, 120, 131, 133–34

Faragher v. City of Boca Raton, and strict and vicarious liability, 172

Farley, Melissa, and prostitution v. sex work, 323, 360–62

Federal Drug Administration (FDA), 259–61, 263–64, 267–69, 272–74, 277–83, 285–86, 288, 291, 296

Female circumcisio. *See* female genital mutilation

Female genital mutilation (FGM), 3, 6, 44, 212, 321, 363–64, 405–6, 408, 419–24, 428–34, 436–41, 451, 458–60, 462–64, 467; as cultural practice, 3, 44, 423, 429–30, 437, 439, 459; and family honor, 406, 458; as a health issue, 319, 423, 430, 464; as human rights issue, 36, 420, 430; legislation regarding, 3, 44, 422–23, 430–31, 439; prevalence estimates, 436; and the UN, 429–34; and Western women, 364, 423, 430

Female infanticide, 208, 419, 421, 444, 465, 475; ultrasound and sex determination, 444

Female sexual purity, 452; and honor crimes, 212, 321, 363–64, 406, 421, 429, 451, 458

Femininity, 1–2, 9, 18, 22, 24, 40–43, 46, 76, 83, 85, 89, 98, 101, 113, 119, 121, 125–27, 129, 133–34, 138, 165, 177, 186, 190, 192–93, 210–11, 227, 234, 239, 242, 254–55, 258, 273, 298, 365–66, 374–75, 377, 384, 396, 398–400, 405–8, 423, 456; blameworthy, 190, 251, 295, 406; commodification of women, 312, 366, 368, 406, 409; constructions of, 1, 43, 76, 121, 133, 210, 227, 239, 374–75,

406; degradation, 41, 69, 82, 84, 88, 90, 96, 99–102, 178, 209, 359, 407, 475; dirty, 76, 108, 149, 177, 212, 237, 402, 406; economic inequality; sexuality, 2, 76, 83, 85, 89, 101, 177, 190, 192, 210–11, 234, 239, 374–75, 406–7

Feminist: perspective, 47, 59–60, 65, 99, 101, 121, 145, 185, 198, 248, 298, 364, 432; scholars, 144, 240, 370

Fen Phen, 256, 278–81, 298; and American Home Products, 256, 278–81, 285, 289; and weight loss industry, 278–81

Filner, Bob, 174–75

Foot-binding, 5, 47, 149, 408, 423–29; demise of, 427–29; and foot fetishes, 424, 426

Freud, Sigmund, 59, 155, 226, 234, 248; Freudian view of family violence, 71, 120, 127

Friedan, Betty, 84, 109, 120, 128–29, 133, 155, 162, 198, 227, 236, 248–49; *The Cult of True Womanhood*, 70, 129, 155, 222; and the problem that has no name, 128

Gang rapes in India, 5, 207

Garfinkel, Harold, 10, 58; "taken for granteds," and *Studies in Ethnomethodology*, 36, 41, 92, 173, 176

Gates, H., 424, 426, 428. *See also* foot-binding

Gender: binary, 2, 24, 133, 374, 399; equity, 228; harassment, 99; socialization, 35, 46

General systems theory, 36

Giarretto, H., and his approach to incest, 32, 37, 61–62

Gilder, George, 123, 134

Gilman, Charlotte Perkins (*The Yellow Wallpaper*), 92, 125, 155

Global Alliance against Trafficking in Women (GAATW), 362

Gordon, Linda, Progressive era and family violence, 119, 132, 134

Grassroots activists/campaigns/ movements, 117, 121, 144, 264

About the Author

Mary White Stewart, PhD, is a professor of sociology and director of the School of Social Research and Justice Studies at the University of Nevada, Reno. She received her MA in sociology from Temple University and her PhD from the University of Nevada, Reno. She writes and does research in the areas of family, identity, gender, and violence against women, as reflected in her books: *Silicone Spills: Breast Implants on Trial* (Greenwood, 1998), *Ordinary Violence: Everyday Assaults against Women* (Bergin and Garvey, 2000), and *Portraits of Change: Unparalleled Freedoms, Unanticipated Consequences* (Hamilton Books, 2013).